Alternative Engines

Volume 1   Compiled and Edited by Mick Myal

Published by Fiesta Publishing
Post Office Box 65106
Tucson Arizona 85728-5106
United States of America

Copyright ©1996
Fiesta Publishing

All rights reserved.
This book, or any part of, may not be reproduced
without the permission of the publisher.

Printed in the U.S.A.

Library of Congress
Catalog Card Number
96-085423
ISBN 0-9643613-2-9

Dedicated to my immigrant parents,
Michael Myal and Frances Urbanski,
and to two special teachers during my formative years,
Stella Adamski Daniels and Edmond H. Borgioli

Contents

Preface viii

Perspective 11

Observations 16

Engine Knock Detection--Parkman 37

Conversion of the Chevrolet 4.3 Liter V/6 Engine--Carter 39

Magnetos: Be Aware 49

E-Racer Profile: a Fast Glass Canard Two Place--Dickey 50

Liquid Cooled Aircraft Installation Aerodynamics--Miley 58

Power and Performance
Small-block Chevrolet Powered Cessna 172--Erickson 65

Subaru EA-81 Turbo Powered Avid Flyer--Hoffmann 77

Ducted Fan Propulsion for Replica Jet Fighters--Jones 80

New Aircraft Engine Development Program--Ostasiewski 91

Belted Air Power: The Buick 215 Engine--Meyers 96

Modifying GM's Aluminum V/8s--HOTROD Magazine 108

Affordable Aluminum V/8s--HOTROD Magazine 116

Understanding Ignition--Kuhlmann 123

Safety in Flight--Parkman 125

A HAPI Magnum Plus Engine Problem--Griffin 126

Ford 351 W Engine Aero Conversion--O'Neill 128

Converting the Mazda RX-7 Rotary Powerplant--Mayfield 146

Mountain Climber: A Piper Pawnee Conversion--Erskine 155

Chevrolet V/8 Longevity Report at 300 Hours--Ward 164

Propeller Drive Systems
and Torsional Vibration--Hessenaur 165

Igniton Coil Failure-Wiley's SPAD Powerplant--Parkman 175

Converting and Flying
the Ford 3.8 Liter V/6 Engine--Schweitzer 176

Orb's Engine Emporium- Parts 1 thru 4--Erb 187

Removing Engine Heat--Eaves 191

Some Observations on the Cooling
of Auto Engines--Hinote 196

High Energy Ignition for Factory Engines--Eaves 198

Tri-Q Renaissance--Parkman.. 201

Six Appeal--CARCRAFT..211

Octane Requirements and Your
Experimental Airplane--Yeakey 215

Ford 3.8 Liter V/6 Engine Conversion Information--Frank............217

Push-rods and Power in the Ford 3.8L V/6 Engine--Frank............220

Converting the Subaru Legacy Engine--Rogers.........................224

Analysis: NonTraditional Engines in KIS Aircraft--Jaqua............232

Some Homebuilding Considerations--Jones.............................238

One Hour Flight Test--Waldmiller..245

Legacy Powered KIS--McCormick...248

Antifreeze and Coolant--Maes and Armstrong............................251

Development of a Turbocharged Subaru EA-81--Clarke.............255

Gyroscopic Forces and Torsional Vibration--Spreuer..................262

Electronic Fuel Injection Simplified--Parkman............................263

Converting Auto Engines--Jones..265

Legacy Power -- Mace 269

Separating BS from BHP--Jaqua...276

Mazda 13B Powerplant Installation
in a LongEZ--Gowan...279

Programmable EFI for Auto
Aircraft Engine Conversions--Farnham.......................................285

Stratus Engine Development--Hoffmann....................................289

The LPE Engine: Alternative High End Power............................295

Contact! Magazine Information..303

About the Editor..304

Preface

My aviation roots go back to my childhood on a small farm in a Michigan county aptly named Arenac, Indian phonetics for sand. My most vivid recollection is of a low flying, fast, silver monoplane which tipped its wings to me one hot summer day. I believe it was a P-35, based at Selfridge Field near the big city of Detroit. From that moment the sky was my TV. During those Depression days it was rare to see airplanes that far Up-North but each sighting was a treat.

A visitor to the farm brought me a beautiful P-39 balsa model. I managed to carve the spinner; however, I had no clue how to begin building it. That plane and its plans gave me many hours of imaginative thinking.

My first plane ride at age nine was in a blue painted Funk; I still remember the thrill! From then on I knew aviation was my first love.

Ken Sevier, my high school classmate and eventually a professor of aeronautical engineering at the University of Illinois, introduced me to that one time great publication called Air Trails. I wrote to every school for enrollment information but when it came time to commit I decided much older WWII veterans then coming home would largely occupy the aeronautical engineering field. Cars were to be my career path.

I joined EAA shortly (EAA 007978) after college and military service. The only regret I have is that I did not join sooner! The early years of EAA were the most exciting times, mainly because of their color, diversity and sense of freedom. Picture a cloud-like fly-by of 50 or more biplanes, not in any semblance of formation and you get the idea! Duane Cole describes the ecstasy and growing pains of those early years in his 1972 book, "This is EAA". Things are very different now.

The Contact! magazine concept began in 1987 with my personal belief that I and other experimenters were being overlooked to satisfy a more diverse audience of aviation enthusiasts. From the beginning I felt that technical content based on first hand information should be the driving force behind this publication. It was relatively easy to establish the reporting format, which is loosely based on the style of SAE (Society of Automotive Engineers) Technical Reports. Realizing that aviation enterprises, with a very few exceptions, are losing propositions, I, along with some local fellows, formed a non-profit educational organization in 1990 to best serve my objective. It is registered in the State of Arizona as Aeronautics Education

Enterprises, a Non-Profit Corporation. AEE received its permanent classification as a 501(c)(3) non profit educational organization by the IRS in 1995.

Copyrights to published Contact! articles were released by the AEE Board to me on February 27, 1996. This book is my attempt to convey useful information to others desiring in-depth coverage of modern auto engine conversions.

I would be remiss if I did not thank again all contributors to Contact! magazine and specially those individuals featured in this publication for sharing their exhaustive and, sometimes, frustrating efforts. Without their contributions there would be no publication. Each one upholds the long EAA tradition of helping the next fellow.

Readers of this book seeking additional, ongoing auto engine conversion information will find Contact! magazine subscription rates and ordering details at the back of this book.

Overview

Innovation and experimentation is at the very core of American life. Not satisfied with the status quo we are driven by the notion that newer is better, that there is always a better approach to any problem, that products, even things like breakfast corn flakes, can be improved. From the beginning, alternative, non-certified engines have played an important role in grass roots experimental aviation.

It began with the Wright brothers. Having no suitable engine they designed their own, a flat inline four weighing 179 pounds and producing 12 HP. As flight fever mounted most any engine was a potential power source. In 1911, the Douglas, Arizona Flying Club equipped its glider with a Buick engine. During the Depression era homebuilt designs such as the Pietenpol Air Camper, the Payne Knight Twister, and the Heath Parasol relied on a variety of car and bike engines. The widely available Ford Model A engine was the powerplant of choice for many homebuilts of that time.

Amateur aircraft building was rekindled in the early 50s when a few individuals began to seek improvements to their light airplanes. It wasn't dramatic or purposeful at first, just a bunch of friends interested in airplanes. Work focused on the modification of existing designs, principally the utilization of certified parts of fuselages and airframes to increase performance for air show work. Fly-ins of these one-of-a-kind aircraft exposed these efforts to more enthusiasts. Such gatherings greatly helped to cement bonds of friendship and paved the way to the formation of an organization. It took an attractive experimental parasol airplane named the Baby Ace to jump start the growth of the Experimental Aviation Association. Baby Ace plans were featured in Mechanix Illustrated magazine. That nation-wide exposure of one man's efforts brought together a clan of experimenters who would stimulate the thinking of many others.

Most every airport around the country had a few tired or damaged airplanes which would provide the raw material for these unique airplanes. World War II surplus materials were available at below wholesale prices. We had three stores in Detroit; Berrys, Silverstines, and Benjamin Sales each had barrels of rod ends, push rods, cables, turnbuckles, instruments and the such. Aluminum stock and aircraft tubing was to be found in most sizes at Factory Steel. One could easily find Sitka spruce spar and plywood web material at John R Lumber. One can only imagine the amount of suitable material harvested near aircraft factory hot spots in California, Kansas and New York, or from Arizona storage!

Certified engines, likewise, were no problem, some coming from airport bone yards and some from war surplus. Overhaul parts were plentiful and relatively cheap. The biggest find for many experimenters was the Lycoming O-290G ground power unit. Its going price in 1962 was $97.50, FOB Montebello, CA! Hundreds, if not thousands, of these 125 HP engines were converted into reliable powerplants and many are still flying today.

In economically depressed postwar Europe, several light weight single seat designs emerged. Powered by the Volkswagen 1131 cc 30 HP (DIN) engine they soon found their way into Canada and the U.S. This engine in direct drive form spawned major experimental developments such as the KR-1, Varieze, Dragonfly, and the Soneraii. Engine conversion specialists, like Huggins, Revmaster, Monnet, Barker and Taylor, were the principal suppliers of this relatively cheap power source.

Burt Rutan's VW powered prototype suffered some engine problems and was quickly redesigned to take advantage of the then still plentiful half-time or near runout Continental engines from 65 to 100 HP. Rutan's economic rationale worked and many of us became airborne through wise shopping (in 1976, a zero timed O-200 engine cost $3000; many used engines in this HP range were available at considerably less than half that figure).

The mildly modified aircooled VW engine has had a lot of interest and some success as an aircraft powerplant. Its reliability record is somewhat spotty, particularly in large displacement versions. Serious attempts have been made to identify problem areas with mixed results. The 1/2 VW engine has also enjoyed a large experimenter following. The basic four cylinder design configuration is fully certified in Europe by Limbach.

The Chevrolet Corvair engine of 145 in^3 displacement and 80 HP received its share of experimenter attention in the 60s. Gil Baker, at that time a Chevrolet experimental engineer, designed and built a planetary reduction drive using Chevrolet Turboglide gears for his conversion. Static tests indicated that the engine would develop 95 HP at 4200 RPM. The weight with two carburetors was 209 pounds. This unit was flight tested by Piper Aircraft in 1962 in the experimental plastic Piper Papoose. The results were disappointing to Piper. The record shows that Cessna also toyed with the 1962 engine. Two engines were shipped, according to a Chevrolet Technical Report dated 1-29-62. Baker also tested the engine in his original design amphibian. The pylon mounted pusher propeller was driven by the vertically installed engine in the hull. This drive arrangement, using a long drive shaft to clear the hull and a 90 degree Gleason gear box final drive, produced severe torsional resonance cutting short the first flight. The pylon drive concept was terminated for a conventional engine arrangement. Baker's findings now lead him to conclude that the Corvair engine is somewhat on the heavy side and is best suited to an airplane with plenty of wing area, such as the Pietenpol. Several of these airplanes are flying today with a Corvair engine. Baker is of the opinion that modern liquid cooled engines offer much better choices.

A year after the introduction of the air cooled Corvair, General Motors came out with the 215 in^3 (3500 cc) V/8 in the Oldsmobile F-85, Buick Special and the Pontiac Tempest (identical to the Buick version). An immediate favorite of the auto and boat racing crowd, this all aluminum engine repeatedly demonstrated its survivablity under highly stressed operations. The Buick version tooling was acquired by Rover in the UK in 1967. Displacements have increased over the years; a 4400 cc engine was built at one time in Australia. The fastback Rover 3500 sedan was the exclusive British police car for many years while the Land and Range Rovers have held an international reputation for engine durability. Experimenters Jess Meyers, George Morse and the late Steve Wittman obtained excellent results with this engine. Homebuilders looking for 150-200 HP at take off will find the 215 a viable choice. Collectors have hoards of these engines and parts are still available 35 years later. The UK is an untapped source for fresh salvage engines.

Ford engines gained their share of experimenter attention in the late 1970s, beginning with the Pinto installation by Dave Blanton. His work throughout the next decade terminated with the development of the Blanton Javelin STOL, a Piper Tri-Pacer airframe modified to a tail dragger configuration. Powered with the relatively light weight, thin shelled cast iron Ford V/6 289 in^3 engine with a cog belt reduction drive, this airplane became very popular with many homebuilders. Controversy surrounded the HP rating method espoused by Blanton in contradiction of established dynamometer determinations. Enthusiasts following this development believe hundreds of completed airplanes are currently flying with still others under construction. A Canadian experimenter, Ed Lubitz, also was heavily involved in Ford engine conversions during this period, along with several others.

Mazda's rotary engine, since its inception in the early 1970s, has always been found to be near the center of alternative powerplant interest. Spurred on by Curtiss-Wright and General Motors licensing agreements, engine experimenters, like Harold Gallatin, began building Wankel type engines. Lou Ross began his redrive design on a 2-stroke 1000 cc engine in 1978. The Ross redrive was adapted to a Mazda 12A engine. Although underpowered it did fly in a BD-4. Unfortunately, the engine has drawn its share of con-artists, causing losses of deposits and a jail term for one operator, well known to all Mazda conversion pioneers. His ads have recently reappeared in a popular kitplane magazine.

The 13B version is proving to be a reliable powerplant in the 150-180 HP range. The advantages of the rotary layout in an aircraft application include its fail safe design-no valves, just seals which fail "softly" giving plenty of warning that power is being lost through poor compression. The dual plug ignition arrangement offers redundancy. The engine's low parts count also strongly suggests that the engine has less failure modes. On the other hand, the engine is noisy and has a higher rate of specific fuel burn than that of contemporary liquid cooled auto engine conversions.

Chevrolet's small and big block engines are being used in a number of experimental airplanes. There are many reasons this is the case. New Mr. Goodwrench long block assemblies come very reasonably priced. Large availability and competitive pricing of aftermarket performance parts are an attractive incentive to engine builders. Proven performers on the racing circuit and in marine applications these 350 and 454in^3 engines are adaptable to large 4-place designs and single place fighter replicas. For applications needing less power the 4.3 liter V/6 engine is being considered for a growing number of airplanes. It is compact and utilizes many small block parts. Aftermarket aluminum blocks and heads offer substantial weight reduction at a price, still well under the cost of new certified engines.

Last, but not least, is the Subaru product line. The horizontally opposed layout loosely based on the VW design is a natural replacement for Lycoming and Continental engines with the exception of the cross flow head design which can disturb the normally clean appearance of the upper cowling. C.G. Taylor introduced his unique Subaru powered Taylor Bird at Oshkosh in 1979. His attention grabbing design introduced many experimenters to the Subaru, creating a wave of Subaru enthusiasts. The engine was quickly adopted by gyroplane designers. Today's gyros are largely powered by Subaru.

The high cost and questionable durability of 2-stroke Rotax power encouraged Avid Flyer builders to look to the Subaru. Reiner Hoffmann flew his with a turbo EA-81 in 1992. Since then, a growing number of airplanes have been successfully powered by this engine. The Subaru family (EA-81, EA-82, ER-27, EJ-22) has proven successful in various airframes. The SVX engine has drawn much interest from builders of four place airplanes. Because of its rarity not many of these engines will be found in aircraft.

The forementioned automobile engines are the backbone of the current experimental engine movement. These engines helped bring forward the modern canard (Varieze, E-Racer), the tanden wing (Dragonfly), the Piper Tri-Pacer conversion (Blanton STOL), fighter replicas (FEW and S-51D) and several other auto engine based airplane designs. As new engines are placed into automobile production experimenters will be challenged to produce additional conversions.

Not satisfied with the wide range of available production engine options some experimenters have chosen to develop powerplant alternatives. Darus Zehrbach, Jim Rahm and George Morse each have developed high HP versions of custom engines, relying heavily on lessons learned from racing technology and availablity of performance parts, forgings and aluminum casting sources. The parts aftermarket (carburetors, fuel injection, intake manifiolds, ignition systems, etc.) is huge, giving custom engine designers, as well as those using stock blocks and heads, a wide selection of engine dress items. Magazines, such as Car Craft, Hot Rod and Circle Track are good starting points for aftermarket parts.

Diesel powerplants at this juncture remain an elusive dream. Structural weight is a prime design consideration in a compression ignition engine. The famous American Packard, which utilized several weight saving ideas, appeared in 1928. A compact nine cylinder radial displacing 407in^3 and weighing 510 pounds, it produced 225 HP at 1950 RPM. Because it used the same port for both intake and exhaust, its ever present engine fumes in those open cockpit days caused its downfall.

Before closing here it would be fair to mention that most every engine, at some time, has been viewed as a potential candidate or has been converted for aircraft use. The historical record is replete with references to industrial, snowmobile, marine outboard, motorcycle,as well as ground and air power units. Not many have been successful conversions for a variety of reasons, none of which can be attributed to failure of internal engine components.

It can be concluded from this overview that automobile based engines are the logical source for affordable alternative aircraft power. Converted properly, installed in a compatible airframe and maintained with the same due care afforded certified engines, today's auto engines, built to precise manufacturing standards, should match or surpass certified engine experience.

Observations

Auto engine conversions are the future of grass roots, experimental aviation. It seems that prices of certified engines and parts continue to increase each year. As time passes, used aircraft engines, once a good source for inexpensive power, become riskier investments. Too many horror stories are being uncovered about used engine bargains requiring complete, checkbook busting overhauls. Cost effective powerplant alternatives are available and eventually will become mainstream as airframe designers bring into focus their talents and energies on the unique requirements posed by liquid cooling.

The pioneers who have flown modern auto engines have paved the way for the rest of us in overcoming negative opinion and sharing their trial and error experiences. This book documents their efforts. It is for us to learn from them and add to that growing store of knowledge.

Much information can be gleaned from past experience. Successful engine conversion is strictly a matter of attention to detail, viewing every aspect of the conversion with a questioning attitude, reaching a logical decision on each element of the conversion after careful study.

Contrary to unsubstantiated opinions, I believe the modern auto engine is fully capable of operating at high power outputs. I base this on the fact that modern engines are tested for durability (many other whole engine tests as well) at wide open throttle for hundreds of hours, the dynamometer load computer adjusted between maximum torque and maximum HP throughout the entire run (saw tooth fashion, 5 minutes peak to peak). Actually, durability testing is a misnomer; testing is completed after 600-1000 hours to examine each engine component for wear or unusual conditions. A single dyno run can easily consume a tanker truck load of fuel.

Engine related components must meet strict specifications. Emissions control items, from spark plugs to O_2 sensors, must survive by law for 100,000 miles without failure or serious degradation under a wide variety of driving conditions. Having qualified modern auto engine capabilities, let's get into the details!

AIR COOLED INSTALLATIONS

Installing a certified or experimental air cooled engine is relatively a minor challenge. The homebuilder may have a set of plans from the designer which walks him through the installation process. These plans will likely include a firewall layout drawing showing location of pass through holes for engine controls and instruments, placement of relays, the breather oil separator, auxiliary fuel pump, gascolator and starter solenoid. A complete set of baffling drawings will be included. If the plans or instructions are not provided, or are incomplete, he can dig out needed information from other builders, aircraft mechanics, Tony Bingelis' book "Fireward Forward" or by copying the layout of most any uncowled factory installation.

Typically, he isn't finished even after his airplane has been test flown. However, even if everything was done according to plan or acceptable aircraft practice he will likely find that engine temperatures are on the high side requiring rework of the baffling. Additional hours will be spent finding that elusive leak in the cooling plenum. External engine elements, such as carburation/ fueling and ignition systems, are normally included in the original engine purchase and will not require special attention (unless a "lemon" is involved-it happens!).

AIR COOLING PRINCIPLES

To set the scene for a successful auto engine cooling installation let's first review the typical air cooled installation. Air enters the cowling through small openings facing the air stream. It is trapped in a plenum made up of the inside of the cowling, the engine itself, and aluminum bulkheads which are tipped by elastomeric/fabric seals. Additional cylinder baffles surround parts of the cylinder barrels forcing the air to flow by the cylinder fins and pick up heat. What makes the pressure cowling work is the old standby, pressure /volume Bernoulli equation, $P_1V_1= P_2V_2$. Incoming air is at atmospheric, static pressure while its velocity is high. The pressure cowl causes the air velocity to approach zero while the pressure increases. Air flow over an airfoil follows the same rule.

To help understand what is actually happening in the plenum let us follow this analogy. Consider just that part of the upper airfoil profile aft of the maximum chord thickness. Assume that the cowling inlet and P_1V_1 begins at the point of maximum chord thickness on the upper surface. Since the equation must hold true the result at the airfoil trailing edge must be P_2V_2. Pressure increases while velocity slows. Similarly, air undergoes that change in a expanding three dimensional space. We want to avoid air separation as happens when a wing stalls. Thus, we can also infer that careful attention to the shape of the intake plenum is essential and will lead to optimum cooling and low cooling drag.

The real world situation is not that different. Looking at existing solutions is another approach to understanding Bernoulli. The T-28 oil cooling layout is one example. The inlet opening is about 4 by 17 inches, or 68in^2. The circular radiator has a cross section area of 143in^2 which results in an expansion ratio of 2.10. The internal ductwork is not optimum although one can see that effort was made to minimize sharp breaks. It would be interesting to know the pressure drop across that installation.

If everything works out the pressure drop across the cylinder fins should be about 3-4 inches of water. That number comes from experiments performed on the air cooled Defiant in Canard Pusher #47, Rutan's excellent newsletter. I am informed that radiators in automobiles do not experience that much drop across the core. That would be expected with the lack of intake duct work seen in most cars.

A simple water manometer is used to make this measurement (see page 138, Terry O'Neill's article). This device responds to simple physics and does not lie. Everyone should use one during development. Surprising things will be learned using this tool.

Assuming the pressure drop is less than that expected let's search for the cause. Any one or a combination of the following problem areas could be the culprit:

Intake blockage
Plenum blockage
Plenum leaks
Heat transfer
Exhaust air into positive air pressure

Intake blockage is caused by sharp inlet openings and poor entrance conditions which create turbulence and reduce the amount of effective expansion volume. Plenum blockage is a disturbance inside the plenum proper. The continuing expansion, if not managed through careful plenum design, limits the amount of pressure rise in the plenum. A smoothly shaped plenum ducting is ideal. Several Formula 1 racers use composite plenums which are shaped internally to minimize turbulence and optimize pressure rise. Plenum leaks are an obvious source of pressure drop loss. Heat transfer from cylinder head fins is well documented in factory airframe installations. However, the air flow must be directed carefully around the cylinder to be effective.

The exhaust air must depart into a pressure area lower than that of the plenum to achieve pressure drop through the cylinder fins. The common exit location is at the bottom of the firewall which may just be a high presure area of the airframe! The usual fix, when that happens, is to add a fixed cowl flap or re-shape the engine cowling so it protrudes below the firewall to produce a local low pressure zone. Some airplanes incorporate engine exhausts into localized bulges below the airframe proper to lower the air pressure at the exit. Here an increase in V_2 of the engine exhaust helps to lower the total P_2! Cooling augmentation is a useful solution in reducing airframe drag since the exit areas can be smaller. On non augmented exhaust systems the exit area must be larger than the intake area to accomodate air expansion due to the addition of heat. For this case noted designer Dave Thurston recommends a 22 percent area increase.

Consider the three dimensional shapes and turning vanes (if necessary) found in a typical wind tunnel design as the ideal model for radiator ducting and you will not be too far off the mark for efficient cooling.

LIQUID COOLING

Liquid cooled engines in aircraft are really no different in that cooling remains the biggest challenge. Essentially, the radiator replaces the cylinder cooling fins. The chief difference and problem lies in the lack of practical information on aircraft radiators, their heat transfer characterisics and their proper installation.

Each Big Three company has its own radiator manufacturing operation. Automobile radiators are engineered and tested over a wide range to provide adequate cooling under severe desert conditions. Seldom does anyone have a cooling problem with a modern, low milage vehicle. Thus, a radiator's heat transfer capability in BTUs can be approximated assuming a percentage of engine HP rejected as heat in a given vehicle. In automobiles, radiators normally face the pressure source. If tilted to the air stream, radiators will lose some efficiency from turbulence caused by turning the air into the radiator core. Radiator efficiency will be severely reduced by any obstruction (check for nests) or by long term dust and debris build up.

Some radiator shops have the capability to build radiators to specific dimensions using existing cores and tanks. The techniques are time proven and are the same as those employed by the manufacturers.

Looking back, there is no difference between air and liquid cooling when considering the basics of heat transfer. However, getting rid of engine heat can be trying. My old college roommate who specialized in aerospace heat transfer work calls it a "black art". The article on beginning on page 58 provides considerable information on managing the engine heat transfer problem. The math might be hard to recall for some but any high school physics teacher should be able to explain what is going on. Other articles provide practical cooling solutions for a number of experimental airplanes.

UNIQUE COOLING PROBLEMS

Other important details must be considered in dealing with liquid cooling. Much can be learned from studying modern automobile installations. We are well beyond the thermal syphon approach of the 1930s.

Normal system pressure ensures that the boiling point of the coolant is not exceeded at typical sport plane altitudes. The average cap is designed to maintain 15 PSI which will prevent boil over up to the top of Pike's Peak. The pressure (filler) cap is typically located at the highest point in the coolant system to ensure that the entire system is completely filled with coolant at start up. Where a submerged radiator is used, a small custom header tank, made from light aluminum stock, is typically built and located above the coolant level of the engine, usually on the firewall. As coolant expands the pressure build up will cause the cap innards to open venting the coolant into a recovery bottle. Upon shut down, the cap vacuum valve will eventually open and allow the coolant back into the system. The recovery bottle is located below the pressure cap, usually on the firewall. A quality cap (OEM) should be checked by a mechanic for correct function before use. New caps have been known be inaccurate or to fail.

Although an expansion tank can work in place of the small header tank and recovery bottle the latter approach seems simpler. Recovery bottles come in a variety of shapes and sizes. By looking at the cold and hot level markings on the coolant bottle used with your engine you can determine what size to use and select a shape that best fits the installation. Polyethylene recovery bottles can be easily repaired should you find one that fits perfectly but has a leak.

The airplane must be instrumented with coolant pressure and coolant temperature gages. If pressure is dropping during flight it is a sure sign that coolant is leaking. Higher than normal coolant temperatures indicate a problem with proper cooling (bird nest again?). As specific coolant pressure gages are not currently available it is quite possible that a 0-30 PSI fuel pressure gage will work. Check with Westach Instruments!

Some late model vehicles are being equipped with low coolant level sensors to help protect aluminum heads from damage or meltdown This is good insurance and should be considered standard equipment for any installation with aluminum heads.

A thermostat should be used to maintain constant coolant system temperatures, its rating following the engine manufacturer's recommendation. Aftermarket thermostats can vary from their stated temperatures. To be absolutely sure it is a good idea to check the opening function in heated water with a candy thermometer or with your local high school lab person. Some experimenters have left these off which defeats the purpose of running an engine at a uniform temperature. If the engine is not being cooled adequately with the thermostat in place the problem lies somewhere else in the system.

Prestone and Texaco brand ethylene glycol (EG) formulations in a 50/50 mix with distilled water are recommended for all modern engines, including aluminum engines. The ratio is adequate for most climates but should be changed to meet severe local winter conditions. Although raw EG comes from two plants the specific additives are what make these two brands superior to less known brands. Polyethylene glycol (PG) has been used in high heat racing applications. It is not as efficient as EG and should not be considered. Water alone is the best heat transfer medium but will not protect the engine. Products which "wet" the cooling system internals and improve heat transfer are used by racers. I haven't seen any laboratory tests that show they are totally compatible with EG, proprietary additives or engine internals.

Experimenters have found through experience that water pump effectiveness is reduced at typical operating RPMs. Although no tests have proven cavitation (akin to propeller action at blade stall) the possibility does exist. Pulley diameter changes to slow the water pump impeller have helped significantly to improve cooling in some applications.

The conversion will likely need a custom cooling system layout to clear the tight cowling but the routing should be the same as that in the automobile. Reverse cooling approaches are being tried but the complications do not warrant such changes in a conversion. Standard coolant hose is adequate. Where straight runs are needed (such as for remote belly scoop radiators) aluminum tube can be substituted. Hoses should be secured over beaded metal connectors; the bead is necessary to resist slippage of the clamped hose end. If the metal connection does not have a retention bead a series of tack welded beads should be added.

The location of the radiator/s has been largely a matter of aesthetics or a best quess. As discussed earlier, location should be also influenced by airframe pressure distribution. Too little information is available on the subject. Reports that come to mind are those documenting location effects on NACA ducts. An article in the March 1996 Sport Aviation magazine offers some information on this subject. If we consider two-dimensional airfoil pressure distributions it appears that a fuselage similarily shaped will exhibit negative pressures on the top surfaces and positive pressures on the lower surfaces. Installations with aft mounted radiators (usually for CG control) should work if these factors are considered. In plan view, tapered fuselage sides before the widest cockpit cross section may generate areas of low pressure. Aft areas of cowl cheeks will likely produce low pressure. The side bulging cowls of the successful Thorp T-18 airplane suggest they generate low pressure areas. The Thorp T-211 and the Arnold AR-5 have flush cowls with fuselage recesses which apparently create needed pressure drops. The experimenter who plans to install an auto conversion in an established kit or plans built airplane has the opportunity to first determine areas of high and low pressure by instrumenting another plane of the same type. All it takes is some duct tape and a home built manometer (and a helpful EAA type who will fly the test).

Auto radiators, heater cores and air conditioning evaporator cores are commonly used in experimental homebuilts. Some buy custom radiators from racing suppliers, such as Griffin, or will have their local radiator shop customize a radiator to fit.

The last five years of Contact! articles and conversations with experimenters suggest that the experimenter should first try using auto parts before investing in custom units. Jess Meyers' Buick 215 powered Swift was initially cooled by a custom radiator in a belly scoop. Jess has since reconfigured his cooling, using a/c cores in the cowl with appropriate plenum ducting. He has found engine cooling has improved and the plane cruises faster without the scoop. There is no simple answer at this stage of radiator location and sizing to make a blanket recommendation. The builder should make it his priority to first learn what others have done in the past to solve his liquid cooling problem. Installation articles in this book should provide the reader with a lot of useful infomation.

INDUCTION/FUELING
Here is where we provoke some honest debate regarding the choice between auto based carburetion and fuel injection. The argument will go on well after the publication of this book.

Certain advantages can be found in each type of fueling system. Rather than talking about advantages it is more important, in my opinion, to lay out the disadvantages which have greater impact on the experimenter.

Here is my list of potential problems or deficiencies with each:

CARBS	INJECTORS
icing	complex
poor fuel distribution	dependent on electrical power
leaning capability	expensive
power compromize	new learning curve
flooding/priming	trouble shooting
engine matching	retrofitting
poor fuel economy	power matching

The basic carburetor is a simple device. Modern carburetors are a maze of added parts and passages to improve fueling control at various power settings. The EFI injector is also simple; its control system is complex. Scores of shop and performance manuals are written on how both work and how they are to be serviced.

Carburetor technology goes back to the turn of the century. Injectors and fuel injection are relatively new to light aircraft. Electronic fuel injection (EFI) is, perhaps, the most complex because of its stringent emissions control function. Which is better for the auto engine conversion? This question is largely answered by a person's personal comfort level with each approach. Both will work if correctly engineered. Neither will work correctly if not understood.

We take for granted the lousy start up performance of an certified HO air cooled engine. The seemingly endless hand propping or starter whine is observed with a cringe at every fly-in. Raw fuel must climb up hill to mate with air in a correct ratio before firing. When initial firing occurs and then quits the fuel/air supply must be replenished. That is not all; once fired up the engine's fuel/air distribution is still in question. To prevent engine damage each cylinder is carefully monitored with EGT probes to determine the lean cylinder. The other three or five cylinders are free to gulp more fuel than necessary.

The fuel consumption of the air cooled engine is famous. Nothing new. Some fifty years ago when gasoline was a dime a gallon it was a common Big Three practice to calibrate their carburetors to run somewhat on the rich side, for better power and engine cooling! Modern auto carburetors are much better calibrated but will consume more fuel than fuel injection systems due to less precise fuel metering.

The carbureted auto engine conversion doesn't have to fight gravity since the far more efficient intake manifold is on top! EFI engines start at the turn of the key. Something is seriously wrong if the engine doesn't start after a turn or two of the prop. Stock downdraft auto carburetors are a good choice but should be modified or retrofitted to allow leaning. Riener Hoffmann uses a auto heater control part to lean his Bing carburetors at altitude, see page 291.This back suction method acts to control the amount of fuel flow from the fuel bowl by modulating the fuel bowl pressure between the carburetor venturi and the atmosphere. At idle cutoff the fuel bowl pressure is the same as that in the venturii, stopping fuel flow.

Aftermarket auto carburetor manifolds are typically designed for high RPM performance. Passages are large; at low speeds fuel will tend to drop out, wet the floor of the plenum and change fuel distribution. For normal aircraft applications the stock manifold, although a compromise, is probably a good choice in that it has undergone much development. Many experimenters, faced with bulging stock intake manifolds go the extra step to keep cowl lines clean. Custom intake manifolds, made from aluminum stock or composite material, are common solutions on Subaru engines. Fuel distribution can be adversely affected when such manifolds are used with carburetors, potentially leading to engine damage from leaning. When so modified, plugs should be checked frequently during development to verify correct fuel burn and distribution.

PVC pipe has been used to prototype intake manifolds! Rubber coolant hose elbows have been used in place of solid peices. Long hose runs will eventually collapse from manifold pressure (vacuum) if not supported internally.

The following information applies to those builders choosing to accept the complexities of electronic fuel injecton. Modern, low milage, recently salvaged EFI engines are ideal for conversion and are the power source for many of the auto powered airplanes and gyroplanes flying today. Their precise electronic systems are warranted for 50-100K miles, depending on model year.

After finding no impact damage and clean internals the purchase should include all of the expensive wiring harness and the electronic control module (ECM). Running changes may be involved so related bulletins will also be needed along with the applicable shop manual. Before doing any wire cutting the electrical system schematics should be studied and compared to the actual hardware. Various sensors, wire colors and connectors should be identified. Broken down into specific functions and repeated several times, this learning process will also benefit the builder in future troubleshooting, plus gaining an understanding how his ground vehicle works. As a general rule, re-programming of the ECM is not necessary for these high revving engines as experienced by several builders. These engines lean automatically.

Adaptation of a stock auto factory electronic engine managment system to an old (pre ECM) engine is possible for those well versed in auto electronics or willing to learn. Here, the key item is to match the fuel injector discharge rate to the specific displacement needs of the engine. Injectors look alike but may deliver differing fuel volumes per standard opening pulse. It is necessary to do some homework to determine which injector will work with what ECM. Re-programming of the ECM may be necessary.

Aftermarket electronic fuel and ignition systems are also available. Primarily designed for marine and racing applications these systems should also work well in auto engine conversions.

Mechanical fuel injection, used on certified aircraft engines, is another viable, but more expensive, alternative that could be considered. Fuel is metered to the intake ports by measuring the quantity of air flowing through the intake and adjusting fuel pressure to result in the correct fuel air ratio. The best source of information on mechanical fuel injection is your local aircraft engine mechanic or a specific shop manual.

IGNITION

Magnetos are fast becoming obsolete. Noted for their poor spark at starting RPMs, bulk and weight and high replacement costs I expect that all newly certified aircraft engines will have standardized on some form of electronic ignition. A few auto conversions used magnetos before the first HEI distributor systems came into production in the 1970s. No recent auto engine conversion has replaced the factory stock ignition with magnetos.

Two magneto articles are included in this book to make experimenters aware of their inherent problems and to show how magnetos can be converted economically into excellent HEI units. The June 1996 Private Pilot magazine reported that a new electronic ignition (with mechanical magneto backup!) developed over several years was certified for use on the Lycoming O-320. This direct replacement for mags and harness was priced at $2500, about 10 times the cost of Leonard Eaves' solution (page 198)!

The prime concern with any electrical system is the matter of redundancy. Two magnetos obviously provide that assurance. Auto based battery ignition systems can be modified to provide redundancy. Two batteries are used in conjunction with diodes to permit simultaneous charging of both, with switches to select either electrical source. Ignition coils have been known to fail (notably Ford units, one with a tragic result). An automatic coil switcher device is available from MSD to eliminate that power failure problem. Some experimenters have gone the extra step in developing dual alternator systems to ensure electrical redundancy.

Switching between DC electrical sources, such as dual battery systems, should be approached with an understanding of electrical spikes and how they can occur in some circuits. Essentially, pure resistance circuits will not generate spikes; circuits with coils, condensers, or both, are good candidates for spike production. Some form of surge protection may be necessary for avionics. DC switches should be used for ampere carrying ability. AC switches are not designed to make and break high amp loads. Since AC current flow reverses every 1/60th of a second, electrical arcing is minimized. DC arcing is more severe due to arc duration.

Dual plugs are not needed in modern engines. They are necessary in large bore aircraft engines, using slower burning, high octane leaded fuel, to ensure complete burning across the cylinder. Auto HEI provides sufficient spark to ignite the most stubborn mixture and total plug fouling is rare. Some auto conversion packages are sold with a choice of either single or dual plug heads simply to satisfy customers who are convinced that dual plugs are necessary, not because the vendors believe in them. If vendors are asked they will admit that dual plug heads are not needed. NASCAR cars don't need them to produce power.

I have seen dual ignition systems which feature siamesed plug wires leading to single plugs. This approach helps to solve the dual plug dilemma for some experimenters. Some people don't recognize that plugs are the most reliable part of the ignition system and need no back-up. Modern plugs are good for 100K miles; EPA certification rules require that they work for that period of use. Plug examination should be made frequently during ground and flight test stages and periodically after that point. Combusion chamber differences affect plug performance. Always begin with manufacturer recommended plugs. What plug heat range works best must then be determined. Incidently, the new batch of aftermarket multi-spark electrode plugs do work in improving combustion. However, what happens to them over the long haul in the real world has not been established.

Distributor HEI is perfectly suited for use on older, pre EPA engines. It delivers a hot spark at all RPMs. Timing advance can be tailored to performance demands. It may be possible to modify some HEI distributors to permit in-cockpit manual timing advance thus optimizing engine operation. Various brands of HEI systems are sold in the aftermarket, claiming superior spark energy levels. Real life ignition demands in the cylinder are adequately handled by modern stock system voltage levels.

Aftermarket spark plug wires now come in a wide assortment of colors! If this appearance trend continues experimenters can expect to see a lot of bright wires in their future cars. Realistically, ordinary factory production wires have advanced considerably over the years, again due to EPA certification/warranty concerns and competition. Unless one is concerned with looks the production wire is perfectly adequate. Insulation breakdown leading to a crossfire condition is rare but it is a good idea to keep wires separated. The firing order of some engines may invite cross firing conditions.

Several custom electronic ignition systems have been developed for the homebuilt market. It is too early to tell which are better in terms of installation, performance or cost. Perhaps the best evaluation one can make is to speak with the people who use these commercial units. The vendor should be sufficiently confident in his product to release the names of his customers. If not, he may be looking for a development engineer to work out the bugs.

I personally believe that original equipment auto electronic ignition systems, proven to EPA durability standards, are the way to go for several reasons. First, dealerships do have qualified mechanics who are knowledgable in their operation and can help sort out problems. Most every community offers adult education classes on these systems. Parts are extremely reliable and, when needed, are within easy reach. Prices are competitive.

TORSIONAL VIBRATION

The unseen killer of engines, torsional vibration occurs in every rotating mechanism that is subject to periodic applications of force. In the piston powered engine each firing causes the crank throw to twist minutely as it rotates under the compressive force of the rod. As the crank continues to turn the load causing this deflection will eventually stop and the crank throw will then unwind in the opposite direction, just like a spring. At certain RPMs the force of the piston/ rod and this deflection will combine and cause resonance which, if unchecked, will over stress the crank.

The torsional damper detunes these forces, essentially adding a shock absorber to the system. Crank torsionals continue to occur but the damper system shifts potential crank resonance to a RPM range not normally seen by the crank. The torsional damper is mounted on the front of the engine crank and typically mounts the accessory pulley/s. Often overlooked, crank torsionals are also present at the flywheel end of the engine. They are damped by the torque converter in automatic transmission vehicles and by the clutch assembly in manual transmission models. Lightening the flywheel or using the flexplate without the weight of the torque converter changes the tuning of the rotating parts. This problem is accentuated as the number of firing pulses per revolution is decreased since the firing pulses are far apart. Broken cranks after a few hours of running three cylinder engines without flywheels are the result. The larger the number of cylinders, the lesser the problem.

Before the invention of the automatic transmission the clutch was the go-between the inertia of the road and the engine. Those of us who drove stick shifts then learned very quickly how to get smooth starts without jerks. The simple clutch disc with its friction surfaces and concentric springs was an excellent damper of engine torsionals! Today, this device is used in many marine drives to dampen varying prop loads. It is used with success in some conversion reduction drives.

Torsional dampers, notably those employed in large World War II engines, were of the pendulum type which incorporated movable counter weights on a crank throw. The shifting inertia of these weights would counter the deflection produced by piston forces. The mathematics to design a pendulum damper have been published. With liquid cooled auto engine conversions already penalized by additional weight the addition of such mechanisms may be regressive.

Cog belt reduction drives are claimed to produce sufficient damping due to belt slack inertia and some undetermined belt stretch. This not been proven by engineering analysis but the results in successful conversions do indicate that damping is effective. A cog belt drive design that also incorporates the clutch damping component was introduced to experimenters by Ron VanderHart. In addition, his design imposes no radial loads on the rear main bearing, a possible drawback in flywheel mounted driver sprocket designs.

Vibratech produces a front mounted viscous damper (Fluidampr) which is a replacement for the crankshaft mounted stock elastomeric damper. These units are used extensively by racers, possibly because the cranks are not stock and probably that the viscous (silicone filled) design damps over a wider range of RPMs. This type of damper does work and should be considered as a replacement for a missing or worn factory damper.

In no case should an auto engine be run without a torsional damper on its front (accessory) end. Careful thought should be given to the matter of torsional vibration at the flywheel (propeller) end, as well.

REDRIVES

Modern high revving automobile engines produce power at RPMs which are not compatible with conventional propellers or airframe designs. Some form of gearing (the generic term) is usually necessary. Analysis of the problem shows that geared engines are better performers than direct drive engines at the low end of the flight envelope, as pointed out in the article by Vance Jaqua, beginning on page 132. Gearing increases take off acceleration and improves climb, much the same as we experience in automobiles at the stop light or going up an incline.

Virtually all high HP certified engines use steel redrives. The WWII era military and commercial reciprocating engines produced high HP at relatively slow turning speeds. These engines featured steel spur, helical, herringbone and 90 degree planetary gears, principally to manage large diameter propeller tip speeds. Today's Lockheed C-130 Hercules prop jet blades turn at about 1300 RPM, the output from a spur/planetary gear box while turbine internals operate at 13,280 RPM. One certified airplane which did not have steel redrive components was the 25 HP Crosley powered Mooney Mite. Four Goodyear "V" belts produced a 2:1 reduction ratio.

The 1960's Corvair engine received its share of attention resulting in several experimental planetary and spur gear redrive designs. Bud Rinker's adaptation of VW Transporter rear end steel gear sets was one of the most popular redrives around. Many plans were sold but the record is void of actual flight experience with this design. A few years ago I received a test stand photo from Australia which clearly showed a Rinker box on a Rover (Buick) 215 engine! It was never flown in that configuration according to my source. Corvair engine experimentation also included work with the cog belt. Several articles by Waldo Waterman were published by EAA in 1969. These described his flying "Chevy Bird" installation. He used a four inch wide, 7/8 inch pitch belt and sprockets resulting in a 1.66:1 ratio.

Today's homebuilder has a wide variety of custom redrive types and vendors to choose from. The axial planetary gear redrive has the familiar look of a direct drive HO aircraft engine(and features a built-in prop extension). The spur gear, chain/sprocket and the cog belt/sprocket designs raise the propeller center line above that of the crankshaft, thus offering more propeller ground clearance.

The question frequently asked is which type of redrive is the best. My answer is that any properly engineered, tested and built with precision redrive type should be satisfactory. Although a few cog belt redrives have been run without lower outboard bearing supports this method is a questionable engineering practice. It is evident the unsupported belt load on the lower sprocket places a cantilever end load on the crankshaft. Each engine revolution causes the crank to complete one fatigue cycle.

With respect to redrives, the devil, as usual, lies in the details. Product quality and reliability is essential. Quality requires only the best materials are used and that part tolerances are maintained throughout the assembly. Machining should be clean. One test that helps sorts out the quality and reliability question is a simple request for some user references. A visit to the vendor's shop is a good idea in that the homebuilder can learn a lot about its unique features. However, the visit should not be a substitute for printed assembly and setup instructions. I think the vendor would be eager to sell his installation and set up instructions separately. If instructions don't exist or are sketchy, seriously think beforehand what steps you would take to assemble and adjust the redrive to your engine. Be prepared to spend a lot of time on the phone asking for that information.

It is a fact that the past has seen a few bad actors who have preyed on honest builders and their enthusiasm. Asking for payment up front for a promised delivery date is a favorite ruse, resulting in a felony conviction in one case. Payment before receipt of goods is a matter not to be taken lightly. Both parties should be certain of the payment terms. Finally, the vendor should have a written warranty, listing warranty terms. If none exist one can be pretty certain that refunds are not in the picture, or will come very slowly.

The vendor has some rights, also. Too often, purchases are made well in advance (maybe years!) of their installation or first flight, obviating any vendor responsibility for possible refunds, missing parts or problems. Probably the best time is to buy a redrive is when the engine conversion begins.

Vendor experience also enters the picture; some redrives are fairly simple mechanisms which tend to invite new vendors into the business. Being a flight development engineer for a new firm is not necessarily bad if that understanding is well established in advance of purchase.

It is refreshing to note that reduction drive vendors, in general, have largely ceased criticizing competitive products and gearing methods, a real problem some years ago. There is plenty of business to go around as demand grows for less expensive powerplants. Redrives are a big ticket item, in some cases the largest single conversion expense. Selection of a redrive should be given ample study.

The choice of redrive ratio is largely dictated by the diameter of the prop, as established by the ground clearance of the airplane. It is a good idea to first establish the maximum take off RPM of the engine. I personally prefer to set limit RPM at a point 150 RPM below valve float or engine redline. Redline can be determined by looking at the engine specifications or HP/torque curves. The prop RPM is calculated by limiting prop tip speed to, say, 850 feet per second, well below the sonic number of 1100 FPS. The result of engine RPM divided by prop RPM is the redrive ratio.

While not essential to flight as proven by hundreds of direct drive KR, Dragonfly and Soneraii airplanes redrives are the direction most experimenters are taking.

PROPELLERS

Propeller selection can start by considering the brand, diameter and pitch recommended by the airframe designer. The correctly geared engine, if its rated power is equal or close to that of the replaced factory engine, should be able to turn the original prop somewhat faster (100-200 RPM) during the full throttle static run up. Using one of the designer recommended props during initial ground testing is a good verification of the claimed conversion HP. It also is a solid point of departure when shopping for the final installation prop.

Another approach is to use the certified engine maximum RPM at the prop and work backwards toward the engine to define the redrive ratio. However, if another experimenter has gone through intial calibration and has good results, these steps can be skipped.

In the case of some popular custom airplanes a lot of prop optimization work has been done, some even for auto conversions. Such prop selection information may be obtained from several sources. Other experimenters are usually very helpful. Also consider checking with the aircraft designer, prop suppliers and the type newsletter editor.

Experimenters leading the auto engine conversion movement have learned that propeller matching can be an expensive proposition, in a few cases exceeding the cost of the engine conversion! Where there is little or no data on a specific airframe/engine conversion combination the best approach is to use a ground adjustable prop currently offered by several vendors. More expensive than a fixed ground adjustable prop in this situation is recommended.

Cut down metal props are not recommended. A rash of in-flight blade separations occured years ago on certified engined homebuilts. Apparently, the prop vibration characteristics were changed such that the blades would suffer a catastrophic fatigue failure. With more interest in auto conversion growing each year no one should attempt to reinvent this wheel!

In-flight prop failures are rare but they do occur. The violence of a broken prop can cause the engine mounts to break, the engine to depart the airplane! As insurance every auto conversion installation should be equipped with a steel safety cable (any 1/4 inch) connecting the crankcase to the airframe, using aircraft style terminations. All Formula 1 and Formula "V" racers are required to have this safety item. Although we are not racing our conversions (not yet, anyway!) this recommendation doesn't cost much and only weighs ounces.

It is appropriate here to mention manifold pressure and its application to propeller matching. Those who fly constant speed propellers know that engine load is governed by the pitch of the blades and that engine load is set and determined by the reading on the manifold pressure gauge. Pilots flying fixed pitch propellers determine approximate engine load using the tachometer. The latter case is well and good for certified airplanes whose power and performance are documented.

Fine tuning of the propeller/engine conversion can be assisted by using a manifold pressure gauge. On a standard day at about 7,700 feet density altitude a full throttle setting should result in a reading of about 22 inches of mercury. The engine RPM varies with the prop load; a too high engine RPM is a sure sign that the prop is not taking sufficient bite assuming that the proper reduction ratio was chosen. Using the gauge, RPM, outside temperature, and barometric pressure readings the power absorbed by the propeller can be determined and compared to factory engine performance charts.

ENGINE MOUNTS

Auto engine mounting points are selected to minimize engine shake, the forces caused by moving engine masses. Depending on the engine cylinder arrangement shake can cause rocking or lateral movement. It is best to use the factory mounting points when possible.

The current focus on NVH (noise, vibration, harshness) is driving engine designers to incorporate balance shafts in their carryover engines. These shafts are rotating masses which counteract the inertia of engine moving parts. Just great for NVH reduction but a heavy burden on the auto conversion. The shake of older engines is not noticeable as compared to most aircraft engines, making them preferable, weightwise, to the newer, heavier versions.

The auto engine has pulleys that are normal to the crankshaft. These come in handy when building the engine mount. As applied by Ross Aero, the engine is simply placed over a plywood mockup of the firewall using the crankshaft pulley to support the engine weight. A wooden firewall spacer and shims are placed under the crank pulley to obtain the desired clearance and thrust angles. A come-a-long, secured to the ceiling, is used to steady the engine during the mount building process. Since this is done over a horizontal flat surface dimensional control is much better than hanging the engine horizontally next to the actual firewall.

USED ENGINES

Cost, in all cases, is the most important factor in auto engine conversions. If cost was no object all of us would be buying factory new, certified engines. One can easily overextend available financial resources if no effort is made to plan for the conversion, to itemize and budget for the cost of parts and materials, additional machine work and testing. The purchase of a complete salvage engine is very likely to be the least expensive portion of a typical engine conversion budget.

Additional dollars will buy a brand new Mr. Goodwrench long block or a rebuilt AC Delco long block (guarenteed for one year or 12K miles). These products are an viable option if the experimenter plans to make extensive ignition and fueling changes from the stock factory configuration.

Most conversions are done on used, low milage engines. Builder reports almost unanimously confirm that wear in Subaru engines is minimal, some with mileage approaching the 100K mark! Improvements in manufacture, rings, lubricants, filters and frequent oil changes have paid off. I personally would have no qualms of using any 5 year old salvaged engine, provided that it was clean internally, top and bottom, had no external engine damage (Subaru engines are specially vulnerable) and was salvaged from a recent accident. Although rebuild parts are cheap I believe there is no better engine builder than the fellow doing the engine assembly in today's engine plant. With today's demands for smoothness and emphasis on precision manufacture it would be difficult to find an engine that isn't balanced. Blueprinting by definition is the measurement and modification of parts to published manufacturing dimensions. The term is still around but is obsolete by today's manufacturing standards. Building up an old engine is a different story. Balancing and blueprinting may be necessary if dealing with aftermarket parts.

ADDITIONAL DETAILS

We have reviewed some areas of auto engine conversion which, to some experienced hands, are elementary. Attention to detail is very important and nothing should be taken for granted. Here are just a few items to keep in mind, not in any specific order.

Some form of engine log should be kept to document the steps taken during the conversion process. Parts and part numbers get lost making replacement difficult. Adjustments and calibrations, such as prop pitch, should be maintained. Photos are a definite assist to record keeping. Performance data should be logged during the flight test phase.

Modern salvage engines should be purchased complete with all electronics included. These components are expensive if bought new.

Engine electrical systems require attention. Computers, are subject to electrical spikes. Care should be taken to eliminate static before handling such items. The engine/ redrive installation should be grounded with bonding straps. Wires should be secured in bundles away from heat.

Hot exhausts should be shielded from adding heat to the entire compartment. The auto practice of locating the inline fuel filter above the engine should not be followed. Fire sleeves (insulation) should cover fuel lines. The upper cowling should have provisions for venting heat after shutdown. This minor modification will increase the longevity of any plastic/elastomeric parts.

Carburetor heat provisions must be installed on carbureted engines. Don't fall for the premise that under cowling heat is enough.

All mechanisms generate vibrations. Engine sensors should not cantilever from the engine block face but should be supported to eliminate fatigue failure from possible excitation. Copper lines are particularily susceptible to work hardening and should not be used in engine compartments for any purpose. Custom support brackets tend to fail from vibration. Alternator brackets are notorious for failure. Their design should be fail safe so as not to affect engine operation if failure occurs. Checking for cracks is a preflight must.

Use of the largest possible air filter is recommended. Pressure drop across the air filter becomes more critical with increase in altitude.

The auto engine should run more smoothly than a Lycoming or Continental. If it doesn't, find the problem first before flying. Sorry to say, some "test" pilots have overlooked some roughness before flying. One magazine article described the flight test of a 215 Oldsmobile conversion in a Tailwind. Roughness was later pinpointed to the use of heads with differing compression ratios. t.

Engine rebuilding should be based on factory shop manuals and, very important, other technical publications. The latter are useful in pointing out parts changes, model year differences and helpful techniques that will save time. The dealer's parts counter man is an excellent source for parts changes and helpful information.

Everyone needs some help, some more than others. Rely on the experience around you but be certain that the experience is qualified. Auto racers know how to obtain the last ounce of power but their recommendations concerning intake manifolds and cams for your conversion may be totally wrong. Some performance shops appealing to the high school hot rodder are a poor source of useful information. Serious engine builders who have extensive machine shop facilities and have been around for some time can be very helpful. Asking around before building up an old engine will uncover the fellows who know their business.

SUMMARY

Converting an auto engine can be a satisfying endeavor. Much of the total time will be devoted to learning what is involved. It can be fun or it can be totally frustrating depending on the individual. People who have the aptitude to build an airplane can also produce a practical engine conversion.

A unique market providing complete firewall forward auto engine installations has emerged in the 90s. For those not having time or inclination to convert or build an engine, purchase of a complete installation is now possible. Brochures and conversations do not tell the rest of the story. To be confident of your choice I recommend that before the actual purchase the vendor be requested to provide a list of prior customers. Instances have occured where trusting builders have been taken for large sums of money, simply accepting false representations! The reputable vendor of firewall forward installations or redrives should be happy to comply with your request. If the vendor cannot provide references you could become his development engineer. That situation is not neccessarily bad and can work if the understanding is reached beforehand.

Some readers will recall that the homebuilt movement always has had its share of controversy. We have witnessed past debates favoring either rag/tubeor wood construction, resorcinal or epoxy glues, or metal as opposed to composite airframes. Today, the factory vs. auto engine issue is emerging as the topic of choice. The argument will blow over as more homebuilders become exposed to the low cost of auto engine conversions and more designers introduce specific auto powered airframes.

Expected growth in demand will create some logistic problems for the homebuilder. Conversions and redrives essentially have been a custom business to this point in time, a side line activity in some instances. It is very likely a few vendors will reach the limit of their production capacity, causing orders to stack up. Either they will establish a wait list as is done by some composite airframe companies or they will tool up or hire more employees to meet their orders. Some competition for salvage engines may result in prices going up.

The following pages are a compilation of important alternative engine activity over the last five years. The reproduced articles represent a cross section of successful auto engine conversions and alternative engine development. At the leading edge of experimentation these authors have made a major contribution to the experimental aircraft movement by sharing their knowledge and experiences.

Although the reader may have special interest in a specific engine conversion article other articles should be consulted. They contain valuable in-depth information which can be applied universally.

I have a simple request concerning the following material in this book. Please be considerate and do not write or leave phone messages with the authors. These experimenters like to help the next fellow but, like most of us, don't have the time or the inclination to answer letters nor should they expend their funds to cover return call conversations.

Regarding my personal overview and observations I will appreciate receiving any comments, corrections, or suggestions. Your inputs are always welcome.

Michael C. Myal
June 15 1996
(520) 881 2232
(FAX) 795 6776

ENGINE KNOCK DETECTION

Steve Parkman
SWAG Aeromotive
2521 North Fairview
Tucson Arizona 85705
(520) 622 6910

The arch enemy of any spark ignition, internal combustion engine is detonation. As a result, virtually all engines until recent times have been designed with considerable safety margins to minimize or eliminate the occurance of engine knock. In Contact! issue #6, Yeakey proposes the use of a knock sensor to improve 180HP Lycoming performance. Eaves in #12 offers his proven, low cost solution to fixed certified engine timing to improve engine efficiency. This article introduces the knock sensor as a useful add-on, stand-alone device for obtaining optimum fuel efficiency and added flight safety. MCM

MIT Professor John B. Heywood[1] defined knock as the sharp metallic "noise" caused by pressure fluctuations during spontaneous release of chemical energy in the combustion chamber. This knock or ping causes a noise that rides on the high-frequency pressure wave which is superimposed on the normal cylinder pressure waveform. Due to the multiple frequency waveforms present at knock, a knock sensor has to be able to discern the frequency that the knock is predominant, typically 5 to 11 kHz and secondary and tertiary signals are present at 11 to 17kHz. When cylinder pressures and temperatures increase abnormally during charge burning, knock results. These high temperatures and pressures induce ignition of the remaining, unburnt air/fuel mixture. The interaction of the two burnings (the spark wave front and the endgas) creates the high pressure wave known as knock.

The following formula shows that the fundamental frequency of the shock wave is a function of the distance it travels (bore diameter) and the local speed of sound (average temperature of the combustion chamber):

$$f_n = \frac{k_c * c}{B} = \frac{k_t}{B}\sqrt{T}$$

f_n = fundamental knock frequency
$k_c\ k_t$ = constants
c = local speed of sound
B = bore diameter
T = combustion chamber temperature

KNOCK DAMAGE

Knock will transmit more heat and pressure to the cylinder walls, pistons and to the valve train causing scored and cracked cylinder walls, burnt and broken valves, collapsed rings and complete failure of the piston tops leading to rod and rod bearing failure. Causes of knock include the following variables:

Water/block temperature: Above normal temperatures can cause preignition knock leading to run away destructive knock.

Air temperature: Extreme air temperatures will cause cylinder temperatures to rise causing the pre-ignition of fuel.

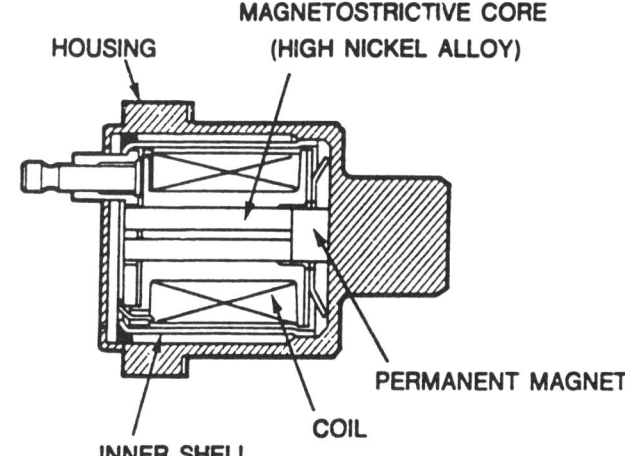

The knock sensor is a tuned magnetostrictive accelerometer.

Incorrect fuel octane: Low octane level will cause a high unburnt fuel/Air mixture that will quickly lead to preignition and then to knock at a sustained power demand.

Contaminated fuel: Contaminates in the fuel will lower the octane rating of the fuel leading to endburn. If the fuel contaminates are not totally mixed with the fuel this can lead to random knock.

Lean fuel mixture: A lean fuel/air mixture will cause hot spots that can lead to run-away knocking.

Over-advanced timing: Incorrect timing will cause a constant ping or knock that can lead to the complete failure of the engine.

Vacuum leak: A port vacuum leak on an carbureted engine can cause a reduced fuel flow that can create an over lean condition. On a electronic fuel injected engine a port vacuum leak will tend to cause a over rich condition.

High cylinder head compression: This can be caused by incorrect assembly of the pistons, heads, or incorrect head gaskets. Also, accumulation of carbon can cause high compression.

KNOCK CONTROL

Now that we have looked at the definition, sources and results of knock we will look at a closed loop knock system that works in conjunction with an electronic ignition system. The drawing above shows a typical knock sensor used by General Motors. Basically, it is an electrical device, behaving somewhat like a magneto in response to specific combustion vibrations. It produces an AC voltage output proportional to the vibration level at the "Knock Frequency".

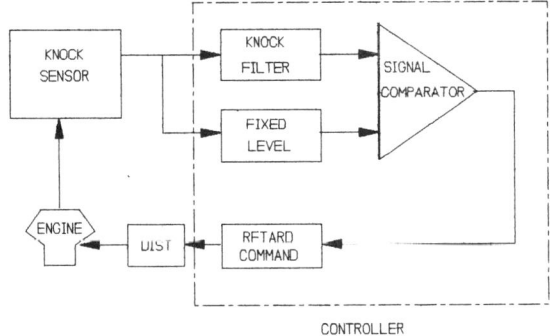

Block diagram of automatic retard circuitry in GM HEI systems.

The drawing in Figure 2 shows a block diagram of a typical automatic retard and advance circuit that is used by GM on their HEI ignition systems. When knock is present in the engine the knock sensor will generate a higher output signal then the fixed side of the comparator signaling the condition to the electronic distributor thus retarding the advance on the timing. When the knock is reduced the timing then is advanced back to the desired amount of advance.

Now for the auto engine conversions that don't have a variable electronic timing we have designed a small knock indicator (see photo) that will give a visual indication via three LEDs. When the engine is started the green LED (left) will light up showing that the sensor circuit is working. if the engine starts pinging the yellow LED will flash, if the pinging gets worse the red LED will start flashing, also. If the engine starts knocking lightly the yellow LED will stay on and the red LED will flash. When the engine knocks hard the red and yellow LEDs will stay on full bright. The knock sensor is powered by 12v. DC negative ground. It can be mounted in any position. The knock sensor will work with any piston engine. It comes with easy to follow step by step instructions.

For Contact! readers who would like to build a simple knock sensor we have also designed a single LED system. When the engine pings the LED will flash at you and when the engine starts knocking it will come on full bright. This circuit can be built using a printed circuit board from Radio Shack, or any other electronic supply house. All resistors are 1/4 Watt carbon film. Mount the sensor securely your engine intake manifold (liquid cooled) or block (air cooled) closest to the center of the crankshaft and to the rear of the engine away from the load on the crank. To set the negative input to the correct voltage measure between pin 4 of U1 and ground and adjust the pot until pin 4 reads .8 volts DC.

If the knock sensor LED is too sensitive to your engine noise you can adjust the potentiometer upwards till the background noise is gone. The knock + wire attaches to the center pin on the knock sensor. The knock - wire attaches to the block of the engine. The negative wire attaches to the frame or ground bus and the positive 12 volt line attaches to the master switch.

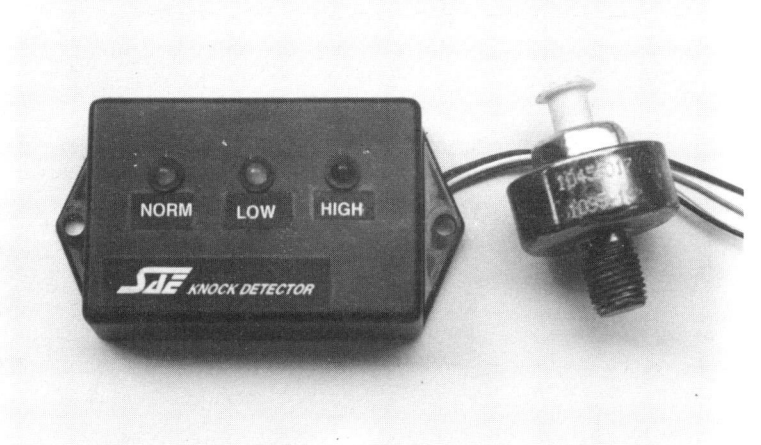

SAE's knock detector, applicable to both certified and experimental powerplants, features three levels of sensitivity.

If you have troubles building or tuning this circuit feel free to call me 8 to 5 MST M-F. We reserve the copyrights to this design and release this schematic to Contact! readers exclusively as a contribution to flight safety and fuel efficiency. **SP**

REFERENCES

1. P. Kingham et al, SAE Automotive Engineering Journal, December 1993

2. J.H. Currie, D.S. Grossman, J.J. Gumbulton, "ENERGY CONSERVATION WITH INCREASED COMPRESSION RATIO AND ELECTRONIC KNOCK CONTROL". SAE Paper 790173, 1979

3. S.M. Dues, J.M. Adams, G.A. Shinkle, "COMBUSTION KNOCK SENSING: SENSOR SELECTION AND APPLICATION ISSUES", SAE Paper 900488, 1990

4. L. Eaves, "HIGH ENERGY IGNITION FOR FACTORY ENGINES", Contact! #12

Parts List

D1 bridge	R3 1k
D2 9.1v Zenier	R4 10k
D3 red LED	U1 LM 358
C1 .1µf	U2 7809
C2 .047 µf	K1 KS2 sensor
R1 47k	(from Standard)
R2 100k pot	

Simple knock alert circuit. Copyright Steve Parkman SAE 1995.

An Elegant Conversion of the Chevrolet 4.3 Liter V/6 Engine

Fred Carter
1641 East Woodman Road
Apt 168
Colorado Springs Colorado
80920
(719) 260 9388

Fred has had a life long love of engines and machinery going back to childhood and go-kart days. He is an electrical engineering graduate of Oklahoma State and works in the field of electrical motor and control design. Development of the Chevrolet 4.3 liter engine to his demanding criteria is outstanding. His extensive re-engineering of an Orion kit will be reported in a future article. MCM

I joined the EAA about 20 years ago. I always had an interest in auto engines and long felt these were the things to fly behind. Some years ago after I finally got situated where I could start a big project, I decided on the Wheeler Express. I wanted the RG model and, of course, I wanted to put an auto engine in it. The company was not too crazy about auto engines. They also said they couldn't ship the RG version for about a year. I kept looking around for a four seat plane to build but the choices were limited at the time. I discovered that an Orion project existed in Atlanta, a French Orion G802. I went over, looked at it, and just loved the airplane! It's a pusher, a beautiful, elegant airplane. It looks somewhat like the Cirrus and Lear Fan airplanes in overall layout.

Both the Orion and Cirrus have a large cavity right behind the cabin, an ideal place for an auto engine. This location is near the CG, a definite plus. If the engine is off a little bit in weight, it will affect the gross weight but won't change the balance much. I thought it was an ideal aircraft for my purposes. So, I just jumped right into it! At that point the main question was what auto engine. I wanted an engine that would put out a good strong 200 HP at a low stress level.

SMALL GM V/8

The first engine that I really studied was the Buick and Oldsmobile aluminum V/8, the old 215 from the early 60s. I had one engine and the more I took it apart the less I liked it. Not to bash the 215 but it's not designed for high horsepower, in my opinion. It's a fairly low performance passenger car engine, the original setup producing very modest power. Olds did make a turbo model but there aren't very many of those around and it still wasn't a powerhouse by my standards.

The first design Chevy V/6 block is lighter than the Buick 215 block by a few pounds. Note the compact size of the V/6 which has 22 percent more displacement.

CHEVY 4.3 LITER

I came upon the Chevy 4.3 V/6 at a swap meet in Carlyle, PA. A racing company was dumping their excess stock. I got a real bargain on a fresh aluminum block and a pair of big valve aluminum heads!

The block weighs about 65 pounds. Newer block designs are beefed up quite a bit for high powered turbo racing. These engine blocks are pushed up to 800-900 HP with pretty good racing success. My block is only good for about 500-600 HP and is now obsolete by current racing standards! However, it has 4 bolt main bearing caps and the outer bolts are splayed. I made my own screw-in freeze plugs because I don't like the pressed in ones. Per the many Chevy Power Catalog pointers I inserted plugs in existing oil drain holes throughout the lifter valley. Under very high RPM conditions producing extreme oil flow the oil typically moves through these holes and falls all over the spinning crankshaft. When these holes are plugged the oil is forced to drain at the front and back of the block avoiding the spinning crank. This simple modification keeps the oil from getting whipped up and helps to save HP. Little tricks like that add up and are common in good race engine building! The Chevy Power Catalog contains many such valuable pointers.

I was targeting this engine to produce 250 HP for the Orion, a fairly conservative number of about .95 HP per in^3. I didn't like any of the stock passenger car cranks. They are cast from nodular iron and seem to perform quite well in mild racing applications. However, I decided to have a forged one made. Mine is a custom crank made by a company in Memphis, TN, which builds these cranks for the Busch Grand National cars. Super high grade 4340 vacuum degassed steel is used to produce the crank. Beautiful machine work and heat treating results in a crank that is absolutely perfect and qualified in many heavy racing applications The other nice feature is that the crank is about a 1/3 the cost of an aircraft crank.

CAMSHAFT

Hydraulic roller camshafts are easy on the valvetrain and absorb less power. I found that the passenger car hydraulic rollers did not fit in the racing block as the lifters were too tall. The racing block is exactly like the traditional small block V/8 design in that the lifter sockets are not tall enough. I had a well known company build a custom hydraulic roller camshaft for this block. That was a big ticket item. The cam grind is mild. Cam specifications are: intake duration of 216 degrees with a .462 inch lift and exhaust duration of 220 degrees with .487 inch lift, on 112 degree centers. For my required power band I knew I didn't need very much camshaft. It would be real easy to over-cam because these heads breathe so well.

HEADS

The aluminum heads are the first design of aluminum heads by Chevrolet and are referred to in the Chevy book mentioned earlier. The combustion chamber is the typical wedge shaped small block configuration, with an 1.625 inch exhaust and a 2.020 intake valve. I decided to go with the most severe duty valves that I could buy. For the intake valves I chose Manley, the highest grade of stainless racing valve available. For the exhaust I chose Inconel valves that are used mostly in offshore turbo boat racing applications run at continuos high power settings. I decided I might want to add a turbo later so I built up the heads with additional performance in mind. The cost of these valves is miniscule compared to the outrageous prices charged for aircraft valves. I cc'd (volume checked) all the combustion chambers to verify that the compression ratios were exactly the same. It was a good thing I did so because the two heads were different yet had the had the same part number. One of the cylinder heads had about a 1/2 point higher compression ratio than the other, a lot in terms of engine smoothness. Now they are all the same after some machining. Incidentally, you may have read elsewhere that a fellow built up an aluminum V/8 engine using both high and low compression heads. The resulting roughness was noticeable and would have been avoided with a little attention to detail.

These heads come with small combustion chambers to produce high compression ratios demanded by racing. Casting tolerances are pretty poor sometimes. The Chevy Power Catalog gives instructions on how to clean up the head ports, the valve pockets and what the contours should look like. It shows how to blend the hardened valve seats blended into the aluminum to get good flow. I followed the book and ground out each combustion chamber to reduce the compression ratio and to "unshroud" the valves for better breathing.

PISTONS

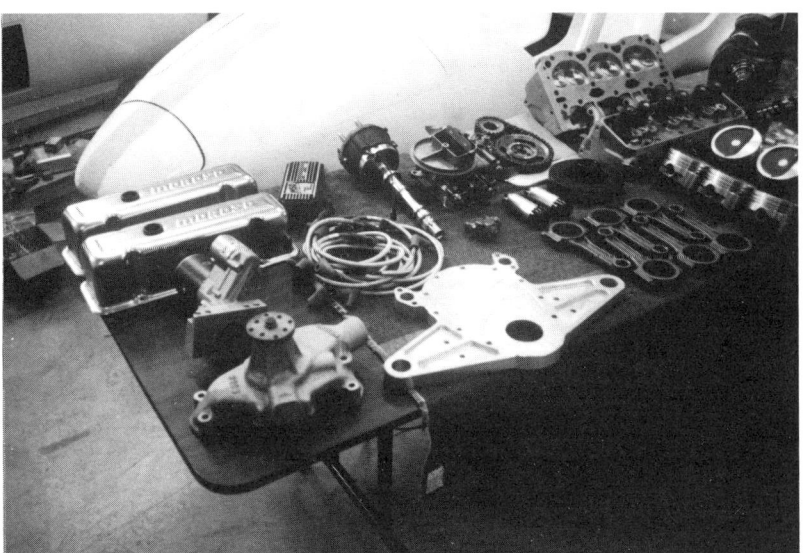

Bench layout of engine parts includes lightweight aluminum valve covers and water pump, lightweight starter, electronic ignition module (1 of 2), custom machined front timing cover/integral engine mount and Holley 500 CFM carburetor.

I chose to use the Chevy 350 TRW turbo pistons which are primarily designed to reduce the compression low enough to permit use of car gas. One of my goals is to operate the engine on car gas, to keep my operating cost down. The resulting compression ratio is around 8.75; that's about as high as I thought I could go and still maintain a reasonable detonation margin. I also the matching TRW "turbo" plasma ceramic rings.

Pistons come in many sizes depending on the crank stroke. When ordering a custom crank you can have any stroke you want for the same price. I've decided after much thought, to stick with the standard stroke. There are several reasons for staying standard. As stroke is increased the top of the piston has to stay in the same place. Pistons made for a stroked

Other parts: true roller chain timing set, "Fluidampr" viscous damper, racing connecting rods, aluminum cylinder heads, TRW # L2441F turbo pistons, custom SAE 4340 odd fire crank, hydraulic roller camshaft and modified aluminum dual plane intake manifold to match high rise heads.

engine move the wrist pin higher up on the piston which crowds the rings higher up the piston where they run hotter and hotter. Chevy 350 TRW performance pistons, which are interchangeable with the 4.3, are hard to beat!

CONNECTING RODS

I bought some aftermarket Sportsman rods intended for entry level racing. They are forged from 4340 vacuum degassed steel. The "pink" rod was what was used on the Z28 and high powered small block Corvettes and the like, the best production rod. Sportsmans are twice as strong as pink rods and they come in a matched and balanced set. They are a real bargain as they don't cost any more than the Chevy rods. Once again, my selection might be viewed by some as overkill for a purpose built, derated engine.

INTAKE MANIFOLD

Based on my research for a pump gas engine, I expected to obtain 230-250 HP at 5000 RPM. I already knew the racing heads were going to breathe real easy. Choosing the correct intake manifold, camshaft, and the headers would result in a broad torque engine. It is hard to mismatch a broad torque engine to an airframe. They're docile, efficient, and also I wanted maximum efficiency and torque at cruise RPM, 3700 in my application.

The only off the shelf manifold that would bolt up directly to the racing heads was the Chevy race manifold. However, it was tuned for too high of an RPM, 4500-9000, my estimate. I looked at other manifolds including Holley, the stock Chevy and Edelbrock. I chose the Edelbrock performer manifold as it looked the best for what I wanted. The intake runners were near equal in length; they were a little bit small but that's what is needed for good mid-range torque. One major problem arose, the manifold ports wouldn't match the racing heads. In fact, you could place the Edelbrock manifold over the heads and see the head openings! These racing heads have large, high ports. When Chevrolet enlarged the ports on the race design most of the increase was added to the top. With a lot of welding to build up the manifold runners and subsequent grinding I was able to match the manifold to the heads.

ODD FIRE CRANK

I decided to build an odd fire engine, firing at both 90 and 150 degrees. Since there is no throw offset between the opposing cylinders the basic crank is much stronger. On the even fire and the semi-even fire V/6, the rods and bearings are narrowed because each journal is split into two parts. I didn't want that and took the race engine route. The odd fire engine uses standard V/8 style rods which are priced much more competitively. I also learned it was cheaper to buy a matched set of 8 rods than it was to buy 6. Some readers may know that the V/8, the most popular small block Chevy engine, has 100s of performance parts choices. They're all priced so low because there is a lot of competition in that market. The rods and the pistons are a real bargain. Sticking with popular engines saves money.

VALVE SPRINGS

The valve springs supplied with the cam kit were way too stiff. They were probably intended for 7000 RPM operation. Since I was not going to turn my engine at that RPM I ordered a different set of springs to cut that pressure down. No sense subjecting the valve train to any more wear than necessary. The other thing experimenters have to watch is allowable valve lift on a given set of valve springs. The original valve springs supplied me were only rated for an 1/2 inch of valve lift, and my cam was right at a 1/2 inches of valve lift. So there was really no margin; the coil springs would almost bind. I did more research at this point and picked a set with reduced pressure that were not anywhere near to their minimum height at my required 1/2 inch; the coils of the spring, even

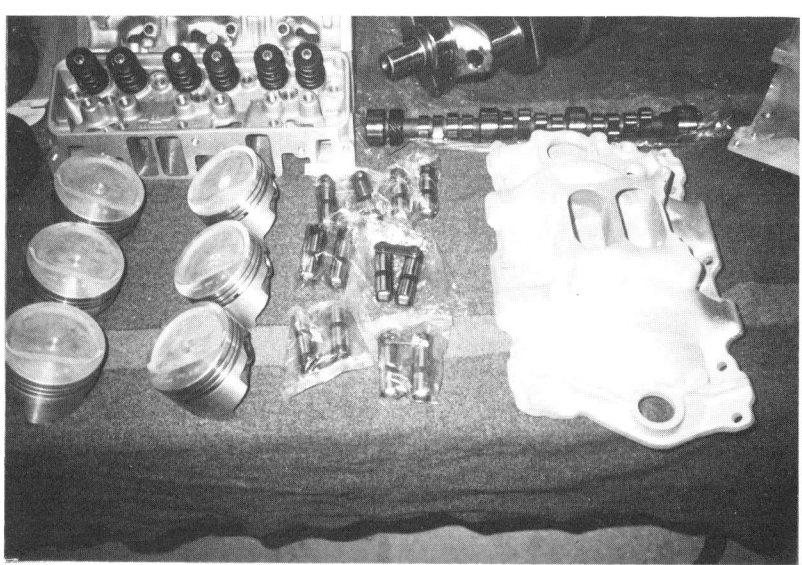

Close up shot of TRW turbo pistons, roller lifters and Edelbrock intake manifold. Relatively small intake runners were effective in producing a wide torque band. Considerable weld build up of intakerunners was necessary to match heads.

at full valve lift, would still be pretty far apart.

I opted for the traditional racing type aluminum roller rockers which work well with the roller cam. Valve guides last longer because valve side thrust is greatly reduced. The new Corvette small block engine incorporates roller rockers.

FUEL SYSTEM

The airplane will have four wet wing fuel tank with a total capacity of about 100 gallons. First, I want a good long range, cross country airplane. It is also because I am cheap. I am one of a few who is not in favor of landing somewhere just to buy some expensive aviation gas. Besides, I am a little leery of buying auto gas at some strange airport. My family lives in Oklahoma and Texas. Being single and flying solo I can load up on fuel and fly home and back and not need to buy gas enroute.

Fuel vapor lock is of serious concern. Here in Colorado, we are forced by EPA to use oxygenated fuel during fall and winter seasons. Vapor lock is a real problem at this high altitude. To reduce vapor lock tendencies I am using the automotive type submersible fuel pumps in each tank. These are recommended in the Chevrolet book for racing applications. They have a 15-18 PSI rating which adequately pumps the fuel up some 42 inches up to the carburetor. Constant fuel pressure to maintain correct fuel flow is necessary under positive G maneuvers. A fuel pressure regulator holding pressure at around 5-6 PSI, is mounted on the firewall at the same height as the carburetor. Tank selection is done manually by turning on the designated fuel pump.

I'm using the Holley 500 CFM 2 barrel, the 34-4412 with the electric mixture control. That's a whole story in itself. We found some design problems with it on the dyno. They were easy to fix but hard to pin point the basic problem.

Cylinder head studs are best for almost any engine but are particularily recommended for aluminum blocks. The Chevy book specifies use of Locktite and torque limits. Fel-Pro head gaskets were used. Note lightweight Tilton starter, double row timing chain.

IGNITION

The distributor that I chose is a MSD racing type distributor. The reason for that choice is that it is a high quality, precision unit. Some may not know that a standard GM distributor is deficient in one respect; its rotor head is swaged onto the shaft. I've had them come loose before. The racing unit is made of high grade steel, its been magnafluxed, it's been heat treated properly, it's TIG welded together properly . . . it's a quality unit.

I opted for electronic ignition. I'm using the MSD ignition system, the multiple spark variety. I have two pick up coils in the distributor, two ignition modules, two ignition coils, and a single distributor. One set of plugs and wires is entirely adequate. If one cylinder should foul or wire fail I still have five running.

TORSIONALS

One important part is the torsional damper. At the beginning of its development it was called a harmonic balancer by General Motors. Its purpose is to dampen torsional vibrations within the crank shaft. The crank shaft and its journals may be compared to a spring. Under firing impulses the crank tends to wind and unwind, acting like a spring. If the engine happens to be operating at an RPM where torque pulses are adding to the springiness of the crank, resonance will occur. Resonance will break a crank in short order.

I called Fluidampr since I was using a custom crank and different material which I believed would have differing torsional characteristics. They build a viscous type of device as opposed to the common inner-outer rings separated by an elastomeric band. They said I wouldn't even need one because the resonance of that specific crank occurs in the 6000 RPM range. Since I would never turn 6000 in my airplane the engine would not see resonance. However, to be safe, I chose the smallest one Fluidampr makes. It has a 6.25 inch diameter and weighs about 6 pounds. I could live with that. The nice feature of viscous damper is that it will dampen a wide range of crank vibration; also, it doesn't have to be tuned to a particular crankshaft. It costs about $200 from a discount mail order catalog.

LUBRICATION

My airplane is not an aerobatic design. As a big four seater I didn't need a dry sump system with a reservoir or an inverted oil system. I kept to the standard automotive type wet sump oiling system. Initially, I made the same mistake that many people seem to repeat. I bought a high volume oil pump. Racers use the high volume unit found on the V/8 and that's a lot more oil pump than needed for ordinary operation. The V/6 doesn't have so many bearings or passages, not a lot of places for the oil to go. The oil volume of the V/6 is less. Excess volume just dumps back into the oil pan and the pumping process uses more horsepower than necessary. So I went back to the standard volume size, a hot rod version of it which has special machining inside the oil pump to produce smoother oil flow, less cavitation but essentially a stock unit. Eventually I'll build a custom aluminum oil pan, but for right now I'm using a plain, stamped steel one.

My oil pressure actually measures about 58 PSI. That's a bit higher than I need. If I were turning 6500-7000 that pressure would be marginal. At my 3700-3800 RPM at cruise, likely less than 5000 RPM at take-off, I could go in there and modify the spring relief which sets the oil pressure and not hurt the engine. I would save a little bit of power but I don't know if the gain is worth the trouble. I wouldn't feel good with it much below 50 so I'll probably just leave it alone.

ACCESSORY DRIVES

Despite the growing use of serpentine belts I chose to use "V" belts. My airplane is all electric and electrical power is needed to keep the engine running because of its electronic ignition. A redundant source of power is necessary, if not desirable. I have two batteries and two alternators, totally isolated. My reasoning was as follows: if the alternator quits when on cross country somewhere the battery may get me to an airport but won't get me home safely. I decided to bite the bullet and install two small alternators and two small batteries. If one system quits I can still safely fly it home. I also have the option of safely flying to an alternative airport instead of a panic emergency landing and repairing the problem in the middle of nowhere.

Since aluminum castings sometimes have porosity problems Fred decided to pressurize his virgin block before assembly. In a recent issue of "Circle Track" one racer trick mentioned was the use of a porous intake manifold to increase the amount of air entering the combustion chamber!

I paid a little weight penalty for that option. I'm using two Nippindenso alternators found on the GEO Metro, Suzuki Sidekick, and the Chevy Sprint. The unit is a beautiful little thing. It does have an internal regulator which some people may not like. It is small, with either 45 amp or a 50 amp output depending on specific model, and weighs about 6 - 6 1/2 pounds.

In my setup each alternator belt also drives the water pump thus providing water pump redundancy. Loss of a single alternator is serious but not critical. Loss of belt power to the water pump is critical thus the weight penalty of the extra alternator and its belt is justified.

I made up custom pulleys because my engine will cruise at 3700-3800 RPM. The alternator's standard, small diameter alternator pulley would mean turning the alternator at about 10,000 RPM. High RPMs are not needed but simply increase wear of the bearings and brushes. I built oversize alternator pulleys to slow them down a little bit, to maintain a more normal operating RPM. I chose aluminum for ease of machining and weight. These were anodized to limit pulley wear.

The degree wheel and dial indicator define the true position of the cam to the crank. Their use eliminates any tolerance build-up in the timing train. Degreeing is also used in cam re-indexing. In general, advance will produce torque at lower RPM, retarding it moves the torque curve up.

OTHER ENGINE COMPONENTS

I used the Cloyes brand roller timing chain set. It is the recognized performance standard for engines. I inserted a Torrington needle thrust bearing set between the upper timing gear and the block. That's important because normally the timing sprocket just rubs against the front of the block. On cast iron engines such contact is OK but on the aluminum block the aluminum will be worn quickly. Actually, my upper timing sprocket is floating between two needle bearings, one on the front and one on the backside.

Most performance people recommend cylinder studs in lieu of head bolts. In my opinion it is the way to go, especially on aluminum blocks. ARP recommends Locktite and a light installation torque of 10 foot-pounds.

Between the reduction drive and propeller is a automotive style driveshaft about 7 feet long. Since I built an odd fire V/6 I didn't know how smooth it was going to be. I decided I could live with a 15 pound flywheel. I wanted as much inertia as I could get in the 15 pounds of weight. There are two fly wheel

Close up views of Carter's engine: (top) twin alternator setup and the dual deep "V" pulley driving water pump; (middle) the high inertia flywheel was lightened with machined slots and (bottom) the Holley on the modified Edelbrock torquer manifold. The intake runners were built up with welding rod about 1/2 inch to match the high rise heads.

sizes you can buy for the small block Chevy, 12.75 inches and 14 inches. I went with the 14 inch size just to get the maximum inertia. I started out with a 30 pound flywheel and machined it down to 15 pounds, leaving most of the weight around the outer edge.

For the head gaskets I chose the Fel-Pro with the embedded wire "O" ring around each combustion chamber. I also chose Fel-Pro for the intake manifold gaskets which come with silk screened silicone rubber seals around each passage opening.

The front timing cover is an light aluminum hot rod part. Stamped aluminum valve covers help reduce weight. The aftermarket starter is about half the weight of the production item. These identical starters are sold under several brand names, from Hamburger to Tilton.

The other thing I did was to chose small tube headers, 1 1/2 inches. The standard small block Chevy would typically use 1 5/8 inch headers, or even a little larger for real high power. I went with 1 1/2 inches because that size boosts mid-range torque. I wanted the broadest torque curve that I could get.

ENGINE ASSEMBLY

I put the engine together carefully spending many days on the assembly process. Precision assembly is not difficult and procedures are explained in detail in performance engine build books. I recommend following the book and you won't overlook any step or have any problem later on. The process is a deliberate one and should take a long time. Checking the clearances on all of the bearings was done at a time consuming "one at a time". The camshaft was degreed in and double checked. When finished with the installation of external parts and assessories I connected the temporary gas tank, the fuel pump and the water tank. The engine started after about two revolutions. I had to adjust the idle speed some and I ran it about 5-8 minutes, then shut it off. My temporary bucket supply of anti-freeze coolant mix was getting hot. That was enough for the first run.

I let the engine cool down. I removed the oil filter, cut it open, and checked it for metal debris, put another oil filter on it, and cranked it up again. The engine ran just beautiful, just perfect. I ran it several times and accumulated about 3-4 hours of running at no load and different RPMs.

DYNAMOMETER WORK

I wanted to dyno test the engine because I wanted

to get the redrive ratio right the first time. Without knowing horsepower and or torque, you really are guessing in specifying the RPM reduction ratio. If your engine is kind of wimpy, then you need to gear it down and turn it a little faster to get the horsepower. If your engine is real strong then there is no point in turning high RPMs. I've been reading hot rodding magazines since the 1960s and I was able to refer to information dealing with small block engines, etc. I found a real good article on dyno testing and build up of the Chevrolet 4.3 V/6 that was published about 6 years ago. It was my best reference. Car Craft magazine took a 4.3, put it on a dyno and started building it step by step, and published incremental horsepower increases. These tests gave me real good ballpark numbers and the types of changes desirable for an airplane engine conversion.

I learned that dynamometer time is generally sold by the day. Dyno shops prefer that the customer bring his engine in the day before, like in the afternoon so they can bolt it up and make sure it runs. This approach minimizes installation hang-ups which can occur occasionally. Then they will crank the engine and run it. Some people will make the costly mistake of bringing in engines that won't run or they will run but not make power. Engines may cut out, they'll bog down, or they'll have some problem of matching to the dyno. In my case it took a couple of hours to set the engine up and get it running. After warm up, the first fully loaded run at a modest RPM resulted in 180 HP. The dyno operator found no unusual noises (a good operator will listen for engine noises) and that the engine would make power. We determined that actual testing could begin the next morning.

Depending on the shop and city a dyno test will cost from $300-$400. If it is more than that, then you are probably getting ripped off. I had mine done here in Colorado Springs on a computer controlled Superflow 901 dynamometer. This shop had huge exhaust mufflers on the roof of the dyno room because this shop is in downtown Colorado Springs. The computer console and the monitor was located outside of the test stand room for safety and isolation reasons.

The console contains some of the necessary gauges. It has the usual analog instruments used by the "human" operator to monitor RPM, torque, HP, temperatures and air flow, all of which when analyzed by the computer program software determine actual and corrected power. The recorded data comes out from the computer printer.

Many dynamometers have several automatic shutdown features. In a typical set-up you will get to preset your limits. If something unusual happens, such as the engine losing oil pressure, exceeding temperatures and especially RPM, the computer instantly shuts down the engine run.

A typical dyno will measure inlet airflow, fuel flow, RPM and torque. Horsepower is a calculated value. Engine load is absorbed by a water brake. Once it is running, you'll see water flow because the water returns to the big reservoir which is open. During these runs we boiled the water out 2 or 3 times and flooded the floor. A dyno shop has headers for every standard auto engine. Unfortunately, this dyno shop did not have any headers for the V/6. I had my own headers but these had to be modified to fit the four inch dyno exhaust system. It was more time and trouble spent. My headers are 1 1/2 inch small tube headers designed for torque. The primary tubes are about 38 inches long from the head flange to the collector.

The dyno test was well worth the money spent on this final stage of engine development. It proved that the engine was mechanically capable of generating sufficient power. It established actual torque/HP values needed for optimizing the redrive ratio. It helped uncover a carburetion problem which might have been difficult to find under ground taxi conditions. It also increased confidence that the engine was ready to fly!

The reader can expect to observe the following steps during the test. The timing is checked and recorded. We started out very conservative, about 34 degrees total. 34 degrees is a little over the factory settings for a small block with a wedge combustion chamber. I had a 1971 Z28, which had a cast iron 350 with 9:1 compression. The factory setting was 32 degrees total. And that was pretty conservative. None of the factories want to set the engine up at its peak because maximum power occurs at the threshold of detonation and destruction. Manufacturers can't afford that problem. They set the timing back, maybe 4 or 5 degrees from the maximum power setting, allowing for carbon build up over time, for lousy fuel, and for various overheating problems.

Aluminum engines tend to run cooler. Thus, one can run about a 1/2 point higher compression ratio with the aluminum engine under the same octane fuel and ambient conditions. Aluminum offers less hot spot problems, better heat conduction and so forth. Actually, racers are concerned with

Computerized dyno console. Analog gages show "real time" test information while the computer stores the data in digital form. Digital switches set the automatic overspeed shutdown limits. The lever on the console table is the throttle lever. Printed results are obtained after runs.

overcooling of the aluminum engines. Some racers will go to the extent of sloshing the cylinder head water passages with a sodium silicate compound to build up an insulating layer.

Most dyno shops want you to bring your own fuel. I took quantities of 87 and 91 unleaded auto pump gas and 100LL av fuel. I made sure to buy the auto oxygenated fuel. I figured if I could get it to run right on that stuff we'd be home free.

TWO DYNO TESTS

There are two kinds of dyno tests. One is called the accelerated dyno test and the other is the step test. I didn't know any of this when I went there and time is money. The accelerated test is the method by which most automotive racing type dyno testing is done. In racing, the object is to pass the other guy. So racers want to know the horsepower that is being delivered while your car is accelerating at a certain rate measured in RPMs per second. Depending on the track length they can program the dyno computer for any anticipated acceleration. In my test, the operator had it programmed for 600 RPM per second. What this means is that one whole test run takes about 4 seconds.

If the beginning RPM is set at, say 2000 RPM the operator will manually adjust the load and throttle until he finally gets the throttle wide open at 2000 RPM. He will then punch a button and the computer will take over from that point and allow it to accelerate up to the preset maximum RPM while the computer is adjusting the load to maintain 600 RPM per second acceleration. Once the preset limit RPM is reached, the engine drops to idle.

The second type of test, the step test, is a steady state test at a fixed RPM. Control is turned over to the computer. The load will be varied over a period of seconds until it determines the maximum HP that the engine can produce at that RPM. Then, it will jump up to the next preset RPM level and it will run there for a while until it determines the most the engine can do at that level. Step by step, the computer works the dyno through the whole RPM power band, until it reaches the preset RPM limit.

That type of test is really what we need for aircraft. A typical step test may take two or three minutes, all at full throttle.

During our step run the V/6 headers began to get red hot. The #6 cylinder would get red hot first, at a medium RPM. As the RPM went up and the test continued that tube would actually cool down a little bit and then cylinder #2 would get red hot. Part of the problem was that I had a two barrel carburetor on a 4 barrel manifold and a 1/4 inch spacer between the carburetor and manifold. My mixture distribution was not good. I needed a 1/2 inch or 1 inch spacer. When running wide open, the throttle blades are vertical and act like guide vanes. With the carburetor sitting almost flat on the manifold, the throttle blades actually stick down inside the manifold. So the air can't turn very easy to get to certain cylinders. I need to move the carburetor a little higher and get that guide vane back up out of the way.

Carter's float bowl test setup. Fuel flows through regulator, flow transducer and filter to bowl. Two return lines fed by the carb main jets have fuel control valves. The bowl has a plexiglass window to reveal float action and fuel bubble formation.

DYNO PROBLEMS

I wanted to get some cruise power and fuel burn data. There is no way in a one shot deal for the operator to program the computer for that type of run. He had to do it manually and wasn't really able to do it. We couldn't get good data without spending another day on it. The other problem was seen at the higher power settings, when flowing quite a bit of fuel. We experienced vapor lock problems. His fuel pump system had to lift fuel out of the gas cans on the floor and push it through his fuel flow metering system. With oxygenated auto gas he could hardly do it. We developed fuel bubbling problems giving us erroneous fuel flow readings.

Once more I must reinforce the idea of being careful with auto gas, especially oxygenated fuel. It is a very gassy, bubbly fuel. Kick an open can of this fuel and you can see bubbles come up. It's like a can of pop. Real gassy, just terrible stuff. This is the reason I went to submersible fuel pumps. Don't try to suck it very far. The fuel should be pushed and kept under pressure. Otherwise, you can incur problems.

CARBURETOR PROBLEMS

At the high fuel flows, at about 15 GPH, we discovered an erratic air/fuel ratio problem. The Holley 34-4412, under steady state conditions, has no moving parts except for the float and needle. There are no rods, no pistons; the only thing in it is the power valve, and at wide open throttle, it doesn't move. Yet the air/fuel ratio was real erratic at high flow/power settings. I concluded the problem must be in the float bowl.

I built my own flow bench for the float bowl using a fuel flow transducer. I could measure the gallons per hour that I was putting through it and perhaps learn what was happening. When you buy a Holley with mixture control you get a different float bowl and float than the traditional "race" float. The problem was the aeration in the float bowl.

To confirm what was happening I installed a plexiglass window on the float bowl and ran a fuel flow test. I discovered the source of my engine problem. The carburetor came with a plastic shield over the needle and seat to disperse the spray but it wasn't totally effective. Fuel was spraying down the sides of the triangular needle body and was shooting through openings stamped in the arm of the float. Through my temporary plexiglass window I could see the fuel spray churning and creating air bubbles. At high power settings, the fuel was going by the needle and seat so fast it was carrying air bubbles clear to the bottom of the bowl. As a result the main jets and the mixture solenoid were ingesting air bubbles at high flow settings. A thin brass sheet from the hobby shop was soldered over the float arm holes which cured the air bubble problem. It was real easy to fix but I never would have found the problem without dyno testing. Finding that problem (which would have otherwise plagued the entire project) was well worth the expense of the dyno runs.

Thus, the 4 second accelerated dyno test is really not long enough to really show up certain fuel flow problems. When we went to running wide open throttle, 3-4 minutes at a crack, we were able to uncover this carburetor fuel/air ratio situation.

Shown is my flow bench for the float bowl system. You don't need the entire carburetor. You don't need the engine. Two hoses pick up the fuel, just where the main jets are. I had two valves here to allow me to extract that fuel from the main jets at whatever rate I wanted. You can watch the aeration of the float bowl. The flow bench is nothing fancy. This is a backyard thing I made! It sure shows the problem. I didn't need any air flow, I just needed to flow the fuel out through the main jets and metering solenoid, then watch what was happening in the float bowl.

The Holley carburetor with the adjustable mixture only allows 20 percent control of the fuel. I wanted more than that because, if jetted properly for sea level, that means that the mixture will go excessively rich above 10-12K feet. Lean as far as it will go but it will still go rich above 12K. I wanted more control than that. So I drilled out the passages to increase the percentages of fuel that goes through the mixture control circuit.

Component Weights	Chevy 4.3	Buick 215
Aluminum block	65	75
Crankshaft	52	40
Pistons/rods	18	20
Cam/sprocket set	16	16
Damper/pulley	10	12
Front cover/oil&water pumps	15	10
Intake manifold	10	12
Valve train/covers/bolts	10	12
Ignition system (1)	8	8
Aluminum heads/complete	40	40
Oil pan/misc bolts	10	15
Carburetor	10	10
Starter	11	20
Flywheel	15	15
Total weight in pounds, dry	290	305

The dyno computer recorded the manifold pressure. At 5000 RPM my engine showed 1.64 inches of mercury drop across the carburetor. That means that the 500 CFM two barrel is really a little too small. I'm losing potential horsepower. Holley recommends not more than 1 inch of mercury drop. I could install a 4 barrel and pick up some more horsepower. We only were able to make 24 dyno runs during that day due to carburetor troubles, tests of three different kinds of fuel, and playing with the ignition timing, and so forth. That was basically a day's work, we quit a little early.

There is very little difference in power of my airplane engine between 34 and 38 degrees total advance. I will run my airplane on the conservative side about 34 degrees. I haven't given up much power but have that important margin over detonation. That safety margin is there for carbon build-up increasing compression ratio, poor quality fuel and engine overheating.

We found no HP difference with the different types of fuel.

With a low compression engine you don't need high octane. When you have excess octane that is actually nothing but resistance to the rate of burning. Higher octane fuels burn slower. Remember, you get the maximum power and efficiency right on the threshold of detonation.

USING DYNO DATA

The importance of dyno test data should not be overlooked. Not knowing the output of a custom built (non stock) engine is a recipe for surprises or worse. The data shows my engine is more powerful than I had expected. Thus, the operating engine RPM will be lower than I had planed. A 1.71:1 reduction ratio would produce 2700 RPM at the prop for an engine speed of 4617. For cruise, the numbers would be 2300 and 3933, respectively. If throttled back to 2200 RPM the engine will turn at 3763 RPM. Using this redrive ratio I am confident the engine should run for a long time at these modest speeds.

The dyno data shows that the 500 CFM 2 barrel carb is dropping 1.64 inches Hg at 5000 RPM. According to Holley catalog information, CFM ratings differ between 2 and 4 barrel carbs. Single and 2 barrel units are rated at a 3.0 inch Hg drop while the 4 barrel carburetors are rated at 1.5 inches Hg.

Thus, more options are open. A few additional HP could be picked up by changing to a larger 4 barrel carburetor having additional flow. Also, the data shows this engine has a lot of low end torque that cannot be used effectively in the airplane. By going to a more agressive cam torque at higher RPMs could be increased. Going further, the intake manifold could be replaced with a unit tuned for higher RPMS, increasing HP. If still more power was needed raising the compression from 8.75:1 to 11:1 would likely increase HP some 20-30 numbers but would require the use of 100LL fuel.

A future Contact! article will document the operation of this engine in my flying Orion. If you are building up a custom engine I will be happy to accept your incoming calls. **FC**

CARTER'S 4.3 LITER (262 IN³) V/6 DYNAMOMETER DATA (raw)

speed RPM	torque ft-#	power HP	fuel burn # per hour	air flow CFM	torque ft-#	power HP	friction HP	volumetric efficiency	mechanical efficency
2500	234	112	68	151	309.5	147.3	18.8	102.8	85.6
2750	245	128	71	178	323.7	169.5	21.7	110.2	85.5
3000	238	136	80	192	315.9	180.4	25	109.5	84.5
3250	238	147	101	207	315.9	195.5	28.4	108.5	83.8
3500	232	155	90	221	309.3	206.1	32.1	108	82.8
3750	230	164	92	234	307	219.2	36.3	106.6	81.9
4000	226	172	97	246	302.8	230.6	40.8	105.2	80.8
4250	216	175	99	263	291	235.5	45.5	105.7	79.4
4500	224	192	109	281	302.1	258.8	50.6	106.5	79.1
4750	225	203	105	296	303.8	274.8	56.2	106.5	78.4
5000	216	205	119	306	292.8	278.8	61.9	104.5	76.8

ADDITONAL COMMENTS

The above chart is a composite of raw and corrected (bold) computer printout data from run #15 made on October 13, 1992. The dyno measured torque, air flow, manifold pressure, atmospheric pressure and air temperature. The computer generated values for HP, air/fuel ratio, BSFC, BSAC, friction HP, plus volumetric and mechanical efficiency. I felt much better after finally seeing the corrected data which took into account the local 8,000 foot density altitude during the dyno runs.

Volumetric efficiency is high which suggests that intake and exhaust dynamics are working very well. Friction HP will come down as oil reaches normal operating conditions. A lighter grade of 100 percent synthetic would also increase HP. Careful selection and matching of camshaft, intake and exhaust system for the engine really paid off. I don't plan to make any additional changes at this time. **FC**

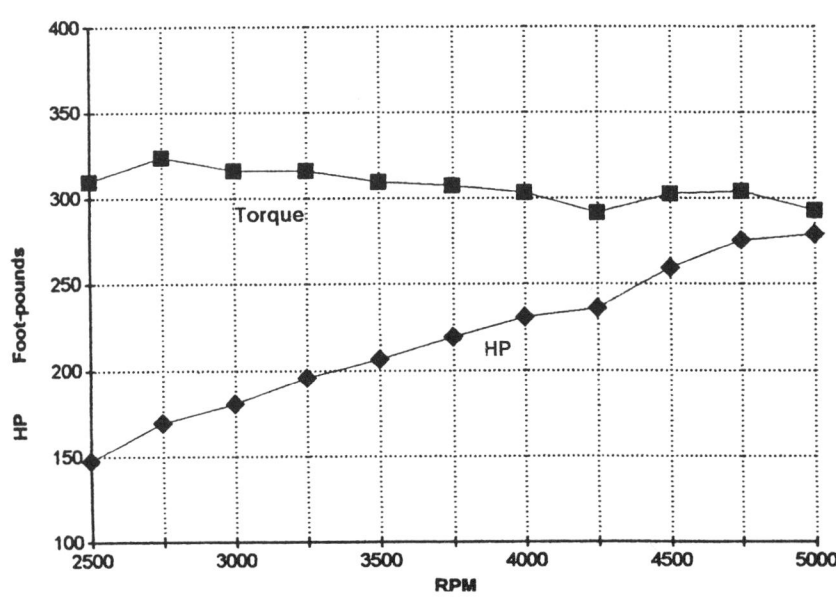

HORSEPOWER/TORQUE PLOT
(corrected to sea level conditions)

MAGNETOS: Be Aware

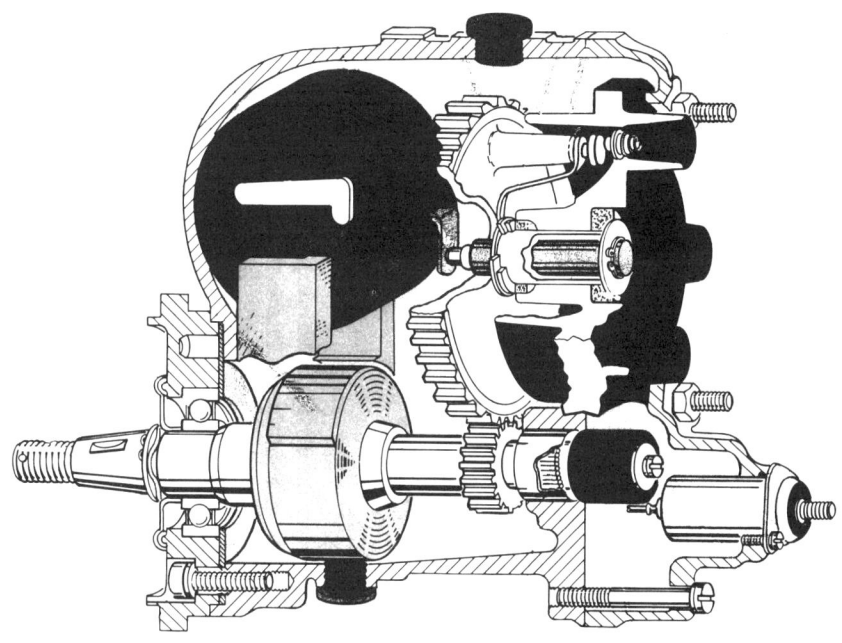

Since 1985, the National Transportation Safety Board (NTSB) has cited magnetos as a cause or factor in 92 accidents involving 22 fatalities and 21 serious injuries. A multitude of Service Difficulty Reports regarding magnetos produced by various manufacturers have been submitted to the FAA during this period. These reports include 130 instances of cracking, burning, arcing, leaking, or other deficiencies in certain magneto ignition coils.

The FAA believes that periodic inspection, overhaul, and replacement of critical components are important fundamental facets of magneto remedial maintenance. However, an examination of accidental reports and Service Difficulty Reports make it clear that the current level of magneto inspection, maintenance, and service is much too infrequent. For example, in 1990, an aircraft sustained a loss of engine power while in flight due to faulty ignition and crashed. An investigation of the magnetos revealed that the same magnetos were installed on this aircraft for 27 years. A review of maintenance records disclosed that the magnetos had been overhauled 21 years ago, but had not been thoroughly inspected since that time. Although annual inspections or 100 hour inspections of the aircraft had been performed by several different inspection/repair facilities, an AD which should have been complied with in 1982 (at the time the aircraft reached 2,000 flight hours) was never accomplished. When the magnetos from the previously mentioned aircraft were mounted on a test stand, both units began to malfunction after 15 to 20 minutes of operation. The obsolete coils in these units were cracked and leaking. Test personnel indicated that the inflight performance of the magnetos would have been worse than experienced on the test stand because of the increased operating temperatures.

When performing annual inspections and 100 hour inspections on reciprocating engine powered aircraft, maintenance personnel are required to run the engine(s) to determine satisfactory performance in accordance with the manufacturers' recommendations regarding power output, static idle, revolutions per minute (RPM), and magnetos. However, this only determines that engine RPM using both magnetos does not drop excessively. The magnetos are not removed and inspected unless a problem is evident. As a result, there is no assurance of the integrity of the components of the magnetos or that the magnetos are capable of continued safe, reliable operation.

Teledyne Continental Motors (TCM) acquired the Bendix ignition system product line and recommends that all of the magnetos in their product line be disassembled and given a detailed inspection at 500 hour intervals. TCM's Service Bulletin No. 632 (as revised), "Maintenance Intervals for all TCM and Bendix Aircraft Magnetos" issued in November 1989, further emphasizes several important inspection/overhaul intervals.

Magnetos are electromechanical devices which use rotating parts and are subject to the same service treatment, environmental conditions, and wear as the engine. Also at engine overhaul, harnesses should be replaced, and ignition switched and starting vibrators should be internally inspected and functionally tested for airworthiness.

Severe environmental operating conditions can affect operating engines as: engine overspeeds, sudden stoppage, immersion, and other circumstances may require complete or partial engine overhaul prior to the overhaul time recommended by the engine manufacturer. The magneto is an integral part of the engine and is subjected to the same degenerating forces as the engine under the abnormal conditions previously listed. In such circumstances, the magneto (regardless of "in service" time) should be overhauled with particular attention focused on all rotating parts, bearings, and electrical components.

There are unknown numbers of airplanes which, because they have been stored or otherwise utilized infrequently, may not have accumulated sufficient total flight time to require that obsolete magneto ignition coils and/or rotating magnets be replaced with more reliable parts in accordance with AD 73-07-04, or other service information. Ignition coils are adversely affected by the environment over relatively long periods of time. They should be replaced and subsequently inspected at conservative intervals of calendar and flight time. (This safety article, attributed to FAA, was published in the January 1993 newsletter of EAA Chapter 81, Tucson Arizona).

The last issue confronted aircraft magneto problems in offering an unique solution which was both practical, effective and inexpensive. Considering that a complete magneto overhaul can cost upwards of $1000 dollars this gross expense is yet another reminder that certified aircraft owners are hostages of the antiquated FAA aircraft type approval certification process.

In view of the present "bogus parts" crisis, a complete overhaul and relaxation of the present regulations relative to the production of alternative engine accessories is necessary and timely. MCM

E-Racer Profile: A Fast Glass Canard Two Place

Shirl Dickey
Shirl Dickey Enterprises
Box 1184
Yarnell, AZ 85362.
(602) 427 6384

Shirl is a 1970 Mechanical Engineering graduate from University of Utah. His long involvement with aviation includes some 15-20 years in the aerospace industry. Working in various capacities on jet engines he also worked on hydraulic systems for Boeing Aircraft, and several other companies. This is a status report on the Buick powered version. Shirl is busy testing his new 4.3 Chevrolet V/6 installation at press time. MCM

I had a lot of interests including boat and motorcycle racing before my beginning in aviation. I got my pilot certificate around 1977; like most people with obligations my pilot training was an on and off situation. I started to build a Varieze from the original plans in 1979 and I finished that plane in 1981. It was an extremely fun, nice little airplane and I developed my flying skills with it to the point where I was actually flying some local aerobatic air shows.

Somewhere along the line, being an engineer and looking for a challenge, I decided that I wanted a little bit more. Basically, I liked the canard layout and Burt Rutan's simple, moldless construction approach. I began by making out a list of design objectives that I would like to have in a new design for a canard type aircraft. That list consisted of automobile engine power, retractable landing gear, side by side seating and several other minor items. I also included cockpit pressurization, floats and a few things that were not too practical. Like most other designers or dreamers, I suppose. We all end up compromising the dream design and rationalize on a few key items. Of great influence on my design criteria was the emergence of the Oshkosh 500 race in the late 1970s. A large cash award was being posted for a high placing, water cooled engine powered airplane called the Downey Prize. The financial incentive of the $5,000 offering helped motivate me to design the basic E-Racer.

DESIGN

The design of the E-Racer deviated from the Rutan tandem designs. I initially wanted a four place. I did a lot of analysis on that, particularly weight and balance, and found that I could not, nor could anyone else, design a four place without weight and balance compromises, which I was unwilling to do. So, when I began the design preliminaries on the E-Racer I essentially stepped back to a two place, side-by-side configuration. I liked the idea immediately. In my opinion it's a sportier aircraft. Since I didn't require the four place seating this alternative allowed me to solve the weight and balance issues by moving the entire cockpit back, closer to the center of gravity. The prototype and the E-Racers being built today by my builders require no special CG management attention because of the aft cockpit location.

The next, most important thing for me to do was to design an acceptable, retractable landing gear system. It was a top priority issue. The airplane would never have been built without this feature. I did not want a fixed gear, Rutan type arrangement or anything else, so the design phase focused on those two criteria. The design of the retracts and the basic layout to solve the weight and balance issue. Those were my two key driving parameters. I did some layouts that looked good. I did some mock-up testing and geometry work and developed the E Racer landing gear to my satisfaction. Thus satisfied, I proceeded with the construction.

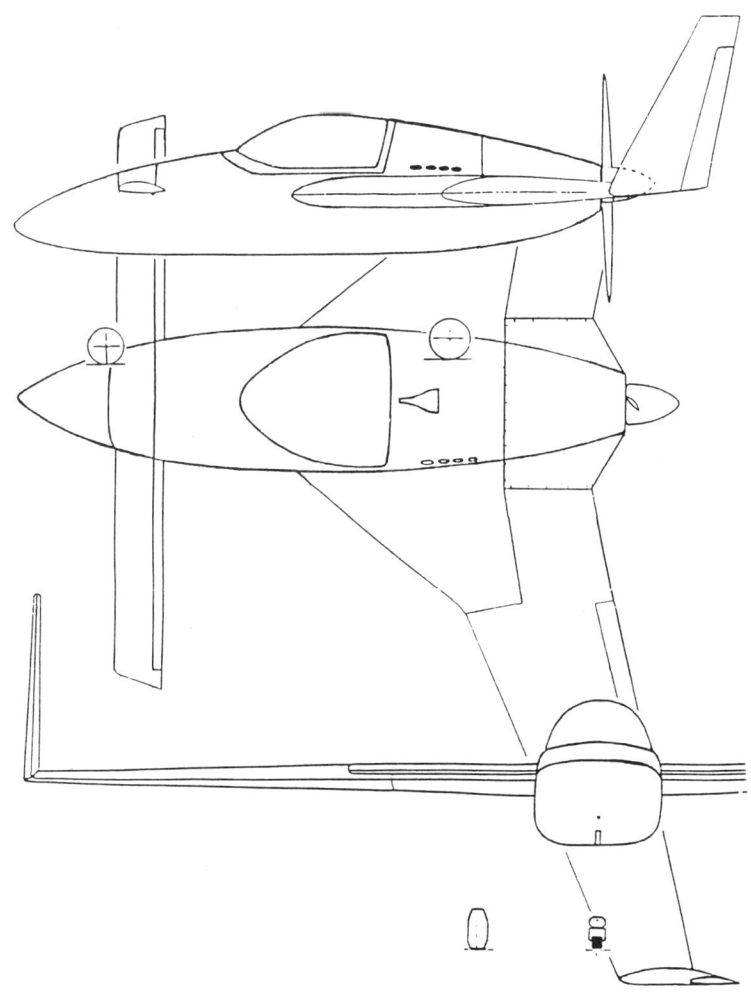

It took me 2 1/2 years to build the airplane from scratch, with no plans, just doing my own engineering as the airplane progressed. The E-Racer is a derivative of a Long EZ; the wing and canard use Long EZ aerodynamics. I did beef up the airframe some, because I wanted a higher gross weight of 1800 pounds. The structural parts of the wings, the spar caps and the shear webs, are now 25 percent thicker than the original Long EZ. Other than those structural changes the wings are essentially the same. I did take the opportunity to take a kink out of the wing trailing edge, which was a compromise on the Long EZ. I didn't feel I needed to keep the original line. I moved the winglets to the forward leading edge of the wings and I eliminated the lower winglet. The basic appearance is not that different from the Long EZ; most people do not see these differences.

The key to the use of an auto engine conversion in this aircraft required an acceptable reduction drive unit. I had a lot of experience with race boats and the use of "V" Drive technology, which is essentially a gear box for high powered race boat applications. I never had a problem with those components. Many of my friends pushing boat racing limits blew engines, twisted prop shafts and drive shafts but they never experienced "V" drive failures. It is an proven power transmission component that has a tremendous history of strength under severe performance demands. I basically took a "V" drive and converted it into what I call a "Z" Drive. I added the propeller extension and the appropriate fuselage structural members to adapt the reduction box for aircraft use. After I was satisfied that this arrangement would work I installed it in the aircraft. For a powerplant I chose the 1961-3 all aluminum Buick V/8. At that time, it was the only available engine that had the features I needed: lightweight, durable, and adequate horsepower. In retrospect it was a good choice for other reasons. Parts and spare engines were readily available as well as a network of people who used these engines in racing applications.

OIL COOLING

The airplane first flew in 1986. My principal problem with the initial test flying were with engine cooling. I had a number of both oil and water cooling problems. Some of those stemmed from design bugs hidden in the engine that I didn't understand at the time. One design inadequacy was the pressure relief valve in the oil pump. This valve caused the engine oil to by-pass the oil cooler; I didn't realize that it was staying open. Very deliberately I went through a number of iterations on cooler sizes, arrangements and other things. Nothing seemed to work until I finally located the source of my problem. I blocked off the pressure relief valve. This change forces the oil to go through the cooler and into the oil filter. The filter now has a bypass in it that will allow it to continue to pressurize the engine if the filter gets plugged up (no filter should but it has happened on rare occasions). With that problem solved it was just a matter of making sure I had adequate air flow and capacity in the oil cooler.

I am very happy with the performance of the oil cooler. Along with that, I am sold on the use of synthetic oils. I find that they hold their viscosity at higher temperatures and they also have a higher temperature capability. I use synthetic oils exclusively in both the engine and the gear box. I have used several different brands. I started off with Amsoil, which I think is a terrific product but has a drawback. It is hard to find outlets for it. I have since switched to Valvoline Synthetic (full synthetic, not the mix), and that is readily available at just about any store. I did that primarily for availability reasons. I believe that they are equivilant to each other, they both have the same capabilities and properties.

LIQUID COOLING

When I began I didn't totally understand what it took to design an engine cooling system. I made some early mistakes such as thinking it was necessary to have a high pressure cooling cap on it. I had a gut feeling that I didn't want to dump anything overboard for any reason so I chose a 20 PSI cap. That was a mistake because the problem with a high pressure cap is that it will store an enormous amount of energy in the cooling system. The result is, as the coolant heats up and expands, it builds pressure. When the cap does blow off it is a violent eruption and a LOT of coolant is lost. So much in fact that the engine no longer has enough coolant to cool the engine. This lack of coolant creates another eruption and at that point the airplane becomes a glider. I was a glider around Utah and Arizona before I figured that out.

The system that works best for me right now is just like the system found in a car. Under engine operation the expanded coolant flows into a coolant recovery bottle which captures anything that would go overboard. When the engine cools atmospheric pressure forces the coolant back into the engine. I use a 12 PSI cap. I always check to see that my cold coolant

SPECIFICATIONS	E-RACER
OVERALL	
span	26.2 ft
length	16.0 ft
height-level	7.6 ft
height-ground	7.6 ft
FUSELAGE	
seats	2+1
frontal area	8.2 sq ft
cockpit width	42.0 in
cockpit height	36.0 in
PERFORMANCE	
Vne	299 mph
Vc, 75% power	210 mph
Va	160 mph
Vs	60 mph
rate of climb	2500 fpm
service ceiling	25000 ft
takeoff, 50 ft obs.	1000 ft
landing, 50 ft obs.	1500 ft
range, 75% power	1000 mi
fuel capacity	46.0 gal
wing loading	19.5 lbpsf
power loading	7.2 php
G load+	9.0
G load -	6.0
WEIGHTS	
gross	1800.0 lb
payload	800 lb
baggage limit	60.0 lb
WING	
span	26.2 ft
area	94.0 sq ft
aspect ratio	8.0
chord-root	Long EZ
chord-tip	Long EZ
CG-fwd	F.S. 97
CG-aft	F.S. 103
airfoil-root	Eppler 1230
airfoil-tip	Eppler 1230
dihedral	0.0 deg
washout	2.7 deg
sweep	23.0 deg
incidence	0.0 deg
AILERONS (each)	
span	5.4 ft
area	2.26 sqft
def-up	25.0 deg
def-down	25.0 deg
type	plain
FLAPS (each)	(none)
span	
area	
type-def	
CANARD	
span	12.25 ft
stab area	8.2 sqft
elevator area	3.0 sq ft
airfoil	Roncz 1145
def-up	15.0 deg
def-down	22.0 deg
incidence	3.0 deg
TAIL (vertical)	
span at rudder	Long EZ
stab area	4.5 sqft
rudder area	1.6 sq ft
airfoil	Eppler 1230
deflection	+25.0, -0 deg
POWERPLANT	
make	Chevrolet 288in^3
HP	260
max RPM	5000
max torque	300 lb-ft
fuel quality	100 LL
PROPELLER	
make	B&T
type	fixed
material	wood
diameter	68.0 in
pitch	88.0 in

level is OK. My header tank has about a quart of air above the coolant liquid level.

Also, I played a little bit with radiator sizing. I now have a radiator that is actually over size which gives me excellent ground cooling. The entire engine cooling system is as reliable as one you would find in any new car. I treat it just like my car; nothing different (except for a thorough annual inspection of the entire system). You really don't have to check the radiator cap every time you fly. I look at my panel mounted coolant pressure gauge to verify the system is intact before take off. I never have had to add coolant and I am extremely pleased with the operation of both the oil cooling and the water cooling.

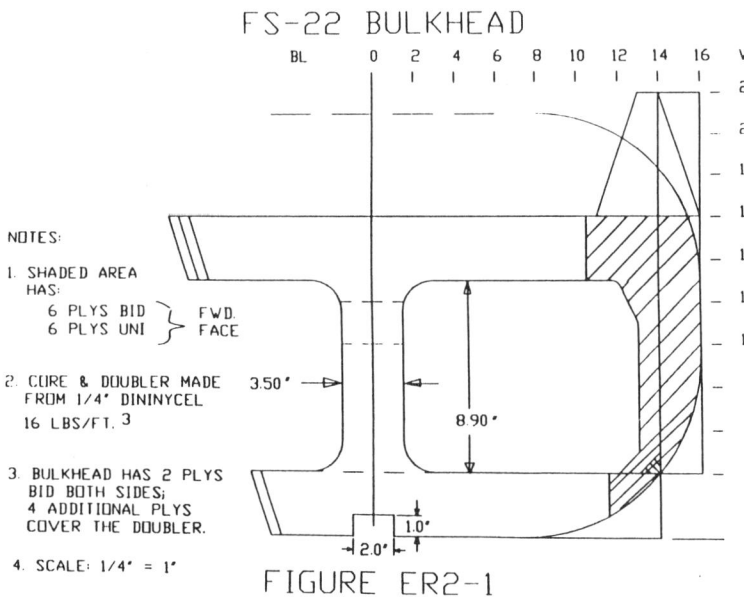

Typical 1/4 scale bulkhead drawing in plans book.

VIBRATION

Early on, I had some concerns about the drive train. It turned out that the drive train was giving me some indications of beat frequencies and harmonics. I was extremely nervous about that so I added a lot of damping features into the drive train. After many flight hours I believe these additions were probably not necessary but I am content I have them anyway. Actually, as it is often the case, I was treating a symptom and not the problem. It turned out that the problem I was having was caused by my straight pipe exhaust system. The engine gases were blowing out of the side of the engine cowling and causing a tremendous disruption to the prop slipstream. The prop was operating in a very turbulent environment, it was very inefficient and it was also creating a lot of drag. The airplane's performance was quite disappointing to me. It wasn't until I changed to a header style exhaust system, that directed the gases in and at the root of the prop, that I achieved a quantum leap in performance. Most will agree prop efficiency is dependent on the air that is running through it. In the case of the E-racer, prop efficiency is adversely affected by the fuselage and the wake of the wing. Further disruption by exhaust gases (think of it as a percentage of engine HP powering the slipstream) will reduce prop efficiency. I found that out in a big way when I changed the exhaust. I had a 20 MPH increase in speed, and my drive train went immediately smooth as a turbo. I now fly a drive train with extreme confidence. It has given me no problems. I have 400 hours on the system now and I am extremely pleased with its reliability.

DRIVELINE

The key to the entire drive system was a rubberized donut device that is found on BMW, Mercedes and FIAT automobiles. These vehicles mount these devices immediately behind the transmission in line with the drive train. They are designed to modulate torsional vibrations. I mounted one of these units from a FIAT vehicle in my drive line at the input to my gear box. That was probably the most important thing that I did. It does not slip, it doesn't generate any appreciable heat. In addition to that, I now have a 16 pound fly wheel that is bolted to the engine crankshaft. It supports the original vibration damper that came with the engine. The entire assembly is carefully balanced. The 26 inch long drive shaft is a simple automotive style shaft, that is 3 inches in diameter, .083 wall thickness. It has a U-joint at the engine end, which is a simple 13-10 series face mount U-joint. There is no vibration isolation to separate these components. The whole system has been trouble free and I have been very happy with it. Those items basically comprise the E-Racer drive system.

The gear box operates in the wake of the radiator at an oil temperature of 160 degrees F. It is a sealed system that is splash lubricated with synthetic oil. I am sure that if it were operating in a cooler area, the temperature would be less than the 160, but of course, 160 is totally adequate. On one of my occasional post flight checks I will go back and lay my hand on the gear box. I find that, by the time that I have taxied and shut down, it is just above body temperature. The only air going to it is the heated air coming off the radiator. No external cooling; it's being heated up. Engineering text books will tell you that a gear train is the lowest loss drive transfer system that there is. I am convinced of that because of my experience with my gear box. There is a little backlash in the gear system, as is with any gear system. That is not a problem provided torque reversals or critical harmonics in the system occur outside the operating range. My system has a critical harmonic at about 300 RPM. At start up, the engine passes through the critical point without any torque reversal and cannot be felt. However, when I shut the engine down, as it passes down through the critical, I do feel one or two torque reversals. It backlashes on the gear.

In flight, there is a positive load on the gears at all times. Absolutely no harmonics, no vibration and no beat frequencies are produced. The situation can be fairly compared to the final drive of your car, the rotational components between the transmission and the tires. You have no sense that these parts are turning. I am very happy with the drive system.

PROPELLER

I use a fixed pitch, wooden prop in order to optimize the auto isolation with a gear reduction. I firmly believe that a variable pitch prop would allow me to obtain better performance but, at this time, I can't afford a variable pitch prop. So I am cruising a little slower than I normally would if I could crank in more manifold pressure and still hold the RPM at my cruising RPM of 4000-4100. My fixed pitch prop limits my performance. During a flight to Oshkosh 1994, cruising at 11,500 feet over Santa Fe, NM, my true air speed varied between 205 and 210 MPH. I was pulling between 17.5 to 18 inches of manifold pressure. That equates to approximately 60-65 percent power. At that power setting I was burning 8 gallons of fuel per hour. That is essentially my cruise set up and I cruise around the country at close to those settings. It will go 240 MPH at sea level at 5000 RPM, but I don't choose to run the engine that fast. With a constant speed propeller these numbers would be improved.

ENGINE

I experienced one engine failure. It was not the engine's fault. I had the desire to have more cubic inches than the small Buick 215 block and I had the block bored out, removing the original steel sleeves. I had them replaced with a much larger diameter, thin wall pressed-in steel sleeve. This modification gave me 298 cubic inches, a 37 percent increase in engine displacement. I operated that engine for about 200 hours before suffering a cylinder wall failure. The cylinder wall cracked from fatigue and lack of sufficient block support. Most engine builders do not recommend going over a 3.7 inch bore on these 1961-63 blocks but I did not know of that experience beforehand.

I then obtained another block. A typical bore clean up is .030 inch over the original 3.5 inch bore. That left me with the original cast iron sleeves, which of course were cast in place with the pour of the 356 alloy block. It also gave me the original substantial aluminum structure that backed that sleeve up. I am back with the original block structure, a very strong cylinder configuration proven in high HP output racing applications. This was a compromise from my original but weak engine. Displacement was reduced down to 266 in2. The compression ratio was reduced from 10:1 to 8.5:1. These changes cost me an estimated 25-30 HP. On the plus side, the aircraft is now much more reliable. I feel a lot better flying it but it's not as fast. I haven't lost anything in cruise because I still run 4,000 RPM but it takes more manifold pressure (throttle) to do it. With a larger engine, I could develop the same amount of horsepower at 15-16 inches of manifold pressure.

The difference occurs at full throttle as evidenced by my Jackpot race performances. At 7,000 foot altitude, the original aircraft was running at about 232-235 MPH. It now runs about 10 MPH less. I ran Jackpot last year at 222 with the smaller displacement engine. I've lost about 10 MPH in top speed but I still can cruise at the same cruise speed as before because I'm still cruising at part throttle. It just takes more manifold pressure to do it. It takes the same amount of fuel to generate the same amount of horsepower. One of the only things I notice with the smaller bore is that it runs a little cooler. The engine operates at a slightly cooler temperature. My plan right now to compensate for the loss in power is to turbocharge the smaller motor. The Buick 215 has strong cylinders. I am very comfortable with every other part of the motor. I am going to use a very conservative setup to regain approximately 30 percent increase in power. At sea level that is only a 2 PSI boost above ambient, a small number which is easily handled. I don't want to get into detonation problems.

ENGINE BUILD

What is in the engine? The only things I kept from the original 215 was the block and the oil pan, both of which were modified. My engine uses a Buick 300 crank, with the main journals turned down. It uses a different rear main seal and support that I bought from Dan LaGrou in Michigan (Contact! issue #25). I use Chevrolet rods, small journal 327 high performance rods, that have to be narrowed 1/10 of an inch, to fit the journal. I'm using TRW forged pistons, 8.5:1 compression ratio. It uses Buick 300 heads, which have bigger valves, and bigger ports. I have an Edelbrock performer manifold that was speced for the Rover V/8 and, of course, it bolts right on. I use a 750 Holley 4 barrel with a mixture device that I invented and Tom McNealy manufactured for me. He collaborated on some of the design as well.

The cam is a Crower product from San Diego. It has about .450 inches of lift, about 222 degrees duration at .050 lift. It is a hydraulic lifter cam. I use the Buick 300 front cover and oil pump, simply because it places the fuel filter in a more favorable location. It also has a timing mark that matches the Buick 300 harmonic balancer. The engine is mounted in the airframe with a very simple four point mount. The engine is isolated from the airframe by .25 inch rubber pads, that's all that is required to dampen the engine. It runs very smooth, and I don't have any vibrations that transfer into the airframe. I use a standard water pump. The only modifications are with the inlet hoses to redirect the hose in a more favorable direction. I use nothing but a new water pump. One reason I don't recommend a rebuilt pump, cavitation erosion occurs around the impellers and in the housing which widen the gaps and make the rebuilt water pump less efficient. A stock water pump is extremely good. Everything else is pretty much standard.

I use a Vertex single ignition magneto at this time. However, I am looking at other ignition options. I have, in mind, concepts that will allow me to have a back-up ignition. The reason I am interested in that is I did have an ignition, actually a tachometer failure, coming out of Dubuque, IA back in 1988. The forced landing tore up my airplane pretty bad. When the tach shorted out it took the ignition and engine with it. It happened during take off, the worse possible time, and

I did an off airport landing. It was within the airport boundary, but it was in the dirt. The aircraft traveled about 60 feet and then the main gear and the nose gear collapsed. It slid the rest of the way on its belly. I walked away from it without a scratch. The strength of Rutan composite construction once again was proven, allowing the aircraft to be rebuilt.

FUEL SYSTEM

The fuel system consists of a stock, engine mounted fuel pump and an electric boost pump. Normally, I only use the boost pump for take offs and landings. I operate in the mechanical pump mode during cruise. The reason I do that is because its a way for me to verify that the mechanical pump is functioning. Also, this method conserves the boost pump. Earlier this year I experienced a fuel pump failure. The actuation rod came loose and would not allow the fuel pump to operate properly. The boost pump brought me home on that deal. I am very critical when selecting a fuel pump, making sure that the pivot point for its rocker arm is not staked in place. I avoid upset metal, where manufacturers stake the aluminum housing to retain the pivot pin. I found a newly manufactured fuel pump available from NAPA that has a pin running through a solid aluminum housing that is removable and does not have any staking. It's the only fuel pump design I would recommend for any this auto engine conversion. Unfortunately, I found that virtually all fuel pumps from different manufacturers use the staking method, which failed on me. That's a caveat for anybody that is using this engine.

The boost pump is a simple Facet unit. It puts out 6 PSI. I am not sure what the flow rate is but it is adequate for my airplane. I've used one on my Varieze for years and found it totally acceptable. A cube like shape, it is commonly used by home builders.

CRANKSHAFT

The crankshaft is machined from a nodular iron casting, specially formulated for the purpose (not pot belly stove cast iron). Experimenters need to understand that a cast crank has higher fatigue capability than a forged crank. In endurance applications fatigue life is much more important than structural strength. Case in point. If you study D9 bulldozers and huge industrial diesels you will see they all use cast cranks. Contrary to popular expectations these engines are not highly stressed. Now if one is producing thousands of horsepower in a drag race car, structural integrity is much more important than endurance. Here, I want to stress one of the most important things about any aircraft application, which uses an automobile or any other engine for that matter. The engine must be built for the application. If you take your engine to a typical Hot Rod shop they will very likely build you an engine that will go good in a hot rod but will probably suffer problems in an aircraft, Endurance and reliability should be foremost before you can even think about horsepower.

LANDING GEAR

The main landing gear design went through a number of iterations before I reached the point where I am now very pleased with its performance. It had some problems early on. I made the legs out of fiberglass layups initially and found that I had some high stress areas and delaminations. I ultimately switched to carbon fiber composite for the landing gear. I have changed the pivot bolt from 5/16 to 3/8 inch. Although the original design was adequate some people may land harder than I do. Also, I no longer specify flange bearings with which some people have had trouble (since I was swapping engines I made these changes recently).

To address the possibility of excessively hard landings, I have structurally beefed up the landing gear to the point now where it is a very strong, very effective landing gear that has no problems. The landing gear was selected by Dave Ronnenberg for the use on the Berkut. I am his supplier; in fact, he inadvertently tested the gear for me that uncovered a slight problem that was occurring around the pivot bolt. He dropped his airplane in from about 15 feet and put 5 Gs of impact load on his meter. The landing gear cracked in a small area around the pivot. As a result of his experience, which goes way beyond anything that one would normally expect, I have changed my design to a solid steel tube insert for the bolt rather than sleeves from each end. I have also increased the bolt diameter to 3/8 inch. Also, I have incorporated stronger mono balls on either side of the pivot, instead of the flange bearings. That describes the configuration being delivered to my builders at this time. I want to make sure that everyone understands that the E-Racer landing gear had some problems and that these problems led to solutions. The production E-Racer landing gear is an extremely fine unit. Ronnenberg has over 1,000 hours on his landing gear system, and can't say enough about it. I feel the same way. Being the designer and tester was a responsibility I assumed when I began to sell plans. I believe I have lived up to that responsibility.

CANARD

Originally, my Varieze used the GU airfoil for the canard surface, like most others built early on. Aircraft pitch trim behavior was unusual in that about 25 percent of the EZs trimmed up, the other 75 percent trimmed down. The severity of the trim varied from airplane to airplane. My Varieze canard had an uptrim. I never considered it to be a problem because the trimmed up configuration was basically safe as far as I was concerned. Besides, it was a small amount, easily trimmable. But because of this problem (I suppose some could call it that) John Roncz and Burt Rutan got together. They went through several iterations on airfoil design and ultimately designed what is now commonly referred to as the Roncz Canard. I used this airfoil without modification on the E Racer. I am extremely pleased with its performance.

PLANS STATUS

At this time (Summer 1995), I am almost right at 271 sets of plans that have been delivered and indications are that others are seriously considering building the E-Racer.

The plans initially started out in pretty rough shape. They have steadily been evolving to the point where they are now a very complete, high quality set of plans. I am also updating plans for people who have bought previously and they also will get, if they haven't already, all of the updates that have been developed up to this point.

Four airplanes have flown at this time, myself and three others with aircraft engines. Two of the airplanes were O-360s and one O-320. Mark I auto powered configuration and the Mark II airplanes with aircooled engines are now flying. A number of other builders getting close to completion; one is a supercharged Chevy V/6 E-Racer that will probably fly later this year. He is out of the Chicago area. There is another Buick V/8 powered E-Racer that will probably fly in a year or less; he is out of the Sacramento area. There are a number of other projects that are not as far along as those.

About 75 percent of the builders are opting for aircraft engines and 25 percent are putting in various automobile engines. I fully support both configurations; each have their own pluses and minuses. The auto engine of course, is going to be a lower cost and higher performance installation. On one hand, it is somewhat limited in its baggage volume. The auto engine installation takes up two major bays in the airplane, thus limits the ability to take a lot of baggage. On the other hand, if a builder installs an aircraft engine on an E-Racer, on the back behind the spar like a Long EZ, he ends up with a huge baggage volume behind the two front seats.

Thus, the individual builder has the option of choosing between aircraft or auto conversion (of which many I support and am interested in). Basic limitations on what engine can be used in an E-Racer are horsepower and weight limitations. I would not recommend any engine in excess of 300 pounds no matter what it is. I would not recommend any engine producing more than 300 horsepower. Those are basically my limiting factors on an auto engine selection.

As far as the gear box is concerned, I have had people ask me if they can substitute a belt drive or a planetary system, or something else. Essentially, the auto engine version aircraft is designed around a specific gear box, which fits the shape of aft fuselage nicely. It has a 4 inch center to center distance between the input and output shaft. It has a structural strength capable 10 times the normal horsepower input. It only weighs 50 pounds. In my opinion, it is absolutely the best choice for an E-Racer. Belt redrives typically have a much larger center to center distance which would cause a big bulge on the back of the aft cowling. Personally, I don't believe a belt has the capability of handling horsepower like my gear box has. I am not opposed to belts; they just don't fit the E-Racer design very well. Obviously, they are extremely successful in other applications and that's fine. A similar situation exists with respect to planetary systems, they're concentric with the crankshaft and their use would result in a 4 inch loss in prop clearance. The Ross unit is great but for higher HP outputs I would like to see a little more structural strength. For those able to use a concentric drive Ross offers several versions of his design.

Long EZ components are commonly used. Keith Outwater's nose gear structure and hardware shows careful attention to detail.

I recommend using the specified gear box. The weight of the gear box includes everything from the input coupler to the prop flange. It does not include the prop, the vibration device which bolts to the coupler or the drive shaft. I have a 26 inch long drive shaft. The gear set has a 4 inch center to center spacing. The helical cut spur gears are 1.5 inches wide. The box is manufactured by Casale Engineering to my specifications. I provide the aircraft version exclusively because internal changes to splines, gears and gear ratios are different than those used in boats. I can provide any mechanical ratio between 1:1 and 2:1 that a builder would like. I also provide the aircraft adaptation parts which include the prop extension shaft, necessary thrust bearings, the external truss structure, the coupler and the flanges.

SUMMARY

The E-Racer is the safest, most advanced and versatile Rutan derivative on the homebuilt market today. It is the only design that will accommodate auto conversions (Mk I) or aircraft engines (Mk II) without compromise. It is the only design that will accommodate large sized occupants (King Racer Version). Its retractable gear offers low drag and pleasing aesthetics without compromising strength or safey. A major safety feature is that CG envelope re-ballasting is not required when flown either solo or as a two-place.

Couple these design and performance advantages with new prefab components (now available from Glassic Composites Company, Dayton, Tennessee) and builders have a superb performing, easy to build airplane that is light years ahead of its competition. **SD**

E-Racer
Powerplant Installation

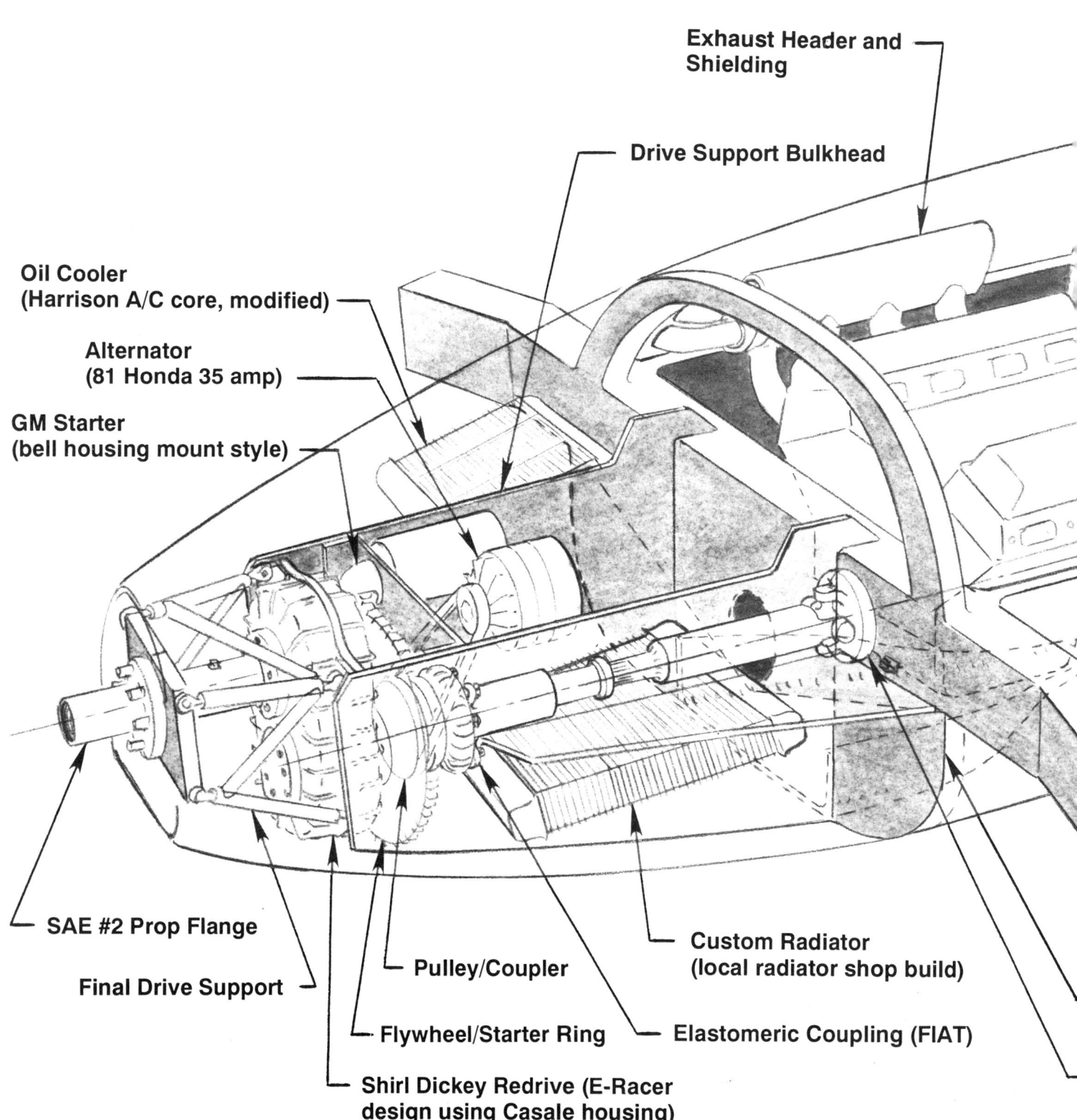

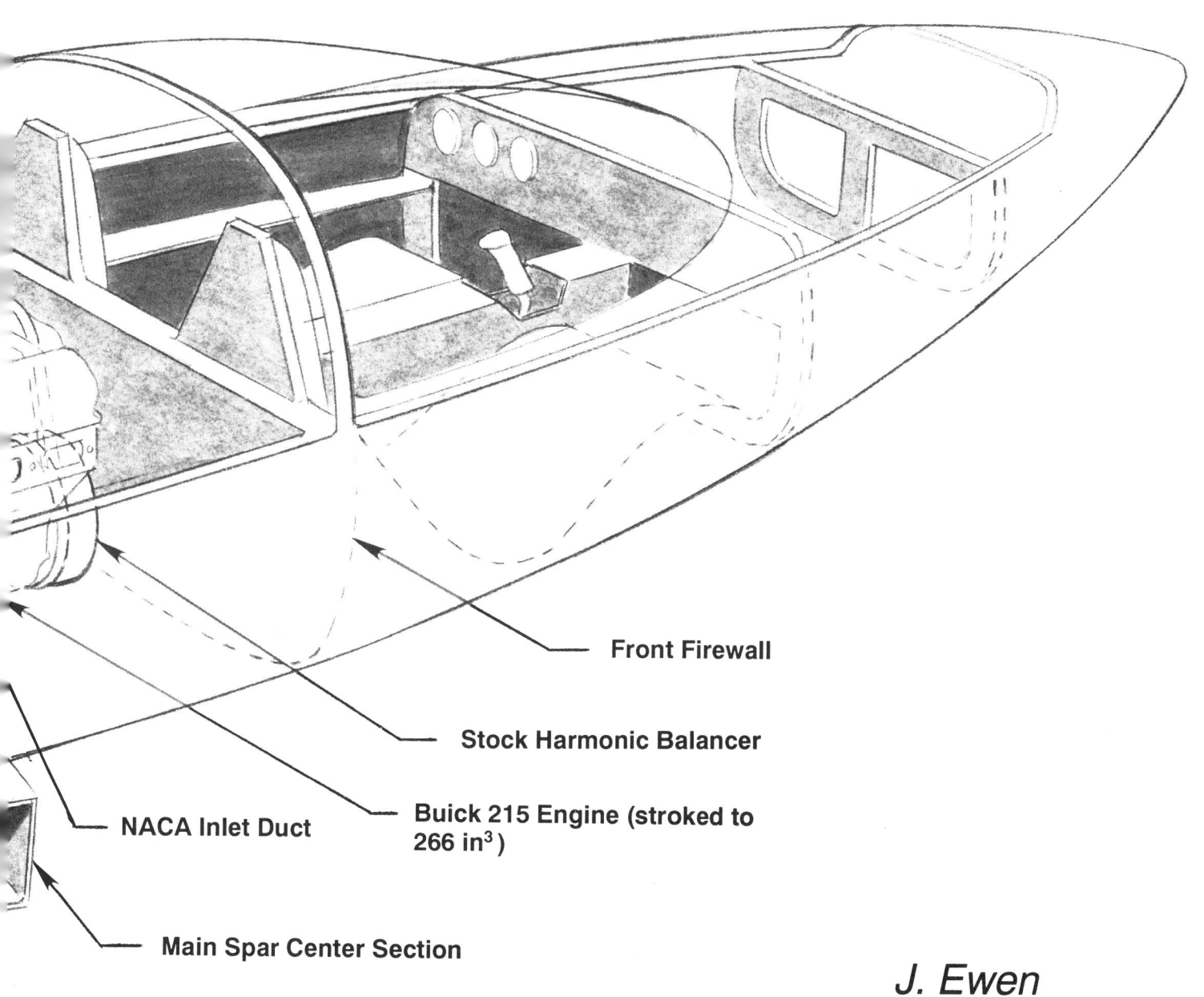

Review of Liquid-Cooled Aircraft Engine Installation Aerodynamics

S. J. Miley
Texas A&M University
College Station, Texas

(Originally published in Journal of Aircraft, March 1988, © 1987 AIAA- Reprinted with permission.)

The aerodynamic behavior of liquid-cooled aircraft engine cooling installations is reviewed. Design considerations for inlets, diffusers, and exists are discussed. It is shown that the design of an efficient liquid-cooled installation is a technically sophisticated problem. This problem should not be underestimated in the development program of liquid-cooled aircraft engines. Questions are raised concerning the availability of suitable radiators for aircraft installations.

INTRODUCTION

To many, liquid-cooled aircraft engines seem to have an aura, a fascination that has not been given to air-cooled engines. Some of this is certainly due to aesthetics. Liquid-cooled engines are synonymous with streamlining and aerodynamically clean profiles. The connection is readily made to the legendary Spitfire, Mustang, and Messerschmitt. The unappealing radial-air cooled engine does not enjoy this subjective attribute. Today's horizontally-opposed air-cooled engines fare no better. The mention of liquid-cooling immediately stimulates designers to visualizing low-drag shapes and improved performance, and stimulates marketing to thinking in terms of lightning-bolt and shark-mouth paint schemes. However, if more objective criteria are applied, the air-cooled engine compares more favorably with the liquid-cooled engine.

It is apparent from literature during the l930's period that each had strong proponents and that it was relatively easy to start an argument over the relative merits of each. Most of the same technical points apply today. The author, though, will separate these points into propulsion concerns and aerodynamic design concerns. From the standpoint of propulsion, the liquid-cooled engine offers better fuel efficiency and longer engine life. Better control of cooling paths and subsequently of component cooling is realizable. On the other hand, the air-cooled engine offers system simplicity and is less vulnerable to system component failure. The weight of the cooling system is less. From the standpoint of external aerodynamic design, the liquid-cooled engine offers reduced frontal area and the potential for reduced drag, particularly compressibility drag. The internal combustion engine aircraft speed record was held by a liquid-cooled engine; however, it is now held by a radial air-cooled engine. Engine power must be factored into the comparison. Ground cooling is more of a problem for liquid-cooled engines. From the standpoint of internal aerodynamic design, the liquid-cooled engine has a definite advantage. Aerodynamically, each component of the system is in theory well behaved, i.e., no separated flows. The liquid-cooling system is more tractable to analytical aerodynamic modeling and design. The horizontally-opposed air-cooled engine configuration leads to large separated flows, because the relatively large internal volumes and ducting necessary to do otherwise are not practical. This is inherent in the geometry of the engine. The radial air-cooled engine configuration is aerodynamically much easier to deal with.

Liquid-cooled aircraft engines are presently available up to approximately 400 hp. There are developmental programs under way that could extend this range. In some cases, these are derivatives of automobile engines; in other cases, these are unique designs, such as the rotary type. The author's recent experience with one of these programs has brought forward an appreciation for the level of technology required to design an effective and efficient liquid-cooled installation. The technical problem of achieving the required cooling for minimum drag penalty should not be underestimated. It is the purpose of this paper to identify and discuss the various design problems of a liquid-cooled installation, indicating, where possible, what is known and what is unknown. Much of the information in this paper is taken from literature, particularly the works of Kuchemann and Weber.

BACKGROUND

The first technical problem one encounters in aircraft liquid-cooling systems is the lack of current information. The state of the art is World War II, and this is where one must look for technical guidance. Immediately it is seen that there is very little available. The United States was far more successful in the development of air-cooled engines than liquid-cooled, and this is reflected in the literature. Success here is defined in terms of military requirements rather then civilian commercial requirements. The U.S. did produce liquid-cooled engine powered aircraft, but the engines were deficient in altitude performance in the European theater compared to their British and German counterparts.

Presently there are only three practical sources of information: the NASA Langley Research Center Technical Library, the Library of Congress, and the National Air and Space Museum. The key to building a data base in this area is to concentrate on foreign technology, principally German. What remains of the American developed technology is covered by the NACA indices. The few other documents that remain from industry and military programs can be found at the NASA library. The foreign programs of interest are the British and German efforts. Much of the British activity is inaccessible from the United States. While references to British documents, are available at the NASA library, a large number of these still carry World War II classified status. Up to this point, there has been no reliable mechanism for determining which have been declassified by the British government; consequently, the WW II classified status is still in effect, and these documents are unavailable. There are two sources of German work, the National Technical Information Service (NTIS) and the "Operation Paper Clip" (OPC) collection at the National Air and Space Museum. There were numerous copies of the OPC collection available after World War II, but the only remaining one to the author's knowledge is in the Air and Space Museum. Concerning German work, the OPC collection is by far the most extensive, containing in excess of 500 documents. The NTIS holdings are less but contain more English translations. Copies of NTIS documents can be obtained from the PB Copy Center at the Library of Congress. A significant part of the German data concern radiator design and testing. The remainder deal with internal/external aerodynamics. A representative summary of the German work in installation aerodynamics can be found in Kuchemann and Weber[1,2] and Hoerner[3]. Regarding Refs. 1-3, they are considered essential by the author if one is to be effective in this area. Kuchemann and Weber provide the basics of the analytical modeling of the various aerodynamic components. Hoerner provides design information, much of it empirical, which is important not only for initial design cuts but also for verification of computational models.

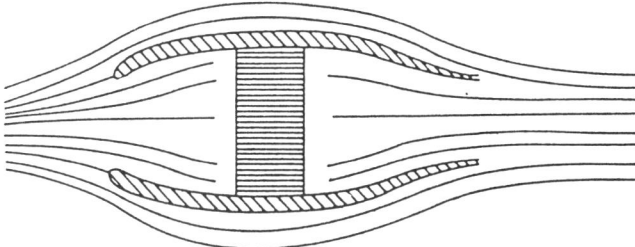

Fig. 1. Simple ducted radiator system

INSTALLATION AERODYNAMICS

The prime component of the liquid-cooling system is the liquid/air heat exchanger or radiator. The purpose of the installation is to convey the required amount of cooling air mass flow to the radiator and then exhaust the heated air to the external flow. A simplified system is shown in Fig. 1. Because of the velocity differential between the external free stream and that required by the radiator; the inlet area may be only 20 to 30 percent of the frontal area of the radiator. The aerodynamic components then consist of the inlet, the diffuser, the radiator, and the exit. Each of these components presents particular design problems that must be addressed if the system is to operate efficiently.

A representative liquid-cooling installation is shown in Fig. 2. Here a common inlet supplies three different radiators, each with different flow requirements and flow characteristics. Many times, restrictions on the available internal volume require slanting the radiators and/or ducting so that the airflow enters and leaves at oblique angles in relation to the radiator core passages. Figure 2 represents the "real world" design problem, as opposed to Fig. 1.

INLETS The aerodynamic operation of an inlet has some similarity to that of an airfoil. The lip contour and the locations of the stagnation point on the lip determine whether the inlet operates with attached flow or separated flow. This is illustrated in Figs. 3 and 4. Consider first an airfoil; as the angle of attach increases in the positive direction, the stagnation point moves to the lower surface and the acceleration of the flow around the nose contour produces a suction pressure peak on the upper surface followed by an adverse pressure gradiant that ultimately leads to separation. As the angle of attack increases in the negative direction, the stagnation point moves to the upper surface, resulting in a suction peak and ultimate separation on the lower surface.

In the case of an inlet, the inlet velocity ratio has a similar effect. Referring to Fig. 4, as the velocity ratio is decreased, the stagnation point moves to the inside of the inlet, producing a suction peak and possible separation on the outer surface. As the velocity ratio is increased, the stagnation point moves to the outside, causing a suction peak and separation on the inner surface. Inlets with relative thick lip contours, like thicker airfoils, have a wider range of operation than those with thin contours. The penalty is similar also in that thicker lip contours lead to increased frontal area and increased drag. A reasonable range of velocity ratios is

$$0.3 < V_i / V_o < 0.7 \qquad (1)$$

where V_i is velocity at the inlet and V_o is the free stream velocity. Values outside this range would require special attention to inlet lip contour design. Relative changes in inlet velocity ratio for a liquid-cooled installation in a fighter aircraft due to altitude are shown in Fig. 5. The data are taken from Katzoff[4]. The curves were

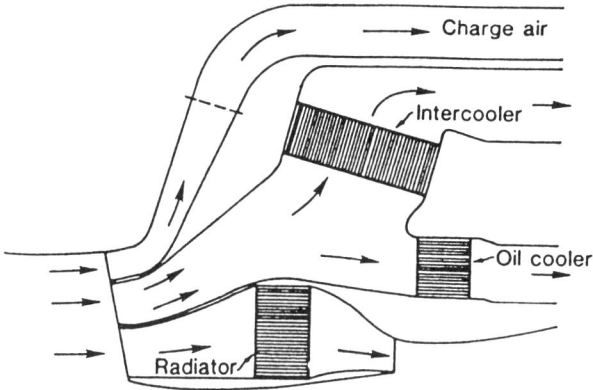

Fig .2. Representative liquid-cooled engine installation

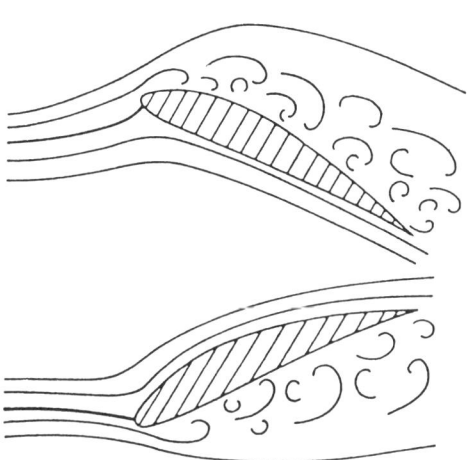

Fig. 3. Effect of stagnation point location on airfoil separation.

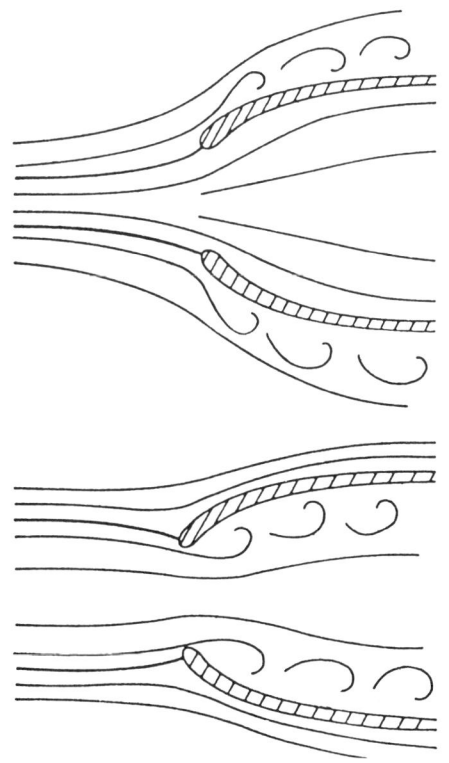

Fig. 4. Effect of stagnation point on inlet separation.

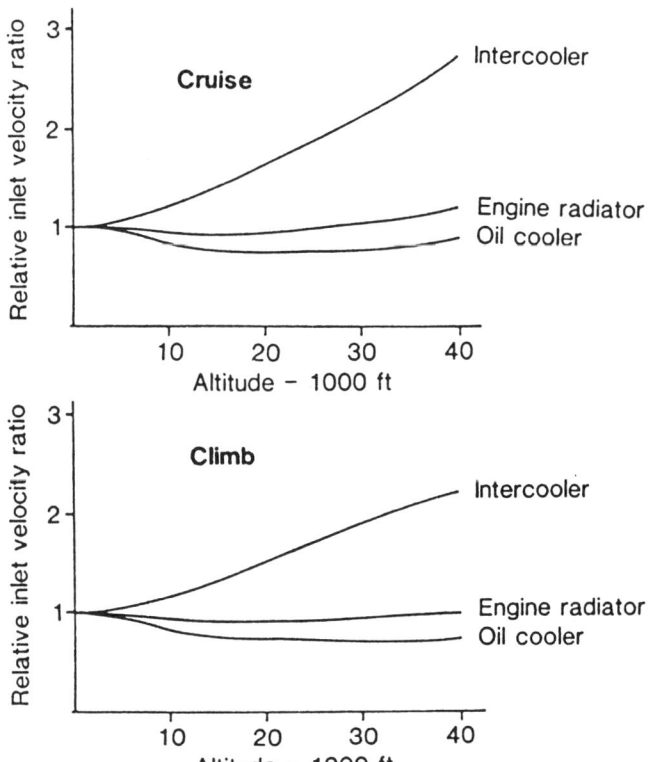

Fig. 5. Relative inlet velocity as affected by altitude.

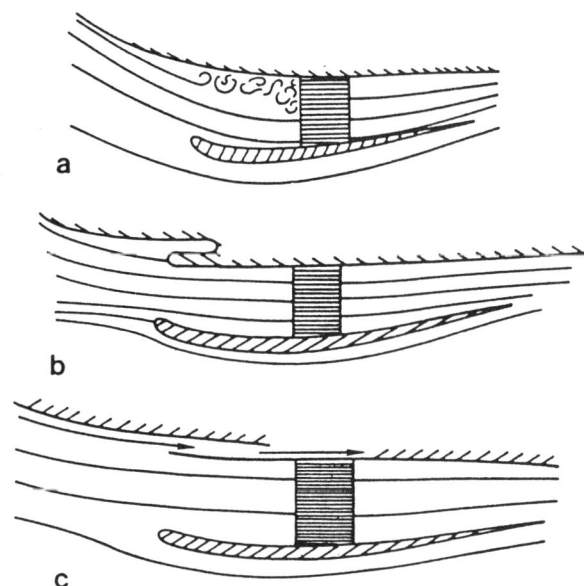

Fig. 6. Underslung inlet installation: a) airframe surface boundary layer separation; b) offset from airframe boundary layer; and c) diversion of airframe boundary layer.

obtained by dividing the radiator-required volume flow by the aircraft true velocity. No information was given concerning the appropriate inlet area. The relative inlet velocity ratio differs from the actual value by a constant which is the reciprocal of the inlet area. For a given installed power, and thus the same cooling air mass flow requirement, the inlet area and therefore the constant will depend on the speed performance of the aircraft. A high-speed aircraft will required a smaller inlet area to pass the necessary mass flow, whereas a low-speed aircraft will require a larger inlet area to pass the mass flow. The issue in Fig. 5, however, is not the value of the constant but the change in the inlet velocity ratio that occurs over the performance envelope of the aircraft. It is seen in Fig. 5 that the engine and oil radiator-cooling air mass flow requirements result in a nearly constant inlet velocity ratio. The inlet(s) for these components could be optimized for a narrow range of operation. On the other hand, the intercooler radiator-cooling air mass flow requirements can alter the inlet velocity ratio by a factor of almost three. Referring to Eq. (1), this will exceed the normal good operating range of the inlet, and one now has an aerodynamic design problem to contend with. The heat rejection load on the intercooler increases with altitude because of the corresponding increase in pressure rise across the supercharger necessary to maintain a given power. Recent design analyses by the author for a liquid cooled intercooler installation on a light twin-engine aircraft resulted in inlet velocity ratios in excess of 2 at 20,000 ft altitude compared to sea level. This relatively wide range of inlet operation called for special attention to lip contour design.

When considering inlets, a distinction must be made between three-dimensional nose or underslung geometries and two-dimensional wing mounted geometries. Each geometry has its own particular aerodynamic behavior, and accordingly, the lip contours will be different. Care should be used when applying 3-D inlet lip contours to a 2-D inlet, and vice versa. The stagger or sweep of the inlet causes changes in the flow such that the forward lip velocity is reduced and the rearward lip velocity is increased. The lip pressure distributions change with the inlet angle of attack, according to the movement of the stagnation point. An increase in angle of attack moves the stagnation point to the inside on the upper lip and to the outside on the lower lip, increasing pressure peaks and the possibility of separation as previously discussed.

Care must be exercised in the use of underslung or protruding inlets. The aerodynamic behavior of 3-D or 2-D inlet depends on the lip geometry. If a fuselage or wing surface is used as one side of the inlet, the original inlet geometry is altered, and the flow over the lip contours may be different than planned. Design procedures for these types of inlets are given by Brodel[5] and Ruden[6]. The relatively thick boundary layer on the airframe surface often separates in the adverse pressure field of the inlet, reducing pressure recovery and increasing drag. This is illustrated in Fig. 6, along with current design solutions.

A summary of inlet design methodology is given by Kuchemann and Weber[1]. A bibliographic listing of inlet related technology is given by NACA[7]. It should be mentioned here that the analytical design procedures given in Ref. 1, 6, and 7, were developed prior to programmable computers. They use classic hydrodynamics formulations. They are amenable to digital programming, but one should have some knowledge of hydrodynamics before undertaking the task.

RADIATORS The operating theory of liquid/air exchangers will not be dealt with in this article. Interested readers are advised to consult Kays and London[8], Fraas and Ozisik[9], and the Military Vehicle Power Plant Cooling Handbook[10]. Aerodynamically, the radiator behaves as a orifice, causing a pressure drop in the duct which is a function of the flow velocity through the radiator. For a specific core configuration, the relationship between the flow velocity and the pressure drop is altitude-dependent, being primarily influenced by the air density. The pressure drop characteristics can often be represented by

$$w = a(\sigma_{ex}\Delta p)^b \qquad (2)$$

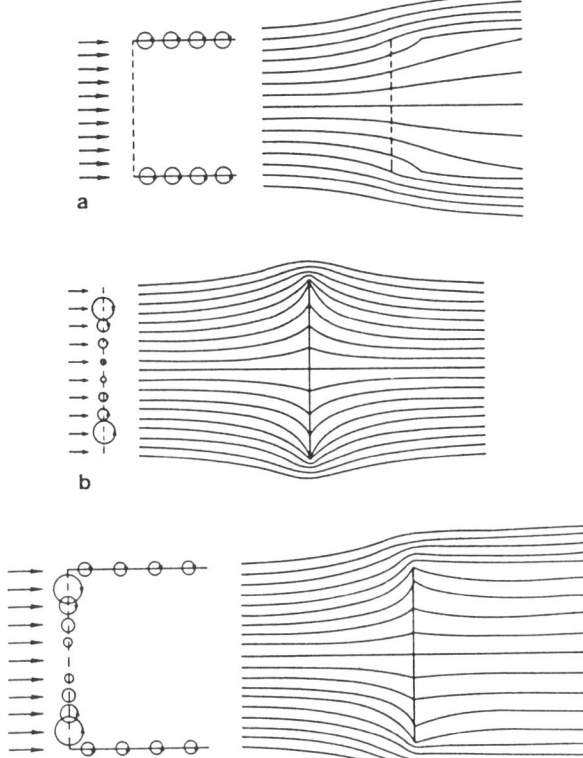

Fig. 7. Singularity models for development of of streamline diffusers; a) vortices on bounding streamtube, b) votices on radiator disk, and c) combined streamline and radiator vortices.

where w is the cooling air mass flow, σ_{ex} is the density ratio of the heated air at the radiator exit, and Δp is the static pressure drop through the radiator. The constants a and b depend on the core design. The selection of the radiator is the central problem of the cooling installation design. Given the operational heat rejection requirements, the selection problem is one of finding the optimum combination of radiator entry area and pressure drop characteristics. A large entry area results in low pressure drop and low internal drag; however, a large internal volume is required, or increased frontal area and high external drag will occur. A small entry area leads to small volume requirements, reduced frontal area, and low external drag; high internal drag, however, results from the associated larger pressure drop. The question is further complicated by the availability of the thermal energy given to the air flow by the radiator. A part of this energy can be utilized to compensate for the increased pressure drop. There is often speculation that the imparted energy is sufficient to overcome the drag of the installation and produce a net thrust. The North American P-51 Mustang is said to have this attribute. The author, however, has uncovered no documentation to support this. The available literature on this subject (Refs. 2, and 11-14) is entirely theoretical and is divided between the British position (pro) and the American and German positions (con). The weight of opinion at present is against realizing a net thrust from the cooling installation.

As stated previously, a large amount of the German research activity was directed toward radiator development. There are a significant number of American publications in this area also. However, many of these are for air/air heat exchangers used as intercoolers for the air-cooled engines. In the author's opinion, an important obstacle to the application of liquid-cooled engines to aircraft is the lack of suitable radiators. The term "suitable" here means radiators designed for operation at flight altitudes and having core geometries compatible with installation aerodynamic requirements. The radiators currently available are ground vehicle designs and are of the large entry area type. It is likely that useful radiators can be assembled from existing core structures; however, provision for this requirement should be incorporated into any liquid-cooled aircraft engine development program.

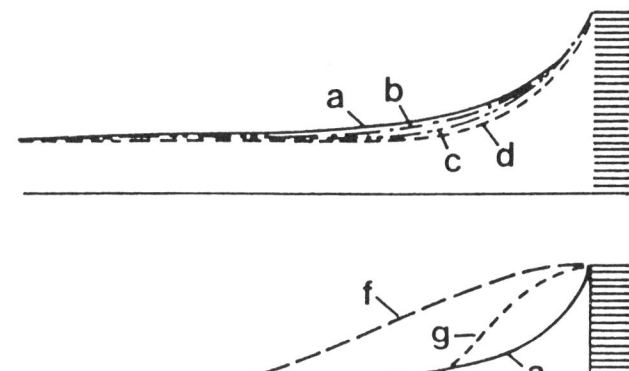

Fig. 8. Comparison of diffuser shapes listed in Table 1.

Table 1 Pressure drop for different contours[2]

Contour	$\Delta p/\Delta p_o$
(1) Streamline	1.08
(2) Exponential	1.28
(3) Circular arc	1.31
(4) Parabola	1.35
(5) Sine long	1.35
(6) Sine short	1.35

The quantity Δp is the pressure drop across the radiator diffuser combination, and Δp_o is the pressure drop across the radiator alone.

INTERNAL FLOW AERODYNAMICS

Design problems with the internal flow ducting concern the use of diffusers, oblique flow entering and/or leaving the radiator, and the exit ducting. Diffusers are necessary to reduce the external air flow velocity to the level necessary for the radiator. Design methodology for diffusers is presented in Ref. 2 and data for different diffuser area ratios are given in Ref. 1. The design procedure simulates a freely exposed radiator block by a distribution of singularities. The singularity strengths are set by the ratio of the velocity at the radiator to that of the freestream. The bounding streamline that results provides the contour of the diffuser. As discussed in Ref. 2, it is necessary to employ the right combination of sources, sinks, and vortices to obtain a solution that will work in practice. The design procedure is illustrated in Fig. 7. Comparisons between the streamline contour and other contours are given in Table 1. The respective contours are shown in Fig. 8.

Often, it is necessary to achieve a reduction in the frontal area of the radiator installation. This is generally the result of limitation of available internal volume. The design problem is one of obtaining a trade-off balance between increased internal drag and increased external drag. Reducing the frontal area of a radiator is accomplished by slanting the radiator so that the entry and/or the exit flow is oblique to the core passages. The core matrix is thus required to function as a turning vane system. The ability to turn the flow is dependent on the leading edge radius of the core plates experiencing the angle of attack, i.e., the ability to support

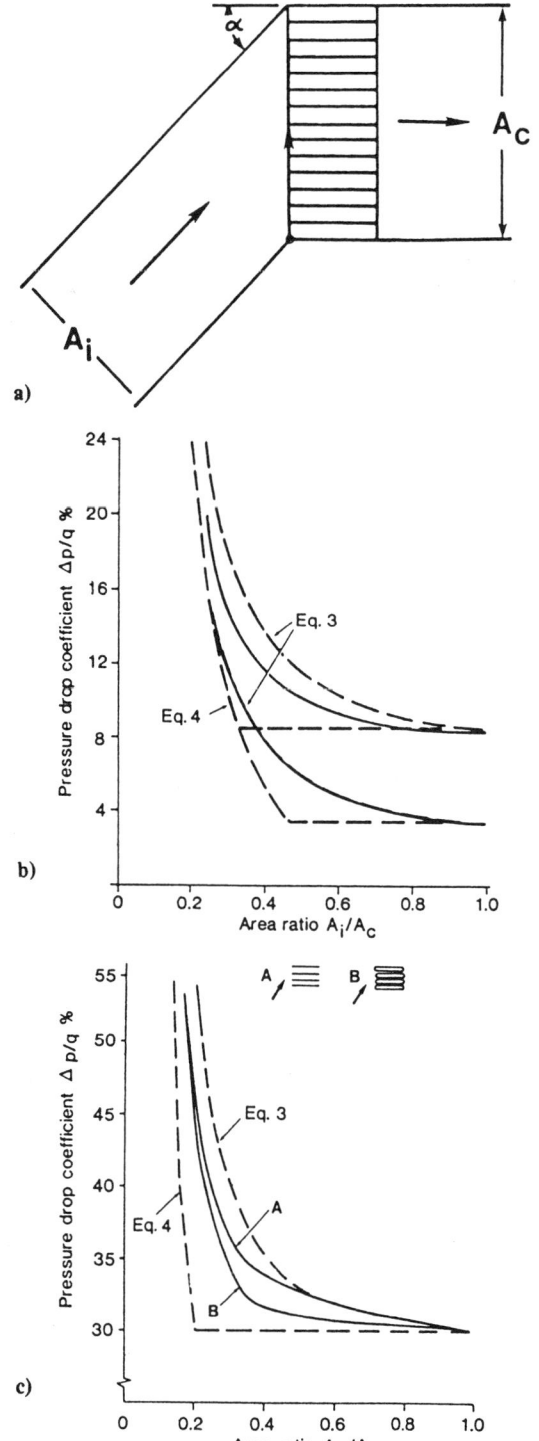

Fig. 9. Oblique flow effects: a) flow model, b) results from Ref. 2, and c) results from Ref. 15.

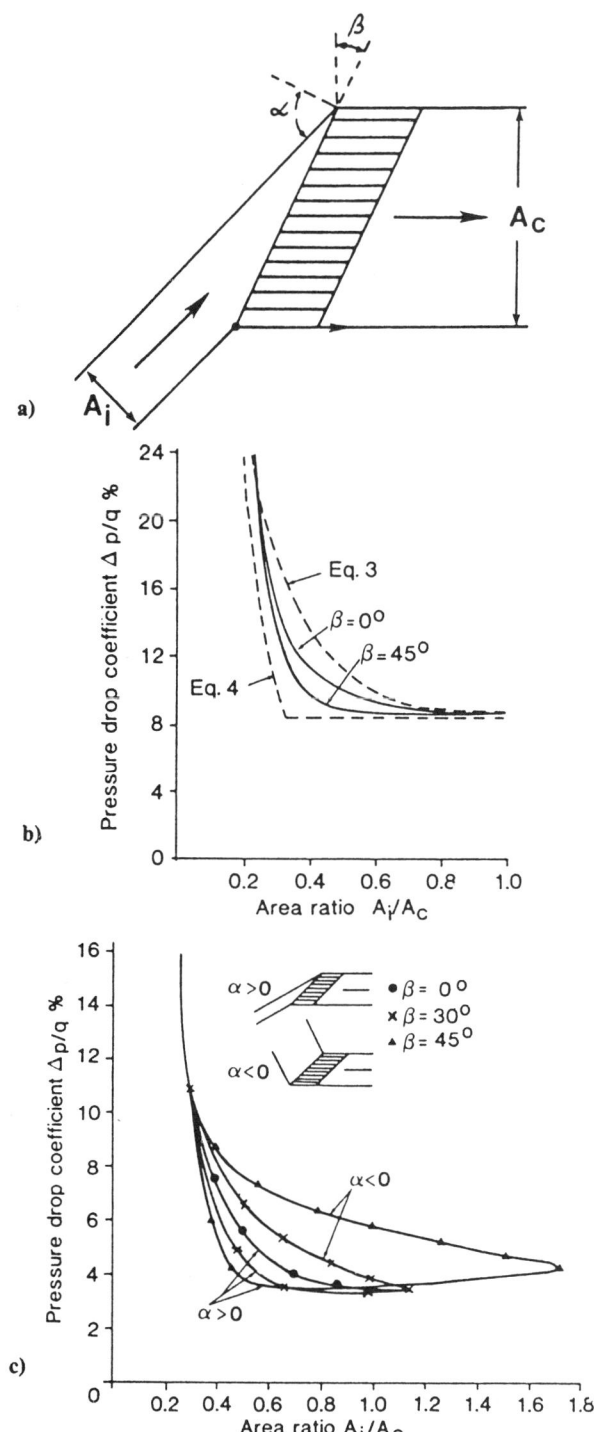

Fig. 10. Effects of staggered radiator on oblique flow: a) flow model, b) results from Ref. 2, and c) further results from Ref. 2.

the necessary suction force. If elliptical or oval coolant passages are used in the core, these should be oriented to function as the turning vanes. Kuchemann and Weber[1,2] developed relations that give the upper and lower limits of the internal drag increment due to oblique flow. These are given as follows:

$$\Delta p/q = \Delta p_o/q + \tan^2\alpha \qquad (3)$$

and

$$\Delta p/q = \Delta p_o/q \quad \alpha < \arccos(A_i/A_c)$$
$$\Delta p/q = \tan^2\alpha \quad \alpha > \arccos(A_i/A_c) \qquad (4)$$

where Δp is the pressure drop due to the oblique flow, Δp_o is the pressure drop due to the normal flow, α is the angle of attack of the flow, and A_i and A_c are the inlet and radiator areas as defined in Fig. 9. Equation (3) assumes flat plate behavior, i.e., no leading edge suction of the core elements, and represents the worst case. Equation (4) assumes some leading edge suction and is based upon experimental data. Results from Nichols[15] and Kuchemann and Weber[2] are given in Fig. 9. Equations (3) and (4) are identified in the figure. Higher oblique flow angles for the same drag penalty can be obtained by introducing stagger into the radiator design. The stagger angle effectively reduces the suction

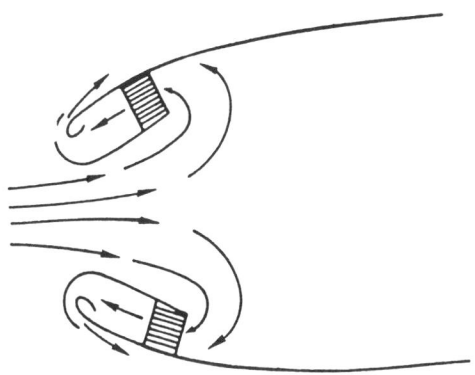

Fig. 11. Nose slot exit in asymmetric inlet cowl.

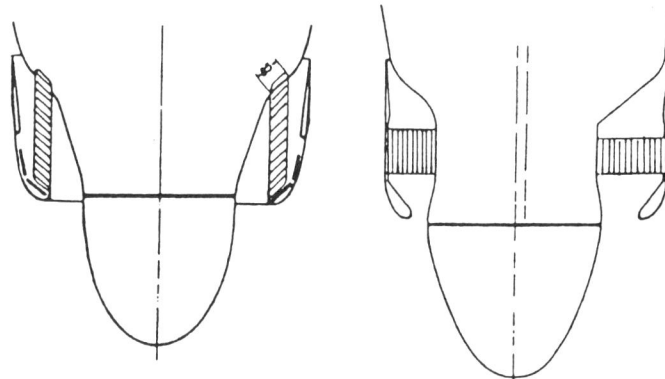

Fig. 14. Ring radiator installations.

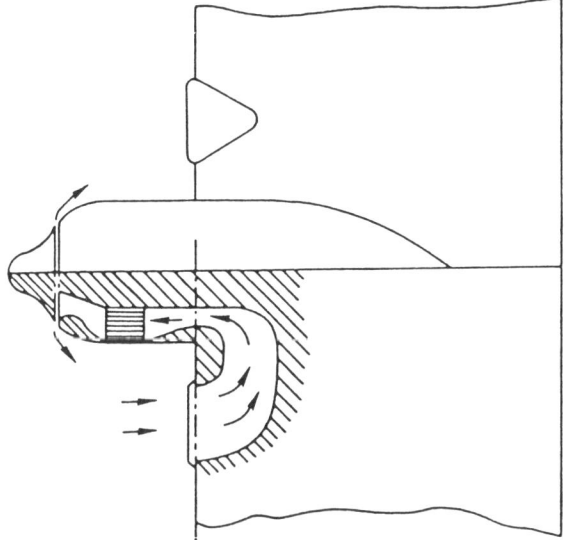

Fig. 12. Nose slot exit with wing leading edge inlets.

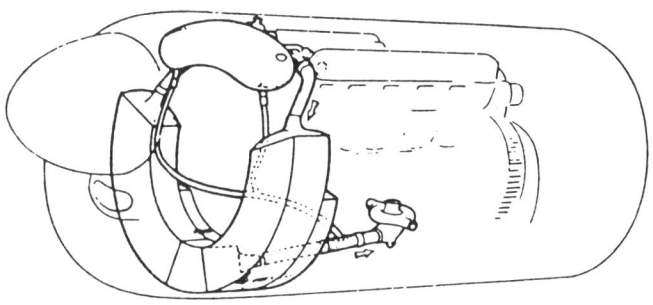

Fig. 15. Internal schematic ring radiator.

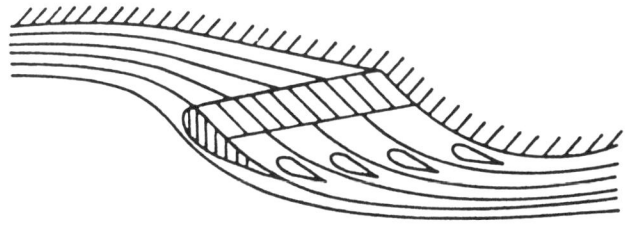

Fig. 13. Cascade exit flap.

load on the core element for a given flow angle. Results from Ref. 2 showing the effect of the stagger angle are presented in Fig. 10.

The shape and angle of the exit duct also affects the pressure drop through the system. There are limits on the exit flow angle and distance to duct converging sections distance to duct converging sections, beyond which increases in internal drag occur.

EXITS The exit has two basic functions: to regulate the cooling air flow and to exhaust the cooling flow into the external flow so as to result in minimal drag penalty. To adequately perform the regulation, the exit must act as both a throttle and a pump. Throttling is necessary in cruising flight to minimize the cooling drag by reducing the cooling flow so that sufficient to meet cooling requirements. In ground operation and in climbing flight, the exit must act as a pump to induce sufficient cooling flow through the system. Both of these functions can be performed by a hinged flap. The fundamental principle here is that for any subsonic flow system, the flow rate through the system will always adjust itself so that the static pressure at the exit will match the local external flow static pressure surrounding the exit. The static pressure at the exit is controlled by the exit area. Thus, regulation is obtained by varying this area. Opening the flap beyond the contour of the airframe creates a low-pressure region that induces additional flow through the system. It became common design practice during World War II to serve the exit flap to a coolant temperature sensor to optimize the system operation.

It is occasionally suggested that the cooling flow exits should be located in a low-pressure region on the aircraft to achieve extra pumping. Experimental results published by Hammen and Rowley[16] and by Miley et al[17] show a net increase in drag for this approach. While cooling flow is increased, exhausting the flow into a low-pressure region leads to increased external friction drag and pressure drag due to subsequent flow separation. Another example of this is the nose-slot cowl developed by Merceir[18]. The cooling flow exit is located near the lip leading edge of anaxisymmetric cowl where the suction peak occurs. Use is made of the suction peak to pump the cooling air. The cooling air inlet may be in the center of the cowl as in Fig. 11 or located elsewhere as in Fig. 12. Investigations by Smelt and Smith[19] and Theodorsen[20] et al showed improved cooling in climb but an increase in drag for cruise and high-speed flight.

An interesting concept reported in Ref. 2 is the cascade exit flap shown in Fig. 13. Low pressure is generated through streamline curvature induced by the flap setting. No experimental data has been found by the author to evaluate this design.

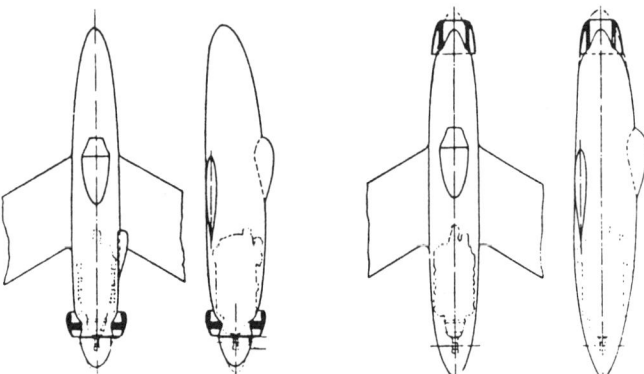

Fig. 16. Fore and aft ring radiator installation from Ref. 2.

INSTALLATION DESIGN

There are many examples of installation designs in the cited references. In particular, Refs. 1-3 and 7 should be utilized. Two additional references in this category are Seddon and Harrison[21] and Hartshorn and Nicholson[22]. However, supporting engineering data are not always given. Most of the designs fall into one of three types: fuselage underslung, wing underslung, and internal wing. Underslung installations locate the inlet, and in some cases the entire radiator system, on the lower surface of the aircraft. The location may be either on the fuselage or on the wing. The internal wing installations utilize two-dimensional leading edge inlets and locate the radiator within the thickness envelope of the wing section.

RING RADIATOR INSTALLATION Ring radiator installations have shown great promise. The inlet is in the nose of the cowl and can be axisymmetric. Two configurations are shown in Fig. 14, and an internal schematic is given in Fig. 15. The ring radiator offers advantages both from the standpoint of location and of design. Little if any increase in frontal area is required. The inlet design is less aerodynamically complicated, and pressure recovery with minimal losses is relatively easy to achieve. The installation is almost identical to that of radial air-cooled engines in appearance, and the design can benefit from this technology. The Focke-Wulf FW-190 fighter flew with both air-cooled and liquid-cooled engines. The ring radiator was utilized with the liquid-cooled installation. Examples of the ring radiator installation from Ref. 2 are given in Fig. 16.

SUMMARY

Liquid-cooled aircraft engines are with us again. The current state of the art of installation aerodynamics has been reviewed in this paper. The level of technical sophistication required to do a good aerodynamic cooling installation should not be underestimated. The technical literature available is fragmented and sometimes difficult to obtain. However, most of the problems have been identified. The use of digital computers allow much more freedom in the development of analytical models. The one major area of concern is the availability of suitable radiators. There are still unanswered questions regarding large-frontal area/low-pressure drop vs small frontal-area/high-pressure drop. Retrofitting existing air-cooled installations forces consideration of the latter because of inadequate internal volume within the airframe.

REFERENCES

1. Kuchemann, D. and Weber, J., *Aerodynamics of Propulsion*, McGraw-Hill, New York, 1953.

2. Kuchemann, D. and Weber, J., "Cooling" (AVA Monograph J_1), British Ministry of Supply, Reports and Translations 914-923, 1946.

3. Hoerner, S.F., *Fluid-Dynamic Drag*, Hoerner Fluid Dynamics, Brick Town, NJ, 1965.

4. Katzoff, S., "High-Altitude Cooling, V--Cowling and Dueting," NACA Wartime Rept. L-775, 1945.

5. Brodel, W., "Theory of Plane, Symmetrical Intake Diffusers," NACA TM 1267, March 1950.

6. Ruden, P., "Two-Dimensional Symmetrical Inlets with External Compression," NACA TM 1279, March 1950.

7. Anon., "Bibliography of NACA and Other Reports on Air Inlets and Internal Flows," NACA Res. Memo. 8J05, Oct. 1948.

8. Kays, W.M. and London, A.L., *Compact Heat Exchangers*, McGraw-Hill, New York, 1964.

9. Fraas, A.P. and Ozisik, N.M., *Heat Exchanger Design*, Wiley, New York, 1965.

10. Anon., "Engineering Design Handbook--Military Vehicle Power Plant Cooling," US Army Material Command, AMCP 706-361, June 1975.

11. Meredith, F.W., "Note on the Cooling of Aircraft Engines with Special Reference to Ethylene Glycol Radiators Enclosed in Ducts," British ARC Repts and Memo. 1683, Aug. 1935.

12. Rauscher, M. and Phillips, W.H., "Propulsive Effects of Radiator and Exhaust Ducting," *Journal of the Aeronautical Sciences*, Vol. 8, Feb. 1941, pp. 167-174.

13. Winter, H. "Contributions to the Theory of the Heated Duct Radiator," NACA TM 893, April 1939.

14. Berton, A.B.P., "The Increase in Thrust Obtainable from a Power Plant Installation using the Cooling-Air as a Propulsive Jet," British ARC Repts and Memo. 2147, May 1945.

15. Nichols, M.R., "Investigation of Flow Through an Intercooler Set at Various Angles to the Supply Ducts," NACA Wartime Rept. L-408, 1945.

16. Hammen, T.F., Jr. and Rowley, W.H., "Factors Pertaining to Installation of Inverted In-Line Aircooled Aircraft Engines," *SAE Journal (Transactions)*, Vol. 54, March 1946, pp. 138-152.

17. Miley, S.J., Cross, E.J. Jr., Owens, J.K. and Lawrence, D.L., "An Experimental Investigation of the Aerodynamics and Cooling of A Horizontally-Opposed Air-Cooled Aircraft Engine Installation," NASA Contractor Rept. 3405, March 1981.

18. Mercier, P.E., "Drag and Cooling of Air-Cooled Engines," Aeroplane, Vol. 61, No. 1571-72, July 1941, pp. 21-22, 24, 48-50.

19. Smelt, R. and Smith, F., "Model Tests of a 'Return-Flow' Cooling Scheme, having a Wing Leading Entry and a Nose-Slot Exit," British ARC Repts and memo, 2403, March 1940.

20. Theodorsen, T., Brevoort, M.J., Stickle, O.W., and Gough, M.N., "Full-Scale Tests of a New Type NACA Nose-Slot Cowling," NACA Rept. 595, 1937.

21. Seddon, J. and Harrison, J.E.A., "A Collection of Wind Tunnel Test Data on the Exit Static Pressures of Engine Cooling Ducts," RAE Rept. AERO 2127, March 1946.

22. Hartshorn, A.S. and Nicholson, L.F., "The Aerodynamics of the Cooling of Aircraft Reciprocating Engines," British ARC Repts and Memo. 2498, May 1947.

Professor Miley's benchmark paper provides automobile powerplant experimenters with an excellent reference on the subject of liquid-cooling. This information is particularly applicable to many on-going engine conversion projects. Contact! wishes to acknowledge and thank the American Institute of Aeronautics and Astronautics on behalf of its readers for its permission to reprint this significant article. MCM

POWER & PERFORMANCE
Small-block Chevrolet Powered Cessna 172!

Roger E. Erickson
Alternative Power
1114 East 4th Street
Fairmont, MN 56031
(507) 238-4134

Several years ago I embarked on a project which would provide me with many challenges. This endeavor has turned into a wonderful learning experience. It all began when my Cessna 172 O-300 (145 HP) Continental engine failed to pass its inspection. I initially considered an overhaul and quickly learned that prices had skyrocketed with the passage of time. One estimate for a complete zero time overhaul locally was $10,000! I was aware others had installed automobile powerplants in their airplanes. I did a fair amount of research on existing auto conversions. Since I have some machinist skills and a shop with all the necessary tooling, including a turning lathe and a vertical milling machine, to produce my alternative power systems I decided to produce the necessary components in my own shop. Ron Gilmore, a retired Coast Guard machinist and friend, assisted me with the cutting and milling of parts which my machines could not handle. My experimentation and development of hardware has progressed to the point where I am confident of producing quality redrives for customers although this was not in my original goal.

To put this effort in perspective I spent over three years getting to where I am now with my airplane. (I already have spent ten years working on my helicopter). Someone once remarked, "you couldn't possibly have a full-time job" and get done what I have done. This is true! I have worked day and night, weekends, holidays, and Sundays. Family life has had to take a back seat to my development of an alternative power source for today's airplanes. Also, I wouldn't care add up the amount of money I have spent in the process of building what I believe to be the most reliable gear box available today. This unit is safe, strong, and visually appealing. Best of all, it fits neatly under the existing cowling of the Cessna Skyhawk!

REDRIVE MARKET

My initial investigation of other available redrive systems indicated that sub-jobbing of key parts invariably lead to long lead times and delivery delays. Also, I had spoken to a number of experimenters who were either in the process of converting their airplanes or had built an experimental airplane of some sort. All of these people had one thing in common: they experienced difficulties with the current conversions being marketed! I learned that some companies offering redrives and conversions have not produced parts on a reasonable timetable and one seemed to be troubled with financial problems. Readers new to alternative powerplant development should be aware that a few redrive marketers have taken customers' money for conversions and then did not deliver what they promised. This has obviously dampened an otherwise active market demand for auto powerplant conversions. I hope to change that!

REDRIVE CHOICES

The construction of a gear drive system for an airplane leads one to try a number of routes--often leading to dead ends and a loss of invested time and money. It took me months to track down the data I required to arrive at formulas which would give me quick, accurate answers to my design questions. Even the engineers I consulted did

not have the answers I so often sought during the construction and development of my gearbox. My telephone calls added up quickly during the research and testing phase of my conversion. The facts presented in my literature and articles already published have come about due to a lot of tough research. Outside help was scarce.

I chose not to design a redrive around the popular rubber cog belt because, in my opinion, they are hard and, according to their manufacturers' specifications, are not intended to be run at RPMs necessary for proper propeller speed. Therefore, I developed a sprocket-chain redrive system. In my opinion, one of the best chains for this

Two photos of the Continental O-300 and 350 Chevrolet small block engines illustrate the relative compactness of the V/8 design. Note Ericson's dual plug heads, dual GM HEI distributors and cast housing chain redrive.

purpose is the one used on the Chevrolet Blazer 4-wheel drive vehicle. It has already proven itself in road tests everywhere and its cost and availability makes it a practical choice for the home builder.

ALTERNATIVE ENGINE

I had already decided to use the Chevrolet 350 powerplant because of its proven performance record on and off the track and its reliability as an automobile engine. Stock and racing parts are readily available and mechanics familiar with this engine regard it as trustworthy. I bought a salvage stock Chevrolet 350 engine and started weighing the block, heads, intake manifold, etc. During this process I realized that I needed to know the exact weight of the Continental O-300 engine on my airplane, complete with accessories. I discovered in reviewing official engine specifications that it is virtually impossible to determine the weight of an aircraft engine due to the many design variations and accessory choices.

Anyone who has attempted to document their airplane's individual component weights can quickly attest to the fact that information of this type is not available. Aircraft and Powerplant mechanics (A&Ps)--"we all know at least one"-- could not give me answers to simply stated questions, like, "what does the complete engine weigh?" It seemed a lot of these guys were "oil and tire changers" who only wanted to do complete annuals or engine overhauls. None I dealt with had any incentive or interest to research this subject or were too busy to bother with me since what I was doing was not documented in their manuals. I finally took the only correct step and removed the Continental O-300 engine. A balance beam scale gave me the answer (if there is a simpler method, please advise!). The entire assembly, including engine mounts, less firewall mounted components, weighed 385.0 pounds on a balance beam platform scale. Now, I had a accurate target installation weight to shoot for!

ENGINE PARTS

I realized early on I would have to go with aluminum heads and an aluminum intake manifold in order to keep the engine weight within the Cessna C.G. envelope. After installing these parts and re-weighing the engine I still was over my target weight. It was clearly evident I could not to use the cast iron block on the engine so I bought a used Donovan block which weighed 91 pounds less than the cast iron block. For the record, my stock Chevrolet block weighed one hundred sixty-nine pounds as compared to the Donovan block's seventy-eight pounds!

I installed a Tilton geared reduction super-starter designed principally for race cars which turns 25 percent slower. My main reason for doing this was to reduce stress on the starter's Bendix drive induced by the inertia mass of the large propeller mass. I knew from my previous

experience that I did not need the speed of the stock starter to get this engine running. I picked up a weight bonus. This starter weighed ten pounds less than the standard Chevrolet unit! I recommend it for any large engine requirement.

My carburetor is a stock Rochester two barrel which is readily available. Although I also considered a four barrel carburetor or fuel injection system, I elected to use components I had on hand because the total dollar investment was necessarily contained throughout this project. Remember, I had a goal to keep this unit affordable for the homebuilder and sport pilot!

I also used a stock Pontiac air cleaner on this engine to achieve clearance under the cowling. Top clearance was necessary in order to replace the stock cowling on the airplane. The photographs show how well it turned out.

COMPONENT WEIGHTS		
	iron	aluminum
Redrive		55.0
Radiator	12.0	9.0
Heads(2)	104.0	50.0
Intake Manifold	42.0	19.0
Exh Manifold(2)	14.0	
Starter	19.0	9.0 (Tilton)
Block	169.0	78.0

REDRIVE DESIGN

The design of the gear reduction box was the biggest challenge. I reviewed all the existing units and decided they were too bulky and wouldn't allow me to utilize the existing airplane cowling. I constructed my prototype gear box from 6061-T6 billet material which was sawed to rough size and then milled to dimension.

As you can see in the pictures I incorporated engine mounting points into my gear box as well. These were drilled into the aluminum and then Lord engine mounts were incorporated into the bolt-attach points to remove the vibration from the frame. My gearbox attaches to the stock Chevrolet engine, utilizing the existing bell housing holes. It holds one quart of gear lube for the chain. It also has a breather to allow for expansion of the oil as the temperature rises.

The gears are all hardened steel. My original gear reduction unit was a 34/25 tooth unit, or 1.36:1 reduction. An engine turning at 3600 RPM producing 350 HP and 345 foot-pounds of torque would give me 351.9 foot-pounds of torque on the prop. In the future I would recommend a 1.44:1 ratio although there will be a 1.84:1 available for V/6s.

ENGINE MOUNT

Next, I designed an engine mount which placed the engine and gear box in the desired thrust line location. This specific engine mount configuration is available for purchase with my gearbox. Finally, after mounting the entire engine assembly on the airplane I was 5 pounds lighter than the original Continental O-300 engine! The original Cessna engine and the Chevrolet 350 engine are shown together so you can compare the size directly. Quite amazing is the size difference and the extra horsepower available!

However, with the additional 55 pound gearbox, the radiator (12 pounds) and coolant (13 pounds) ahead of the design C.G. I had to add ballast weight in the tail. From the Cessna Service Manual I calculated this was approximately a 3:1 ratio so I needed 30 pounds to offset the weight in the front. I also moved the 40 pound battery to the tail cone and added 28 pounds of ballast in the tail of the airplane.

COOLING/COWLING

It was my original intent to keep the cowling on the Cessna 172 original to reduce the conversion workload. However, as experimenters often find, desires differ from reality. As it turned out, I kept the top of the cowl original and virtually destroyed the lower section in the process of designing an efficient cooling system for my airplane. Several times I butchered into it only to find it was still ineffective for cooling such a large engine. I even added louvers to the cowling at one point hoping to dissipate heat through the cowling sides.

The most troublesome part of the entire project was to find a location suitable for the radiator to get rid of the heat. After several unsuccessful attempts I installed the radiator at a 36 degree angle which is now operating perfectly. Perfect but not pretty at this point in the development process.

The redrive, the stock HEI distributor, dual plug heads and added HEI distributor/adapter are shown. Another option is the use of a single plug head and siamesed plug wires from both distributors.

Although some have suggested that I incorporate a blunt nose shape (like the one on the Bonanza) to hide the radiator behind a grille I am considering another alternative. My next modification to the Cessna will NOT involve any cowling rework. I intend to mount the radiator vertically in the vertical fin of the airplane. As I envision the design, it will receive plenty of air from the prop wash while on the ground which and provide the same cooling ability. Besides, with some additional ballast needed in the tail anyway, this would be a logical place to put it. Appearance is not definite yet, but may resemble a ducted radiator once the shroud is constructed and plans completed. Watch for this as my next enhancement.

INSTALLATION DETAILS

Carburetor heat is not needed with the down-flow carburetion on auto engines. Icing should be a thing of the past. Oil circulation has been sufficient to keep the engine well lubricated and the spin-on type filters can be easily changed. Remember, when one installs this conversion on their airplane, the original mounting bolts are utilized as a "bolt-on" stock unit. Reinstall the cowling after fitting the radiator and it is complete.

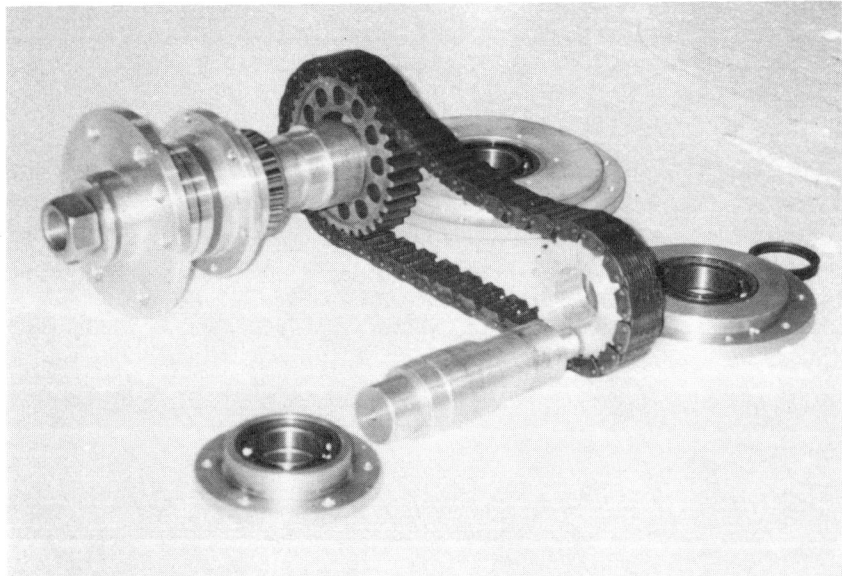

The durable Chevolet Blazer roller chain is the heart of the redrive. Precision bearings and hardenedsteel sprockets are fully adequate to handle engine and prop loads. Self contained simple wet sump lubrication is used.

It is then necessary to change a number of cockpit interior components. For instance, automobile manufacturers do not use heat off a hot manifold to warm the interior. A small hole in the muffler could render a pilot unconscious. Carbon monoxide detectors? A thing of the past! Why would anyone continue using such an outdated and dangerous mode of heating the cabin anyway? I simply installed an automobile heater core and a small fan and presto, safe and adequate cabin heat to satisfy our needs for creature comforts!

The old magneto switch can be replaced with an ignition key switch readily available at all auto parts houses. Costs vary but are a steal compared to the outrageous prices charged by aircraft suppliers. I simply open the door, sit down, turn on the switch (like in my car). I warm up the engine, as you would normally do in an airplane, before adding power for take-off.

Some gauges, which operate off the vacuum system, still require an aircraft style vacuum pump. Therefore, I modified the alternator to drive this vacuum pump. It is quite obvious to anyone who is driving a late model car that the automotive industry has perfected their ignition systems far beyond the ancient magneto setup. All electrical gauges are still operative as usual. I did install a digital tachometer to get more accurate readings. You cannot use the aircraft unit as is since the RPMs are higher than the gauge is calibrated to indicate.

DUAL IGNITION

With millions of automobiles running everyday, properly maintained single HEI distributors have proven themselves to work well. However, for those "flat earth" people who subscribe to the notion that two plugs are better than one, I also designed and constructed a dual ignition system for the Chevrolet small block engines. In some instances as in large bore aircraft engines dual ignition is necessary. According to several conversations with the Mercury Outboard Motor people, the addition of two spark plugs per cylinder gives a substantial power gain of 8 to 12 percent. Their result may be due to the unique configuration of their combustion chamber. It is obvious that the Mazda rotary engine with its long flame front requires two plugs to operate efficiently; otherwise, the engine would only have one plug. In addition to the dual ignition HEI system I designed new aluminum heads with provisions for dual spark plugs. This combination has not been flight tested yet but will be very soon.

FUTURE CHANGES

In addition to the tail mounted radiator mentioned earlier, future developments and enhancements will include a complete muffler package for the Cessna 172 and other planes. Mufflers are commonly required in Europe and the United States usually follows the regulatory trends set overseas. Although I had two small mufflers installed along the sides of my engine during my early tests I do not have these installed at the present time. Noise is not a factor at altitude and it was convenient at one point during the conversion to leave them off. I plan to incorporate a complete muffler/lag-pipe system which will appear as a neat package tucked neatly along the side of the fuselage. I believe factory airplanes are extremely noisy but need not be.

PERFORMANCE SPECIFICATIONS
Propeller: 76 inch diameter 64 inch pitch
1.36:1 Ratio Gearbox

Engine Speed	3800 RPM
Torque	469.2
75 percent power	351.9
HP	244.6
Tip Speed	631.8
Airspeed	169.3

PERFORMANCE SPECIFICATIONS
Propeller: 76 inch diameter 64 inch pitch
1.44:1 Ratio Gearbox

Engine Speed	4000 RPM
Torque	496.8
75 percent power	372.6
HP	257.5
Tip Speed	628.1
Airspeed	168.1

The optimum performance from the Chevrolet manual, a stock 250 HP Chevrolet V/8 2 barrel with a 4.0 inch bore and 3.48 inch stroke with a compression ratio of 9:1 puts out 250 HP maximum brake at 4800 RPM and 345 maximum foot-pounds of torque at 2800 RPM. Therefore, with this information the best gear ratio would be 1.44:1.

I wrote a simple BASIC program to help with "instant calculations" of various gear ratios and propeller performance. You may like to try it with your current power configuration and use it to verify your numbers! I have included the program here for you to experiment with, as well. The program works well for most light airplanes and you can determine what size propeller your powerplant will turn.

TEST PROGRAM

In the process of testing components, Ron Gilmore and I started out with a USED chain with 60,000 miles on it to document the durability of this chain. This used chain is still in use today in the prototype unit! I have 130 hours of flight on it as well! I am fairly confident of its durability and do not expect any problems with the Blazer chain.

To address the problem of backlash, I installed a spring loaded slipper on the slack chain side of the gear box. I stress-tested the prototype gear box with an oversized 94 inch power prop with 44 inches of pitch. This propeller came off a Cessna Ag Wagon. In order to minimize the stress of this size of propeller imposed on the gear box system, I installed a 10 spring 10 spline, 1.750 inch clutch center from a semi truck between the engine and the gear box. In my present design, this part is no longer needed since it does not react with the same forces as it did during testing. Many tests were run with used and worn components on rough running engines. These runs also proved how essential smooth engine operation is in the aircraft environment.

The tests were essential to the building of a safe and reliable conversion gear box. I have saved all future prospective pilots from anxiety over whether this conversion is safe and reliable. One need only FLY this airplane to recognize the quality built into it. I tested and checked everything beyond expectations.

For instance, after three engineers recommended the Ramsey chain with half-moon pins, I installed one in my prototype gearbox. Within two short hours of running I had totally destroyed it! Here was a case where the numbers (which don't lie??) proved inaccurate. From this experience I learned to trust my knowledge of parts and consider raw strength rather than simply relying on published engineering data. I relied upon the industrial world's experience with high-stress components to help determine whether a component had the strength to work in my gearbox. I believe I now have the ideal chain drive system which is strong, quiet, and safe. The chain has also been stress tested and I have NOT destroyed one yet!

A simple solution for a challenging problem. The aircraft vacuum pump is coupled to the alternator shaft thus eliminating the weight and complexity of additional brackets and pulleys. Note large alternator pulley.

My flight tests have shown the following performance specifications with my configuration. I have a 76 inch long fixed pitch propeller with a 60 inch pitch. It flies better than a Cessna 182. I have a rate of climb of 1400 feet per minute with this configuration. Someday I would like include provisions for a variable pitch electric propeller in order to fully utilize the horsepower available in this engine.

PERFORMANCE COMPARISON		
	before	after
Fuel Burn g/hr	8.5	10
Range in miles	546	576
Speed in mph	130	159
Rate of Climb	645	1400
Take off Distance	865	540
Normal landing(flaps)		20 deg

REDRIVE FACTORS

Another thing common to the people working on alternative power systems is that they are OVER-PROPPING their engines! Comments from people in the conversion business are disturbing. It seems that all of these folks recommend a propeller way too large for the power they have available. These are big propellers with a lot of inertia and they require big horsepower to turn them. They recommend too much pitch and too long a blade for the alternative powerplant. In my opinion, experimenters should be simply re-pitching their existing propeller and flying the conversion at the recommended speed. Consider this: does anyone have a problem with the usual certified factory engine 2700 RPMs? That is the optimum speed and recommended performance for maximum efficiency. I suggest that we turn the propeller at the speed it was designed for so our factory airplanes will perform! It also appears the composite propeller presents some problems for the homebuilder. In my view, their long term reliability is questionable at the present time--especially coupled to the high HP powerplant I am proposing with my alternative power system. Therefore, I cannot recommend anyone using one with my conversion at the present time.

The pilot who is converting his aircraft to auto power is not fully informed when it comes to making an educated decision. I see this due to a number of factors: First, the pilots and owners have not adequately researched the wealth of information available out there and secondly, they are looking for a "fast-fix".

AUTO RACE ENGINES

I have also learned the RACE CAR motor cannot be utilized in the conversion of airplanes to automobile power! Unlike the race car, which is built expressly to function at very high power settings and high RPMs, the airplane engine needs to run smoothly at all power settings. Proof of this is in the idle speed and prop inertia after you start up a cold engine. I have seen the results of this interaction and I can positively report you would definitely not like the results if you had an engine cammed for performance. These engine conversions must idle smoothly! If you want to increase horsepower it must be done with cubic inches, carburation, fuel injection, compression ratio, supercharging or some other method other than performance camming.

The use of an auto engine in the airplane results in one needing a combination of smooth performance and high power at all throttle settings. I have spent a great deal of time researching this aspect of the conversion process and feel it cannot be done with RACE CAR approaches. These are airplanes we are dealing with, folks, and we should utilize the power at much lower RPMs than the current breed of conversions vendors have been marketing. There should be no need to turn these automobile engines at 5000 to 8000 RPMs. This range of engine speed is not conducive to long-life expectancy in the engine.

Early photo of Cessna 172/Chevrolet 350 engine installation. The proof-of-concept redrive housing was built up from aluminum plates. Automobile mufflers were innstalled during initial stages of development.

AIRCRAFT CERTIFICATION

Dealing with the maintenance people of the FAA was very rewarding. I found them easy to work with, offering suggestions, and even assisting with the documents. However, the administrative department was quite different. The Minneapolis FAA District Office signed off my airplane for experimental category twice, upon my presenting them with a "Letter of Program." I was initially certified under *EXPERIMENTAL-RESEARCH AND DEVELOPMENT* and now am licensed under the *EXPERIMENTAL-EXHIBITION* category. This has allowed me to accumulate a lot of hours and show this conversion off at a number of airshows throughout last summer.

If someone converts his own certified airplane to alternative power it is very likely that the FAA will place the airplane into the *EXPERIMENTAL-R&D* category. Flights will be limited, perhaps to a total of 25 hours and to a 100 mile radius of his home airport. After successful completion of the test program, a Special Airworthiness Certificate will be issued (likely *EXPERIMENTAL-EXHIBITION*) for one year in effect for the Continental U.S. and no longer renewed yearly, according to the Minneapolis FAA Maintenance office. Subsequent modifications to the conversion may require new operating limitations and re-issuance of the Certificate. Nothing changes relative to the airframe; rules applying to annual inspections still apply. I have included copies of my FAA paperwork in this article to help those who plan to follow this effort with their experimentation. (see "Program Letter" which I submitted to the FAA and the FAA Special Airworthiness Certificate). FAA field offices have total responsibility for these procedures (as for Form 337 field modifications on certified airplanes). It is advisable to seek out those FAA individuals who have a broad range of experience with homebuilt aircraft activities. They can be a big help to you.

```
10 REM ******BASIC PROGRAM***************
20 REM CALCULATIONS USED:
30 REM (KNOWN TORQUE * RPM) / 5252 = STD HORSEPOWER (UNCORRECTED)
40 REM ((KNOWN TORQUE * GEAR REDUCTION) * (RPM / GEAR REDUCTION)) /5252 =STD HORSEPOWER (UNCORRECTED) ***
50 REM *********************************
60 REM E = ENGINE RPM
70 REM GR = GEAR RATIO
80 REM D = PROPELLER DIAMATER (LENGTH)
90 REM P = PROPELLER PITCH (STAMPED ON PROP)
100 REM T = ESTIMATED TORQUE
110 REM TT = STD HORSEPOWER (UNCORRECTED)
120 REM PL = POWER LOSS DUE TO GEAR REDUCTION
130 REM CH = STD HORSEPOWER (CORRECTED)
140 GR=0
150 CLS
160 PRINT " (1) V8 400 = 420 FOOT LB TORQUE"
170 PRINT " (2) V8 350 = 345 FOOT LB TORQUE"
180 PRINT " (3) V6 230 = 155 FOOT LB TORQUE"
190 PRINT
200 PRINT" DO YOU HAVE ONE OF THE ABOVE ENGINES (Y)ES OR (N)O";:INPUT R$
210 IF R$="Y" OR R$="y" THEN GOTO 250
220 PRINT " ENTER ENGINE TYPE (IE. V8 CHEVY 406) ..";:INPUT M$
230 PRINT " ENTER FOOT POUNDS OF TORQUE.. ";:INPUT F
240 GOTO 260
250 PRINT " SELECT NUMBER OF ENGINE / FOOT LB DESIRED ";:INPUT A1
260 PRINT " ENTER GEAR RATIO IF KNOWN, ELSE ENTER 0 ";: INPUT GR
270 IF GR = 0 THEN GOTO 300
280 IF GR > 0 THEN GOTO 310
290 PRINT
300 PRINT " ENTER 1.80 OR 1.44 AS DESIRED GEAR RATIO AVAILABLE";:INPUT GR
310 PRINT " INPUT ENGINE SPEED IN RPM's:";:INPUT E
320 PRINT " INPUT PROPELLER DIAMETER (LENGTH) IN INCHES:";:INPUT D
330 PRINT " INPUT PROPELLER PITCH (IN INCHES STAMPED ON PROP)-";:INPUT P
340 PRINT
350 PRINT " IS THE ABOVE DATA CORRECT (Y)ES OR (N)O";:INPUT A$
360 IF A$="Y" OR A$="y" THEN GOTO 370 ELSE GOTO 150
370 CLS
380 E$=M$
390 T=F
400 IF A1=1 THEN E$="V8 - 400 - "
410 IF A1=1 THEN T=420
420 IF A1=2 THEN E$="V8 - 350 - "
430 IF A1=2 THEN T=345
440 IF A1=3 THEN E$="V6 - 230 - "
450 IF A1=3 THEN T=155
460 TT = ((T*GR) * (E/GR)) / 5252
470 PL = TT * .02
480 CH = TT - PL
490 PRINT:PRINT " ENGINE SELECTED = ";E$;:PRINT T;:PRINT " FT LBS TORQUE"
500 PRINT" GEAR RATIO SELECTED = ";GR
510 PRINT " PROP DIAMETER (LENGTH) ";D
520 PRINT " PITCH (IN INCHES STAMPED ON PROP) =";P:PRINT
530 PRINT "ENGINE SPEED (RPM) = ";E
540 PRINT
550 PRINT "CALCULATED PROP RPM =";E/GR
560 PRINT
570 PRINT "ESTIMATED TORQUE = ";:PRINT T*GR;:PRINT "FOOT LB "
580 PRINT
590 PRINT "USABLE TORQUE (75% OF TOTAL) = ";:PRINT T*GR*.75;:PRINT " FOOT LB "
600 PRINT
610 PRINT "ESTIMATED HORSE POWER AT PROP =";:PRINT CH
620 PRINT
630 PRINT "PROP-TIP SPEED IN MPH = ";: COLOR 2,0:PRINT (E/GR)*(D * 3.14159 * 60)/(12*5280)
640 COLOR 2,0
650 PRINT
660 COLOR 7,0
670 PRINT "ESTIMATED AIR SPEED FROM PROPELLER =";:PRINT E/GR * .00947 * P/10
680 SOUND 178,10
690 PRINT
700 PRINT"*** PRESS F2 TO CONTINUE OR TYPE SYSTEM THEN <ENTER> TO EXIT ***"
```

FIREWALL FORWARD

My on-going research and testing has taken me to the production of a complete package for the Cessna owner. I have built everything from the engine mount to the interior wiring. The actual installation of my conversions can be achieved with bolt-on sub-assemblies. Remember, the simplification of my construction allows one to use all existing mounts.

To assist customers I have produced a video tape of the entire construction process of my gearbox and conversion. I have documented the flight characteristics and performance figures on my airplane throughout the long and sometimes tedious testing routine. It contains a wealth of information that is NOT AVAILABLE from any other source.

HELICOPTER ACTIVITIES

Some readers may recall that my original experimental work in aviation was in the development of a helicopter rotor head and a gyroplane rotor for an original design helicopter. These units flew, are Alternative in production and work very well. However, due to the unavailability of affordable blades (they are ridiculously expensive) I will be extruding my own leading edges. Many of the blades currently on the market do not appeal to me--partly due to cost--but mostly due to the lack of good construction techniques. I will develop the die necessary to make the best blades available! In addition, I have constructed the ONLY ninety-degree angle transmission for the small-block Chevrolet engine which makes helicopter flight practical and affordable for the homebuilders. I have SOLVED the "heat problem" so often encountered with automobile engine conversions in helicopters.

CONVERSION COSTS

I have listed a range of estimated costs of a typical Chevrolet 350 conversion. Please note that the single largest cost item is the Donovan block. My Cessna required the use of an aluminum block. Some airframes may tolerate the use of a Mr. Goodwrench factory block, reducing the overall cost considerably. If one were to do this type of conversion to an existing airplane, he would have an engine to sell. A used Continental O-300 currently sells for approximately $3600. When this price is factored in the Chevrolet 350 makes for a very inexpensive conversion! Low cost rebuild parts also are part of the equation.

FINAL HORSEPOWER CALCULATIONS

There seems to be an enormous amount of confusion among the aviation community concerning the definition of horsepower in relation to torque. Calculations and formulas provided here use these calculations extensively to determine what horsepower is delivered from their engine. Hopefully, after you work out a few calculations you will find these numbers beneficial in your own experience. The following will tell you how these calculations were determined.

The definition of horsepower is the amount of power it takes to move 33,000 pounds one foot in one minute. This is not to be confused with TORQUE. Torque is defined as the force required times the distance moved. Therefore, horsepower is TIME dependent and torque is FORCE dependent!

Standard horsepower is recognized as:
HP = TORQUE X RPM / 5252

Alternative power
350 Chevrolet Conversion

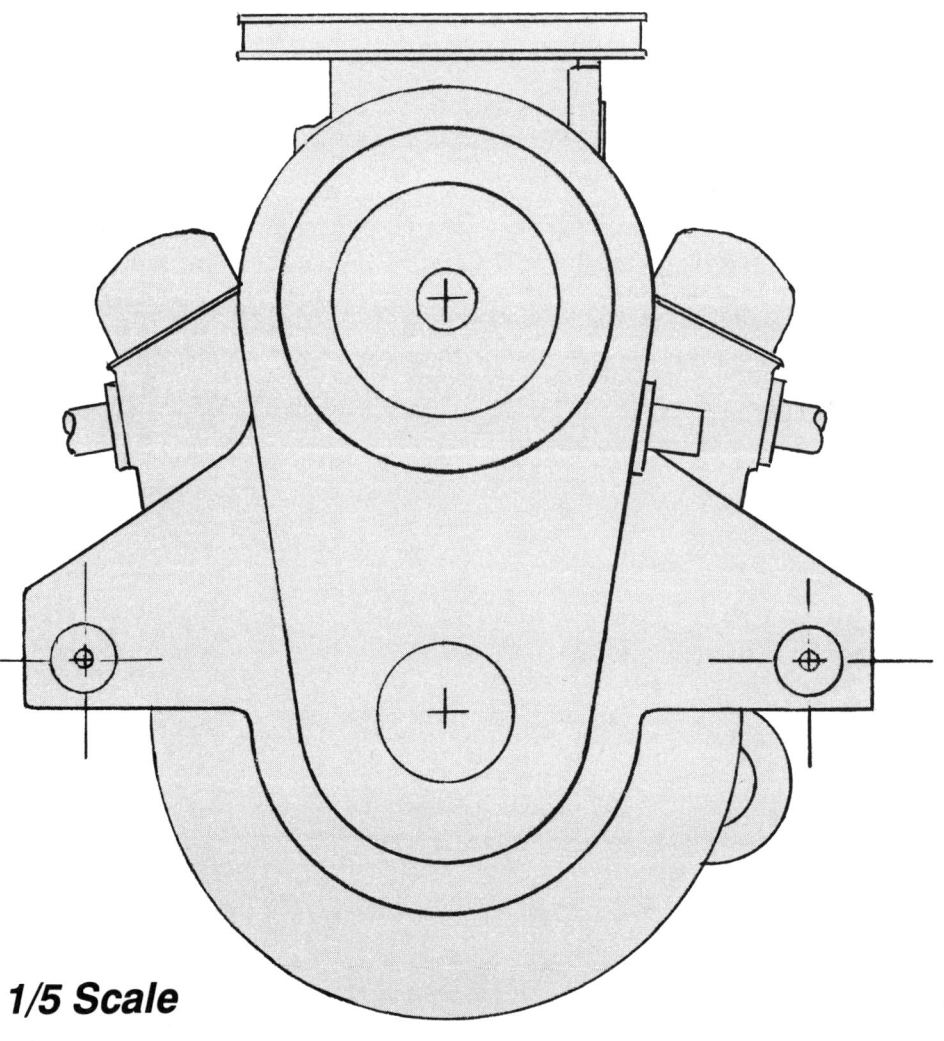

1/5 Scale

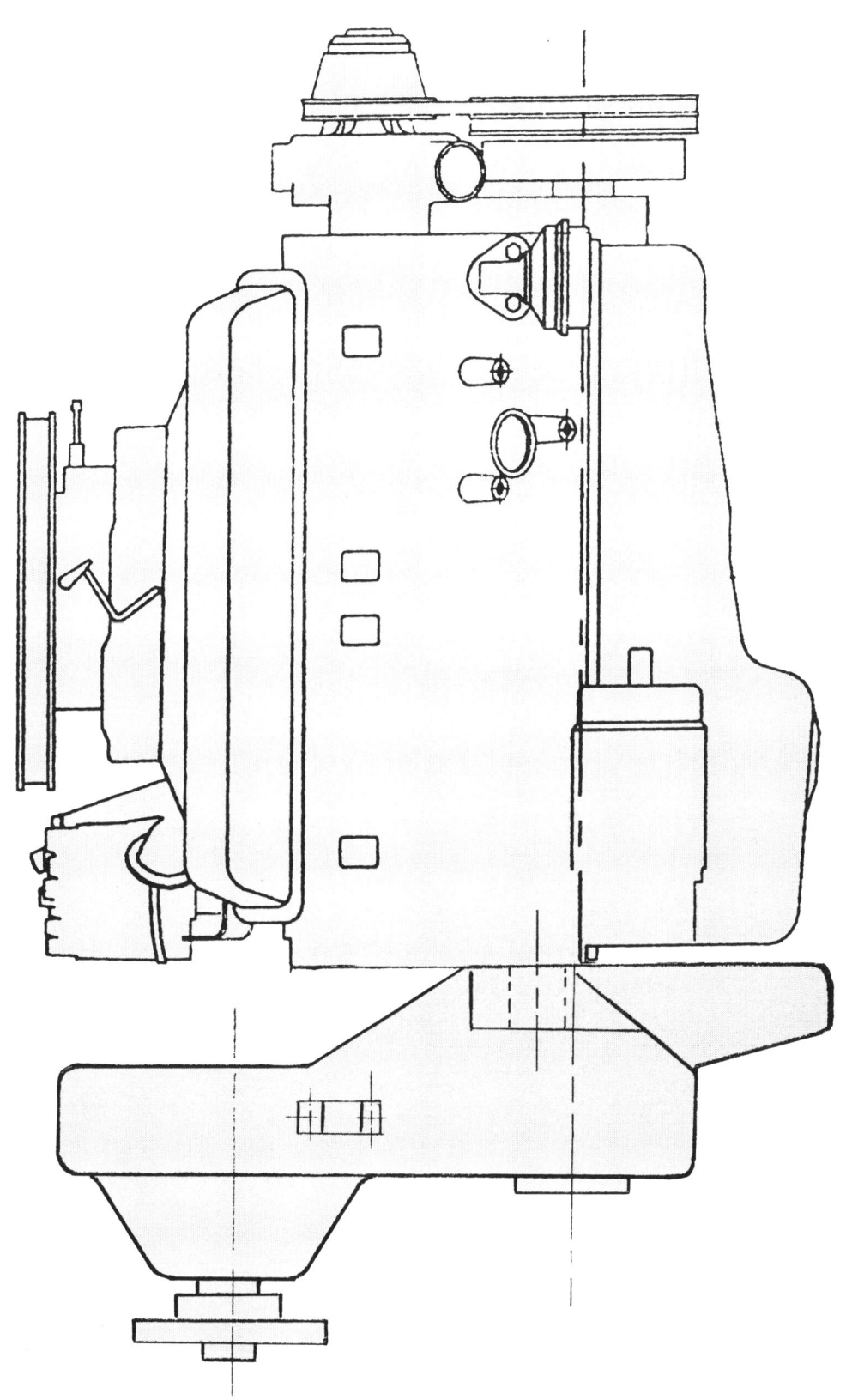

U.S. Department of Transportation
Federal Aviation Administration

Manufacturing Inspection
District Office
6020-28th Avenue South
Minneapolis, MN 55450

EXPERIMENTAL OPERATING LIMITATIONS-EXHIBITION   #4

MAKE: Cessna   MODEL: 172II   SERIAL NO. 17255794
REGISTRATION NO.: N2594L   REGISTERED OWNER: Roger A. Erickson
OWNER'S ADDRESS: 207 Fairview Avenue - Fairmont, MN 56031

PHASE I. INITIAL FLIGHT TEST IN RESTRICTED AREA:
1. No person may operate this aircraft for other than the purpose of flights to accomplish the flight tests outlined in the applicant's program letter dated 9-20-93 , describing compliance with FAR section 21.193(d), and made available to the pilot in the aircraft. Additionally, this aircraft shall be operated in accordance with applicable air traffic and general operating rules of FAR 91, and all additional limitations herein prescribed under the provisions of FAR section 91.319(e).

2. The initial 10.0 hours of flight shall be conducted within the geographic area as follows: Within a 25 Statute mile radius of Fairmont, MN.
* See reverse, Phase II, Item 2, for approved locations for Exhibition.

3. No person may be carried in the aircraft during flight tests unless that person is essential to the purpose of the flight.

4. All flight tests will be conducted under the provisions of FAR section 91.305, that is, no person may flight test an aircraft except over open water, or sparsely populated areas, having light air traffic.

5. Unless appropriately equipped for night and/or instrument flight in accordance with FAR section 91.205, this aircraft shall be operated day VFR only.

6. The pilot-in-command of this aircraft must, as applicable, hold an appropriate category/class rating, have an aircraft type rating, have a flight instructor's log book endorsement or possess a "Letter of Authorization" issued by an FAA General Aviation or Air Carrier Operations Inspector.

7. Acrobatic flight in this aircraft is ~~permitted~~/prohibited. When acrobatic flight is permitted, acrobatics or violent maneuvers should not be attempted until sufficient flight experience has been gained to establish that the aircraft is safely controllable. Only those acrobatic maneuvers which have been satisfactorily demonstrated during the flight test period and documented in the aircraft log, are permitted after leaving the assigned test area. All acrobatics are to be conducted under the provisions of FAR section 91.303.

8. This aircraft shall contain the placards, markings, flight manual, etc., required by FAR 91.9.

9. The person operating this aircraft shall advise each person carried of the experimental nature of the aircraft.

10. No person may operate this aircraft for carrying persons or property for compensation or hire.

11. The operator of this aircraft shall notify the control tower of the experimental nature of this aircraft when operating into or out of airports with operating control towers.

12. The cognizant FAA office must be notified and their response received in writing, prior to flying this aircraft after incorporating a major change as defined by FAR 21.93.

13. Compliance with FAR 91.319(b) shall also be recorded in the aircraft log with the following or a similarly worded statement: "I certify that this aircraft is controllable throughout its normal range of speeds and throughout all maneuvers to be executed; and the aircraft has no hazardous operating characteristics or design features." The entry shall include the aircraft total time-in-service, the name, signature, pilot certificate type and number of the person making the certification, and the date.

14. No person shall operate this aircraft unless within the preceding 12 calendar months, it has had a condition inspection performed in accordance with Appendix D of Part 43 and found to be in a condition for safe operation. Additionally, this inspection shall be recorded in accordance with limitation 15 listed below. Only FAA certificated and rated airframe and powerplant mechanics and appropriately rated repair stations may perform condition inspections in accordance with Appendix D of Part 43.

15. Condition inspections shall be recorded in the aircraft maintenance records showing the following or a similarly worded statement: "I certify that this aircraft has been inspected on _____ in accordance with the scope and detail of Appendix D of Part 43 and found to be in a condition for safe operation." The entry will include the aircraft total time-in-service, the name, signature, and certificate type and number of the person performing the inspection.

PHASE II - UNLIMITED OPERATIONS:

1. Limitations 5, 6, 7, 8, 9, 10, 11, 12, 14 and 15 from Phase I are applicable.

2. This aircraft is authorized for flights or static display at aviation events conducted under a waiver issued in accordance with FAR 91.903. (Waivers are not required for motion pictures, when in compliance with FAR 91.) Flights to and from these events are also authorized. Sun-N-Fun, Florida; SWPC Convention, Wanachee, WA; EAA, Oshkosh, WI; EAA, Albuquerque, NM; and EAA, Killeen, TX. XXXXXXXXXXXXXXXXXXXXXXXXXXXXXX
3. This aircraft shall not be operated for parachute jumping or glider towing operations.

4. Except for take offs and landings, this aircraft shall not be operated over densely populated areas or in congested airways.

These operating limitations are a part of a special airworthiness certificate issued 10-26-93 and will expire 10-25-94
Date of issue: 10-26-93   Issued by: Stephen _____

TO: Federal Aviation Administration
Manufacturing Inspection District Office
6020-28th Avenue South, Room 103
Minneapolis, MN 55450

Please accept this as my Program Letter.

I hereby request an experimental airworthiness certificate to operate an aircraft for the purpose of flight testing within an area described as follows:

Within a 25 Statute mile radius of Fairmont, MN for 10.0 hours. * See below for approved locations for Exhibition. XXXXXXXXXXXXXXXXXXXXXXXXXXXXX

I estimate that these operations will be completed in
one year.
(days) (months)

Aircraft Make Cessna
Aircraft Model 172II
Aircraft Registration Number N2594L

Date: 9-20-93
Signature: Roger A. Erickson
Title: Owner

* Sun-N-Fun, Florida; SWPC Convention, Wanachee, WA; EAA, Oshkosh, WI; EAA, Albuquerque, NM; and EAA, Killeen, TX. XXXXXXXXXXXXXXXXXXXX

LETTER OF PROGRAM

I. Purpose of Experiment
   A. To design an engine mount which will allow a Chevrolet small block engine to power a Cessna 172.
   B. To develop a torque box to use power of engine.
   C. To allow for an increase in speed which does not exceed airframe limitations.
   D. To maintain weight and balance so we do not change the handling characteristics of a Cessna 172.
   E. To increase performace on take-off and climb for hauling parachute jumpers.

II. Pre-test evaluations
   A. Chevrolet small block all-aluminum engine best suited to application.
   B. Torque box has run over 94 hours without failure of any components.
   C. Weight and balance falls within the existing envelope--verified with scales.
   D. Engine mount does not change the basic position of the propeller with respect to the cowling.
   E. Total conversion falls within my projected affordability group for a majority of pilots.
   F. Handling characteristics will allow all 172 pilots to fly this aircraft without updating their certificates.

III. Proposed Experimental Testing Certification Requirements
   A. Strictly NORMAL category operations
   B. Non aerobatic configuration
   C. Flight Test area of 5 states, IA, MN, SD, ND and WI, including Market Survey Trips to TEXAS and return.
   D. Flight approval for day and night operations
   E. VFR operations
   F. Waiver of engine hour running requirements due to the already proven track record of the small block Chevrolet engine.
   G. Flights to major General Aviation events or shows for the purpose of marketing said conversion(s).
   H. Certificated individuals can pilot this aircraft as configured after the conversion.

IV. Additional considerations for approval as requested
   A. Propeller
      1. Sensinich 60 inch pitch propeller.
   A. Engine mount
      1. Four-bolt pattern mates to existing fire-wall on standard Cessna 172
      2. Constructed from 4130 steel tubing
      3. Shock mounted rubber grommets to absorb vibrations.

This formula assumes a 1:1 gear ratio or direct drive. In situations where you are using a gear reduction box, the formula is:

HP=TORQUE X GEAR RATIO X ENGINE RPM/ 5252

The common denominator for these calculations (5252) is derived from the classical engineering division of 33,000 feet per minute by 2pi, or 6.2832, in order to convert James Watt's definition of linear power to rotational power as measured on a dynamometer. Incidently, The universally used 5252 denominator is found in any college engine design textbook. Decades ago during the horsepower race era manufacturers would maximize their HP numbers by elimination of accessories and perform testing under optimum ambient conditions. To put engine performance on a comparative basis SAE Recommended Practice 1349 was developed. SAE 1349 does define gross and net horsepower rating methods based on engine configurations (accessories, optional equipment). Mention of SAE horsepower ratings in advertising merely refers to these methods; no specific SAE defined horsepower calculation formula is published.

This is considered an "uncorrected horsepower" which must be reduced by 2% to compensate for power loss through the gearbox. Remember, you will NOT change the available horsepower, just the amount of torque available and the propeller revolutions per minute! As I have stated before, there is no magic associated with the use of automotive engines. Many automobile engine converters try to "over-prop" their engines without first checking the torque available and come up far short of what they expect.

These are examples I have run from the above formula. You can see you don't have to incorporate any RACE CAR devices in these engines to get the necessary horsepower we need in our airplanes! These engines must idle extremely smooth and with these numbers you can see what you can get with a normal stock engine. These engines can also be run at a sensible RPM and still perform extremely well. For example:

ENGINE: V8 - 400 CU. IN. -- WITH 420 FT. LBS. TORQUE
    GEAR RATIO: 1.8:1
    PROP DIAMETER: 76"
    PITCH IN INCHES: 90

    ENGINE SPEED: 4500 RPMS
    CALCULATED PROP RPMS: 2500
    ESTIMATED TORQUE: 756 FT. LBS.
    USABLE TORQUE (75%) 567 FT. LBS.

    ESTIMATED HP @ PROP: 352.7
    PROP-TIP SPEED IN MPH: 565.2
    ESTIMATED AIR SPEED: 213.1

This is using a Chevrolet 400 engine! Another example:

ENGINE: V8 - 400 CU. IN. -- WITH 420 FT. LBS. TORQUE
    GEAR RATIO: 1.44:1
    PROP DIAMETER: 76
    PITCH IN INCHES: 64

    ENGINE SPEED: 4000 RPMs
    CALCULATED PROP RPMS: 2500
    ESTIMATED TORQUE: 604.8 FT. LBS.
    USABLE TORQUE (75%) 453.6 FT. LBS.

    ESTIMATED HP @ PROP: 313.5
    PROP-TIP SPEED IN MPH: 628.1
    ESTIMATED AIR SPEED: 168.4

Note, the differences in gear ratios used and the change in propeller pitch. The second example could be with a "stock" propeller from many light airplanes that could be repitched to these specifications!

These figures are for FIXED PITCH PROPELLERS! Imagine the performance with constant speed propellers or variable pitch propellers! In the future I am going to build an electric powered variable pitch propeller system. I think this would apply to the general aviation public to both enhance performance of their airplanes and still be affordable. Watch for this development in future news from Alternative Power.

SUMMARY

The Cessna installation will continue to be tested in the future. I have plans for a "ducted-fan" type tail cooling system to eliminate tail ballast. I perceive the addition of a hydraulic system in the future (remember, I have 300 HP to deal with) which can run floats, gear, etc. Since I am the sole proprietor of my operation, I am responsible for the TOTAL construction phase from beginning to end. To achieve this level of self-sufficiency I needed the ability to cast my parts. Recognizing the need for a foundry, my life-long acquaintance, Chuck Paden of Bingham Lake, MN, offered to help with my construction and teach me the foundry business. I spent a year and a half with him on this project. He is in the early stages of constructing 2-4-6 cylinder hortizontally opposed direct drive liquid cooled engines based on Chevrolet small block engine components as his alternative power source. The final machining of all these components will be done on my mills and lathes.

Throughout the engineering, research, development, and construction process, I have had to learn bits and pieces one at a time. I attempt to spell out, sometimes in minute detail, the entire project. I want the reader to know the who, what, why, where, when these items were constructed. The decisions I had to make during the construction were never taken lightly--this is the safest gearbox flying today!

Flying is the real test of my labors. Many people have flown in my converted airplane and remark not only on its performance but also on its very normal flight characteristics. One need only take a "test drive" and feel the extra margin of comfort and safety afforded by having power available when it is needed. After flights in my airplane it is hard to return to the lower powered airplanes flying today. My observation concludes: all civilian airplanes flying today are under powered with obsolete motors! Military and commercial aviation has enjoyed this extra power for years. We would not drive around today with automobiles with 1940 model engines--so why should airplanes be stifled? Let's work together to achieve some real performance for all pilots.

I have attempted to incorporate as much information as possible into this article. Hopefully, these documented facts are helpful for ALL experimenters building planes. I trust you will find this information accurate and beneficial to your own construction process. Some articles have generated a number of misconceptions which experimenters have assumed were true. My experience and data has proven otherwise. Even though this information has been difficult at times to come across, I am willing to share it with all the flying public in the hopes we can work together and build affordable, flyable airplanes! **REE**

COMPONENT PRICES	
Aluminum Heads (2)	$ 1200.00
Dual Plug Heads (2)	1600.00
Drive, 2nd Distributor	695.00
Aluminum Block	4200.00
Freeze Plugs	70.00
Water Pump	125.00
Starter	269.00
Custom Built Pulleys	125.00
Plug Wire set	129.00
Distributor (1)	197.00
Correct cam (removes valve overlap)	90.00
Gear box	3600.00
Typical cost of an operating Engine: $ 9500.00	

SUBARU EA81 Turbo Powered AVID FLYER

Reiner Hoffmann
Stratus, Incorporated
7750 12th Avenue N.W.
Seattle Washington
98117-4135
(206) 784 8376

Experimenters are paving the way for general acceptance of auto power conversions in amateur built aircraft. Modern auto water cooled designs such as the Subaru EA81 offer more power in stock form than the once popular, souped-up VW conversions. Redrives, cooling and propeller developments are major areas of focus.   MCM

In late 1991, after flying my Avid Flyer with Rotax 532 power for about 15 hours, I was already tired and wary of the screaming two-stroke Austrian hand grenade. Another powerplant needed to be found. I immediately researched what was available in the automobile engine market. I searched for a lightweight small engine that would fit my Avid. First, I studied the three cylinder one liter Suzuki engine which powers the Geo Metro (the original Canadian Airmotive CAM 90 was based on this engine but did not make it to production). I test drove a Geo for some time but was not pleased with the engine's rather rough idle and its dimensions which did not seem to fit the cowling lines of the Avid. I also checked out the Subaru EA81. It was a bit heavier, but its dimensions and configuration seemed to suit the cowling shape better. The fact that the engine had a good record of reliability in street use was the prime reason for my decision to go with the Subaru.

I began a search for a suitable reduction drive and came to the conclusion that a belt reduction drive was the best choice. I called all over the country to learn more about belt drives. I spoke to several people and learned, for example, that a few certified aircraft powerplants do include gear reduction systems. I also learned that planes containing these engines had a placard mounted on the instrument panel that prohibited pilots from operating the engine at certain rpm readings. No one, on the other hand, had experienced any bad situations associated with belts. My investigation concluded that the belt drive would give me a smooth running drive, that would be relatively easy to inspect periodically for wear or cracks, and that could easily be serviced for adjustment or replacement. Since I planned to fly the Avid on floats into high country lakes and would need altitude performance, I decided that the EA81 Turbo version would be best for my purposes. This engine has hydraulic valve lifters that are an asset in reducing engine maintenance.

I bought the engine and its accessories for $500 (it was a Japanese inspection reject; in effect, Japanese vehicle inspection regulations force car owners to replace their engines after some 30,000 miles of driving). The engine was bulky so I stripped off the large offending intake manifold with its fuel injectors. I fabricated a custom intake manifold using steel sheet metal and stainless steel tubing that was 1.5 inches in diameter. Beacause I hoped to use leftover Rotax components wherever possible, I first used the Rotax Bing carburetor. This design did not work to my satisfaction. The slide cutaway was too small, which made the engine run very rich during idle. I modified the carburetor in an attempt to improve the situation, but to no avail. I then tried a 34 mm constant velocity Mikuni carburetor, which was originally on a Kawasaki 250 motorcycle. This solved the bulk and idling problems and reduced the weight by approximately 25 pounds. The Amax reduction drive I ordered finally arrived and, to my

The Avid Flyer at an early stage of engine installation. The turbo version was initially chosen for altitude work. Because of its complexity and critical pilot demands, it is not recommended for more typical fun flying.

dismay, was damaged rather seriously during its travels from Australia. The heavy flywheel banged against the machined engine mating surface of the reduction housing in transit. The small sprocket belt guides were bent. The big sprocket was also dinged from contact with the flywheel. AMAX sent me a new housing. I was able to make the other parts serviceable with a little straightening and filing to remove the damage. I soon discovered that this redrive combination did not have any provisions for mounting the starter. My first task was to fabricate a starter mounting bracket. Thanks to my tool and die training, the fabrication of this part was of no consequence. The bracket is seen in the above photo, above the right cylinder bank.

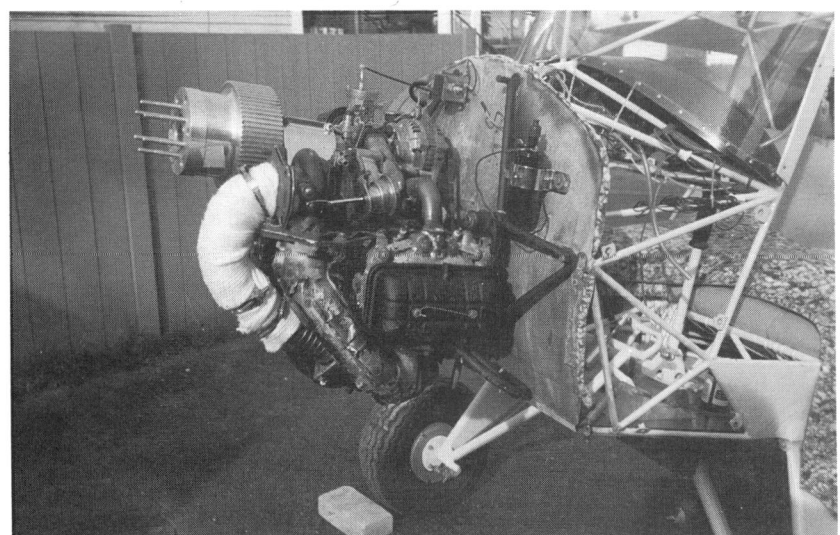

Another view of the installation with the AMAX belt reduction drive visible. The stock auto components were removed.

Fabricating the engine mount was the next project. The Avid engine compartment was bare, so I leveled and blocked the fuselage. Then I placed the Subaru engine in position next to the firewall and leveled it on a wooden base. This was easy to do since the engine's oil pan is the lowest point of the engine and can support its weight. Factory engines are normally hung from overhead because their bottoms are occupied by carburetors and the like. An A & P friend and I cut, tacked and later welded the engine mount tubes. An additional welded attachment point was incorporated in the fuselage for the support of the heaver engine; the point is located on the bottom center of the firewall just above the floorboards. We decided to change the angle of the vertical fin from its factory offset of 2-3 degrees for the Rotax engine rotation to zero degrees. I modified the factory cowling to house the Subaru conversion.

I spent much time in adjusting the ignition timing to match the engine boost requirements. Since I knew I could easily damage the engine I asked experienced engine people for their advice. After considerable testing I arrived at 24 degrees BTDC advance. My boost was mechanically limited to 5 psi by use of a "popoff" wastegate. I originally used a highly modified Mazda RX7 oil cooler as my radiator, which worked very well until the temperature reached 85 degrees F. The radiator permitted the engine to overheat. To correct this problem, I selected and installed an all aluminum VW Rabbit radiator. It lies parallel with the bottom of the cowling and the leading edge is faced with a scoop. This arrangement worked very well cooling the engine to 180-195 degrees while running on the ground at over 100 degree ambient temperature. Once these installation problems were resolved there wasn't any excuse not to fly.

On a nice 60 degree Friday afternoon at the Arlington Washington Airport, I lifted off using very little runway in comparison to past flights with the Rotax. The airplane flew very well,I but was felt to be slightly nose heavy. After an uneventful flight I found that the CG was off the optimum location by one inch. Two pounds of lead added to the additional tail load of strobe and battery solved the problem. Testing resumed. The maximum continuous rate of climb turned out to be 2000 feet per minute. Top speed on my Avid (built with the STOL wings) is 130 mph, indicated. Since I was concerned with altitude performance, I also climbed to 15,000 feet and obtained 800 fpm climb at that altitude.

At the local airport, my airplane is called the "Stealth" because it is so quiet. At 85 mph, indicated, the engine turns at 3400 rpm; the Stinger muffler and the turbocharger are also very effective. At this point in the project the airplane has almost 100 flight hours, all trouble free. The fuel burn is 2.8 gallons per hour at an 80-85 mph cruise setting. Slow flying for sightseeing reduces that figure to about a 2.0 gallonper hour burn rate.

Since the reaction to my conversion has been very positive, I have decided to design and build reduction drives and engine conversions, incorporating the many improvements defined during my test program. Work began shortly after Oshkosh 1992. With the assistance of a Boeing engineer I have configured a dual 30 mm belt reduction drive arrangement using HTD belts. The crankshaft/propshaft centerline offset dimension is 7.0 inches. The driven sprocket diamenter is 8.4 inches, which defines at one point the upper cowling centerline profile. HTD belts run much smoother than

The original cowling required modification. This was done after the installation was completed. The radiator is visible forward the gear struts.

Closeup view of the VW Rabbit radiator and motorcycle muffler. Very effective noise reduction without any appreciable loss in power.

First public outing at Arlington 1992. The modified cowling fits in with the overall appearance of the Flyer. The adjustable Warp Drive propeller came in handy during flight tests.

Flight above the crater of 14,410 ft Mt. Rainier; the goal is reached!

Polychain belts. The dual belts offer a measure of redundancy if one belt breaks. I replaced the stock induction system with a custom intake manifold with dual Bing altitude-compensating carburetors. The engine is now dressed with a light weight 12 ampere alternator. The total weight of the entire engine, including reduction drive and flywheel, starter, alternator, carburetors and intake manifold, ignition, exhaust headers (less the weight of engine mount, engine oil, engine coolant and radiator, which will vary with differing airframes) at this stage of development is approximatwely 180 pounds. This engine configuration develops around 100 hp on my dynamometer which is adequate for a number of custom airplanes now using less reliable powerplants.

As of this writing (December 1992) my prototype reduction drive has accumulated 26 hours of flight time without any major problems. Sometime in January, I expect that another Avid Flyer should be flying with my reduction drive and conversion of a normally aspirated 100 hp Subaru EA81 engine. A third conversion (normally aspirated) will be assembled for extensive dynamometer testing to determine horsepower, torque, and fuel consumption figures. Testing of the prototype engine and redrive configurations should be completed by the end of the first quarter of 1993. Hard tooling will be updated accordingly. Shipping of production conversion assemblies should commence thereafter.

Avid Flyer (STOL)/Subaru EA81 Turbo Performance

Empty weight (with parachute)	632 lb
Cruise speed	95 mph
Stall speed	32 mph
VNE	135 mph
Rate of climb	>2000 fpm
Take-off distance	80 ft
Landing distance	150 ft
Service ceiling	> 15,000ft

Ducted Fan Propulsion for Replica Jet Fighters

Ernest R. Jones Ph.D
Embry-Riddle Aero University
600 South Clyde Morris Blvd
Daytona Beach FL 32114-3900
(904) 226 6000

The following article was originally presented May 24-25, 1994, at an AIAA/FAA Joint Symposium on General Aircraft Systems at Mississippi State University by the authors[14]. Interest in amateur built replica aircraft has grown over the last forty years with the appearance of many designs, ranging from wood and fabric WW I "crates" to highly crafted metal WW II machines. This unique study addresses the concept of jet fighter replicas utilizing auto engine power. It challenges experimenters to go forth and further explore the possibilities of ducted fan propulsion. MCM

Scale fighter plane replicas are becoming increasingly popular in Sport Aviation, which is one important aspect of revitalizing general aviation. However, no suitable propulsion systems exist for jet sport aircraft. The technology for ducted fan propulsion of larger aircraft has been established, but applications to light aircraft have been few. The feasibility of using ducted fan propulsion for a 2/3 scale replica of the Douglas A-4 "Skyhawk" fighter plane was determined by performing a complete conceptual design of the aircraft. Results of the study show that such a design is feasible and that the performance in all flight regimes is acceptable if a readily attainable power loading is used.

Compared to conventional aircraft, the advantages of such a design are: (1) ownership of a unique and exciting aircraft, (2) quiet operation, (3) enhanced ramp safety due to enclosed propeller, and (4) performance exceeding most general aviation aircraft. Disadvantages include: slightly increased weight and cost (both initial and operating), limited fuselage volume and center of gravity travel and more difficult engine accessibility.

A complete ducted fan propulsion system concept has been developed, including design of the fan, inlet ducts and outlet ducting. A structural design concept is also shown accounting for all of the required systems, a version which would permit fabrication of a prototype at low cost.

DESIGN PROGRESS

Sport Aviation has grown steadily since the mid 1950s and has now reached a level of maturity such that a greater number of homebuilt aircraft are taking to the air each year than production aircraft by the major manufacturers. Some high performance homebuilts are also exceeding functionality and performance of production aircraft, and they are gradually shedding their former slightly disreputable status.

The FAA is even encouraging the development of new light aircraft by simplification of the certification process. A number of homebuilt aircraft are being certificated for production under these new regulations. The future of sport and light aviation looks brighter than it has for years. Many new aircraft are under development to try to catch the resurgent wave of popularity for sport flying whether it be fixed wing, rotary wing, sailplanes, aerobatics, warbirds, or restoration of classic and antique aircraft,

Replica fighter aircraft are a popular alternative for the average pilot without the means and training to own and operate one of the increasingly rare "Warbirds." However, these are almost entirely propeller driven aircraft since jet powered sport aircraft are, and will continue to be, very rare due primarily the high cost of purchasing and operating gas turbine engines.

However, the thought of flying around in a jet fighter aircraft is an intriguing one. A possible method for achieving much of the "look and feel" of a jet without the associated high cost is to use a ducted fan propulsion system powered by a conventional reciprocating engine. The purposes of this design study were to (1) investigate whether a ducted fan propulsion system is a feasible means of powering a replica jet fighter and (2) to determine if adequate performance levels are attainable. The results of that design study are summarized in the following report. Interested readers may contact the authors for more detailed information. (Mike Stevens and Adriano Almeida have completed their studies and are no longer at ERAU-MCM).

DESIGN REQUIREMENTS

The proposed aircraft is a single seat sport plane which will be flown only for pleasure and display purposes. It should be a subscale replica of a jet fighter aircraft having wide recognition and appeal and maintain the scale appearance in so far as possible. The aircraft would be designed using FAR 23[1] regulations as a guideline but would certified in the experimental category. The structure would be designed for the aerobatics although there is no intent to make the aircraft competitive in aerobatics.

A reasonable high level of performance would be required to make the airplane attractive. The following performance goals were specified:

    Stall speed = 61 kts maximum
    Cruise speed = 175 kts minimum
    Range = 450 nm plus reserves minimum
    Payload = 170 lb pilot plus 35 lb baggage
    Take off and landing = 3000 ft over 50 ft obstacle.

REPLICA AIRCRAFT SELECTION

The selection of a suitable aircraft for scaling is partially governed by the size of the cockpit relative to the overall external dimensions. When a large aircraft is selected as a candidate, the size must be reduced sufficiently to accommodate a reasonable sized, low cost powerplant. However, the cockpit must remain large enough to fit the pilot. A subtle change in the geometry should not offend the replica enthusiast but, as seen in the case of the BD-10, the required cockpit size tends to be larger than is aesthetically pleasing. Other complications arise with mid-mounted wing configurations, especially if the landing gear retracts into the fuselage. The internal fuselage volume is important in ducted fan design since the thrust and efficiency are dependent on the fan diameter.

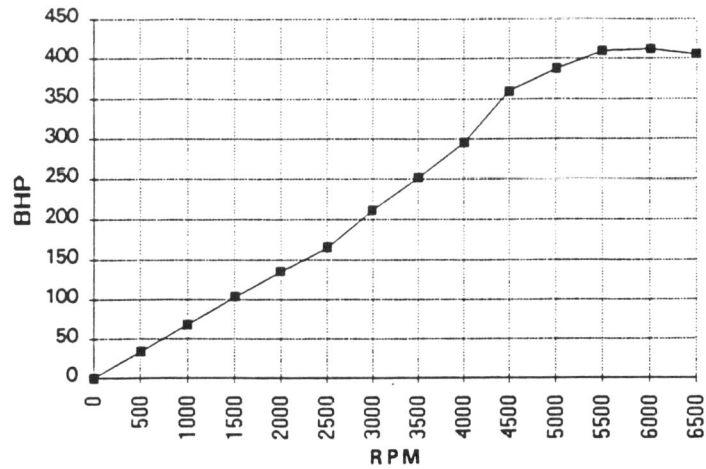

Figure 1. Performance data for the Chevrolet 350 in^3 V/8 engine.

The F-15, F-16, F-4, F-18, and the A-4[5] were among the many aircraft considered. The A-4 Skyhawk was found to present the minimum number of problems in terms of powerplant installation and pilot integration. Moreover, the A-4's low wing allows for easy engine access, wing mounted landing gear, and ease of fuselage to wing integration.

All of the low aspect ratio fighters have similar problems in the lower speed and high angle of attack regime since the induced drag is high for this type of configuration. In addition, as the vortex flow begins to dominate at the higher angles of attack, the maximum lift is typically delayed to the angles beyond 20 degrees for symmetrical airfoils. Although low aspect ratio invokes a large penalty in terms of induced drag and minimum lift, the effects can be minimized by having a light span loading. If the wing loading is sufficiently low, the penalties imposed by the low aspect ratio are bearable. Examples of successful low aspect ratio sport aircraft are the Dyke Delta and the Rutan Variviggen, which have reportedly pleasant flight characteristics and attractive performance levels.

CONFIGURATION LAYOUT

As shown in the 3-view drawing, the 2/3 scale replica A-4, dubbed the "Minihawk" has a wing span of 18.3 feet, a total length of 27 feet, and a height of 5 feet at the nose. With the exception of a thicker wing section, a slightly larger canopy, and modified ailerons the replica has dimensions scaled precisely from the original aircraft.

AERODYNAMIC SURFACES

The wing section is a NACA 0012 symmetrical airfoil and tail surfaces are NACA 0009 sections. Longitudinal control is provided by a stabilator while roll and yaw are provided by a rudder and conventional ailerons.

LANDING GEAR

The landing gear system for the Minihawk is similar to the original configuration. The replica's landing gear features some key changes which make the system more affordable. The primary changes are the incorporation of a castoring nose wheel and a simplified retraction geometry. The increased wing thickness and slightly larger retractions pods allow the main gear to be retracted forward without having to undergo a 90 rotation as the A-4 does. The retraction system operates on manually actuated hydraulic pumps and the up and down locks are cable actuated for overall simplicity and ease of design.

The landing gear legs consist of telescoping steel tubes that use a system of rubber donuts between each tube for proper shock absorption. The gear doors will be sequenced with the retraction through mechanical linkages. The nose gear retracts forward into the cockpit such that the gear leg is positioned beneath the seat and the wheel fits between the rudder pedals. Emergency gear extension will rely on G-loading and flow induced forces such as on the original A-4.

During low to intermediate taxi velocities directional control is provided through the use of differential braking. During takeoff and landing the rudder provides sufficient authority for ground control due to the higher velocities. The primary drawback of a castoring nose wheel is that during pushback operations, there is a tendency for the wheel to cock sideways.

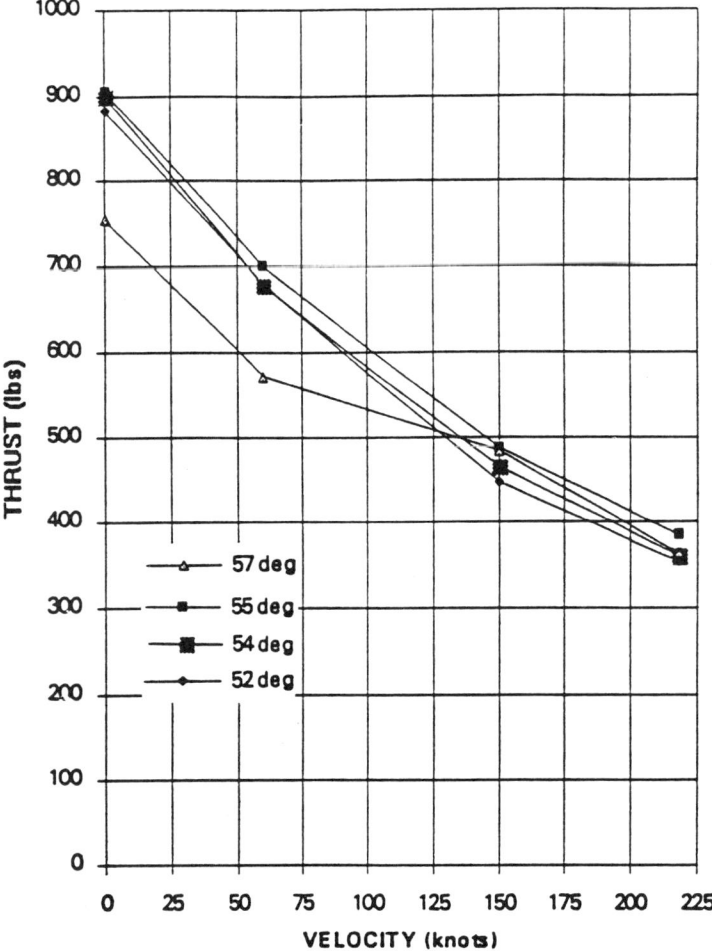

Figure 2. Thrust versus velocity for different pitch angles at .75 radius.

The fact that the Minihawk sits fairly high on its gear and has a relatively large fuselage area could create some difficulties during cross wind operations. The operator will have to ensure that the established cross wind limitations are not exceeded for safe flight.

WEIGHT AND BALANCE

The gross and empty weights, as well as the center of gravity position and range, were calculated using the methods given by Raymer[4] and available in Raymer's Design Software (RDS). The initial weight estimates were somewhat low at approximately 1500 pounds whereas the revised weights of 1829 pounds gross and 1407 pounds empty seem more reasonable for this size aircraft. Due to the internal ducting requirements associated with this type of aircraft the conservative weight estimates were used as given by the general aviation category in the RDS software. At a cost of $100 per pound saved an additional 70 pounds can be saved by substituting an aluminum block engine for the conventional cast iron block.

The static margin changes from 11 percent to 16 percent of the mean aerodynamic chord depending on the fuel load and pilot weight. The baggage allowance of 35 pounds has little effect on the aircraft CG because of the proximity of the load to the aircraft CG.

The replica configuration is very susceptible to pilot weight however since a relatively long moment are exists between the cockpit and the aircraft center of gravity and since the pilot weight makes up a higher percentage of the gross weight than in the original A-4. If the pilot weight is increased by 30 pounds the CG is shifted forward by one inch, corresponding to a 2 percent change in the static margin. The shift in CG resulting from changes in the cockpit weight is not a major problem for a single seat version, but would probably create the need for ballasting in a two seat variant. Table I summarizes the resulting weight estimates.

Structures Group (lb)		Equipment Group (lb)	
wing	150	flight controls	28
horizontal tail	26	hydraulics	2
vertical tail	55	electrical	54
fuselage	225	avionics	25
main gear	97	total	109
nose gear	39		
total	592		
Propulsion Group (lb)		Useful Load Group (lb)	
installed engine	683	pilot	170
fuel system	23	fuel	210
total	706	oil	7
		cargo	35
		total	422

Distance from nose
Empty Weight 1407 pounds
CG 162.5 inches (no fuel)
Gross Weight 1794 pounds
CG 158.5 inches (gross weight)

Table 1. Weight and balance summary

COCKPIT

The cockpit was one of the important criteria considered during the aircraft selection process. The published minimum acceptable dimensions for the 90th percentile pilot were used as the guide lines in selecting the aircraft scale factor. The cockpit dimensions arrived at should be comfortable for the average pilot. The proposed mission of the aircraft is mainly for sport flying. Therefore, the required instrumentation is minimal. Basic VFR flight instruments, navcom, transponder, and handheld GPS would be more than adequate for the mission requirements. The minimal instrumentation helps keep weight and cost down but, if desired, one could capture the jet image by making use of one of the recently developed heads up display units that provide performance and navigation data all in one location. Available heads up displays sell for as low as $5000, depending on the navigation capability.

The use of a sidestick controller is employed in order to

establish more precise control during slow flight, when the stick forces are lower. Moreover, it helps to reduce the required cockpit depth. The flight control system is simpler than in many general aviation production aircraft, such as that found in the TB-9.

The entire nose and cockpit of the aircraft is seen as being a cohesive structural unit that maintains its integrity in the event of an incident, with the canopy frame and forward bulkhead providing the required roll over protection.. Recent data published by Cirrus Aircraft Corporation indicates that seat energy absorption requirements can be achieved through the use of TemperfoamTM, which greatly simplifies the design of the seat and associated structure. The canopy design replicates that of the original but the requirements for impact and battle damage are less severe.

STRUCTURAL CONCEPT

The basis for the prototype Minihawk structure is foam and fiberglass composite sandwich construction using a wet lay up technique. The wing has three spars which were designed to handle the flight loads as well as loads imposed by the retractable landing gear during ground operation. In order to accommodate the complex spanwise taper geometries the wing spars are constructed from foam stabilized graphite composite. Instead of using a solid foam core, ribs are cut from foam and spaced at approximately 12 inch intervals. A solid foam core was found to produce a large weight penalty which could be overcome by using the more conventional built-up approach. The entire wing structure is covered with 1/16 inch plywood and 2 layers of very light weight glass cloth. The plywood is equal in strength to fiberglass in terms of capability to transmit shear loads,but it also reduces the amount of filling and sanding required for a suitable finish when compared to a strictly glass over foam construction, The two layers of 3/4 ounce glass fabric serve to seal the surface and to protect it from the environment. Another advantage of the plywood is that the structure can be painted any color with no risk of losing strength at elevated temperatures, such as with a typical wet lay-up. The control surfaces are cut from a single piece of foam, a spar is installed, and the assembly is skinned with plywood and fiberglass.

Detailed design of the fuselage structure is a challenging task. The prototype will utilize two frames to support the fan-engine integration, as well as to transmit the wing shear loads. The forward fuselage bulkhead is a focal point for the loads imposed by the nose gear and the pilot, and it also acts as the firewall. The ducting is a thin walled fiberglass construction inside the tall which is designed to withstand the hoop stresses resulting from elevated pressures. The fiberglass inlet ducting needs to be reinforced since there will be negative air pressures in that region during takeoff and acceleration. The inlet ducting will follow similar paths to that of the original A-4, except for the addition of a large cheater hole in the bottom of the fuselage. The cheater hole is necessary for providing the fan with sufficient mass flow during takeoff.

The horizontal stabilizer consists of a plywood skinned foam core, with a spar and torque tube along with several ribs made of light plywood. The rudder is virtually identical to the ailerons in construction and hinging.

PROPULSION SYSTEM

The propulsion system is the key technology of the proposed concept, and consists of an engine, ducted fan, drive shaft, fuel tank and system components, intake and exit ducts and cooling system (radiator). Each of these propulsion system components is discussed in the following sections.

ENGINE SELECTION

A number of engines were considered for the Minihawk, including small gas turbojet engines. However, it was quickly obvious that no suitable jet engine exists that can be purchased for any reasonable price. Thus, the ducted fan propulsion system, powered by a reciprocating engine was selected.

Both aircraft and automotive engines were considered for the powerplant. Aircraft engines in the required power range (300 to 400 hp) were very expensive as shown in the table below. Also shown in the table are two of the many automotive engines considered. The usual drawbacks of automotive engines for propeller driven aircraft are actually advantages in a ducted fan design. The operating range of the fan is in the vicinity of 4,000 to 6,000 rpm, which is about the same as the average V-8 automobile engine. It is probable that a direct drive system could be utilized without problems, making the propulsion system simple and light weight.

Engine	Cost	Weight(lb)	BHP	Fuel(gph)	Overhaul Cost
Lyc IO-720	$70,000	568	400	18	$8000
Ward V/8	$20,000	535	475	15	$800
ZR-1 V/8	$3,000	605	350	13	$800

Table 2. Comparison of a typical aircraft engine to automotive engines.

From Table 2 it is seen that a ZR-1 V/8 engine (Chevrolet small block) is slightly heavier than a Lycoming IO-720, but it has a lower fuel consumption and is much cheaper. The aluminum block Ward V/8 saves 70 pounds in weight but adds approximately $7000 to the acquisition cost. Since the ZR-1 is relatively inexpensive and comes ready to run from the factory with an output of 350 HP at 5600 RPM, it was used as the baseline for the replica propulsion system.

The Chevrolet small block is one of the most popular engines in the hotrod market so numerous after market options are readily available at reasonable prices. For example, a Paxton supercharger is available for $4000 complete. Using a supercharger would allow the replica jet to maintain rated power to 10,000 feet where the increase in true airspeed would be a significant factor in the overall aircraft performance. Also available are automatic mixture control carburetors and fuel injection systems. Figure 1 shows the performance of a slightly modified ZR-1 engine. Other

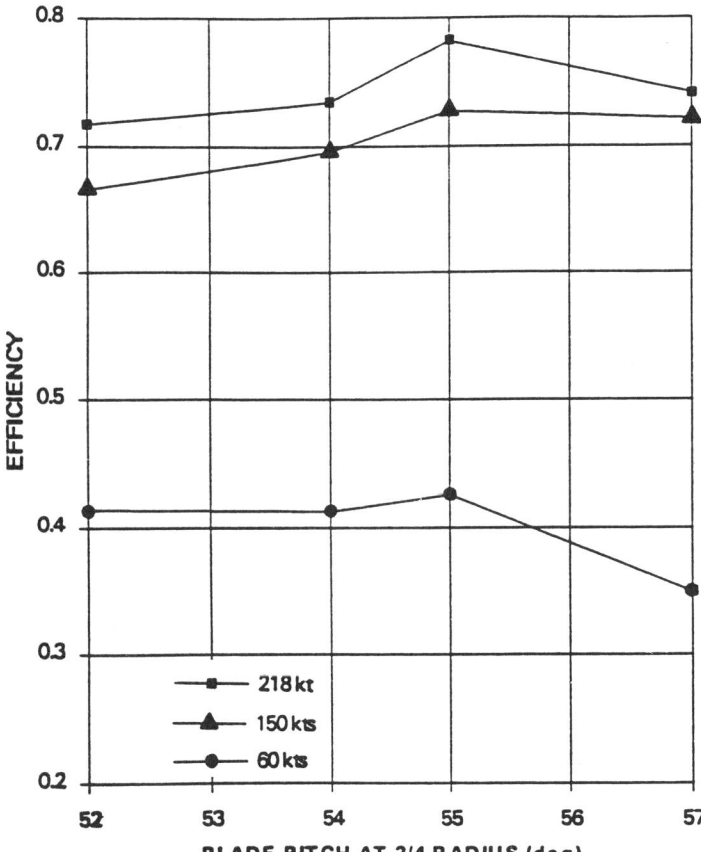

Figure 3. Propulsive efficiency for different pitch angles and flight velocities.

engines considered, but not reported here, were the Mazda rotary, Ford SVO group, and the Cadillac Northstar engine. The Northstar[6] is of particular interest due to its ladder style block support construction, low weight and numerous safety features to prevent engine failure; e.g., the "limp home" mode which provides alternate cylinder firing in order to maintain acceptable cylinder head temperatures in the event of coolant loss.

The use of the liquid cooled engine adds complexity to the aircraft since it requires a radiator, but the technology to cool engines in aircraft is well proven and should not present major difficulties. Of greater concern is the dependence of the automotive engine on battery power for the production of spark. The majority of the converted auto engines flying today utilize a backup system which is used to provide an alternative source of power in the event of alternator or other electrical failure.

ENGINE LOCATION

The location of the engine is governed to a great extent by the need to maintain a scale vehicle appearance and acceptable CG range. Its center of gravity needs to be located approximately 168 inches aft of the aircraft nose in order to attain the correct aircraft CG location. The pusher configuration is the best design from an internal aerodynamics point of view and for ease of engine to airframe interface. Since a direct drive shaft is used to rotate the fan the engine crankshaft must be aligned with the thrust line. The crankshaft on most V/8s is approximately 18 inches below the top surface of the engine which leads to conflicting requirements in engine placement. Since the fan needs to be as large as possible without interfering with the wing carry through structure, the engine clearance from the tip of the fuselage must be minimized. Susceptibility of the room temperature cured composite materials to high temperatures places a limit on this clearance. The drawing which shows engine placement with structural details can be studied.

ENGINE COOLING

The ZR-1 engine is cooled by the usual 50/50 mixture of ethylene glycol and water. The cylinder head temperatures and specific fuel consumption of the liquid cooled engine are typically much lower than for an equivalent air cooled engine. The primary advantages in the operational characteristics of the liquid cooled engine are the reduced sensitivity to shock cooling, as well as the increased resistance to overspeeding. The heat rejection rate of the internal combustion engine can approach 30 percent of the total energy of the fuel consumed. In the case of the Minihawk the heat rejection rate will approach 4000 BTU/min for the engine coolant and 1000 BTU/min for the engine oil.

An accepted cooling configuration is to use an aluminum core custom made radiator with a built in heat exchanger for the engine oil. Preliminary calculations show that an inlet capture area of 45 square inches for engine cooling should be sufficient. An 18 x 31 inch radiator is incorporated such that the required capture area is in the duct inlets. After passing through the radiator, air passes over the engine and is then bled back into the internal slipstream just forward of the fan guide vanes. The requirements for a clean, cool source of induction air is met by designing the Minihawk with a pair of 12 square inch flush NACA inlets, as shown in the inboard profile drawing.

FAN DRIVE SHAFT

The drive shaft from the engine to the fan is of critical importance since poor shaft design has been the downfall of several promising designs. The V/8 engine coupled with the short shaft promises to be free from the effects of torsional resonance. The detail design of the stator and rotor shows that the thrust and gyroscopic loads will be handled entirely by the stator, which consists of four streamline steel tubes. The engine is isolated from the rotor and stator by the use of a splined sliding shaft and universal joints. The drive shaft material used is mild steel with a thin walled tube making up the bulk of the shaft.

FUEL SYSTEM

The prototype Minihawk design utilizes a single fuel bladder installed in the area just behind the pilot. The race-car style fuel cell is adequate for 35 gallons on internal volume. The system will need an electrical fuel pump as backup to the usual engine driven pump. The fuel compartment will also be isolated from the engine and cockpit by firewall bulkheads. Since engine fire would be catastrophic for the Minihawk, precautions have to be taken to ensure safety. The fuel cell, emergency fuel shut off, and Halon fire extinguishers should provide sufficient protection for the prototype. Kit produced versions of the Minihawk would employ the familiar wet wing concept. In addition to being safer, a wet wing configuration would ease the CG travel due to fuel burn, improving the operational characteristics of the Minihawk.

FAN DESIGN

An extensive literature search was required to find the information required to design and analyze the fan. Very little information was found when searching using the DUCTED FAN keyword. Most of the useful information was found by using reports written for the design of wind tunnels10 or for the aerodynamic design of axial flow compressors8. Two older reports were found which provided a complete design methodology using cascade theory. A very useful and extensive source of current information was provided by Dr. Terry Wright, et al, at the Georgia Institute of Technology in Atlanta, Georgia. After some study, all of these reports were found to contain the information necessary for the design and analysis of ducted fans.

	Current Propeller	Q-fan
Diameter (in)	78.0	36.0
Number of blades	3	9
RPM	2700	4060
Sea Level Thrust @ 66 kts (lb)	880	880
Sea Level Thrust @ 218 kts (lb)	316	329
Weight (lb)	77	175
Noise Level (dB)	99.5	79
1980 Cost without engine	$803	$1650
Required Engine Horsepower	286	387

Table 3. Comparison of propeller and Q-fan criteria.

However, the method finally selected was based on a 1973 report[9] entitled "Q-Fans For General Aviation Aircraft" by Rose Worobel and Millard Mayo of Hamilton Standard in Windsor Locks, Connecticut. This report examined the use of ducted fans powered by either piston or gas turbine engines where the primary emphasis was on reduced noise, hence the term Q-FanTM.

The Q-fan is a low noise propulsor concept which was developed in the early seventies to meet the expected noise restrictions of the future. Although Q-fans require more engine power in order to match current propeller performance at low speeds, this penalty is compensated by the fact that it provides cleaner airframe design alternatives.

The report is an extensive design study for ducted fan propulsion for several classes of general aviation aircraft aimed at improving safety, utility, performance, and cost. Complete analytic methods are given, as well as a tabulated step by step procedures for designing a ducted fan, including numerous design charts. Although not reported here, several checks were made using the methods of the previous reports in order to validate the Q-fan method and to ensure that the results were realistic.

A comparison of a Q-fan design and a conventional propeller system is provided in Table 3. From this table it is seen that in order to match the thrust of a propeller driven by a 285 HP engine at sea level and 66 kts, a 387 HP engine is required for the fan. The penalty associated with using a Q-fan design is not as severe at higher flight speeds where the 387 HP engine can be used to produce higher thrust levels than the propeller system driven by a 285 HP engine.

The design charts developed by Hamilton Standard combine propeller analysis theory with experimental data obtained from tested Q-fans of various configurations. Factors such as fan diameter, blade total activity factor, blade structure, tip speed, geometric pitch at 3/4 radius, inlet to exit area, duct length, advance ratio and engine power were all considered in order to arrive at a working design. An iterative approach was taken such that the power required by the fan at each condition was equal to power supplied by the engine. A summary of the fan design process and a sample calculation are given in Appendix 2 of the original paper. The values used for calculating the fan performance are also given in Appendix 2. The numbers extracted from each chart were entered into a spreadsheet template which was programmed to solve for the thrust, power required, and efficiency.

The engine output at the design point was fixed at 330 HP at 4330 RPM and a tradeoff study was conducted by determining the performance for different pitch angles at 3/4 radius. Once the RPM and blade pitch were established at the design point, the total blade solidity was varied until the power required by the fan was equal to the power available by the engine.

To calculate the fan performance for off design conditions, an iterative approach was taken which involved selecting a fan RPM and calculating the power required for the given flight speed and blade activity factor. If the power required did not match the power available by the engine, as given by the manufacturer, the RPM was adjusted until the condition was met.

Higher pitch angles, such as 57 degrees, produce minor benefits at higher velocities and result in significantly lower thrust levels at low velocities as a result of blade stall. Propulsive efficiencies were calculated for different pitch angles by dividing the product of thrust and velocity by the engine power input. As can be seen in Figure 3 the propulsive efficiency of the fan peaks at a pitch angle of 55 degrees for all flight velocities studied. For structural purposes, the pitch angle selected for the preliminary fan design was 54 degrees, which requires four blades with an average chord of 4.0 inches each.

Although 55 degrees pitch produces slightly higher efficiencies, it requires a lower blade activity factor, which would result in a smaller blade width if four blades are used. Of course the activity factor could be reduced without reducing blade width if three blades are use instead of four, but a lower number of blades increases the noise level due to flow pulsation.

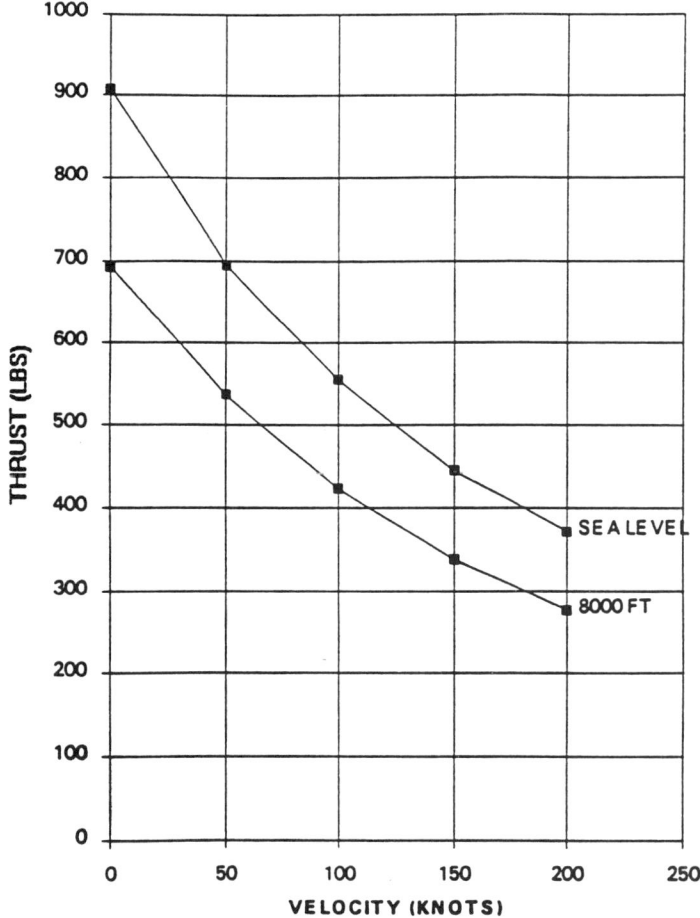

Figure 4. Performance of selected Q-fan configuration.

Having established the blade pitch angle at 3/4 radius, the actual blade design is governed by the condition of obtaining constant lift coefficients of 0.7 throughout the blade at the design point. As recommended in Hamilton Standard's report, the proposed Q-fan uses NACA 65 series airfoils of varying thicknesses.

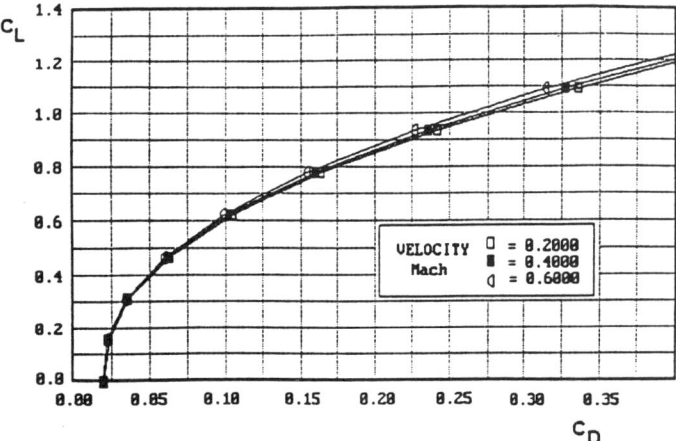

Figure 5. Drag polar for different flight speeds.

The thrust produced by the fan at different flight velocities is given in Figure 4 for a standard sea level condition and for an 8000 foot altitude. At higher altitudes, the output of normally aspirated engines is reduced but the power required by the fan also falls. As mentioned previously, the use of a readily available turbochargers or superchargers would result in very attractive performance figures at high altitudes.

Fabrication of a fan with ground adjustable pitch angles would be highly desirable, since the performance is, like and propeller system, sensitive to blade pitch. Slight disturbances in the internal flow caused by the engine or inlet ducting could result in a fan which is not optimum and a means of adjustment may be better than making new fans until the correct pitch is obtained by trial and error.

PERFORMANCE

Performance estimates were obtained by entering the Minihawk's design parameters, such as weight, thrust, and geometry into Raymer's Design Software. The internal ducting concept used in the Minihawk design represents a large increase in wetted area as compared to a conventional propeller driven aircraft. It is estimated that 30 percent of the total parasite drag is due to the ducting. In order to minimize friction drag, the wetted surfaces must be made as smooth as possible and number of protruding members and gaps must be kept to a minimum, The drag polar shown in Figure 5 assumes a friction drag coefficient of 0.005 for the internal ducting. The resulting minimum parasite drag coefficient for the aircraft is 0.0195 and the maximum lift to drag ratio for level flight is 8.5 at a CL of 0.3 and a velocity of 122 kts.

The Minihawk's flight envelope includes a maximum level flight velocity of 207 kts and a 56 kt stall speed. With 80 percent cruise power setting, the Minihawk's airspeed is 185 kts. Assuming 15 gallons per hour fuel consumption, a range of 450 nautical miles and an endurance of at least 2.3 hours can be attained. The large power to weight ratio enables the Minihawk to break ground in less than 600 feet at standard sea level conditions, Total takeoff distance over a 50 foot obstacle can be accomplished in less than 1200 feet. Total landing distance, including a 600 foot flare, is less than 1320 feet, which is adequate for most airfields. The maximum rate of climb at sea level is 2300 feet per minute at 125 kts. This rate decreases to 1250 feet per minute at 8000 ft altitude (Figure 6). The specific excess power plot shows that the maximum continuous load factor for sustained level flight is 2.1 Gs at 150 kts. (Figure 7). As indicated in Figure 8, the maximum turn rate is 43 degrees per second at a comer speed of 150 kts.

STABILITY

Radio controlled models of the A-4 are stable and easy to fly for intermediate to advanced R/C pilots, thus no problems are expected with the 2/3 scale Minihawk. Static stability of the Minihawk was calculated using the methods of Torenbeek[12], Perkins and Hage[13], and Etkin[11], resulting in a neutral point at approximately 37 percent of the mean aerodynamic chord. The as-drawn center of gravity is 158.5 inches aft of the datum (aircraft nose), yielding a static margin of 15 percent with a 170 pound pilot.

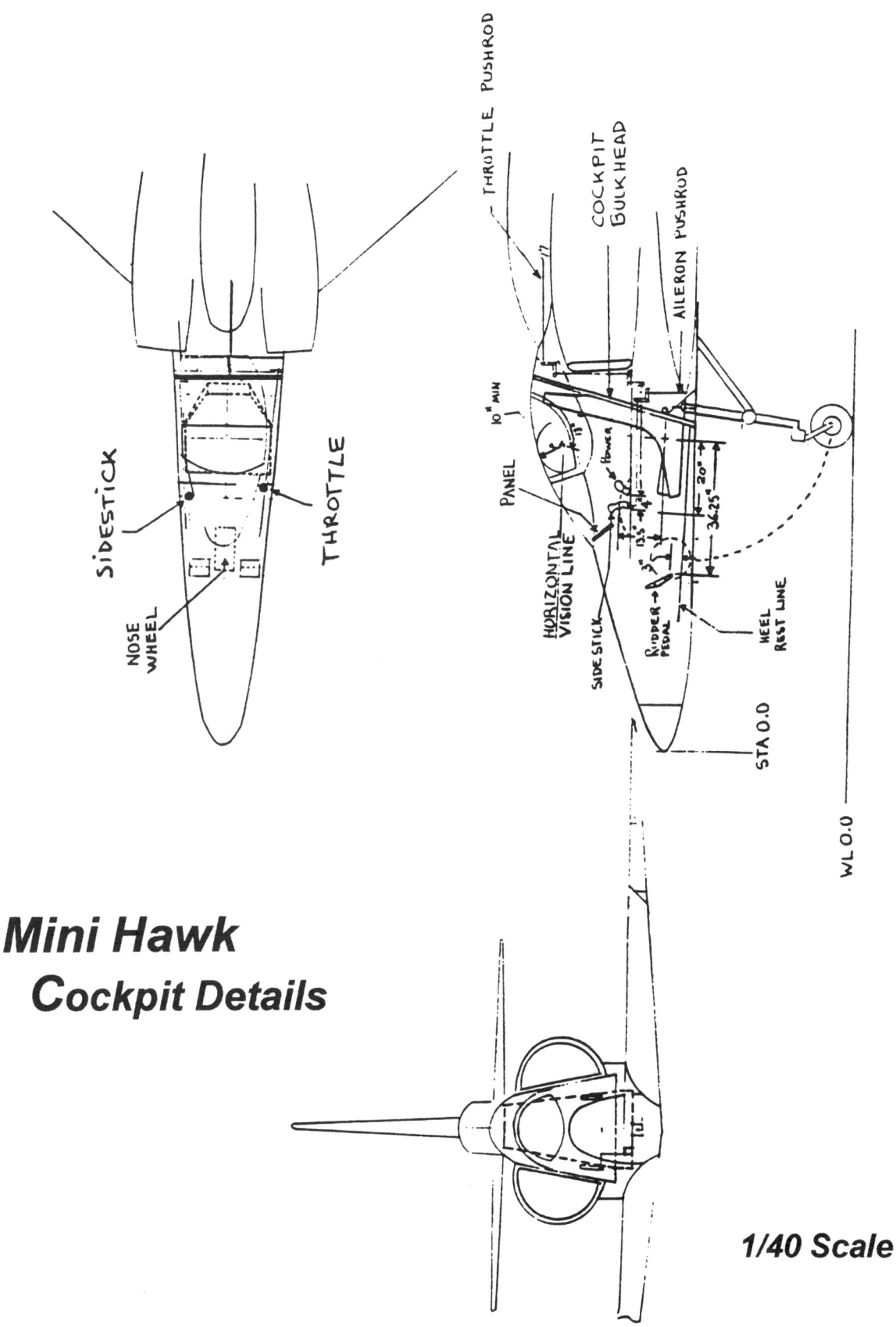

Mini Hawk
Cockpit Details

1/40 Scale

Mini Hawk

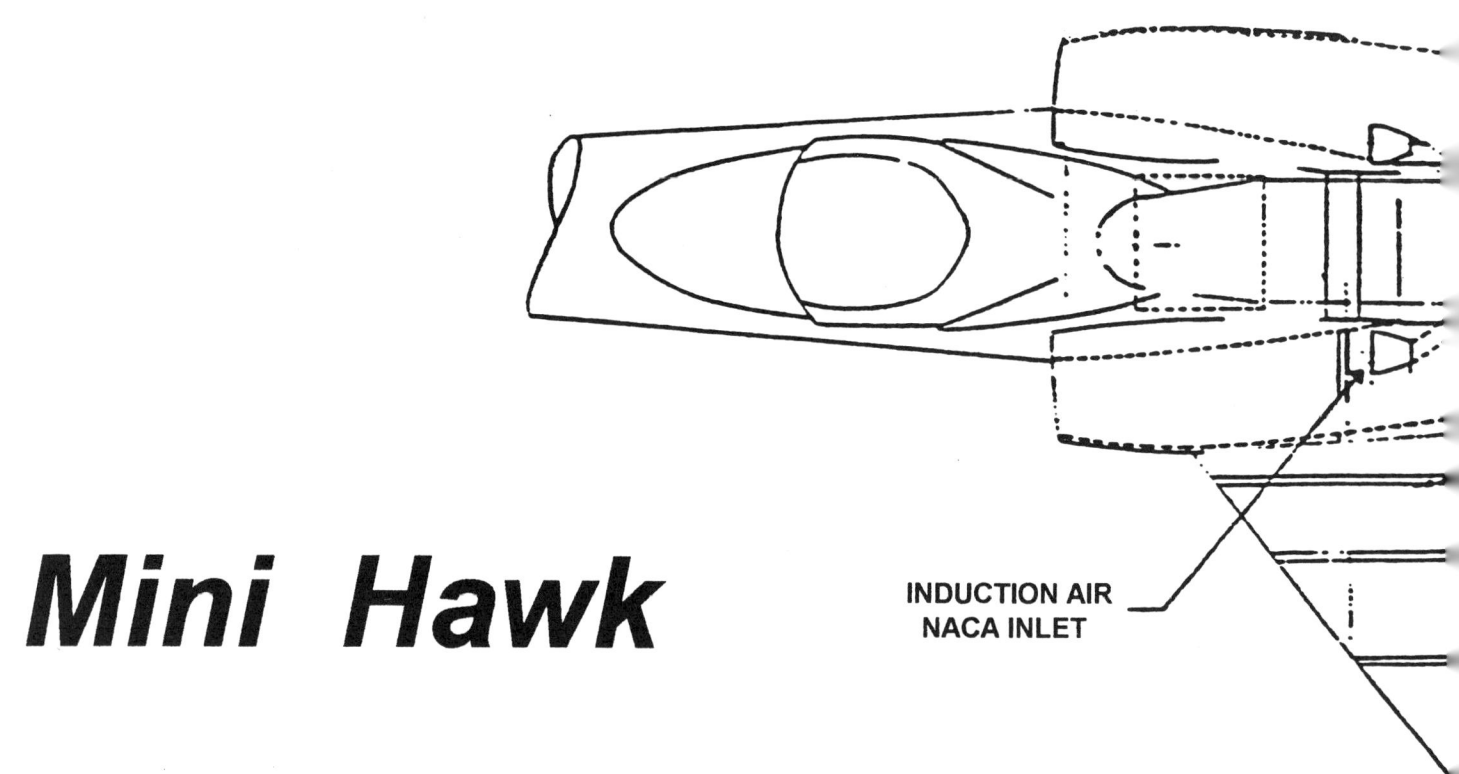
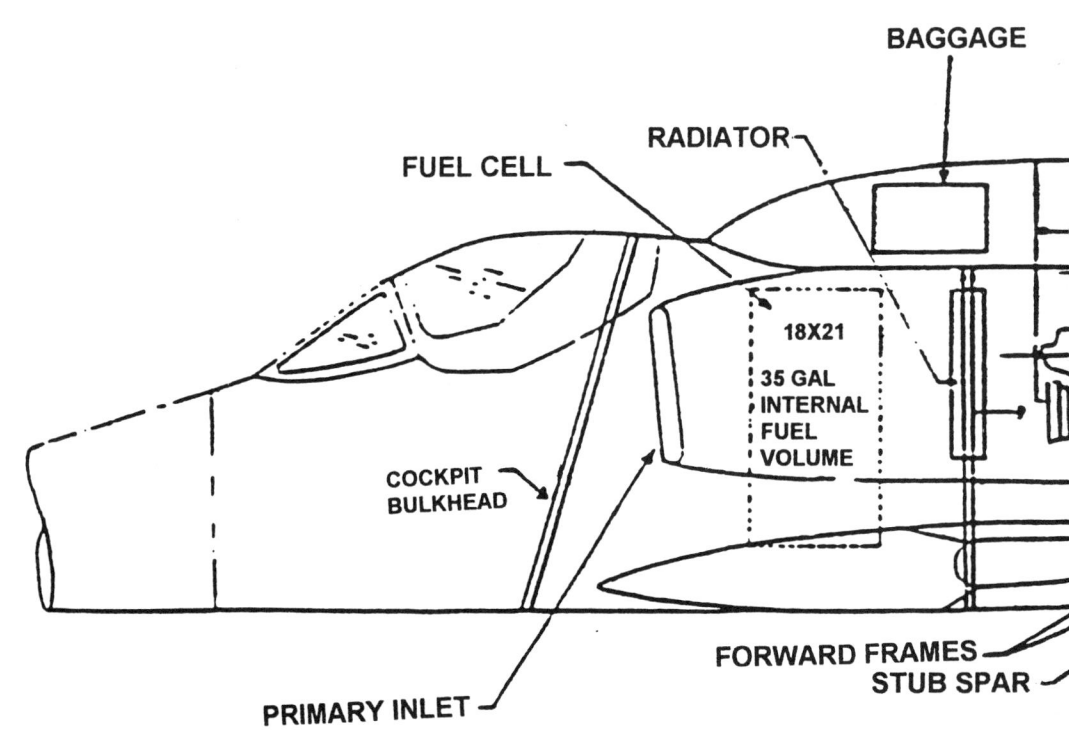

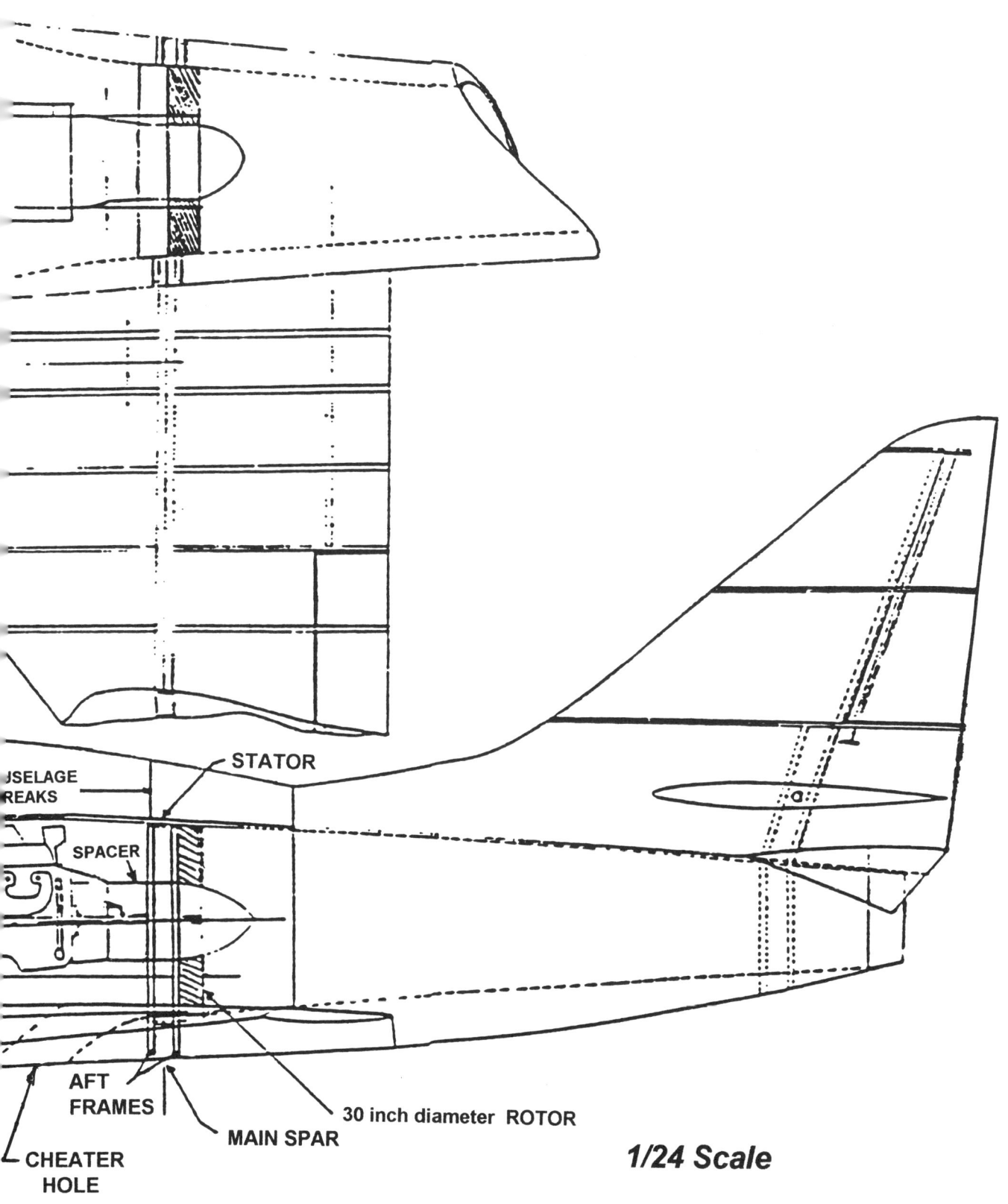

The Minihawk was found to sensitive to pilot weight due to a long moment arm from the crew station to the center of gravity. The proposed CG envelope for the Minihawk gives static margins of 5 to 15 percent of the mean aerodynamic chord. This static margin results in an allowable CG travel of 8.7 inches. If the nominal CG location is positioned in the mid range of the static margin, the acceptable range in pilot weights covers the 25th to 75th percentile.

A check of lateral stability characteristics was also made, The directional stability derivative with respect to sideslip (C_{nb}) was found to be .0005 per degree which is acceptable.

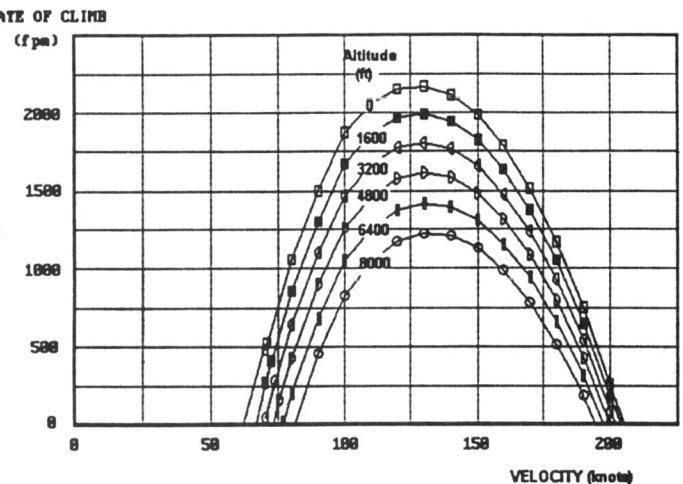

Figure 6. Rate of climb versus speed from sea level to 8000 feet.

COST

The estimated cost for building the prototype is approximately $80,000. This includes minimum required avionics, engine and fan, and assumes labor costs corresponding to 3000 man hours.

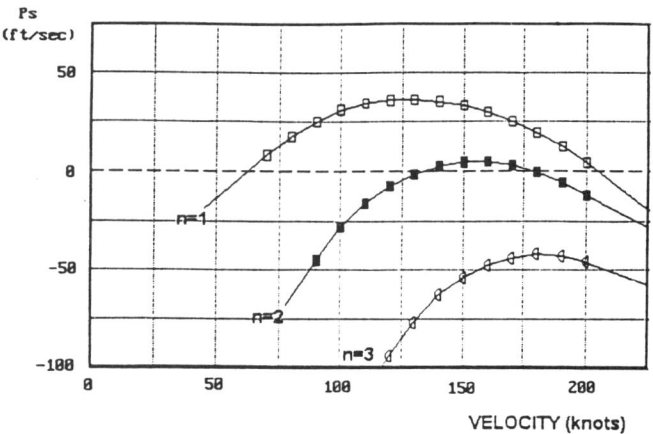

Figure 7. Specific excess power for different load factors.

CONCLUSIONS

The design study summarized in this report has shown that it is feasible to make a 2/3 scale replica of the A-4 fighter aircraft which is powered by a ducted fan propulsion system. Sufficient technical information on ducted fan design is available in the literature to approach the project with a high degree of confidence in the resulting performance.

The resulting aircraft would have a very realistic appearance and would provide the owner with a unique and enjoyable sport aircraft. The resulting aircraft could be expected to have excellent performance and normal flight characteristics. However, more power is required compared to conventional aircraft due to the increased wetted area and limited fan diameter; this is somewhat offset by the ability to use a direct drive automotive engine. Other disadvantages include a sensitivity to pilot weight range, more complex structure, and more difficult engine access. Major advantages of the ducted fan propulsion system include ramp safety from the enclosed propeller and significantly reduced noise. **ERJ**

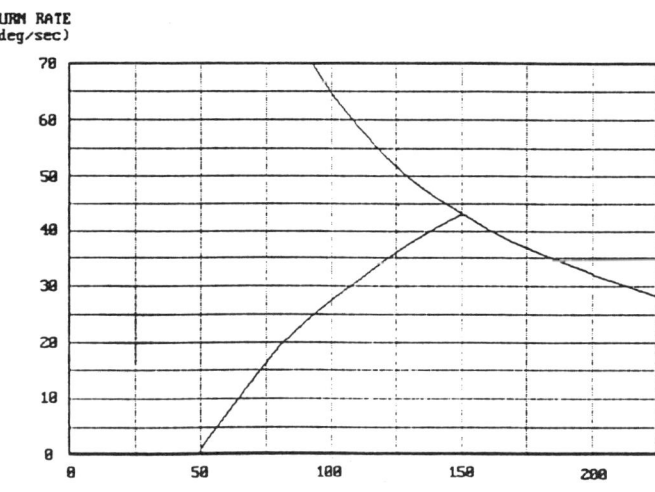

Figure 8. Maximum turn rate at sea level

REFERENCES

1. FAR Part 23 "Airworthiness Standards: Normal, Utility, Acrobatic, and Commuter," 1991
2. Niu, Michael C., "Airframe Structural Design," Technical Book Co., New York, 1988.
3. Roskam, Jan, "Airplane Design, Part I," Roskam Aviation and Engineering Corp., Ottowa, KS., 1990.
4. Raymer, Daniel P., "Aircraft Design: A Conceptual Approach", AIAA Press, Washington D.C.., 1989.
5. Bell, Danna, "A-4 in Detail and Scale," Aero Press, Blue Ridge Summit. PA, 1986.
6. Stevens, Mike, Personal conversation with local GM Dealer, Daytona Beach, FL, 15 OCT 93.
7. Collar, A.R., "The Design of Wind Tunnel Fans," NASA Report No. 1889, 10 AUG 40.
8. NASA SP-36, Aerodynamic Design of Axial Flow Compressors," NASA Lewis Research Center, 1965.
9. Worobel, Rose, "QFANS for General Aviation Aircraft," Hamilton Standard, NASA CR 114665, 1973.
10. Pope, Alan and Rae, H. William, "Low Speed Wind Tunnel Testing," John Wiley and Sons, New York, 1959.
11. Etkin, Bernard, "Dynamics of Flight," John Wiley and Sons, New York, 1959.
12. Torenbeek, Egbert, "Synthesis of Subsonic Airplane Design," Delft University Press, Delft, The Netherlands, 1986.
13. Perkins and Hage, "Airplane Performance, Stability, and Control," John Wiley and Sons, New York, 1946.
14. Jones, Dr. Ernest R.; Stevens, Mike and Almeida, Adriano, " Ducted Fan Propulsion for a General Aviation Replica Fighter Aircraft", Embry-Riddle Aeronautical University-Daytona, 1994.

New Aircraft Engine Development Program

Thomas S. Ostasiewski
Light Power Engine Corporation
165 Scott Avenue Suite 102
P.O. Box Drawer 3350
Morgantown WV
(304) 291 2376

New product opportunities abound in the ever changing and highly competitive custom aircraft world. The LPE initiative in the high end powerplant sector is a high risk capital venture, initially dependent on the degree of customer response relative to cost/benefits and ultimately on the performance of its products. Modern engine technology employing electronics, coatings, as well as advanced engine design concepts offers many advantages. On that basis alone the LPE concept should prove to be technically sound. The company plans to attend Sun N Fun and Oshkosh. MCM

A new aircraft engine design is being introduced to the general aviation market. This engine takes technology from the automotive racing, military drone and aircraft engine manufacturing industries and applies it to the specialized requirements of the modern aircraft industry. These engines are designed for maximum reliability and performance as demanded by the aviation consumer. A power range of from 230 to 600 hp has been demonstrated and suggested time between overhauls (TBO) is projected at 2200 hours. The engines, complete with accessories, weigh from 370 to 496 pounds dry, depending upon the model and power output.

COMPANY DESIGN GROUP

AAC International is the parent company of Aircraft Acquisition Corporation (AAC) and Light Power Engine Corporation (LPE). The companies have sales offices in Morgantown, West Virginia. AAC was responsible for producing the Taylorcraft aircraft in 1990-91 and certifying the F 22 A and 180 GT models. AAC is currently conducting negotiations to begin building another line of aircraft. LPE was formed in mid-1990 to market Avia propellers and engines, keeping the engine group separate from the aircraft manufacturing entity.

Three people are directly involved in the design and construction of these engines. They are Darus H Zehrbach, Lester Gireth, and Thomas S. Ostasiewski. Each of the above has formal education and/or experience in the area of engine design and mechanical engineering in general.

Mr. Zehrbach is the President of LPE and AAC, the creator of this concept, and the designer of the engines. He possesses a BSBA in management (WVU '70), MBA (WVU '75) and course work towards a Mechanical Engineering Technology degree. Mr. Zehrbach, former president of Taylorcraft Aircraft and current president of Helio Aircraft, also has significant experience in engine building in relation to automobile and motorcycle racing.

Mr. Gireth is the engine co-designer and the President of Hawk Power Technology, which manufactures major LPE engine components. He holds an MSME (1965) from Cal Tech. Mr. Gireth built the first standard automotive engine to qualify for the Indianapolis 500. Of significance to the LPE project is his experience in designing and building the first automotive all aluminum engine. During his career he ran the Granatelli operation which manufactured Paxton superchargers and Precision Machine, a manufacturer of ultra precision fixtures and tooling, among other related activities. Gireth Bros. has a record of 237 consecutive drag racing wins, was the first to reach 190 mph in the quarter mile.

Mr. Ostasiewski is a mechanical engineer at LPE and possesses a BSME (WVU '91). He works closely with Mr. Zehrbach in the design and selection of components and systems for the new engines.

PRODUCT CONCEPT

Many customers desire new, innovative designs. In contrast, existing aircraft engine manufacturers maintain a very unaccommodating original equipment manufacture (OEM) pricing and delivery schedule while commanding exorbitant prices for antique designs. Although these products do perform fairly well, many customers expect more from their investment. With these factors in mind, LPE began investigating the market and aircraft engine design problems in depth.

The research, conducted as to whether or not to proceed with a new engine design, was based primarily on prior AAC aircraft manufacturing involvement. AAC's Taylorcraft and Helio experience indicated that the existing manufacturers were not very accommodating to low volume aircraft manufacturers. AAC also realized that unless they drove down the cost of engines they could not sell many aircraft (a Lycoming or Continental engine is 50 percent of the cost of producing a certified aircraft). In addition, customer contact at air shows provided the ultimate in what was needed and why. It was at these shows that customers stated that they wanted reliability and low cost along with honest power output and technological improvements. FAA certification was regarded as a nice added feature, if possible, but certainly not necessary at first. Armed with this information, LPE decided to begin the design process and fill the engine gap.

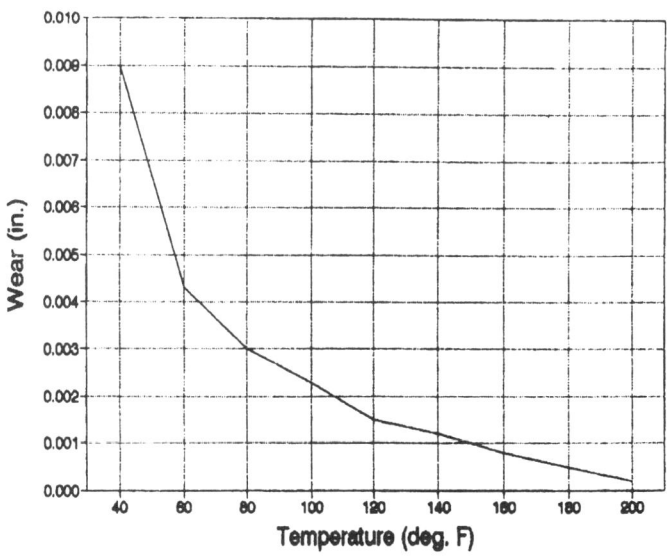

Figure 1
Cylinder Wall Wear vs. Operating Temp.

Courtesy Continental Motors

The starting point was the inline 4 and 6 cylinder aircraft engines sold sold by LPE. Chosen as the design reference these engines had undergone testing to extremes. The smaller horizontally opposed engines (6 and 4 cylinders) are already mass produced and used engines of this size (< 230 hp) can be readily obtained. Larger engines (V12, etc.) weigh too much for the types of applications that LPE wants to cater to. A 90 degree V8 engine provides a proven and very efficient layout and was chosen due to the ultimate considerations of weight versus cubic inches and power.

WATER COOLING
Water cooling has several major benefits that pilots desire. Of these, the most important is the elimination of temperature shock due to rapid cooling of the engine. Secondly, water cooling provides safe hot water cabin heat and maintains the engine at a constant, efficient operating temperature throughout flight in all installations. By maintaining the engine at its optimum operating temperature at all times, component wear is kept at a minimum as noted in Figure 1. It is not evident in the figure; however, it is well proven that increased engine temperature causes wear just as does insufficient temperature. An excessively hot or cold engine causes undue wear on contacting parts as they are designed and installed to operate at a constant temperature. An air cooled engine is very difficult to keep operating at its optimum temperature.

The power range of from 270 to 600 hp was chosen due to the ultimate consideration of weight versus cubic inches and power that the final design allowed. Marketing considerations also came into play as the market below 230 hp is full of used engines. Very few engines are being produced in the power range over 350 hp even though many customers desire this power and some applications require it. Of the manufacturers that do produce engines in this range, the prices are such that the average kit builder can not afford to buy the engine. To become an certified OEM, the restrictions and qualifications are so extensive that only a select few high volume manufacturers can obtain this status and even then, one must contend with the stringent delivery schedule.

DESIGN PHILOSOPHY AND PROCESS
Several design considerations must be addressed in aircraft engine design:

Reliability - Risk of Loss of Life
Develop Power at Low Engine Speeds
Contain Majority of Weight at the Firewall
Control Torsional Vibration / Loading
Improve Visibility Around Nose
Reduce Noise Output
Easier Operation than Current Engine
Lower fuel specifics

Given that the idea was to follow the company's inline engine experience and make the most compact configuration possible, the designers considered various bore/stroke/number of cylinder combinations in various configurations. Vibration ruled out certain combinations, others were eliminated by the fact that the plumbing for the induction and exhaust of the correct tuned lengths bulked up an otherwize compact design. The size and placement of accessories also entered the picture. The combined weight of standard accessories remains fairly constant regardless of the power rating of the engine. This weight is a constant that will drive the power to weight ratio down at lower power ratings. Lastly, the cost of production had to come down. In the end a 90 degree V8 was chosen as the optimum, most flexible design. The engine had to run as an inverted direct drive or as a geared upright installation. A significant departure from "normal" aircraft engine design exercises it was decided to limit the financial risk of the project. The decision was made to produce two sets of drive end molds. One set would have a mount for the direct drive nose; the other would serve a dual purpose. Thus, the block end was designed with the mounts for the gear drive and provisions were made for bell housing mounts to fit the engines in boats. Since boats have nearly the same operating parameters the extra casting molds would allow LPE to have a backup market.

In designing the engines specifically for aircraft use, a great deal of research was necessary in order to not repeat historical failures. This research was conducted by Mr. Zehrbach personally; a review was made of all aircraft engines produced since WWI along with an analysis of auto racing systems and motorcycle engines. To ensure a thorough study of this field, recent auto conversions and their results were also analyzed. It was found that in most cases, failures occurred in the crank shafts, connecting rods, and speed reduction units. This finding is in line with common engine life fundamentals - the parts that endure the most stress will fail first. Valve train failures were known by the designers as a problem area, a fact substantiated by Chevy Racing [1] and by Ford. It was with these considerations that LPE proceeded to design and specify the internal parts and systems that make up the engine. The major components of the engine (block, heads, crank shaft, connecting rods) are all designed and manufactured by LPE and Hawk. By making the major parts internally, the utmost in quality control can be ensured.

ENGINE COMPONENTS
The engine block is designed for a low connecting rod angle and low side thrust forces which leads to longer engine life. The four bolt, cross-bolted "Y" block design (a given from the certified inline engines) exhibits the strongest bottom end design as evidenced by Indy and Formula 1 race teams. This component is made of A-356 aluminum that is heat treated to T6 condition. The LPE / Gireth design calls for a dry sleeve installation. The cylinder sleeves are centrifugally cast from ductile iron which yields a nearly defect free casting. By using this design, these sleeves can be replaced for $27.00 per unit. The sleeves are designed to be easily replaced in the field with a slide hammer. In order to ensure cylinder head sealing and bore roundness a 5 bolt pattern was chosen. A very high deck height is required to accommodate the long rods. The total weight of the 436 in^3 block, with studs and and bearings, is only 86 pounds.

The crank shaft is cut from a billet of double degassed, double heat treated 4340 steel. This material resists torsional fatigue far better than any automotive crank shaft and is relatively defect free due to the manufacturing process. The actual design of this piece is based on personal experience and the ruggedness of the inline 4/6 engine design. The propeller mount is an integral part of the design as specified by LPE rather than a bolt on adapter.

The company's experience with the inlines showed no crank problems with a 4.53 inch stroke, bores of 4.13 to 4.25 and a 7.25 center to center rod. These dimensions became the parameters for the base engine models. Optional bores are available to 4.62 and strokes to 5.75.

The connecting rods are also made from 4340 steel billet. Long connecting rods create a longer duration at TDC which provides more time to build combustion pressure. This increases fuel usage efficiency. The longer rods also reduce the side thrust forces on the cylinder walls which lengthens the life of the engine. The H-beam connecting rods are designed and constructed with emphasis on relieving all stress concentrations and eliminating or reducing all points of wear. The interface between the two halves is machined to inhibit movement.

The all roller valve train increases the life span of the engine and reduces total power loss due to friction. With less side thrust on the valves, valve seat and guide life is increased. By virtue of their design, roller valve trains are more durable than flat tappet designs because of the rubbing action on the valve tip. Rollers require less lubrication than conventional valve trains and so more oil is available for other engine areas. One significant characteristic of roller cams that LPE and Gireth have taken advantage of is the ability to use more cam profiles. The cam design in these engines takes full advantage of this phenomena to obtain the required power out of an engine at low speeds. The cam shaft is driven by the crank shaft through gears, not a chain or belt. This design provides the engine with less points of wear - a reliability and durability issue coupled with accuracy of movement.

A dry sump oil system is chosen due to its many advantages over wet sump systems. Dry sump systems separate and cool the oil supply which generally doubles bearing life. Generally, dry sumps are mounted to the firewall but can be mounted elsewhere. The aircraft designer thus has more flexibility in controlling the installation C.G. by shifting the weight of the dry sump.

ENGINE ELECTRONICS

Electronic systems have been a long time coming to aircraft engine management. In fact, studies done by both the Navy, Air Force and NASA state that costs could be lowered and reliability could be improved by substituting electronics for mechanical or hydraulic systems.

The automotive industry has produced two very efficient and reliable engine management systems that are put to use in this engine. The first of these is the electronic fuel injection system. This system provides improved fuel atomization over carburetors and mechanical injectors while increasing fuel economy drastically. Automatic mixture control also adds to the fuel economy because of the elimination of human error in determining mixtures. With the elimination of a carburetor venturi throat, the possibility of carburetor ice is eliminated. LPE offers dual, redundant fuel injection, an industry first. The primer or choke is also eliminated.

The second electronic engine management system utilized in this design is the electronic ignition. The LPE design uses two of these systems to reassure the customer who is used to magnetos. This distributor-less, high energy system has no moving parts, much greater accuracy of spark timing, and eliminates the need to pressurize the ignition system to avoid arcing at high altitudes. The system specified by LPE is not a capacitor discharge system. It uses two systems of four coils each. Each coil fires two cylinders.

ENGINE ACCESSORIES

The accessories that are included in the design are as follows:

One Alternator
One Dry Sump Pump
One Water Pump (driven by the cam directly)
One Starter (located on engine nose)

Optional accessories (not included for pricing or weight calculations) are:

Propeller Governor
Second Alternator
One Geared Accessory Drive
Air Conditioning Compressor

The drive mechanism for these accessories is a flat, toothed, reinforced belt system. These systems are in use in a wide variety of industries and applications. LPE specifies that these belts be rated at 50 times the actual expected applied load on the engine. These quiet, strong, and light belts are easily inspected for wear and replaced. With this design, all accessories except the starter are mounted on the rear of the engine (firewall end).

This system offers many advantages over conventional accessory drive systems. The belts are quieter, produce less heat and less vibration. Drives are added as needed to reduce cost and weight; no idlers are needed. But most important, the belts are chosen for one primary reason; the accessory drives do not use engine oil for lubrication.

ENGINE TORSIONALS

Aircraft engines must endure a significant amount of torsional vibration and gyroscopic loading due to the propeller movement. This engine design uses hydraulic dampers that are not frequency specific to damp the vibrations. Similar units have been featured on various heavy equipment and are proven industry wide. These damping units are located on the rear ends of both the crank shaft and the cam shaft. The gyroscopic forces are dealt with in the design of the nose piece and in the design of the crank shaft and supporting bearings.

FINAL DRIVE

LPE wanted a flexible design engine in both direct drive and geared versions. The unusual nose design can be rebuilt without disturbing the engine proper. The nose is long to eliminate prop extensions and unsupported loads as commonly seen on conventional engines. The geared engine uses a gear box with unusually wide gears of ultralight design.

In the case of the higher powered, geared engines, the prop speed reduction unit is of a primary concern. Failures have been reported. In LPE's view, a major contributor to this is the use of engine oil as a gear lubricant. The gear reduction drive and the engine are two very different machines relative to tolerances, heat and vibration; thus, they require very different treatment in regard to proper lubrication. While LPE and Hawk are in the final stages of development in this area, they have zeroed on two very important design elements. The reduction unit must have its own lubrication system and it must have a cooling unit for this lubrication. The wear characteristics and general environment inside a gear box is radically different than that in the engine itself. By maintaining two separate lubrication systems, emphasis can be placed upon using the correct lubrication for each system, not in making a compromise between the engine and gear box lubricants. The LPE / Gireth gear reduction drive weighs 87 pounds dry, has interchangeable gear sets to facilitate various reduction ratios, has a separate lubrication system, and keeps the oil cool.

ENGINE TEST RESULTS/EXPLANATIONS

Test engines have run since 1982 to determine the feasibility of parts and designs. Several components, such as a variable cam-lift/duration/lobe center system was found to be unnecessary. The oldest running engine has over 3000 hours with only a fuel pump and water pump replacement. The primary reason for testing was to see if more power could be produced per weight and displacement at a lower fuel burn than conventional engines.

421, a 422 and a 500 in^3 engines have been run to substantiate the design. The 421 engine pulled 320 hp at 2750 rpm and 435 hp at 4300 rpm (non-geared). Based on the tests the standard engine displcement is now increased to 436 in^3. The 500 in^3 engine is at the very bottom of its range of displacement, the 421 was at the maximum; therefore, the 500 was expected to do poorer given that its cam was designed to handle 672 in^3. This engine pulled 346 hp at 2750 rpm and 498 hp at 4500 rpm. The 422 engine pulled 400 hp at 2750 aand 570 hp at 4500 rpm. Engine builder results prove that that the claimed power of the final LPE designs is, in fact, achievable. Engine differences are noted to "normalize" the test auto engines. At this point in the development every part of the engine itself has been tested extensively. Only the direct drive nose and the gear box tests are limited in nature. However, these parts are based on components tested at 300 percent of the predicted aircraft engine power. Figure 2 shows 230 hp at 2750 RPM. Assuming that power output is proportional to displacement (keeping everything else the same):

$$\frac{230 hp}{406 CID} = \frac{247 hp}{436 CID}$$

Advancing the cam shaft timing yields a power gain of near 5 percent [2]. Increasing the compression ratio of the engine yields an increase of 5 percent for every 1/2 point increase in CR [3]. The engine in Figure 1 has a 9:1 CR and LPE / Gireth engine has a 10.5:1 CR. This gives a 15 percent increase in power.

$$247 + 247(.05 + .15) = 296 hp$$

Figure 2 also shows 375 hp at 4300 RPM. Assuuming that power output is proportional to displacement (keeping everything else the same):

$$\frac{375 hp}{406 CID} = \frac{403 hp}{436 CID}$$

Figure 2
Power Curve of 406 CID Engine

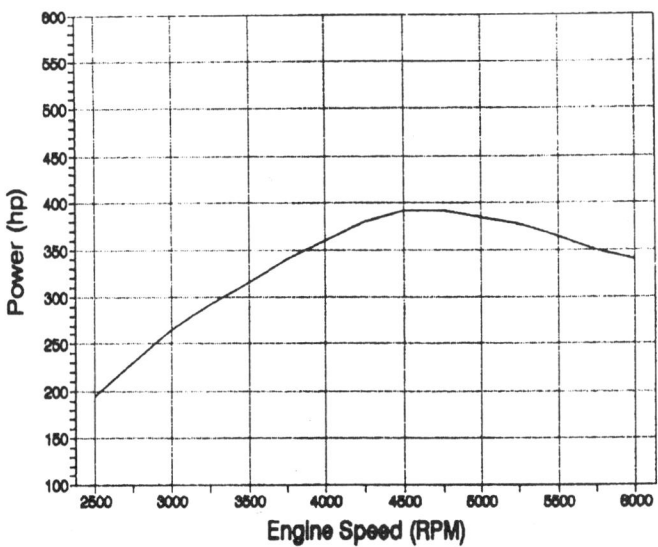

A relatively new technology, anti-friction coatings, is used extensively in the LPE / Gireth engines. These coatings have been shown to increase power output by 5 to 15 percent at high engine speeds while reducing component wear at all speeds. The results of this type of engine treatment are indicated in Figure 3. For the power calculations being discussed here, the 5 percent value is used for an added measure of certainty.

Advancing the cam shaft timing yields a power gain of near 5 percent [2]. Increasing the compression ratio of the engine yields an increase of 5% for every 1/2 point increase in CR [3]. The engine in Figure 2 has a 9:1 CR and LPE / Gireth's engine has a 10.5:1 CR. This gives a 15 percent increase in power. In addition, a 5 to 15 percent increase in power can be realized by

$$403 + 403(.05 + .05 + .15) = 504 hp$$

Figure 4
Power Curve of 421 CID Engine

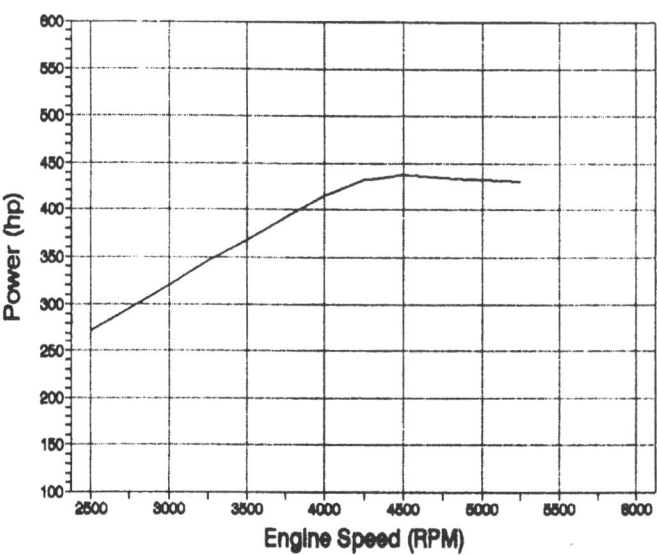

using internal engine coatings (see Figure 3). A 5 percent increase is used here.

Figure 3
Coated & Uncoated Engine Curves

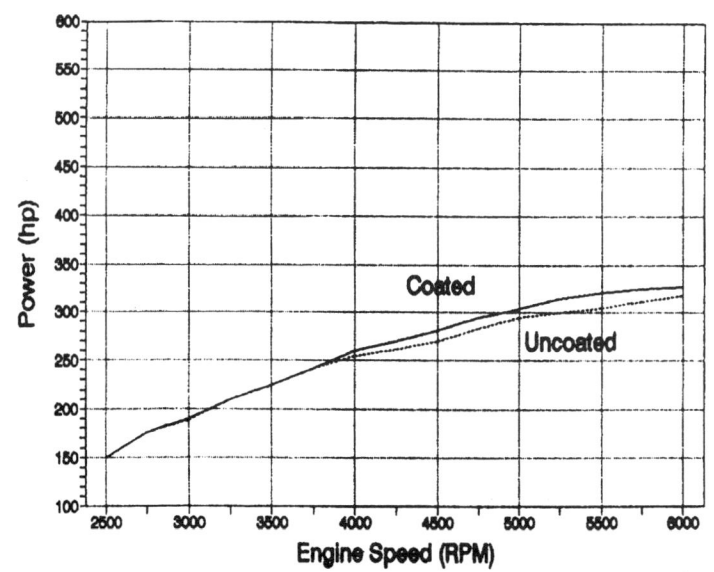

Figure 5
Power Curve of 632 CID Engine

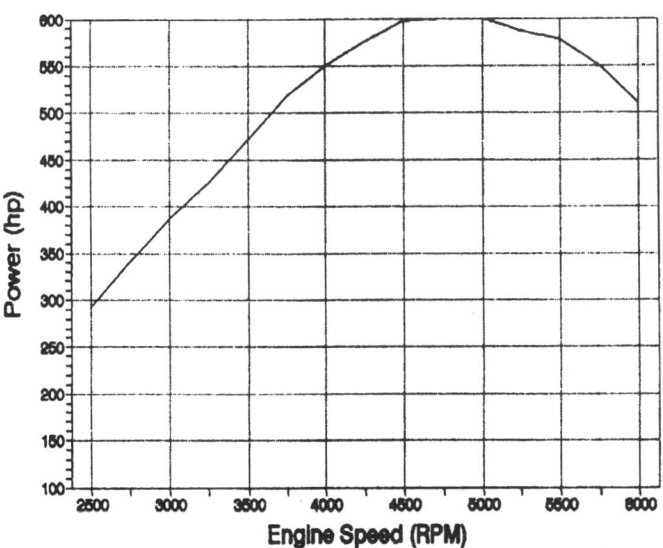

$$296hp - 10\% = 266hp$$
$$305hp - 10\% = 275hp$$
$$\frac{266hp + 275hp}{2} = 271hp$$

$$504hp - 10\% = 454hp$$
$$435hp - 10\% = 392hp$$
$$\frac{454hp + 392hp}{2} = 423hp$$

The engine represented in Figure 4 is also representative of the LPE / Gireth engine. As noted, this engine produces 305 hp at 2750 RPM and 435 hp at 4300 RPM. These values are considered to be "proven" values for the sake of this discussion. To arrive at the advertised power ratings of the LPE / Gireth engines, both the calculated and proven values were reduced by 10 percent and then the average of the two taken as shown.

The above calculations do not take into consideration the effects of using a roller valve train (+7 to 15 hp) or tuning the intake runner lengths to a specific engine speed (up to 50 hp gain). With these LPE / Hawk modifications, the engines could produce much more power than is advertised. The above numbers are used to provide a safety margin for designers.

For the "big block" design, Figure 5 is closely representative of the actual LPE / Gireth design in performance expectations. Base values of 330 hp at 2750 RPM and 598 hp at 4500 RPM are used as noted on the graph. For the direct drive engine, the only LPE / Gireth modification affecting power output is the tuning of the intake runners for optimum operation at low engine speeds. The tuning of intake runners has been shown to increase the power output at a specific engine speed by up to 50 hp. With this done, a power rating of 380 hp at 2750 RPM is projected.

In regard to the geared version of the engine, the only modification affecting power output is the application of internal anti-friction coatings. The effect of this ranges from a 5 to 15 percent increase in power as noted in Figure 3. For this engine calculation, a 5 percent increase is used giving 603 hp at 4500 RPM. While the engine in Figure 5 is very similar to the LPE / Gireth engine in power output, it should be noted that the design of the internal parts and other parts and systems that have little effect on power is significantly different. One major example of this is the design of the crank shaft, the vibration handling equipment, etc.

CONCLUSIONS

With the introduction of this engine design the aircraft industry now has another option when selecting an engine for a certain application. The LPE / Gireth engine, while not yet aircraft proven, certainly offers substantial improvement over both the auto-conversion and conventional aircraft engines.

REFERENCES

1. Chevrolet Motor Division, Chevrolet Power Catalog, 6th edition, 1988, "Rocker Arms", P. 5-46.

2. Interview with Darus Zehrbach, LPE Corp., Morgantown, WV

3. Walordy, Alex. Popular Hot Rodding, September, 1992. "Taming Godzilla - The Inner Workings of Bill Mitchell's Big-Inch Chevy Engines", P. 78.

DATA SOURCES FOR FIGURES

1. Monroe, Tom. How to Rebuild your Ford V8, Fisher Publishing, Inc., 1980 "Inspecting and Reconditioning the Shortblock", P. 5-46.

2. Summit Racing: 406 CID Engine, Flat Tappet, Stock Chevy TPI, 9:1 CR

3. Saueracker, Peter. Circle Track, October, 1992. "The Max Sportsman Engine", P. 56.

4. Air Sensors, Inc.: 421 CID Engine, (Tested at Race Cars and Engines of Crossville, TN)

5. Walordy, Alex. Popular Hot Rodding, September, 1992. "Taming Godzilla - The Inner Workings of Bill Mitchell's Big-Inch Chevy Engines", P. 79.

Belted Air Power: The Buick 215 Engine

Jess H. Meyers
Belted Air Power
1408 Western Avenue
Las Vegas Nevada 89102
(702) 384 8006

Jess Meyers' romance with aviation began in the late 50s. He worked as a helper for a Las Vegas FBO, Alamo Airways, earning money for his flying lessons. He soloed in 1961 and now holds a Commercial (SMEL) license and an Instrument rating. In 1965, he graduated from Northrop Institute of Technology and has held an A&P rating since then. This span of time also included a 6 year tour of duty with the Air National Guard working on C-97s and 7 years with Bonanza Airlines, operating F-27A and DC-9 series aircraft. Well known in Globe Swift circles, Jess developed and holds STCs on the smooth skin installation for the Swift GC-IA and -B series. MCM

Let me begin this article with a parable. "In the Beginning", Quote the Experts- "Auto Engines cannot be used for Aircraft...". Why Not? cried the tumultuous crowd of engine needers. "Because...", answered the Experts... and so it was for 60 years. Only a few of the strange and curious ventured off the beaten path, some with success, some not, but all judged to be a bubble off center. Why would anyone reject technology introduced at the turn of the century; after all, Had not the FAA given out their official blessings?

Auto engines in aircraft had been tried in the 30s but like the autos of that era they powered they were heavy and not too reliable. The Wiley Post A with its Ford Model A engine received Airplane Type Certificate 561. A Studebaker engine powered the unusual tailless Waterman Aerobile, a working roadable aircraft. The SF-2 Plymacoupe designed by Ole Fahlin and Swen Swanson weighed in at 900 pounds empty and cruised at a comfortable 85 MPH. Perhaps the most recognized by enthusiasts the Arrow Sport F strut braced low wing airplane was powered by a Ford V/8 of 82 HP at 3075 RPM. The M18 Mooney Mite first featured a 22 HP Crosley overhead cam engine with a V-belt reduction and cruised at 110 MPH at a 1.5 GPH fuel burn rate. Not many experimenters know that David Blanton, pioneer belt redrive developer, was one of the original test pilots on that project in 1948 while working full time as an engineer at Boeing.

Resurgence of auto engine conversions today cannot be credited to any specific design, event or individual. The post-WWII movement toward the use of direct drive air cooled VWs began in Europe. In the U.S., the 1960 introduction of the air cooled Chevrolet Corvair engine encouraged designers like Pietenpol, Huggins, Waterman and many others to develop its possibilities. More recently, liquid cooled conversions have come to the forefront with the availability of low HP, technologically advanced and aluminum block engines.

THE GM 215 ENGINE

In 1961, General Motors introduced its baby V/8. An all aluminum engine of 215 in^3 and conservatively rated at about 150 HP this engine was specifically designed for the GM "Y" body vehicles (Pontiac Tempest (option engine), Oldsmobile F-85, Buick Special). During its three year production run about 750,000 cars were built. Customer demand for the larger 1962 Chevolet CHEV II "X" body vehicles prompted GM to combine the four name plates in 1964 using the new "A" body design and drop the relatively expensive engine.

Enthusiasm for the engine did not die. Popular with hydroplane and sports car designers the engine was bored, stroked, cammed, injected and blown to extreme limits.

The Buick 215 engine in its stock form puts out 150 HP at WOT and 3500 RPM. Cruise fuel burn at this RPM setting is around 7.5 gallons per hour. These engines are still available from collectors or in imported Rover vehicles.

Modified versions appeared at LeMans, Sebring and other famous racing and road rally events. Numerous articles in racing magazines of that era document these developments. Tooling for the Buick engine version was purchased by the British Rover company in 1965 and went into production with minor changes in 1967 as the Rover P5 Saloon. The engine is still in production and is used in the current Range Rover utility sport vehicle import.

Most readers are aware of pioneer Steve Wittman's successful development of the Olds 215 conversion in his

Tailwind. His engine was turned upside down to raise the propeller thrust line. It used the stock bell housing in conjunction with a direct drive input shaft and propeller hub. Chris Beachner introduced his Special at Oshkosh in 1983. A stock, direct drive, upright Buick configuration, it produced approximately 125 HP at 3600 RPM.

The firewall end of the Buick 215 engine. The assembly here is supported by a pipe member sliding over the crank stub. The unique "front cover" incorporates the distributor, oil pump, oil filter, fuel pump and water pump.

There is no question that a direct drive configuration is simple and straightforward. The major drawback is that auto engines, in general, generate rated horsepower at higher RPMs than their air cooled aircraft counterparts. However, propeller tip speed is limited by efficiency; a maximum tip velocity of 800 feet per second is recommended by William A. Welch (*author of recommended Lightplane Propeller Design, Selection, Maintenance, and Repair-Tab Books-MCM*). Methods for increasing engine RPM while limiting tip speed include the use of small diameter propellers or ducted fans or a mechanical gearing interface (redrive).

Realizing the need for additional power at the propeller, experimenters have used power transmission belts, gear boxes, and chain reduction systems for their respective redrives. Each redrive system has its unique advantages and its detractors. There are some naysayers to the belt, they may break, they whine etc. These are the fence setters, having read and commented but never actually done. In fact, belts can crush steel bearings, bend mighty propellers and still function for years; the whining is a factor of tensioning. For smoothness, reliability and serviceability we chose to use the cog belt approach.

We at Belted Air Power have been flying a Belted Buick for 11 years, accumulating some 500 hours on the engine in flight and many more on the dyno. We have NEVER had a drive failure.

THE BUICK 215

We chose the all aluminum Buick 215 V/8 powerplant primarily for its exceptional performance in racing applications and its relatively light weight, availability of engines and parts. These engines have been pushed beyond the limit in auto and boat racing proving conclusively that the original factory block and head design was very conservative and fully capable of powering an aircraft. The stock Buick/Rover V/8 offers 200 HP at 5000 RPM with 220 foot pounds of torque available at 2800 RPM. This engine is one of the few that produces its maximum torque at such a low RPM and remains flat throughout its operating range. Coupled with our belt reduction unit the engine produces 160 HP and 340 foot pounds of torque at the prop shaft while only turning only 3500 RPM; this output equates to 70 MPH in an early 60s automobile.

Our first engine was obtained from an abandoned auto which we purchased for $50. The engine was pulled and the rest was sold for scrap; net cost of engine was $15. The complete overhaul cost $1500 and included the cost of new cylinder sleeves. The only original parts kept were the block, heads, and crank. At the same time we priced out Lycoming exhaust valves. One-half inch valves cost $450 each at that time so for the price of four aircraft engine valves we had a remanufactured zero time engine.

COMPONENT WEIGHTS

The engine weighs 272 pounds bare (block, heads and manifold). Aircraft engine weights are always listed bare, with accessories listed separately, such as magnetos, carburetor, fuel pumps, etc., to allow for engine specification flexibility by the airframe manufacturers. Any complete installation weight is dependent on the choice of components. The Swift has the custom radiator made by Griffin (Griffin Race Radiators 1-800-RACERAD) while the RV-6A uses two GM air conditioning evaporator cores.

engine long block	261.0
intake manifold	11.0
carburetor	11.5
air cleaner	1.0
stock starter	22.0
Tilton starter	10.5
Mallory distributor	1.5
ignition harness	1.0
spark plugs (8)	1.0
generator	15.0
Motorola alternator	8.0
exhaust manifolds	18.0
exhaust headers	8.0
custom Al radiator	6.0
2 A/C type radiators	11.0
Al coolant tubes	3.0

IGNITION

We chose to use the stock distributor and added another set of points 180 degrees from the original. This setup allows for one or the other to be used (see drawing) for ignition redundancy. The reason we use this older technology is two fold; one, it is time proven and two, it is safe. Aftermarket manufacturers of solid state ignition and fuel injection systems have stated that a high energy discharge such as lightning can damage or incapacitate solid state devices, such as found in modern electronic ignition systems. In our opinion, an airplane in flight can also be viewed as an object trolling for lightning. The "limp home" mode of typical automobile electronics may not provide enough RPM to maintain flight and may be totally disabled. Those of you who have flown near or around thunderstorms will agree that this is not the place to find out the truth of a "might be or maybe". This could be the worst time to lose one's ignition or electronic fuel injection unit.

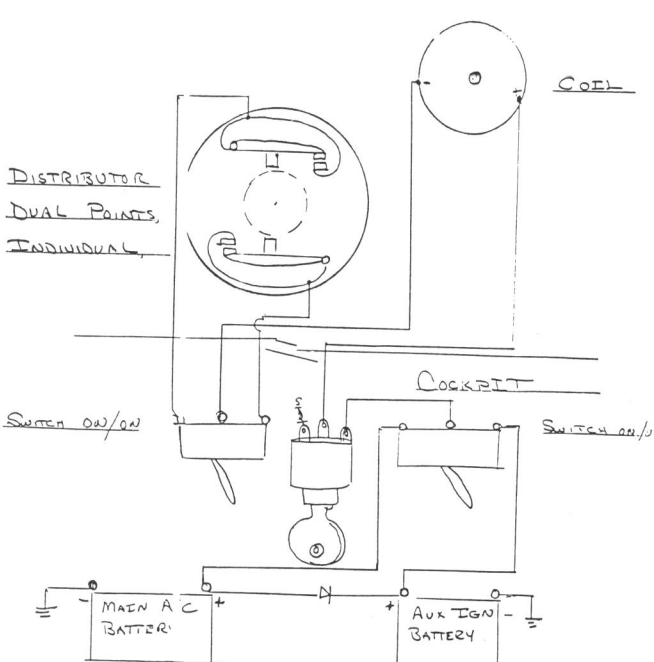

Back-up Ignition System

Aircraft ignition systems use grounded cables to the spark plugs; that is, they are grounded at the magneto and at the plugs. This shielding provides suppression of electrical noise that would be a nuisance when a spark plug is fired. Auto engine ignition spark plug cables do not have this type of construction. Typically, a spiral wrapped core performs the noise suppression function. The aircraft practice of bundling the plug cables is completely safe because of the external grounded shield. However, innocently carrying this practice to auto engines will result in CATASTROPHIC FAILURE of their engines. The problem is cross-firing and is caused by an electrical force known as inductance. One wire will be energized by others in the bundle to fire its plug in a cylinder that may have just taken on a charge of fuel/air and not be in proper firing position in relation to crankshaft travel. The result is a bent or broken rod and, or, combined with a shattered piston followed by rapid engine failure. We have seen many such improper ignition cable installations. When the wires start to age and lose their insulation properties disaster can occur at any time. When this happens the engine itself is unfairly blamed.

Another fallacy is that if the stock automobile ignition system is good, mega volts at the plugs would be better. Keep in mind that during WWII aircraft went to low tension ignition systems to prevent problems as aircraft started flying higher. The higher in altitude one goes the less air pressure and the more chance of a spark to jump. The same physics apply to auto engines. Stock auto ignition systems are perfectly adequate to handle density altitudes found at the top of Pikes Peak.

We did not skimp on the ignition harness and bought the best available. We use the Jacobs brand which sells for about $50 for the set of eight cables. The spark plugs are AC R-43CFS which list for about 1.17 each. We have tried Champion L-93 and L-87Y which are less in cost but show a drop in performance in dyno tests.

When we talk of auto engines for aircraft please bear in mind that the main reason we did this project was for economy. If you plan to fly at extremely high altitudes and require shielded ignition systems and constant speed props then this may not be the way for you to go. It was intended for the flyer who wants safety and economy along with high reliability. We encountered another phenomenon with unshielded auto ignition. Our all metal aircraft became invisible to radar with even the primary and secondary target disappearing during certain RPM ranges of operation. It was explained to us as something to do with the electricity generated. So much for Stealth technology, confirmed by Wichita, Phoenix and Las Vegas radar!

FUELING

We used the stock automobile carburetor that came with the engine. A overhaul kit which cost $6.95 at the time was installed. The overhauled carburetor has performed as intended since 1982. The stock fuel lines of the Swift were connected to the stock engine diaphragm fuel pump. The line from pump to carburetor is 1/4 inch I.D. stainless braided Teflon. The RV-6A uses line sizes specified by Vans Aircraft feeding an Edelbrock 500 CFM four barrel carburetor jetted for performance. A stock automobile air cleaner is used.

Some will argue that modern electronic fuel injection and solid state ignition timing are superior to old technology points and carburetors. I will agree with them for over the airport flying and for strictly VFR flying but not for long journeys from the airport. I also believe that the use of the solid state ignition system is OK but, to be conservative, a backup system is incorporated. An electronic fuel injection system can be used but, in that case, we prefer the additional installation of a manual fuel dump valve to allow fuel flow into the manifold in the event of a electronic injection failure.

ENGINE MOUNTS

We chose to use the cradle style of engine mounting, patterned after the type used on the early Cessna airplanes with the Continental engines. In a manner we copied Cessna's method of mounting, incorporating the stock auto engine mounting points into the Cessna cradle configuration. Provisions for the two front mounting points were designed into the rear redrive housing.

COOLING/RADIATORS

The black art of cooling has been tucked away in the archives for many years now as the military went to jets in the 50s. Frequently today one can see radiators on ultralights hung out in the breeze with only marginal cooling. The radiator seems to be as large as the engine it is trying to cool. Others lay the radiator flat under the engine and cannot understand why it fails to provide cooling. After all, the radiator is exposed but there is no cooling, what is wrong? The answer was found after reading "Fluid Dynamic Drag" by Dr.-Ing. D. F. Hoerner. According to his text, air, like most of us, will choose to take the path of least resistance and tends to only bend 5 degrees maximum without help of turning vanes. So while a large radiator hanging in the breeze looks great, more air is going around it than through it.

The same occurs with a radiator mounted below the engine, air tends to roll over the top and back out the opening and also adding engine temperature to the radiator face increasing the temperature of the coolant trying to be cooled. The Messerschmitt Bf-109 with its underslung radiators was an example of bad airflow. Before all of its problems could be worked out the war was over. The Spitfire suffered similar deficiencies but, due to short ground runs and climbs to very cold operating altitudes, it was a relatively minor problem. Even the P-51 with the best and most efficient radiator ducting was limited to minimum ground running. What is required is proper planning of radiators, positioning, ducting and size. In general, the radiator should be aligned to have its face facing the relative airflow, this will allow the best cooling for the least effort. There are some airframes that will not allow this and will call for much duct work and turning vanes to get the proper airflow through the radiator.

The radiator material is also important, aluminum being the best and the lightest. An opening of 30 percent less than the frontal (normal) area of the radiator with less than 5 degrees of bend to the radiator surface will work great. This configuration will allow the air to enter the radiator at a slower than scoop entry speed. After departing the radiator the heated air will need just about double the inlet area for the outlet. We have always used a thermostat in the engine. While it has been suggested that we modulate the cooling with a cowl flap in the radiator air outlet we have not found it to be necessary.

On the subject of radiators we have also used auto air-conditioning evaporators with great success. They are of the correct package size, are made of aluminum and, most of all, are inexpensive. They can be purchased usually from $5.00 on up, a great buy. We have used a two row, 26 x 6 inch custom built radiator on our Swift. Our maximum temperatures run 100 degrees above ambient. The configuration of this radiator will allow extended ground runs. Our cooling capacity is the same as that of the automobile requirement, 2.5 gallons. Some people

The lower rear redrive housing is designed to support the front end of the engine. Note engine mount tubes are attached to stock RV-6A upper and lower firewall hard points. Additional struts support the A/C cores.

recommend using a coolant system pressure gage. We do not; instead, we use two temperature gages. One indicates the coolant temperature coming out of the engine while the other indicates coolant temperature after it leaves the radiator. This method eliminates the chance of a leak in the cockpit. Hot steam is not a pleasant thought. If one gage reads normal and the other "zero" you have probably pulled a wire from the sender. If one reads hot and the other very low or zero, you have probably lost your coolant and should plan on a landing. In our system we typically see a 20 degree difference in the gages, with the return being the cooler of the two.

Radiators are an interesting subject for study. Very little information is published. We have found they work best when placed directly in front of the relative wind. Ducting is important along with the matter of correct angular entry. Radiator builders are sensitive to the product liability issue; it is best not to mention airplane but use words like "off road" or "snow plow" or something other than your project when asked for the application. By using quality hoses and fittings you should avoid problems with leaks. We have used a cooling system pressure tester with air before adding the coolant. This is a cleaner and cheaper approach. The entire system can be checked with soapy water and a brush without any spills. A 70:30 mixture of distilled water and Prestone II brand coolant, respectively, is our recommendation for best cooling results. We avoid de-ionized and purified water.

ENGINE OPERATION

We have established a level of complete engine reliability with our Buick installation. The engine itself has proven to be a champion. In the last 500 hours of operation aircraft 100LL seems to be the only glitch. Its high lead content leaves large build ups in the combustion chambers and on the piston tops. This can be cleaned up periodically by the use of water while the engine is at operating temperatures and being run at approximately 750-900 RPM. We have been using a Alcor TCP additive with good results for the lead scavenging but it still builds up on the valve and head area, hence the water treatment.

We have chosen not to use auto fuel in our local area due to the large amounts of alcohol being added to the fuel. The engine runs great on this fuel but the rubber hoses in our aircraft swell up like a poisoned pup causing fuel starvation to the engine resulting in shutdown. Replacement of these hoses with alcohol tolerant material would solve that problem. Also, we are aware that any aluminum fuel tank that was sloshed with a tank sealing compound of the 60s and 70s would have this problem. This sealer will come off the tanks in sheets clogging the fuel screens causing engine stoppage, again resulting in the comment " they were using auto fuel when the failure occurred".

REDRIVE

Belt drives also offer the absorption of any prop vibration to the engine or vice versa. With belts you don't have to worry about backdriving the engine at low speeds; something you must consider with chain drives or gears. On the RV-6A we use the propeller reduction as a beta unit. When we slow the engine to 500 RPM the prop acts as a brake. No more overshooting; if the glide path begins to appear too short just pushing the throttle to zero thrust corrects the situation.

Belted Air Power units are designed to use standard propellers that use the SAE #2 hub design. We have used many propellers and find that the standard propeller for a rated horsepower can be used with our ratios The auto engine seems to have the power and the torque to turn it through its range up to max RPM, or 2700, with the position of the throttle. The is unlike most aircraft engines that cannot turn the prop to their full RPM unless at sea level and on a standard day. We offer four ratios at the present time; 1.43:1 for the Buick/Rover V/8 engines, 1.71:1 for the 350 Chevy and the 4.3L Chevy V/6. A 2.34:1 ratio is available for some of the scale fighters and a 1.86:1 for the 2.2L Subaru Legacy is still under development. Prototype development and production work is performed in our shop in Las Vegas. We do not offer redrives for sale that have not been tested unless it is agreed upon beforehand by all parties.

DYNO TESTING

By studying the Buick engine and its torque curves we initially decided on a 1.43:1 ratio. This would allow ample amounts of torque and let the engine produce ample horsepower at moderate RPM. When dealing with any redrive it is well to remember that only torque can be multiplied, not horsepower. The HP=33000 foot pounds per minute number was established when the King's old Dobbin was traveling in a straight line but to get rotational numbers it is divided by 2 pi. This gives us the 5252 number that is used today and is programmed into all engine dynamometers. Torque times RPM divided by 5252 equals Horsepower. We were fortunate enough to have access to a dyno to get the information on our engines. The engine

The stock distributor is reworked include a dual point/condenser setup which provides ignition redundancy along with a backup battery and wiring. Top quality spark plug wires and wire spacing prevent cross firing.

we flew for 11 years had a low compression ratio and a smog cam but still turned a respectable 147 HP at 3500 rpm. Our present engine sports a cam very comparable to what Buick originally specified and the compression ratio is the stock 8.8:1. The out put of this engine is in the neighborhood of 165 HP.

A dyno can be considered a truth machine. It will only show what you are getting regardless of the super pistons and cam combination you install. For example, we received a new cam fresh off the manufacturer's shelf with the key cut 6 degrees in error. Yes, the error could have been discovered by dialing the engine when building it as the hot rodders do, but we didn't. On the dyno the engine made all of the fury of a 300 HP monster but the dyno only said 70 HP. After much head scratching and mild oaths being muttered about the weasley dyno we found the error. It hurts more when you do it to yourself.

V/6 ENGINE CONVERSIONS

Belted Air Power continues to recommend the use of V/8 engines. If a V/6 is desired the engine must be balanced for its operating range with the drive unit somewhere in the 3800-4800 RPM range. This will assure smoothness in the range that it will operate with the 1.71:1 unit for the Chevy series. Our unit for the Chevy 350 will also fit the 4.3L V/6. The 90 degree V/6 cannot be balanced for its entire operating range therefore its imperative to decide which ratio is being used and balance accordingly. As used in an auto the V/6 is balanced somewhere in the 2800 RPM range and would be out of balance in the range used in aircraft. When having your engine balanced be sure to take all of the rotating parts to your machine shop. That includes the harmonic damper, the rods, pistons, crank and the starter ring gear/flex plate. Also when completed the redrive components may need to be safetied to prevent looseness of parts on the engine. With V/8 engines harmonic shake does not seem to be a problem.

I address this problem for the benefit of those who may elect to use the V/6. People who believe any engine produced is a conversion candidate should be aware that each engine configuration has its unique characteristics. We have ventured into these realms at times but with the V/6 engine we elected to leave it stock. We believe that those who designed it are far more knowledgeable than we are regarding torsionals. For the more adventurous, articles in HOT ROD MAGAZINE cover this subject.

There are some pitfalls in dealing with auto conversions in general. Ignition wires should never be bundled together; bundling is a sure recipe for cross-firing and internal engine damage. Auto hot rod harness setups are good examples to follow. Engine internals should be left stock unless you have done it before or know exactly what you want. Introduction of changes without benefit of knowing the beginning point of the engine output is expensive and may be non-productive. The best place to start if you plan to increase engine output is with experienced hot rodders, such as the folks who sell cams for a living.

BUILDING YOUR BUICK

Although some of the following information may be "old hat" to some engine builders I would like to share my experiences with this project. Some unusual things have happened which may be new to some and may save you some grief.

First, a reality check. It is not as simple as pulling the engine out of the car and dropping it on an engine mount. Prices. Although my first used engine cost $15 you may find a similar deal. These engines are not rare and large caches (or hoards) are around the country. Complete engines are available from collectors for 200 to 400 dollars. Of course, the UK and Australia are other areas of the world where these engines are sold today. You should also acquire technical information on this engine. Old shop manuals are available through Hemmings ads. Local libraries should have copies of Motor's Manual for 1961-63, the source for technical specifications, serial number locations and year codes. These codes are important as you may wish to avoid the 1961 engine. It has lower torque values than the succeeding years which suggests that the engine may have been poured with a "softer" grade of aluminum. The published torque values will be needed for assembling your engine.

Owner and RV-6A. Typical GPS measured cruise performance at 7,500 MSL with power set at 3500 engine RPM is 168 MPH. Note growth in cowling cross sections at cowl opening and radiator location.

Unless your engine is clean to the touch steam cleaning is next. The plugs should be removed next and the cylinder walls sprayed with WD-40, or similar cleaner to help loosen the rings. An engine stand of 750 pound capacity is a useful investment. During this phase take plenty of photos to have a record of component bracket locations and bolt arrangements. These shots are also valuable information and should become part of your engine logbook. Also at this time, set up a inventory control system so you know (label) what parts are in each bag or box . Be sure to make a note where you store these parts. It is a good idea to include your wife, girl friend or the fellow who drops in occasionally on your storage plan. I found out after several frustrating experiences that outsiders seem to remember such things clearly.

View of the RV-6A engine compartment looking toward firewall. Air cleaner housing has unusual shape and baffling. Right valve train cover includes breather and oil filler cap. Redrive belt and driven sprocket are also seen.

RV-6A ignition wires are properly spaced to prevent crossfire. Stock automobile carburetor is used. A custom log type exhaust manifold occupies minimum space. Light weight automobile starter is seen below the manifold.

MANIFOLD ORIENTATION Remove the carburetor. If it's a four barrel save it for your project. The ID number is on a small metal tag attached to one edge of the carburetor. This number is cross-referenced to the required float setting value. If you elect to use this carburetor we recommend using a #48 for the primary and #54 for the secondary jets. Carefully remove the intake manifold and note that two bolts are longer than the others. These are at the raised portion of the manifold, near the thermostat location. Note also two sizes of intake holes, the primary inlets being smaller. We rotate the manifold 180 degrees to orient the carburetor float chamber in the proper direction for acceleration. We have tried it both ways and, let me put it this way, a two-stage takeoff can bring on some quickening of the pulse. The airplane will accelerate up to a point when the carburetor bowl is emptied; the engine quits and a moment later, fuel again flows and the airplane continues on. Obviously, we do not recommend using the stock manifold orientation. When the stock manifold is re-oriented the stock water ports are exposed. These must be welded closed and small #40 steam holes drilled through the aluminum cover plates. New coolant holes must be cut into the block corresponding to the new manifold orientation. At this point it is a good idea to check the manifold and block for areas needing repair. Some corrosion damage may be present as a result of using non-distilled water.

VALVE DRIVE TRAIN Be prepared for a shock when you remove the valve covers. What you will typically see is 20 years worth of solid grime which indicates the engine has had a long rest. The mess will probably make you want to change your car engine oil more often. This is the time to take some more photos or sketch the relationship of the springs and spacers to the rocker arms. Remove the rocker shaft, loosening the bolts a little at a time so as not to bind the shaft or bend it. Be careful not to lose the tips of the rocker arms as they come out. Note the wear on the rocker tips. If they are grooved they should be discarded. Also note the position of the oiling holes relative to the rocker towers. This engine oils the rockers through the rocker towers. The pushrods are solid, unlike other General Motors engines. Be sure to remove the plugs in the ends of the rocker tubes and clean these thoroughly. If you happen to forget the grime WILL eventually trash your valves and rockers. Another point. The rocker tube position relative to the towers is critical. It is very easy to install these parts backwards causing no oil to get to the rockers. This misstep WILL also trash valves. For the novice builder it is better to take this overhaul in small increments, to take time and do it once. You may recall the old saying which applies here, "There is never enough time to do it right, but always enough time to do it over".

The next step is the removal of the heads. While removing the bolts note the differing lengths. Their positioning is listed in the Motor's Manual. Inspect the water passages in the ends of the heads; now is a good time to have the openings Heli-arced or otherwise repaired. Your local machine shop can be called on to re-surface the heads, install new valve guides, springs and valves. The valves should be dressed to the same length since the hydraulic lifters are not adjustable. You may wonder here why we do not mention porting, polishing and flow benching. In the context of an airplane engine that will operate at relatively low RPMs the power gains from these procedures are minimal. In our experience the stock heads do quite well.

ACCESSORY CASE The front accessory case is removed next. The torsional damper is keyed to the crankshaft. Its center retainer bolt is removed and a puller is used. Since the case is a die casting, is expensive and will break don't pry on it to pull the damper. Once it is off, the timing chain, gears and the fuel pump cam are exposed. The chain is removed by pulling both gears at the same time. The shop manual describes the procedure. The engine block valley cover when removed exposes more engine grime! The push rods are removed, cleaned and checked for equal length and straightness. The latter is done simply by rolling each piece on a flat surface. Reject those that wobble. The lifters are discarded and will be replaced by new parts.

CAMSHAFT Exercise care in removing the cam. Opinions vary as to the choice of replacement cams for any engine. You should not choose a replacement cam on the basis of "torque", "half-race", or other simple labels. Keep in mind that virtually all aftermarket cam manufacturers have devoted their design talents to the development of high RPM engines, not primarily focused with the improvement of low RPM horsepower. So, if you are set on re-camming your engine do some research beforehand. Considering the reduction ratio of our redrive and the airplane application we find that the original factory grind or one close to its specifications performs well and recommend this approach.

BLOCK VARIATIONS This engine was designed and built with unique cast-in iron cylinder liners, machined with grooves for maximum retention. We have found that some engines show a slight shift of the sleeves with respect to the machined bore, seen as a round bore in a somewhat egg-shaped sleeve. Apparently, the sleeves would shift during the cooling process causing an uneven distribution of sleeve material and would cause uneven cooling during engine operation. Although the factory allowed for 0.060 inch overboring some engines could only be opened up to 0.010 inches before entering the aluminum substrate. This much distortion is unacceptable for our application so we recommend that blocks with visible eccentricity be bored out

Overall view of the RV-6A installation. Note use of piano hinge stock for attachment of the upper cowling.

Similar view of Jess Meyers' Swift. The larger stock cowl of the Swift completely hides the Buick installation.

and re-sleeved with the step at the bottom. The Chevrolet Vega has a top stepped sleeve but it is only 0.0625 inch thick as compared to the 0.125 thickness of the bottom stepped parts. It is a good idea to have the new pistons on hand before cylinder work begins. Each make of piston requires specific cylinder wall clearances for proper operation. Actual piston dimensions and clearances establish the finished

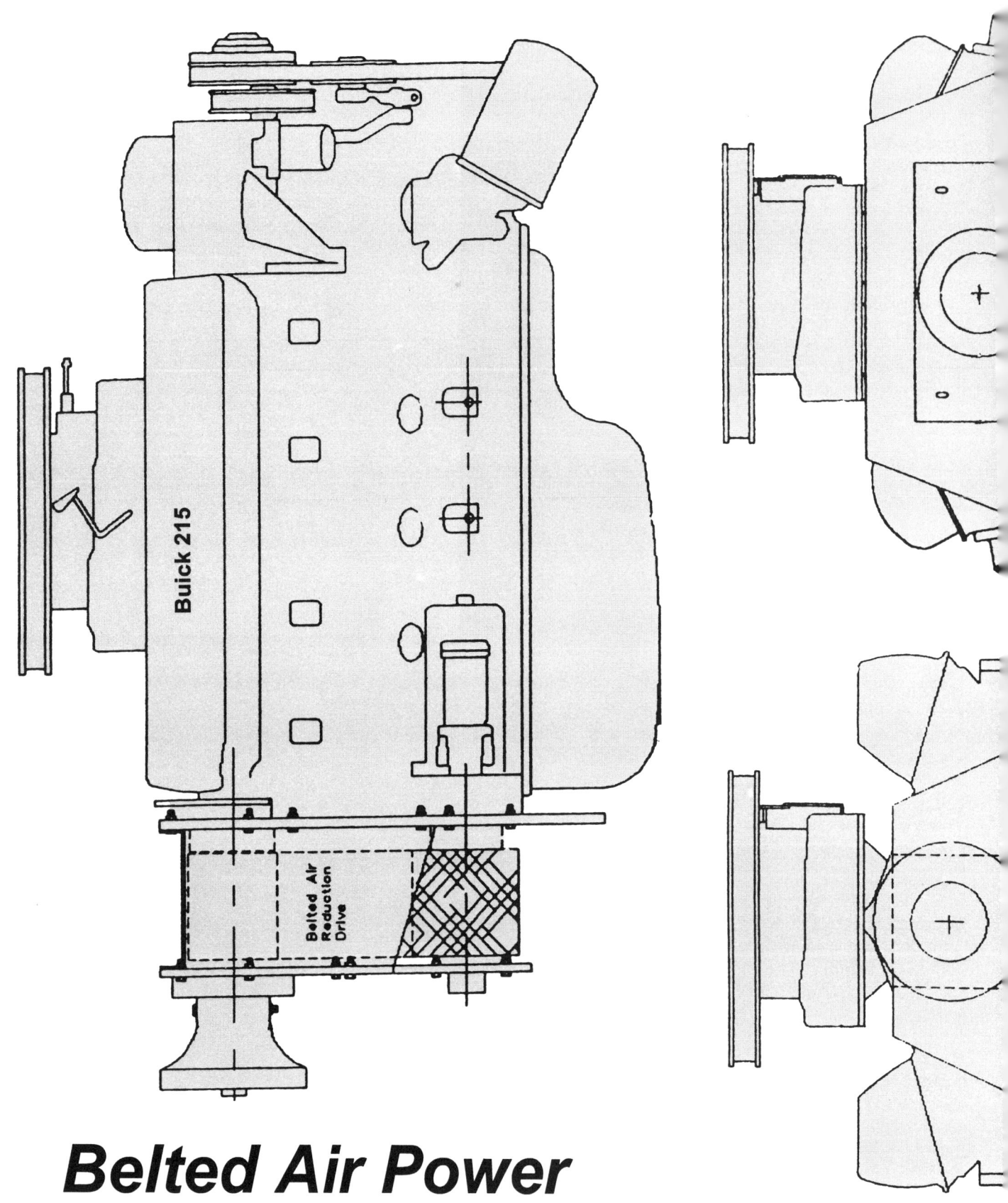

Belted Air Power Aero Conversions 1/5 Scale

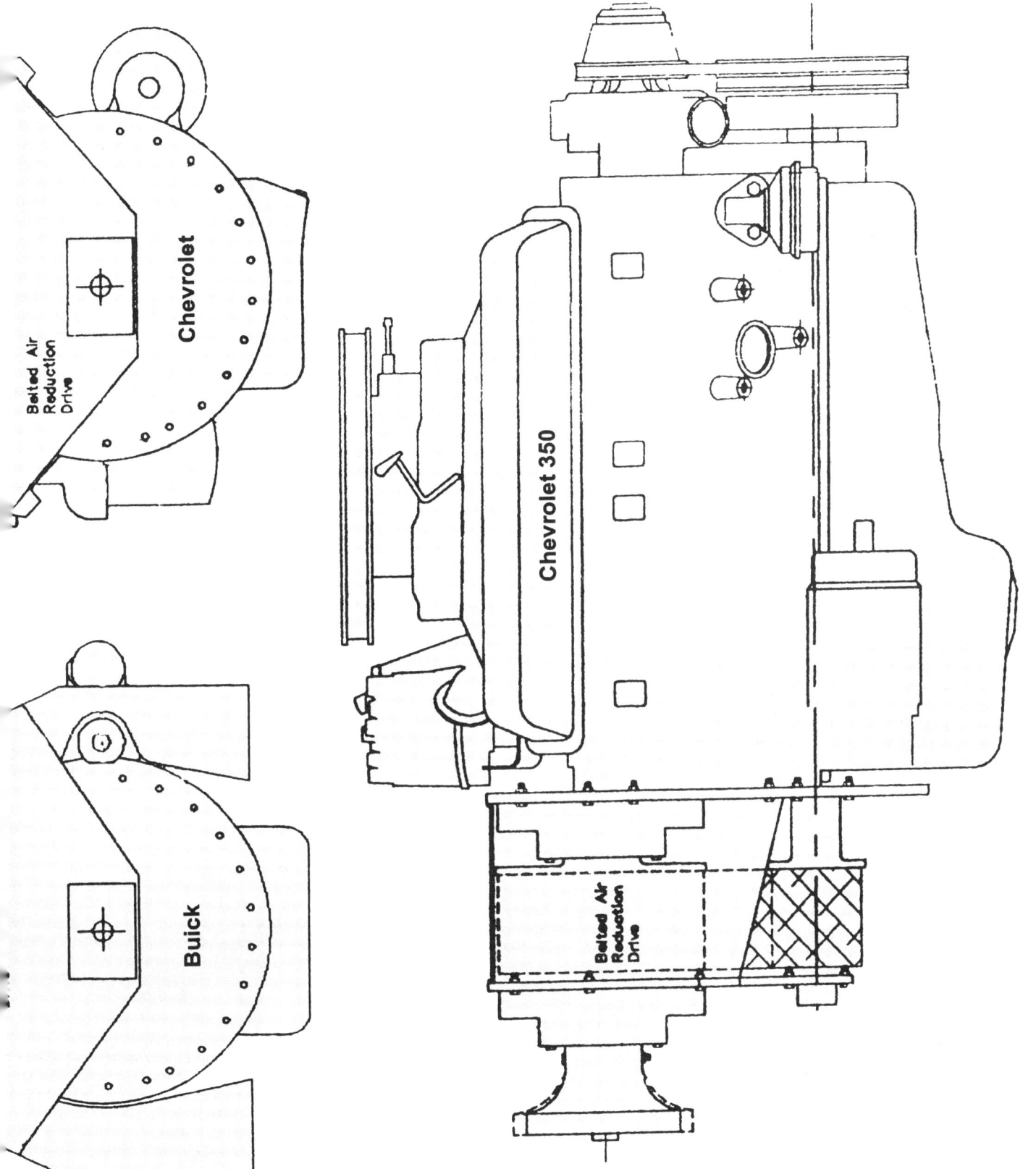

bore diameters. A well equipped machine shop can relocate and true the bores for new sleeves before installation thus ensuring you of maximum cylinder cooling. The block should be decked to provide a flat head gasket surface. The machine shop will also line bore the main bearing bores and give you new main bearings. The return of your block is just the beginning if you choose to complete the build process.

Cleaning the block is extremely important. A bucket of hot, soapy water, liquid dishwashing soap or Tide and a variety of brushes to reach minute crevices are the tools of choice. Freeze plugs are punched and twisted out. Oil passage plugs are removed (gun bore brush here) and passages cleaned out. The cleaning process should be repeated several times to make CERTAIN all dirt is gone. GM 215 blocks have their share of flashing and roughness which act to retain engine oil. It is a good idea to grind off these obstacles to oil cooling with a Dremel type of grinder or air tool. The crankshaft is also cleaned with particular attention given to oil passages which are usually gummed up. Shop air is used to remove moisture and to dry off all parts.

Swift belly scoop with custom radiator and external aluminum coolant pipes.

A side view of the Swift belly scoop. This setup handles Las Vegas summer desert temperatures quite effectively. Photo taken at Prescott Copperstate.

RE-ASSEMBLY The front accessory case needs to be checked. First note how the front seal retainer fits and retains the seal and then remove both. Use carburetor cleaner to remove varnish and dirt. The case is then checked for alignment. Install the oil pump gear with the long shaft in place and the distributor In its hole. Turn the distributor shaft by hand and note the freedom of movement and alignment with the oil pump shaft. If you feel some binding a new front housing is needed.

V/8 engines run smoothly. Although the original 215 connecting rods and the crankshaft are fairly well balanced and better than the typical aircraft parts you may want to get the moving parts balanced to within grams. Piston rings are gapped and fitted according to Motor's Manual instructions. You may elect to replace the original head bolts with studs of the proper length. If any threads in the block have been damaged or are in question use Heli Coil inserts.

Assembly of the engine begins with the installation and staking of new freeze and oil galley plugs and follows published instructions with particular attention to torque values.

Heads require special attention. We have found that by spraying the head gaskets with aluminum lacquer prior to installation that this procedure resists leaking. We recommend that you follow the steps outlined in Motor's Manual but torque the heads in 10 foot pound steps, from forty to the final value. This approach ensues that the heads pull down evenly. Make a mental note to run your engine a short time or up to 180 degrees F., then let it cool overnight and retorquing the heads again. Some of the bolts will take up slightly but with this follow up step your engine should be good until the next major inspection and overhaul.

Our airplanes use the Mallory aftermarket distributor which has an extra set of points added 180 degrees from the

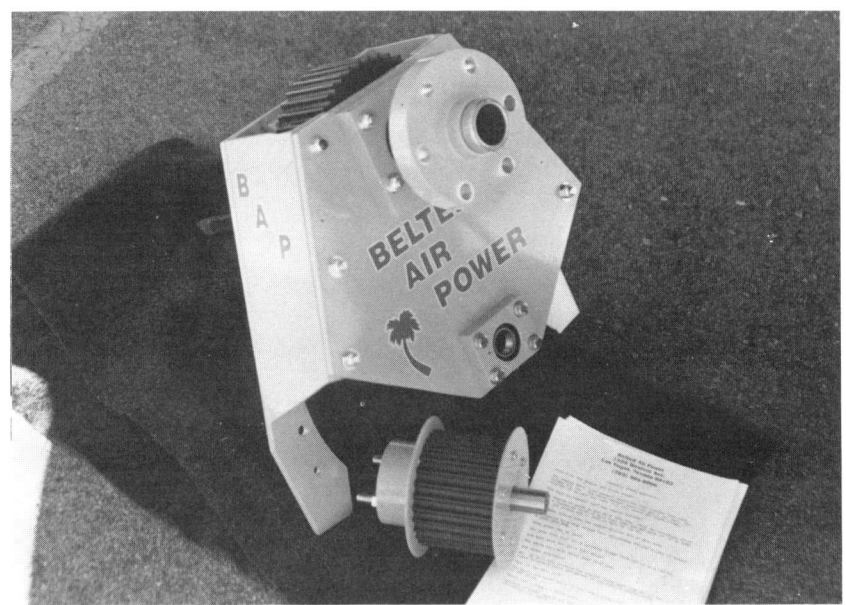

One of Belted Air Power's redrives. The 215 Buick 1.43:1 ratio unit weighs 38 pounds; the 350 Chevrolet 1.71:1 ratio version weighs 55 pounds.

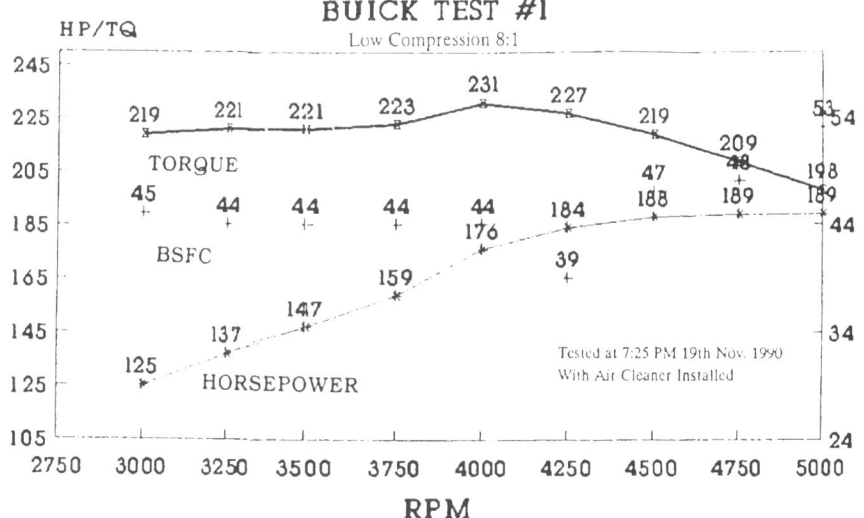

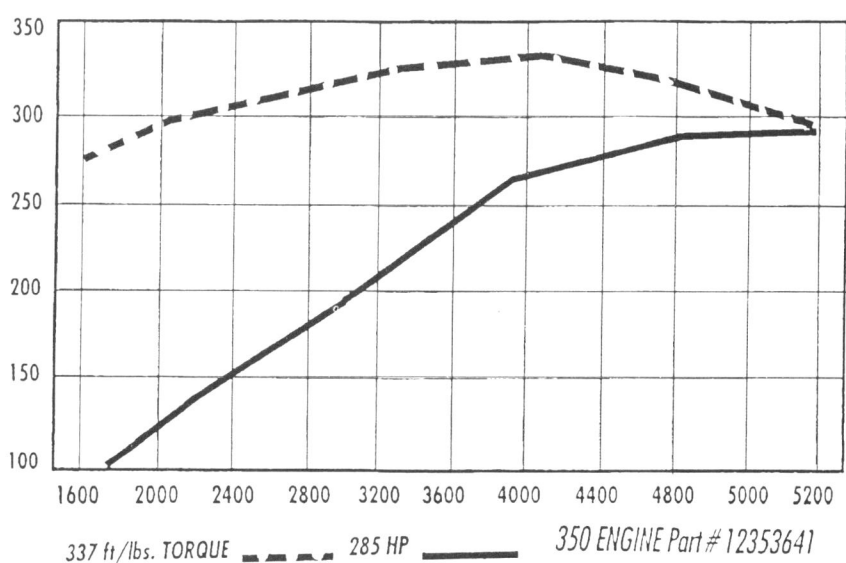

337 ft/lbs. TORQUE ---- 285 HP —— *350 ENGINE Part # 12353641*

standard set. This dual point arrangement is wired to a backup battery through a cross tie switch for redundancy. The Mallory also has a tach drive. The stock 215 distributor can be used and an extra set of points added. Other aftermarket pointless systems are available. The tach can be of the inductance type, clipping over a spark plug wire. We use a point ignition system instead of solid state devices to avoid any failure due to lightning.

COOLING Responsibility for a homebuilt airplane lies completely with the builder. Proper cooling is a essential element of this responsibility and must be taken seriously. Air cooling of certified engines is no simple task; try comparing baffling designs for a given factory engine installation! Liquid cooling has no established benchmarks from which to begin but we have found the following to work for us.

Using an aluminum radiator, single row tube area of 1x 125 in^2 we have determined that a frontal area of 1.43 in^2 will cool 1.0 in^3 of engine displacement. Thus, a 215 in^3 engine will require 150 in^2 of a two row frontal area radiator. Any radiator is adversely affected by its duct design. A leak free duct is essential; air is like water in that it seeks the path of least resistance. The intake opening is important. We found a opening 55 percent that of the radiator frontal area to work. The intake duct should not diverge more than 5 degrees. Radiator tanks must not be exposed to the flow, to avoid piling up of the air. The air scoop should face free air, not exhaust stacks. Ideally, the scoop must be exposed, not located behind a bend in the fuselage. The inlet length should be about 1.23 times that of the xhaust length. The outlet area should have twice the area of the inlet opening. Strange things happen to air flow; the Bf 109 actually had reverse flow due to insufficient inlet length causing it to overheat during ground runs. A simple manometer is ideal for trouble shooting. **JM**

Modifying GM's Aluminum V8s

This article by Ray Brock, with photos by Eric Rickman, was originally published in the June 1961 issue of HOTROD magazine. Contact! expresses its thanks to the publisher for the express permission to reprint this technical report of interest to experimenters. Thanks also to Bruce Johansen for use of his reference copy.

The second year of the "compact age" is in full swing now and at least two of the engines in the latest crop show qualities which should make them extremely popular among those with an outlook for performance. The two engines referred to are the new aluminum V/8s used in the F-85 Oldsmobile and the Buick Special. Pontiac Tempest also offers an optional V/8 but it is purchased from Buick and is identical in all ways to the Special engine. So, everything that applies to the Special engine in our story is ditto for the Tempest V/8.

Our first look at the aluminum V/8s came when the small Olds and Buick cars were introduced last fall but our observations were restricted to what we could see by lifting the hoods of the cars. Our second look came last December when we saw a pair of the engines being uncrated at the Edelbrock Equipment Company in Los Angeles where they were planning to make a series of dynamometer tests. We were invited to participate in these tests to develop speed equipment for the engines. In so doing, we were able to really get a thorough picture of the little engines as we witnessed and even helped tear the engines down, swap parts around, put them back together and then check results of the experiments on the dyno.

ENGINE COMPARISON

Olds F-85 and Buick Special V/8s are quite similar. Both use a 3.50 inch bore and 2.9 inch stroke for 215 cubic inches. Both are rated at 155 horsepower for their standard engines although the Olds rating is at 4800 rpm while Buick's peak power rating is at 4600 rpm. In the advertised torque department, the Olds is rated at 210 pound/feet at 3200 rpm while the Buick is rated 220 pound/feet at 2400 rpm. A 10 pound difference in torque is easy to understand but the big difference in maximum torque rpm doesn't make sense especially when engines are so nearly identical. A power and torque curve we found in an Olds manual leads us to believe that the Olds rating at 3200 is correct while the Buick maximum torque speed of 2400 rpm is probably a typographical error. Tests made on Edelbrock's dyno showed Buick maximum torque to be between 3100 and 3200 rpm.

Comparing the two engines part for part, we found almost everything below the cylinder heads interchangeable. Cylinder blocks are aluminum with ridged iron liners cast into the block. Everything else about the blocks is aluminum with no inserts for cap screws, etc. Part numbers are different for the Buick and Olds blocks but except for a minor difference in the exterior surface around the rear of the blocks, they appeared identical. All interior measurements were the same. Olds blocks use a six-hole pattern around each bore for cylinder head cap screws while Buicks use only five but the Buick block had the extra tapped holes required by the Olds even though they weren't used. Steel main bearing caps were fitted to the "Y" type block which has the bottom skirt well below the center line of the crankshaft for added main bearing support.

Crankshafts for the Olds and Buick engines share the same GM part number so are obviously identical. They are cast of Pearlitic malleable iron with 2.3 inch main bearing journals (less clearances) and 2 inch rod journals. Main bearing inserts are steel-backed Moraine with a babbitt overlay; number three main is fitted with thrust surfaces. Suggested main clearance is .0005 -.0021 with crankshaft end play .004 -008 inch.

Connecting rods for the two engines share the same GM part number so are identical. Automobile Manufacturers Association specifications indicated a difference of one third ounce (17.89 oz for Olds versus 17.55 oz for Buick) in rod weight but when the two engines were balanced by Edelbrock during the test program, they checked out within .1 ounce between engines. Rod bearings are also Moraine 100-A steel-backed babbitt with recommended

Bottom view of both Olds and Buick appear the same with nodular iron crankshaft and steel main caps. Cast iron cylinder liners are cast directly in the block, otherwise no inserts are used. All bolt holes tap into the aluminum.

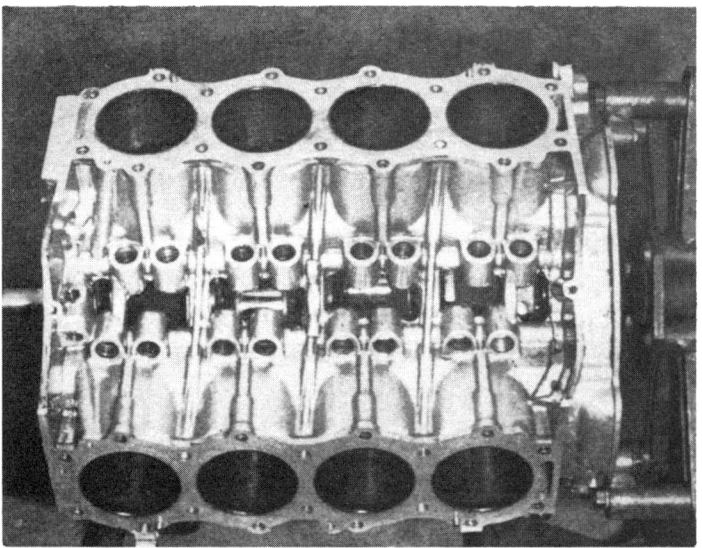

Top view of blocks is also the same although Buick does not use the bolt holes at the top of each cylinder to hold down the heads like Olds. There are two main oil galleries, each intersecting a row of lifter bores while supplying bearings.

Cylinder heads for the Olds and Buick engines share the same spacing for the intake ports, also the same for the exhaust, so their intake and exhaust manifolds are interchangeable. Olds head (front) is fitted with taper-wound valve springs, Buick uses straight-wound but pressures for both are close.

Crank is well supported in deep block. Drive gear for distributor and oil pump is keyed to camshaft and held in place by bolt. During dyno tests, rapid wear was noted on the drive gear.

clearances of .0002-.0022 inch and .006-.014 inch end play for two rods.

It's not until you get up to the piston department of the engines that you see a visible difference between the small V/8s. Olds uses a flat-top piston while Buick's piston is a dished-top variety. Piston weights vary somewhat too with the Olds piston almost 3/4 ounce heavier than the Buick. Piston pins for the two engines are another common item as they have the same GM part number and are a press fit into unbushed upper rod ends.

Cylinder heads for the engines are completely different, both Olds and Buick used a variation of their larger V/8 chambers. The little Olds head has a definite wedge chamber while the Buick head uses an oblong hemispherical chamber. Olds intake and exhaust valves are side-by-side across the center of the cylinder bore while the Buick valves, also side-by-side, are crowded over more toward the upper side of the bores. Buick's spark plug location is almost in the center of the cylinder while Olds is in the top of the wedge, nearer the bottom edge of the cylinder bore. The larger capacity of the Olds chamber teams with the flat-top piston to give a compression ratio of 8.75:1 while the small Buick chamber and extra volume of the dished-top piston add up to give a 8.8:1 ratio.

Both cylinder heads use the same pattern and spacing for intake and exhaust port openings. Intake ports are close in design for the two engines but the Buick exhaust is typically Buick in design with a small, restricted port beneath the valve, flaring out as it reaches the manifolds for the two engines are almost the same in appearance but have slightly different flange designs where they enter the exhaust pipes so use different numbers. Except for the flange difference, they are interchangeable.

Valve trains for the two engines start out the same at the camshaft but change as they reach the head region. Both engines use the same camshaft and hydraulic lifters. Although timing figures on the AMA specification sheets released by Buick and Olds do not jibe, part numbers were the same on the camshafts in the two test engines as well as in the parts books. Evidently, one manufacturer listed total timing including clearance ramps while the other listed effective timing at the valve. Using this theory, we will choose the lesser timing figures as effective and they are: Intake opens 22 degrees BTC, closes 58 degrees ABC for 260 degree duration; exhaust opens 60 degrees BBC, closes at 20 degrees ATC for 260 degrees duration and 42 degrees overlap. Total lift for both intake and exhaust valves is .384 inch.

Pushrods, although of the same solid forged design with upset radiused ends, are slightly different in length. This is due to valve length and rocker arms with a ratio of 1.6 to 1 and a slight offset between pushrod and valve ends. The aluminum stands which support the rocker shaft are held in place by four long cap screws which go completely through the head and into the block helping to hold down the heads as well as the rocker shafts. Oiling for the rockers comes from the main oil galleries, one on each side of the lifter chamber. These galleries run the length of the block and intersect the lifter bores with passages drilled to camshaft and crankshaft main bearings. Rocker oil passes through a passage up to the top of the block, then into a groove across the face of the Olds cylinder head where it then goes up through the head, around the front rocker stand cap screw and into the hollow rocker shaft.

Oiling for Buick rockers is similar except that the oil passage between the block and the front rocker stand is via a slant-bored passage in the Buick head. The Buick rocker arms are also 1.6:1 ratio but they are forged aluminum with pressed-in steel buttons on the valve end and sockets on the pushrod end. Buick rocker-shaft-stand assemblies fasten directly to the cylinder head, instead of on through into the block.

Valve sizes for the two engines are of similar dimensions although the Olds does use slightly larger intakes (1.522 vs. 1.500 inches) and exhausts (1.353 vs. 1.313 inches). An interesting item in the valve department of the engines is the fact that both use tapered valve stems but they each have their own ideas on the matter. Buick uses tapered valve stems on both intake and exhaust valves so they have .0005 inch more assembled clearance at the bottom of the guide than at the top. Olds tapers only the exhaust valve stem but they give .001 inch extra clearance at the bottom of the guides. AMA published valve stem sizes are .002 larger on the Olds and this plus about 1/4 inch extra length cancels any ideas of interchangeability between the engines. One last difference, Olds uses a flat headed intake valve and tuliped exhaust while Buick reverses the order with a tuliped intake and flat exhaust.

Valve seat inserts are used by both Buick and Olds in their cylinder heads but each evidently has its own preference in material. Olds calls their seats steel, while Buick refers to theirs as sintered iron. The Olds seat seems to be pressed into the head and then the aluminum head material (is) crimped down over the top edge of the seat to lock it in place. Buick's seats appear to be pressed into place without any crimping. During the tests, a Buick head was ported too far in an attempt to improve breathing and had to be replaced. Just to check how secure the seats were, we popped a couple of them out but not without considerable difficulty. We tried to heat a spot on the seat red hot, then cool it quickly with an air hose to crack the insert but the aluminum head carried the heat away so fast that we had a hard time getting the seat hot enough. After this episode, we predict that the valve seats will not present any problems in normal service - they are in to stay.

Intake manifolds are different in appearance between the two engines but they will interchange from engine to engine since the intake port and bolt pattern in the Buick and Olds heads are the same. Olds uses a cast dam around the top of the manifold which matches a stamped steel air cleaner top that completely encloses the carburetor. Buick uses a conventional type air cleaner which covers only the top of the carburetor so does not use the raised dam.

The rest of the engine components are interchangeable; water pump, oil pump, fuel pump, timing sprockets and chain, timing cover, flywheels, etc. Even the starter and generator will interchange although they do have different part numbers. Comparing the Buick and Olds engine(s) in broad terms, they are the same except for cylinder heads, piston design and part of the valve train.

Getting into the actual dynamometer test section of the comparison, we made more than thirty runs on various combinations of compression, carburetion, cam timing, exhaust systems, ignition timing, porting, etc. We had first one, then the other engine on the dyno over a three-month period and accumulated a number of reports which we have sorted through to get facts for this story. Some of the tests did not prove anything or were repetitious so we discarded them. We also changed the order in which the reports were complied so we don't have to jump back and forth from one engine to another.

The performance figures were compiled on Edelbrock's 700 horsepower Clayton dynamometer. The dyno is located in the rear of Edelbrock's large machine shop and we found the temperature to always be within a couple degrees of 70 degree F. during the middle of the day when we made our runs. Barometric readings were recorded from a barometer mounted next to the dyno and variations were very slight. Since atmospheric conditions were so uniform during our tests, we made no attempt to correct readings for temperature, barometric pressure and humidity, they were recorded just as observed on the dyno gauge.

TEST PROGRAM

We started out with the Olds engine first on the dyno so we will lead off with the Olds results and then follow up with the Buick. By checking the horsepower chart on this page, the results of the various changes we will describe can be noted throughout the entire rpm range.

BUICK SPECIAL V8 HORSEPOWER

Test	2000	2500	3000	3500	4000	4500	5000	5500	6000	6500
1	73	93	113	128	137	139	136			
2	73	96	121	135	147	153	156			
3	69	94	122	140	161	174	177			
4	69	93	116	140	166	189	207	214	215	
5	70	93	118	146	171	197	213	222	226	220
6	73	93	115	146	173	198	217	226	230	226
7	71	93	114	148	173	198	218	230	233	233
8	72	93	114	148	171	197	215	229	231	231

Rocker arm assemblies for the two engines vary widely. Buick rockers, front, are aluminum with stands that bolt directly to cylinder head. Olds has steel rockers and stand bolts extend through head into block. Both type rockers have the same ratio, 1.6:1.

OLDS F-85 V8 HORSEPOWER

Test	2000	2500	3000	3500	4000	4500	5000	5500	6000	6500
1	69	90	110	122	130	135	130			
2	68	87	110	125	134	140	137			
3	70	91	112	133	149	156	155			
4	75	98	118	134	146	150	150			
5	74	94	123	140	159	170	172			
6	68	86	112	133	163	179	189	194		
7	60	77	103	130	154	175	187	192	192	187
8	68	83	109	145	161	181	197	201	200	191
8A					164	183	198	208	213	208
8B					168	187	202	208	213	208
9							203	212	217	223
10			109	144	165	188	205	211	217	213
11	63	85	104	136	156	177	191	200	203	199

OLDS #1 The 215 cubic inch F-85 engine was completely stock for the first test but did have 6 1/2 hours of run-in time on the dyno at various loads. No fan or generator was used but the water pump was operating. The vacuum line to the distributor was disconnected since full throttle tests would not provide any vacuum advance anyway. Since our objective was for the best possible power, not economy, the primary jets on the two-barrel Rochester carburetor were changed. Stock jets were .046 inch. We tried both .048 and .050, finally choosing the .048 inch jets since they gave the best power.

Ignition was power timed at 4000 rpm with a full load and proved to be 13 degrees initial advance. Coupled with the 22 degrees centrifugal advance in the stock distributor (AMA specs call for 26 degrees), the total advance used was 35 degrees. We checked the power readings in 500 rpm steps and recorded a maximum observed reading of 135 hp at 4500 rpm. Although some 20 hp less than the advertised 155, this is very good for a production engine with normal manufacturing tolerances and not too much break-in. Power fell off at 5000 rpm and an attempt to get a power reading above this speed was not successful as the valves started floating audibly at about 5300 rpm.

A subsequent check of the combustion area with a piston at top center and both gasket and cylinder head in place showed the actual compression of our test Olds to be 8.6 to 1 instead of the advertised 8.75. This figure, too, although slightly low, is very close compared to various production V/8s we have checked in the past.

OLDS #2 For the second test, we made a simple change, one which any F-85 owner could easily make, and picked up a quick 5 hp at 4500 rpm. The change was to install a slightly larger Rochester carburetor. The stock Olds Rochester has two 1 inch venturis while the one we installed was designed for a 283 inch Chevy and has 1 3/22 inch venturis. The extra venturi area gave more power at all steps above 3000 rpm and provided the necessary extra intake charge to keep the power from dropping off rapidly above 4500. With the larger carburetor, power was 7 hp better at 5000 rpm. Although this doesn't sound like much, remember that this is a small displacement engine and we are not starting out with a lot of power. Jets in the larger Rochester were juggled a bit but worked best with stock .057 jets.

OLDS #3 For this test, the engine was left completely stock except for the installation of Edelbrock's new dual intake manifold and two stock Olds 1 inch venturi carburetors. Jetting was adjusted by trial .002 larger than stock with .048 inch jets in both carburetors. This move really confirmed the suspicion that the little V/8s are well restricted for fuel economy reasons as the engine responded with increased power throughout the entire range. The maximum power reading was 156 hp, 21 more than stock. Compare test #1 and #3 on the Olds horsepower chart to see how much difference the dual manifold made throughout the whole rpm range.

OLDS #4 Back to stock again for this next test except that a set of JE experimental high compression pistons were fitted and the crank assembly rebalanced for the new pistons. Although the JE pistons had a raised head to increase compression, they were slightly lighter than the stock Olds pistons. Again the compression was checked by positioning a piston at top center, using wax to seal the gap between piston and wall, then bolting on a head with gasket and measuring the amount of light oil needed to fill the combustion chamber through the spark plug hole. The compression ratio was increased from 8.6 to 12.3 to 1 with the pop-up type pistons. Everything else in the engine was exactly as it was for test #1, a single stock carburetor with .048 jets, 35 degree total timing, stock exhaust etc.

The increase in compression helped throughout the entire rpm range reaching a maximum horsepower reading of 150 at both 4500 and 5000 rpm. Power was up about 10% all the way from 2000 rpm to 5000 rpm.

OLDS #5 The next obvious test to make was a combination of #3 and #4,

TOP-Olds chamber is wedge design with valves side by side across center of bore. Six bolt pattern around each cylinder ensures very good seal.

CENTER-Three pistons used during test were: Stock Buick, left, which has dished top; stock Olds with flat top; JE high compression for Olds with pop-up top which boosted ratio to 12.3:1

RIGHT- Buick's aluminum 215 chamber is semi-hemispherical in shape with small pockets for valves. With flat top Olds pistons, ratio was 12:1. Stock ratio is 8.8:1

the high compression pistons and the dual intake manifold. The rest of the engine was left stock and spot checks made to see how well the stock AC 46FF spark plugs would stand the increase in pressure. They showed signs of blistering so were replaced with a set of colder Champion J 63R side electrode plugs.

Carburetion and compression really made the little engine start to produce. Maximum power was jumped to 172 hp at 5000 rpm, an increase of 37 hp or 27 percent above the maximum power reading when stock.

OLDS #6 The next step we took was to further improve the breathing ability of the engine. This we did by installing a camshaft reground by Iskenderian to his E-4 grind. The stock hydraulic lifters were also replaced with Isky solid lifters and a set of adjustable pushrods used. Dual valve springs were installed in place of the single progressively wound stock spring. Another addition at this point was the installation of a Spalding dual-coil ignition in

Stock exhaust manifolds for both Olds and Buick are similiar in design but have small area in some places which restricted engines after intake had been opened up. Manifolds were reversed with outlet facing forward for use on dyno. The four-quart pan holds plenty for the engine; temperatures never got hot.

place of the stock distributor. We had not experienced any trouble with the stock ignition up to this point but with extra compression and speeds anticipated, we knew that we soon might.

So, as we prepared for the dyno test, the stock engine had been modified to the following degree: High compression (12.3:1); dual intake manifold with two stock carburetors, Iskenderian E-4 can and kit; and a Spalding ignition. We power timed the engine at 4000 rpm and ended up with 32 degrees total advance. As we expected, the increase in camshaft timing cost us some power at the lower engine speeds but by 4000 rpm, the extra breathing started paying off as power went up at a rapid pace. We reached a maximum reading of 194 hp at 5500 rpm. Attempts to get a steady reading at 6000 rpm were unsuccessful as there was audible valve float just below 6000. Again, we had improved the power but the comparatively mild E-4 cam and springs would not reach the rpms we wanted.

OLDS #7 Another cam was sent over by Iskenderian, this time an E-2 grind with a stronger set of dual valve springs. We installed

them but everything else was left exactly as it had been for test #6. The increased timing on the E-2 cam again shaved its share off the lower rpm power but started picking up above 4000 rpm. Power did not quite match the E-4 grind at its maximum, falling 2 hp short with 192 at 5500 rpm, but the engine could be turned an extra 1000 rpm with good power. A full load check was made at 7000 rpm and no audible valve float could be heard but power was off substantially.

OLDS #8 A set of special Hedman headers were installed for this test with everything else left exactly as it had been for test #7. Power was improved throughout the entire rpm range with a maximum reading of 201 hp reached at 5500, 200 hp at 6000 rpm. An interesting notation was that the low rpm power was improved more, percentage wise, than was the high rpm power. At one point, 3500 rpm, the difference between test #7 and #8 was an unbelievable 15 hp but we double checked it twice more and found it correct.

At this point in the test, we double checked ignition timing again and found that we had lost about 3 degrees total timing and had actually made this last run with only 29 degrees total timing. A thorough check was made to find just what had happened and it was found that the distributor and oil pump driving gear which bolts on the front of the camshaft and is not part of the cam billet, had worn badly and caused the retardation. We checked with the local Olds dealer and learned that they too had had this problem. We installed a new gear and rechecked for power.

OLDS #8A and #8B For test #8A, we reset the total advance to 32 degrees and started our checks at 4000 rpm. Power was up slightly at 4000 but improved quickly above 5500 rpm, showing 13 hp better at 6000 rpm with a maximum reading of 213 hp.

For test #8B, we added another 4 degrees initial timing to give 36 degrees total and repeated the previous checks. Power was up an appreciable amount at 4000 and 5000 rpm, then equaled the readings of test #8A above 5000 rpm. This setting, 36 degrees total advance, was determined the best setting for the ignition.

OLDS #9 The drop-off in power above 6000 rpm with no audible signs of valve float indicated that perhaps the engine could still use a little extra breathing so a pair of the Chevy Rochester carburetors with 1 3/32 inch venturis were installed in place of the stock Rochesters with 1 inch venturis. Spot checks proved stock .057 jets were best for maximum power. Since the effect of this change would not be noticeable at the lower speeds, we started our checks at 5000 rpm. Power was improved 4 hp at both 5500 and 6000 like it had with the smaller Rochesters and was 15 hp better at 6500 rpm. We made further attempts to increase the power at this point by using larger .059 jets in the carburetors and increasing total timing to both 40 degrees and 45 degrees but could not improve on the 223 hp maximum reached with .057 jets and 36 degree total timing.

OLDS #10 In an attempt to improve the breathing through the Olds heads, we modified the chamber slightly, extending it .150 inch farther into the quench area to try to cut down on any shrouding effect this part of the chamber might have had on the valves.

Everything else was left exactly as it had been for test #9. Checking the combustion chamber with a graduate after the modification, we found that we had lowered the compression ratio from 12.3 to an even 12 to 1. The modification evidently upset the turbulence in the cylinder because we had to richen the mixture up to regain power (.062 jets were finally used) and then fell off at 5500 rpm, probably because the mixture was too rich at this point.

OLDS #11 For the final test on the Olds, we reinstalled the stock pistons (after the chamber modification, the new compression ratio checked out at 8.3:1) so that we could find out just how much power could be gained strictly through bolt-on items that don't require pulling the pan off the car. Bolt-on equipment used included: Edelbrock dual intake manifold with two Chevy 13/32 inch Rochester carburetors; Isky E-2 camshaft with lifter, pushrod spring kit; Spalding Flamethrower ignition; and Hedman headers.

With these comparatively easy-to-install items, a maximum power reading of 203 hp was recorded at 6000 rpm. This represents a 68 hp or 50 percent increase over the 135 hp reading recorded for the completely stock Olds F-85 engine.

Now, for you owners of Buick Specials and Pontiac Tempest V/8s, here's what we did to the little Buick engine and the results of these experiments.

BUICK #1 For this first test everything was strictly stock except that we had determined the carburetion needed richening .002 inch for best power. Spark setting was power timed and checked to be 36 degrees total. The Buick engine also had several hours break-in time on the dyno.

Like the stock Olds engine, the Buick reached its maximum power at 4500 rpm with 139 hp recorded. As with the Olds, valve float was audible at about 5300 rpm. The Buick compression ratio checked out at 8.65:1 instead of the advertised 8.8:1 but this is very close and just a half point more than the Olds. Since the only difference between the Buick and Olds engine is in chamber and port design, the indication was that the Buick engine gets slightly better results from the larger quench area in the chamber and a resultant slight increase in power. Confirming the Buick's claim of 10 pounds/feet more torque than the Olds, we registered 10 pounds more than the Olds at both 3000 and 3500 rpm.

BUICK #2 Since the stock Buick piston has a dished top, we installed the complete set of stock Olds flat-top pistons in the Buick block (everything fits perfectly) and jumped from 8.65:1 to an accurate 12:1 c.r. Everything else was left exactly as it was for the first test; stock carburetor with .048 carburetor jets, 36 degree total advance etc.

The power increase was good throughout the entire rpm range with a maximum of 156 reached at 5000 rpm. With stock Olds pistons probably retailing at about $8 a piece, they look like a good investment for Buick engines although they are about 3/4 ounce heavier and the crank assembly should be rebalanced to make the job correct.

BUICK #3 Edelbrock's dual intake manifold with stock carburetors was installed next with everything else left just as it had been for the last test. As with the Olds engine, the extra breathing unlocked a nice chunk of hidden horsepower as the maximum reading of 177 at 5000 rpm was 21 hp more than it had been in test #2. From 3500 rpm on up, the extra carburetion really helped.

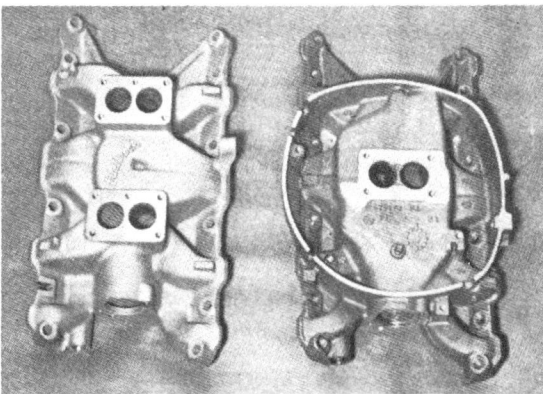

ABOVE- 215 inch Olds F-85 engine modified with 12.3:1 compression ratio, Edelbrock dual manifold with two Chevy Rochesters, Hedman custom header, and Spalding Flamethrower ignition registered high of 223 horsepower, 88 more than stock. TOP RIGHT- Stock Olds intake manifold has raised air dam to match air cleaner, Edelbrock dual fits both engines. BOTTOM- Olds chamber modification attempt failed to improve performance (left one completed, right one marked).

Two changes, the Olds pistons and the dual manifold had increased the maximum power output of the Buick 38 horsepower. Not bad for a start.

BUICK #4 Next, we skipped some of the small changes we had made in the Olds tests and went directly into a search for maximum power. The larger Chevy carburetors were installed on the dual manifold with .059 jets, the Isky E-2 cam and kit were installed, Headman headers were bolted on and Spalding dual-coil ignition used. Again, timing was set under full power at 4000 rpm and checked to be 36 degrees.

As expected, the power increase was quite good with a maximum reading of 215 hp recorded, but power flattened out just when we thought it should be strong. Checks showed the mixture was too lean and the Champion L 10 plugs being used were too hot.

BUICK #5 Jets were changed to .062 (.003 larger) and colder Champion L 63R plugs installed. One other change was made strictly as a precautionary step, the oil pump relief spring was shimmed 1/16 inch to raise oil pressure 10 pounds to 60 psi at 6000 rpm.

This time the power was more like we had expected with a maximum of 226 hp reached at 6000 rpm. The richer jetting had also raised power throughout the power range.

BUICK #6 Iskenderian sent over another cam for us to try, this on a modified E-2 grind, so it was installed and everything else left as it had been for test #5. The new grind gave slightly better power, 4 nore at 6000 rpm, and didn't hurt the lower speed readings so seemed an improvement. We tried to get a steady reading at 7000 rpm but ran into valve float at 6800.

BUICK #7 For this test, the Buick heads were ported out and the valve seats moved out slightly on the inserts. As we mentioned earlier, the first head we tried to port was ruined when we went too deep in the exhaust port. There is not too much material around the ports and if you try to exceed 1/16 inch, you run into trouble. It was impossible to heli-arc the hole due to the thin walls so a new head was purchased and much more care taken on the second attempt. Actually, the amount of porting gained was hardly worth the effort, the valve job probably helped more.

Power was increased slightly at 5500 and 6000 with the best increase, 7 horsepower, shown at 6500 where power had previously dropped off. This indicated breathing ability of Buick heads and ports is probably pretty well taxed.

BUICK #8 A roller camshaft and kit were installed for this test, Isky's RR-2 grind. Everything else was exactly as it had been for test #7. The cam change did not help the power at all, in fact it was almost identical to the modified E-2 grind at low speeds and actually fell off slightly at the top.

The 223 horsepower reading we reached with the Buick was the highest achieved during the tests and although our maximum with the Olds engine was 10 hp short of this, don't forget that we didn't have the modified E-2 grind in time to try it in the Olds. All things considered, we found the two engines quite evenly matched. The Olds ports appear a little less restrictive than those in the Buick but the Buick seems to have the edge in chamber design.

Both of the engines are very light and for use in competition cars or boats (and) could be trimmed down to some pretty impressive figures in the weight department. Although GM advertises the engines as weighing 350 pounds complete, we did a little checking on Edelbrock's Fairbanks platform scales and came up with following weights. The stock Buick engine ready to rum including flywheel and starter but no generator or exhaust manifolds, weighed 289 pounds. The flywheel weighed 23 pounds, the starter 17 pounds. The Olds was weighed complete with starter, flywheel, clutch, cast iron exhaust manifolds. air cleaner etc., and totaled 326 pounds. Minus exhaust manifolds, it was 302 pounds.

All the work we did on these little engines produced no unusual problems. Despite turning them as high as 7000 rpm, the standard steel-backed babbitt bearings looked perfect at the completion of the tests. We used the same shim steel head gaskets from start to finish of the tests and never had a sign of gasket leakage. In fact, we never used any sealing compound either, just wiped off head, block and gasket with a clean rag and put them together. Despite all the teardown and reassembly, we only stripped two threads in the aluminum engine, one head bolt hole in the block and one manifold bolt hole in a head. These we quickly and easily repaired by dragging out the Heli-Coil kit and installing steel inserts. For someone who is going to work on these aluminum V/8s often, it's a good idea to keep Heli-Coils around. Although we followed the torque charts religiously, we stripped a couple.

The tests we made are just a hint of what will happen in the future because there are many enthusiasts in this country who will probably soon have these engines in racing boats, sports cars and other types of competition cars in the near future. When you turn loose a whole country loaded with hot rodders who are full of ideas, things start happening. Already, we have shown that it's easy to exceed one horsepower per cubic inch; it won't take much more to get one horse per pound. After that, a little boring and stroking plus a little more weight trimming should see an unheard of figure for automobile engines of one inch per pound. Just imagine, one of these little lightweights could conceivably be opened out to 260 inches, weigh 260 pounds and produce in excess of 260 horsepower all ready to go! Sound good? END

Olds F-85 sedan was used to street test dual manifold and acceleration was improved with slight change in mileage for average driving. The finned cast aluminum rocker arms covers are another Edelbrtock item. They are also available for Special.

The General Motors aluminum 215 engine has had a successful history in racing and performance applications. It has powered its way into desert sand rails, power boats, dirt track racers, dragsters, and airplanes. Of the latter, the extensive work done by George Morse with his Auto Aviation Olds powered Skybolt and Prowler airplanes and the Tailwind by Steve Wittman are most notable.

Designed specifically for the compact 1961 Buick and Oldsmobile "Y" body cars, the engine was also available as an extra cost option in the Pontiac Tempest. An Olds turbo charged "Jetfire" version producing 215 hp was also offered. Some 700,000 engines were built during the 1961-3 model years. The popularity of the 1962 Chevy II "X" body size led to the introduction of the larger 1964 "A" body which consolidated the four nameplates.

The Buick version surplus tooling was sold to Rover of England where, according to Autocar and Motor magazine, extensive funds were spent on new production equipment. One principal change was the use of cast aluminum blocks and pressed in cast cylinder liners. The engine reappeared as the powerplant for the 1967 Rover P5B sedan, with British accessories. This version of the engine was rated (gross) at 184 hp at 5200 rpm, 226 foot pounds torque at 3300. The engine was used in a wide number of British sourced vehicles. It is still in production.   MCM

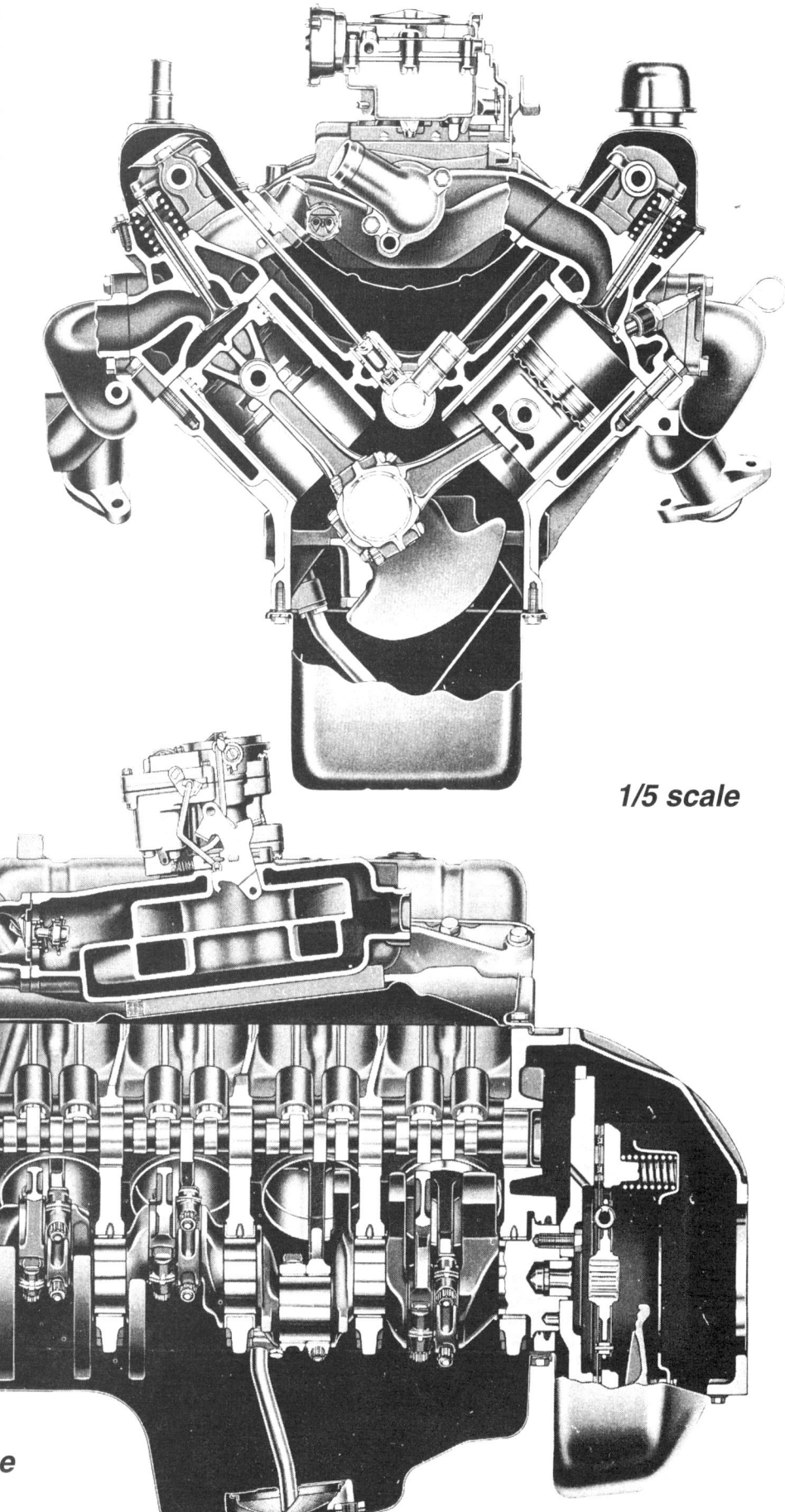

1/5 scale

GM 215 Aluminum Engine

Affordable Aluminum V/8s

This article/photos by Marian Davis was originally published in the March 1985 issue of HOTROD magazine. Contact! expresses its thanks to the Publisher for his permission to reprint this information which is of interest to experimenters. Minor additions and changes were made where appropriate due to the passage of time.   MCM

Have you priced a Chevy aluminum small-block lately?

Whether procured from factory or aftermarket sources, expect to pay somewhere in the neighborhood of $2500 to $3000. And that merely gets you a bare block. No crank, rods, pistons, camshaft, or valve gear. Not to mention the aluminum cylinder heads, which will run around $1000, bare. No wonder most of us make do with the old "iron horses."

It doesn't have to be that way. For well under the purchase price of the Chevy bare block, you can build an affordable aluminum V/8 with

Phil Baker and Buick (left) and Olds 215 engines. Note identifying valve cover angles.

displacements up to 305 cubic inches. Unbelievable? Not really. We are speaking of the 1961-'63 Buick/Olds 215 aluminum motor, an often overlooked granddaddy of the Buick V/6, that unfortunately was about 15 years ahead of its time.

With over 3/4 million built, blocks are relatively easy to locate at the local boneyard. Since the motors had cast iron cylinder liners, corrosion is not nearly the problem it was on the liner less Vegas. While it's true that parts on the out-of-production motor are not exactly plentiful, many parts from more modern motors can be substituted with little or no reworking. Two individuals Phil Baker (Baker's Auto Repair, 19552 40th Place. NE, Seattle, WA 98155, (206) 363-5088) and Dan LaGrou (D&D Fabrications, 8005 Tiffany, Almont, MI 48003, (810) 798-2491(8-5pm))-backyard-build strong-running 215-based motors using amalgamated parts from a variety of engines. Both these individuals also hoard tons of hard-to-find 215 parts. Additionally, D&D offers a completely integrated Vega swap kit that will be covered in detail in a future issue.

WHAT IS A 215?

Before there were Buick V/6s, there was a lightweight aluminum V/8 installed in many Buicks and Olds, and some Pontiacs. Designed originally as an economy engine, it found its way into several quasi-high-performance applications, including Olds' turbocharger applications. Because the aluminum castings cost too much money to produce, the cast-iron Buick V/6's replaced it in the economy role, with the 300/340 Buicks taking over in the moderate performance category. Later, the tooling was sold to Rover, where a descendant powers that company's products to this day.

There were two major 215 variants: the Buick version and the Olds version. Olds engines may be identified by their angled 5-bolt valve covers; Buicks have flatter 4-bolt covers. (Pontiacs used the Buick versions) The late British Rover motor is based on the Buick, and except for different accessory mounting bosses on the cylinder heads, it is considered universally, dimensionally, and functionally interchangeable with the Buick design. However, the imported parts are quite expensive.

Olds cylinder heads are bolted to the block using six bolts per cylinder, while Buicks use only five bolts. The extra Olds head bolt also retains the Olds rocker shafts. Valve train pieces from the pushrods on up are not interchangeable between the two versions.

Buick blocks don't have the extra head bolt hole drilled in them, and the casting has insufficient thickness to add it. For this reason, an Olds head cannot be installed on a Buick block, although a Buick head (and its associated valve train components) will bolt on an Olds block using only five bolts per cylinder. (Head bolt holes are blind, so water jacket seepage from the empty hole isn't a problem.)

Combustion chamber design also differs, with the Buick using a slightly more open-type design. The Olds head runs better on low-octane gas, but the Buick makes more power in racing trim. Buick has only one type of cylinder head, varying compression by changing piston design. Olds, conversely, uses only one piston, altering compression by

Compared to the 300 crank (right), the 215 crank is slightly shorter, has smaller main journals and larger rear main seal. Because of these differences, special mods are required to install the 300 crank in the 215 block. Depending on the specific piston used with the 300 crank throws may need to be kissed for clearance.

Baker installs 300 crank in the 215 by machining the block rear face to accept an aluminum adapter. The adapter seals to the block using a GM TH-350 front pump O-ring gasket; to the crank using a Chevy rat motor neoprene rear main seal.

Rare Olds "turbocharged engine" blocks had taller, beefier main caps retained by twelve point fasteners. They're not neccessary for street use, even if you could find them.

Buick 300/340 cast iron engines (right) can be distinguished from the 215s with a magnet -and by their "B-O-P" bell housing and one piece intake manifold/valley cover. The 1964 300 heads were still aluminum, and offer a performance boost on the 215.

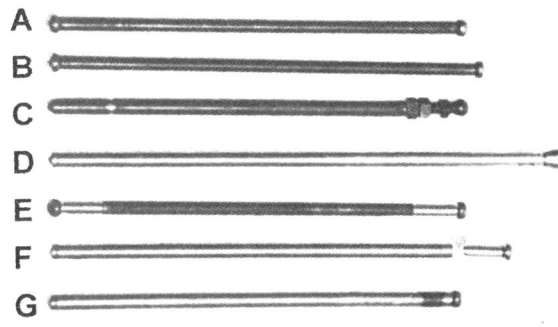

Pushrods: Stock Buick(A) is shorter than Olds(B). Non-stock lengths are often required to maintain non-adjustable valvetrain geometry. Baker fabricated an adjustable checking pushrod(C). MOPAR 225 slant six(D) is hollow and much longer. Baker turns the stock 215 rod ends down to .230inch(E). They are then cut off and pressed into cut-down MOPAR(F), finally resulting in the correct overall length piece(G).

Olds rocker shaft (below,left) is retained on block by extra head bolt and mates with cast-iron rockers. Buick rocker shafts bolt to the head with small 3/8 inch bolts and require aluminum rocker arms with steel inserts.

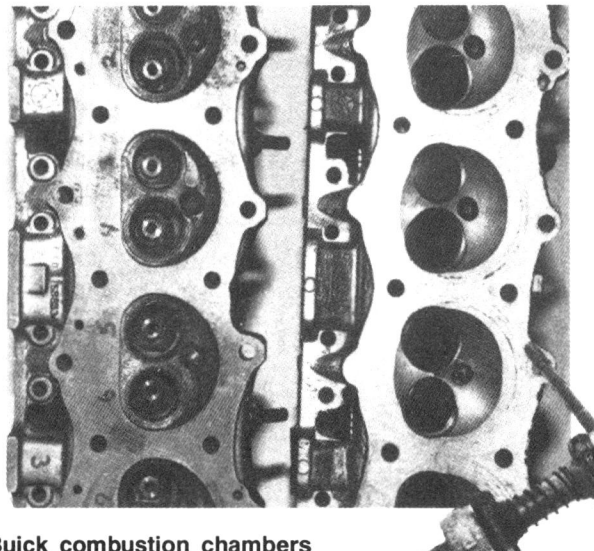

Olds (left) and Buick combustion chambers differ significantly. The Olds head also requires an extra head bolt, so it won't bolt onto Buick blocks.

varying combustion chamber volume.

Since the Olds had a unique valve train not shared by later Olds engines, while the Buick version gave birth to later Buick V/6s and V/8s, parts for Buicks are much more plentiful than for the Olds. Also helping tilt the scales in the Buick's favor is its greater production numbers, outnumbering the Olds as it did by about a 3:2 ratio.

BUILDING THE 215

Once unbuttoned, the 215 is not really unfamiliar at all-it looks like a Buick V/6 with two extra cylinders. As a Buick V/6 relative, it shares that engine's oiling system problems. The same fixes apply to it as on the V/6: for high-performance street use, use a bigger pickup, high-capacity oil pump, increased pan capacity, and larger diameter block oiling passages (see photos). For racing, adopt the various external systems developed for the Buick V/6.

The bottom-end presents no particular durability problems on the street. For high-performance work, bearing clearance should be kept around .002-.0025. Overbore potential is limited to around .030 (.040 if you're brave) with the stock sleeves. But since there is ample aluminum thickness around the sleeves, much larger bores are possible via the installation of bigger aftermarket sleeves. Baker uses Ohio 231 sleeves, SL 4150 or SL 1121_the former ones being cut in half and used to produce two sleeves for the price of one.

Externally balanced 300 cranks require special 300 balancer (right), plus appropriate weights added to flywheel or flexplate.

To mate a late GM automatic with the 215 block/ 300 crank combo, Baker uses a 1964 Ford C4 flexplate (A) to mesh with the 215 starter. A spacer bolts to the C4, and in turn accepts a Buick 300/ 340 flexplate (B), needed to bolt up the late torque converter. Differing block trans adapters are then used for different vehicles.

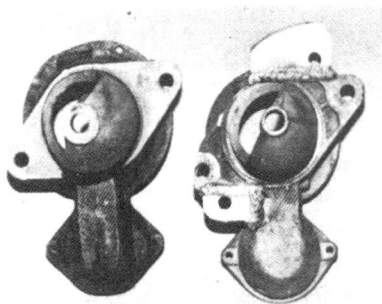

Modified starter nose (right) is needed when using Baker's 300 crank adaptation system. Detailed fabrication instructions and illustrations for all necessary parts are available from Baker.

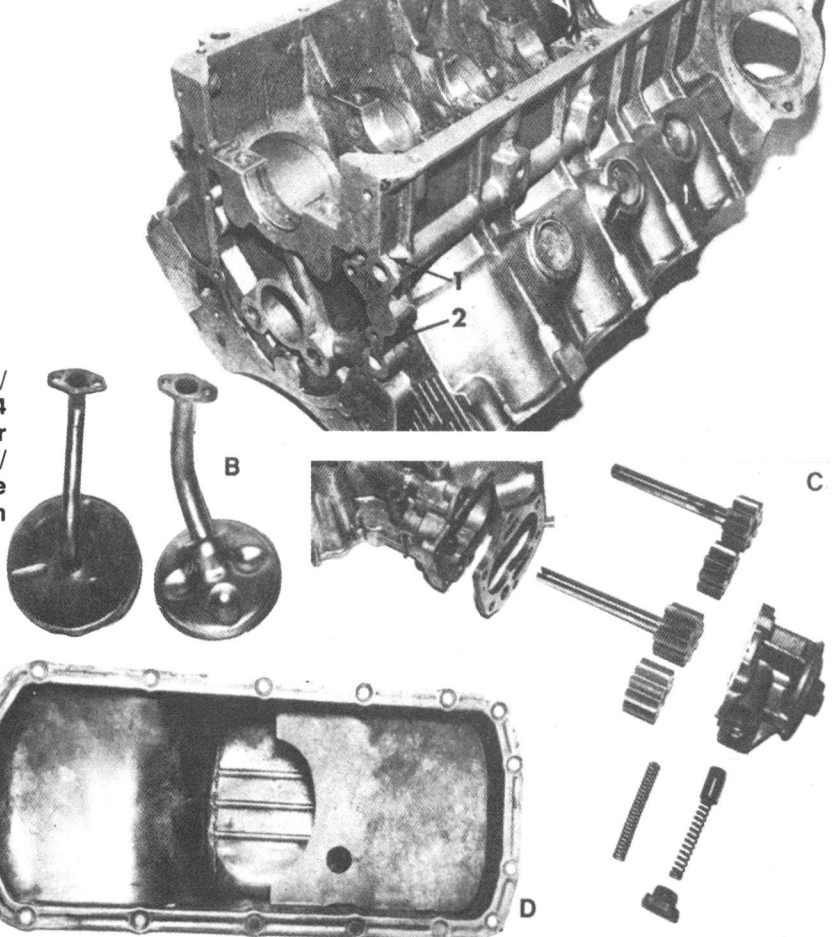

Oil system fixes: Open up block oiling passages (A, 1 and 2) and oil pickup tube pilot hole (A,3) to 1/2 inch ID. Use a 5/8 inch tapered reamer to mate top of passage 3 to larger 1980 up Buick V/6 pickup (GM 25505644) (B). Mellings high capacity pump with larger gears, spacer, and stiffer pressure relief spring replace stock pump (C). Finally, oil pan is deepened and baffle added.

Stock piston availability is severely limited. Only Silvolite (United Engine & Machine, 4909 Goni Rd., Carson City, NV 89701, 702/882-7790) offers new pistons of the dished-type 8.8:1 CR Buick variety. These can be used with Olds 4-barrel heads, producing a nominal 8.6:1 ratio. Compression is way too low with Olds 2-barrel heads.

If new connecting rods are required, the 1967 and earlier Chevy small-block pieces may be substituted. Their 2.0 inch rod journal size is the same as the Olds; however, the Chevy big ends must be shaved approximately .100 inch on their offset sides for correct fit in the narrower 215 journal. Nominal center-to-center lengths are nearly identical - 5.7 inches for the Chevy compared to the 215's 5.660.

Moving up to the valve gear, the aftermarket still carries camshafts and lifters, which interchange between Buick and Olds. Cams from the 300/340 engines also work, as do Cloyes Buick V/6 double-roller timing chains. As noted above, Olds/Buick valve train similarity ends above the lifters; pushrod, rocker arms and shafts, valve springs, keepers and retainers, valve head sizes and valve stem lengths all differ. Olds stock replacement valves are nearly impossible to find. Phil has come up with substitute valve, spring, keeper and retainer packages (see chart). Due to the small combustion chamber and required separate valve seat inserts, radically oversize valves will not fit in stock bore 215s.

Non-stock valves often require different length pushrods to maintain correct geometry with the stock, non-adjustable rocker arms. There are a number of alternatives; build your own by grafting solid Olds pushrod ends onto hollow 225 MOPAR slant-six pushrods (photo), use Olds ends on

Oversize Parts Combinations

In the combinations listed below, bear in mind that Olds heads fit Olds block only; Buick fits either. Small-ends of rods and piston pinholes may have to be bored or bushed, as necessary, when using non-stock combinations. Always check deck height and piston-to-valve clearance. Dimensions in inches, or fractions thereof. Equivalent pistons other than specific part numbers and manufacturers listed may be substituted.

CID	BORE	STROKE	PISTON	ROD	HEADS	COMMENTS
217	Stock 3.5 +.030	Stock 2.8	215 +.030 Buick (Silvolite 1718+.030)	Stock 215	215 Buick or Olds 4-barrel	Buick heads: 8.8:1 CR. Olds heads: 2-barrel loses too much compression. 8.6:1 with 4-barrel heads.
245	3.736	Stock 2.8	305 Chevy L69 (GM-14044069)	'64-'67 Buick 300	Olds 2-barrel, Olds 4-barrel, Buick 215	Install sleeves 3¾×3/32-inch. This engine for max mileage using 4-barrel Olds or Buick heads. Crower mileage cam a must, 5-speed T-50 or T5 recommended. Hone piston pinhole from .927 to .940. CR: Over 11.5:1 with 4-barrel Olds or Buick heads; 9.7:1 with Olds 2-barrel heads.
247	3.750	Stock 2.8	265 Chevy flat-top (Perfect Circle 224-2860)	2" journal early small-block Chevy	Olds 2-barrel, Olds 4-barrel, Buick 215	Olds 2-barrel heads give 2.0:1 lower CR than 4-barrel Olds or Buick heads. 2-barrel Olds CR with .020-thick gasket: 8.54:1. Install sleeves as per 245-cid.
262	Stock 3.5	'64-'67 Buick 3.4	140 Chevy Vega (TRW L2401F) or 267 Chevy (Sealed Power 8456P)	2" journal early small-block Chevy	Olds 2-barrel, Olds 4-barrel, Buick 215	140 Vega piston, 4-barrel Olds or Buick heads: 10¼-10½:1 CR. 2-barrel heads 2.0:1 lower. 267 Chevy piston: ½ ratio lower than Vega. Must deck 267 piston .050.
266	Stock 3.5 +.030	'64-'67 Buick 3.4	170 Ford 6 +.030 (TRW L2142CF+30)	Stock 215	Olds 2-barrel, Olds 4-barrel, Buick 215	For racing or ultimate Crower Mileage System. (Crower CMS-1 cam recommended for mileage.) Hone rod from .875 to .912. CR w/.040-thick gasket: 4-barrel Olds heads, 13.4:1; Buick heads 13.3:1; Olds 2-barrel heads, 11.4:1.
289	3.68	'64-'67 Buick 3.4	255 Ford (Sealed Power 9039P)	Stock 215	'64 Buick 300	Port heads, use oversize 5/16-stem valves. Install sleeves 3 11/16 × 3/32-inch. Hone rod for pin (.875 to .912). CR 10.38:1 with '64 Buick heads and .040 gasket.
292	3.721	'64-'67 Buick 3.4	2800cc Ford V6, 1.516 comp. hght., +.060 (Perfect Circle 224-1999+.060)	2" journal early small-block Chevy	Olds 2-barrel, '64 Buick 300	Different manufacturer's Ford 2.8L V6 piston compression heights may vary; must use 1.516 for this combo. Sleeves as per 289-cid. Hone piston for Chevy pins. CR: 10.8:1 with Olds 2-barrel heads and .020 gasket.
298	3.736	'64-'67 Buick 3.4	305 Chevy dished LG4 (TRW L2432F)	2" journal early small-block Chevy	Olds 2-barrel, '64 Buick 300	Install sleeves 3¾×3/32. Olds 2-barrel heads and .040 gasket: 9.2:1 CR. '64 Buick heads and .040 gasket: 8.7:1 CR. Mopar slant-six modified pushrods recommended.
305	3.780	'64-'67 Buick 3.4	2.3L Ford Turbo 4 (TRW L2455F)	2" journal early small-block Chevy	'64 Buick 300	Ultimate combination for street high-performance. Ford turbo piston has .400-thick deck, allowing variable CR's from 8.0-11.5:1 Use oversize 5/16 stem valves, ported heads, big cam, chrome-moly tubular pushrods, '74 Buick 350 HEI distributor. '67-'69 Javelin AFB carb (Carter 4660) has 1 1/16 primaries × 1 9/16 secondaries, bolts to stock intake with no adapter required.

the Chrysler Direct Connection build-your-own-pushrod kit (Chrysler P4007284) or order custom (and expensive) aftermarket pushrods. To determine the new pushrod length, Baker recommends installing the head and used head gasket with the mounting bolts torqued to specifications. Rotate the crank to No. 1 firing position so the lifter is on the heel of the cam. Using a fabricated or aftermarket adjustable pushrod, adjust the unit to achieve zero lash. Add .040 inch more to this derived figure to obtain the required overall length.

Adjustable rocker arms are required when using solid or roller cams. Kenne-Bell offers custom Buick roller rocker arms and solid lifters. Crane has both solid and roller lifters available. No adjustable rockers are offered for the Olds but Dave Smith Oldsmobile (112 N. Manchester Ave., Anaheim, CA 92802, 714/635-3100) does have adjustable pushrods and rebuilt, hard-chromed rocker arm shafts available.

Front covers from later 300/340 engines and Buick V/6s are a direct bolt-on to the 215, although timing marks may not correspond. This is easily solved by degreeing the balancer. Late-model front covers have different oil filter mounting angles, shorter water pumps, and are generally more compact overall, which can be a real advantage in tight engine swap situations.

Engine mount hole spacing is identical to the Buick V/6, opening up several intriguing possibilities (215-powered Skyhawk, anyone?). Unfortunately, the bell housing bolt pattern is unique and not shared by any 1964 or later engine. Trans-Dapt offers a replacement bell housing that works with conventional mechanical linkage. D&D has a bell housing setup for cable linkage. Both Baker and D&D offer adapters to mate modern automatic transmissions to the 215. D&D uses early 60s 166-tooth Olds Roto-hydramatic or Buick Dualpath flex plates. When combined with a crank pilot spacer, torque converter spacers, and block spacers, it allows the late GM autos to bolt directly to the Olds using the stock 215 starter. Baker retains a stock 215 flex plate to actuate the starter. A spacer is used behind the 215 flex plate to mate with a Buick TH-350 flex plate, which in turn hooks up to the late torque converter. Naturally, a block spacer/adapter is required as well. All this adaptation is necessary because most later GM starter bodies will not interchange with the 215 block and starter nose. An exception are those 215 starter noses made from aluminum; they'll bolt directly to Vega or Chevette starter bodies.

While the foregoing may sound interesting, you're probably thinking, "215 just isn't enough." Never fear. Phil Baker and D&D have come up with several combinations that enable displacement increases all the way to 305 cubic inches (see chart)! The largest engines require both the big aftermarket sleeves and a Buick 300 crankshaft to increase the stroke by .600-inch (from 2.8 to 3.4 inches). The 300 crank's larger main journals must be turned down to the 215 size. Due to rear main seal differences and longer rear crank overhang, special mods must be performed to the rear of the block. Baker has developed detailed modification plans which are available for a nominal fee, or his machinists, Palmers Four Wheel Drive Center (710 S.E. Everett Mall Way, Suite A, Everett, WA 98204, 206/355-8902), will perform the mods if you send them a block. Basically, Baker modifies the rear of the block to accept an adapter plate that in turn mates with the 300 crank. D&D also offers an adapter plate.

To solve the crank overhang problem when using an automatic transmission, Baker again uses the dual-flex plate approach (photo), along with a modified starter nose. D&D uses a late Buick V/6 flex plate that bolts directly to the 300 crank and meshes with the stock 215 starter. When used with the required transmission case-to-block spacer/adapter, the late flex plate bolts right up to the late torque convertor, due to the 300 crank's greater rear overhang. If using a manual transmission, D&D recommends a 166-tooth 300 flywheel. The ring gear must be removed and the flywheel's OD reduced to accept the 215's 156-tooth ring gear. Use the 215 bell housing and the transmission will bolt right up.

The 300 crank isn't the only Buick 300 part that's useful for hopping up the 215. While the block is cast iron, only the 1964 300s had aluminum heads with larger ports and valves that bolt right on to 215 blocks using four head bolts per cylinder (sealing is not a problem). The 1964 heads also feature the modern Buick V/6-V/8 style accessory bosses, allowing the use of the most current mounting brackets, including those designed for "shorty" air conditioning compressors.

Valvetrain Substitutions

Since some valvetrain parts have been discontinued, and you may wish to add oversize valves, Baker has developed the following valve, valvespring, retainer, and lock combinations. These work with stock or near-stock cams, except for the Buick 300/oversize valve combo, which will work with most aftermarket cams. If using a healthy aftermarket cam in other combinations, inform the cam grinder of the valves being substituted and follow his recommendations for the rest of the valvetrain combination. Non-stock combinations must be substituted *in their entirety* for stock parts.

CYLINDER HEAD	RECOMMENDED SUBSTITUTION	MODIFICATIONS REQUIRED
OLDS	Ford 260 valves, springs, retainers, and locks.	Depending on head design (2 or 4-barrel), Ford valves are up to .040-OS, requiring valve seat machining. If stock guides are acceptable for reuse, use '64-'65 260 valvetrain combinations. If guides unacceptable, use 5/16-inch stem '62-'63 Ford 260 with Precision bronze guides, B-5038.
BUICK 215	Stock or aftermarket replacement parts still available.	
BUICK 300 with stock 1.625-intake, 1.313-exhaust valves	Stock or aftermarket replacement parts still available.	
BUICK 300 with oversize valves	Exhaust valve—Manley VW 38mm (1.496-inch); intake valve—TRW Volvo V2927X (1.723-inch); 360 Chrysler springs; Chrysler Hemi or Crane 99947 retainer; standard VW locks.	Use Precision B-5038 guide and grind out seats as necessary. Shim rocker stands to accommodate .040-inch longer Volvo valve. Grind VW valvestem to Volvo height.

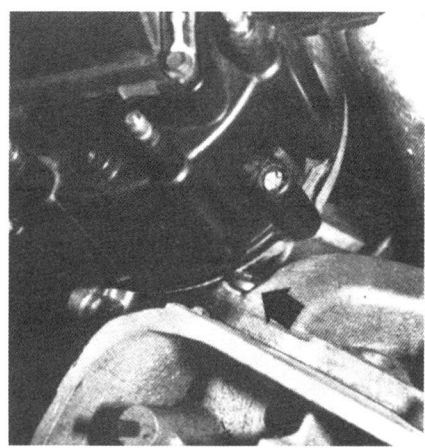

Post '74 Buick 350 HEI distributor bolts right into a 215. Left front intake manifold bolt hole is trimmed for clearance (arrow) and Buick V/6 "Torx" screw is used.

We'd probably all be driving this combo today if GM hadn't prematurely sold out to Rover. But as hot rodders, we don't have to fret over "might have beens." What the factory didn't do, we can: A 215-based motor will provide superlative handling, fine power-to-weight ratios in today's downsized autos, and won't cost you your life savings to build. **HR**

The following comments were requested to provide readers with additional information on the 215 engine based on more recent experiences. MCM

JESS MEYERS

His Buick powered Swift was featured in Contact! issue #19. Originally configured with a P-51 style belly scoop housing a Griffin radiator the airplane now has two GM A/C cores behind the cowling inlets. Aircraft performance has been improved with this lower drag installation. Jess has a little over 600 hours on this stock 215 engine. Main and rod bearings at 500 hours showed no wear. Valves were touched up as the 8:1 compression engine operates on 100LL aviation fuel. Las Vegas auto fuel has high alcohol content which will attack the Swift's tank linings and hoses. His parts list for the Buick conversion follows:

Item	Brand
Timing Gear	Cylent S-323
Timing Chain	Cylent C-359
Cam Gear	S.P.* N-36-3-534-6
Lifters	Crower/S.P. HT-96
Valley Gasket	Victor MS-15806
Pistons(8)	Silvolite(Cast) 8:1
Pistons(8)	Venolia(Forged) 782 10:1
Manifold	Offenhauser 5165 (Milled level)
Water Pump	RepcoRebuilt 1353 or 1353A
Motor Mount(2)	TRW 83166
Intake Valve(8)	S.P. V-1551
Exh Valve(8)	S.P. V-1550
Cyl Sleeve(8)	SL-407-SF
Valve Guides(16)	1871-A Bronze
Head Stud Kit	ARP 124-4002
Distributor	GM Stock Dual Plate
SS Ignition	for Stock Distributor
Perlux Ignitor	1181
Fuel Pump	Carter M-3643
Starter	Tilton 122

* S.P. -Sealed Power

JM

PHIL BAKER

The '64 Buick 300 heads are used only on big bore (3.7+) versions of the 215. These heads have four head bolts per cylinder and do not seal as adequately as the '61-63 Olds heads. Since the HOTROD article was written we have limited the overbore to 3.720, preferring 3.700 to minimize bore wall flexing.

Rumors persist that a few '64 Buick 300 blocks were produced in aluminum. There are none! The 262 engine is built on a Olds block with .030 overbore. Heads are of the two barrel variety, best identified by casting number 1358746. Rods are '64-67 327 Chevy first magnafluxed then narrowed .075 on the wide side and .025 on the narrow side. Pistons (cast) are Chev 267 V/8 which in stock form are dished out about 15 cc to result in a CR of 9:1. Chev rod bearings are narrowed .020 on each side and then sharp corners are rounded to clear crank journal fillets. Buick 300 rods are cast, thus not used.

We use moly rings, the Cloyes roller timing chain set and the Chev 427 rear seal. Guides are replaced with PEP bronze parts. Valve springs are 350 Olds Diesel for normal RPM operation or MOPAR 340-360 springs for 7500+ RPMs. Chev 327 valves are installed along with Martin Wells alloy valve seats. Most engines are equipped with Chev hydraulic lifters which cost less than Olds parts. We build our own pushrods (see HR article) as the Chev lifters sit lower in the block. Replacement Olds rocker assemblies are not available. We use good salvage parts; rockers are refaced and rocker shaft plugs are removed for thorough cleaning.

The inadequate stock timing cover rope type seal is replaced by a Victor 49649 which requires a slight bore job for fit. We use Crower cams in our engines and find the #50231 works fine for mild street use, the #50232 has a little more lift and duration for lightweight sports cars and street rods. Cam bearings are always replaced as is the oil pump with a Melling high volume unit, # K20- IVH. The distributor is updated to HEI, Unilite or MSD units. Plugs are Autolite #275 gapped to .050 using 8 mm wires for best performance. Wire separators are always used to prevent

Critical Blueprinting Information

CYLINDER HEAD VOLUMES
'61-'63 Buick 215..........37cc   '64 Buick 300......54cc   Olds 2-barrel......51cc   Olds 4-barrel........38cc

HEAD GASKETS

Head type	Holes/cyl.	Manufacturer/type	Part No.	Compressed thickness
Buick 215	5	*Victor/steel shim	1174BS	.020
		Fel-Pro/composition	7984 PT	.040
Olds 215	6	*Victor/steel shim	1169BS	.020
		Fel-Pro/composition	7995 PT	.040
Buick 300**	4	Fel-Pro/composition	8172 PT	.040

*Some late production gaskets are composition, although part number remains the same. Compressed thickness figures do not apply in that case.

**Use with all 300 heads on any block, or with any heads when running 3.625-inch or larger bores; punch extra bolt holes in gasket as required.

crossfiring. We found the best intake combination is the Edelbrock #2198 manifold with Carter carburetors. We find Carters are light and they don't leak.

Ignition is set at 12 degrees with 12 degrees built into the distributor (24 crank degrees) for a total of 36 degrees.

We enlarge oil pans where possible to increase oil capacity since operation over 4000 RPM is insufficient. We prelube the rebuilt engines by driving the oil pump with a 12 inch tanged shaft. Engines are run non-stop for 30 minutes; carburetion and engine timing should be carefully set before starting. After run-in and engine is at ambient temperature we retorque the head bolts to 50 foot pounds. **PB**

DAN LAGROU

As a former GM engineering technician I have been involved in building and testing engines for about 35 years. I think GM's 215s are really neat motors, well ahead of their 1960s contemporaries. When the Northstar program group was formed a few years back I gave them a block for study. They were interested in the cast in place cylinder liners and eventually adopted that design. Incidentally, the Northstar has the lowest warranty claim rate of all current GM engines.

In my opinion, Buick 215 versions are better then the Olds for several reasons. More Buicks were built. Parts are more available as the engine is still produced in England. Olds wedge combustion chambers are less tolerant of high compression effects as opposed to the polyspheric shape of the Buick design.

Buick 300 heads are not a good fit to the 215 block since the bores are different. The 1/8 inch difference causes turbulence around the valves and the combustion chamber volume (54 vs. 37 cc for the 215) reduces the CR 2.0 full points. Forget building up the chambers; welding aluminum after 30 years of carbon impingement is not a good idea as any good welder will tell you.

Use of the Buick 300 crank is a very good idea, particularly in an aircraft application operating all day at 3600 RPM. Low end torque is a major improvement. I like using Vega, Chevy 267, or 3.0 liter Ford ('86-89 Taurus, Sable) pistons. I personally don't like the 327 Chevy rod/bearing rework. It's just too much effort for the end result. In my 22 years of fooling around with 215s I have yet to see a broken rod so the need is just not there, in my opinion. A 300 crank and a .030 overbore results in 266 in^3. Don't build anything bigger. Bigger bores can result in cylinder wall blowouts or liner cracking. The latter is evidenced by coolant coming up between the liner and block. Bigger here is not better.

Stock Buick pistons are available from Silvolite in 9.0:1 and 9.5:1 compression ratios. CR can be increased 1.0 point by milling the heads or decking the block. For each .010 inch removed CR goes up by 0.20 points. Allow for Fel-Pro head gaskets; they are .040 thick versus the production .020 gaskets. If you use Buick pistons in an Olds block CR goes down 2.0 points.

My company, D&D Fabrications, carries 215 engines, parts and special items. Inventory is the largest in the U.S. Special 300 crank rear seal spacer kits are produced. This superior design eliminates block machining. Custom flywheels and one piece flex plates for automatic transmissions are also available. Olds valves and rocker assemblies are scarce but I do have a limited supply. **DL**

ROVER

Thanks to the Rover Company and the then managing director, William Martin-Hurst, the basic design of the GM 215 is still in production. The 1995 Land Rover utility/sports vehicle is the latest in a long line of vehicles powered by this engine beginning in England with the introduction of the 1967 Rover P5 saloon. Engine development has not stopped; as one example, a prototype P8 design featuring 4.4 liter displacement (268 in^3) was sold to Leyland Australia and was used at one time in the Leyland P76 cars and Terrier trucks.

The basic engine was used in a number of BL vehicles, including the Range Rover, the Land Rover, the MGB GT V8, the Rover 3500 sedan (SD-1) and the Triumph TR8, the latter two, rare U.S. imports. Limited production vehicles, such as the Morgan Plus 8, the TVR, the Marcos and a number of kit cars took advantage of the basic powerplant capabilities. The V/8 was very popular in racing and rally applications, again for its light weight and robust structure. At least eight British custom engine preparation shops have been involved in pushing the V/8 performance envelope. The V/8 has performed well in races run on short and endurance courses (a 1-2-3 win at Monza one year). Perhaps the most demanding test of an engine is the tough, annual Paris-Dakar rally of some 7-8,000 miles. Always a top contender with outstanding reliability, the V/8, in a privately prepared Range Rover, won the1981 event.

The block was modified 4 times. Following the 4.4 project a stiffer block was engineered in 1984. The block was revised again in 1989, opening the bore from 3.5 to 3.7 inches, increasing the displacement to 3.9 liters, and then to 4.2 liters in a longer (3.0 inch) stroke version. Two oil pumps (pre and post SD-1) have been in production, the latter having increased size for more oil volume. Three front covers evolved over the engine's lifetime, principally to improve the original crank seal installation. Several camshafts have been used during the ensuing 34 years.

Rover information was gleaned from two comprehensive books on the subject. Both authored by David Hardcastle, "The Rover V8 Engine" (208 pages) and "Tuning Rover V8 Engines" (190 pages) are available from Classic Motorbooks, 1 (800) 826-6600. MCM

UNDERSTANDING IGNITION

Kurt Kuhlmann
Empire Development Corp
307 N. Gertruda Avenue
Redondo Beach, CA 90277
(310) 318-2788

I first met Kurt at the 1995 Copperstate Fly-In. An electrical engineer, Kurt owns his own company which manufactures an EI system with an optional integrated knock sensor, a 3-axis GPS auto pilot and other products designed for the homebuilt aircraft market. He also is a distributor for the IVO propeller and is currently working with the designer on an electric cockpit controlled variable pitch version. Kurt can be reached by mail, telephone direct or via modem. Addresses are: WWW: http://user.aol.com/chanik/ed; Email: ChaniK@AOL.COM. MCM

One major shortcoming to aviation engines is the use of magnetos as ignition systems. With weak spark energy and no variable advance, mags substantially limit the efficiency and power output of these power plants. EI (electronic ignition) systems are relatively new on the aviation engine scene. Borrowing from the automotive world, they offer enhanced performance and reliability for a relatively low cost and are easy to retrofit to aviation engines. Well, for the homebuilt community, anyway.

MAGNETOS

The main strength of a magneto lies in the fact that it is a stovepipe system, self-contained and self-powering. It basically consists of a point ignition system with a built in distributor. Compared to an EI, a mag delivers 1/4 the spark energy at roughly 25 degrees BTDC (before top dead center) fixed timing, with up to +/-8 degree variability due to component wear and gear lash. Collectively, these specs are poor for a number of reasons. Here are a few: Large bore aviation engines ideally need to be sparked between 50 BTDC and TDC depending on engine MAP (manifold absolute pressure) and RPM in order to run efficiently. The faster an engine turns, the earlier in the compression stroke a spark needs to be initiated. In order for an engine to burn fuel effectively, the flame front needs to be well under way before the piston reaches the top of the cylinder. Another problem arises when the MAP is lowered; the engine requires additional timing advance. The pressure of the gases in the cylinder is directly related to the density of the fuel/air mixture, which in turn determines the speed of sound in the medium, and because flame propagation is directly proportional to the speed of sound, less manifold pressure translates into an even earlier spark. Also, small spark energy mandates a small plug gap to ensure the spark can make the jump. This leads to poor flame kernel initiation from low current and a small kernel due to the small spark length. Magneto driven spark plugs need to have a small gap, typically 20 thousands. With more energy, one could go with a 40 or 50 thousands gap. A longer, hotter spark initiates a better flame front which also permits less advance. Also, the wider gap is less likely to foul, which can short out the plug electrodes.

EI SYSTEMS

The intrinsic problems with magneto ignition systems has led the automotive world to first develop point ignition systems around 1927 and finally EI systems to which they have been devoted for over 20 years. Since auto engine manufacturers are mostly driven by the need to lower pollution, in particular hydrocarbon emissions, they have developed EI systems to optimize efficient fuel burning which in turn optimizes fuel economy. Originally, all EI systems were capacitive discharge (CDI), although recently all have been microprocessor based inductive ignition. The performance difference is minimal, but the newer types are more reliable as they do away with the large capacitors and their associated charging circuitry. The easiest way to make a more reliable electronic circuit is to reduce the number of components and beef up the power components. High power components that get hot like SCRs and MOSFETs usually are the first to go. Vibration is another killer, so encapsulation is necessary for all circuit modules. The reason the inductive types came second is that they require a microprocessor to figure when to recover the coils, while a CDI may be built out of discreet components. Essentially all EI systems on the market are direct crank triggered which permits more accurate timing of the spark. Variations on this theme include counting teeth on a gear bolted to the crankshaft and magnet triggered sensors with trip magnets located on the crank. Both types offer continuously variable spark timing and hot sparks. The only exception to the rule of throwing a single, whopping spark is at idle.

MULTI SPARK

For ordinary run speeds, the air flow through the manifold into the cylinders is so fast that the resulting turbulence ensures even mixing of the air and fuel together. At idle, with slow flow, the fuel can separate out as droplets and the resulting mixture can therefore be either too rich or too lean at any spot inside the cylinder. This leads to problems since the spark may not initiate a flame if it does not have the right stoichiometric fuel/air ratio between electrodes. Most magneto systems misfire significantly below 600RPM because of this condition. The solution is to send a quick series of slightly weaker sparks to the plug. Separated by a few milliseconds, the multiple sparks give the cylinder several chances to "find" a decent mixture and fire the fuel/air charge. Multispark permits a lower, smoother idle with less fouling by mostly eliminating misfires.

EI APPLIED TO AVIATION ENGINES

In the case of aviation engines, the standard installation arrangement is to use a distributorless, waste-spark system with multiple coils, which is also becoming the preferred approach on modern automobiles as well since it eliminates some moving parts. The basic idea is to fire pairs of cylinders from a single coil when both are rising up towards TDC. Each revolution, one of the pistons rises on its compression stroke while its opposing number rises on its exhaust stroke. The spark is wasted on the exhaust stroke; this is a negligible amount of energy to throw away to achieve a simpler system design. In fact, only about 15% of the total spark energy is dumped on the exhaust plug since its breakover voltage is lower. The energy spent on a spark is proportional to the voltage induced in the gap multiplied by the current.

Under compression, this voltage follows a logarithmic function of pressure, $V=K*P0.8$ where K is a constant. Although the current is the same in both plugs, the one under compression has 6 or 7 times the voltage and, thus, most of the energy goes to that plug. One can generally get hotter sparks distributorless, as well, since the work is shared by more than one coil, and this approach has the added advantage of allowing some of the cylinders to continue to fire even if a coil or its driver stage is lost. Whether an automotive EI fails totally or partially really doesn't matter much with a car, because people can walk pretty well. In aviation EI systems, however, this ability to "limp home" is an important feature . The other thing a robust EI system must do well is prevent detonation, which can occur from firing a cylinder either too early or too late. If too early, the burning fuel/air charge can go into runaway auto-ignition creating excessive pressure spikes on the piston while it is still rising on the compression stroke. Ironically, if the charge is fired too late, it does not burn completely during the power stroke. This leads to prolonged burning that can continue through the exhaust stroke. Instead of powering the engine, the exhausting gas, still burning, causes the cylinder, and especially the exhaust valve, to overheat. Eventually, this condition will lead to runaway pre-ignition which can only be stopped by aggressive leaning of the mixture. A properly timed EI is not likely to get into the second condition unless the mixture is obscenely rich, but a number of factors can lead to the first: low octane fuel, oil in fuel or contaminated fuel, high inlet air temperature, improper leaning, excessive compression from carbon buildup on and under the rings. If allowed to persist, detonation will usually burn the electrode off the spark plug. This is especially true with automotive plugs, which is actually a good thing since replacing a plug is typically cheaper than replacing a jug. However, chronic detonation can also burn holes in pistons, break cranks, burn valves, crack cylinder walls, collapse rings, many bad things. It would be a nice safety feature to detect detonation and then retard the timing to try to suppress detonation while warning the pilot of the condition. Enter the knock sensor.

KNOCK SENSORS

Knock sensors let the microprocessor or CPU know when the engine is detonating by measuring the high frequency vibrations on the crankcase. It takes some work to get them to function on aviation engines since they are inherently vibration-noisy. An automotive EI system would think the engine was constantly knocking. But the knock sound is distinct from the ordinary vibration signature, so with the proper filtering, the sensor can be made to work. Even though only one knock sensor is used, the CPU knows which jug it just fired. So if it detects a knock, it knows which one is the problem. This is important since often only one cylinder is the culprit. It is undesirable to retard them all, especially since over retarding can also lead to detonation. By limiting the retard authority of the knock detector circuit and retarding cylinders individually, the knock sensor can provide an extra degree of safety while ensuring optimum spark timing. This permits more aggressive advance timing of the EI and compensates for lower fuel octane (up to a point).

THE NUMBERS

So what does all this translate to in real terms? The difference between ideal spark timing and a magneto's fixed 25 degrees advance is most pronounced at around 60 percent cruise. Here the timing can be off by as much as 20 degrees, and it's here that the main advantage lies. A single EI system typically offers an 8 percent improvement in fuel economy over a mag (10 percent if using dual EI). Maximum power output increases by a more modest 3 percent (4 percent if dual EI). Partly this is because mags are timed pretty well for full power settings. EIs also draw slightly less power off the engine, saving another 0.2 HP per mag removed. However, since it is easier for mags to degrade, be mis-timed or have degraded plugs, actual measured improvement may be much higher. EIs weigh about the same as mags. Now, if we could just get a decent after-market, multi-point fuel injection system for aviation engines...

MAGIC PIXIE DUST AND OTHER MYTHS

There is some nonsense out there concerning EI systems, enough so that I feel compelled to try to dispel some of it. I confess I haven't done a tremendous amount of hands-on research into these things myself, partly because I'm an electrical, not automotive, engineer, but principally because there is a group of people who already have, members of the Society of Automotive Engineers, or SAE. The same people who gave us metal grades and propeller bolt patterns have, in fact, spent millions researching all of the nuances of EI systems. Not all of the research makes it into cars, since auto manufacturing is more of an economic, than technology, driven system, but the collective engineering done by SAE members is tremendous. There is a saying: 50 million car engines can't be wrong.

Here's some collective wisdom:

Hot sparks: Increasing spark energy is a good idea but only up to a point. It's a matter of diminishing returns, as energies over 80milliJoules or so are more than adequate to initiate a solid flame kernel in a typical 40mil plug gap under even 10:1 compression. Most EIs work with about 90 to 130mJ (0.022 to 0.031cal) energies as a margin, but over that, one just burns up the spark plug electrodes faster.

Spark pulse shape: There is no evidence to support the notion that special wave-shapes of the high voltage surge that drives a spark have any appreciable effect on engine performance. Once the voltage exceeds breakover, the energy is dumped as a current spike through the ionized path between electrodes. This pulse can be stretched slightly by using shielded harnesses, which have high capacitance or by simply adding a few picofarads to the coil secondary terminals. It can be stretched or changed in other ways as well; there's just no point in it.

Various systems' performance: There are a number of features to evaluate prior to buying an EI system, but performance isn't one of them. Properly timed, and with a spark energy over 80mJ, any EI system will work about as well as any other within a percent or so. There is only so much one can do to engine performance by "perfecting" the sparking part. Added features like knock sensing, multispark, output displays, component reliability are the only substantial differences between systems. Oh, and cost.

Fusion metalloid lubricants: Generally, these are a class of compounds added to engine oil to increase lubricity. Common ingredients are Zinc Ditheiophosphate (ZDP) and Manganese Disulfide (MnS2). They bond directly to the metal surface and work pretty well. Their drawback, and the reason these compounds are not recommended by engine manufacturers, is that they are very effective octane inhibitors. Even the small amount clinging to the cylinder sleeves is enough to drop several points off of the gasoline octane rating by catalyzing the formation of unstable hydrocarbon radicals which are prone to autoignition. Typically, the power savings from reduced friction loss is thrown away to reduced combustion efficiency. If coupled with other factors, these compounds can reduce the octane rating to dangerous levels in some engines, leading to detonation.

Spark plugs: Both auto and aviation plugs can work fine with an EI system. The auto plugs have the advantage of being less expensive and easier to gap open. There has been some concern lately over improper heat ranges of auto plugs (if the range is too high, it can lead to an overheated electrode, thus inducing detonation). The concern was with Bosch plugs. This type of detonation quickly leads to the destruction of the plug center electrode. I don't use the Bosch plugs but, since I'm not aware of any incidences where people running these have been going through new ones every hour, I have to conclude that it is not an issue. Incidentally, Splitfire plugs, and other split electrode types, are not really worth consideration in aviation or automotive engines. This is an old racing trick which adds maybe a percent of power (real figure), at the cost of greatly reducing plug life since the spark jumps between electrode edges, which are quickly eroded, instead of between plates, which hold up better. Fine for racing, where plugs are changed every few hours and they need every last drop of power, but a waste of money for general use. The same is true for the alleged advantages of fine wire electrode plugs. Look, if a simple change to the spark plug electrodes could really add 8 percent (!) more power and fuel economy to an engine, these things would be standard equipment on every single compression ignition engine made, period.

Safety in Flight

Steve Parkman
SWAG Aeromotive
2521 North Fairview
Tucson AZ 85705
(520) 622 6910

What does Paul Poberezny making a gear up landing in a P-64 and a very good friend of mine making an off field landing in his auto engine powered plane have in common? Mistakes can happen to even the best of homebuilders.

My friend's airplane uses the stock factory electronic multiport fuel injection system and electrical charging circuit. A master circuit breaker was added per aircraft practice. Separate circuit breakers were used for all the other circuits. Recently, new lights were wired in through the master circuit breaker. When the light wiring shorted out it tripped the master circuit breaker cutting off the power to everything downstream of the master. The only thing heard was the sound of silence as the engine quit running and all electrical circuits quit working. Resetting the master breaker didn't work as the lighting circuit still had the short in it. Shutting off the lights didn't help as the short had effectively taken the switch out of the circuit.

An uneventful off field landing was made. After the plane had been brought back to the hanger the wiring harness was examined and the problem identified. All circuit breakers are now being wired separate through the master circuit breaker.

The lesson here is that each electrical load grouping should have its own circuit breaker and should be wired through a separate switch. If a switch shorts out it will not take out the master circuit breaker. The newer computer controlled engines have an excellent "limp home" mode provided there is power to the computer. **SP**

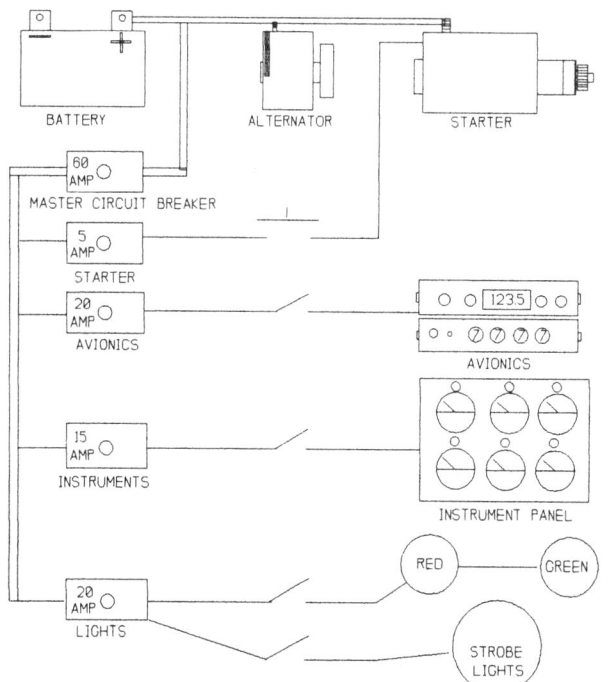

A HAPI Magnum Plus Engine Problem

Len Griffin
2316 Johnson Road
Silver City
New Mexico
88061
(505) 388 5414

Robert Catrambone
Division Automotive
1938 North Anita
Tucson Arizona
85705
(602) 622 6640

Safety and craftsmanship is paramount when dealing with auto engine conversions. This article goes beyond the usual anonymous "buyer beware" admonition. Some 15 years of VW engine preparation and racing experience back up the findings in this case. Catrambone's performance engines and turbocharger applications are known in the Southwest for their power and longevity. His turbocharged VW sand rail placed second in a field of 140 cars in a 250 mile race at Puerto Penasco (Mexico). He is now preparing a twin turbo Olds aluminum V/8 package. MCM

Griffin: This is the story of HAPI Engines Model 82-2 DEH, S/N 00518 (Magnum Plus) which came to an early demise at 83.2 hours. I took delivery of a Dragonfly November 17, 1989, complete with a new HAPI engine.

Built up and installed under HAPI supervision in Dragonfly N826DB in late 1989 (likely the last engine built at Eloy) this engine failed as a result of poor design and sloppy workmanship. Initally covered by a HAPI warranty and contrary to HAPI's original assurances, Mosler Motors does not recognize this as their responsibility. No point in beating a dead horse. The intent here is to call attention to potential problems facing owners of like model engines.

The first sign of trouble at 14.1 hours was rough running on ground runup to check alternator operation, necessitated by a change in wiring to correct a HAPI design error. The problem was traced to an intake leak. The riser tube hoses were too short and had pulled loose. The fix was simple; longer hoses were installed. I was glad this occurred on the ground.

Next incident occurred at annual. A blued steel washer, 5/8 OD and 3/8 ID, bent and a portion missing, was found in the oil screen along with some brass filings in the oil filter indicating some prior interference with the distributor drive gear. The washer was not a VW part. The next ten hour oil change showed no further filings.

At 48.6 hours three cylinders were indicating low compression. Caused by lack of valve guide clearances and sticky valves this problem was acknowledged by Mosler but covered by their warranty only on North Carolina assembled engines. A top overhaul, including valve replacement, was performed locally.

At this point I was somewhat upset but my nightmare was just beginning. At 83.2 hours, and again on the ground, zero compression on one cylinder was measured. One exhaust valve hydraulic lifter had come apart (broken wire retainer clip) and the corresponding valve guide was completely shot. The engine had seemed to develop power in the air but upon landing did not sound right and idled roughly.

The required tear down revealed signs of overheating in all P/Cs (pistons and cylinders). Further examination led to the finding that the POSA Ultra Carb had been set up with the mixture control at 50 percent lean at the full rich stop! To make the engine run someone compensated the setting by turning the main needle to maximum rich. The over lean condition was not seen by the instrumentation. The only subtle clue to this screw up (pun intended) was an occasional sputter if the throttle was opened too quickly. The need to split the case raised a serious problem. The HAPI design of the front seal and retainer (one piece, epoxied to the case) was such that it had to be broken loose and removed with the crank. Those who know VW engines will agree the concept is entirely wrong. We found physical differences in the lifters leading to our conclusion that the engine was built up of spare parts.

Rex Taylor's book states (page 38) he doesn't care for shrink fit propeller hubs because they cannot be removed without possible damage to the hub or the crankshaft. Yet this was the situation we encountered. Obviously, no serious thought was given to the replacement of the front oil seal on this HAPI creation. When the hub was pulled we found that the reduced diameter of the crank was built up by a sleeve and was spot or tack welded in place. Instead of a proper keyway and key a 1/4 inch hole was drilled lengthwise at the hub/sleeve interface. An easily removable, loose fit 1/4 inch pin engaged the two pieces.

I contacted Steve Bennett at Great Plains Aircraft. He was able to rework the SCAT crank for his Force 1 hub and bearing. However, when the case was machined for the Force 1 bearing it was found that HAPI had removed some 1/4 inch of material presumably to glue on their seal retainer. This and other modifications made the case unserviceable.

The cam and distributor drive gears showed evidence that the washer mentioned earlier had made violent contact with them. The SCAT crankshaft was an eight dowel design but as the flywheel used had only two holes six of the eight dowels were cut off. The two remaining dowels showed scars from the amputation process! The case had 8mm studs but most VW experts specify 10mm studs for 94mm bores.

To conclude, this aircraft was purchased with the understanding that HAPI would install a new engine along with a fresh annual. Other owners of HAPI engines should be aware that their engines are not likely to survive a complete overhaul.

Catrambone: Initial problem we ran into on the HAPI Magnum Plus engine was burning valves. After performing the second valve job to cure the valve burning problem we discovered that the lifters were not functioning properly. Upon examination we found three different part number Chevrolet small block hydraulic lifters. Also, we found that one of the lifter caps came off which apparently increased the effective lifter length causing one valve to become bent in contacting its piston.

The sloppy build of the engine seen thus far led us to a complete tear down of the engine. The crankshaft propeller shrink fit hub was doweled to the crankshaft (SCAT brand as used in many VW high performance racing applications) and was further retained by a 9/16 inch bolt.

To remove the propeller flange from the crankshaft required some 30 tons of pressure. We found that the crank was sleeved and welded presumably to increase the crank end diameter to fit the standard propeller hub. In the process of removal the sleeve peeled off like a Pillsbury dough bread can. Obviously, this design was not meant to be serviced at any time in the future.

The front bearing surface of the aluminum crankcase was found to be highly modified. The front bearing seal was epoxied onto the case. The front bearing set appeared to be a Toyota part of unknown vintage. A week was spent in an unsuccessful attempt to locate a duplicate set to save the modified case.

It appears that the modification was an attempt to pattern the Magnum Plus after the successful Great Plains Force One design. However, use of that specific Toyota bearing required that a 1/4 inch spacer be epoxied to the original crankcase surface. On the opposite half of the case a Dremeled oil passage was opened in the spacer. This, in effect, destroyed the integrity of the crankcase.

We remachined the case to adapt it to the Force One bearing and found that the case in its reworked state did not have sufficient metal to properly support the gyroscopic propeller loads. Over 1/4 inch of unsupported bearing projected beyond the face of the case which if not corrected could precipitate the ripping out of the front end of the case. A major welding rework to restore the case to its original configuration was judged to be uneconomical after reviewing all the possible fixes.

In general, the engine as received was thrown together with parts at hand. The rear of the case lacked welded reinforcements which are a must for high performance or racing applications. This opinion is backed up by 1000s of hours of durable running time in VW sand rail races. The propeller hub retaining bolt was of insufficient thread length to secure the hub to the crankshaft.

We are trashing the HAPI case and starting anew. The SCAT crank is salvageable. The flange end has been reworked to replace the lost metal. It is now remachined to fit the Force One hub and includes more thread grip length for the propeller hub retainer bolt. The hub and crank now have a three degree, lapped to fit, taper. Local case reinforcements will be added. We can expect a 1000 hour TBO when operated conservatively as a certified engine.

Force One bearing overhangs the Magnum Plus crankcase. Rework to provide full bearing support was judged to be uneconomical, thus requiring purchase of a new case.

The screwdriver tip points to the Dremeled oil passage feeding the bearing of the original HAPI configuration. Epoxy fill can be seen as a layer in the bearing support area.

Reworked SCAT crank is tapered and double keyed to retain FORCE ONE hub. Insert shows faulty lifters, original short threaded hub retainer bolt and its replacement.

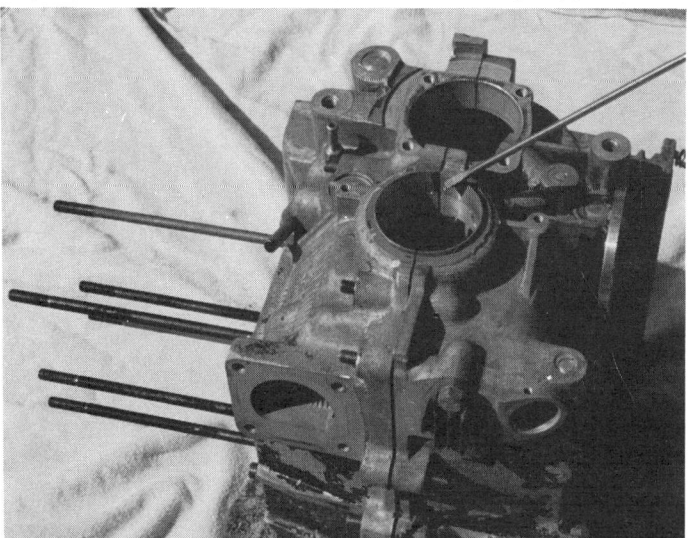

Another view of this specific HAPI engine oil passage and crankcase modification which was apparently designed to locate and feed the special Toyota bearing installation.

Ford 351 W Engine Aero Conversion

Terrance O'Neill
791 Livingston Street
Carlyle IL 62231
(618) 594-2681

After flying the Magnum back from the 1984 Oshkosh EAA Convention I modified my radial engined design, changing the prototype's fuselage from "swing-wing" to a "fast back" for more cabin headroom and adding the "swing-tail" for cargo loading. These modifications were completed in 1986. When I taxied out to test fly it, the carburetor began leaking gas, just another problem with an engine installation that just wouldn't cool to my satisfaction after about three years of prior cooling modifications. The carburetor was now leaking for no good reason and the eternal wiping-off of exhaust-blown oil finally combined to make my frustration complete. I sold the old oil belcher to a grateful I95 owner.

I needed a 400 HP replacement to make Magnum's 3800 pounds gross weight move. A fresh look through the latest Trade-A-Plane revealed sobering prices for used airplane engines. I had also considered converting another auto engine (I had earlier converted a Ford/Javelin 231 Windsor V6; but that is another story).

Rumor had it that Ford would soon build a high-performance version of its solid 351W, a "crate motor" for racers. I decided to investigate further. I looked the stock 351W engine over, liked the big crank bearing diameters, priority oiling, the quality of its materials, and its service reliability, knowing that some of Ford's engines are made of excellent materials and are well proven. Without really getting into the conversion details I was confident it should be able to make 400 HP pretty reliably, without many expensive changes. I made the plunge to convert the 351W.

In 1992, after I was already flying my converted 351W, Ford started delivering their new 351 HO, a 385 HP (by private dyno-tests) mill for $3,995. The 351 HO specifications and tests are impressive. The engine looks a lot like mine, is <u>brand-new</u>, the price is right and the power is perfect for my application. I was just 4 years too early; I couldn't wait for the promised engine since my Magnum was engine-less.

Still, there are those who might want to build their own 400 HP airplane engine. My 351W conversion offers experimenters another option and may be an inexpensive way to do it for those with skills and tools.

DESIGN GOAL

The goal was an affordable 400 HP engine. To me, "affordable" meant around $5,000. An overhauled Lycoming or Continental in this HP range costs over $20,000, plus a run-out engine (as seen in recent Trade-A-Plane ads). A factory new engine goes for much more. An auto conversion costs much less initially. Future repair and maintenance costs can be expected to be much lower than for factory aircraft engines.

As far as power potential is concerned I learned much from exhaustive research of "endurance racing" engines, performance product offerings, and from the B&M Supercharger Technical Manual. This excellent reference, a valuable guide for any engine experimenter, contains the

The clean cowled front end of the Magnum airplane was designed to increase effectiveness of the 100 inch Prince propeller. Note the two flush latches which allow quick inspection and servicing of the powerplant.

results of many dyno tests of 350 in^3 size engines with various modifications evaluated.

I learned that I could get 400 reliable, continuous horsepower on premium auto gas with about 350 cubic inches of displacement, even if I stuck with the manufacturer's engineering intent for the entire engine; i.e., its rated RPM. I decided to avoid the temptation to go for higher power through higher RPMs, simply because high RPM parts cost a lot more, and introduce a lot of unknowns. It is no secret that racers on too many occcasions blow their engines.

My goal was KIC (keep it cheap) and as stock as possible, using the factory production block, crank, pistons, etc. Instead of employing racing tricks I wanted to get simpler, cheaper and more reliable power through better breathing and through "the squeeze", increasing the charge density by changes to compression ratio and/or supercharging. I wanted maximum reliability at 250 to 275 HP cruise power and I wanted about 400 HP for a short time at takeoff. I decided to honor the manufacturer's design RPM (rated at 5400) so all the major stock parts would be usable. The RPM range decision and my propeller size established the redrive ratio. My 400 HP bush aircraft design was originally configured to swing a nine foot prop. With a 2.68:1 ratio, 5400 engine RPM gives me 2022 prop RPM, for maximum thrust.

These early decisions controlled the whole development of the design. Looking back, I still maintain they accomplished what I wanted.

Side hinged clam shell cowlings provide complete access to the engine compartment. The cog belt redrive housing and the carburetor air box are visible along with two rods which actuate the side cowl flaps.

ESTIMATED ENGINE COST

Next, I estimated my costs to build up a 351W for this aircraft application. Including the cost of a redrive, if I did it all myself, it would be about $6,000 for 400 HP, including engine accessories and cooling system. However, being 62 years old at the time, I didn't really want to learn how to rebuild or modify engines. I wanted to concentrate on my first love which is airplane design. I decided I would try to buy a "nearly done" engine.

When I reached this point in my analysis Javelin Aircraft advised me that the demand was too small, that they were not in the position to do the conversion or the big redrive at that time. I was beached up the DIY creek. Looking at the bright side I thought I could learn as I went. I got more "learning" than I had expected.

TECHNICAL EDUCATION

I had searched the local area for two months for a low mileage salvage engine, gave up the search much too quickly and bought a salvage yard "core", a dirty, greasy worn block of junk from a 1974 Torino, for $125 (It makes me laugh to think of that "bargain" now). I also bought "How to rebuild your SMALL-BLOCK FORD", with 160 pages jammed full of small-block Ford information. I also borrowed overhaul manuals from the local Ford dealer, my source for Ford parts. The rebuilding manual is a must for building up a Ford small block 351W. Unfortunately, this literature did not mention the 351W's main shortcoming: restricted exhaust ports.

Using that information I began making expensive decisions about what to do to this V/8 to get it to make 400 reliable HP as cheaply as possible.

There were only certain ways to get more power once I had selected the 5400 RPM limit and exclusive use of premium unleaded auto fuel. Most common auto "performance" modifications are not effective at RPMs below 5500. These mainly take advantage of higher velocity flows at higher RPMs. By limiting the RPM and choosing auto fuel I eliminated the use of all high strength items in the engine's lower end like special rods, forged cranks and pistons, and top-end higher RPM related items such as lighter valves, valve springs, pushrods, special rockers, and roller lifters.

Available performance options for an engine that would always operate under 5400 RPM included the following: (1) new engine parts, including a larger carburetor and spacer, a performance intake manifold, and a cam to put the peak torque at 4500 RPM (about cruise power); (2) optimum compression ratio (and/or supercharger) "squeeze" to get the maximum possible brake mean effective pressure without detonation; (3) good exhaust porting (which I did not realize for two years) by either by porting the existing heads or by installing better aftermarket heads and free-flowing headers and pipes...possibly cruise-tuned; and (4) to cool the extra power, an aluminum water pump with a cast centrifugal impeller for more coolant flow and a custom radiator.

According to my manuals and other dyno tests on similar and same size engines, I expected about 285 HP (had there not been the exhaust restriction) from my initial non-supercharged version with an 8.7:1 compression ratio, (this engine configuration was flown and evaluated). I would later add the supercharger - easy to do with a Paxton bolt on unit to get power up 40 percent to about 385 HP, at least for takeoff. Maybe even 400! This was my basic plan.

Final external engine compartment configuration includes two air intakes to propeller redrive. Belt temperatures are kept within recommended limits. The large intake opening feeds air to the engine block, the large air filter, and the custom Griffin radiator.

Entire engine is accessible for inspection. Note upper portion of clam shell is hinged clearing the engine completely. The prop extension creates a streamlined nose. Small rod projecting by supercharger actuates cowl flaps.

SALVAGE ENGINE CONDITION

What I found by buying a $125 salvage "core" was disappointing and costly in the long run. The 351W crank design is excellent with big bearings and priority oiling. A low mileage crank I surely could have used as-is but my high mileage crank journals were galled requiring replacement. A new stock Ford crank would have been a good alternative if I could have gotten a good discount. This would have allowed me to use stock new bearings with perfect factory clearances. However, I bought a rebuilt crank and the bearings which came with it. I could have, but didn't, specify the crank-bearing clearances to be .0027 to .0028 although anything between .0025 and .0030 would have been acceptable. I am told these are the best tolerances for endurance racing.

The 1974 block was good and "seasoned". I found no cracks and the cylinders were evenly worn. The block was basically dirty, in dire need of a boiling out and steam cleaning, including the oil passages. This step was done by others but I had to check everything and redo some spots better, particularly the oil passages at the front of the block, above the cam. The shop did not pull that plug and left the dirt. I cleaned up the missed spots.

The heads were not repairable (valve seat damage) but even if they were they would require considerable porting because of the stock exhaust restriction. Probably I could have kept the existing valves, rockers and lifters. but stock springs would have been too weak for the new cam.

In spite of some wear and carbon build up the pistons were in good shape. I considered forged pistons, but everything I read stated that if the RPMs were standard, there was no advantage to forged pistons. However, well after that primary stage of engine conversion, I learned that the 1974 Ford cast pistons were not hypereutectic (high silicon alloy), were brittle, and were likely to crack in the skirts under prolonged high load (as in "supercharger") which would increase oil consumption, noise, and possibly worse. Piston casting and metallurgy have improved a lot since the early 70s. The new hypereutectic cast pistons are not brittle and are much stronger. Uninformed, I kept my old pistons.

For moly-faced rings the cylinder bores have to be "very round" and as smooth as possible, for relatively fast break-in. The only way to get such bores is with an automatic power hone. As a veteran race-engine builder told me, "If the holes are not round, you're just throwing 25 HP away". The cylinder bores were all less than .004 oversize so I had them all made round and sized to .0045 larger than the pistons. This I thought would be about right for stock pistons and the power level that I was shooting for.

ENGINE BREATHING

My high mileage cam and its lifters were trashed but even if they had been like-new I would have replaced them because the stock cam timing was not suitable. Since I always intended to install an old McCulloch (now Paxton) supercharger I had in my garage, the cam I selected was a B&M Street Charger for a Ford 302. This selection made it necessary to swap around four plug wires to 1-5-4-2-6-3-7-8, a different firing order than used in the 351W (1-3-7-2-6-5-4-3). This is a standard Ford performance modification; many rodders do it. This cam shifts the torque peak up to about 4000 RPM. Cars cruise at about 30 percent power; this cam is designed to raise the valves for best torque at this RPM. Airplanes normally will not maintain altitude on a 30 percent power setting; most need about 45-50 percent power to be able to hold altitude (think of how a twin-engine aircraft struggles on one engine). So the cam has to be designed to peak the torque at cruise RPM, in this case, around 4000-4500 RPM.

I was seriously interested in hi-cruise, because at 25,000 ft. my indicated airspeed of 135 is transformed into 200 MPH true. Valve timing for a supercharged engine is different from a normal-aspirated or turbo-charged engine. Another point about cams is that the valve springs must be strong enough to seat them at high RPM. B&M recommends 100-110 pounds seating pressure for this specific cam's valve springs. The springs must be able to allow full cam lift (about .471 inches in this case) without going solid. Also, the pushrods must not bind against their passageway through the heads. I eventually had to abandon my rail type rockers and go with TRW 49009 guideplates. They had to be moved around a little to get the rocker arm ends centered over the valve stems. The rocker point of contact has to be kept at least .020 inboard from the edge of the valve stem so the valve stem tip is not mushroomed by rocker pressure and to ensure that the rocker does not slip off the stem which would make very expensive noises. Most of this adjustment was checked visually with valve covers off and spark plugs out.

The intake manifold is an important breathing component. The stock 2 hole iron intake manifold weighed 50 pounds. It would not work with the new carburetor I wanted to use so I discarded it and replaced it with a 15 pound aluminum Edelbrock Torker II. This design has a low profile and performs well for the anticipated 4500 to 5500 RPM range. I blocked off the under-carburetor crossflow passage with thin stainless plates since in my aircraft installation and operation there is plenty of heat available to vaporize fuel in the incoming charge.

CARBURETOR SIZING

Planning on eventually using my old supercharger I originally calculated that the carburetor size I wanted had to flow about 750 cubic feet a minute. I preferred carburetor to fuel injection because, in my personal view, a carburetor is less likely to quit instantly. The basic performance Holley carburetor, an O-3310, requires a 4 hole intake manifold which had to be suitable for flow at 5500 RPM. At the time I did my build-up, Wise Speed Shop had both the carburetor and the appropriate low-profile Edelbrock Torker II manifold on sale. Currently, the Victor Jr. is reportedly a little better but sits higher on the engine. Due to a large propeller

Cooling air flows through the radiator into the engine compartment and exits through the side cowl flaps. The supercharger also taps into the ambient air flow (lower hose) and pumps air into the carburetor air box. Coolant over flow is managed by the round firewall mounted header tank.

diameter requirement there is no room to spare between my engine and the top of the cowling.

The small Ford carburetor was replaced with a 750 CFM Holley 34-3310 double pumper, to supply enough flow for up to 450 HP. A better choice (but more expensive) would have been a 34-4779 Holley with mixture control. The latter has mechanical secondaries and an adjustable jet for each of the four barrels. The secondaries of the -3310 open at around 2500 RPM, as they respond to a vacuum differential between the carburetor's ambient air and the primary throats' venturis increasing pressure as the blower begins to spool up. The secondary barrels of the 34-3310 erratically vary the RPM without any additional throttle movement. Odd behavior but I got used to it.

OTHER ENGINE PARTS

The timing chain and sprockets were excessively worn. I selected a chain set that was "heavy duty", whatever that means. I installed a new oil pump and a new Ford distributor with large top. I should have (but forgot) modified the original water pump by adding a plate to the impeller to increase flow. Stock spark plug wires suppress the spark so I purchased "wire" wires. I selected Belden 8mm stainless wire. Eventually this set will be replaced with wires that have spiral-wire winding about the core wires, in order to suppress EM field propagation and the dreaded cross-firing popping off a cylinder half-way up its compression stroke! To shortstop the crossfire problem I used some old WACO ignition wire braided sleeves.

Before assembling the engine I had all reciprocating parts balanced for around 4500 RPM. I eventually installed a Ford Motorsport aluminum water pump and cast impeller which works fine.

HOW SHOULD I "SQUEEZE" IT?

My next decision focused on the power options, between raising the compression ratio or supercharging. Two considerations were weighed at this point:

> **(1) For altitude flying I definitely wanted a blower. A centrifugal supercharger makes less engine compartment heat than a turbocharger and is much simpler to install. It is more efficient than a Roots-type.**
>
> **(2) A supercharged engine will make more power than a high CR (compression ratio) engine, even when both have exactly the same peak cylinder pressure (which determines detonation). The reason is because the blown engine with low CR gets more than 20 percent more fuel/air pumped into the cylinder (instead of drawn); compared to the high CR engine, with smaller combustion volume and less but tighter-squeezed fuel/air mixture in it. The blown engine has a higher <u>average</u> cylinder pressure, high pressure for a longer time. That makes more power.**

Here are some additional comments about superchargers for homebuilt airplanes, based on my collection of reference material on the subject.

First, as I am old enough to remember World War II, I can point out that every one of some 100,000 Allied or Axis warplanes that went to altitude used a centrifugal type blower; not one had a Roots type. Was this some kind of prejudice? No, engine designers long ago recognized that the centrifugal type blower is more efficient. A centrifugal type does not heat the air as much as the Roots-type does (the older Paxtons would do 63 percent adiabatic; scarcely any Roots type can make 50 percent efficiency). The Roots type beats and heats up the air a lot in order to build up pressure at lower RPM with its overlapping rotors.

The availability of boost pressure at low RPMs makes the Roots type the blower of choice in automobile applications. Airplane engines, however, run all their adult lives at about 70 to 100 percent RPM so they are perfectly happy with centrifugal blowers and can take advantage of the greater efficiency.

Makes of superchargers now available, besides Paxton, include the Vortech, also a centrifugal, the Whipple compressor and the Latham axial-flow (like a jet-engine compressor section). B&M, Weiland, Camden and a host of GMC Roots-types are also available (see Hot Rod August 1993). The Paxton and Vortech "blow through" the carburetor and can be mounted about anywhere the accessory belts will go. However, they will create fuel flow problems. The blow-through type allows maximum flexibility in achieving a lower cowling top-profile. The Roots-types usually "draw through" the carburetor and are installed and sit on top of the intake manifold, with carburetors sitting on top of the supercharger. Not an optimum aerodynamic solution for airplanes.

COMPRESSION RATIO SELECTION

The B&M Supercharger Manual assumes that for practical supercharging (automotive use) one should start with a 7.5:1 compression ratio and then select pulley diameters to gain boost to about 8 PSI. The manual contains a chart that shows how much boost is allowed. It depends on the engine's compression ratio and is based on the assumption that an engine can run a CR of about 11.25:1 without detonation on automotive premium gas.

For example, if your CR is only 7:1 you may wish to supercharge up to 13.5 PSI without detonation, on premium auto gas. If the CR is 7.5, a 11 PSI boost can be tolerated without detonation problems. If it is 8.7:1 (like mine was when I flew it with stock heads), the boost limit is 6 PSI. With 64 cc combustion chambers on some aftermarket heads (like my World Products Windsor heads) the CR is about 8.5:1 so the boost limit is about 7 PSI. At 10:1 CR (like the

351 HO "crate motor") max boost is about 2.5 PSI. If the CR is 11.25 you cannot supercharge without encountering detonation unless you are in rarified air.

In an aircraft engine conversion with relatively high CR you may still want the supercharger to maintain your "no-boost" sea level manifold pressure up to high altitude. Just do not fully open the throttle at low altitudes. The solution in that case is to redline your manifold pressure gage to match your engine's limits. Two-inches of MP equals about 1 PSI boost.

SUPERCHARGED MAGNUM 351W

Magnum's V/8 prototype engine compression ratio is 8.5:1. I am using an old McCulloch VS-57 supercharger with a snowmobile variable speed pulley. It is set it up to not exceed engine MP (about 40 inches Hg) and the compressor's design redline rotor RPM limit of about 42,000, produced when the 351W is turning 5400 RPM. The blower drive pulley has a minimum diameter of about 3.5 inches and a maximum diameter of 5.62 inches. I blocked the moveable pulley sleeve so it could not open far enough to overspeed the impeller while using the old drive pulleys. Also, I redlined the manifold pressure gage accordingly. If I planned a lot of flying at maximum altitude (over 20,000 MSL) I might increase the compression ratio to about 10:1 during the next rebuild by going to forged pistons. I then would redline the MP gage at about 2 PSI boost or 34 inches MP (maintaining the same BMEP as a 8.5 CR at 42 inches MP). I would need a blower pulley that would give me that 2 PSI boost all the way up to altitude.

The old McCulloch Supercharger Efficiency Chart shows the blower efficiency for various boosts and air flow. The chart shows airflow in pounds per hour. Since a cubic foot of air weighs about .0751 pounds I take my engine displacement of 351 in^3 and divide it by two, since four-strokes breathe every other rev. The 351W's unsupercharged flow at rated RPM (5400) is as follows:

0.10 ft^3 displacement x 5400 rev/min. x 60 min./hr. x .075 /ft^3 (unsupercharged) = 2432 pounds of air per hour.

If I want 40 percent more power, I supercharge the air density up 40 percent and the weight of the engine-breathed air goes to about 3400 pounds. The engine behaves nicely only when the right amount of fuel mixes with the additional air. The chart and blower design are both are 40 years old but have since been much improved...witness the Paxton ads for 45 percent boost their units make for 351W Ford V/8s and 350 Chevys these days. Both Paxton and Vortech are now offering blowers with increased capacity (efficiency).

A Paxton representative told me that blowers which used to be limited to about 35,000 RPM are now turning up to 48,000 and have more drive capacity. The current Paxton car kits are reported to supply 6 PSI boost to 350 in^3 Chevys and Fords at 6000 RPM, which calculates to equal about 5500 pounds per hour, comfortably more than I need. Paxton has a policy of upgrading older VS57 McCulloch (pre-Paxton) blowers. I sent my blower in with instructions of what I needed. The inspection and evaluation fee was $65. A technician called and advised what could be done and what it would cost. For about $200 I got new O-rings, seals, and springs shimmed so the older model blower can turn up to about 42,000 RPM without the planetary drive-balls slipping. These changes make 6 PSI boost available. The old VS-57 has a solenoid control which varies the pulley radii so I can select lo or hi boost. I can get 38 inches MP static with hi boost, and 31 inches MP static with lo boost.

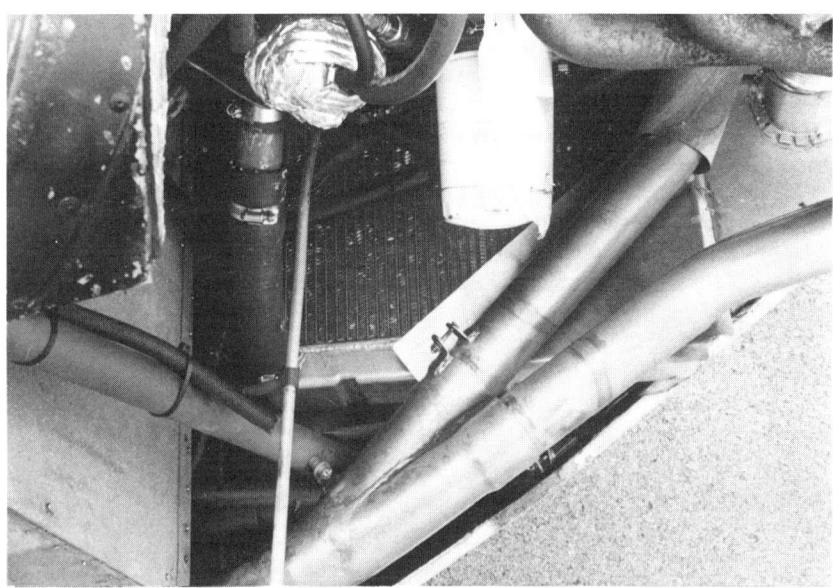

Right side of engine looking down on left and right exhaust pipes, radiator and radiator hose from water pump, shielded oil filter and cowl flap actuator rod. A portion of the header is seen at the top of the picture.

The new Paxton units are improved and cost about $1,000 (as of 1990) for the blower only; the custom pulleys, brackets and carburetor boxes, etc., are extra. No hi-lo boost feature is currently offered. Both Paxton and Vortech are introducing new, bigger blowers in 1993.

POWER LIMIT: DETONATION

The B&M SuperchargerManual explains that a "normal" engine designed for 91 octane unleaded premium fuel can handle the equivalent of about 11.25:1 compression ratio. My translation: maximum power is possible without trashing the engine! If you get some bad gas in your car you can listen for the ping or rattle of detonation. Unfortunately, airplanes are usually so noisy you will not this warning noise. One worry-reliever now available from auto speed shops is a "Knock Alert" unit which for about $100 senses destructive engine detonation and flashes lights and beeps at you when pinging starts so you can back off the throttle and save your engine. I screwed my Knock Alert sensor into a flange on the block near the alternator, and attached 12 v. DC. Oh, what a relief it is, to know my engine is not going to blow up as I see the runway pass beneath me and I am climbing away at 90 MPH with full throttle.

Horsepower in the low 400s is about the maximum possible, given these pre-selected and adhered-to limits of operation of RPM and premium auto fuel. With the 351 in^3 I could not safely get more than 430 HP with supercharging. B&M says to expect a slightly lower power charge density if not pre-squeezing with a supercharger. If I squeeze the charge only with compression ratio nothing but atmospheric pressure is pushing the fuel air mixture in through the carburetor-manifold-valves and I don't get as much fuel-air charge into the cylinder. I estimate 410 HP with an 11:1 CR, or surely 385 HP "out of the box" with a new Ford 351 HO "crate motor" and a little over 400 HP after the run-in period.

THE STOCK CONGESTED HEAD

More than a year after I had completed my prototype's engine and was flying it, unsatisfied with its "modest" performance, I learned about Ford's "congested head" problem-the restriction built into its exhaust ports. According to experts the stock Windsor heads dam up the exhaust, beginning around 4000 RPM, making the power curve go flat. This occurs on the exhaust side of the combustion chamber so my engine output was not helped by a better cam, a new intake manifold and a 750 CFM carburetor. Turning the engine faster than 4500 RPM only reduced the power. Even pumping supercharged air into the cylinders would only (and dangerously) raise the exhaust temperature.

The stock head exhaust passages must be flow-ported (enlarged and smoothed out) unless one is content with about 230 HP at 4500 RPM. With only 230 HP, Magnum's measured rate of climb is only about 500 ft./min. at 2800 pounds. Not real bad, but that would limit me to half of my design payload. To haul full gross (3800 pounds), or six people, full fuel and some cargo a la Beaver, I needed another 100 HP. That addition of power, with the same prop, the 2800 pound gross weight would increase the rate of climb to about 2000 ft./min. Ignorance on my part at the start of the project, about the head "congestion" was especially aggravating because as it turned out I had to buy rebuilt heads anyway. For a few bucks more, either for a professional porting job or for aftermarket heads, I could have avoided this problem and anxiety entirely.

Super Ford Magazine ran an article with tests comparing the un-supercharged flow of Ford small block heads before and after porting. The comparison was between stock Windsor heads, the Ford L302 (GT40) heads, and the J302 Ford aluminum heads.

Flow, before and after professional porting:

Head	Stock	L302	J302
As cast	116	128	142
Ported	139	188	213

The flow numbers are in cubic feet per minute, with .50 inches of valve lift, at 28 inches of water pressure.

This means that if I had my stock heads ported, the flow would increase from 116 to 139 CFM, or the same volume as the hot Ford Motorsport aluminum heads. The flow increase is about 20 percent, which equates to about a 20 percent fuel/air charge increase which is about the same as a 20 percent power increase, or 230 HP (at 8.5:1 CR) x 1.20 = 276 HP. With that flow, then, all I had to do was either squeeze it more (i.e. 10:1 CR), or pre-squeeze it 40 percent with a supercharger to 6 PSI boost, and I would have increased the output to about 400 HP.

I looked at the B&M Supercharger test chart for the 351 Windsor and noted that they encountered the Windsor head "congestion" problem when they applied about 8 PSI boost and pumped the stock heads up to 340 HP before the curve went flat. That is about a 48 percent jump but was also the "congestion" limit.

So B&M's dyno testers yanked off the stock heads and bolted on the Ford Motorsport aluminum J302 heads. At 4500 RPM the power jumped from the stock 230 HP up 74 percent to <u>400 HP At 5000 RPM</u> - from 220 HP stock up 95 percent to 430 HP. With this Motorsport J302 "Sine-Aide" the relieved Ford heads peaked output at 5500 RPMs at 439 HP, up some 119 percent from 200 HP stock, at the same RPM. Is that interesting or what!

BOLT- ON RELIEF

The cheapest way to relieve congestion is by porting. Unfortunately, porting is an art, as well as a science. To have the flow improvements verified the engine performance artist needs an expensive flow bench so he can see what effect his grinding produces. Also, he will want to do a valve job -- for better flow test numbers. And he'll try to talk you into more expensive trick parts, which you don't really need. It also may signal one could be dealing with a machine shop that is not always straightforward in its promises or estimates, as in my case, an expensive experience. In retrospect, a better alternative might be new heads. There are eight or more excellent heads available now, including the Ford L302 (GT40), Ford J302, Ford (full race) K302, World Products aluminum head, World Products iron Windsor head, and three Goldcoast (stages of flow) heads. Edelbrock is coming into this market, also. Prices start around $500 for bare heads, and go upward to over $1,500 for assembled and ported aluminum heads by World Products or Ford. After trying stock rebuilt heads unsuccessfully I eventually went with World Products iron heads, which were a few hundred dollars cheaper than Ford GT-40 heads.

REBUILT "HEAD" ACHES

Unless you really know heads, spring pressures, machining, etc., avoid buying rebuilt stock restricted flow heads as I did. I eventually abandoned them. I then bought World Products Windsor heads and had Wise Speed Shop "assemble" them, for my early 351 Windsor engine. I had assumed these guys knew that all small-block Ford engines used rail-type rockers from 1967-77. Wrong. As the Wise guys loaded my assembled heads with their 1.6 inch exhaust and 2.02 inch intake valves into my car I asked, "are you sure these are going to work with my original rail-type rockers and pushrods?"

This question caused them some concern because they took the heads back out of my car and upon checking the heads for clearance with my rockers they announced, alas, that since they used Chevy stainless valves in their heads (which valves had stems too short above the spring keepers to clear the rail-type Ford rockers) they assumed they would work in the World Product heads! They had assured me they would before I ordered. I was not pleased.

I wound up buying non-rail type rockers, along with the additionally needed pushrod guideplates and assembled them on the engine, to find -- guess what -- these speed-shop bozos sold me Chevy rockers for their Ford heads! Chevy rockers! Chevy rockers are about a quarter-inch shorter than Ford rockers, so that they only came half-way out over the valve stem, and would have failed surely, probably on an attempted start up. I had to make yet another trip back to St. Louis.

Upon return to the Speed Shop I showed them the Ford and Chevy rockers so they could see the different lengths, and asked to exchange the Chevy rockers for Ford non-rail rockers. I also asked them why they were selling Chevy rockers for Ford aftermarket heads. Would you believe they could not find a single set of Ford rockers in the store! They were selling big-buck heads for Fords and had no Ford rockers in stock! Or pushrods. Further, the pushrod guide plates were not the right ones for the World Products Windsor heads, as I found out by calling World Products in California. The speed shop finally ordered me the right guide plates for exchange, and a set of rockers, with apologies. Since the new rockers were non-rail, I also needed chrome-moly pushrods because, as I found out after about 20 seconds of engine running with the original pushrods, the soft rods wore about a third of the rod thickness through! I found the right Ford pushrods from Ford Motorsport in Houston (an 800 number).

Finally, after much confusion, I had heads which would flow enough for 285 HP normally, and accommodate supercharging to about 400 HP later. This situation illustrates what can happen when dealing with speed shop people. Some are knowledgeable, but most are just clerks, and/or have big gaps in their areas of "expertise". Moral of this episode is clear: Recommendations of others may not apply in all cases. Look out for pot-holes regardless of your choice of engine brand. If building up a similar Ford engine buy completely assembled heads from the head manufacturer, not a distributor. Explore all options, like going with Ford GT-40 heads and everything else from Ford Motorsport because then everything will fit.

I had to learn all this about building up my own engine. I got a lot of valuable help free from the neat guys on Ford Motorsport's technical assistance telephone line. The hard part was learning enough to be able to ask the right questions.

ACCESSORIES AND MOUNT BUILD

I built my own redrive using the PolyChain belt and sprockets (a story in itself) and bolted it to the engine. I made a more compact alternator mount and exchanged my junk alternator and starter for rebuilt NAPA units. With the help of my son I got the engine assembled, jigged it up to the old radial engine mount position and fabricated new engine mount tubes. The original firewall Lord shocks and attach points were from a Cessna T50, originally designed for the Jacobs R755. Since that engine weighed about the same as the V/8 I assumed the existing hardware would be sufficient. I later noticed the mounts were transmitting vibration and were considerably deflected while static. I called Lord and asked for the static load rating. Would you believe 175 pounds? How Cessna got that small snubber into production in WW II is beyond me. I changed to the Lord H5020 which has about three times the capacity and the same diameter so it easily adapted to my installation.

The new engine mount is bolted rigidly to the threaded hole on the side of the block and to the threaded holes at the end of the heads. A header tank sits high on the firewall. The radiator, a 19x31inch aluminum Griffin, is under the engine oil pan. Cooling air comes in the front cowl opening, goes up through the radiator, and then over the oil pan, feeding the carburetor as "sheltered source" air, and outside through cowl doors.

With the engine assembled on the mount, with attached radiator, coolant, accessories, less exhaust headers and

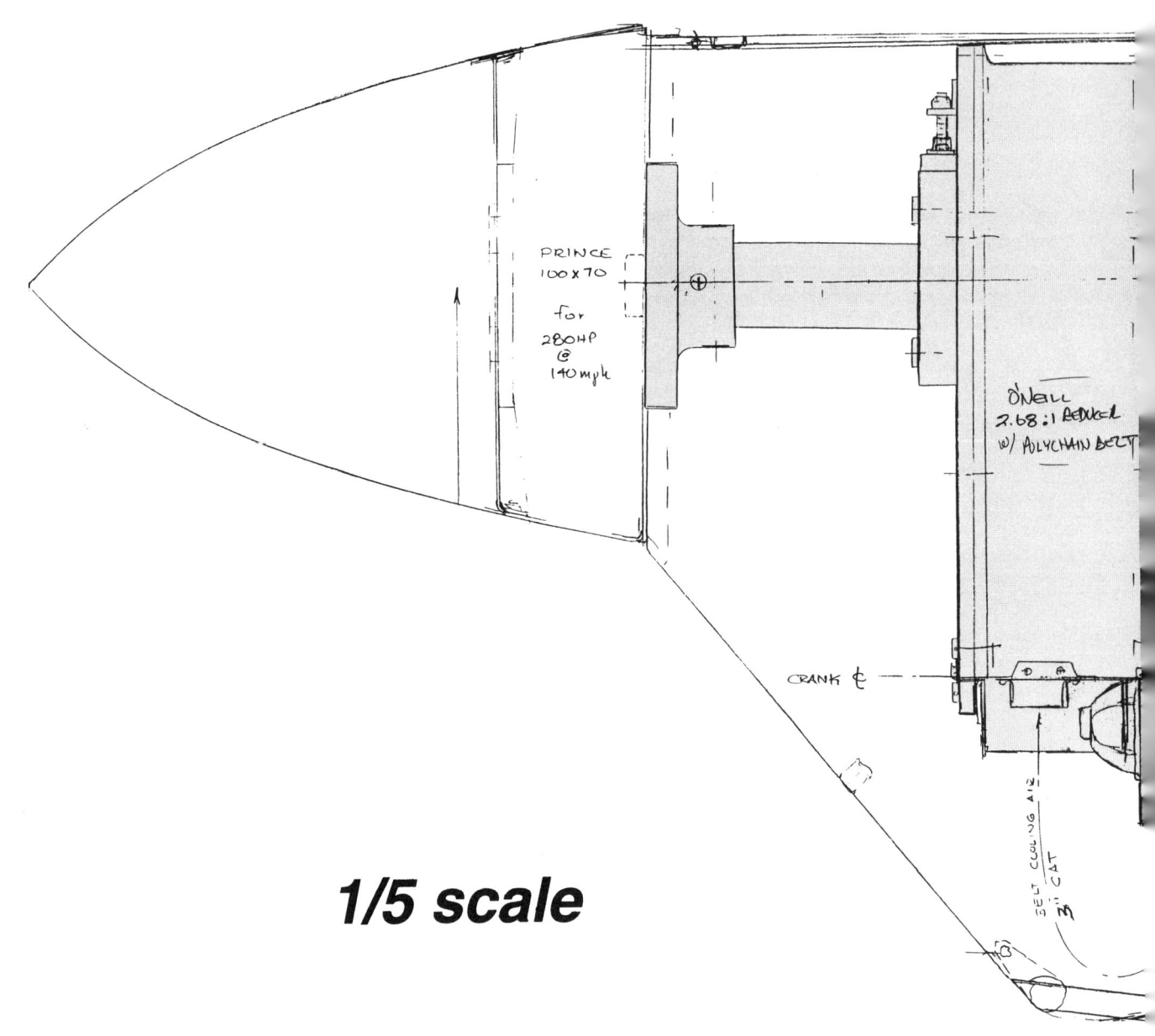

1/5 scale

O'Neill
351 W Ford
Aero Conversion

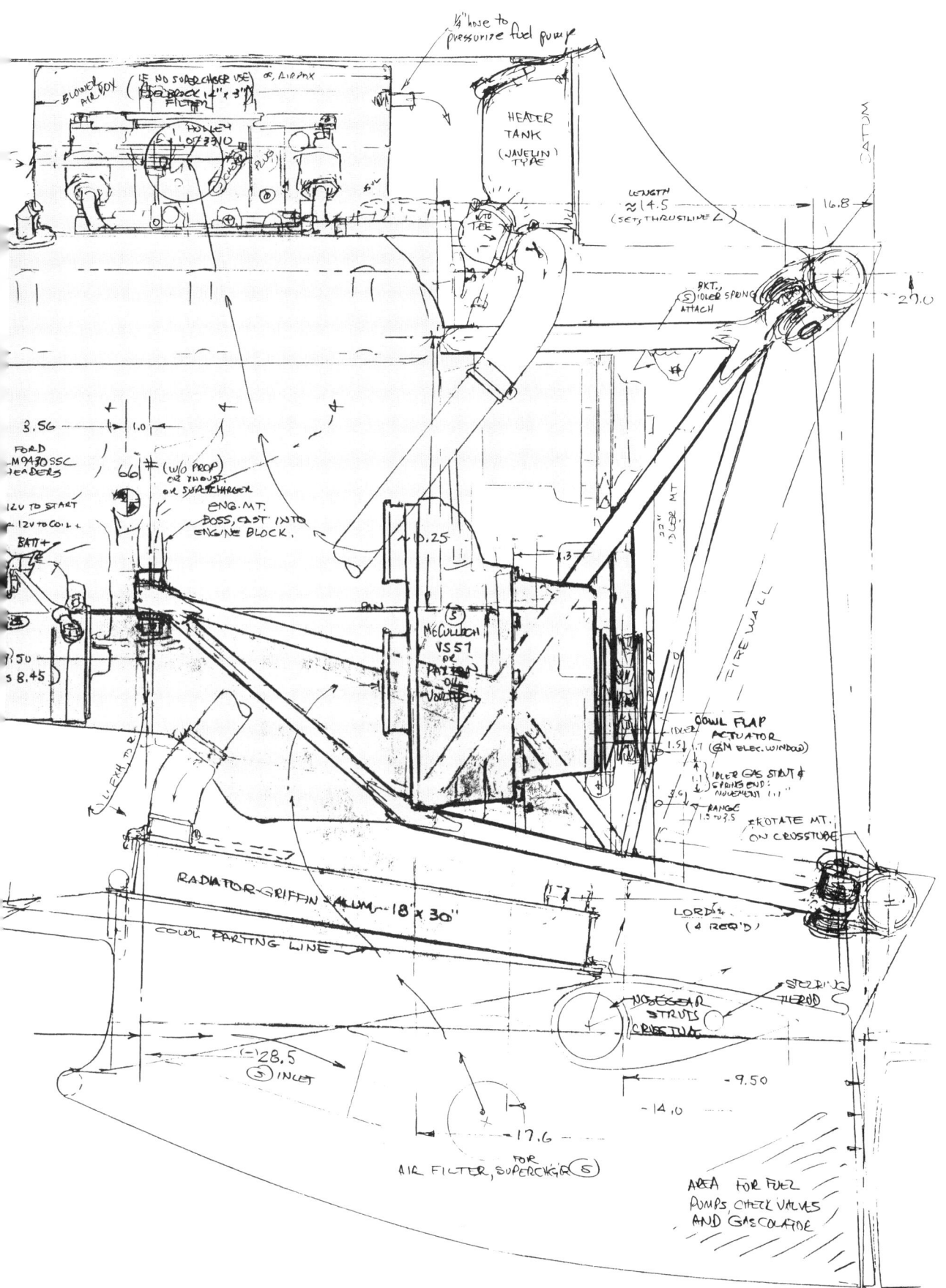

prop, the completed assembly weighs 661 pounds. The prop and headers weigh an additional 40 pounds. If I had used aluminum heads I could have deducted about 50 pounds. An aluminum water pump would have reduced another 10 pounds. A different aluminum redrive top-pulley (not used) would have reduced the total weight by another 35 pounds (95 pounds total).

Summing up, the 25 pounds additional for the supercharger and the above weight savings I would have produced a 400 HP (351 HO) supercharged conversion weighing 590 pounds, including radiator and coolant. However, as my engine (351W modified) now is configured, it is at about 675 pounds, including the supercharger, aluminum water pump and iron redrive prop pulley.

ENGINE COOLING

I built a cowling to fair the airflow streamlines from the 17 inch diameter spinner back to the existing firewall. I made a wild guess on cooling and cut out inlets and outlets for the cooling airflow. The first engine runs of the new engine showed gradual heating reaching redlines, at which point I shut the engine down. The overheating occurred a lot more gradually than with an air-cooled engine, an advantage when doing development. My coolant would climb to over 250 F. with oil about 30F. higher. I added cooling fans on the radiator, then two more fans in the cowl outlets. No problem during taxi but the fans blocked airflow in flight.

Cooling inlet and outlet configurations were modified at least seven times. At that point desperation, exasperation and flights limited to minutes forced me to read through about 10 years of back issues of Sport Aviation, trying to find something that would help me understand what was going on, how to cool my 351W. Finally I found an excellent article (August 1989, p. 39) which established some basic cooling rules.

Rule #1: There <u>absolutely must be</u> a pressure drop from front to back of the radiator, of about 6 to 8 pounds/ft^2 (converts to 2 inches of water differential pressure) which can be easily seen by means of a cheap and simple "manometer", a 1/4 inch diameter plastic tube, bent into a "U" with some liquid in the bottom of the "U", hanging on the instrument panel. One end of the tube goes in front of the radiator and connects to a little piece of brass, copper or aluminum tubing pinched shut, with a half-dozen .063 holes drilled in it to sense the pressure. A similar probe is used on the other end of the plastic tube and is situated just behind the radiator. My youngest engineer-son designed this manometer, a simple device which took us all of 5 minutes to make and install. I knew about "manometers" but I thought they would be expensive, tricky, and complicated.

I soon found out that "scooping" the air does not always get it to flow. We taxied out to the runway with the problem cooling system, made a fast-taxi run, only to find the pressure was not <u>plus</u> 2 inches, but was <u>negative</u> 1/4 inch! The air was actually flowing <u>backward</u> through the radiator, even though the inlet opening was right in front in the prop blast. The side outlets were in the curves of the cowl, with flanges to "help". By now I knew that the inlet and outlets were too small, which lead me to Rule No. 2.

Rule #2: Make the inlet and outlets big enough. You can reduce them later. How big? About 15 percent of the engine power is in heat that must be removed from the cylinder walls, by coolant, oil, or air flow. The mass of airflow required to cool 100 HP (at rich mixture) is 1.7 pounds/sec. and air weighs about .075 pounds/ft^3. Ergo, as my prop pulled the cooling inlet and outlets through the air, that amount of air had to flow into the inlet, go on through the radiator, and then out the outlet. The radiator flow area (area of the holes through the radiator) should be two to three times that of the cowl air inlet area (call this Rule # 2A): to cool 280 HP ("ordinary" speeds assumed) I would need about 140 square inches of inlet area and two to three times that in hole area through the radiator. The outlet needs 1.2 to 1.5 times the inlet area. This is a conservative ratio but is a starting point.

The NAPA starter is heat shielded from the left header and exhaust pipe which crosses under the oil pan (more shielding). Note use of flexible aluminum ducting to protect air intake hose. Header design requires additional spark plug protection.

Rule #3: The outlet absolutely must be in a lower pressure area than the inlet even if one has to get the pressure drop by use of a deflected cowl flap. Pressure differential (See Rule #1) is what powers the flow. No power? No flow.

Both outlet cowl flaps are about 20 inches high and can open to about 4 inches wide. They could be a little larger, but they work, so far. Armed with solid advice and saber saw, I enlarged my cowling openings, added ramps to the outlets to help the heated air to accelerate outward. Tim and I taxied out again. On static run-up we got about 1 inch of water pressure positive differential (air was flowing the right way) and on the fast taxi we were up to 1.7 inch at 70 MPH...an amazing improvement! Coolant cooling was accomplished.

The coolant temperature sender is in the intake manifold near the 160 F. thermostat, just before it goes out to the radiator. The pressure sender is located in the header tank. Dave Blanton suggests the most important cooling system information is the coolant pressure. I obtained a liquid-filled gauge from a store that sells hydraulic components. Heavy but cheap and accurate. The pressure cap on my reservoir is 22 PSI. My coolant pressure usually runs around 9-12 PSI, though it sometimes goes as high as 20 PSI if I have just filled the reservoir too full. This happens since I think excessive filling creates vapor pressure behind cooling fluid. Eventually, the coolant cycles through, gradually bleeding off the vapor and pressure. A Griffin aluminum custom-made racing radiator measuring about 19x31 inches with about 400 square inches of airflow (holes) is used. This size of radiator installed on Magnum should be able to cool up to about 600 HP, according to my estimates. It would take a pretty highly-modified and blown 351W, running about 6000 RPM, or so, to produce 600 HP.

The right side view of the engine shows the stainless Ford Motorsport "shortie" exhaust manifold, stainless steel exhaust pipe, shielded oil filter and the cowl door actuator rod (left center).

COOLING PERFORMANCE

I finally switched to Texaco ETX 6024, which does not suffer from anti-corrosion additive fallout if things get too hot...which would result in aluminum corrosion and a clogged radiator...a good Dave Blanton tip. I got my supply from Olin Brown of Texaco Research in Texas, and I think it is the same stuff as used in the Saturn cooling system. An old race engine builder suggested trying for 200 F. where the coolant goes to the radiator...not more than 220 F. I agree with that. However, I have seen Magnum coolant temperatures above 270 F.(before we made our manometer) without steaming my 22 PSI radiator cap. These levels are not going to hurt anything, at least not until all the coolant turns to steam. If you have a problem with that think about those air-cooled "airplane engine" cylinder heads running nearly double this temperature!

Since modifying the cooling airflow I have been able to run the engine for an hour straight at maximum static power, about 28.5 inches MP and 4600 RPM, without overheating anything. The run just got a lot of bugs on the prop and was a good confidence builder, demonstrating engine reliability.

OIL COOLING/PRESSURE

Oil, in addition to its primary function as lubricant, is an important part of the engine cooling system. The combustion chamber walls pick up heat which is partially removed by oil. To keep the engine oil cool I installed a Ford heat exchanger (Ford # E3ZZ-6B856-A and bolt E3ZZ-6L626-A). This setup cools the oil with radiator system coolant from the water pump auxiliary outlets. The result is that the oil runs only about 30 degrees hotter than the coolant. Some engine people take the oil temperature in the gallery near the oil pump, using the oil pressure tap accessed by the auto builders. According to Ford Motorsport experts, measuring oil when it is pressurized causes readings higher than actual because the pressure of the oil causes the oil to heat up. A cylinder head temperature (sparkplug) thermocouple on the oil drain plug is used. The stock oil pressure tap is fitted with an electric oil pressure sensor.

I found a variety of limits being used for allowable oil temperatures. Not comfortable with ball park figures I did some research. Some veteran auto racers advise keeping the oil temperature between 220 F. and 260 F. For them, 285 F. is the absolute limit in racing-type applications since mineral oil will flash at 340 F. For light (automotive) use the common passenger car oil temperatures commonly go over 300 F. Unfortunately, oil warning "idiot" lights do not react to oil temperature. In response to my call, Ford Motorsport telephone service consultants said to the effect, "if it gets up to about 340 F. that's cause for alarm". I am of the opinion that the old race-engine builders know what they are talking about: keep engine oil temperatures between 220 and 260 F. if using petroleum oil for "endurance racing" ... i.e., continuous high power settings, as seen in airplanes.

Synthetic oils will stand perhaps 500 F. which is a temperature seen by aircooled engines. But synthetics are very expensive...over $8.00 per quart. Polyester-based synthetics are claimed to be the best. Next best is good quality racing oil. I have been satisfied with Blanton's advice on this and use only Valvoline 50W racing oil. Relative to oil pressure the Ford manual states 40-65 PSI at 2000 RPM, hot. An old race-engine builder suggests...10 PSI per 1000 RPM. I have 40 PSI at 2000 RPM near idle, 45 PSI at 4000 RPM (hot), or more than 10 PSI per 1000 RPM.

REDRIVE TEMPERATURE

Another important item of cooling for an engine with a belttype RPM reduction unit is the belt temperature. PolyChain and HTD belt catalogs include mention, in rather small letters in the beginning pages, that belt limit temperature is 185 degrees Fahrenheit. Somewhere above this number the belt teeth melt. To achieve my redrive cooling I found it necessary to get fancy with cooling air ducting because my entire engine cowling is completely sealed for engine cooling and minimum drag. My design has all of the air coming into the cowl going through the inlet to the coolant radiator first, including the carburetor air. My wife's meat thermometer (stuck through the firewall) tells me that the outlet air temperature on the other side of the firewall can be as high as 140 F. to 150 F. That sampling includes post-radiator air along with engine radiated and convected heat from the block and pan, from the redrive, and a large portion of the heat shielded exhaust system. Thus, the engine block runs a bit hotter, and the aluminum redrive housing bolted to it acts like a big heat sink. The redrive soaks up heat and expands causing the dimension between crankshaft centerline and prop shaft to grow about .030 inches. The belt tension increases as a result of this growth and because of a quirk of Kevlar (as Kevlar gets hotter it shrinks a little). The net effect is severe belt tightening, to the point of causing belt whine and a large load on the bearings.

So, to keep the redrive and its belt cool, I bring in cool air from openings under the spinner through two 3 inch diameter expandable aluminum (clothes dryer) heater ducts up to the redrive where it must circulate around the belt and housing before escaping through holes in the assembly. On the last flight this exhaust air indicated 160 F. with an OAT of 90 F. To compensate for some redrive growth the belt is adjusted to be a little loose before start-up.

IGNITION

I am using standard Ford Duraspark II ignition, with two separate ignition modules (Ford # E8PF12A199AB with blue plastic) with a left-off-right (about $50!) switch to select the module and route its output to coil and distributor. I also have an alternate battery source in case the alternator or related elements go pfft! I modified my ignition distributor by removing the vacuum advance. I could have (should have) bought an aftermarket distributor without a vacuum advance, since I was buying a new distributor anyway. But I was trying to stay as "stock" as possible. I set the ignition timing so that the spark advance is limited to 28 degrees, which results in 9 degrees at idle. Idle is smooth at about 500-600 RPM, warm, with the prop whopping quietly at about 200 RPM. Neat to watch the blades.

The B&M Supercharger book shows a graph of where maximum power usually comes in, at about 35 degrees ignition advance. But by reducing my advance to 28 degrees I only gave up one percent of power (3 HP) but gained seven (7) degrees protection against possible detonation. When I switched to the World Products Windsor head I selected the coldest plugs. Recently with the supercharger setup I changed from #68 to #71 jets and from the Accel 272 cold plug to the Accel 276 (hotter) to stay clean with the richer mixture.

Plug wires need to have solid wire (stainless steel preferred) cores. They should be shielded to prevent cross-firing, or else have spiral winding on the core to prevent propagation of the electromagnetic field when passing spark current. Great effort should be taken to assure the wires stay a half-inch from each other (to avoid the dreaded cross-firing) and any metal. This also prevents spark loss through grounding. My coil needs external ballast (a resistor) so that it only gets 7 or 8 volts of the total battery potential, except when starting. My ignition and electrical system is the result of research, trial and error, and (finally) following the correct Ford diagram exactly...and it works.

MINOR CHANGES

Alternator: I am using a 63 amp. NAPA auto alternator, with a $15 off-the-shelf 5 inch diameter Moroso aluminum pulley with 17mm bore, from Wise Speed Shop in St. Louis, to reduce the high RPM the alternator would otherwise suffer, at airplane-cruise (about 11,000 RPM plus). I also made a special little aluminum bracket to hold the alternator close to the block, for a shorter belt and revised the bracket that adjusts belt tension. I have an alternate (motorcycle) battery just for the ignition system, in case the charging system should fail. The alternate battery will serve the ignition system for about an hour, time enough to find an airport and land. The charging system keeps the alternate battery charged through a diode. The pre-flight checklist during engine run-up includes switching to each DuraSpark and each battery source, and noting the available static RPM at start of takeoff.

Carburetor: It's a Holley 34-3310. Extras include a custom insulating base of several laminations of gaskets and better. Hold down bolts are safety-wired. Using an EGT gage was, until recently, about the only way to monitor the jets, besides inspecting spark plug electrodes. The inexpensive $129 oxygen sensor now reads mixture directly.

When initially flying without the supercharger I safety-wired the carburetor air-cleaner hold-down screw. Javelin mentions they even safety-wire the jets. I have not done that but I do install them snugly, lest one fall into the engine and punch holes in its innards. Also, I installed a semi-coarse aluminum safety screen under the carburetor to keep any foreign objects from getting chewed up in the engine. Backfires instantly melted the aluminum screen and I am installing a stainless steel screen. The carburetor vacuum lead serves the Manifold Pressure gage. The carburetor throttle return spring was removed and one was added to pull the throttle to full-open in the case of throttle cable failure. Also, a spring was added to the choke lever to hold it open in case of choke cable failure. The engine was run about 40 hours with a small Edelbrock triangular-type "Free-Flo" air cleaner. The filter element came closer than 3/4 inch to the carburetor air vents which distorted the carburetor's flow sensing ability. I replaced it with a 14 inch diameter by 3 inch deep Edelbrock air cleaner which should also extend time between changes. With

The enclosed carburetor is supercharged. A tube (top) connects to the fuel pressure regulator which automatically sends 6 psi more to the carb bowls than supercharger pressure, thus maintaining proper float level.

supercharger installed I use a very large intake filter with a finer air filter inside of it.

At 55 hours I added the electronic Holley mixture control which controls fuel flow and is claimed can vary it 20 percent, or 5 jet-sizes, at least on the two primary jets. I can get 125 F. EGT rise from best power to peak but cannot get a lean drop off. I yearn for a Holley 34-4779 carburetor which varies all 4 jets at the same time. It costs more.

Fuel: I have been flying on Marathon 91-92 octane unleaded premium, mostly. The fuel flows from the tank through a Parker quick-disconnect (with that $14 part I can drop the tank with all fuel in a second), then to the electric pumps and bypasses, then through the strainer-drain, then to the fuel line regulator and "Y" connected to the two carburetor bowls.

Starter: The starter is supported by a clamp around the rear end to brace it against engine vibration and the clamping strap has a tab on the end which is bolted to an existing tapped hole in the block just above the rear of the starter. This stops vibration that results from not being supported by a full transmission bell housing at the geared end. The starter bolts to the redrive housing. Tooth gap is adjusted with a rod end on a tube that goes across the engine under and behind the flywheel to the bottom block lug on the other side.

Redrive: Several cog belt units are available. Mine has a 2.67:1 ratio, for a maximum prop speed of 2000 RPM, to turn a 108 inch diameter propeller for STOL flying. I added a temperature sensor to make certain it stays under the 185 F. limit.

Installation Details: To prevent vapor pockets building in the heads I vented the two high points by drilling and tapping with 1/8th inch pipe threads on a brass 1/8 inch hose fittings. These were "T" connected to a hose back to the water pump inlet. I used brass and auto-quality hose for this as aircraft aluminum plumbing fittings were exorbitantly expensive and unnecessary.

With the supercharger, the intake air comes from the cowl inlet, through a large 2-stage filter (from a farm tractor) and then to the supercharger inlet. It is "unsheltered" now but the blower action will heat it up about 70F. Since the air is heated in flight the exhaust crossover under the intake manifold is blocked off with two thin pieces of stainless when the intake manifold was installed on the head/block.

I had to complete the attachment of the cooling system to the airframe, wire up the accessories, alternator, ignition, and sensors to the instrument panel, route and attach the controls and switches and gages. Spark plug wires had to be kept separated from one another by a half-inch, and anchored so they did not flop around, wear and short out, or cook to death on a red hot header. Plus, they had to be protected from radiation from the red hot manifold tubing, no small hazard. In some places the wires are silicone, routed inside of fire shielding or thin steel tubing. The exhaust system had to be built up in-place, to clear oil pan, radiator, landing gear tubes, engine mounts, etc. I cut and tack-welded exhaust pipes to attach to the headers. I then fitted additional pieces as I routed them underneath the oil pan and past the radiator and aft toward the firewall on the right side, and down to the right bottom corner of the cowling. The tack-welded pipes were removed, finish-welded and eventually chrome-plated to prevent rusting. In many places exhaust pipes would radiate heat that would damage wires or hoses or cowling fiberglass, so additional shielding was required. Thin sheets of aluminum were trimmed to block heat radiation toward wires, hoses or cowling. Where the headers are about 1/4th inch from the cowl, stainless sheet shielding is used.

The nuts holding the exhaust pipes to the headers kept loosening. The problem was solved by a NAPA suggestion that brass nuts be used. They now stay tight. To protect the inside of the fiberglass cowling I used upholstery spray-adhesive to glue ordinary kitchen aluminum foil onto the inside of the cowling to reflect the heat.

To retain most of the radiant heat from the exhaust pipes I slipped expandable aluminum 3 inch heater ducting over the exhaust pipes from the headers to the cowling outlet but this has occasionally melted through (aluminum melts around 1100F). In some places the .016 aluminum shielding runs close to the aluminum radiator so those areas are shielded by an extra piece of .015 stainless sheet.

My original standard item headers were made by Hedder but unfortunately the thin steel does not last long in an aircraft-type high heat-condensation installation. The first Hedder headers only lasted about 40 hours rusting completely through, probably due to the hangar condensation plus excessive heat from being Insul-wrapped which keeps moisture in when cold and high heat in when hot. The Hedder gaskets to the downpipes lasted even less time and I replaced them with steel-wire-reinforced gaskets from NAPA. The Hedder headers have now been entirely replaced with Ford Motorsport SSC stainless "shorties" and two 2.5 inch diameter pipes to the collector for the 3 inch tailpipe, then back to the 5 inch Supertrapp muffler.

ENGINE TESTING

I tested the engine at the airport. One overlooked advantage of a liquid-cooled engine is that high power testing can be done before flying; full throttle runups on the ground are possible without overheating. I tethered Magnum to my hangar concrete foundation and measured 600 pounds static thrust at 4500 RPM and full throttle (about 28 inches). On 230 HP this equates to 2.6 pounds thrust/HP, the same ratio I got with the turbocharged 350 HP Jacobs radial, or 900 pounds on 350 HP. I have made static maximum MP test runs as long as an hour at WOT without overheating, about 4600 RPM at 28 inches MP, as I mentioned above, and for a few minutes at 5200 RPM at 38 inches MP with the Paxton supercharger.

FLIGHT PERFORMANCE

I had Lonnie Prince design the prop for a design maximum speed of about 140 MPH at 5400 RPM, absorbing about 285 HP. With more power from supercharging the prop will likely need repitching. With the carbureted engine, stock heads and the Prince P-Tip 100 x 70 inch pitch prop, climb at 90 MPH is around 4850 RPM and 28 inches MAP. Coolant temperature (70 F. day) is about 190 F; coolant pressure is 9-12 PSI. Oil temperature is at 212-230 F. Normally, upon reaching cruise altitude, the nose is trimmed down to maintain altitude as airspeed builds to about 115-120 MPH; throttle is reduced to about 22 inches and RPM comes down to 4200.

With stock heads I got 230 HP at takeoff (28.5 inches MP), which reduced to 26.5 inches at 3000 ft., or about 205 HP. Power for cruise at 3000 MSL is estimated at 205 x 22/26 inches=173 HP. On one flight at 2400 pounds I maintained altitude at 85 MPH on 3800 RPM/18 inches MP, or about 140 HP. At this time I feel fairly confident the engine will run continually at cruise power (20-22 inches MP and 4100-4200 RPM). I recently flew a 2.3 hour flight at about this power setting. This included a full power climb to 3000 MSL and further climb to 6500.

HP COMPARISONS

Note that when I have 385 HP (like the 351 HO, or with supercharger), the Magnum V/8 (3800 pounds per 385 HP, or 9.9 #/ HP) weighs less per horsepower than the DeHavilland Beaver (5100 pounds per 450 HP, or 11.3 #/HP). Bettering the Beaver was my design goal. When I fly with only 280 HP (no supercharger) I chose to reduce the allowable gross of Magnum to a 4-seater equivalent of about 3000 pounds to avoid too sluggish performance. Accordingly, the Magnum V/8 with two people and fuel (2600 lbs. flying weight) and 385 HP up front will have a power-weight ratio better than an RV-3, Glassair or Kitfox. Even at 3800 pounds gross, each horsepower lifts less weight than a 2+2 or STOL, and should climb about 1500 ft./min., all hauled up by a Ford V/8.

SUPERCHARGER EFFECTS

I subsequently installed my supercharger and ground tested it. To initially check the mixture, I watched the EGT as I adjusted the electronic leaning while the aircraft was tied down and the engine running at about cruise power. My old KS EGT probes are about 2 inches out from the heads on the front and back of the engine and sometimes read erratically. With most intake manifolds and 4-barrel carburetors two corner cylinders on each bank are mostly served by the nearest carburetor barrel when all four barrels are open (which is most of the time at airplane power levels).

I eventually ran at maximum (supercharged) manifold pressure (38 inches, or about 380 HP) to see how much static power would develop with the Prince prop, and whether it would hold this power for about two or three minutes maximum (simulating climb out). This may have pushed the stock pistons a little, but it was better to find out any problems on the ground rather than at 100 feet above the runway. Definitely, there will be no problem with high power cruise at 4500 RPM and 24 inches with hypereutectic pistons. This is where the big Ford-engined marine inboards normally run with hypereutectic pistons...4500 RPM...all day long.

This power level should pull Magnum along at about 140 MPH at sea level; and, if the blower will still produce the 22 inches at 25,000 MSL (according to the charts), that equates to 200 MPH true airspeed, a great cruise speed for my draggy airframe.

I now experience fluctuating EGT readings with my 34-3310 vacuum-secondary type-carburetor. To make sure I don't trash the engine with detonation I could not hear I am installing a new Air-Fuel Mixture gage which Edelbrock just introduced... as a back-up to my Knock Alert gage. Mixture is really what I want to know, anyway. That and incipient detonation.

FUEL DELIVERY PROBLEMS

When I started generating more than 230 HP the little Facet pump could not keep up, nor could the engine mechanical pump. So I bought a Holley-Red electric pump, and also a Holley-Street pump with 3/8 inch ports. This gave plenty of flow at the carburetor, which needs inlet pressure between 3.5 and 6 PSI.

When I installed the supercharger and ran the engine up to power, it simply quit. I started it again and watched the gages. At about 31 inches MP it quit again... sounded like it just ran out of gas. The blower pumped boost air into an airbox which surrounded the carburetor. As the blower spooled up and the pressure rose to about 4 PSI in the box, the fuel pressure (about 7 PSI) dropped to around 3 PSI and the bowls just ran out of fuel. The manifold pressure was still there...I could push it up to 38 inches but there wasn't any fuel to burn with it. The fix suggested by the speed shop that sold me the Holley pumps was to plumb a pressure line from the airbox into the top of the mechanical pump diaphragm chamber. This trick adds 6 PSI (boost) push to the pump spring pressure. Together, they automatically keep the fuel pressure where it should be. This worked briefly.

The mechanical Holley pump has a seal that is designed to keep crankcase pressure and oil out of the fuel pump but the fix introduces supercharger boost pressure trying to blow past that seal and back into the crankcase. The seal, in addition to being distorted, does not get the little bit of oil that seals need to live. At first, I tried to reverse the seal, double it, and that did work, at least for a while. I considered adding a drip-oiler to the fuel pump diaphragm and vent the top of the oiler to the boost linebut I would have to remember to keep the oiler full.

Coolant header tank is at installation high point. Engine breather hose taps into valve cover. (Bottom) Prop flange has additional holes for a special propeller. Spinner has front and rear bulkheads. Muffler is outside the fuselage.

A better idea might be to tap the engine oil system somehow, perhaps like the old external oilers used on Ford V/8s which had the rocker oil-passage worn closed as it passed the camshaft. Or maybe make an Oilite bronze bushing for the diaphragm pull-up shaft. Finally, calculations showed that boosting the mechanical pump's load by 6 PSI was stressing it too much so I replaced it with a Mallory 140 gal/hour electric pump, a regulator vented to the carburetor air box and two fuel check valves to allow either or both fuel pumps to run.

The engine is running great now, and the supercharger moves the maximum static RPM from 4500 up to 5200, and the static thrust now pulls 750 pounds, which was only 600 when unsupercharged at 4500 RPM. More power is always better.

COSTS

Repairs are cheap. Thus far I have had to replace the $35 starter which had a cracked lug. I just ordered a new set of sparkplugs, which cost less than $20...for eight (8). Now that I'm switched over to stainless, no more exhaust system costs. My old Facet electric fuel pump was only good to about 250 HP. With the supercharger, I had to go bigger, to the Holley+Red electric pump, and the Holley 3/8 NPT mechanical street pump costing a total of $120. The Mallory fuel pump and associated parts cost about $150. I got my O-3310 Holley carburetor and Edelbrock Torker II intake manifold on sale at Wise Speed Shop in St. Louis, saving a couple of bucks, at about $140 each and the Dial-A-Mile for carburetor mixture cost another $129, converting the O-3310 into a 34-3310. Doing it again, I would buy a Holley 34-4779 carburetor, with mechanical secondaries (instead of vacuum) and the Quarter Mile Dial option which varies all jet mixtures simultaneously.

The Griffin aluminum radiator was $300, custom built to my specification. I'm using automotive hose, clamps and tubing. Ford also gives me a price break, for distributors, plugs, oil heat exchanger, etc. Linkon's Auto Parts just sold me a $55(retail price) air cleaner for $34.

Costs are one of the biggest advantages of DIY auto conversions when compared to certified engines. If my Ford 351 Windsor V/8 engine continues to be aero-reliable, then I have produced 400 HP of flying power, that is affordable and sustainable, operationally and money-wise, for a total cost of about $6,000.

This is one way to get affordable 400 HP. Today, I personally would opt for the Ford 351 HO "crate motor" and save myself all that work, worry and spend my time enjoying the airplane designing part. The alternative costing $20,000 was not in my price range.

RELIABILITY

Of course, the most important feature of any aero-conversion is reliability. Hours of trouble free operation is the only proof. I'm beginning to get those now and expect the hours to build up rapidly. My confidence goes beyond my experience with the Magnum installation. The 351W engine and its components have huge amounts of service experience running at much higher power levels than my installation so I am looking forward to enjoying many hours

Overall views of the Ford 351W installation in the Magnum airplane. Photos were taken by the author last month during a maintenance and inspection session. Note round pocket in spring loaded cowl door for actuator rod.

of flying my aero-Ford.

Anyone performing this specific aero-conversion must understand that each <u>differing</u> airframe installation makes <u>different demands</u> on the engine so specific reliability must be verified. But doing many of the same successful things that a prior "converter" like me did should reduce the problems considerably.

Experimenters should anticipate problems occurring and plan accordingly. When I first went to WOT the radiator steamed, the oil pressure went down as the oil got hot and, in a few short runs, the engine ran rougher or backfired. Components started to disassemble themselves when not wired, clamped, Locktited, etc. All of the above due to experimentation and the learning process.

Just like people, engines have a tendency to come apart under severe pressure. Each need to be prepared by "good upbringing", learning how to get one's act together, and to do it right. However, when things are balanced, assembled right, matched, safetied, cooled, and properly fed and sparked, it is a truly awesome, unforgettable "happening" to see your 20 year old engine that was designed for a car and output of maybe 150 HP hunker down and roar out 380 HP smoothly and with great determination. Man! You can just barely hear the whine of the blower as the supercharger sings upward and pumps 40 percent more atmosphere into each firing cylinder, and the tachometer pushes up to 5200 RPM...some 700 RPM higher than it would have twisted that same prop at full throttle normally-aspirated. And it just keeps running, with no overheating, while blasting propwash back around the fuselage. You don't have to worry about thermal shock as you pull the power back and listen to the smooth exhaust tones, idling smoothly at 600 RPM, just waiting to be run hard again. Makes you want to smile big, and give your Ford V/8 engine an encouraging pat on the head.

Aero-ized automobile engines can certainly make big power for unbelievably small bucks. Readers can tell that I really like the 351W conversion. I bet the 351 HO would be even better.

Over 54 flight hours on the 280 HP version and over 17 hours on the 400 HP supercharged version have been logged as of September 1. Countless ground test hours, many at high power settings, are not included in the 71 hour total. I plan to give Contact! readers a follow-up story after the next 100 hours, concentrating on performance and operation. **TO'N**

Terry O'Neill's aviation interests go back to 1953. Freshly graduated from Notre Dame he entered Navy flight training, becoming carrier qualified, completteting his service as P2V commander. He is no stranger to the experimental aircraft movement (EAA #5572). Some readers may recall seeing his unsual PeePod at Rockford, a minumum size (8 foot span) canard configuration which featured use of Styrofoam and fibergass composite structure. To be flown by a prone pilot the project was terminated for lack of a suitable engine. He re-engineered and flew the last Waco factory AristoCraft pusher to Rockford in 1964. In 1967, he began work on a 6 place design which received a provisional TC from FAA. Plans were also sold for a homebuilt version. Design of the Magnum bushplane began in 1970 while still employed. Current retirement involvement also includes experimentation with the flying wing to improve roll/yaw stability, applying a O'Neill patented device.

A most informative project review, this article also illustrates the pitfalls in dealing with "experts". If heeded, these warning signs will surely save someone a lot of aggrevation. Time and effort that went toward the preparation of the article is much appreciated. MCM

Converting the Mazda RX-7 Rotary Powerplant

Jim Mayfield
Arizona Rotors Project
10556 West Avalon Drive
Avondale Arizona 85323
(602) 977 9760

A twenty-five year veteran of the Marine Corps Jim has accumulated about 10,000 hours in fixed and rotary aircraft. In addition to all of the fixed wing ratings he also holds a CFII in rotorcraft. His involvement with gyroplanes goes back to 1965. He has founded and is principal owner of the Arizona Rotors Project which has at its foundation a flight training program for rotorcraft. It is uniquely designed to transition gyroplane pilots into helicopters. A full line of rotorcraft services will eventually be offered. MCM

Some background to this article is necessary. Because of the horrible safety record of open frame gyroplanes, the FAA granted an exemption 4 years ago to allow the conduct of commercial flight operations, including flight training, in experimental gyroplanes. Once that decision was reached, I decided that I would form a company that offered flight training and examiner services for open frame gyros. We got started on the design and build of the aircraft in January of 1993. The machine was completed in December 1993 after about 1,000 hours of work. We received the operating exemption and actually started flight training operations on January 27, 1994.

ENGINE SELECTION

One of the criteria I had for the gyro was the requirement for a high output powerplant because of the added weight of the two place design. Also, I wanted the engine to be smooth as possible because the gyroplane rotor, particularly on a two bladed rotor system, inherently generates substantial vibrations in of itself. By selecting a smooth running engine I would be able to isolate rotor vibrations from airframe engine vibrations. The decision to chose the Mazda 13 B was based on my research over the years, reading Lou Ross' material, and other sources of information that were available to me. I was particularly impressed with the performance of Mazda 13 B engine on the race car circuit, on the power race boat circuit, and the fact that the reliability under these conditions seemed pretty high.

The completely rebuilt engine long block was purchased from Adkins Aviation, which is a subsidiary of Adkins Racing in Washington. Their successes with racing engines was the determining factor in selecting their engine. I decided to keep the engine add-on components as simple as possible. For the ignition system, I chose the stock Mazda 13B mid year model 1985 unit because it is based on a simple electronic ignition configuration. Engine fueling cannot get any simpler than carburation so I decided to go that route with a large 650 cubic foot per minute, Holley 4 barrel mounted on a Mazda Marine aluminum intake manifold. Lou Ross helped me reach a decision on the starter. I ended up with a Subaru geared starter because it is very powerful and relatively light.

Overall powerplant package is relatively compact. This installation has accumulated over 300 hours of running time since December of 1993.

EXHAUST SYSTEM

The Mazda rotary exhaust system is known for its extremely high temperatures, in the neighborhood of 1650 degrees F. There is no manifold as such; a thermal reactor was used on this model. But the Mazda unit is very heavy and bulky, so I

Right side of aircraft tail boom structure supports engine muffler. This Super Trapp design is quite effective in reducing the rotary's exhaust noise.

elected not to use it. Instead, a custom header design coming directly out of the block was fabricated. Based on input from Adkins Racing, and also Chris Ross, we determined that the optimum length for the headers before entering into the collection chamber should be about 21 inches, and that dimension is critical to within about 1/2 inch.

The first mild steel unit of .062 wall tubing lasted a grand total of 41 hours before a hole was blasted right through the side of it. (In the automotive application there is, in fact a manifold, and also a heat exchanger, which reduces some heat problems in the automotive application). So, I went to an all stainless steel exhaust system which has sustained 250 plus hours and still looks new. It is not only able to absorb the heat, but the extreme temperature changes associated with the typically short training periods of the gyroplane instruction program.

Because the combustion chamber is long and narrow each rotor requires two plugs. Steel braided lines carry oil between engine and oil cooler.

Rotary users find an abundant amount of engine block mounting points. This shock mounted arrangement further reduces low engine vibrations.

ENGINE COOLING

Cooling this engine has probably been the greatest challenge of the entire project. Going in, I had personal knowledge of three other rotary engines in a comparable gyroplane application - all three have had engine failures before 100 hours, perhaps because of coolant overheating. Some background may be useful to others. In conversations with Chris and Lou Ross in June of 1993 we began to analyze our cooling situation. I was aware of the high internal temperatures generated by the Mazda. It is an engine that has approximately 80 cubic inches which is capable of putting out 160 to 180 horsepower in the 6,000 RPM range. At higher RPMs, since it is not a torque limited engine, the horsepower keeps climbing. I know that the engine in racing applications can run at 12,000 RPMs with a fair amount of reliability.

Chris' recommendation to me was to use Harrison heat exchangers, a fancy way of saying the evaporator section of GM automotive air-conditioning systems. Chris has done some experimentation with the Harrison heat exchangers on his test bed and also on The Ross Aero Mooney. The problem I have in my application is that I don't have a closed cowling; any ducting or baffling to create a low pressure area behind the radiator to draw air through. It is my opinion, contrary to popular belief, that air is not pushed through a radiator, but that air is pulled through a radiator and that demands a low pressure area behind it. My design does not have that capability.

I initially used a Diesel Rabbit radiator; it has relatively small capacity, about 5 1/2 quarts. When the ambient temperatures were down around 50 to 70 degrees Fahrenheit, cooling was adequate, running 195-200 degrees F. temperature, which is quite good, since the thermostat was fully open at 200 degrees. (You have two choices of thermostats 185 or 195 degrees Fahrenheit.)

Along about March of this year, we had a little heat wave and ambient temperature got up to around 88 degrees. Our coolant temperature climbed right up to the edge of red line shortly after take off so we landed and went back to the drawing board.

To fix this emerging problem I obtained some after market automotive cooling fans, two eleven inch diameter fans and installed them behind the Diesel Rabbit radiator. The thermostats were set so the fans cut in at 150 degrees F. as measured in the radiator. It helped a fair amount but still was not adequate at high power settings. At that time the gyroplane had a relatively small diameter main rotor system, which meant that I was operating at a minimum of 80 percent power. That level of power in itself generated quite a bit more heat. We decided at that point that cooling was not enough.

The 650 CFM Holley four barrel carburetor has been proven to be a correct match for this engine. This gyroplane is typically operated above 5000 RPM.

The Mazda Marine aluminum manifold supports the carburetor in car attitude minimizing float problems. Exhaust headers are by Burns Stainless.

Another problem with cooling this engine application is that the engine was running at extremely high RPMs, much higher than the RPM seen in a typical automotive application. The automotive crank shaft pulley, the alternator pulley, and the water pump were running at high RPMs, defined as over 5000 RPMs for purpose of illustration. One of two things could happen according to two schools of thought:

> 1. Water is moving through the heat exchanger so rapidly with the stock automotive pulleys at high RPMs that the water does not have time to exchange heat with the atmosphere through the cooling fins.
>
> 2. The water pump actually begins to cavitate at sustained RPMs above 5000, and therefore does not pump the coolant efficiently through the cooling system (this is Chris Ross' explanation).

My personal opinion was that stock automotive pulleys at high RPMs move the coolant too fast through the heat exchanger. The coolant does not have time to exchange heat with the atmosphere. To find out I performed a check of coolant flow. I hooked up a "T" in my outlet radiator hose. To do this I actually cut the radiator hose in half and put a "T" fitting in it with a 1/4 inch line that came out of it into a bucket. I started the engine and statically ran it at 5000 RPMs and measured the coolant flow, the amount of coolant I got in the bucket in a minute. Then I changed the pulleys to decrease the water pump speed by 25 percent. I had less water in the bucket with the smaller pulleys. While changing pulleys I also performed a check of the temperatures with the big pulleys and the little pulleys. The temperature with the reduced water pump speed was about 15 degrees F. cooler at a given ambient temperature because I did this within about a two hour period. Temperatures were measured on the outlet side of the pump. The ambient temperature was fairly constant, in the low 90s.

Two facts emerged from this simple experiment. One, the temperature went down about 15 degrees F. with 25 percent smaller pulleys and the water flow obviously went down. Which lead me to conclude that with the use of stock pulleys at high RPMs coolant was passing through too fast through the system. The volume was too great and the velocity was too high to allow it to exchange heat to the atmosphere.

However, I was still dissatisfied with the cooling modifications. The primary mission of Arizona Rotors is to use this aircraft for flight training. I am required to travel around the country. I go to Fly-Ins and Air Shows and give instruction. Some of the airports that I visit are at high density altitude and usually warm. For example, the outside air temperature at Dalhart, Texas, in May of this year was 94-95 degrees, and the density altitude was up around 6500-7000 feet. Once again, overheating reared its head, which meant, that although I kept very busy, I had to confine my flying to early in the morning or late in the evening. In mid-day I could not keep the engine cool enough at those density altitudes.

MORE COOLING

At this point the machine had a Diesel Rabbit radiator, and two after market automotive cooling fans thermostatically controlled. I next piggybacked a Harrison heat exchanger plumbed in series with the Rabbit radiator. This has given me the necessary cooling margin for operations in hot Arizona summer weather. For example, I was flying yesterday (July 14, 1994) when it was 108 degrees, at gross weight and at 75 percent power. The engine was running about 195-200

F. coolant temperature. So the extra radiator capacity coupled with the reduced diameter pulleys help a lot. It is obvious that the present cooling system is not applicable to fixed wing airplanes. I would question the use of cooling fans, for example. Certainly, the amount of radiator surface needed here is largely due to the lack of effective cowling. Again, I have to emphasize that I have absolutely no way to direct airflow or drop air pressure without designing a ducting system, which I'm unwilling to do because of weight and complexity.

Cooling has evolved through several combinations: the Rabbit radiator and the stock pulleys; the Rabbit radiator, stock pulleys, and cooling fan; the Rabbit radiator, modified 25 percent smaller pulleys and fans. We then ran the previous combination with a piggyback Harrison heat exchanger; and we ran the Diesel Rabbit radiator, the Harrison piggyback and no cooling fan. The only combination thus far that has given me acceptable cooling has been all of those modifications. Without the fans and the piggy back Harrison and at high temperatures (between 90-100) I would reach 220 degrees F. very quickly at 75 percent power. Incidentally, along the way I changed the alternator pulley to maintain the stock alternator speed.

TEMPERATURE LIMITS

Here is an interesting aside before I get into hoses and weights. It is extremely difficult to find concrete numbers on what the maximum and minimum operating temperatures are for this engine. Not just in this application, but in this engine, period. One of the automotive technical magazines mentions that if you have two thermostats 185 and 195 degrees you can get information that says, "Don't run this engine too hot or it will vomit" but I could not in my research find a number or anyone to tell me not to run it hotter than 215 degrees, or 230 degrees. So I use a conservative approach. If the thermostat does not begin to open up until 195 degrees and is fully open at 200 degrees, then I am attempting to stay within 10 percent of that number. In other words, I am trying to stay under 220 degrees. Where did I come up with 10 percent? It's a number I felt comfortable with and I can't be more precise than that.

With manufacturing tolerances in mind I bought and tested four thermostats in my deep fat fryer. One 195 degree thermostat, for example, did not start to open until 200 degrees and opened fully open at 215. The other two, a small sample admittedly for thermostats, started to open at 196, and finished opening at 203 and 204. The latter thermostat is the one I am using now, limiting operations to 220 F. I don't know if excursions to temperatures like 230 degrees would hurt it. I don't have that data. It is a good idea to run function tests to make certain you are installing the correct value of thermostat.

HOSES

The plumbing of this installation is not very complex. It was time consuming trying to find the correct hose elbows. Since I have an open airframe and I'm not constrained to a cowling I chose to use flexible hoses available from NAPA. The

This view shows the reduced diameter crank pulley, stock distributor and leads, oil filler pipe, engine mounting and the integral seat/fuel tank.

outlets from the water pump, outlet and inlet, are 1 1/2 inches O.D. The outlet/inlets on the Harrison heat exchanger are 1 1/4 inches O.D. Some adaptation to make the hoses fit both ends was necessary. I ended up buying a couple (very short, so I could get the cheapest ones I could get) 1 1/4 I.D. radiator hoses, and simply cut off two inches off the ends of

One ignition coil for the "leading" spark plugs and one for the "trailing" plugs. Note vertical coil orientation and secure mounting to rotor mast.

them and used them as sleeves inside the 1 1/2 inch diameter hoses. I could attach them to the smaller pipes of the radiator's inlets and outlets, it was the easiest way to do it.

WEIGHTS

The cooling system weights, the easiest way for me to do it right now, is that I know that I am running a total of 16 quarts of coolant. That includes the coolant in the engine, in the two radiators, and in the hoses. I started pouring in the top and measured. Sixteen quarts, two pounds per quart, so we have 32 pounds of coolant. The Rabbit radiator is quite heavy at 23 pounds, the Harrison heat exchanger is very light at 6 1/2 pounds; so that totals to 61 pounds. The hoses are short runs so we can add another three pounds. So we are running about 65 pounds for cooling.

The heat exchanger is a GM large car air conditioning evaporator core. I do not have engine component weights at this time. I did weigh them but lost my notes. The installation weights mentioned in Contact! issue #1 seem to be reasonable.

PROPELLER

Propeller choice was difficult and it was application driven. Let me illustrate. If I were going to hang this engine on a Long EZ or on another relatively high speed aircraft of any kind I would need to consider an operational window from 60 calibrated air speed to 160-180 calibrated airspeed, a 100 - 120 knots flight envelope requiring adequate efficiency. My rotorcraft has a minimum speed of about 20, and a maximum safe speed of about 70 (the retreating blade stalls). So I have half the operational window and a different set of requirements. A gyro by definition, is an extremely high lift, high drag device. Climb and acceleration performance is paramount, as in a car leaving a traffic light. As in a car maximum torque at low speed is essential. A prop that produces high cruise speed performance is worthless since the gyro cannot, by definition, operate at high cruise speeds.

I chose Warp Drive simply because they have an impeccable reputation in the low speed arena(gyroplanes and ultralights). Looking at the prop design it has a very heavy backing plate; it is 5/8 inch, 2024 T3 aluminum on both sides. The blades are carbon fiber over a wood core. In my opinion it is a very strong prop and blade. The maximum prop diameter allowed by the airframe was 68 inches. I am running a 160 horsepower powerplant (the number I've worked out with Adkins and Ross since I do not have dynamometer capabilities). That is not a lot of propeller disk area to absorb that much horsepower. I felt that a Warp Drive propeller would solve that problem. They have an infinitely ground adjustable pitch in the prop. It is relatively easy to do and takes about 20 minutes to change the pitch on the ground.

The prop had to produce maximum static thrust, the reaction product of engine torque. The reason is simply because the gyro flies so slow. Even though there is some difference in the amount of available thrust, at 50, than there is at 0, it is a relatively small difference so I tuned the propeller for near maximum static thrust. Since I have been flying these things for 30 years I realized that as the airfoil blade moves through

Oil is supplied to the Ross redrive from the oil pressure outlet and returned (bottom line) to the unpressurized oil filler pipe.

the air it would pick up efficiency and pick up some additional RPM. Although my first computations were to achieve maximum static thrust I increased the pitch just enough (in my opinion, 3 degrees on a four bladed prop) that I loaded

Business end of the Mazda rotary. Geared starter is mounted to Ross adapter housing. Warp Drive 4 blade prop and rotor head flex drive are seen.

the prop down at zero to some RPM value under maximum static thrust. At 50 MPH this propeller setting governs the engine to exactly 7000 RPM at wide open throttle. This is the maximum RPM that I have chosen to run this engine, which gives me the maximum thrust at that RPM. I was able to experiment with different pitch settings to slow the engine down enough with that much horsepower to maintain the operating RPMs that I was comfortable with. Right now I am running the pitch at 16 1/2 degrees, that is as referenced to the crush plate on the prop. Sixteen degrees from the crush plate. The crush plate, of course is perpendicular to the propeller drive shaft.

Custom crank pulley is used to reduce watr pump impeller speed. Adjacent to hose clamp, a small plate covers tip seal oil pump drive access.

REDRIVE SELECTION

It is not the smartest thing in the world to select an engine first, later select a redrive and finally select a propeller. Aside from the factors of installation packaging and weight and balance I find one of the hardest things to do is to integrate mechanical systems, to have all parts work together in harmony. I looked at the history of high output automotive engines equipped with redrives and found instances of component failure, particularly at the juncture where the redrive starts and the engine ends, caused by not having harmony between those two, not having proper damping vibration, isolation etc. That being said, I wanted a smooth engine, a reliable redrive and a propeller combination for the above mentioned reasons. Those considerations lead me toward the Mazda engine conversions by Duncan and Ross.

I gravitated toward Ross Aero for a couple reasons, one of them rather pragmatic. Ross was physically closer for me to go look at his offerings. On the other hand, I had heard that the thickness of materials in the Duncan cog belt redrive system, particularly the redrive backing plate, which holds the assembly together, as being relatively thin material. Secondly, I was disturbed at some specific fuel consumption claims made by Duncan, that did not seem reasonable to me.

I decided to purchase a Ross redrive because I wanted the reliability and smoothness of the planetary gear system. I chose the 2.85 to 1 ratio. For every 2.85 crankshaft revolutions, I get one propeller revolution, 2456 propeller RPMs at 7000 RPMs. The prop turns relatively slow as compared to a Lycoming on a Cherokee 140 on takeoff, turning at 2700 RPMs with a fixed pitch propeller to get maximum power.

TIP SEAL PROBLEM

Simplicity and the ease of servicing was a worthy Mazda objective. The stock engine as it came from the factory had one major drawback due to that fact. Owners familiar with other automobile engines and not aware of Mazda's approach to engine lubrication would on occasion "cook" their engine. A problem with low oil supply was not expected and rotor tip seal burnout was a typical occurrence as a result. Mazda tip seals are normally lubricated by an external oil pump on the side of the engine. Looking at the engine from the transmission end, it is located on the right side near the crank shaft pulley. This pump feeds crankcase oil up into the tip seals to lubricate and cool them. The combustion chamber is a very harsh environment and there is no real way to run an oil line to that point to cool it. Oil is literally dripped on the tip seals, much in the same way that oil is fed to a bench grinder. Since some owners did not keep their crank case topped off the result was inevitable.

Seventy AMPalternator provides power for ignition and electrical system. Pulley size was changed to limit alternator RPMs.

I made an decision early on that I was going to take the pump off and throw it away (I put it on a shelf) and use premix fuel. There are numerous reasons that I made this decision: First, in my application it is not inconvenient to do so - most of my flight missions are only 30-40 minutes long and I normally refuel between flights. I use automotive fuel rather than aviation gas, mainly because its an automotive engine and is designed to operate on an automotive grade of fuel and because it is far less expensive. There is yet another reason I chose to operate without the tip seal oil pump. I have a vague memory of an earlier Mazda aircraft application and a problem with the pump; Chris and Lou may have some more information on this. It sheared the shaft driving the tip seal oil pump. The failure was not catastrophic but would eventually require an engine overhaul. With pump failure the tip seals dry out and simply erode away; the engine becomes very noisy, starts using a lot of oil and loses power.

We operate the engine using a fuel premix with two ounces of high quality two stroke oil per gallon of auto fuel. Following

Coolant recovery bottle is level with engine water jacket. Optimum recovery would require placing bottle slightly higher.

One oil cooler and two radiators. Cooling is a challenge in this typically low speed application.

that simple method I can rest assured that those tip seals will always be lubricated. I think that is one of the main reasons I have run the engine for over 300 hours with no problem. This may explain why some experimenters have had poor results with their conversions. The oil capacity including the cooler, is 7 1/2 quarts. I use the Mazda stock oil heat exchanger.

LUBRICATION

Past problems with the Mazda engine lubrication system were of serious concern to me, requiring more decisions. One-third of the total cooling of the engine core is by oil and the remaining two-third is done with coolant, according to the RX-7 Haynes Manual section on engine cooling. I reached a decision early on that I was going to use a full synthetic oil. It is much more expensive. I pay $3-4 a quart for it but I only change it every 75-100 hours depending on what it looks like and if I am picking up any particles in my magnetic drain plug. I have over 300 hours of operation thus far with no signs of metal particles. I made a decision to go with a full synthetic formulation after Adkins Racing assured me that it would not damage the internal seals in the engine. I am convinced that synthetics have a very good lubrication value and are less susceptible to breakdown under high operating temperatures.

REDRIVE LUBRICATION

The redrive is lubricated by the stock engine oil system. A fitting near the oil pressure pick up, actually parallel with the oil pressure pick up outlet, is the oil source. A pressure line from that fitting feeds oil into a fitting in the top of the redrive through a .040 drilled orifice, limiting the amount of oil in the sealed redrive housing. The oil drains out the bottom of the redrive and returns to the stock wet sump via a fitting on the oil filler neck. It is an unpressurized location and obviously does not create any back pressure in the redrive.

Some development background to this arrangement is appropriate. One of the early problems I had was a failure of the oil seal. I was doing a full power run during one of my early flight tests. Suddenly the tower told me I was on fire. As a matter of fact, I had just taken off runway 21 at Goodyear. I was at about 100 feet and unaware of any problem when the tower called and said I was on fire. I landed, cleared the active and got out of the gyro very rapidly. No fire! The cause - the oil seal had popped out of the rear of the redrive allowing engine oil to spill over the exhaust system. Just like a smoke generator there was this huge cloud of white smoke above slowly dissipating in the breeze as I sat next to my machine.

After taking the redrive off and taking it back to Ross Aero we found out that it required a .040 of an inch diameter restrictor orifice on the inlet side of the redrive. Planetary gears do not require an oil bath; an oil spray or mist is sufficient. Without the orifice and the pressure fed 1/4 inch oil line the redrive was a pretty strong oil pump. I was filling the redrive so my redrive was in a bath of oil. As the planetary gears turned the pressure blew the seal out. Since we put the restrictor in it, the .040 orifice, I haven't had any problem at all.

WEIGHT AND BALANCE

As gyroplanes go, my aircraft is on the heavy side. It weighs 758 pounds with the rotor. Gross weight is about 1330. That is the computed gross weight based on the strength of the rotor and rotor head components. This machine is essentially my design, based loosely upon a design made by William Parsons in Flagler County, Florida. Mr. Parson is a real pioneer in gyroplane construction. He built the first two seat powered trainer. I do not want to take any of his glory away. I had my own set of needs but I did base my configuration on his original design and he truly deserves this acknowledgment.

The only problems the Mazda engine caused me in weight and balance terms was it was so much heavier than the typical engine for this size of rotorcraft that my gyro became tail heavy. With my engine, I estimate that the all up running weight is about 320-326 pounds (including brackets). The airframe before my modifications to it, was designed for an engine weight of about 110 pounds. It was a pretty simple modification, I simply had to move the rotor head back 6 inches in order to shift the CG forward to be within the CG limits for the rotor. This shift does cause some interesting controllability problems because in shifting the rotor head back the distance or moment arm between the vertical stabilizer and rotor is reduces, or shortened. Obviously, the size of the vertical stabilizer is a function of the moment arm. The longer the arm, the smaller the area of the stabilizer. The arm on a rotorcraft is measured from the center of lift, usually just behind the rotor head. I had to increase the vertical stabilizer area approximately 40 percent to give myself adequate rudder control in power out situations. Power on , the lack of vertical area is not a problem because the Mazda engine produces a tremendous amount of thrust. However, in power out situations the stabilizer has to be big enough to maintain directional control with no propeller wash. So that was the only weight and balance problem.

Engine installation was very straight forward. We bolted it to the engine mount. It is essentially a stock engine in a stock automobile orientation. That is, the stock oil pan is on the bottom and exhaust manifold (header) is located on the right side of the aircraft as does the intake manifold. It is very much a stock installation and is bolted on using existing studs and holes on the block.

GROUND TESTING

Although the airframe was completed earlier, we finished the entire system in December of 1993. I had the engine installation complete about a 1 1/2 months earlier than that date and was able to start my ground testing and run the engine. The very first time I put power to the system, I turned on the battery only switch, punched the start button, and it started and ran smoothly. We began using the standard crankshaft pulley which had the factory timing marks. Later, we simply extended those lines on to the smaller modified crankshaft pulley using the keyways as references in order to use standard timing techniques and a timing light.

While timing this engine one has to be really careful. The engine has four spark plugs; each chamber has a leading and trailing spark plug. The engine has two coils and two pick ups in the ignition system. The leading and trailing spark plugs are timed separately and the Haynes shop manual contains complete instructions. I soon discovered that when I timed the ignition somewhere in the middle of the specified range it would start and run every time. At first, until I could figure out how to time it, I flew almost 60 hours, just rotating the distributor cap until it ran the smoothest at idle. My engine has a single distributor with two pick ups, one each for the leading and trailing plugs.

We ran the engine on a makeshift test stand, to Chris Ross' amazement. Instead of a closed coolant and radiator setup we ran the engine with city water. We pumped the water through the engine block and flowed it out on the ground in of my back yard. Initially, I ran the engine slowly, for about 1 1/2 to 2 hours, slightly above idle because I wanted to break in my tip seals and other seals. Total ground running time was about ten hours at about 5000 RPMs, non continuous, with a club prop providing the requisite load. I had no problems with running tap water through it for cooling. This approach saved me a lot of time.

ENGINE CONTROLS

Since I have a Holley carburetor that is not altitude compensated my fueling and induction system makes for a simple installation. Although mixture controls are available for this family of carburetors, I elected not to choose one. I have ample power from sea level to 7000 foot density altitude and I have not found the need to do any leaning, which supports my original analysis. It was not just " Hell, I don't need it", it was a conscious decision to eliminate leaning capability. In my view, heat is the principal enemy of my engine. It has two cast iron sections and three alloy aluminum sections that clearly expand and contract at different rates. Heat is the enemy. Gas is cheap compared to engine cores. And I think any pilot knows that one of the ways to cool an engine is to dump excess gas through it. I made a conscious decision not to run this thing lean.

I use stock spark plugs gapped to specifications (Haynes); Spitfire, AC, Pep Boys are some of the off-the-shelf brands I have used. The Mazda spark plug is a little different in that it does not have a big electrode which goes across the top; it has a little short stubby one that has a very strong spark.

I find it necessary to change plugs every 50 hours at a modest $1.39 a plug. The reason I change them is that I do notice erosion. Physical manifestation of plug erosion is noticeable. The engine started to develop a miss at idle at about 50-60 hours. Full power operation was still fine. I could not determine any perceptible power loss. But there would be a miss at the 1000 RPM idle setting. Every once in a while the engine would run and then it would sputter. So I pulled the plugs to check them. They were all of a nice color but the electrodes were eroded. So I changed the plugs. It was pretty

Closeup of piggyback A/C core over Rabbit radiator. Two 12 v. fans are also necessary to pull air through the radiator.

Primary and secondary fuel pumps are used instead of mechanical pumps. Note careful attention to detail throughout entire powerplant installation.

clear to me that I need to change them so now I make plug replacement a part of my routine maintenance. At 50 hours they come out.

This engine in this application, other than sustained high RPMs, does not know it is not in a RX-7 car because all of its internal components are essentially stock. It is the simplest way for me to go. So far, we have over 300 hours on our 13B with no significant problems. The cooling requirements in the early developmental phase were challenging, but not insurmountable. The process did not cost a bundle of bucks.

ENGINE SOURCING

Why did I decide to go with Adkins? I can go down to a corner lot in Phoenix and buy a 1979-1985 RX7 sports car from $800-1500, and pull the 13B or 12A engine out of it. Some empirical information first: I have personal knowledge of four engines in the application that I am running. Three were salvage yard engines and have failed. Mine has not. What that means, I'm not sure.

I went with Adkins based on his reputation and on the recommendation of Lou Ross. When I started talking to Mr. Adkins and asked questions with my Haynes book in my lap, I found he was very patient and provided answers. $1500 delivered was the price for his engine. It did not include exhaust, intake, carburetion or pulleys or alternator. In other words, a long block and nothing more. After the engine block arrived we had it down at Ross' to match it to the adapter and redrive. Lou, who I trust implicitly, stated was that the engine was essentially new inside. All tip seals were replaced. "O" rings were new. The exhaust inserts were apparently also new. The engine is a stock or four port Mazda 13B. I truly don't know, I don't have enough data, the sample is not big enough to know why my engine has not failed and the others have. I do know that Mazda mechanics I have talked to have stated that these engines do not sit well in junk yards. The tip seals and "O" rings decay, that the corrosion on the rotors, side seals and the rotor facing plates causes interference and problems. Obviously, when engines in that condition are started up, scoring on these contact surfaces is quite possible.

The results speak for themselves. I am happy that I spent the extra bucks for my engine. This is not a bargain basement engine when considering the following: $1500 for the core, $2500 for the redrive, $2000 for running accessories, so this is a $6000 engine. I could have bought a half time Lycoming O-320 for $6000 (buyer beware-some of these with an unknown history may end up to be scrap). But I choose not to do that because I wanted to do some development for my application with a Mazda, because of the size of the package, and because of perceived reliability.

RELIABILITY QUESTION

Readers and fans of the Mazda rotary engine have likely considered this but I would like to explain my thinking. Engine reliability is not linear; X number of engine hours at 12000 RPM cannot be equal to 2X hours at 6000 RPM. Now, whether it's twice as long or not, I don't know. I suspect it's not linear, I think it will be exponential; I think that I will probably get 1200-1500 hours before losing performance. I don't expect any catastrophic engine failure, thanks to this inherently simple design. **JM**

MOUNTAIN CLIMBER
A Piper Pawnee Conversion

Jed Erskine
1553 West Avenue, H11
Lancaster, CA 93534
(805) 949-6718

Designing and building a home built airplane requires broad knowledge and experience in a variety of disciplines. My knowledge and experience gave me the depth of understanding to know how much help I needed. I flew fighters in the Air Force, I have a CFII and I am an operations engineer in a flight test program at Edwards AFB. To design and build an airplane, and do a credible job of it, required far more expertise than I possessed. I needed help from several people. I am lucky enough to have great friends who are expert in fabrication, electrical design, automotive engine modifications and a host of other skills. My wife learned to apply fabric, stitch wing ribs, operate a power metal sheer, a metal brake, a drill press, make brackets by making cardboard patterns and then building the part out of aluminum. Without all of them, this aircraft never would have flown.

I have liked the Piper Pawnee, from afar, for years. It seemed to me that a forward cockpit in the hopper area and dual controls would make a great "going fishing" airplane. The back-country of Idaho and Montana have several remote strips that are next to great fishing and camping spots and I wanted to visit them in a strong, tough aircraft. The opportunity finally came for me to try out my ideas. This is the account of a conversion of a Pawnee to a home built experimental airplane.

CERTIFICATION

The first thing to do was to find out about the certification process. I discovered that there is as much difference between one FISDO and the next as there is between one country and another. (I mentioned this observation to one particularly obnoxious FAA inspector, and he agreed with me). I found, through several phone calls, that there are some FAA people who are truly interested in aviation, rather than their retirement, and will sincerely try to help.

FAA Circular 20-27D explains the certification process in detail and how to qualify for a Home Built Air-worthiness Certificate. However, there is an FAA ORDER 8310.18 and its Appendix 1 that provides a check list to follow that will calculate the amount of amateur builder participation. This ORDER will establish and document the "51%" rule that is required to qualify for the Home Built certificate.

If you live in a FISDO area where there are no helpful inspectors, you may have to move! I know of no way to force the FAA to follow their own rules or to be reasonable in evaluating a home built project. In my view, the Research & Development (R&D) certificate is not a very usable way to go. With the R&D, you have to re-certify each year and you have to be working toward an STC and a return to a normally certified aircraft. Also, you are required to perform several tests such as EPA noise test, a drop test, design reviews, etc. These tests must be witnessed by the FAA at your costs. If you don't progress toward an STC, you have to scrap the project. So, if you don't have an understanding with an FAA

inspector beforehand, don't start a project. I was very fortunate to find an inspector who is the experimenter's dream. After I found him all I had to do was invest large quantities of time and money.

I began checking the Trade-A-Plane for a cheap, early model 150 HP Pawnee. I found one for $8,700 and bought it. The belly was rotted out, the engine was run out, the fabric was rotten and it otherwise was in pretty bad shape. I sold the engine, fire wall forward, and stripped the complete aircraft down to the tubes. The wings were also disassembled.

PROJECT GOALS

The objective was to convert the Pawnee to a two-place, rugged airplane powered by an automobile engine conversion. In order to install a small block Chevy 350 HO ZZ2 engine with a cog belt reduction drive, the engine would be installed as far aft as possible to reduce the forward moment arm, the existing fuel tank would be removed from the fuselage and new ones installed in the wings, a radiator would be installed behind the rear cockpit, the battery moved to the aft fuselage, dual controls would be installed, the forward cockpit would be the command cockpit and the existing canopy would be redesigned to cover both cockpits. This concept was penciled out and checked to keep the CG within allowable limits.

FUSELAGE

After the frame was sand-blasted and painted, it was modified to change the forward section for a redesigned firewall. This change allowed for the change in engine shape and the new nose bowl and cowling. Also, the canopy frame was welded in place to allow for four hatches and a new windscreen. Provisions for the front seat, consoles and instrument panel, were built. The redesigned flight control system was installed.

The Pawnee has a large stick throw in roll. I wanted to reduce this stick displacement, so we made the new flight control aileron control horn longer. This would make the stick loads higher but I planned to install servos to reduce the loads if that became necessary. Other mods to the frame included many panel frames, tabs for skin panels, brackets for fuel pumps, radiator inlet and exhaust ducts, battery box, electric trim actuator, 1.5 inch coolant tubes, replacing/adding chrome moly tubes for additional strength, moving the flap handle to the front seat and other minor changes.

Another modification to the fuselage was to build two baggage compartments. One is just behind the firewall. It has an outside door and is large enough to carry sleeping bags, tents and other high volume, low weight items. There is another baggage area behind the back seat. This is where we carry the rest of the camping stuff, clothes, etc.

WING MODIFICATIONS

The wings were taken apart for modification also. Two 25 gal fuel tanks were built and installed outboard of the lift struts. This makes for a large roll inertia with full tanks, but there is a lot of aileron surface and I didn't think it would be a problem. Advantages of having the tanks outboard is they do not interfere with flight control cables and with the large amount of dihedral in the wings, they are closer to the height of the engine driven fuel pump. The tanks were built to be the wing surface in the tank area. It is a "wet wing" section at that location. It is interesting to note that the wing section containing the fuel tanks divided by the total wing area is close to the same value as the weight of the fuel divided by the weight of the aircraft. This would indicate the fuel tanks can lift their own weight. This is not pure science, but a point to ponder.

The interior of the tanks have several baffles to prevent slosh. One inch openings are cut in the corners of the baffles to allow fuel to flow to the outlet. The openings should have been much larger. Refueling is slow because of this. That is a minor problem which I am accustomed to now. Also, the inboard compartment has a fore-and-aft baffle with a one way gate to prevent forward slosh in a steep descent. We

Stripped Pawnee fuselage was sand blasted and thoroughly inspected for damage and rust. Repairs were made as necessary to bring airframe up to airworthiness standards before beginning major revisions.

used the flush type fuel caps that work like an old thermos bottle cap. These have a large rubber seal that is compressed when the locking lever is stowed for flight. That rubber seal swells when wet and the cap will not come off. The seal eventually dries and then leaks. I will never use that type of fuel cap again.

I did, however install wing spar doublers. These doublers are 7075, .090 inch aluminum strips that are bonded and bolted to each spar. The shear strength of these doublers is 20K pounds. The bonding material is Type V EA934 and has a shear strength of 20K PSI.

Nearly all the wing ribs were either repaired or rebuilt because of previous damage. Landing lights were installed in each wing and new leading edges were installed. The wing tips were redesigned with electrical conduit used as the bows, rather than the wood type used in older aircraft. Wiring in the wings included the stall warning switch, nav lights, landing/taxi lights and fuel quantity sender wires. The last effort on the wings was to cover them with STITS fabric.

ASSEMBLY

The fuselage was assembled with new sheet metal and fabric, new Plexiglas and windscreen. The nose bowl was built by shaping a foam block that was glued in place at the front of the engine. This formed shape was then placed in a large wooden box and concrete was poured over it. The

Highly modified fuselage details include two place canopy, enclosed baggage locker, strobe lights, new wiring. Radiator and portion of cooling duct work is seen at bottom center of photo.

Business end of Mountain Climber features Chevy 350 HO. The cradle type engine mount uses the reduction unit and rear point attachments. Engine exhaust stacks appear to be cut to tuned lengths.

cement block was turned over and the foam shape removed. The mold was then used to form a fiberglass part.

The new windscreen was formed in an oven we made out of plywood. The form was made by placing cardboard in the place of the windscreen and cutting out cardboard ribs that conformed to the curve of the windscreen. Plywood ribs were then cut using the cardboard ones as a pattern, and a frame was constructed. A piece of aluminum was nailed over the ribs and this was the form for the new windscreen. This form was placed in the oven, a flannel sheet was put over the aluminum and the Plexiglas was laid over this. I used a large plumber's propane torch to provide the heat. A glass pane in the top allowed us to watch the Plexiglas droop over the form as the temperature came up in the oven. It took three or four attempts before we got it right, but we finally produced a good windscreen. I found that a die grinder with a rotary grinder bit worked the best to drill holes for the attachment screws.

The landing gear is stock, but everything was rebuilt, including brakes, new bearings, new tail wheel and all new hydraulic lines. New rudder pedals and brake master cylinders were built and installed in the front cockpit. The gear has typical shock cord over a shock absorber type suspension. I should have changed to a better shock cord arrangement. A PA25-150 shock cord ring is not strong enough; my gear is now sagging. I will have to either install PA25-235 rings or go to the new oleo strut system.

REDRIVE

Of all the reduction drives I considered, the Belted Air Power redrive by Jess Meyers looked the best. I went to Las Vegas to see Jess and he had a prototype unit for the 350 HO that was not complete. I bought it in the "as is" condition. I had to do some work on the sprockets to fit them to the 350 "new" crank shaft design. We then took the sprockets to a plating company in West Los Angeles to have them anodized. I believe the hard anodizing job I got there was not hard enough and the belt eventually eroded through to the aluminum. I would point out here that Jess has not had any such problem and he is a most reputable person to do business with. I recommend his product even though I had a problem with the one I had.

At about 80 hours of operation I had a belt fail. My analysis of the cause was: the belt wore through the anodizing on the drive sprocket and the drive sprocket then wore into the belt cogs. The cogs then were cut off, and several cogs log-jammed at the drive sprocket and as they went around the sprocket, they parted the belt.

I am now putting together a new belt system, a Gates Poly Chain 14MM pitch, 90MM wide belt and steel sprockets. There will be a weight penalty, but I am willing to pay it for dependability. The new system has a drive sprocket with 30 teeth and a driven sprocket with 50 teeth. The small pulley I ordered is made of ductile iron and has a max RPM of 6090. So, a reduction drive can be designed for just about any engine speed; but, this is one more thing to consider.

The prop shaft has two thrust bearings that support the shaft, the driven sprocket and the prop. It is a 50MM diameter steel shaft. The only interference fit bearings I could find are metric sizes. All inch size shaft/bearing combinations are a slip fit. There are no penetrations into this shaft. The prop flange is heat shrunk onto the shaft and the driven sprocket uses a QD bushing. There are no keyways, taper pins or other devices that could produce a stress riser. The small sprocket is bolted to the crank through a spacer that aligns it with the top sprocket. The small sprocket has a carrier bearing that is located at the outer end. This bearing is supported by the forward plate. (More on the small sprocket bearing later). Belt tension is an interesting challenge. The aluminum drive plates expand some as the engine heats up and the belt may get slightly shorter when it is hot. This all adds to a change in belt tension during operation. This is another balancing job. Heat has other effects as well.

The small sprocket that is bolted to the crankshaft will eventually come up to the temperature of the engine. This will transfer heat to the belt. This heat may cause damage to the belt. We are trying to solve this with a cold air duct from the nose bowl into the drive. This will help with another problem as well. It is difficult to inspect the inside of the belt on preflight. The cooling hole in the nose bowl and a bore scope can now be used, on a frequent basis, to look at the belt and see how it is faring.

If I was to start from scratch I would use the 125 MM wide belt. With a 30 tooth small sprocket turning at 4000 RPM, the 125 MM is rated at 511 horsepower. With the same conditions, the 90MM belt is rated at 368 horsepower. RPM and sprocket size must be considered. There is a limit to sprocket rim speed. Speeds over 6,500 feet per minute are prohibited with their gray cast iron sprockets. Higher speed sprockets are available but those also must be factored into your design.

OTHER REDRIVE FACTORS

Another major consideration in the reduction drive design: A small block Chevy develops about 350 foot pounds of torque. With a 5 inch pulley, there is a 2.5 inch lever arm working on the belt. This results in something around 1680 pounds of pull on the belt. The Poly Chain belt can handle it but this force is also being felt by the pulley, which is, also to say, felt by the pulley support system. I have a very robust outer carrier bearing to help support the outer end of the pulley. This will reduce the force on the main engine bearing; but, how long will the main engine bearing last? In an attempt to mitigate this concern, I have changed the oil pump pressure control spring so that I am running over 65 PSI oil pressure at 3500 PM. As a minimum, I believe one should have at least 10 PSI for each 1,000 RPM. At 3500 RPM, the minimum oil pressure should be 35 PSI. The higher pressure that I am running may help to increase the oil film pressure in the main bearing and prevent metal to metal contact between the crank shaft and the bearing surface. I replaced my engine main bearing at 80 flight hours and found some slight indication of wear at

Left side of fuselage structure showing side mounted radiator, upper defuser panel, hose connector and AI lines routed to forward engine. Baggage locker, instrument panel and rudder controls also seen.

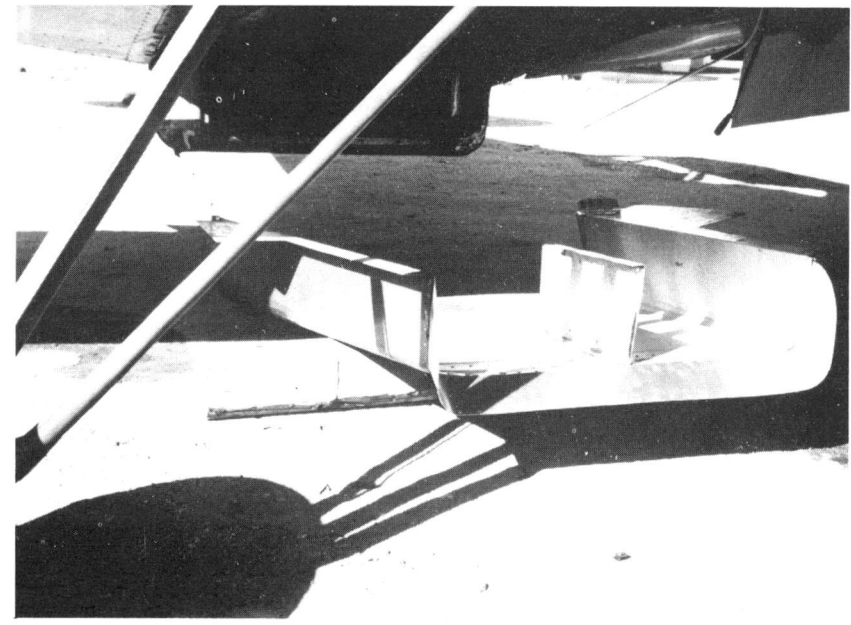

2024-T3 aluminum belly scoop and exposed 1/3rd lower portion of radiator (in shadow). Note center stiffening rib and addition of aluminum sheet to increase volume of inlet air. This type of diffuser design is used in the P-51.

the 12 o'clock position. A spur gear drive would have the same problem at the 3 o'clock position unless the crank shaft flange end is supported by some other means. When these drives start getting to the one thousand to two thousand flight hour range, we will know a lot more about these factors. We may find out the drive pulley, or gear, needs to be completely supported and driven by a separate shaft coupled to the crank shaft.

Belted Air Power redrive as installed on Chevy 350HO. Note relocated engine timing pointer next to engine flexplate, outboard bearing support and belt adjustment at prop flange.

ENGINE
The engine is a Chevrolet 350 HO with a 1.6:1 belt reduction drive. The prop is a metal 88/63 McCauley on a SAE 4 hub. I have repitched the prop twice to get the prop RPM I want which is about 2100 RPM at cruise. I started out using a Holley 750 carburetor with "out of the box" jets and the spark plugs that came with the engine. The timing was set at 35 degrees BTDC at 3200 RPM. The engine mounts use the stock mounts on the block and a Lord mount type setup on the reduction drive plate. The structure for the engine mounts is a chrome moly tube design that bolts through the firewall to the fuselage frame and extends to the engine mounts.

COMPLETION
Finally, two years later, and more money than I want to admit to, the project was finished. We managed to get all the paper work taken care of and we could finally start flying!

The first few flights went well except the water temperature was running higher than I liked. I spent several short flights working with this problem. The temperatures were not over 225 F., but I wanted it to run closer to 200 F. I discovered that the thermostat was too restrictive to the flow and removing it all together solved the problem. The question of removing the thermostat and the resultant increase in speed of the coolant flow is very interesting. A lot of articles have been written on the subject. My experience indicates that removing the thermostat will lower the operating temperature of the engine. With a slow moving water flow, there is a large temperature drop across the radiator. When the water is moving faster, the temperature drop is less; but, the entire cooling system runs cooler. The coolant may run too cold. This must be controlled by air flow or some other means. The oil temperature runs a little higher than the water temperature. I have never seen anything over 245 F. There are lots of possibilities. Using Mobil 1 solves many of the oil temperature concerns, but bearing life will suffer with temperatures above 290 F., or so.

The max RPM I could get static was 3400 RPM. However, on takeoff roll, I could get 4200 RPM on the engine. This prop RPM should not go over 2500. The tips go supersonic much above that. To figure max prop RPM to keep it efficient, the following method can be used. The prop diameter in feet times pi (3.1416) gives circumference of the prop. Multiply that times the RPM of the prop, multiply that by 60 for feet per hour then divide that by 5280 to get MPH at the prop tip. If that is over 600 or so, the prop is getting very inefficient.

I am burning super-unleaded auto gas for fuel. On occasions, I have burned avgas 100LL. The avgas burns cooler and leaves a gray deposit on the plugs. Otherwise, it seems to run well on avgas and switching back and forth is no problem.

PROBLEMS
The real problem started when I began operating for longer periods. I checked the plugs after a 2 hour flight and found metal specks on the center insulator! It looked like pepper specks. This is an indication of aluminum and could be an indication of detonation. Also, there were other indications of over temperature. The center insulator looked like it was boiled. If it truly was detonation, the engine could have failed in a matter of seconds. The metal deposits must have been caused by pre-ignition. The most likely cause of this was a combination of too lean a mixture and too hot spark plugs. The lesson to heed is: start flying with 2 or 4 jet sizes larger than stock and do not use the AC 14-904 plugs that come with the engine. These plugs are for street use and are much too hot for aircraft applications. I think you should at least start flying with Champion S57YC. They are a much colder, protruded tip plug and are much closer to the correct heat range. It would be even better to start with a Champion S53C plug that is very cold. You can then work up to hotter plugs as conditions permit. The variables in a combustion chamber are plug heat range, fuel mixture, spark timing, octane,

compression ratio and head temperature. Some of these we can not change easily, so you have to change the things that you can for the best combination.

My recommendations for initial settings for the 350 HO are: use a 16 PSI radiator cap, 4 jet sizes larger than stock, Champion S53C plugs, timing at 35 degrees BTDC at cruise RPM, and no thermostat. These settings come from boiling down lots of articles written by race engine builders and my own tests. It's all a balancing job. I recommend always changing one thing at a time and try it. I have changed jets and timing at the same time and the change was so great I couldn't tell what caused the change. I then had to restore one item back to the pre-test condition and run another test.

For some reason, I have found if the timing is too retarded, the center four plugs (3,4,5,6) run black (rich) and the corners (1,2,7,8) run clean. When I bring the timing up, the fuel distribution changes for the better, but I have to go richer on the jets to keep from detonating. If anyone knows why timing changes fuel distribution, please let me know.

I have chased this uneven distribution of fuel to the cylinders for a long time. I have used two Holley four barrels, a Predator and I now have a 500 CFM Holley two barrel with a "Dial A Mile" electronic mixture control. The fuel distribution is the best with this setup, but the mixture control has a too narrow band to allow for efficient operation at all altitudes. I have been told that if the holes in the carburetor base are slotted, you can move the carburetor forward and aft a slight amount and solve the distribution problem. I have not tried that yet. I have tried larger main jets and removed the power valve to get a rich enough mixture at sea level and still have a clean burn at 10,000 ft. This has not worked all that well. I use a six cylinder EGT gauge to determine best settings. 1550 degrees F. is the temperature I look for. I have used a 2.5 inch Hg power valve in an attempt to keep the power valve closed except at wide open throttle, but at 10,000 feet, I need full throttle to climb at a reasonable rate. The size of the carburetor is important. If you multiply the RPM times the engine displacement and divide by two and then divide by 1728, you have the CFM the engine is using if the volumetric efficiency is 100

Preparation, covering and finished wing utilizing wing airfoil contours in fabrication of fuel tanks.

percent. This is a good place to start for selecting a carburetor size. The intakes on these HOs are designed to run at a much higher RPM. I don't want to change manifolds, but if there is no combination that will work, I may have no choice but to go to an RV type manifold.

An unique, low cost concrete female mold was made from a male pattern to produce the airplane nose bowl. Concrete has stiffnes and shrinkage properties ideal for such parts.

Fuel injection may be the answer, but I haven't found one I like yet. I don't like the electric fuel pump needed for fuel injection, I don't want high pressure fuel lines in the engine compartment and injectors are intolerant to particles in the fuel. All these complaints with fuel injection can be taken care of but a good carburetor is what I am looking for.

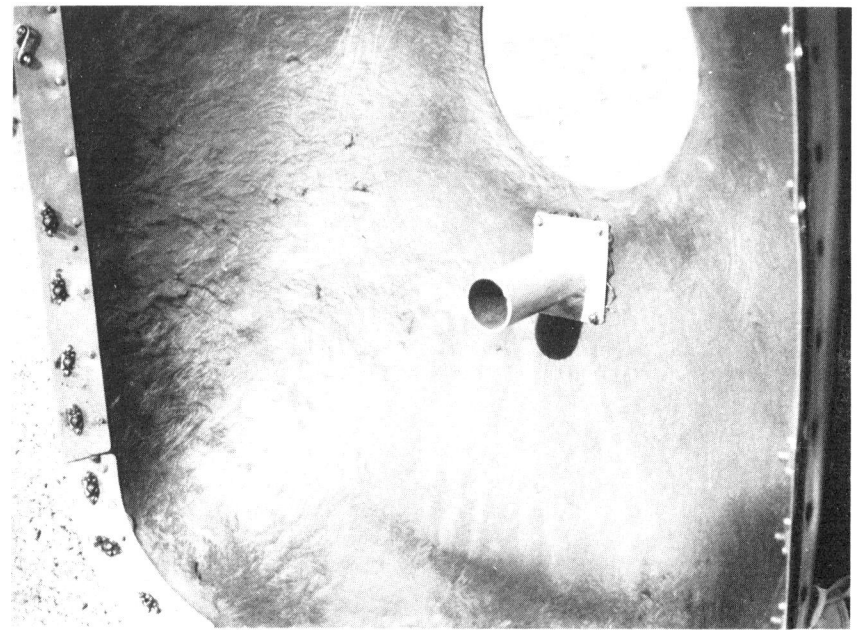

The nose bowl was laid up using chopped fiber mat which provides excellent strength in this type of application. Note the blast tube installed to cool the belt; considerable internal heat is generated during operation.

ENGINE CHECKS

When checking the health of an engine, a compression check is one way to see how well things are holding up in the top end. The aircraft type of check uses the pressure differential method. The interesting thing about this is there is usually no specific pass/fail criteria. Most inspectors have their own limits. If there is 80 PSI going in and there is less than 65 PSI, or 60 PSI, or some other pressure showing on the second gage, the engine fails the test. This checks the pressure at the top of the stroke only. This is the area of max crush on the rings. A trick to get a low cylinder to pass is to carefully move the prop so the piston goes off Top Dead Center (TDC) then pull it back to TDC. Sometimes this will help to seat the rings in the groves and get the minimum reading. The real way to do this test is to get a calibrated metering block from the engine manufacturer for the particular engine and use that to calibrate the compression tester. This then is the pass/fail pressure reading for that engine. On the other hand, the old automotive type compression tester works for me. To find out what this reading should be, first look at a manifold pressure gage (MAP) without the engine running and take the reading. This is close to the barometric pressure in inches of Hg. Divide this by 2 and you have about the PSI of the local atmospheric pressure. If you have a ten to one compression ratio engine, you should have about ten times the atmospheric pressure. An example :on a standard day at 2500 MSL field elevation the MAP should read 27.3 inches. This is 13.4 PSI. A 10 to 1 compression ratio engine would produce 134 PSI on a compression check. I find I get a little more than that probably because some heat is produced by compression of the air in the process. If you get a very low reading, it is time to worry, especially, if there is a large difference between one cylinder and another. If you get a much larger reading, throw away the tester and get a new one.

While we are talking about engines, I am told there is a GM LT1 marine engine available that is much like the 350 HO and has a four coil bullet proof ignition, a geared reverse flow water pump, fuel injection and set up to operate at 3500RPM for hours on end. This could be the answer to a turn-key aircraft engine. A stroker kit in one of these engines would likely put out 350 HP at 4200 RPM.

IGNITION

The ignition is the stock HEI with a motorcycle battery as a back up power supply. The emergency battery is charged through a diode to prevent reverse current flow. There are two ignition switches in the cockpit. I always start on the emergency battery to check it, then switch over to the main battery for normal operations. I don't use any vacuum advance on the distributor. I took the distributor to a racing shop and had them open up the mechanical advance to 35 degrees. I changed to lighter springs to get the advance all in by 3000 RPM. I can start the engine with about zero advance and have the full advance curve in at cruise RPM. An aircraft engine runs at a higher power setting than an automobile. If the you leave the vacuum advance hooked up you may not know where you are on the vacuum portion of the advance curve. At high altitude with wide open throttle, all the vacuum advance would be removed. Therefore, the total advance may be less than you want for cruise. I think a mechanical advance system takes away all the guess work in knowing what advance you have at a particular RPM. If you do use the vacuum advance, a vacuum gauge may be a good instrument to use. It also would be useful for knowing when the power valve opens in the carburetor. A MAP does not provide manifold vacuum information unless you know what the atmospheric pressure is in the engine compartment.

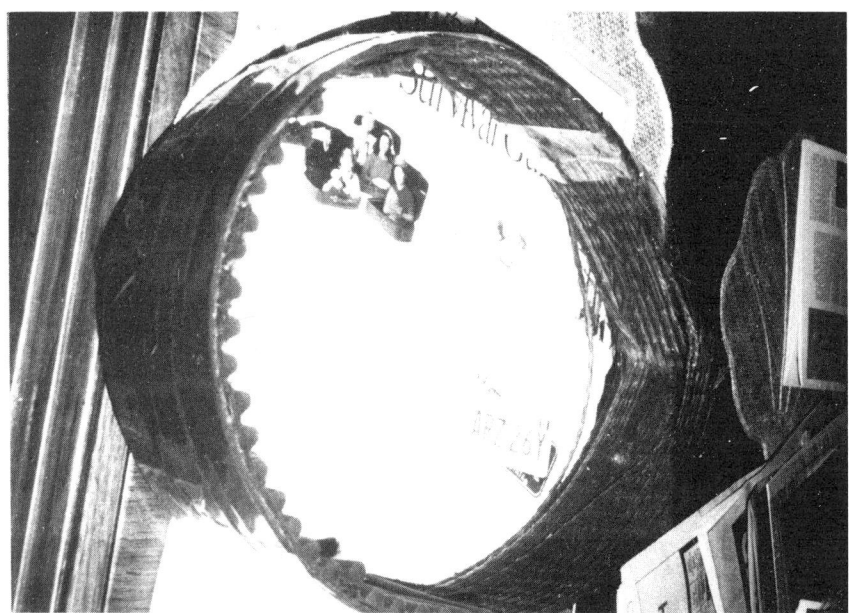

Belt failure after 80 hours of operation. Evidence points to the lack of sprocket hard anodizing causing the sprocket cogs to cut through the belt fibers allowing the belt cogs to be stripped off the belt.

COOLING

The water pump that comes with the engine is a long shaft type. I traded it for a short type at a local parts store to reduce the overall length of the engine. The starter is a Hamburg geared unit that is much lighter and smaller than the stock OEM part. I put on a 7 quart Moroso oil pan that has a baffle and a windage tray to prevent slosh in the base. The exhaust system are stacks that come out and turn back 45 degrees.

The cooling system used a GM cross flow radiator, engine thermostat is removed, a one pint expansion tank located high in the firewall and a automotive type recovery tank that is vented overboard. The radiator was modified by removing the transmission cooler, moving the outlet to a lower location and installing a petcock on the top to let out trapped air. There is a normal temperature gage in the intake manifold plus an additional temperature gage in the radiator return line. I can watch the engine warm up, see the water from the radiator begin to warm up and monitor the temperature change across the radiator during flight. This has worked very well. I do not monitor pressure. The higher pressure cap on the expansion tank helps to keep steam pockets in the head smaller. This is protection against a hot spot causing detonation.

The ducting in and out of the radiator is important. The inlet is 5.5 by 22 inches. This totals 121 in^2. The inlet scoop gets wider as the air passes aft, toward the radiator. Also, the radiator has only one third of its vertical dimension below the original aircraft "mole" line. The two thirds is up in the aircraft. The top of the air duct slopes up to the top of the radiator. This forms a large expansion chamber in front of the radiator. The reason for this is to slow down the air as it flows through the radiator. The exhaust duct is shaped to create a low pressure area behind the radiator to increase air flow across the radiator. I have tufted the intake and exhaust and taken videos in flight. The air flow seems to be very smooth in front of the inlet scoop but the air coming out the outlet is a little turbulent. I believe I can reduce the size of the exhaust opening and clean up that area some.

WEIGHTS

The weight worked out as follows:
Engine, dry, complete with redrive- 465 pounds
Total aircraft ready to fly, no fuel- 1675 pounds
CG 10.8 inches aft of leading edge

With me, my wife, 60 pounds baggage, full fuel, gross weight is 2330 pounds
CG is 16.8 inches aft of leading edge

That loading places me at the top aft corner of the box.

DATA

Data accumulation is a an essential aspect of the experimental auto engine conversion movement. A data base takes the place of, and in some ways is better than, a controlled test. To give you an idea of what it would take to conduct a controlled test consider a 2,000 hour test on an engine and drive that is conducted by starting the engine and warming it up for 15 minutes, then run at full power for 15 minutes, then reduced to cruise power for 2 hours and 15 minutes then reduced to idle power for 15 minutes then shutting down. This would simulate a 4 hour flight. If this was repeated until the 2,000 hours was accumulated, and if the

NOMENCLATURE	MAKE	MODEL	PART NUMBER	COST	SOURCE
ALTIMETER	KOLLSMAN	TYPE C-12	671BK-010	on hand	PA-25
AMP METER				on hand	PA-25
C/B		RESET ONLY	8803K	$104	NEWARK
C/B		IOA,20A	W58XB1A4A	$22	WICKS
CARB	HOLLEY	BRL-750	4778-2	$274	SUMMIT
COG BELT	POLY	966-14M-85	9293 0102	$266	BELTED AIR
ELT	ACK		E-01-TSO-C9	$225	SUPERFLITE
ENCODER	AMERI	AK-350	AK-350	part of IFF	EASTERN AV
ENGINE	CHEV	350HO	10185072	$3,000	RALEY
ENGINE PAN	MOROSO	7QT CHEEK	20205	$172	R & E RACING
FAN BELT	DAYCO	DYNAFLEX	15423	$5	PEP-BOYS
FUEL GAUGE	STEW-WARN	ELECT	82303	$35	SPRUCE
FUEL PRESS	KOLLSMAN	0-30	0-30	$65	CENTURY
FUEL PUMP	AIR	MECHANICAL	AIR 40987	$24	CENTRAL
FUEL PUMP	CARTER	ELECTRIC	P4070	$56	R & E RACING
FUEL SENDER	BORG-WARN	UNIVERSAL	R8925	$35	SPRUCE
GENERATOR				$172	CENTRAL
IAS	AFROMARINE	40-180		on hand	PA-25
INTERCOM	VAL	DUAL P-T-K	801010	$90	VAL
LIGHT FLASHE	NORTH AMER	HT-BEAM FL	AFK-12S	$50	J.C. WHITNEY
MAG COMPAS	ATRPATH	WISKY	G-2300	on hand	PA-25
MAG-WIRE	PEP-BOYS	SPITREL STA	1273	$30	PEP-BOYS
MAP	U.S.GAUGE	10-35	AW2 3/4	$75	CENTURY
MTR MOUNT	RPM	FRONT	RPM 31-2123	$3	CENTRAL
OAT	ROCHESTER	OUTSIDE	A006000	$28	WAG-AERO
OIL PRESS/TE	PIPER			on hand	PA25
PROP	McCAULEY	IA200	FM9047	$1,200	PROPELLA MAN
RADIATOR	GM	CROSS-FLOW		$40	RON
RDTR HOSE	GAT	PUMP INLET	GAT 20390	$12	CENTRAL
RED STROBE	NORTH AMER	CHEAP		$30	J.C. WHITNEY
REDUCTION	BELTED AIR	350	350 SB	$1,800	BELTED AIR
SHOCK CORD		GEAR	128OHD	$54	UNIVAIR
SLAVE CYLIND	CLEVE	FRONT BREA	10-20	$150	SPRUCE
SOLENOID		CONTTNOUS	T214001	$26	WAG-AERO
STARTER	HAMBURGER	GEARED	5000	$187	BEDDANT ENG
STROB LIGHT	UNIVERSAL	UNIVERSAL	FS4400-14V-	$100	SUPERELITE
TAIL WHEEL	SCOTT	SPRINGS	3239	$19	UNIVAIR
TECH	AUTO-METER	0-8K	ATM-1799	$74	SUMMIT
TIRES	MCRY	800X6	800-6	$124	SUPERFLITE
TRANSPONDER	NARCO	AT 150	03606-0300	$1,039	EASTERN
TURN & BANK	R.C.ALLEN	12V	12P61	$165	CENTURY
VHF ANTENNA	COMANT	BOTTOM MOU	805002	$90	VAL
VHF TRANSCEI	VAL	COM 760	801000	$495	VAL
VHF TRAY			802000	$100	VAL
VOLTMETER	AUTO-METER	10-16 DC	ATM-2591	$26	SUMMIT
VVI	GARWIN	4K+-	22-200	$115	CENTURY
WATER PUMP	GM	SHORT	OEM 1354	$21	CENTRAL
WATER TEMP	AUTO METER	60-240	ATM-2533	$30	SUMMIT
WHEEL BEARIN			1-825-TO446	$100	MOTION IND
BATTERY, 12 VOLT, 25 AMP HOUR				on hand	

Builder's parts summary.

oil was changed ever 50 rs, and if this was accomplished during a normal 40 hour week work schedule, it would take a year, cost $1120 in oil, $30,800 in fuel at $1.40 per gallon, plus a $3,000 engine and a $3,000 reduction drive. When this was finished, it would have cost one man-year, $37,920 and the outcome would be statistically insignificant because it would be a sample of one. The point is that field use and a good data base, would be of great value. We are planning to gather as much information as we can with our own tests, gather as much data from other people as we can and build a reliable total package. The entire auto conversion community needs to work toward and participate in this development effort.

PERFORMANCE

The airplane now has more power but is heavier. According to Piper, a production 150 HP Pawnee will cruise at about 95 MPH. Take-off roll is about 500 feet empty and much longer fully loaded. Climb rate is about 600 FPM, as I recall. My airplane is draggy and built for toughness, not speed. However, with half fuel and one pilot, it will get off in about 400 feet, climb at 1200 FPM, and easily cruise at 120 MPH. At full gross, the take-off roll is about 500 feet and climb is less than 1000 FPM but cruise remains the same. The fuel consumption is not to my liking. It is up around 11 GPH at the present. I expect some improvement when I solve the carburetor mixture problem. I can land at 60 MPH and get it stopped in less than 500 feet. The flaps act as speed brakes. They reduce stall speed 1 MPH but are very effective in steep approaches and short rollouts. The plane has an unusual characteristic during slips with flaps. With about half to two-thirds rudder, speed at 80 MPH, the nose will hunt in pitch and act like it wants to depart normal flight. This is a benign condition and is mentioned in the production Pawnee handbook as a "normal" condition.

SUMMARY

The 350 HO from the manufacturer is a great engine. I know it can be developed for aircraft use. I hope I have impressed on anyone planning to use it that it is not a turn key operation. My conversion still needs some additional development. These problems have not resulted in any major incidents, but I have melted aluminum inside the engine and I have had it belch black smoke trying to get into Big Bear at 8,500 ft. More exciting than that, it was about three flying hours after I left Deep Creek in the mountains of Idaho that the belt broke. We were over open terrain and there was no problem landing. I am continuing to develop my installation and will be happy to pass on any lessons I have learned to anyone who is interested. I also hope this article will result in people who have solutions to my problems calling and sharing their knowledge with me. **JE**

	MOUNTAIN CLIMBER	OLD PAWNEE
EMPTY WEIGHT	1675	1250
ENGINE WEIGHT	465	360
CG EMPTY	10.8" AFT	10.8" AFT
FULL GROSS WEIGHT	2330	2330
CG AT GROSS	16.8	16.8
T.O. ROLL LIGHT WEIGHT	250FT	700FT
T.O. ROLL AT MAX GROSS	500FT	TOO SCARY
CLIMB	1200FPM	500FPM
FUEL CONSUMPTION	11GPH	7.5GPH
LANDING DISTANCE	500FT	440FT
CRUISE	120MPH	95MPH

Performance comparison.

Chevrolet V/8 Longevity Report at 300 Hours

Ray Ward
8607 Southwest Freeway
Houston Texas 77074
(713) 777 0133

Engine problems at 300 hours prompted a tear down and inspection of the 475 HP Chevrolet V/8 installed in my BD Super Sport (as seen at Oshkosh and reported in Sport Aviation, February 1993.

During a flight in March of 1995 a rough engine prompted a precautionary landing at Sinton, Texas. An EGT check while still in the pattern revealed only six cylinders firing. More on this incident later. Over the last four years of operation this was the fourth time that a serious problem occurred with the engine. In all four cases the airplane continued to fly to a safe precautionary landing with six or seven cylinders flying. On two occasions, a cylinder was out of action when a rocker stud broke. This problem was finally fixed when it was discovered that the push rods were originally installed with incorrect lengths. Being too long by 0.40 inches, they caused the rocker arms to sit too high toward the top of the studs which caused instability and eventual stud failure.

Two other times, including the current incident, the valve spring retainer broke, allowing the valve to drop and be hit by the piston. The intake valve then broke off at the stem and finally punched a hole in the piston. Metal chips sucked back through the intake manifold grounded the spark plug in an adjacent cylinder; thus, I landed with a V/6. To its credit, the engine continued to run for the time (some 5-10 minutes) that it took to descend to the landing at Sinton. Multi-cylinder V/8 engines do offer an additional measure of safety under such emergency situations.

It would be pointless to continue experimentation with my Chevrolet conversion unless we could be sure this valve spring problem could be solved. Fortunately, I came across an experienced engine machinist who pointed out the solution to my recurring problem. It amounts to this: All race engine builders are sold on the idea of after market 10 degree keepers on the valves because they have a bigger footprint, or contact area. This type of keeper is needed only on powerful, high RPM engines with high pressure value springs. The bigger footprint prevents the keeper from extruding though the valve spring retainer on these powerful engines, By powerful, I mean 4 to 5000 horsepower V/8s! However, when a larger hole is cut in the valve spring retainer to accommodate the 10 degree keepers less metal remains for sufficient strength on the smaller diameter valve spring retainers as found on the small block Chevy. I believe the answer to my problem is to go back to the standard Chevy 7 degree keepers and retainers which will be about twice as strong as the original setup.

In some of my previous articles (BD 4 newsletter) I mentioned that it was important to find a good engine machine shop to build the engine. These four valve train problems attest to the truth of that statement. In my opinion, the auto engine conversion approach is still a valid one despite the serious mistakes made by the original engine builder. I fully expect that the Chevrolet 350 HO engine as factory built by Chevrolet is free of these development problems and I recommend that anyone needing 345 HP and willing to accept 70 pounds more weight consider using the stock engine.

Inspection also showed that the custom flexplate had stress cracks terminating at the three slots. A custom .25 inch thick solid part eliminating the slots is now on order. This problem is similar to that seen in 3.8 liter Ford engine conversion flexplates flown by Blanton STOL builders and Bayard DuPont in his Defiant. It is believed by some that runout and gyroscopic forces interact to cause this phenomenon. An additional steel disk bolted to the Ford flexplate is being tested by various builders. The flexplate in the automobile application is stiffened by the attachment of the transmission torque converter and does not exhibit this problem.

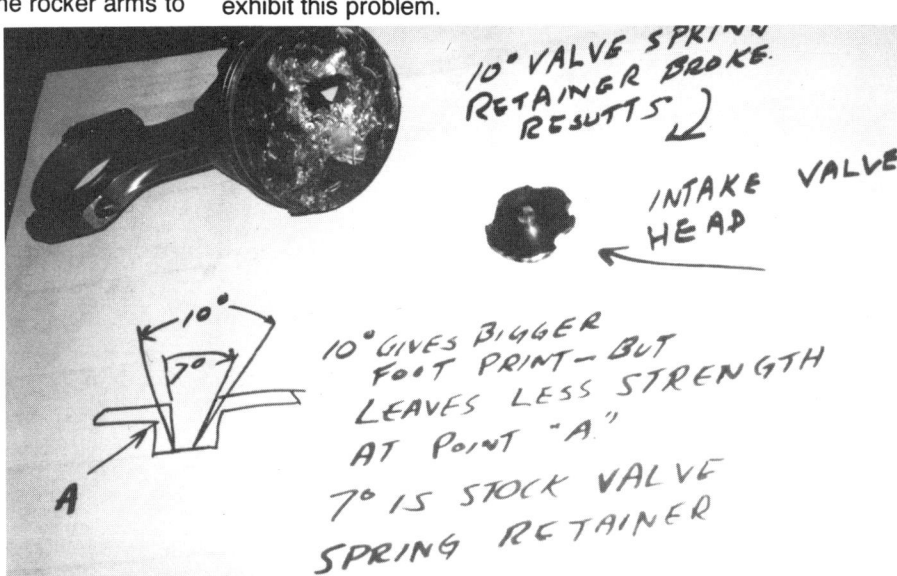

One goal of this long term Chevy experiment is to determine if this engine is economically competitive with the certified aircraft engines which cost about 3-4 times as much (see Sport Aviation February 1993). Time between overhauls has not been established on this engine but we have a better idea now after 300 hours of field testing.

In conclusion, I still believe the conversion of the Chevrolet to an aircraft engine is viable because at 300 hours the bearings and other parts of the engine and chain redrive were examined and given a clean bill of health. I cannot help but assume that a stock factory engine or one built up correctly the first time would go to 1000 hours before the first major overhaul, with top overhauls performed at 500 and 1500 hours. When compared to the 2000 hour TBO of a certified powerplant, the end cost of four Chevy overhauls should only be about 25 percent that of the comparable certified aircraft engine. **RW**

Ray advises he will provide additional articles to Contact! and will be giving a forum presentation at Oshkosh 95. He also publishes a 40 page guide covering his 4 years of experience, covering sources, part numbers, graphs, redrives.,etc. ($32) For more on keepers and retainers read pages 123-125 of David Vizard's book on camshafts and valvetrains-Motorbooks (1-800 826 6600). **MCM**

PROPELLER DRIVE SYSTEMS AND TORSIONAL VIBRATION

Donald P. Hessenaur
Antelope Hills
16 Cienaga Drive
Prescott Arizona 86301
(602) 778 0707

Don brings his unique experience in testing of aircraft to these pages. A graduate of Northrup University and life long interest in new aeronautical concepts, his concerns for safety and progress of auto engine conversions prompted this article. Hopefully his information will create a better awareness of the engineering challenge facing experimenters in modern aircraft powerplant development. We welcome additional articles on the subject. MCM

As aircraft engine prices continue to rise beyond the reach of most who would like to build and fly their own aircraft, many are turning to alternate power sources. This is not a new phenomena. From the Wright brothers on, many have designed, built or converted engines to aircraft use. At one time or another engines have been used from automobiles, motorcycles, outboard motors and even snowmobiles, with varying degrees of success or failure.

AUTO ENGINE CONVERSIONS

Today many automotive engine conversions are appearing on the aviation scene. They are definitely a viable alternative. The automotive engine today is very advanced technically and relatively low in cost when compared to Lycomings and/or Continentals. Unfortunately, automotive engines are designed and optimized for the automobile and not for aircraft. Generally, auto engines operate at a much higher RPM. The torsional vibration characteristics of a given engine, connected to a transmission, drive train and wheels, are quite different from that of the same engine, connected to an aircraft propeller. The damping action of the tires on the road and the inertia effects of the mass of the automobile are not even close to the damping/inertia effects of a propeller turning in air.

TORSIONAL RESONANCE

In recent years, I have developed a concern that many of the individuals and/or companies involved in the development of auto conversions do not seem to have an understanding of the problem of torsional vibration. I'm not saying that this is true in every case. Some appear to have a profound knowledge of torsional vibration but others seem to dismiss it as a minor problem. They feel all they need to do is just stick in a rubber damper, freewheel clutch or some other quick fix and maybe the problem will go away. My experience has been that torsional vibration just doesn't go away. It can be the life or death of an entire project, not only technically, but it can also lead to a financial black hole for the individuals or company involved! The potential for success in such a project would be much higher if the individuals involved knew what they were dealing with and would use valid aircraft engineering procedures during the design and development of an engine. Creativity and experimentation should be encouraged but one must also realize that 9 times out of 10, what was thought to be a new and original solution to a problem has probably been tried by a number of people in the past. The same laws of physics, dealing with torsional vibration, are still in effect today, as they were 20 to 50 years ago. I would be the first to admit, I do not have all the knowledge on vibration in rotating systems. Nevertheless, I have had some unique experiences with torsionals and other associated vibration problems. It is my hope that by relating them, someone will be saved from some grief.

FIRSTHAND EXPERIENCE

In the past I have had the opportunity to have worked on three interesting projects, each of which involved torsional vibration problems to one degree or another. The first was the Avian 2-180 gyroplane which was developed in Georgetown, Ontario, Canada in the early 60's. The performance and handling of this gyroplane has not been surpassed by any other in its class to this day. The second was the BD-5 "Micro" kit aircraft developed in Newton, Kansas by Jim Bede in the early 70's. The third was the RotorWay RW-133 helicopter engine developed by B.J. Schramm in the mid-70's.

AVIAN VIBRATION ENCOUNTERS

The Avian gyrocopter was a pusher design with a ducted Hartzell propeller. The rotor was an articulated, 3 bladed, semi-rigid, high inertia design. For this reason, a substantial drive system was required for rotor spin-up. On the original prototypes there was a 3 inch wide, heavy duty, square toothed belt that transmitted engine power from a smaller DriveR sprocket to a large DriveN sprocket at the base of the rotor hub. Occasionally, during a spin-up, this belt was stretched by some horrendous load so that the belt teeth would no longer engage the teeth on the DriveR sprocket, causing the belt to ride up on top of the sprocket teeth. The resulting high load on the sprockets caused the structure that supported the bearings to collapse. (A round toothed HTD type belt would have eliminated the riding up problem of the square tooth belt but it had not as yet been developed in the early 60's.)

About this time, Avian started to develop and build their last prototype. It was totally redesigned and much improved in every way over the previous prototypes. One area of improvement was the rotor spin-up system. The upper belt width was increased to 4 inch and the structure that supported the sprocket bearings was made more substantial. A new hydraulic multi-plate clutch was designed with more torque capacity and mounted over the engine near the propeller end. This improved drive gave the new prototype absolutely phenomenal jump take-off performance. The gyroplane was capable of jump take-offs to

50 ft. The problem of the upper belt drive had been solved by the brute strength approach, using a stiffer support structure along with a wider belt and sprockets. Nevertheless, as time went on other problems started to show up. The lower belt drive, that took power off the engine, seemed to flop a lot at various times. After a few spin-ups the clutch would become very hot and eventually turn blue in color. If the cowling was removed, immediately after a spin-up, the clutch would appear to have been red hot. The torsional loads going through the drive system appeared to be much higher than the original analytical numbers indicated. I had heard about torsional vibration during my college years but at the time it never hit me that the problem with the drive system involved torsional vibration. As far as I know, the clutch problem was never solved.

FLUTTER & VIBRATION TESTING

While at Avian I was assigned to work with a consultant who was hired to do ground vibration testing and a flutter analysis on our new prototype. This was a relatively new technology and he was the only person who did this kind of work at the time. Although he was from Toronto, Canada, he worked throughout the American aerospace industry. His equipment included a number of vibration shakers that were attached to the airframe, making it vibrate at various input frequencies. The shakers were controlled from a control panel. A number of magnetic vibration sensors were attached to the airframe, along with one that was hand held, so it could be moved around. These pickups were used to sense the resulting amplitudes of vibration at various points on the airframe. This information was then displayed on an oscilloscope. He was able to adjust the input frequency, so that various parts of the airframe would vibrate at their respective resonance frequency. The needles on the instruments, the door handle, the plexiglass in the side window, a duct support strut or the rudder could all be made to vibrate at their individual resonance frequencies. It was really weird. In fact, it appeared downright mysterious to see this engineer adjust the input frequency and shake any part he wished on the airframe. He made a frequency survey of everything that resonated on the gyroplane. This was used to determine if anything resonated within the operating frequency range of the engine, drive system or rotor, that might cause a failure in the future. With this analysis, we found a number of parts that needed to be stiffened or redesigned so they would not vibrate or flutter in flight.

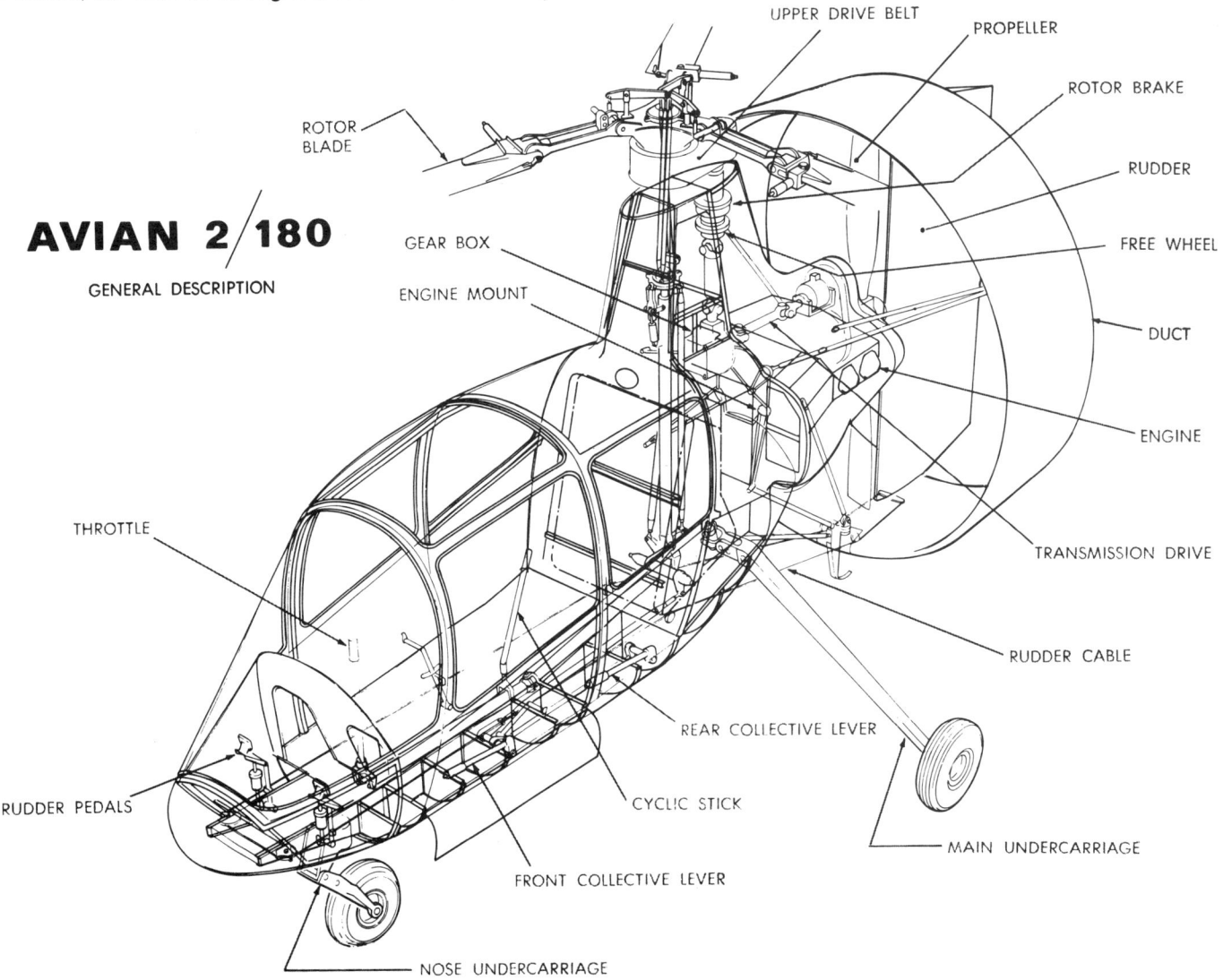

AVIAN 2/180
GENERAL DESCRIPTION

During the 3 days I worked with this engineer as his assistant, I received a wealth of knowledge about vibration and resonance in aircraft.

BEDE AIRCRAFT

I was interviewed and offered an engineering position with Bede Aircraft by Burt Rutan. My employment started on July 6, 1972. After the Avian years, my interest in the entire subject of vibration expanded and I became fully aware of torsional problems in rotating systems. Many spare hours were spent hitting engineering texts and reading numerous articles on the subject, including many by Molt Taylor. I was really curious as to how they had solved the torsional vibration problem in the BD-5.

During the first week at Bede, Les Berven was flying the BD-5 every day. When it would come down after a flight, the mechanics would open up the engine compartment to take a look to see what was going on. It wasn't long before I realized there were a number of problems they were trying to deal with. The engine was having cooling and mixture problems, while trying to maintain the EGTs and CHTs below redline. The problem that really caught my attention was the overheating of the belt and sheaves. At that time they were running a snowmobile belt on variable ratio sheaves. The overheating clutch at Avian came to mind when I noticed these sheaves were quite discolored from the high temperatures involved.

TORSIONALS AT BEDE

During the following weeks they seemed to be doing a lot of ground testing. I had been assigned the responsibility for the weight and balance control for the BD-5 program, as I had done at Avian. Like the Avian 2-180, the BD-5 had a severe aft CG problem. One day, they had been running the BD-5's engine on the ground for a period of time and all of a sudden there was a big explosion. The belt had disintegrated, with pieces all over the tarmac. These pieces of belt were as hard and brittle as bakelite plastic. As soon as I saw what happened, I knew the problem was torsional resonance. I mentioned this to the other engineers and they looked at me sort of strange. They thought I was joking and did not pay too much attention to my comment, since I was just the new engineer.

HTD UNIROYAL BELT

Soon after the belt incident, some belt people were invited to come and look at our situation. The representatives brought a number of belts such as standard V, poly V and various toothed belts. One belt that I had never seen before, caught my eye. It was a unique round toothed belt, an 8mm HTD belt. After all the problems associated with square toothed belts at Avian, when I saw that round toothed belt, I knew this was an exceptional design. It could be used on an aircraft and give much more reliability than one with square teeth. Best of all, the power loss was extremely low, since it ran at low friction levels, resulting in considerably less heat buildup.

About this time I was asked to start investigating various belt systems and get involved in the drive system and engine installation problems. Along with this assignment, I continued to head up a weight reduction program, particularly in the aft part of the ship. It was my intent to not only solve the drive system and engine installation problems but to save weight in those areas as well. Anything that could be done to remove weight, aft of the CG, would permit lead to be removed from the nose. So I started working on a new drive system, using the 8mm HTD belt. Once it was put together and running, it seemed at first to perform quite well, but I soon noticed there was a lot of flapping of the belt at certain RPMs. We tightened the belt as much as we could but the flapping just seemed to persist. Nevertheless, it seemed to solve the problem for the moment and Les Berven put in a lot of flight time. Every once in a while we would have a failure but we would replace or repair the part and keep going. During this time we actually had more of a problem with the snowmobile engine. Various magazines were coming out with articles on the BD-5. It was becoming very popular and kit sales were climbing.

ENGINE MOUNT FAILURE

One significant event that occurred was the failure of the engine mount due to fatigue. The mount was welded up chrome-moly tubing and had a strange crystallized break. When I saw it, I knew it had something to do with the torsional vibration that was still in the system. A new, heavier piece of tubing was welded in to make it stronger and beefier but during the next few flights it proceeded to break again. At this point a new heavier engine mount was fabricated and installed but soon after another failure occurred. This time the engine mount survived but the sheet metal channels that transferred the engine load into the fuselage, along with portions of the fuselage itself, were severely cracked. Also, numerous rivets were starting to work loose in the airframe. All that we had accomplished was to transfer and chase the problem from one area to another. The torsional problem was still with us. The biggest problem I had was that no one would believe me. At least the belt was holding up and no longer a problem.

MYSTERIOUS SHAFT FAILURE

The drive system difficulties were totally overwhelmed by the problems with the two stroke engine. To keep the planes flying for demonstrations and air shows, we were forced to place the highest priority on keeping the engines running. (If only the Rotex 582 had been available, we might have eliminated a major problem with the BD-5!) Cooling was a real difficult problem and one evening I and many of the engineering personnel stayed almost all night to find a solution. Burt was really frustrated with this cooling problem. In a last ditch effort, he got one of the giant

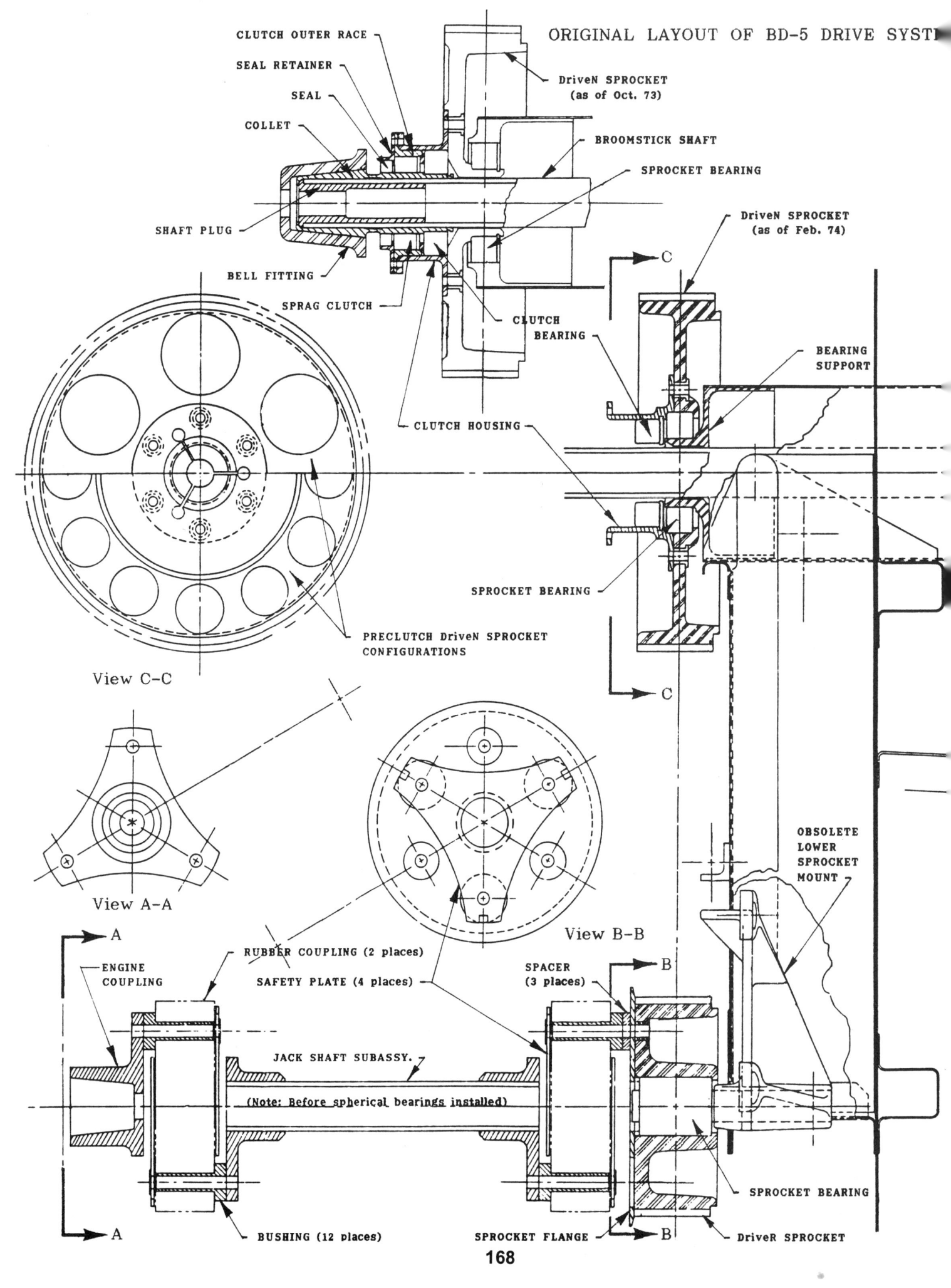

portable electric shop fans, hooked it up to a large duct and then attached the duct to the open BD-5 engine compartment. He felt if we couldn't get the engine to cool properly with this fan, there was no way we were going to get it to cool in the air. We ran the engine at full power and cycled the engine off and on a number of times. All of a sudden, during one of the runs, something broke loose and the engine immediately went up to a very high RPM and seized. We found the propeller could turn freely without turning the drive belt or the engine. We looked all around and through everywhere and couldn't see where any break had occurred. No shaft had broken, nothing had failed that we could see. It was a real mystery.

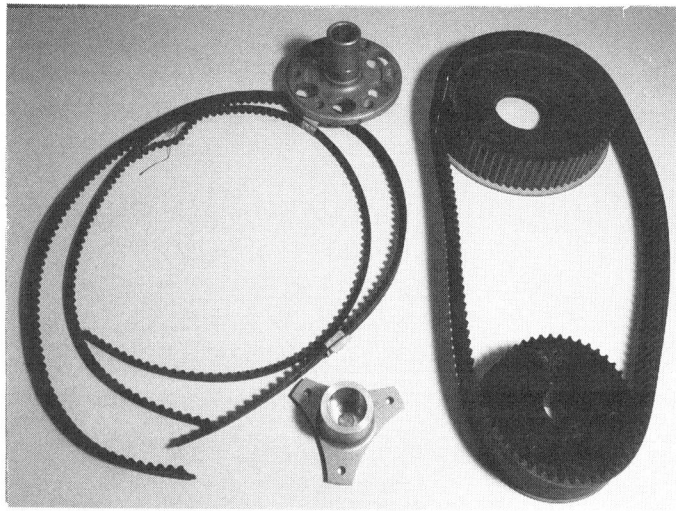

BD-5 HTD belt drive components. Tests were run on various belt widths to establish useful life recommendations.

The drive system we had at that time used the HTD belt with the original upper main shaft. If I remember correctly, the O.D. of this shaft was about 3 inch and approximately 4 foot long. I am not sure of the wall thickness but it may have been .125 inch. This shaft had a machined bearing support fitting on each end, with the propeller mounted on the rear hub fitting and the HTD sprocket mounted on the front sprocket fitting. These end fittings were mounted to the inside diameter of the shaft, with three AN-4 bolts on each end, screwed radially into the shaft. The bolts were quite short so the threads went right up to the head, placing threads right in the shearing intersection between the fittings and the shaft itself. It was these 3 bolts at each end that transferred the torque from the HTD sprocket to the propeller hub at the rear. This was the configuration of the upper shaft when I arrived at Bede. Having bolts transfer torque in shear through the threaded area is not exactly a textbook design procedure but it had held for a year or more.

TORSIONALS STRIKE AGAIN

So we got the mechanic and started taking everything apart. When we pulled out the upper shaft, we found that all 6 bolts, 3 on each end, had failed precisely at the same time. Now this was weird or like black magic. You would think that if something was going to fail, maybe the rear end would be ready to go but the front end might break loose first, relieving the load, then the back end would not fail. But no, both ends of the 4 foot shaft failed precisely at the same time, with all 6 bolts failing the same way. They were all crystallized and appeared to have been working in there for sometime.

By this time, Burt and the others had become believers in torsional resonance. Immediately we got on the phone, woke Jim Bede up and clued him in on what had happened. Within a week or so, Jim brought in Al Beaufrere, a vibration expert from Long Island. I was assigned to work with him to solve the torsional problem. He came up with two different test drive systems. They were quite heavy and complicated but they did give us a direction in which to go. While Al was at Bede, I tried to learn all I could from him. This knowledge, combined with what I had picked up previously, gave us the insight that eventually led to a solution to our dilemma.

THE MOLT TAYLOR DYNAFLEX SYSTEM

After Al left, I started to design a new drive system, using the principles learned. It was about this time that many of the engineering staff were moved into the new Bede Product Development building. I was given an office with another engineer named Larry Heuburger, who I believe helped design the Derringer twin engine airplane. Larry knew Molt Taylor quite well and was able to persuade Jim Bede to let him design and build a small dynaflex coupling out of aluminum. I must say he did a beautiful job and came up with a real neat small dynaflex, which mounted right onto the engine. They used it with the HTD belt system and large upper shaft that I had running at the time. It appeared to successfully dampen out the torsional vibration. At the same time they were testing the dynaflex system, I was coming right along with the design and fabrication of my new drive system.

I forget just how long they flew the Molt Taylor system but one day an inflight failure occurred and Les had to dead stick the plane in. With all the engine problems, this was quite a common occurrence, so it was no big deal. It was found that the dynaflex had broken loose from the engine. A closer examination revealed that the crankshaft had broken clean off. The break was completely crystallized and it was difficult to discern whether it was a torsional break or a lateral break. We were not able to determine why this failure occurred. It may have been due to the rocking couple of the engine. Unfortunately, this failure ended further work on the dynaflex system.

THE BROOMSTICK SHAFT

I had come to the conclusion, based on the information from Al Beaufrere, that we needed to drastically lower the torsional frequency of the drive system by lowering its torsional spring constant. Stan Welles, our stress analyst, came up with a 6061-T6 aluminum shaft, with an outside diameter of 1 inch and a .095 inch wall thickness. This shaft came to be known as our "broomstick shaft". The same tubing size was used for both the upper main shaft and the lower jackshaft. Very soft rubber, donut type flexible joints were mounted on each end of the jackshaft. This lower shaft assembly transferred the power from the engine to the lower HTD sprocket while allowing for engine motion. The sprockets were made of a rag-filled bakelite type plastic by the Budd Corporation and are no longer available. They had wear characteristics, designed to be compatible with the HTD belt and had considerably less wear than anodized aluminum sprockets. Also, they were lighter in weight. The lower sprocket was mounted on an adjustable casting that was mounted on the rear bulkhead of the engine compartment. The belt went up to the upper sprocket, which was attached to the forward end of the upper shaft.

The drive ratio was 1.6 to 1.0. Bearings within the sprockets took the belt loads, which were relatively low since the belt was not preloaded. There was no need to have a tight belt with a torsionally soft system. Since the upper main shaft was only 1 inch OD, two bearings were mounted along its length to tune out lateral vibrations. Another bearing was mounted on the rear hub to take out the propeller loads. (Later, after I left Bede, Dan Cooney added another bearing towards the rear, to more effectively take out gyroscopic propeller loads.)

FRICTION JOINTS

The shaft end fittings on the lower jackshaft and the propeller hub on the upper shaft were attached with press/shrink friction fits. The fitting for the upper sprocket on the forward end of the upper shaft was a removable collet type friction fit. These friction fits were more than sufficient to carry the torque of the engine and were one of the design guidelines given to me by Al Beaufrere for joints subject to torsional vibration. This was a very, very lightweight system. The weight of the entire drive system was reduced by over 40 percent and this went a long way towards solving the aft GC problem in the BD-5. For test purposes, the prototype drive systems were designed and fabricated with zero safety factors. The first version of the "broomstick" drive did not have a freewheel clutch and when we first ran the system, we found out there was still much to be learned before the torsional problem was solved.

LOW FREQUENCY TORSIONALS

The vibration characteristics of the new prototype system was quite different from the previous systems. One could tell something radical had changed. The resonant point had been lowered below 600 RPM, the starting RPM of the engine. With such a low frequency and high amplitude of vibration, it was possible to visually hear and see the resonance occurring. One could see torque reversals occurring at the prop. The aircraft would violently shudder and shake itself apart, if allowed to continue. As the throttle was advanced, the RPM would get hung-up at the torsional point. Les could give it full throttle and it would just soak up all the energy from the engine, preventing the RPM from going through the torsional barrier. Occasionally, more by chance than anything, the RPM would pass through the resonance and then become super, super smooth. Likewise, when the engine was shut down, the RPM would momentarily hang-up at the resonance point. All of a sudden, the plane would shudder and shake until all the energy of momentum was used up. Then the propeller would stop rather abruptly. It was the weirdest thing.

Although we were successful in moving the torsional resonance point to a lower energy level, we had not eliminated the problem. Numerous experiments and tests were tried. At times, we were able to go into resonance with the ignition and fuel off, using only the electric starter. About the same amount of shudder and vibration was produced through the aircraft when excited by the engine compression alone, as it did when the engine was running under its own power in resonance. At this point, we started to realize we had something here that was really mysterious. This led to an experiment where we replaced the two spark plugs with compression release valves, hooked up to a common control handle. With the engine and system turning over using the starter alone, the vibration and shudder in the plane instantly disappeared and became as smooth as silk, as soon as we opened the compression release valves. As soon as we would close the valves, the vibration and shudder would return. We could start and stop the resonance at will. Clearly, it could be seen that the resonance could be excited by compression strokes alone. The thing that blew our minds was, that even when the input energy was low, the output loads were still as destructive to the airframe as when the input energy was high.

INFINITE LOADS?

When we started to look into torsional resonance theory we found an explanation. Without any damping in the system, theoretically the peak load at resonance reaches infinity. That's why the input load had very little effect on the output load. Now many have said that it was just theoretical and there is no situation where any material would have zero damping qualities. Well, how much was the damping effect? We do not really know at this point. If the damping were to bring the load down to one tenth of infinity, that would still be a big load. What I am getting at is this. The loads are very high during resonance and are not entirely dependent on the input load.

THE FREEWHEEL CLUTCH

The idea for the freewheel clutch came from our machinist, Ray Johnson, and I must give him the credit.

He came in one day and told me that when he was a kid, his dad had a thrashing machine on the farm. They would run the belt from the tractor to the thrashing machine and it had a freewheel device on it, so that any vibration coming from the old two cylinder John Deere would be somehow taken care of. The minute he said "freewheel clutch", it rang a bell. After previously seeing the oscillating torque reversals of the prop, I knew we needed some way to allow a torque reversal to occur without the bounce back. I had been looking at centrifugal clutches, manual clutches, etc. that could be used to disengage and allow some slip. We even tried a test with a super loose belt with idler pulleys but the slop still wasn't enough. The torsional amplitude was just too great at the low system frequency we were dealing with.

Immediately after Ray mentioned the freewheel clutch, I started investigating and found a Borg Warner clutch that was used in automatic transmissions. It was a double cage, full phasing, sprag clutch. The double cage caused all the little cams inside to engage precisely at the same time. I had previously had experience with freewheel roller type clutches at Avian but we had problems with the brinelling of the clutch races, when one roller would engage before the others and momentarily take the full torque, causing eventual clutch failure. The double cage, full phasing, sprag clutch solved this problem.

It took a month or two to design and have the clutch parts made. The clutch itself was mounted on the front of the upper plastic sprocket. It had its own bearing to maintain the clutch concentricity. The inner clutch race was integral with the collet that transferred the torque to the upper 1" shaft. The heat treat for the clutch races and collet was somewhat complicated and expensive but at that point we weren't looking at the cost, as much as just trying to find something that was lightweight and workable.

At that time, I was under tremendous pressure at Bede to try to get this system working. After a lot of hard work the parts were made. Everything went together beautifully and the clutch was mounted in the airplane. About that time, our engine company had some problems and we could not get any engines. I had the drive system in the ship shortly after New Years but it sat until sometime in March, before we were able to get an engine to test it. So, I was sitting that whole time wondering if it would work. Finally the engine arrived. The mechanics installed it and started it up. It was super smooth. There was no sign of any shudder or vibration in the aircraft due to torsionals. The first tests were so successful that Les took the plane up. He came back with a big smile on his face and told us it was the smoothest drive system he had ever flown. Jim was relieved and happy, like, real happy! We had solved the torsional problem.

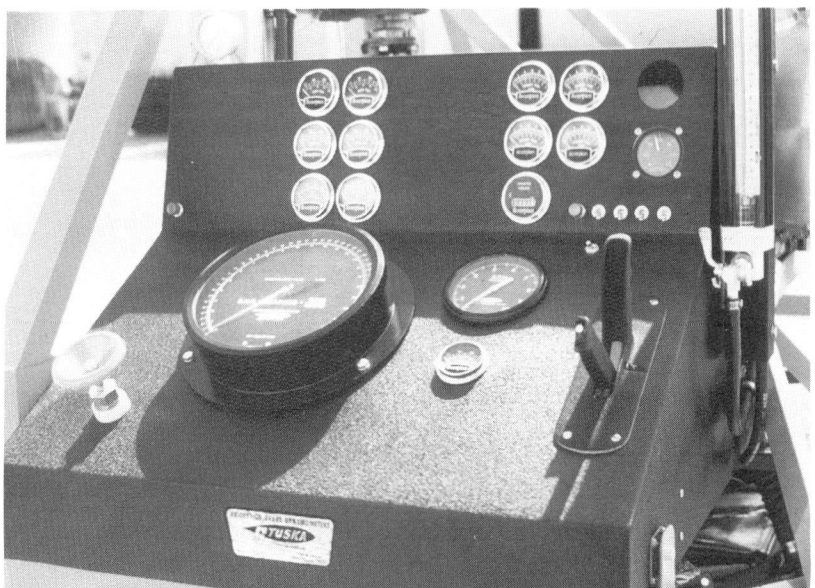

Dyno test stand used for RotorWay engine development, air show demonstrations, and production engine run-ins.

DUAL FREQUENCY SYSTEM

According to theory, when the stiffness of a given system goes to zero, the resonance point also goes to zero RPM. With the freewheel clutch, the torsional frequency would go to zero whenever a torque reversal occurred. For that moment in time, the RPM would then be above the resonance point and the engine would have no problem powering up into the operating RPM range. In this regard, the BD-5 soft system with the freewheel clutch was a passive dual frequency system, that functioned much like the active dual frequency system used in the Continental Tiara family of geared aircraft engines.

FREEWHEEL CLUTCH - PARTIAL SOLUTION!

It must be understood that the freewheel clutch is only part of the solution to the torsional resonance problem. Lowering the resonant point below the starting RPM of the engine is the other essential part of the solution. Simply installing a freewheel clutch in a system, where the torsional resonance point is still in the operating range, may give the appearance of success for the short term but not for the long term. In a low frequency, torsionally soft system like that developed at Bede, the clutch chatter frequency is low and the amplitude of rotational vibration is high, as the RPM passes through the resonance point. Also, this occurs at the point when the engine is just about to start and the energy level in the system is quite low. It is true, the loads can be very high at the resonance point, but this occurs during a torque reversal which disengages the clutch and causes these loads to go to zero. These characteristics are good for long clutch life, which means a smaller clutch with a lower capacity is all that is required. This saves both weight and cost. On the other hand, in a higher frequency, torsionally hard system, the clutch chatter frequency is high and the amplitude of rotational vibration is low. With this type of system, the energy level is high. These characteristics tend to shorten clutch life. A system of this type will require a clutch with a much higher capacity, since torsional resonance is still a problem. The clutch and all other drive system components will then be subject to limited life considerations. I know of many who have tried using a freewheel clutch in a hard system as the solution to the torsional resonance problem, but I do not know any who have succeeded in the long term! For these reasons, I can not recommend the use of a freewheel clutch with a torsionally hard system.

LATERAL VIBRATION PROBLEMS

Although we had solved the torsional vibration problem at Bede, lateral vibration problems still needed to be addressed. They had set up a test stand in an old gutted mobile home beside the Bede shop and the engine mechanic, who was an expert in two-cycle engines, was doing a lot of experimenting to improve the engine. One day he and his assistant were working right beside the engine, in front of everything. The lower jackshaft was turning about 6000 RPM and he was adjusting the carburetors when he stepped aside slightly to get a wrench. All of a sudden there was a big explosion and a hole appeared in the wall of the test stand building. The lower jackshaft had broken loose from its rubber couplings and was hurled like a missile through the wall. It travelled almost to the next building, nearly going through the wing of a Beech 18 and then burying itself in the Kansas gumbo mud. The energy involved was just unbelievable. If the mechanic had been standing where he had been just seconds before, he would have been killed. Once the system was put back together, we ran it with a strobe light on the jackshaft. Immediately, we saw that the lower jackshaft was not maintaining its concentricity with the engine crank on the forward end nor

Exerpt from professional Rotorway operation and maintenance manual which contains detailed step by step instructions. This photo shows a setup for checking drive pulley run-out. A model publication for auto conversions.

161 photos and 10 drawings throughout the manual fully illustrate the operation and maintenance of the RW133 engine. This picture suggests a acceptable method for installing the engine in the airframe.

the sprocket on the aft end. The rubber couplings were too soft. The system was modified to use spherical bearings on each end to locate the lower jackshaft so it would not start this lateral vibration due to the centrifugal force acting on the shaft. This change solved this problem.

There was also a lateral vibration problem with the lower sprocket. After hooking up the strobe light, we found the lower sprocket support was putting an undulating wave of vibration into the rear bulkhead of the engine compartment. This explained why all the rivets on the outside skin at that bulkhead were always coming loose. One day this vibration was particularly bad and we had Burt come by to take at look it. When he saw it, he just looked sort of shocked, turned white and went off mumbling something about not letting Les see this because we'll never get him to fly it again. I think it was at that point that he sort of gave up. This, along with the many other problems with the engine, seemed to be the last straw as far as Burt was concerned. It was about a week or two later that both Burt and I left Bede Aircraft. Before my last day, I turned the design responsibility for the drive system over to our landing gear man, Al Thompson. I gave him instructions on how to redesign the lower sprocket mount. He did a superb job and the new mount solved the lateral resonance problem in the lower sprocket.

ROTORWAY
While at RotorWay, B.J. Schramm assigned me the job of designing and building a water dynamometer test stand for the RW-133 helicopter engine. The engine was mounted vertically, just like it was in the helicopter. The dynamometer had a fairly heavy, high inertia rotor and was connected to the engine by a drive shaft with two universal joints. This test stand was used not only to develop the engine but to later fully test and run each customer's engine before delivery. The test stand was designed and built with a good appearance so that it could be used at Oshkosh and other airshows to demonstrate the engine, showing the actual torque and horsepower output to potential customers.

One day, while testing the engine, all hell broke loose. The jackshaft with the two universals had broken off the engine and was flailing around, shaking the test stand quite violently. If I had been anywhere close, I would not be among the living today. We found that the upper part of the crankshaft had broken off. The break was all crystalline and it had the characteristics of a torsional fatigue failure. I mentioned to B.J. that the crank material sure looked strange. That was when I found out the crank was cast iron. The RotorWay engine was based on the Volkswagon engine but was highly modified to produce the power required for the helicopter. Although the Volks engine had a forged crank, the RotorWay engine required a special crank with a long stroke. Since the engine was only in the development phase, B.J. used a cast iron crank. Soon after this failure, B.J. had new forged crank developed to replace the cast iron crank. One thing for sure, a cast iron crankshaft is not the best way to go, when trying to deal with torsional vibration.

CLUTCH SPRING SOLUTION
B.J. got in touch with the people who manufactured the dynamometer and found out that hooking a 4-cylinder engine to one of these dynos can be a problem. Any engine that produces 2 power strokes per revolution is bad news when it comes to torsional vibration, we were told. They suggested installing clutch springs, from an automobile clutch assembly, between the engine and the water dynamometer to solve this torsional problem. (This is the same idea Lou Ross uses on his gear boxes.) We also put a guard around the jackshaft so that if another failure occurred it would be contained. I saw the test stand a few years ago and it appeared to be in good shape and still in use. The spring idea seemed to have worked out.

DRIVE SYSTEM CONFIGURATIONS
Any time a propeller is connected to an engine in any way other than directly to the crank, it would be wise to realize that torsional vibration can be a problem. Basically, there are three propeller drive system configurations:

1. Propeller speed-reduction unit alone
2. Propeller speed-reduction unit with a shaft drive
3. Propeller shaft drive alone

TORSIONAL RESONANCE FREQUENCY FACTORS

$$k = \frac{T}{a} = \frac{\pi d^4 G}{32L}$$

Where k is the torsional spring constant, i.e. the torque (T) required to produce an angle of twist (a) of 1 radian in the shaft to which the propeller is attached.

Where d is the diameter of the propeller shaft.

Where G is the shearing modulus of elasticity of the shaft material.

Where L is the length of the shaft in inches.

$$f = \frac{1}{2\pi}\sqrt{\frac{k}{I}} = \frac{1}{2\pi}\sqrt{\frac{\pi d^4 G}{32IL}}$$

Where f is the frequency of the torsional vibration.

Where I is the mass moment of inertia of the propeller.

From the above formula it can be seen that:

- The torsional frequency can be lowered by:

    1. Decreasing the diameter of the shaft/s (d).
    2. Decreasing the shearing modulus of elasticity of the shaft material (G).
    3. Increasing the mass moment of inertia of the prop (I).
    4. Increasing the length of the shaft (L).

- The torsional frequency can be raised by:

    1. Increasing the diameter of the shaft/s (d).
    2. Increasing the shearing modulus of elasticity of the shaft material (G).
    3. Decreasing the mass moment of inertia of the prop (I).
    4. Decreasing the length of the shaft (L).

- Torsional resonance frequency is affected, more or less, by the propeller, engine crankshaft, connecting rods, pistons and every part in between such as a flywheel, gears, belts and to a lesser extent, the valve train and accessories.

TYPES OF DRIVE SYSTEMS
1. A dampened system is one that uses a vibration damper to lower the resonant loads to more acceptable levels, while leaving the torsional resonance frequency within the operating RPM range of the engine. A dampened system can be used with a propeller speed-reduction unit and/or a drive shaft. (i.e. Molt Taylor)

2. A hard system is one that has a high torsional spring constant (k) and no slop from the propeller through to the engine crankshaft (maximum rigidity). The torsional

problem is overcome by brute strength and maximum stiffness. If a belt is used it should be tensioned as per manufacturer's recommendations. (i.e. Dave Blanton type belt drive system) A hard system becomes prohibitively heavy when used with a shaft drive because of the high torsional loads involved.

3. A soft system is one that has a low torsional spring constant (k) from the propeller through to the engine crankshaft so as to move the torsional resonance frequency below the operating RPM range and preferably below the starting RPM of the engine. A soft system, using a propeller speed-reduction unit alone (no drive shaft) with a sufficiently low torsional spring constant, would be difficult to design because of space, weight and engineering limitations. A soft system with a drive shaft, if properly designed and tested, has the potential of being the lightest and most reliable of all the systems discussed. (i.e. BD-5 belt/shaft drive system)

DESIGN CRITERIA RECOMMENDATIONS

1. The more cylinders the better!

2. Engine Crankshaft:
- 1st choice > forged
- 2nd choice> machined billet
- Not the best choice > cast iron

3. Joints in Rotating Parts:
- Use joints that transfer torque by friction where possible (i.e. shrink, press &/or tapered fits)
- Splines are not the best choice in hard systems.
- If bolted joints (i.e. flanged) are used, do not use the allowable bolt shear strength to carry the engine torque through the joint. Instead, size the bolts so that they can be tightened to produce sufficient bolt tension so the engine torque can be transferred through the joint by the resulting friction between the flanges (Note: It would not be a good idea to have any bolt threads in the vicinity of the joint.)

4. System Slop:
- In a "hard system" (i.e. Dave Blanton type system) avoid any slop in the system. Use a belt with proper tension as per manufacturer's recommendations.

- In a "soft system" (i.e. the BD-5 system) some slop can be tolerated. If a toothed belt (i.e. HTD) is used, it can be run loose. Also, gears and splines are less critical (i.e. the Continental Tiara aircraft engine). If a silent link type chain is used, chain tension would be less critical.

5. Torsional Spring Constant of the System:
- In a "hard system" (i.e. Dave Blanton type system) the main design criteria should be to achieve a high torsional spring constant, without adding excessive weight. The torsional problem is overcome by brute strength and maximum stiffness.

- In a "soft system" (i.e. the BD-5 system) the main design criteria should be to achieve a low torsional spring constant while meeting the torque requirements of the engine with a moderate safety factor. The torsional spring constant should be low enough to move the torsional resonance frequency below the starting RPM of the engine.

- The torsional spring constant can be lowered by decreasing the diameter of the shaft/s, decreasing the shearing modulus of elasticity of the shaft material, increasing the mass moment of inertia of the propeller and by increasing the length of the shaft/s.

6. Freewheel Clutch:
- Use only a double cage, full phasing, sprag type clutch. This type of clutch works well with a "soft system".

- Roller and uncaged spring-loaded type freewheel clutches are not recommended.

- It is not recommended to use a freewheel type clutch with a "hard system". The higher energy level of resonance, in this type of system, will eventually destroy the clutch, even though the engine RPM only passes through the resonance when going up to or down from the normal operating speed.

7. Cantilever Shafts:
- Mounting overhung belt sprockets or gears on cantilevered shafts should be avoided, particularly on a "hard system".

- If a design requires an overhung sprocket, keep the offset and the belt width to a minimum.

SUMMARY

BECOME FULLY INFORMED BEFORE TACKLING TORSIONALS! It would be advisable to develop a good base of knowledge before becoming too involved in torsional problems. Most intuitive solutions are the opposite of what should actually be done when torsional resonance is involved. It is my hope that this article will bring a degree of caution to experimenters and will encourage them to seek out more knowledge on the subject before they jump in and waste a lot of their time and money.

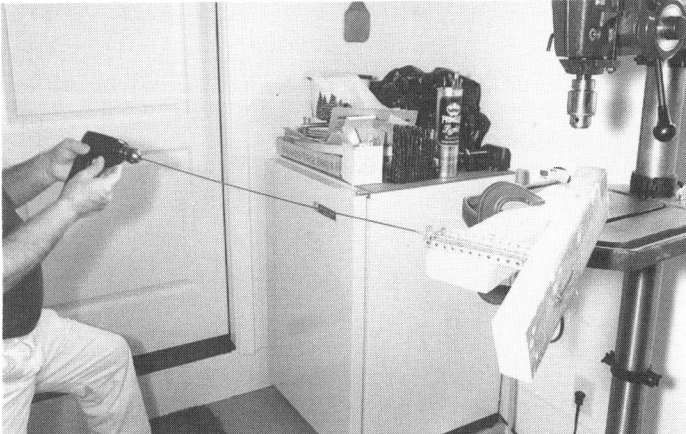

Demonstration of torsional resonance effects. A 2X4 representing the inertia of a propeller is powered by a cordless drill motor through a 3/32 inch piano wire ("soft" system). One end of the rod is bent 90 degrees and stapled securely to the wood. Energy is applied by short, rapid trigger squeezes to simulate engine power pulses. Torsional effects are visual and are heard from the slippage of the shaft in the chuck and torque reversal clicking of the gears.

Ignition Coil Failures
Wiley's SPAD Powerplant

Steve Parkman
SWAG Aeromotive
2521 North Fairview
Tucson Arizona 85705
(520) 622 6910

SAFETY ALERT It has been brought to my attention that most of the automobile engine conversions are using either the stock ignition system or a replacement high performance coil. This by itself is not a major problem if the manufacturers' mounting procedures are followed. Two types of coils are in basic use. The first and most widely used is the dry coil. This coil can be mounted in any position as it uses ambient air for its cooling. The first suggestion would be to duplicate the stock position and orientation as it was mounted in the automobile. If this is not possible due to cowling constraints then one should try to keep the coil assembly away from high heat sources. It is highly advisable to keep a flow of cool air across any coil assembly.

When this type of coil overheats it will break down and start misfiring or not firing at all. This can also lead to a overload condition on the ignition electronic module and cause failure of the switching electronics. In plain English, it will stop running.

The second type of coil is the oil filled version that looks like a cylinder. Quite a few different cooling oils are being used but they all have the net result which is to keep the wire windings cool. The other difference is that this coil must be mounted in the upright position as this keeps the highest current draw portion of the coil covered with oil. It is also highly recommended to keep a cool air flow across the coil to prevent it from misfiring and causing the electronic ignition from failing. Remember you are the design engineer when you install a automotive engine in an airplane. Do all of your research on the ground so you don't have to look for a off-field place to put it down.

SPAD EARLY BIRD Dennis Wiley, designer of the Early Bird Jenny, is at it again. He is now well under way with a new design of a tube & fabric 80 percent scale SPAD. I have seen the preliminary drawings for this airframe and am very impressed with the straightforward layout and the construction techniques.

With this new airframe design he wanted to have the top speed quite a bit faster then the Rotax powered Jenny and also wanted to have a light weight four stroke engine that could be bought and maintained for a reasonable price. Dennis investigated the various possiblities and came up with the Geo Metro 3 cylinder engine. This engine is quite small in size and light weight for the 68 HP it produces.

The total engine weight with a new intake manifold and Lou Ross' new gearbox came out to 100 pounds. The overall height is 24 inches, width is 12 inches and the length is 24 inches with the gear reduction.

There are several drawbacks to using this engine as is. The first is that the distributor is mounted on the transmission end of the head in a horizontal position. The second is that the intake manifold extends out 16 inches from the head. The last problem to overcome is that this engine produces its horsepower at 4800 RPM.

To reduce the RPM at the propeller Lou Ross has designed a smaller redrive unit for the Geo Metro. It is the typical Ross planetary gear reduction design layout as his other other units except that it is reduced in size and is designed for 100 HP engines. For more information on this unit give Lou or Chris a call at their shop.

The distributor/space problem was solved by its removal and replacement with a simple aluminum plug. The overall width was reduced by a new manifold, fabricated from aluminum using a air body for multi-port fuel injection. This manifold extends only 5 inches from the head leaving more then adequate side clearance. The fuel injectors mount directly into the head on the bosses that Geo was kind enough to include in the original castings. To replace the distributor, crank fired ignition is being used, taking timing off the flywheel. This gives up to 36 degrees of advance under full load and automatic retard when needed for load conditions. The multi-port fuel injection is the SWAG standard unit that also is being used on 4, 6, 8, cylinder engines. It uses a Manifold Absolute Pressure sensor for altitude compensation, a Throttle Position Sensor for RPM desired, a Coolant Temperature Sensor along with an Air Intake Sensor and an O_2 Sensor to determine the fuel ratio. With the SWAG multi-port fuel injection this engine will produce 68 Horsepower at 4800 RPM consuming 2.8 GPH, estimated using the manufacturer's figures.

Al tube manifold, SWAG electronic injection and ignition, and the Ross redrive/adapter housing make the Geo engine a strong competitor. A bare A-65 weighs 171#. With addition of geared starter, alternator, radiator, and electronics the Geo engine weighs 130 #.

Converting and Flying the FORD 3.8 Liter V/6 Engine

Jerry and David Schweitzer
504 Jefferson Street
Box 66
Bedford Iowa 50833
(712) 523 2772

Jerry Schweitzer, EAA # 30570, has been involved with EAA and experimental aircraft since 1968. After earning commercial and instrument ratings, Jerry completed a plans-built Pitts Special in 1972; this first effort is still flying in Sweden. Since that time, he has pursued a variety of aircraft and aviation interests. During the past six years Jerry has devoted his time to the conversion and flight testing of the Ford 3.8 L V/6 engine. This effort required the exclusion of all other aviation interests but has resulted in the completion of N21S and the pending completion of a RV-6 which employs the latest innovations in the Ford 3.8 L V/6 conversion. MCM

Since the original research and test flying of the 3.8 Liter Ford V/6 began some ten years ago under the direction of David Blanton of Javelin Aircraft the evolution of this powerplant from automotive to aircraft use has been a persistent and productive effort. Many builders and experimenters have willingly shared their data with others in an unselfish manner, their efforts are truly representative of the spirit of EAA. The early history of this effort has been recorded and is available as a builder's manual from Javelin Aircraft. It is a very "informal" presentation which reads much like a diary. It is a record of the immense effort to sort out reliable information. It documents both successes and failures in the conversion process. This approach is useful since documentation of failure helps define the direction of new inquiry; thus, time and resources are conserved, and the learning curve remains steep.

Blanton's original research combines with the recent experimentation and innovation of dedicated builders throughout the country to form the foundation for the successful conversion of the Ford 3.8 L V/6. Mr. Brantley Harrison, owner of Engines by Brantley, markets a second source for a builders manual. His effort is very concise, deals only with the current state of the art, and is quite complete in describing each powerplant modification required to produce a flyable 3.8 L V/6. Many enhancements have become available and have been satisfactorily test flown in N21S in the past two years. These changes make this powerplant and redrive combination a viable option for use on airframes requiring 170-200 H.P. All of these innovations are available through Mr. Harrison in the form of complete ready to fly engines or individual components. Builders who incorporate all the recent 3.8 L V/6 innovations can expect to invest a total of approximately $4,000 in a completed powerplant.

The total list of aftermarket components used internally to convert the 3.8 L Ford V/6 is very short. Michigan Bearing main and rod bearings, anti-pump up lifters, longer push rods, and Roush forged pistons complete the list. The Roush pistons produce a 9:1 compression ratio, the same ratio now utilized with this block and crankshaft in the Ford Taurus. All other internal components are stock Ford parts. At this time, there appears to be no Ford component in use that is not adequate for long-term service in this application. Factory original standard "unground" crankshafts are used exclusively and are fitted with standard sized main and rod bearings. We have yet to find or hear of any crankshaft which has worn out of standard tolerance. This speaks very well for the durability for the bottom end of this engine.

ENGINE WEIGHT

Engine weight is often alluded to as a deterrent in the use of the Ford 3.8 L V/6 engine. It is indeed a concern and it is an issue which must be considered when choosing an airframe. There have been several weight saving changes during the past two years including the lightweight reduction drive from Northwest Aero, a lightweight geared starter from Ford, availability of machined aluminum pulleys, etc. More recently, a 3.8 L V/6 engine and 1.6:1 redrive have been prepared for a new RV-6 airframe. This package employs these weight saving components. To illustrate considerable progress the engine and redrive complete with wiring, carburetor, oil filter, block heater, vacuum pump, starter, 60 amp. alternator, motor mount, and radiator weighs 393 pounds.

Individual Accessory Weights	
Starter	7 lbs.
60 Amp. Alternator	10 lbs.
Vacuum Pump	7 lbs.

It is appropriate to compare some of the performance and physical data of N21S to the factory specifications of the PA 22 from which it was, in large part, derived. It should be noted that the increased empty weight of N21S is a combination of the effect of a published unequipped weight of a new PA 22 derived from the Piper Owner's Manual and the rebuilt salvage which incorporates considerably more structure. The N21S additions include: full gyro panel with 35 pounds of radio gear, a second battery, heavier sound/heat insulation and interior trim, plus the increased weight of the engine and propeller combination. Since so many questions concerning weight and balance arise when this converted engine is employed the actual weight and balance chart for N21S is provided in this article.

In addition, it should be noted that N21S retains the basic size of the salvage plane from which it was built. The popular notion that the fuselage must be lengthened from 24 to 36 inches suggested in earlier reports to properly balance the heavier Ford V/6 is without factual basis. The only concession to the added weight mounted in the engine compartment was the relocation of the batteries to a location immediately behind the rear wall of the baggage compartment. These batteries and solenoids are accessible for service by hinging the rear wall upward.

COMPARATIVE PERFORMANCE DATA

	PA22-150 Landplane	N21S V-6 STOL
Engine	Lyc. O-320	Ford 3.8L V/6 232 in^2
HP & RPM	150 @ 2700	NA @ 4800*
Test Weight	2000	1890
Empty Weight	1100	1358
Wing Span	29.3	30
Wing Area	147.5 ft^2	159.5 ft^2
Length	20.6	21.5
Propeller	74 in	84 in
Wing load	13.5lbs/in^2	11.85 lbs/in^2
Vc(MPH)	132 @ 7k MSL	142 @ 8k MSL
Rate of climb	725 fpm	1076 fpm (avg. from 1190 - 8190 MSL)
Fuel Burn	9 GPH @ 75%	8 GPH @ 65%

*The author has no method to accurately determine horsepower; therefore, no number value has been assigned. Examination of this data which has been honestly and accurately collected and presented will be more meaningful than an arbitrarily chosen and presented value.

Many sets of existing plans for the V/6 STOL direct builders to lengthen the fuselage. This fuselage extension is appropriate if the builder understands that such a procedure is necessary to satisfy weight and balance requirements in accommodating a coolant radiator located behind the baggage area. Cooling problems associated with a rear fuselage radiator location are quite common considering the number of calls seeking help. While it may be possible to solve these problems a proven solution is to move the radiator under or behind the engine within the engine compartment!

PISTON FITS

All factory approved tolerances for internal engine components are maintained in this conversion with the exception of the cylinder-wall-to-piston clearance of the aftermarket Roush pistons. Roush publishes a required clearance to be observed with each set of pistons supplied as these these pistons require more clearance to operate efficiently. Therefore, the published Roush clearances must be observed for satisfactory operation and heat dissipation.

N21S had flown some 100 hours using stock Ford 8.8:1 pistons and cast iron rings before the author was aware that the forged Roush pistons were available. Although the engine had a completely successful operational history during this period, a decision was made to convert to the Roush product. This disassembly of the engine and measurement of all bearings and bores disclosed no appreciable wear. There was no sign of measurable wear or damage to the Ford pistons. The installation of the new Roush pistons occurred after the cylinders were honed to the correct diameter prescribed by Roush for this piston size. The engine was reassembled and has run satisfactorily thereafter with an average oil consumption of one quart per eleven hours of operation. At this date N21S has accumulated more than 200 hours with the Roush pistons.

In the past year it has come to my attention that several builders have chosen to ignore the published Roush tolerance requirements while assembling their engines with tighter cylinder to piston clearances. In every case, these engines have run excessively hot and have produced less than acceptable power as demonstrated by static RPM tests. In some cases cylinder wall damage resulted. If you have an piston fit in this manner, I encourage you to disassemble it now, hone the cylinders to the correct tolerances, and reassemble. This situation is applicable to other engine conversions. Experimenters replacing pistons should observe the recommendations of the piston manufacturer since piston designs and materials do vary considerably.

ENGINE WIRING

The electrical schematic illustrated on page 9 is typical to the systems in use. It seems to offer good reliability and redundancy. Some can argue that a system with a single distributor, even though that distributor operates on a simple magnetic pick-up system and has no ignition points, is a compromise in redundancy when compared to two magneto configurations common to certified, air-cooled engines. However, those of us who ride behind the Lycoming O-320-H2AD and many of the IO-540 and IO-720 engines are dependent on the single gear and shaft to operate dual magnetos.

ENGINE TIMING

An early entry in the Blanton Builder's Manual which was later corrected by him in his revised manual of 1991, advised builders to use a combination of mechanical and vacuum advance to accomplish a 28 degree total advance condition when under full power or at cruise RPM. Although this advice was recognized as flawed and every effort has been made to clarify the issue I continue to receive inquiries from builders who are unable to achieve a reliable advance. In each case the solution has been to abandon the use of vacuum advance, block off the vacuum port, and accomplish all of the advance to the maximum of 28 degrees BTDC with use of standard counterweights and lighter springs. This process is well documented in the revised Blanton manual and The Engine Builder's Manual by Brantley Harrison. Engine builders working with the early Blanton information should avail themselves of the revised edition.

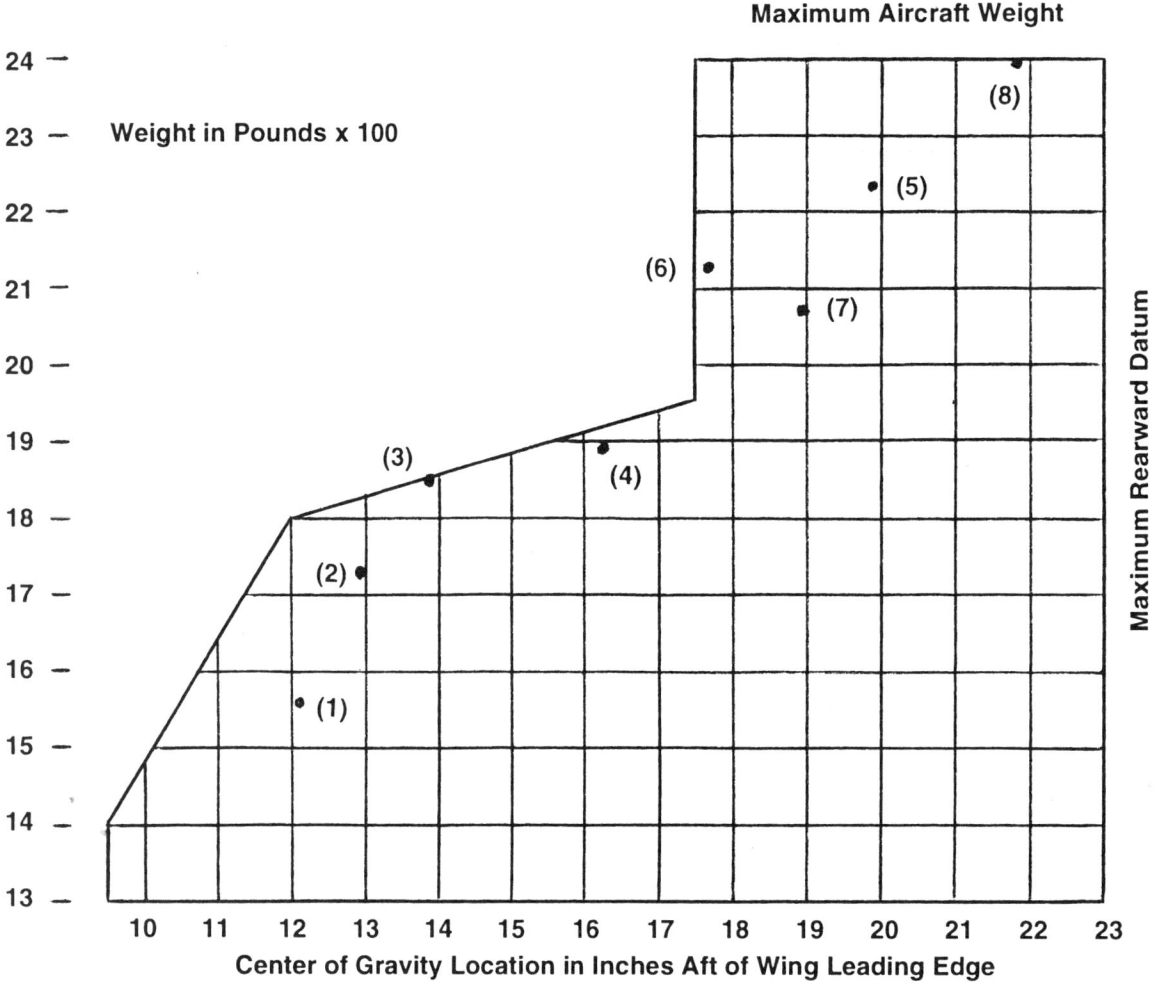

	WEIGHT	ARM	MOMENT	WEIGHT	ARM	MOMENT	WEIGHT	ARM	MOMENT	WEIGHT	ARM	MOMENT
A/C empty	1358	(#1)	14661	1358	(#2)	14661	1358	(#3)	14661	1358	(#4)	14661
P/Pass	170	21	3570	340	21	7140	340	21	7140	340	21	7140
Pass 1/2										170	49	8330
Fuel (main)	24	24	576	24	24	576	156	24	3744	24	24	576
Fuel (aux)												
Baggage												
Total	1552	12.11	18794.72	1722	12.99	22368.78	1854	13.77	25529.58	1892	16.21	30669.32
	WEIGHT	ARM	MOMENT	WEIGHT	ARM	MOMENT	WEIGHT	ARM	MOMENT	WEIGHT	ARM	MOMENT
A/C empty	1358	(#5)	14661	1358	(#6)	14661	1358	(#7)	14661	1358	(#8)	14661
P/Pass	340	21	7140	340	21	7140	340	21	7140	340	21	7140
Pass 1/2	170	49	8330	170	49	8330	340	49	16660	340	49	16660
Fuel (main)	216	24	5184	216	24	5184	24	24	576	216	24	5184
Fuel (aux)	48	49	2352	48	49	2352				48	49	2352
Baggage	100	67	6700							100	67	6700
Total	2232	19.87	44349.84	2132	17.66	37651.12	2062	18.93	39033.66	2402	21.93	52675.86

**Weight and Balance Calculations
for Differing Loading Conditions**

REDRIVE

The most recent advancements in belt-driven reduction drives available for this engine have come from Mr. Elwyn Johnson, owner of Northwest Aero Products. At this time, Mr. Johnson is continuing his research in a very aggressive effort to improve an already reliable system. These improvements include weight reduction through the use of lighter, more durable aluminum alloys, state-of-the-art machining techniques and streamlining for a more aerodynamically correct frontal profile. Many other innovations are under study and will be publicized as they prove viable through trial and testing.

While several reduction ratios are available the two most common found in use on the Ford 3.8 L V/6 are 1.6:1 and 2:1. Obviously, each ratio has a specific operational range which dictates the appropriate redrive-to-airframe combination. The 2:1 ratio is normally used on slow moving (100-125 knot) airframes which can accommodate propellers from 76-90 inches in length turning at 2000 to 2300 RPM in cruise configuration. These units would have good short-field, and rate-of-climb characteristics. Some examples would include most float planes of 2500 pound gross weight or less, the Skybolt, Sportsman 2 + 2, V/6 STOL, etc.

The 1.6:1 reduction drive is used with lighter and faster airframes. Examples of this application would include the Glassair, the RV series, BD-4, etc. These combinations would utilize propeller lengths of up to 74 inches turning 2500 to 2700 RPM in cruise configuration.

The driver sprocket must run true to the crankshaft centerline to prevent adverse bearing and belt loads. A dial micrometer as shown is used to check runout and to determine the amount of materal removal from the sprocket's flywheel face.

This photo shows the surpentine belt routing of Schweitzer's RV-6 engine. Clockwisee from the crank is the smog pump (converted to produce instrument vacuum), alternator, idler and water pump. Note redundant water pump belt and FORD oil intercooler.

Assembly of the reduction unit to the engine block requires no machining and is accomplished with the use of six 10mm bolts. The bottom sprocket will be mounted interfacing with the front of the flywheel using the original Ford flywheel fastener locations. Only very minor alterations are made to the back face of the sprocket to correct any run-out or "wobble" exceeding .001 inch at the front face of the sprocket when it is attached to the crankshaft flange and the assembly is turned. This run-out can be easily identified with the use of a dial micrometer and is corrected by removing small amounts of metal from the sprocket until the proper mounting fit is achieved. A typical installation would involve mounting and removal of the sprocket 6 - 8 times while making small adjustments with a file or emery cloth thus bringing the assembly into acceptable tolerance. The total time to mount the drive unit and alter the bottom sprocket would not exceed 8 man hours.

Left side of the Schweitzer STOL engine compartment. Except for the redrive and propeller the engine installation looks entirely automotive. Engine is supported by a aircraft tube bed mount. .

Close up of the right side of the engine compartment. The horizontal mounted radiator and coolant hose is seen directly below the oil filter. Top quality spark plug wires eliminate electrical noise. Cabin heat is installed using automobile parts.

BELT REDRIVE AJUSTMENT

Adjustment of the reduction drive belt for correct tension and alignment is accomplished by the manipulation of two adjusting bolts. This process is not normally necessary after the initial setting, since the belt used in this application will not shrink or stretch. However, it is a very simple process and can easily be accomplished in a few minutes.

The Blanton Builder's Manual suggests a belt alignment procedure which has created some adjustment errors and damage to redrive bearings. A procedure which has been demonstrated to be appropriate is as follows: the belt must have some "slack" when the unit is in a cool down or pre-flight condition. This proper degree of looseness can be described as a condition whereby the operator can move the belt edge at least 3/16 inch with his fingertips. Observing safety precautions (such as solid footing, clear area, assistance, etc.) the engine can then be run to determine the track of the belt with reference to the front and rear driver sprocket stops. With the prop installed and the engine at full power, the position of the belt to the sprocket stops can be observed. In a full power condition, the belt should not run up against either stop. At very low power settings, the belt can run against a stop without damage. If the belt tension is checked after shut-down, it will be obvious that the drive sprockets and redrive frame members have expanded due to heating since most of the slack has disappeared. The redrive is cooled down completely. The belt tracking and tension is readjusted as needed so that after operation and while still hot the belt retains a small amount of "slack." Failure to allow for the expansion of the redrive components will result in damage or total destruction of the front engine main bearing and drive bearing. Flow of fresh air through the redrive will obviously minimize this expansion.

A pusher model of these reduction units is also available as well as other reduction ratios which have special applications for projects such has scaled Warbirds and vintage aircraft. All use the same ball bearing output shaft support systems which also supply thrust protection.

All engine attach points used in this conversion are also utilized in the automotive application. Machined aluminum adapters which bolt to these support positions are delivered as part of the reduction drive package. These adapters are attached to the engine block using three bolts each and will, in turn, be the support points which will mate with the builder supplied 4130 welded tube mount. Rubber insulating washers used with conical engine mounts are employed to combat vibration. Less than 1/4 inch of rotational movement will be noted between idle and full-throttle RPMs. Very little vibration is transferred through this mount to the airframe with this system.

Accessories used on this conversion are stock Ford items consisting of an alternator, light-weight geared starter, water pump and mechanical fuel pump, and for those who choose, a Ford smog pump reworked to produce vacuum for gyros is available. These accessories are surpentine belt driven. One belt is dedicated to the water pump while the second turns the water pump (redundancy) and all other accessories in use. No V-belts are used in the system. Stock Ford accessory brackets are suggested for use since there is a natural harmony between bracket and accessory necessary to achieve proper belt tension and alignment. Manufacturers spend considerable resources during engine packaging to eliminate fatigue cracking of brackets.

A second precaution must be observed to preserve the service life of these units. Since the operational envelope of the engine requires RPMs of 3900 to 4300 in cruise configuration the unaltered accessory system will cause the individual units to over speed and significantly shorten their useful life span. The solution to this problem is the installation of a lightweight, undersized, aluminum pulley. This pulley replaces the original much heavier and larger crankshaft pulley, thus reducing the speed of all accessories. The alternator and water pump benefit most. The alternator gains longer, smoother service from reduced RPMs. The water pump produces pressure and flow in the design RPM range, thus eliminating the likelihood of pump cavitation and decreased cooling performance.

OIL INTERCOOLER

A Ford intercooler is used in series with the full-flow oil filter to adjust the oil temperature. This unit has an application in both hot and cold environments. The oil cooling capacity of such a device is widely recognized, but of equal importance is the adjustment of oil temperature to a warmer value in cold environments. The intercooler on N21S adjusts the oil temperature to coolant temperature plus 44 degrees F. (measured at engine block high temperature site). This measured result suggests the intercooler has lowered lubricant temperatures 30-35 degrees F. This has, in fact, been documented by the use of a second temperature sensor located in the intercooler return galley. With operational temperatures stabilized in cruise configuration oil temperatures at this cool site will be coolant temperature plus or minus 10 degrees F. It is a system beautiful in its simplicity and effectiveness.

ENGINE COOLING

When used in any airframe, the Ford 3.8L V/6 will require the equivalent of an aluminum radiator with a two row, 1inch tube core measuring 320 in^2 exclusive of tanks and frame. This dimension assumes:

1. a 100 MPH climb speed is used when the ambient temperature exceeds 80 degrees F.
2. a mixture of 50% ethylene glycol coolant is used.
3. a minimum air inlet area of 80 in^2 is supplied.
4. a minimum air outlet area of 160 in^2 which is located in a low pressure area is utilized.
5. air inlet areas used originate in relatively undisturbed air flow.
6. the radiator is 100 percent baffled and not more than 2 in^2 in total air leaks exist.

Stabilized cruise values with horizontal radiator installation in N21S are:

Coolant Temperature = Ambient Temperature + 120 degrees F.
Oil Temperature = Coolant Temperature + 44 degrees F.

This oil temperature value is measured in the lifter galley at a point where the lubricant has passed through entire length of the block. This site is located on the engine block behind the flywheel. The removal of a 1/8 inch plug exposes the galley. This site was chosen since it will produce one of the highest oil temperature readings available. Other sites such as at the intercooler will produce oil temperatures 30 - 40 degrees F. cooler. These statistics assume:

1. **Full rich mixture (1400 degrees F. EGT) used with power settings of 70 percent or more.**
2. **Lean mixture (1550 degrees F. EGT) used with power settings less than 70 percent.**
3. **All engine specifications are as per <u>Harrison Builder's Manual</u>.**

COOLING CONFIGURATIONS

There are two radiator configurations with which the author has had personal experience:

1. the horizontal under engine location, and
2. the vertical behind engine, in front of firewall location.

This horizontal radiator employed in N21S utilizes air brought to it by directing fresh air into the bottom of the cowl and air brought into the front of the cowl, passing over the engine and exhaust pipes and finally through the radiator. The vertical position uses air brought into the cowl forward of the radiator. In both configurations, air having passed through the radiator core exits the cowl at the bottom rear.

Installations that have cooling air entering the cowling next to the spinner, directly forward of the front face of the drive, will have much of the potential airflow blocked by turbulence at the cowl opening. Installing a device to disrupt the turbulence formed against the front face of the drive will allow more air to enter the cowling. The device used on N21S is illustrated here as a suggested remedy.

Cooling air will enter the lower cowl much more efficiently if that opening originates in relatively undisturbed air. The "chin" visible on the lower cowling opening of N21S was a remedy for the turbulence at the entry point of this opening. While this may seem petty, the results of these changes were startling. The total reduction in coolant temperature at cruise was 15 degrees F. while the area of the lower opening was reduced 30 percent.

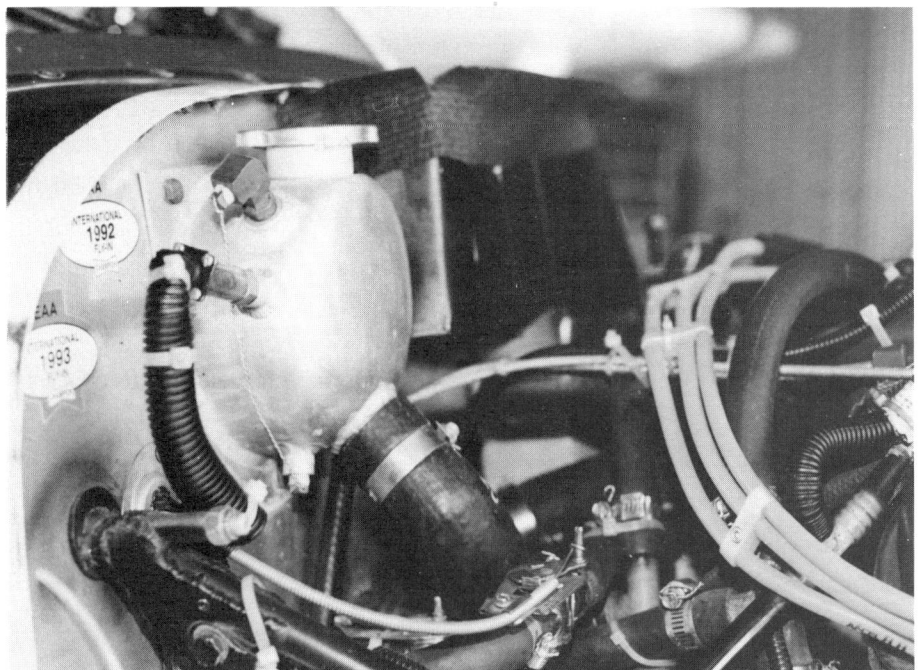

The surge tank is mounted on the firewall at the highest point of the installation. It eliminates the vapor lock problem discovered during the early development of the Ford 3.8 engine conversion.

As measured on N21S, air passing over the engine <u>before</u> exiting through the radiator core has a temperature of ambient plus 34 degrees F. Therefore, utilization of a fresh air source supplying cooling air at ambient temperature (passing through the radiator core before exposure to engine and exhaust pipe heat) would create a more efficient system, all other things being equal. The result could be a smaller inlet area, thus reducing cooling drag. At this time, the vertical position seems to be the most efficient configuration, however not all airframes can accommodate a lengthened engine mount which could provide the 6 inch space required for this configuration.

Vapor lock of the cooling system has been a major cause of inadequate cooling which affects some installations. The resolution of the problem is very simple since the cause is always poor or inadequate system design. The most common flaws encountered are:

1. **a coolant hose which rises above the level of the surge tank which will cause air and vapor to be trapped at the high point, which in turn will restrict passage of coolant at acceptable volume.**

2. **a surge tank installed lower than the water pump discharge point causing vapors to be held in hoses thus restricting coolant passage as above. Good design will accommodate accumulation of all vapors in the surge tank. To accomplish this, the surge tank must be the highest point in the system.**

CARBURATION CHANGES

The test aircraft was originally equipped with a 500 CFM Holley float-type carburetor utilizing an electronic leaning device which made it possible to adjust fuel-air mixture for smooth operation at lower altitudes (8,000-9,000 MSL) maximum when jetted for 2,000 MSL fields. Recently, a change to a 350 CFM model equipped with a manual leaning device has been responsible for a substantial reduction in fuel consumption and an even greater capacity for mixture adjustment as this device can be adjusted all the way to idle cut-off. It is now possible to operate the engine at 65 percent power while consuming 8 gallons/hour. No reduction in available power has been noted.

This powerplant installation utilizes a sheltered air source for combustion air. The system has been unaffected by exposure to moderate rain for extended periods of time and it has never been subject to carburetor icing even in the most suspect conditions (i.e.; outside air temperature 55 degrees F., dewpoint 53 degrees F., fog, etc.) Therefore, we believe the sheltered source is more practical than a fresh air source and carburetor heat even though the latter would result in the availability of additional power.

ENGINE OPERATION

Operation of this powerplant is quite straightforward. Start-up requires fuel valve on, electrical activation of one of the modules, a small amount of choke or prime with the carburetor accelerator pump in cold weather, and activation of the starter. The powerplant always starts on the first compression stroke. Climb and cruise operations require only manipulation of power and monitoring of engine instruments. Essentially, engine operation differs little from that of factory air-cooled engines.

Often test flight data gathered from powerplants and airframes, both "well used", is very enlightening and occasionally disappointing.

A test flight was conducted 5/21/93 specifically to document performance for this report. The following tables contains the pertinent information gathered during this flight.

GENERAL INFORMATION

Test Flight Site	Bedford Municipal Airport, Bedford, Iowa
Test Pilot	Jerry Schweitzer
Field Elevation	1190 MSL
Surface Temperature	70 degrees F.
Barometric Setting	29.90
Time	00.30 Z

AIRFRAME DATA

N21S	Conventional Gear High wing Monoplane - PA22/20
Configuration	very average aerodynamically.
Test Weight	1890 pounds
Propeller	MaCauley 84/72-Metal-Certified
Powerplant	Ford 3.8 L V/6 with 2:1 belted redrive
Radiator	Aluminum 320 in² inch core - two 1 inch tubes thick Griffin Racing Radiators
System Capacity	3 U.S. Gallons

TEST FLIGHT DATA

CLIMB DATA
Climb from 1190 MSL to 8190 MSL
6 min. 29 sec. @ 90 MPH IAS
Average rate of climb
1076 FPM
Maximum Oil Temp. Observed
245 degrees F. (hot sensor site)
Maximum Coolant Temp. Observed
205 degrees F.
Maximum Coolant Pres. Observed
9 psi
EGT
1450 degrees F.

CRUISE DATA

Altitude	8000 MSL
OAT	42 degrees F. 5 degrees C.
MP	22.5 inches Hg
RPM	2350 (Prop) / 4700 (Engine)
EGT	1550 degrees F.
Coolant Temp.	185 degrees F.
Oil Temp.	231 degrees F. (hot site)
CAS	122 statute MPH
Ground Speed	142 statute MPH (avg)

Ground speeds were computed using north and south headings with Loran position readout to determine 10-mile leg lengths and stop watch for time. Additionally, Loran ground speed readouts were noted.

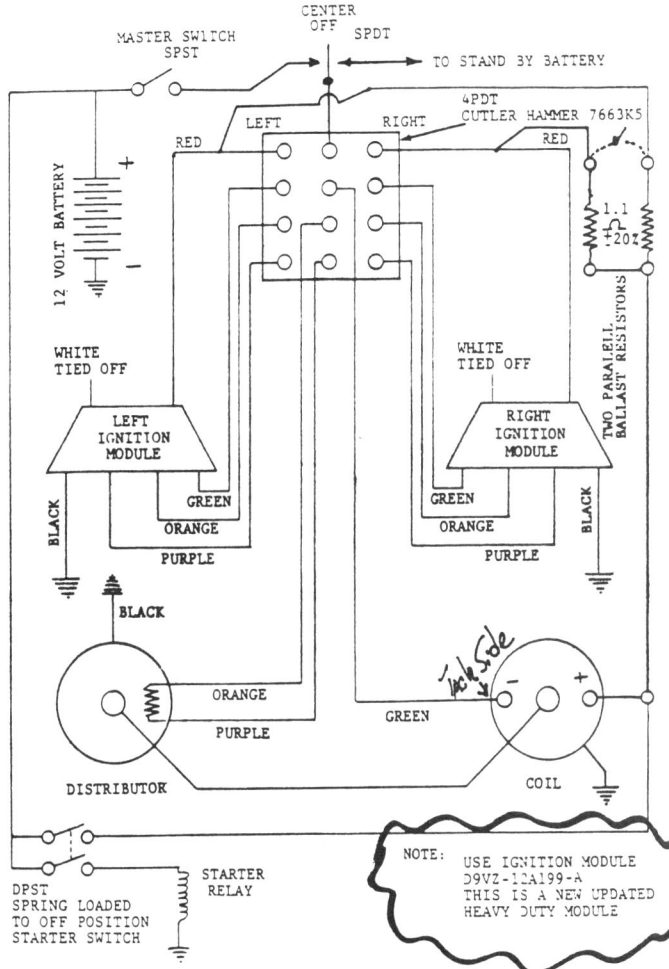

Dual module ignition system schematic as configured in the Schweitzer STOL airplane.

POWERPLANT EXPERIENCE

If there has been any deterioration of this powerplant within its first 300 hours of operation it is not evident to me from this recent evaluation. The data appear to indicate a discrepancy in the application of the coolant temperature and outside air temperature formula outlined earlier. This discrepancy is normal for this installation when it is being operated at 4700 RPM at or near full throttle while leaning to 1550 degrees F. EGT. Coolant temperature readings during operation while using a propeller which limited RPM to 4400 at 8000 MSL were lower and in keeping with ambient air temperature formula used above. This

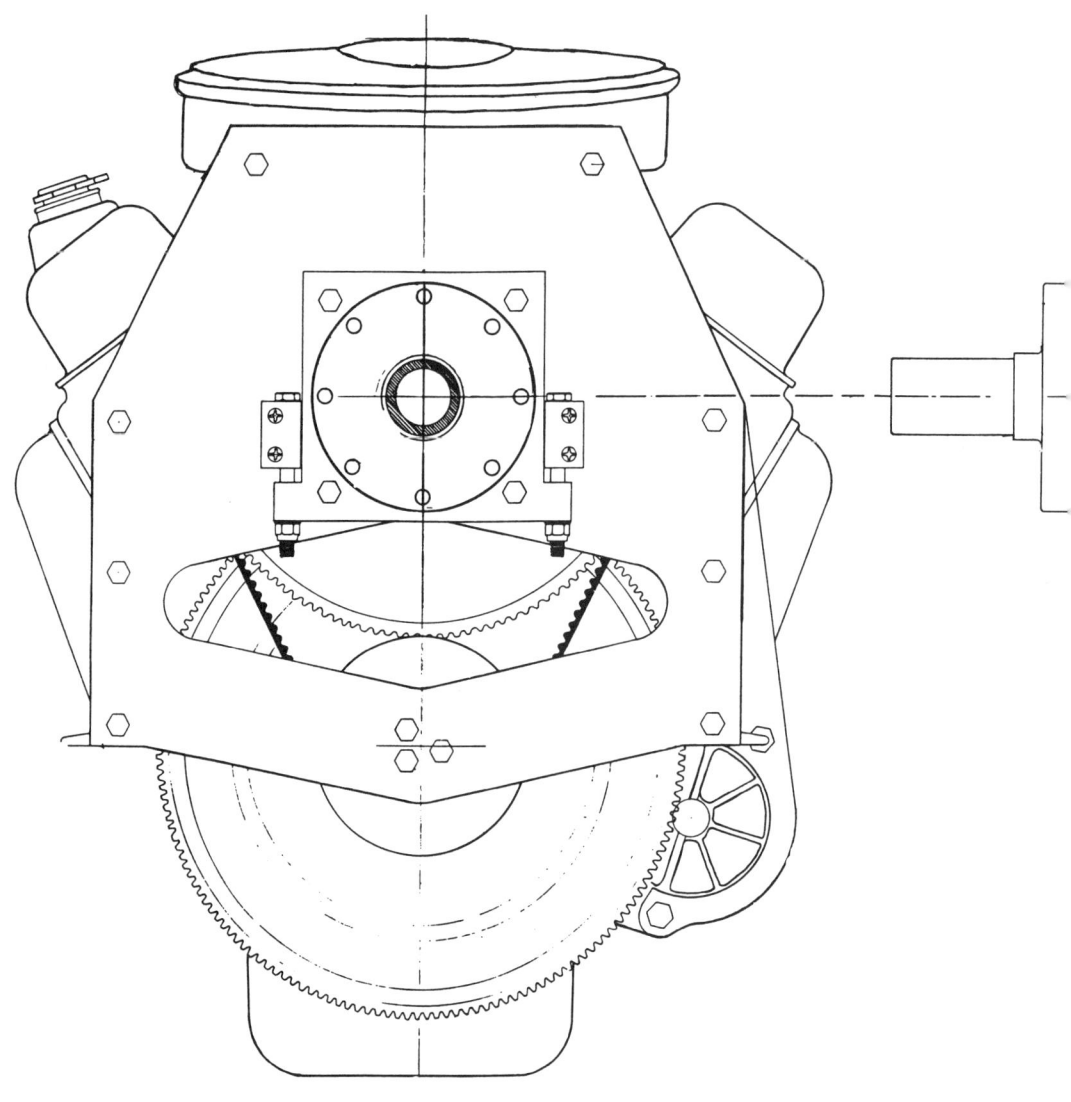

Javelin Aircraft
3.8 Liter Ford Conversion
1/5 Scale Drawing Courtesy of David D. Blanton

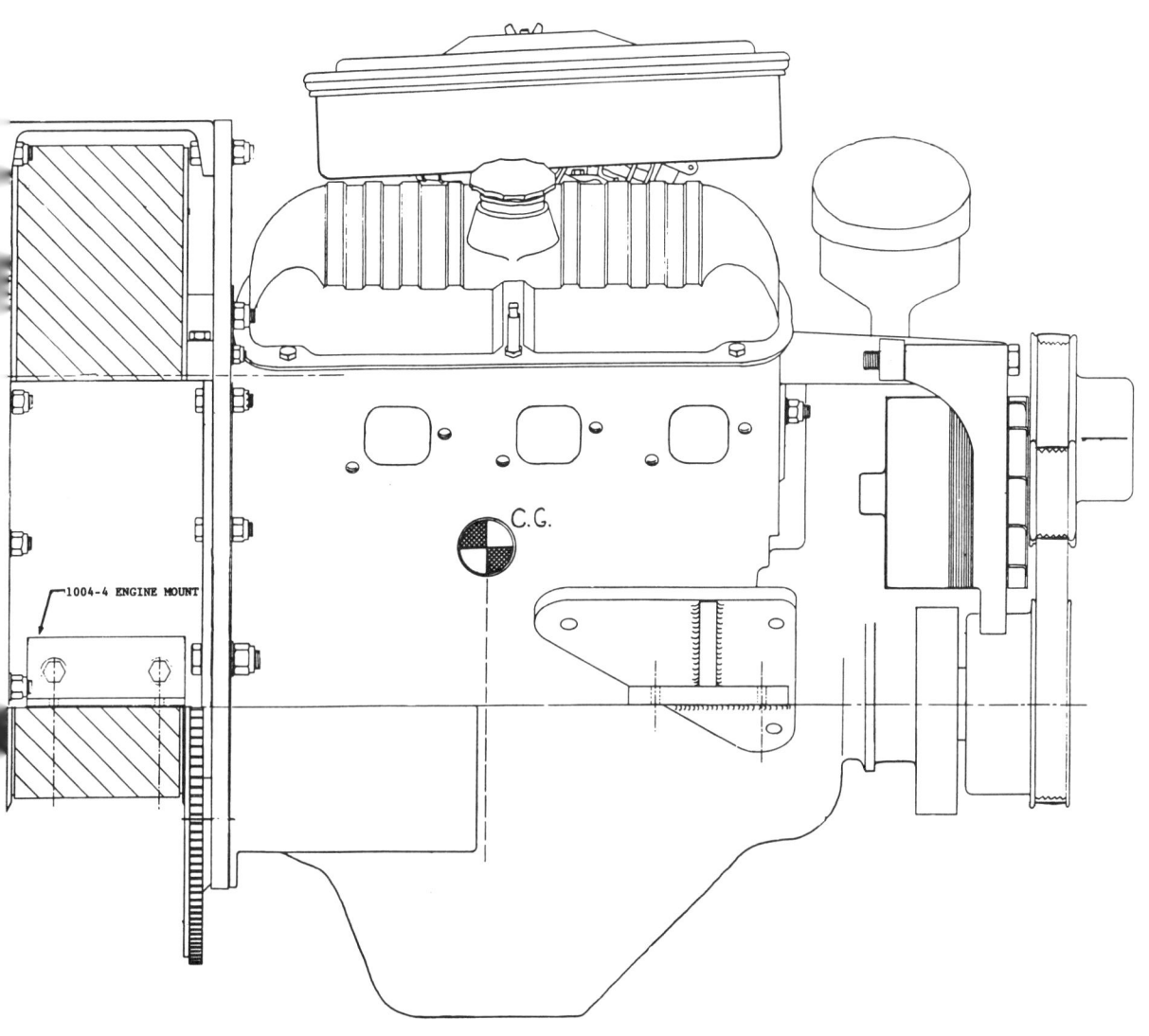

information may indicate the onset of water pump cavitation at RPMs exceeding 4400. However, with cruise RPM at 4700 the powerplant operates very smoothly and there is no pilot perception of maximum effort or strain.

Ready-to-run Ford 3.8 engines are offered by Engines by Brantley. Northwest Aero Products CNC light weight machined redrives are featured. A narrow front support frame design is now available for tight cowling installations.

During the first 300 hours of operation the reduction drive has required no maintenance or adjustment. The powerplant had replacement spark plugs installed at 300 hours and has required the replacement of an alternator at the 250 hour mark. In summary, the 3.8 L Ford V/6 has demonstrated no operational limitation to date which differentiates it from the current crop of certified air-cooled aircraft engines. It does however have several distinct advantages.

During the early development of the 3.8L V/6 process there were no manuals. Information was shared by the builders for the mutual benefit of all. Early manuals contain information which in some cases is outdated, but a comprehensive evaluation and description of these areas is beyond the scope of this effort. Thus, I recommend what I consider to be the most comprehensive and timely engine builder's manual available at this time, The Engine Builder's Manual, published by Mr. Brantley Harrison.

From my involvement in this project and with other builders I find that there is no single source for the design and installation information required for successful liquid cooled system function. This is primarily due to the infinite variety of airframes and engine options available. That not withstanding, when the established principles of liquid cooling are understood and applied, the result will be a predictable and successful installation. Enough "knowns" exist at this time so that air inlet and outlet areas, radiator size and location, and acceptable building materials have all been defined and documented.

Some of the most unused resources at the builders' disposal are the successful experimenters already operating these Ford engines. Successful projects are operating from Maine to California, Florida and Texas to Alaska. Without exception, these people are willing to help those who ask. Find someone in whom you have confidence, with a successful project which is similar to yours. Learn from this person. If you cannot get in touch with anyone you may contact me and I will help you find an appropriate resource person.

CONCLUSION

The previous text is an overview of the information gathered and applied during the past six year period. It is by no means a comprehensive discussion of the subject. Rather, it is intended as an introduction for those who have an interest in specific Ford automotive engine conversions, or in the exciting possibilities of automobile conversions in general. Automobile power is rapidly becoming the choice of more homebuilders. Current engines are a far cry from the technology employed during the 1930s when certified versions of auto engines were employed in factory airframes.

The author received no monetary consideration of any kind as a result of sharing this information. In addition, there is no consideration given, or expected, from any vendor of goods or services mentioned herein. **JS**

Considering the vast resources expended to design, develop and test modern automobile engines to meet durability, reliability, fuel conservation and environmental goals it would seem that Lycoming or Continental would find it financially attractive to take on the conversion challenge rather than adapt automotive technology to obsolete engines. Jerry Schweitzer has again proven that an individual applying a logical engineering approach, limited resources and sustained effort can produce successful aero power. Builders following his ground-breaking lead will find the Ford 3.8 engine conversion task much easier. We appreciate the time taken by Jerry and his son, David, to prepare this article and the gracious offer to provide assistance to others. **MCM**

Erb's Engine Emporium: Part I

Russell E. Erb
5445 Slickrock Drive
Colorado Springs CO 80918
(719) 472 4010

Aero majors and homebuilders alike tend to spend a lot of time talking about airframe issues. For instance, we have sheet metal workshops, composite workshops, fabric covering workshops, welding workshops, and workshops on many other subjects. Rarely do we talk about engines, and when we do, it's primarily about how to attach them to our airframes.

However, engines are a very important part of the aircraft. If the engine ain't working, the airplane don't go anywhere (gliders excluded, but then there always is the tow plane to consider...). A look at the history of aircraft shows that development has mostly been limited by engine technology. This has a lot to do with why an F-16 can carry the same bomb load as a World War II B-17.

The inspiration for this set of four articles was discussions amongst chapter members and in Sport Aviation about modifying automotive engines for aircraft use. As an Aero major, I had some propulsion classes in college, but these were heavily slanted toward, if not exclusively, turbine engines (turbojet, turbofan, turboprop). Virtually no one talked about the engineering principles and design of reciprocating engines. This isn't a problem when dealing with Air Force aircraft, but look through Sport Aviation and what do you find? With the exception of the BD-10 and BD-5J, virtually all homebuilts use reciprocating engines. Many people have shown that this is the appropriate technology for aircraft under about 300 horsepower.

Excellent articles on auto engine conversions appear in Contact! (September-October 1992) and Sport Aviation (April 1993). I highly recommend that you go back and re-read either. The major point that I got out of this article, other than someone was doing this, was that you can't just take a car engine out of the local salvage yard, slap a reduction drive on the front of it, stick it in your airplane, and go fly. (This point is also reinforced in the April 1993 Sport Aviation about installing two Javelin Ford V-6 conversions into a Defiant). He said that the first step was to totally tear down the engine and rebuild it, replacing many parts with competition or racing parts. Of course, after doing that, I purport that you no longer have an auto engine, but a custom built aircraft engine.

A major point that was almost glossed over was that he changed the camshaft to adjust the torque and horsepower curves. This tweaked a question that had been flopping around in my brain but had never come out: "How do you set the engine speeds for maximum torque and maximum horsepower?" Or, if you prefer: "What factors of engine design affect the rpm that the maximum torque and horsepower occur at?" Having renewed access to a university library (namely, the U.S. Air Force Academy library), I went in search of some books that would answer this question. I did find several good textbooks on reciprocating engines, but unfortunately none of them simply answered my question directly. As a result, I had to read many sections and synthesize the information together to get the answer. Along the way, I learned more than I had bargained for, which answered a lot of other questions I hadn't though to ask.

OBJECTIVE My objective is to help you be able to understand the reciprocating engine beyond the basic cycle of intake, compression, power, exhaust. When you consider the speed at which these strokes take place, the reciprocating engine is a very dynamic environment, and cannot be fully understood from a static analysis. These articles aim to help you understand why there are differences between otherwise similar engines. For instance, can you answer these questions:

a. Why does an IO-360 (fuel injected) have a higher peak power than a O-360 (carbureted)?
b. Why is the compression ratio of a TSIO-520 (turbocharged) less than an IO-520?
c. Why can a Rotax 582UL produce as much power as a Continental A-65 with 1/5 the displacement?

This first article will deal with the basic concepts of reciprocating engine design. The second and third article will seek to answer in reasonable detail the original question of what affects the speeds for maximum torque and horsepower. The fourth article (the "bonus" article) will analyze design parameters of actual engines and their effects on engine performance. Let me first start out mentioning two assumptions that I had starting this study:

Assumption 1: Auto engines would not be good for aircraft use because the higher speeds (RPM) required would cause the engines to wear out faster.
Assumption 2: The speeds for maximum torque and horsepower are affected by the bore of the cylinder. This would be why aircraft engines typically ran slower than auto engines. The first assumption is true only in a limited sense, and the second assumption would prove to be FALSE.

TERMINOLOGY REVIEW Three words are typically used to characterize the output of an engine. These are torque, thrust, and power (or horsepower). Torque is simply a moment, or a force times a distance. This is similar to what you measure with a torque wrench when tightening the propeller hub bolts (You DO use a torque wrench, don't you?). If you prefer, it is a measure of how hard is the engine twisting the prop shaft. Well, our buddy Sir Isaac Newton said that for each action there was an equal and opposite reaction. The propeller is typically modeled as a rotating wing, and, like any other wing, it creates drag. In this case, the drag on the propeller blades is trying to slow down the propeller. At a constant RPM, the moment caused by this drag is balanced by the torque generated by the engine. Of course, to spin the propeller faster would require more torque. A well-designed propeller is designed to produce the maximum possible thrust while absorbing the torque of the engine at a specified RPM. It is the drag of the propeller blades that keeps the engine from over-revving.

Thrust, of course, is what moves the airplane forward. Since the propeller blades have a particular lift to drag ratio, or a thrust to torque ratio (this is not a particularly rigorous concept, but only meant to hopefully increase comprehension), an increase in thrust requires an increase in torque. The main point is that while we are used to thinking of the thrust of a propeller, the engine is actually working against the torque required of a propeller. The thrust an engine produces depends heavily on what propeller is mounted on it. It is much more convenient to characterize the engine by its power.

Power, in engineering terms, is defined as thrust times speed. For spinning things, it is equivalently expressed as torque times RPM. The thrust available from the engine/propeller combination will change with speed, as will the thrust required (drag). If the torque of an engine could be held constant the power output would increase linearly with the RPM. It is possible, and in fact is usually the case, that the torque can decrease with increasing rpm, but if the torque decreases at a slower rate than the PRM increases, the overall power will still increase.

Consider an example: Which takes more power, to move a car at low speed or to move the same car at a higher speed? You probably said more power is required as the speed goes up. Now go out and push your car around the street. First push it at a slow speed. You can produce a lot of force (torque) at a slow speed. Now try to speed it up. You will probably find that even though you are producing more power (you said so up above), each push does not have as much force, but they are coming along much faster. So the power output can continue to go up with higher speeds even though the torque is dropping off.

ENGINE SPEED Ask someone how you measure engine speed, and they will probably tell you by the RPM of the output shaft. And in many applications, you would be right. There is another important measure of engine speed, particularly when looking at engine performance. This measure is average piston speed, or how fast is the piston moving up and down. The two are related, as average piston speed is equal to twice the stroke times the RPM. The factor of two comes in because the piston moves twice the stroke (once up, once down) in one revolution. This number will be important when considering how fast the engine is demanding the fuel/air mixture.

THE BASIC ANSWER Most people think of an engine as a device coupled with a propeller used to produce thrust. This idea works well for determining aircraft performance. However, to answer questions like what determines the speed for maximum horsepower, the engine must be considered from a totally different view. The output of the shaft is ignored, and the engine is looked at as an air pump. The purpose of the engine is to pump air from the intake to the exhaust pipe. The shape of the torque and power curves are indications of how well the engine can breathe. When its ability to breathe drops off, the power output will drop off.

According to Obert, "Even for a real engine, the IHP [indicated horsepower can be considered as being closely proportional to air consumption."[1]

If you thought the engine power depended on how much fuel it was using, remember that an engine at full rich runs slower than an engine at the same throttle setting with a properly leaned mixture. The ability to move air through the engine is the important factor; the amount of fuel just needs to be in the right proportion to the air.

Again, we can relate this to another example. Go out and run a long distance. After a short period, you will notice that your speed is not limited by your leg strength (fuel). After all, you can sprint to first base at a speed much faster than you can run five miles. You will find that your maximum speed is limited by how fast you can breathe and supply oxygen to your body. Likewise, the engine is limited by how fast it can move the air from the intake to the exhaust pipe.

In the next Part, we'll look at the dynamics of the air flowing through a reciprocating engine, and see how it changes as the engine speed changes. We will then see how this affects the power and torque outputs. **REE**

REFERENCE
1. Edward F. Obert, Internal Combustion Engines, 3rd ed. (Scranton, PA: International Textbook Company, 1968).

An EAA member and AF Academy graduate, Erb's military career includes M.S. studies at Texas A&M, AF test pilot school, Chief Engineer of the MC-130H special ops project at Edwards AFB. He currently teaches aero engineering subjects at the Academy. MCM

Custom Intake Manifold

Stock Subaru intake manifolds infringe on the top cowling centerline of many homebuilt aircraft designs. Most experimenters have solved this space problem by fabricating custom manifolds from aluminum plenums, angled tubes and flexible hose connectors/worm clamps.

Taking a cue from the auto manufacturers which have used engineering plastics for this purpose (Cadillac Northstar, Olds Aurora, Plymouth Neon, etc.) experimenter Neil Obert, (410) 956 3308, has developed a composite manifold which offers builders another conversion option.

This design utilizes portions of the stock aluminum manifold bases which incorporates mounting and fuel injection provisions. The stock bases are machined to lengths. Composite fibers are initially wrapped around the mechanically grooved ends. When cured the curved tubes of the manifold are laid up, in this case, over plastic pipe insulation. The result is a structural bond between aluminum and composite. The unit pictured features carbon fiber bidirectional fabric. The plenum incorporates a flange for the air throttle body and bosses folr fittings.

This may very well be the first composite manifold developed for auto engine conversions. Years ago, Burt Rutan's Varieze featured fiberglass air induction components (air cleaner cover, carburetor inlet) which were fabricated over shaped urethane foam armatures.

This EA82 manifold is shown with EFI fuel injector plumbing and wiring. The conversion belongs to Gene Nelson, (602) 742 5937. Gene is nearing completion of his RV-3 and was in the process of fitting his Ross Aero redrive and manifold when the photos were taken. **MCM**

Erbman's Engine Emporium: Part II

Russell E. Erb
5445 Slickrock Drive
Colorado Springs CO 80918
(719) 472 4010

In this installment, we will look at the dynamics of how air (or the fuel/air mixture, if you prefer) flows through an reciprocating engine, and how this affects the speeds for maximum torque and maximum horsepower. The first step to understanding this is to realize that, for these purposes, a reciprocating engine cannot be analyzed statically. It must be looked at dynamically. So what does that mean? Here is the Otto cycle described from a static analysis:

> **a.** With the piston at top dead center (TDC), the intake valve opens.
> **b.** The piston moves down to bottom dead center (BDC), drawing the fuel/air charge into the cylinder. The intake valve closes.
> **c.** The piston moves up to TDC, compressing the fuel/air charge.
> **d.** A spark ignites the fuel/air charge, which burns and expands, driving the piston down to BDC.
> **e.** The exhaust valve opens, and the piston moves up to TDC, pushing out the exhaust gases.
> **f.** The exhaust valve closes.
> **g.** Repeat.

As it turns out, none of these things happens exactly when the piston is at TDC or BDC. Valve openings and sparks are timed either ahead of or behind the dead center positions to take maximum advantage of the dynamics of the flow.

VOLUMETRIC EFFICIENCY

An important concept to understanding the variations in power and torque is the volumetric efficiency, which depends on the current engine speed. Volumetric efficiency is defined as the ratio of the amount (mass or volume, depending on who you talk to) of fuel/air mixture drawn into a cylinder on the intake stroke to the maximum amount of fuel/air mixture that could be drawn into the cylinder at the intake density. Alternatively, "Volumetric efficiency is the ratio of the volume of fresh charge taken in during the suction stroke to the full piston displacement. The volume of the charge is taken at atmospheric pressure." (Ref. 1) You can think of this as how much less is the amount of fuel/air charge in the cylinder compared to the maximum that could be there. Of course, the more fuel/air charge in the cylinder, the greater the force will be on the piston during the power stroke. This is how throttling reduces an engines power output. The throttle valve reduces the pressure in the manifold, such that the change in pressure caused by the piston's downward movement is less, thus drawing in less fuel/air charge. For discussion purposes, for finding the maximum torque and horsepower speeds, the throttle will be assumed to be wide open.

So it would seem that the way to get the maximum torque out of an engine would be to get the maximum amount of fuel/air charge into the cylinder. The maximum fuel/air charge will create the maximum pressure on the piston, which would create the maximum torque at the propeller shaft. This is true, but under what conditions does this occur?

INDUCTION SYSTEM EFFECTS

Two real world effects determine how much fuel/air charge gets into the cylinder. The first effect is that air is compressible. The second effect is the dynamics (acceleration/deceleration) of the air. The compressibility of the air becomes a factor when the air enters the intake port around the intake valve. The intake port/valve forms a constriction, much like the throat of a nozzle. Because air is compressible, it can only be pushed through a constriction so fast. Regardless of how much pressure you apply, the maximum velocity possible through the throat of a nozzle is a velocity equal to the speed of sound (Mach=1.0).

The same effect happens at the intake valve. "For convenience, the ratio of the typical velocity to the intake sonic velocity is called the inlet Mach index. From the science of fluid mechanics we know that the controlling velocity in a compressible flow system is usually the intake valve opening." (Ref 2) For a given cylinder and valve design, the inlet Mach index is proportional to the piston speed. This seems reasonable, that the fuel/air charge flows in faster when the piston moves down faster. Of course, at some point the constriction of the valve opening starts to limit this. When the inlet Mach index exceeds 0.5 (intake velocity equal to half the speed of sound), the volumetric efficiency falls rapidly with increasing speed. Therefore, engines typically are designed such that the inlet Mach index does not exceed 0.5 at the highest rated speed. (Ref 2)

The effect of this constriction shows up as a pressure drop through the intake valve. So why don't we just open the intake valve further? Because when the valve is lifted a distance equal to 1/4 its diameter, the area of a cylinder around the valve (that the fuel/air charge passes through, not the engine cylinder) is equal to the area of the valve face and intake port (ignoring the valve stem). See Figure 1.

Mathematically, the area of the cylinder is $(2\pi r)(d/4)$. Since $d = 2r$, this evaluates to πr^2, which is the area of the intake port. Experimentally, the amount of additional flow through the intake port increases very slowly as the lift of the valve increases beyond 1/4 of the valve diameter.

Because of the dynamics of the fuel/air charge, the intake valve normally closes at some time after the piston passes bottom dead center. As the piston moves down, drawing the fuel/air charge into the cylinder. This movement builds up momentum in the intake manifold. When the piston reaches bottom dead center, the fuel/air charge is still flowing into the cylinder as a result of this residual momentum. Thus, at the speed desired for maximum torque, the intake valve closing is timed to correspond with the velocity of the fuel/air charge through the intake port dropping to zero. This closing will occur at some time after the piston has started the compression stroke, and will result in the maximum amount of fuel/air charge being drawn into the cylinder. This maximizes the volumetric efficiency, and maximizes the torque delivered to the shaft (ignoring friction effects). The angle of the crankshaft at the time the intake valve closes is called the intake valve closing angle.

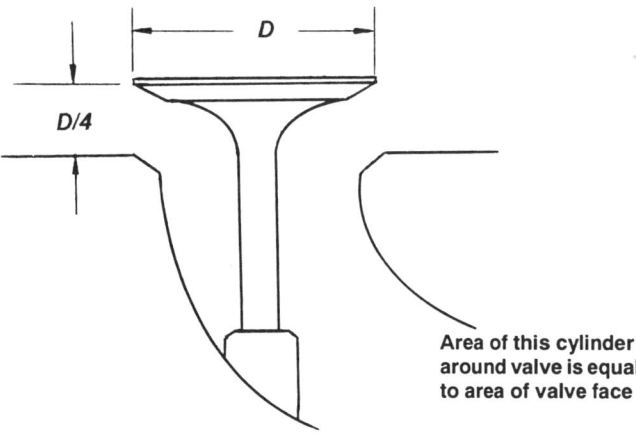

Figure 1. Valve Lift

So what effects does this later valve closing have at other speeds? At low speeds, the momentum built up in the intake manifold will be small, such that part of the fuel/air charge will be pushed back into the intake manifold as the piston starts up prior to the intake valve closing. At speeds above the speed for maximum torque, the constriction of intake valve opening will cause a pressure loss which will reduce the amount of fuel/air charge entering the cylinder. In either case, the amount of fuel/air charge in the cylinder is reduced, and thus the torque is reduced.

The design of the intake manifold also affects the amount of momentum built up in the flow of the fuel/air charge. The momentum of the fuel/air charge is the sum of the effect of standing waves built up from previous intake strokes (remember any tube will have a resonant frequency, just like you hear blowing over the top of a coke bottle) and the effect of the transient wave caused by the current intake stroke. While the standing waves contribute to the overall effect, there are no sudden changes in the volumetric efficiency when the RPM of the engine is an even multiple of the natural frequency of the intake manifold.

Long, skinny intake manifold pipes give high volumetric efficiencies at low piston speeds because high momentum (lots of velocity) is built up in the pipe during the intake stroke. At high piston speeds, the small diameter of the pipe causes a constriction and the volumetric efficiency falls.

So why don't we use long, fat intake manifold pipes to avoid the constriction? Fat pipes show a maximum volumetric efficiency at intermediate piston speeds. However, at high piston speeds, the larger mass of the fuel/air charge in the fat manifold is slow to accelerate, and thus the volumetric efficiency falls off.

As the manifold pipes get shorter, the maximum gain in volumetric efficiency over having no intake manifold at all decreases. However, the gain you do get with shorter pipes happens over a greater range of piston speeds. (Ref 2) Basically, it comes down to the intake manifold should be designed according to the engine requirements. If you need high torque at slow piston speeds, use long, skinny intake pipes. For high torque at intermediate piston speeds, use long, fat intake pipes. For high torque over a wide range of piston speeds (i.e. a flat torque curve), use shorter intake pipes.

EXHAUST SYSTEM EFFECTS

Part of getting a large fuel/air charge into the cylinder (high volumetric efficiency) has to do with getting the combustion products of the previous cycle out of the cylinder. At first thought, it would seem that simply making the exhaust valve bigger would help get the combustion products out. As it turns out, the exhaust valve can be as small as 50 percent the size of the intake valve without affecting the volumetric efficiency over the usual range of inlet Mach indices. Normally, though, exhaust valves are at least 60 percent the size of the intake valve. (Ref. 2) While I did not find this in print anywhere, this effect may arise because the combustion products are "pushed" out of the exhaust port by the piston, while the fuel/air charge is "sucked" in the intake port, pushed only by the manifold pressure.

To enhance the removal of the combustion products, the intake valve is opened prior to the end of the exhaust stroke. Since both valves are open at this point, this is referred to as valve overlap. If the pressure in the intake manifold is greater than the pressure in the exhaust manifold, the inrushing fuel/air charge will help scavenge the remaining combustion products in the cylinder as the piston reaches top dead center by pushing them out the exhaust port. While some of the fuel/air charge may go out the exhaust port, the engine designer tries to design the timing such that the exhaust valve closes just as the last of the combustion products leave the exhaust port. An additional benefit of valve overlap is that the intake valve is essentially fully open at the start of the intake stroke, thus reducing the pressure loss through the intake port during the intake stroke. (Ref 2) The angle that the crankshaft turns between the intake valve opening and the exhaust valve closing is called the valve overlap angle.

Of course, scavenging does not occur at all speeds. At low speeds, the throttle valve reduces the pressure in the intake manifold, such that the intake manifold pressure is less than the exhaust manifold pressure. In this case, a small portion of the combustion products enter the intake manifold, to be pulled back into the cylinder on the intake stroke. Additionally, the combustion products in the space above the piston at top dead center are not scavenged. Even so, at low power settings this is not a problem.

SUMMARY

In general, we have seen that the torque, and thus the horsepower produced by an engine depends on the amount of air that can be pumped through the engine. The more fuel/air charge drawn into the cylinder, the higher the volumetric efficiency. The higher the volumetric efficiency, the higher the torque. The biggest factor affecting the volumetric efficiency is the valve timing, specifically the valve overlap angle and the intake valve closing angle. Volumetric efficiency can also be improved by the intake manifold design. Since the camshaft used determines the valve timing, changing the camshaft will change the shape of the torque curve, and thus the horsepower curve. This is echoed by C. Hall "Skip" Jones in his articles in Contact! and Sport Aviation. (Refs. 3 and 4). In Part III we'll talk about other factors affecting engine performance, including fuel injection, stroke/bore ratio, compression ratio, spark timing, and supercharging.

REFERENCES

1. V.L. Maleev, Internal-Combustion Engines: Theory and Design, 2nd ed. (New York: McGraw-Hill Book Company, Inc., 1945).
2. Charles Taylor, The Internal Combustion Engine in Theory and Practice, 2nd ed. (Cambridge: The M.I.T. Press, 1966), I.
3. C. Hall "Skip" Jones, "Converting Auto Engines For Aircraft Applications," Contact!, September-October 1992 (Issue 10)
4. C. Hall "Skip" Jones, "Converting Auto Engines For Aircraft Applications," Sport Aviation, April 1993.

Removing Engine Heat

Leonard Eaves
3818 NW 36th Street
Oklahoma City OK 73112
(405) 942 6339

Homebuilders focus a lot of effort making certain that their engine installation receives adequate cooling. Relatively little thought is given to the vast amount of heat remaining after engine shutdown.

The ingenious little gadget shown here takes the work out of removing damaging hot air from an engine cowl. When the propeller turns, the door closes. With the engine off the door opens letting hot air escape. Roger White of Owasso, OK introduced me to this 'handy dandy' simple solution to a significant problem. I have used this gadget several years on my two seat N1111V "Skeeter" (Contact issue #12, magneto to HEI conversion) with complete satisfaction. Letting hot air escape from the engine compartment reduces the deterioration of electrical components, such as your alternator, regulator, internal magneto coils and assorted wiring. These items are expensive!

If you are powered by a factory aircooled engine always place your two "bean doors" over the hot cylinders to create a chimney effect. Removing heat quickly and directly from the cylinders in this way will cause less heat build-up at the rear and sides of your engine. My doors are about 8x2 inches in size. I used light guage aluminum, short lengths of piano hinge, and aluminum opening stiffners. The picture shows one door and a portion of the right rear cylinder.

Auto engine conversions operate cooler. Nevertheless, venting engine heat is a good idea and will protect electrical components, sensors and wiring from heat soak. **LE**

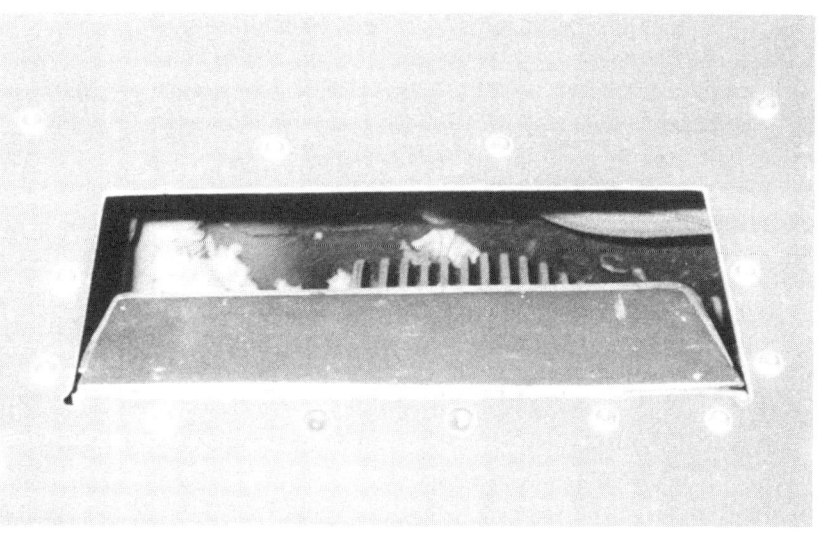

Erbman's Engine Emporium: Parts III and IV

Russell E. Erb
5445 Slickrock Drive
Colorado Springs CO 80918
(719) 472 4010

In Contact! issue 21 we determined that the key to producing high torque from a reciprocating engine was to get the maximum possible amount of fuel/air charge into the cylinder. How well the engine does this is measured by its volumetric efficiency. In general, the more air we can pump through the engine, the greater the torque we will get out. Last time we looked at the two biggest factors affecting volumetric efficiency, valve overlap angle and intake valve closing angle. These are directly related to the choice of camshaft for your engine, and changing the camshaft will change the torque curve, and thus change the power curve. This time we will look at other lesser factors affecting the torque output of the engine, and then look at how the torque output affects the power output.

FUEL INJECTION

So why does an IO-360 (fuel injected) have a higher peak power than a O-360 (carbureted)? The answer is that fuel injection reduces losses in the intake system. The first reason is that the venturi in the carburetor is another constriction in the flow, which manifests itself as a pressure drop in the intake manifold. This pressure drop is eliminated with a fuel injection system, thus allowing a higher pressure to reach the cylinders, and thus a larger amount of fuel/air charge to enter the cylinder.

The second reason is that the fuel/air charge is colder, and thus denser when it reaches the cylinder, again allowing a larger amount of fuel/air charge to enter the cylinder. Just like when you add carb heat, the density of the fuel/air charge is reduced when it is heated. So you're asking "Why would it be heated?" In some carbureted engines, the intake manifold is heated to assist distribution. Even without intake manifold heating, the intake manifold will be hotter than the ambient air simply because it is attached to the engine. Heat transfer studies have shown that the liquid fuel on the walls on the intake manifold increases the rate of heat transfer. (Ref 1) Thus, in a carbureted engine, the small drops of fuel in the fuel/air charge cause the charge to heat up more passing through the intake manifold than dry air would passing through the same intake manifold. Therefore, the density of the fuel/air charge is decreased, reducing the amount of charge entering the cylinder. Experiments have shown that volumetric efficiency may be increased by 10% by direct injection of the fuel into the cylinders. This also prevents loss of fuel because of valve overlap. Fuel injection into the intake port (just outside the intake valve) shows a smaller, but appreciable improvement. (Ref 1)

SPARK TIMING

If you've ever set the timing either on your aircraft engine or your car engine, you've probably noticed that the spark fires before the piston reaches top dead center. At first glance, it would seem that the force of the burning fuel/air charge, which is supposed to push the piston down, would be fighting the piston which is still coming up. Of course, this will happen if the spark is advanced too much. Once again, we must remember that nothing happens instantaneously. It takes a finite, though very small, amount of time for the fuel/air charge to burn and reach a maximum pressure. To get the maximum useful work out of the expanding gasses, the maximum pressure should occur just as the piston reaches top dead center. Thus, the burning must start prior to the piston reaching top dead center. (Ref 2)

So why is a spark sometimes retarded from the position for best power? Within limits, a retarded spark is a powerful way of controlling detonation. This allows use of a higher compression ratio than would be possible if the spark were always set for best power. When high power is required of the engine, such as during a climb, the spark can be retarded to control the detonation. At lower power settings when detonation is not imminent, such as cruise, the spark can be advanced to the best power position. The result of this setup is a better over-all fuel economy than with a lower compression ratio.

STROKE/BORE RATIO

As it turns out, the stroke to bore ratio has no relation to the speediness of the engine. "Low-speed engines with a short stroke-bore ratio are about as common as long-stroke high speed engines." (Ref 2) The size of the bore does not affect the volumetric efficiency, assuming the valves are properly sized. The big factor with regards to the stroke is not the length of the stroke, but the piston speed (because the inlet Mach index is proportional to piston speed). An engine with a short stroke running at high rpm can have the same piston speed, and thus similar performance, to a long stroke running at a low rpm. We'll see examples of this in next month's article.

COMPRESSION RATIO

Why are engines built with the highest possible compression ratio? Higher compression ratios give a higher thermal efficiency, allowing the engine to get more useful work out of the heat energy in the fuel. Compression ratio has only a small effect on the volumetric efficiency of four-stroke engines. (Ref 1) The upper limit on compression ratio is set by detonation, where the fuel/air charge is heated sufficiently in the compression stroke to self ignite. Higher compression ratios can be used by using higher octane fuel.

SUPERCHARGING

Supercharging increases the volumetric efficiency of an engine simply by providing the fuel/air charge to the cylinders at a higher pressure, thus allowing more of the fuel/air charge to be drawn into the cylinders. However, supercharging cannot simply be added to an existing engine without considering the other factors that have been discussed.

As just mentioned, the upper limit on compression ratio is detonation. When supercharging is added, the starting pressure of the fuel/air charge is higher, and thus the compression pressure will be higher if nothing else is changed. At this point, one of two things must be done. The first possibility is to increase the anti-knock characteristics of the fuel (i.e. higher octane). This may be fine if you're racing at Reno, but to the average pilot higher octane fuel means more buck$ at the pump, and the question of fuel availability for anything higher than 100LL. The other possibility is to reduce the compression ratio so that the compression pressure will be the same as before supercharging. This can be done simply by increasing the volume in the cylinder head. This will result in a slightly lower thermal efficiency, but the power output will be increased, since more fuel will be burned. "An engine operating with natural aspiration with a compression ratio 7:1, when supercharged should have a compression ratio about 6:1." (Ref 2)

Another consideration arises when supercharging a carbureted engine. If the valves are overlapped, as they generally will be, some fuel may be lost out the exhaust manifold during the overlap period. Even so, many supercharged aircraft engines use considerable overlap to achieve high values of volumetric efficiency under take-off conditions. The fuel loss is not important because the take-off covers only a short time. In cruising flight, the pressures in the intake manifold and exhaust manifold are close to equal (because of the back pressure from the turbine on the supercharger), and little fuel is lost due to the overlap. (Ref 1)

HORSEPOWER

So far we've talked about volumetric efficiency and torque produced by the engine. Even so, you probably don't remember ever asking someone about the torque rating on his engine. The reason I haven't talked about horsepower specifically is that volumetric efficiency is directly related to the torque, and the torque is related to horsepower simply by RPM. Specifically, torque X RPM = horsepower (with the appropriate units conversions).

The torque will always peak at a lower RPM than the horsepower. As RPM is increased above that for maximum torque, the indicated horsepower will continue to increase as long as the rpm increases faster than the torque decreases. Note that I said indicated horsepower, not brake horsepower. The difference between these is the friction horsepower. Friction horsepower is the power required to overcome the friction from sliding pistons up and down in cylinders and turning shafts in bearings. The friction horsepower increases rapidly at high speeds. As a result, the brake horsepower (the power available at the output shaft of the engine) will eventually peak when the friction horsepower increases faster than the indicated horsepower.

Since high power requires high RPM, this is why your engine produces its maximum horsepower generally at the redline RPM. The maximum torque typically occurs at about half the RPM of maximum horsepower. (Ref 2)

In the following sections, we'll look at actual engines past and present, and see how the topics we've discussed affect their performance. We'll also finish answering the questions raised in Part I.

So now that we are all self-proclaimed experts in reciprocating engine design, lets look at some actual engine data and see how the engine design factors affect the engine performance. Table 1 is an accumulation of data for many different types of engines, including World War II V-12s, radials, current horizontally opposed engines, auto engines, and even a chainsaw and motorcycle engine.

PISTON SPEED

We have seen previously that piston speed is proportional to volumetric efficiency up to a limit, with higher piston speeds allowing higher torque. Near the far right side of Table 1, the piston speeds are listed. Several interesting trends can be noted. The three highest piston speeds at rated power listed are the Chevy 350 V-8 (58.96 ft/sec), the Allison V-1710-F (50 ft/sec), and the Packard V-1650-1 Merlin (50 ft/sec). This seems to be the upper limit for piston speed. Also note that to keep up with these piston speeds, these cylinders each have 4 valves; 2 intake and 2 exhaust valves. While this increases the complexity of the engine, it also allows more area in the ports. Consider two equally sized valves in a cylinder (See Figure 1). Draw one large circle, then draw the two largest equally sized non-overlapping circles inside this circle that you can. Each of the inner circles (valves) has half the radius of the large circle, and thus has .25 the area of the large circle. Now draw four equally sized circles in a square formation tangent to each other and tangent to the inside of the large circle. The radius of the small circles (valves) is .414 the radius of the big circle. The area of two of these small circles is .34 the area of the large circle, an increase in area of 9% the area of the large circle, or a 36 percent increase in valve opening size. I have not heard of anyone using more than 4 valves per cylinder.

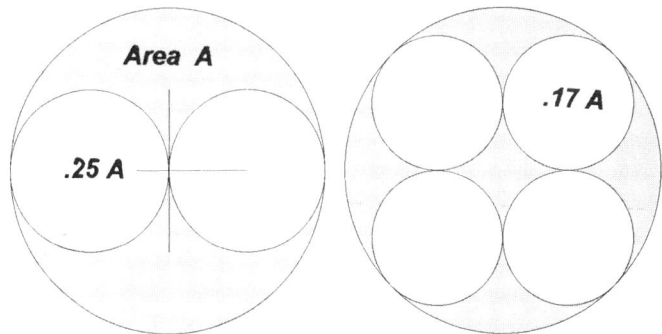

Figure 1. Cylinder heads with 2 and 4 valves

The highest piston speed for an engine with only two valves per cylinder is 49.09 ft/sec for the very large radials. So if auto engines produce their maximum horsepower at 3500 to 6000 RPM, while aircraft engines produce their maximum horsepower at about 2700 RPM, are auto engines running faster? Not when you look at the piston speed. The piston speeds for auto engines are comparable to the piston speeds for aircraft engines. So will the auto engine conversion wear out faster than an aircraft engine? It depends on which part you are talking about. The pistons/cylinders? Probably not. The piston speeds are comparable. Shafts and bearings? Probably, since the rotation speeds are much higher. Even so, consider this: To drive a car 100,000 miles at 50 MPH would take 2000 hours, typical TBO for a Lycoming or Continental. On the other hand, the car engine in this case is at a much lower power setting, so this may not be a fair comparison.

Consider the Rotax 582UL. This engine produces the same horsepower as a Continental A-65, but has only 1/5 the displacement. How can this be? Remember the horsepower is made up of torque multiplied by RPM. The Rotax 582UL must turn at 6200 RPM, while the Continental A-65 only turns at 2300 RPM. Additionally, the Rotax is a 2-stroke engine, so it is producing a power stroke on each rotation rather than every other stroke. If you multiply the number of power strokes per minute times the displacement for each of these engines, the Rotax actually pumps slightly more air per minute than the Continental. The Rotax produces more of its horsepower from rpm than torque. The down side of this is the Rotax must be geared down to turn a propeller at an appropriate speed. Even though the Rotax is running at 6200 RPM, its stroke is so short that the piston speed is only 43.4 ft/sec, which is comparable with other engines listed. The TBO on the Rotax is only about 400 hours, which is much smaller than 2000 hours for a typical Lycoming or Continental, but this is offset by a significantly cheaper price per overhaul. The accumulated cost by 2000 hours for both types of engines is roughly equal.

Also interesting to note is the chainsaw and motorcycle engines listed. While these turn at 11000 and 8500 rpm respectively, the piston speeds are only 42 and 54 ft/sec. These engines are also comparable to the other engines listed.

BORE AND STROKE

As we saw in an earlier article, the stroke/bore ratio does not affect the torque or horsepower. Even so, we can note some interesting trends. The stroke/bore ratios range from 0.72 to 1.12. The 0.72 belongs to a Ford V-8, and the second highest stroke/bore ratio (1.11) belongs to the Packard Merlin V-12. There does not seem to be a definite trend between engine type and stroke/bore ratio.

What is interesting is that the Allison, Packard, Pratt & Whitney, Wright, and Lycoming engines use larger cylinders than Continental and auto engines. For instance, for an O-360 class engine, the Lycoming has 4 cylinders, while the Continental uses 6. It can be shown that using more, smaller cylinders will result in a lighter engine. However, more cylinders means more complexity, and may result in an overall larger engine. The Rotax 582UL uses 2 small, fast cylinders for the same horsepower as the Continental A-65, which uses 4 larger, slower cylinders. However, the Rotax requires a reduction gear, which adds extra weight. I don't have any figures to compare the fuel consumption.

For high RPM engines and high horsepower engines, a reduction gear must be used. Looking at Table 1, the fastest propeller RPM numbers are 2700 - 2800 RPM. Why is this? One of the everlasting laws of propeller design is that for high efficiencies, the propeller tips must remain subsonic. At 2700 RPM, the tips of a 72 inch propeller would be moving at 0.76 Mach at sea level on a standard day. At tips speeds much above this, shock waves will start to form, the torque required to drive the propeller increases significantly, and the propeller efficiency drops. (Not to mention the noise increase--I have heard the reason that T-6s are so loud on takeoff is the propeller tips are supersonic, producing shock waves.)

The largest engine shown with direct drive to the propeller is rated at 450 horsepower. For high horsepower engines, such as the Pratt & Whitney R-4360, the propeller RPM is as low as 1012 RPM. To absorb this much power, large diameter propellers are required. As the diameter of the propeller goes up, the limiting RPM of the propeller drops to keep the propeller tips subsonic. This is why high horsepower engines are geared to such low propeller RPMs.

COMPRESSION RATIO

Does a higher compression ratio increase the horsepower output of the engine? Yes, because the thermal efficiency is increased. Compare the Lycoming O-320-A2B and the Lycoming O-320-B2C. The only apparent difference between these engines is upping the compression ratio from 7 to 8.5. Since the bore and stroke are identical between engines, this was presumably done by reducing the volume of the combustion chamber above the piston at top dead center. This results in a 10 horsepower gain. The down side of this is the fuel required changes from 80/87 to 100LL.

Also note that the WW II engines all have compression ratios between 6 and 7. All of these engines were equipped with gear driven superchargers, and generally were used with external turbo-superchargers, hence the lower compression ratios. After 1935, 100 octane fuel was available in commercial quantities and was used by the military in WWII. The higher octane fuel allowed the use of supercharging without having to reduce further compression ratios.

FUEL INJECTION

Looking at the Lycoming and Continental engines, the larger engines are fuel injected (as indicated by IO in the designation instead of just O). While this will increase volumetric efficiency, it may also be that fuel injection is simpler than designing a large carburetor that would be required to supply fuel to this large of an engine.

SUPERCHARGING

As previously discussed, when supercharging is added to an engine, the compression ratio normally will be reduced. Three examples of this are shown in the table: Lycoming GO-480 to IGSO-480, Lycoming IO-540 to IGSO-540, and Continental IO-520 to TSIO-520.

SOME HISTORICAL SPECULATION

Close inspection of the engine parameters, primarily those built during WWII, leads to some interesting speculation and meaningless facts. The stroke and bore of these engines were designed before the metric system was in vogue, and before decimal measurements were popular either. I say this because the bore and stroke measurements are all even inches or end in multiples of 1/16, 1/8, 1/4, or 1/2 inch. Interesting, but not real important.

At the beginning of WWII, many smaller radials were available, but there was an immediate need for larger, more powerful engines. A quick way to get an engine of double the horsepower would be simply to stick two existing engines together to make a two row radial. The following speculations are based simply on the bore and stroke dimensions:

The Pratt & Whitney R-2800 is two rows of R-1340 with a slightly longer stroke (longer crankshaft throw).
[The Wright R-2600 is two rows of R-1300.
The Wright R-3350 is two rows of R-1820, perhaps with a R-2600 crankshaft.

To reduce the number of parts required to build numerous sizes of engines, Pratt & Whitney only had three sizes of cylinders (bore): 5.1875, 5.5, and 5.75 inches. Wright used two sizes of cylinders: 5 and 6.125 inches.

THE EMPORIUM IS CLOSING

Well, this brings to an end this series of articles. If you started reading this to figure out how to set your timing or change your spark plugs, then you're probably still looking. Hopefully you have gained some insight into the engineering principles of how your engine is designed, and some of the design changes required for converting auto engines. **REE**

Manufacturer	Type	Primary Use	Cooling	Number of Cylinders	Valves per Cylinder	Bore (inches)	Stroke (inches)	Stroke/Bore Ratio	Displacement (cubic inches)	Compression Ratio	Max Horsepower	RPM for Max Horsepower	Gearing	Piston Speed	Propeller RPM
Allison	V-1710-F	Aircraft	Liquid	12	4	5.5	6	1.09	1710	6.65	1475	3000	0.5	50	1500
Packard	V-1650-1	Aircraft	Liquid	12	4	5.4	6	1.11	1649	6	1300	3000	0.477	50	1431
Pratt & Whitney	R-985	Aircraft	Air	8	2	5.1875	5.1875	1.00	985	6	450	2300	1	33.14	2300
Pratt & Whitney	R-1340	Aircraft	Air	8	2	5.75	5.75	1.00	1344	6	600	2250	0.67	35.93	1507
Pratt & Whitney	R-1830	Aircraft	Air	14	2	5.5	5.5	1.00	1830	6.7	1200	2700	0.56	41.25	1512
Pratt & Whitney	R-2000	Aircraft	Air	14	2	5.75	5.5	0.95	2000	6.5	1450	2700	0.5	41.25	1350
Pratt & Whitney	R-2800	Aircraft	Air	18	2	5.75	6	1.04	2804	6.65	2000	2700	0.5	45	1350
Wright	R-760	Aircraft	Air	7	2	5	5.5	1.10	756	6.3	350	2400	1	36.67	2400
Wright	R-975	Aircraft	Air	9	2	5	5.5	1.10	973	6.3	450	2250	1	34.37	2250
Wright	R-1300	Aircraft	Air	7	2	6.125	6.3125	1.03	1300	6.2	700	2600	0.67	45.59	1742
Wright	R-1820	Aircraft	Air	9	2	6.125	6.875	1.12	1823	6.7	1200	2500	0.56	47.74	1400
Wright	R-2600	Aircraft	Air	14	2	6.125	6.3125	1.03	2603	6.9	1900	2800	0.56	49.09	1568
Wright	R-3350	Aircraft	Air	18	2	6.125	6.3125	1.03	3347	6.85	2200	2800	0.44	49.09	1232
Pratt & Whitney	R-4360	Aircraft	Air	28	2	5.75	6	1.04	4363	7	3500	2700	0.375	45	1012
Lycoming	O-290-D2C	Aircraft	Air	4	2	4.875	3.875	0.79	289	7	140	2800	1	30.14	2800
Lycoming	O-235-C1B	Aircraft	Air	4	2	4.375	3.875	0.88	233	6.75	115	2800	1	30.14	2800
Lycoming	O-320-A2B	Aircraft	Air	4	2	5.125	3.875	0.75	320	7	150	2700	1	29.06	2700
Lycoming	O-320-B2C	Aircraft	Air	4	2	5.125	3.875	0.75	320	8.5	160	2700	1	29.06	2700
Lycoming	IO-360-B1B	Aircraft	Air	4	2	5.125	4.375	0.85	361	8.5	180	2700	1	32.81	2700
Lycoming	GO-480-G1D6	Aircraft	Air	6	2	5.125	3.875	0.75	480	8.7	295	3400	0.64	36.59	2176
Lycoming	IGSO-480-A1F6	Aircraft	Air	6	2	5.125	3.875	0.75	480	7.3	340	3400	0.64	36.59	2176
Lycoming	IO-540-61A5	Aircraft	Air	6	2	5.125	4.375	0.85	541	8.7	290	2575	1	31.29	2575
Lycoming	IGSO-540-A1D	Aircraft	Air	6	2	5.125	4.375	0.85	541	7.3	380	3400	0.64	41.31	2176
Lycoming	IO-720-A1A	Aircraft	Air	8	2	5.125	4.375	0.85	722	8.7	400	2650	1	32.20	2650
Rotax	582UL	Aircraft	Liquid	2	2 cycle	2.99	2.52	0.84	35.44	5.75	66	6200	0.388	43.4	2405
Continental	A-65-8F	Aircraft	Air	4	2	3.875	3.625	0.93	171	6.3	65	2300	1	23.15	2300
Continental	C-85-8	Aircraft	Air	4	2	3.875	4.0625	1.04	188	6.3	85	2575	1	29.05	2575
Continental	O-200-A	Aircraft	Air	4	2	4.0625	3.875	0.95	201	7	100	2750	1	29.60	2750
Continental	O-300-D	Aircraft	Air	6	2	4.0625	3.875	0.95	301	7	145	2700	1	29.06	2700
Continental	GO-300-D	Aircraft	Air	6	2	4.0625	3.875	0.95	301	7.3	175	3200	0.75	34.44	2400
Continental	IO-360-A	Aircraft	Air	6	2	4.44	3.875	0.87	360	8.5	210	2800	1	30.13	2800
Continental	IO-520-A	Aircraft	Air	6	2	5.25	4	0.76	520	8.5	285	2700	1	30	2700
Continental	TSIO-520-D	Aircraft	Air	6	2	5.25	4	0.76	520	7.5	285	2700	1	30	2700
Continental	GTSIO-520-D	Aircraft	Air	6	2	5.25	4	0.76	520	7.5	375	3400	0.67	37.77	2278
McCulloch	M2-10	Chainsaw	Air	1	2 cycle	1.75	1.375	0.78	3.3	7.1	6.5	11000		42.01	
Honda	450	Motorcycle	Air	2	2	2.8	2.28	0.81	28	8.5	43	8500		53.83	
Chevy	Corvair	Auto	Air	6	2	3.44	2.94	0.85	164	9.25	140	5200		42.46	
Chevy	Corvair Supercharged	Auto	Air	6	2	3.44	2.94	0.85	164	8.25	180	4000		32.67	
Chevy	230 I-6	Auto	Liquid	6	2	3.75	3.25	0.86	230	8.5	140	4400		39.72	
Ford	289 V-8	Auto	Liquid	8	2	4	2.88	0.72	289	10.5	271	6000		48	
Ford	2.5L I-4	Auto	Liquid	4	2	3.68	3.3	0.89	153	9.7	90	4400		40.33	
Ford	3.0L V-6	Auto	Liquid	6	2	3.5	3.14	0.89	183	9.1	140	4800		41.87	
AMC	232 I-6	Auto	Liquid	6	2	3.75	3.5	0.93	232	8	100	3600		35	
AMC	258 I-6	Auto	Liquid	6	2	3.75	3.895	1.03	258	8	110	3500		37.86	
Ford	4.9L I-6	Auto	Liquid	6	2	4	3.98	0.99	300	13.5	145				
Ford	5.0L V-8	Auto	Liquid	8	2	4	3	0.75	302		185				
Ford	5.8L V-8	Auto	Liquid	8	2	4	3.5	0.87	351	12.9	210				
Ford	7.6L V-8	Auto	Liquid	8	2	4.36	3.85	0.88	460	10.8	230				
Chevy	350 V-8	Auto	Liquid	8	2	4	3.48	0.87	350	9.5	250	4400		42.53	
Chevy	350 V-8	Auto	Liquid	8	4	3.9	3.66	0.93	350	11	375	5800		58.96	

Table 1. Engine parameters

Some Observations on the Cooling of Auto Engine Applications in Experimental Aircraft

Bill Hinote
P.O. Box 390
San Luis Obispo
California 93406
(805) 461 1455

Bill Hinote has been a pilot since 1974 and enjoys competing in sailplane events. His aeronautical interests go beyond mere piloting. He has done some tuft testing of sailplane wing/fuselage junctions and is now pursuing the concept of a two place original design incorporating design and construction features of other experimental category airplanes he finds best define his personal aircraft. Working in the auto parts industry Bill has formed lots of opinions relevant to auto engines and components. MCM

One of the biggest problems related to the installation of auto-engine conversions in experimental aircraft appears to be that of successfully cooling the engine - meaning of course the proper sizing, location and ducting of liquid-to-air radiators.

Of the successful conversions, there is a small percentage achieving success using crude and inefficient locations such as flat (horizontally) above or below the engine, or flat (vertically) near the firewall, behind the engine. The occasional successes of these installations seem to be based on sheer cooling area, rather than on any high degree of cooling efficiency.

For those desiring the cooling efficiencies available from a well-designed liquid-to-air system, a few specifics must be kept in mind:

1) The primary advantage of the liquid-to-air heat transfer concept is its ability to be moved to an optimum location on the airframe. Conversion of the inlet velocity to pressure must occur at the cooling fins of an aircooled engine; with the liquid cooled engine many options are open to the designer.

2) In "conventional" airframes (with tractor engines/ propellers) the most common mistake seems to be the use of the traditional air exit into the freestream at the junction of the engine cowl and the firewall, on the bottom of the aircraft. If we stop (for a moment!) and consider the circulation pattern around a wing of finite span (typically extending in all dimensions to a distance equal to the span of the airplane wing), we find that the up-flow under the aircraft creates an unsuitable location for a cooling air exit - the relative air pressure is too high to be correct... remember, we want high pressure going into the front of the radiator, and a low pressure region for the radiator exit air to be pulled into. In this writer's opinion, the best location for an exit air opening in a "conventional" airframe is at the sides of the fuselage. Alternatively, and with potentially greater effect, an exit at the top of the cowl should create the maximum delta P(pressure change)- and thus the best airflow though the heat exchanger! Another consideration - at a high angle of attack /low speed aircraft attitude the pressure on the bottom of the airframe is even higher than normal - making this an even worse location for a cooling air exit. The best illustration of a successful, efficient cooling air exit would seem to be the side ducts on Mike Arnold's AR-5.

3) Again in "conventional" (tractor) applications, another common mistake appears to be in the design of the intake duct work; there seems to be a gut-feeling (error!) that more inlet area equals more cooling: the mistake here is that the high-energy inlet air behind the prop must be managed properly to convert its velocity to the required pressure to feed the cooling system. The two most important parameters appear to be: 1) a correctly designed inlet opening (with an "airfoil-shaped" lip - so no stalled airflow is occurring!), and 2) a duct with the right length/diameter to convert the inlet air velocity to pressure. (Note: an excellent article appeared in Sport Aviation several years ago . . . look it up!)

Remember to look at the successful Lancairs, and the Lo Presti speed cowls for Comanche, etc; these designs are proof that "less is more" in cooling inlet area.

4) Another unexplored possibility in "conventional" airframes is the placement of the cooling system somewhere in the tail cone. This is normally wasted space - the tail cone has to be there to hold the tail feathers where they need to be - why not use it for something else too? This concept has been suggested by Richard Finch for his "Finchbird" design.

Problems associated with this concept include routing the hot coolant through the cockpit area and increased pumping losses due to the length of plumbing between engine and radiator.

5) For "pusher" engine installations (such as Long EZ, Cozy, E-Racer) the problem is somewhat simpler - this configuration forces a more intelligent placement of the cooling system. In this writer's opinion the E-Racer is the aircraft to look at! The inlet is placed on the (high pressure!) bottom of the fuselage and responds correctly to changes in angle of attack; the exit is into the "dirty" low-pressure region at the rear of the fuselage and around the prop centerline. This would appear to be a "can't miss" cooling system - the pressure differentials in the E-Racer cooling duct work must be tremendous.

6) There is a trend in cooling system design in current autos which is opposite to the direction I believe we should be going: with the low values of Q (dynamic pressure!) experienced by cars, designers are forced to use radiators with maximized frontal area, but minimum depth. Modern aluminum radiators are very thin, having only 1 or 2 rows of tubes; traditional brass radiators had 3 or 4 rows, or more.

To take advantage of the much higher Q available in airplanes, I believe we should be using much thicker radiator cores; the popular VW Rabbit radiator is light and efficient, but thin; stack 2 of them together in a (sealed) duct - they're cheap! Or have a specialty manufacturer make you a thick core radiator that fits your application. This writer prefers to use heater cores for cooling applications for the following reasons: 1) they offer the most cooling area per dollar spent. 2) they are typically very thick, with 4 tube rows appearing to be the average. 3) they have smaller frontal areas than radiators, allowing them to be placed optimally in the air stream.

Most applications of heater cores in aircraft seem to be two cores with the plumbing putting them in parallel flow; there would seem to be no reason why multiple core installations for larger engines couldn't be used. It should be practical to "gang up" 4 or even 6 cores if needed.

Even at this early period of development in installing auto engines in aircraft, we should be looking at the successes and failures in cooling systems already flying. It's the easiest way to avoid making the same mistakes again. Keep your eyes open, and ask lots of questions!

The following items will drive my design approach to engine cooling. Perhaps you will find these elements a starting point for your auto conversion.

HEATER CORES
I am going to use two heater cores to cool my Subaru EA-81 engine. These units are found in mid 80s Jeep Grand Cherokee SUVs. They were the largest I could find with the appropriate shape and hose locations. They measure 10.5 x 6.0 x 2.5 inches and should equal the ubiquitous VW Rabbit radiator in cooling area. I will be able to place them vertically near the firewall and exiting into the free airstream along the sides of the fuselage, similar to the arrangement found in Mike Arnold's AR-5. The Carquest part number is 279482 and you should be able to talk the manager down to less than $50 each.

THERMOSTATS
All thermostats are not created equal! I believe in the use of a thermostat to provide constant temperature over a wide variety of operating conditions. That's one of the properties of liquid cooling we should take advantage of. A thermostat can be very reliable if it is of good quality and properly cared for. Why would anyone spend years of time and effort getting their creation in the air and then chance a powerplant problem induced by a $2.50 thermostat.

If your thermostat is silver colored and has an exposed steel coil spring throw it away. These units are poorly designed and built and self-destruct with regularity. Cooling problems occur when they jam closed or send their parts downstream to create blockages or damage. Use a premium brand (I personally like the Robertshaw) and replace it if you experience any overheating problems. Thermostats are not designed to take thermal abuse and still provide reliable service.

OVERHEATING
If the engine is overheating do something about it. It is likely that more cooling is needed. Aluminum engines (like the Subaru designs) are not capable of handling over temperature conditions as compared to those built from cast iron. The engine will let you down(literally) if you happen to "cook" an aluminum powerplant. If overheating has occurred one should consider the possibility of a partial teardown to inspect critical components and replace appropriate seals and gaskets.

COOLANT
Heat transfer is what keeps engines alive. A reputable brand of ethylene glycol compatible with aluminum is essential for today's modern engines. Considerable research and development has gone into the incorporation of additives to protect coolant passages against corrosion and blockage (Texaco's information is published in Contact! issue #17). Although water is the best heat transfer medium it does not have the protection and lubricity of a good glycol/water solution.

Use of anything but distilled water in the coolant mix is foolish. Tap water contains chlorine in differing amounts; it is very good for health reasons killing off unseen bugs but it also reacts with aluminum and iron; it's in the same chemical family as oxygen but it eats metal even faster! Most every supermarket carries it. The recommended mix is 50:50 by volume which is a good balance between heat transfer, anti-corrosion additives and anti-freeze qualities. Also, I recommend the use of "Water Wetter", a Red Line product available at knowledgeable auto parts stores or performance shops. This additive is used by racers to increase cooling system efficiencies.

RADIATOR MOUNTING
I believe that radiators should be mounted to the airframe, not on the engine. It is obvious that a radiator is not a strong structure by virtue of its vast surface area and number of individual parts joined by solder or brazing. Engine vibrations are rampant. They occur unexpectedly as experienced by many experimenters flying with custom alternator mounting brackets. Mounting the radiator to a solid, non-vibrating area of the airframe minimizes any damage from engine vibrations. Also, it is a good idea to provide additional support for hoses attached to the radiator assembly; one can expect early failure of radiator inlet and outlet tubes if this is not done.

RADIATOR SIZING
Sizing is based on several factors; the two most important would seem to be the power output of the engine (or its heat rejection) and the range of airspeeds expected from the aircraft. As an example, consider two very different airplanes using an 100 HP engine: the first is a very efficient cross country airplane that will cruise at 175 MPH; the second is the traditional high wing taildragger with plenty of wing area that cruises at about 100 MPH. Since the available energy varies as the square of the velocity it is obvious (everything else being equal) that it would take $(175/100)^2$, or about three times less cooling capacity for the faster airplane.

The above example dealing with sizing is offered as a thought starter. The experimenter must also consider other variables as the outside ambient temperature range (are we in Death Valley or in Northern Canada?), ground running time (the aircooled engine having higher operating limits is not greatly affected), the size of the inlet/outlet areas, velocity /pressure effects and engine oil cooling requirements. Don't forget the manometer!   **BH**

High Energy Ignition for Factory Engines

Leonard Eaves
3818 N.W. 36th
Oklahoma City OK
73112
(405) 942 6339

Experimental aircraft are exempt from the regulatory and legal strangle hold imposed on General Aviation. The U.S.A. is the only place on earth where it is virtually impossible to improve any portion of a factory airframe or engine, to make running design changes, without being faced with law suits. I chose Skeeter to prove or disprove existing ideas. It is a one of a kind, experimental, two place, side by side aircraft that was first flown in 1966. It has over 1500 hours.

High energy ignition (HEI) systems have been used on automobiles for years. Sorry but true, general aviation

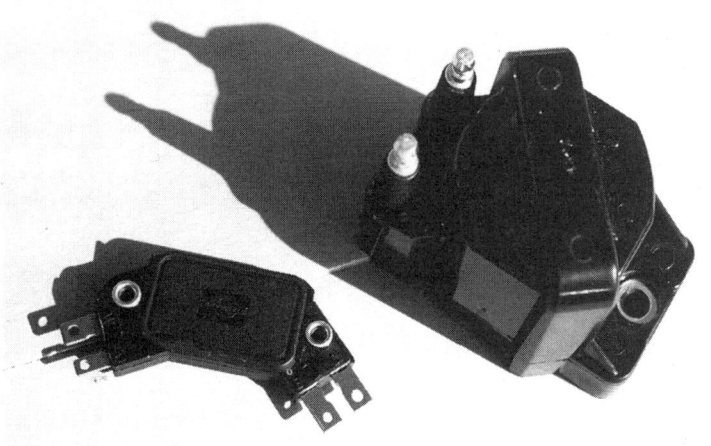

aircraft are still using antiquated methods of ignition, as applied to the first automobiles and farm tractors. One only has to compare a typical aircraft magneto to one found on a 1930's tractor to understand just how little aviation engine technology has progressed.

The HEI system I have devised uses proven auto components. I have incorporated a manual ignition advance and retard feature which replaces those functions built into the conventional automobile distributor. Essentially a bolt on replacement for a magneto, this unit is lighter, less expensive, has minimal inertial drag (less wear) and offers the pilot the means to optimize engine operation through advance/retard control. What could be better?

TEST PROGRAM

My unit has had two years of intermittent testing on an O 290 Lycoming test stand and now has over two years of in-flight operation on Skeeter. The unit is not any better than that used on most automobiles built before the last changes to the EPA implemented Clean Air Act (.41 HC, 3.4 CO, 1.0 NOx). Basic component reliability and durability is established by the stringent rules requiring the auto manufacturers to develop and build 50,000 mile/5 year emissions related engine components. Considering its advantages, I believe the unit fully outperforms the aircraft magneto.

During the extensive period of testing and use one failure did occur. As is many times the case blame is placed squarely on the operator, in this case it was the designer. Here is what happened (in seconds!). Over the mountains at 11,500 feet, fuel was being transferred from the tip tanks to the main tank when the engine suddenly slowed to 1500 RPM. Carburetor heat was applied but no change. With full rich the engine slowed more. The HEI switch was flipped; no presense of HEI was felt. Meanwhile, altitude was being lost causing "concern" but no panic. The mixture was brought to very lean and the engine came to life. In time it was determined that that fuel was not being transferred (the fuel pump reset fuse had popped). The fuse was quickly reset and flying resumed. I had installed the HEI and fuel transfer pump on the same fuse. It was a failure, no less, and the problem was remedied with a separate fuse for the HEI.

In the future I plan to develop a HEI system similar to the one described here that will fire both upper and lower spark plugs. The impulse magneto will be retained purely as a non-battery powered back-up. My experience with aircraft ignition systems has been both educational and convincing. At this writing I do not plan to go back to magnetos as a primary source of ignition.

HEI DESIGN

The main feature of this design is the use of certain magneto parts to mount and initiate the ignition. I used the Bendix S4LN-20 non-impulse magneto; any other magneto make can be converted to HEI with a little study. As the illustrations show this HEI system is fairly simple to fabricate. I used no drawings to make the parts, finding it very easy to take dimensions from existing magneto parts. Magneto cores list for about $180.00; I suggest looking for beat up cores which are unserviceable. An observation: if someone wished to go into production it would not be difficult to fabricate all the necessary parts.

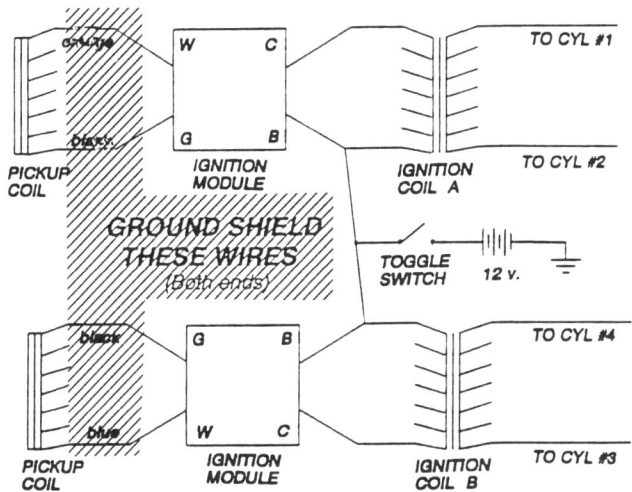

WIRING DIAGRAM

The first step is the dissassembly of the magneto. Parts to be retained are the front housing and the main shaft/drive gear assembly. I replaced the front bearing and seal (202 SZZ B.C.A.). The heavy armature is pressed off the shaft. The front housing is machined parallel with the magneto/engine mounting surface, removing all but one inch of the metal as shown by the dashed lines on sketch (A).

Sketch (B) shows the retained magneto parts, a new rear bearing and new sensor trigger welded to the magneto point cam. The idea at this point is to replace missing housing, provide for shaft bearing, and establish a suitable surface for the HEI sensors.

Sketch (C) shows the parts to be fabricated. At the right is the stationary shaft housing. I made mine from steel. The plate is 1/8 inch. Holes are drilled to attach the plate to the housing and clearance for the shaft. The tube is 1 1/8 x .035 wall, approximately 1.5 inches long. The two are welded together making sure that the tube is square to the plate. With the tube located concentric with the shaft the attachment holes are marked, drilled and tapped.

The next part is the rotating shaft housing. Its tube is 1 1/4 x .032 wall, approximately 2.0 inches long. Before being welded to the 3 3/8 inch circular 1/8 inch plate its end (nearest in sketch) must be swaged to accept a bearing (for the S4 magneto, SKF 2RS/B6). This done by using another bearing or steel bar turned to the correct diameter as a swaging tool. Simply, the ends of the swage and tube are clamped in a vise, heat is applied to the tube and the vise is tightened to expand the tube over the swage to bearing depth.

At the left of Sketch (C) is the pick-up sensor assembly consisting of the Chrysler pick-up sensors (NAPA MP816), a circular mounting plate 2 1/2 inches in diameter and attaching screws (not shown). The location of the pick-ups must be 180 degrees apart and at a distance of .010 inches to the soft iron tab which is welded to the magneto cam. Use a feeler gage and sensor adjustments to make the gaps precise.

Sketch (D) illustrates the assembled HEI magneto replacement unit. Shim stock can be added between the inner and outer tubes to snug up any excess play. A Bowden cable is attached to the moveable shaft housing to advance or retard the ignition timing by rotating the assembly. The shaft housing is prevented from moving laterally along the shaft by the Bowden cable clamp (not shown in the sketch for clarity). I fabricated a right angle clamp bracket from 1/2 inch aluminum stock and bolted it to the stationary housing. The Bowden cable terminates in the cockpit where a simple quadrant lever calibrated in degrees of advance/retard is situated.

OTHER SYSTEM COMPONENTS

The pick-up sensors are wired to the two ignition modules using early GM components (GM part number 1976907) which electronically open and close the primary ignition circuit. Because of the heat involved I mounted my units on a Radio Shack aluminum heat sink. Any aluminum extruded section with fins will do the job when located away from engine heat.

You will need two modern ignition coils. I used the 1986 Buick V/6 coils (GM part number 1103608) which I mounted on the firewall. I selected these components at random. Most any pick-up coils, ignition modules, and two castle coil units firing two spark plugs simultaneously should do the job.

Wiring from pick-up coils to the ignition modules should match the pick-up wires for size and color. All wires from ignition modules to the coils should be #12-16 gage. The spark plug wires from coils to plugs should be top quality automobile resistor wire. I have not experienced any radio noise with my solid state electronics. You may experience noise if you have old vacuum tube radios or magneto wire leaks. Correct your original installation for noise before installing your new HEI system. I do not use the conventional magneto switch to operate the ignition. Instead, I use two toggle switches independently.

SPARK PLUGS

I have found it practical to change to less expensive platinum or gold plugs from the aircraft type specified for my engine. Platinum plugs are the wave of the future for their extreme durability; the Cadillac Northstar engine using platinum plugs is tune-up free for 100,000 miles. I simply used the designated numbers of the shielded aircraft plug and a cross reference guide to find the appropriate unshielded platinum or gold wire plug. Most industrial, commercial stationary powerplants or older trucks should have cross reference manuals. Things to observe are: proper thread size and depth, heat range (must be a cold plug!, otherwise detonation can occur), and correct seating in the head. Since aircraft plug specifications vary with individual engine models I cannot recommend any specific plug that will work with your particular engine.

SYSTEM DURABILITY

The cooler any electrical unit operates, the longer it will last. A cold air blast tube similar to a magneto blast tube aimed at the ignition module assembly is recommended. The ignition coils, although not as sensitive to heat, should also be treated to cold air. A low firewall location can help protect these parts from heat after engine shutdown.

SCHEMATICS AND TIMING

The wiring schematics show the necessary hookups. You will note that coil A is wired to cylinders #1 and #2 while coil B feeds #3 and #4. This type of firing is commonly refered to as "waste spark" ignition since the firing occurs both during the compression and exhaust portion of each cycle, the "waste spark" having no effect on exhaust gases.

Spark occurs as the sensor trigger passes the last bit of the permanent magnet in the pick-up coil. As the magnetic flux collapses it sends a signal to the ignition module which allows the coil to discharge at the spark plug. The HEI replacement for the magneto should be timed initially to fire at top dead center (TDC) which prevents engine backfire at engine start. As the engine begins to run the ignition must be advanced for optimum power. To advance ignition timing the rotating plate must be moved in the direction to make the spark occur before the piston reaches TDC. Safety is paramount. In establishing HEI timing (or magneto timing, for that matter) the engine should be free of fuel when adjusting the HEI. The rotating plate should have sufficient freedom of travel to move from 0 degrees (retard) at TDC to 40-45 degrees advance BTDC. Some temporary taped-on graduation marks on the rotating plate will be helpful during the setup. As mentioned earlier cockpit control of this movement is made possible by the Bowden cable attachment. Marking the cockpit lever quadrant plate in degrees of advance is recommended. LE

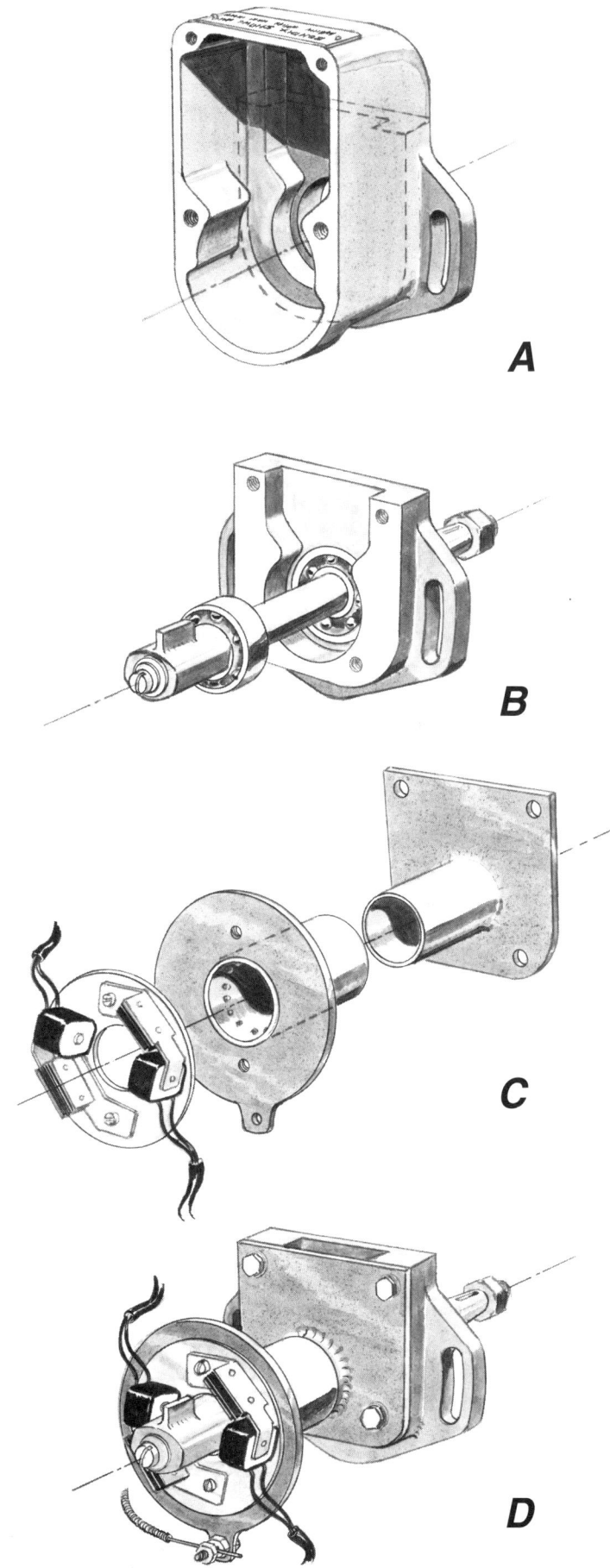

TRI-Q Renaissance

Steve Parkman
SWAG Aeromotive
2521 North Fairview
Tucson Arizona 85705
(520) 622 6910

The large variety of homebuilt designs either in plans or kit form never quite satisfy the creative homebuilder. Modifications, the bane of designers, are honest expressions of individual desires. In more than a few cases design deficiencies are discovered by the lead builders. Inevitable changes improve the basic design but these may also frustrate the conservative homebuilder. Delays become inevitable; the pace of confident building is lost. Inertia sets in; other situations take precedence and the project is not completed. Magazine ads, EAA Chapters, and builder newsletters are good sources for these projects. Before buying become knowledgeable about the design and its construction so that your decision is based on information, not emotion. MCM

I quickly discovered when I got the building bug that I could not afford a new two place 160 MPH plane without taking out a major loan. Paying off that loan would have meant no money for flying the airplane! My desire unabated, I created a paper budget and ballparked some performance requirements. My preferences: a 160 mph cruise, 4 gph fuel burn, two place side by side seating and "take it home" trailerability, all this for a $5000.00 investment. I didn't want much more than the next guy.

I mentally analyzed what type of construction should be used to keep the building time and costs down.

(Wood) Ok, so my father calls me a wood butcher and I don't have a lot of wood working tools so I think I will pass on this construction.

(Aluminum) This construction medium is good and I have a small brake and shear and most of the hand tools I will need though the construction time is quite long.

(Composite) I have put a lot of Corvettes back together and the only basic difference is that the glass cloth is much lighter and stronger. Also, much care must be taken to reduce the amount of resin matrix.

(Tube & Fabric) I didn't want to go as slow as a Cessna 150 so that this construction was out, although new kits, like the Avid Flyer, looked appealing.

Limiting myself to aluminum and composite designs I did some research in issues of Kitplanes magazine to determine availability and costs. I found out that aluminum kits were out of my pocketbooks reach. Other issues contained information on canard type composite planes. Like many before me I fell in love with the canards.

After reading up on the types of planes I wanted to build I found it would still be out of my price range to buy a new kit. At that point I started to look for a kit that someone had bought and not finished. It turns out that about 80 percent of the composite kits purchased by builders are unfinished. For example, I found a classified ad for a Dragonfly in a 1990 Kitplanes issue. Checking back issues I found the same plane for sale in 1986. It looked like not much more work had been done on it in the interim. The price had come down quite a bit in the four years in between the ads.

In the meanwhile, I reached my decision to go with the Q2

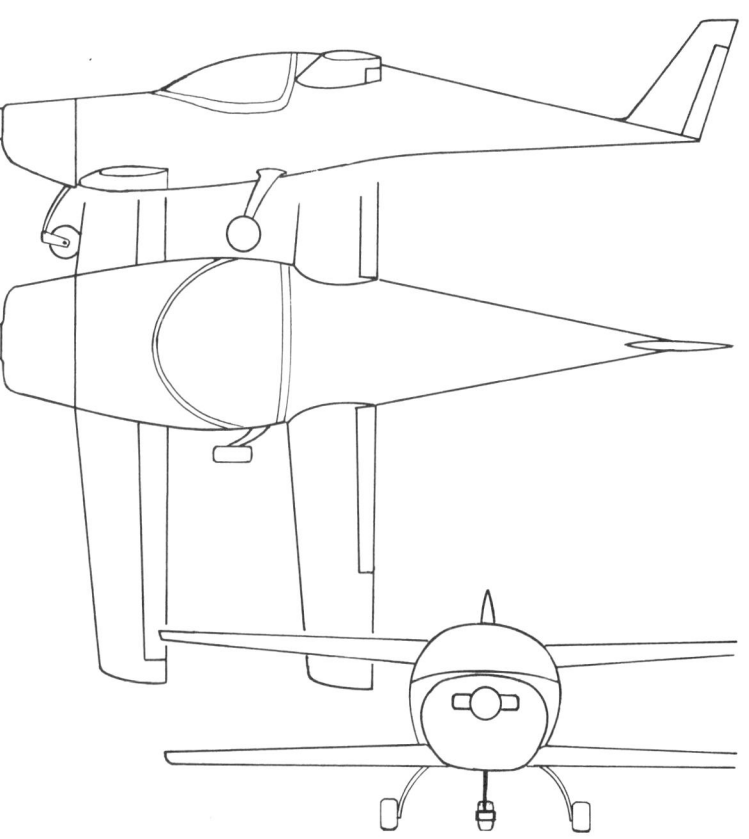

design. It was time to do more research. I was looking for answers to its construction, flying characteristics, and safety record. The best place I found to do this research was found within the Q2 builders group. As with factory type societies or organizations most airplane type builder groups publish newsletters. The letters from the builders let you know real quick what the main complaints are. Another excellent source is the NTSB library of homebuilt accidents accessible by computer (1-800-426-3814). A future issue of Contact! will take you through the process step by step (believe me, it can save you much grief).

According to some builder reports the Q2 design I selected had very bad ground handling problems. Their reports said the Q2 liked to bounce on landings if one wasn't right on the money which caused tail wheels to break, among other things. The other major problem was the GU canard. It would lose lift in the rain and cause pitch down. Trim would not completely correct the pitch problem. This lead to take off and landing problems that would give some pilots gray hair.

Buying into a homebuilt design that has had a track record for some time can save you time, money, aggravation, and possibly more. Thus, I would strongly suggest that if you are not an engineer that the plane you select should have the problems corrected by the manufacturer or by someone with the knowledge on what to change and how to make the changes without effecting the safety of the plane.

Now you are probably asking where did I find my bargain? Again, it was in the classified section. Most every aviation magazine has a classified section. Newspaper style publications such as General Aviation News and Flyer also carry homebuilt ads (pink sheets). The one thing that drew me to this ad was that it was a Q2, the canard type plane I was looking for and it was a 98 percent unbuilt kit. Thus, I could make the necessary changes to correct the reported safety problems without reworking the entire kit. The next thing it said really stood out (No reasonable offer refused).

This kit was a complete kit minus engine and epoxy as the epoxy was about 8 years out of date. The kit included the disc brake upgrade and all VFR instruments. Also included were all of the manufacturers newsletters and all of their upgrades and changes. The offer I made included shipping so I would not have to worry about getting it here.

My next problem was sourcing the tricycle landing gear and the new LS1 canard. Back to the builders group newsletter! One quick call to the editor and he came up with a name of a builder who might know someone who had the design upgrades I needed. To make a long story short I ended up finding a wrecked Q200 in Montana for which I ended up trading a new computer. This trade gave me the main wing & LS1 canard, the tricycle landing gear plus the wheels and disc brakes and the master cylinders. Also included was the main wing reflexer and an epoxy pump. A great trade for both of us; shipping was included.

We cannot fly far without radio these days. Again back to the phone and calls to some of the small FAA electronic repair shops. On the second call I found two Narco Escort 110 nav/com radios. Yes, I realized these units are not supported by Narco any longer. However, if you call some of the smaller repair stations you will find as I did they will check it out for you and make sure that they are within factory specs and also do the repairs necessary. After checking out both of the units I found that the receiver on one unit needed to be retuned which brought it back to specs.

Now here are the totals spent so far:

Plane	*$1000.00*
Landing Gear & Canard	*$440.00*
Com/Nav Radios	*$106.00*
Epoxy	*$177.00*
Misc Aluminum	*$8.00*
Throttle Quadrant	*$45.00*
Micro Balloons	*$21.00*
Feather Fill	*$45.00*
Spot Putty	*$4.00*
Sand Paper	*$20.00*
Primer	*$48.00*
Acrylic Lacquer Paint	*$38.00*
Repair Manual Narco 110	*$24.00*
Total	*$1976.00*

One thing I found out about all the people I talked to that they were all friendly and willing to talk about the problems about the plane I selected and what had been done to correct them. If you want to build a budget plane spend a few dollars on the phone bill and talk to some of the people who own and fly the plane you want. My next project will be a four place so I can take all of my kids along. Hmm! I wonder if anyone needs a computer system?

POWERING THE TRI-Q

Now that I have a plane that is capable of 160+mph I need an engine that is capable of dragging it through the air and still be efficient at cruise speeds, be reliable and last of all not cost a fortune to buy & maintain. I will now go through the three types of engines available for kitplanes.

(Certified Engines) This is *the* first choice if you want a tried and proven engine. We all realize the technology is forty years old. These engines are not fuel efficient. Rebuilding them becomes very expensive as the O-200 (my preference) is no longer in production. If your plane is weight sensitive you could have a CG or flight performance problem when you start adding alternators and starters and all the other options that we can't seem to fly without. When you buy a used engine the possibility exists you may not get a complete engine so be prepared to pay (plenty) for all the miscellaneous parts that are missing. Magnetos, wiring harnesses, and carburetors can quickly punch a hole in your budget.

Here are some vital statistics on several certified engines:

Continental O-200 100 hp @ 2450 rpm, 275 pounds. Average fuel consumption at cruise is 6 to 9 gph; asking prices for used mid time engines ranged between $3200.00 and $7000.00 (Trade-A-Plane).

Lycoming O-290-F1 125 hp @ 2800 rpm, 300 pounds. Average fuel consumption at cruise is 6 to 9 gph; prices for used mid time engines ranged between $3700.00 and $6500.00

(Two Stroke) This could be a good choice. It takes care of the weight problem but still leaves you with poor fuel economy. Dependability is good on the newer engines but the price on 100 HP versions are as high as a certified engine. I have not found any bargains on used 100 HP engines at this time. Too bad I couldn't use a 65 HP engine as there are quite a few used ones at very good prices and the overhaul costs are reasonable. The most noted 2-stroke manufacturer does not have a 100 HP rated two stroke engine but does have a four stroke rated at 79 HP.

Rotax 912 four cylinder four stroke water cooled 79 hp @ 5800 rpm, 123 pounds, 113 watt alternator, electric starter, dual electronic ignition, dual spark plugs, gear reduction box. Price is $7329.00

Hirth F-30 four cylinder, two stroke, air cooled, 95 hp @ 5700 rpm, 123 watt alternator, electric starter, single electronic ignition, single plug, dual carbs. Price is $4164.00 excluding the following options:
Tuned exhaust system $438.00
Dual ignition and heads $491.00
Belt reduction system $1100.00
Baffle air guide $404.00

Arrow GT 1000 four cylinder, two stroke, air cooled, 100 hp @ 6800 rpm, 180 watt alternator, electric starter, single electronic ignition, single plug heads, 4 in 2 exhaust system with aluminum silencers, gear reduction, dual carbs. Price is $6450.00, excluding the following option: Dual electronic ignition with dual plug heads. $550.00

Now that we have looked at the commercial built engines let's take a look at what is available in auto conversion market.

Canadian Air Cam-T-90 Suzuki Conversion, 3 cylinder, 4 stroke, liquid cooled, 97 hp @ 5300 rpm, turbocharged, chain driven redrive, dual electronic ignition, 144 pounds. Price is $6475.00. Options: carb heat adaptor $105.00, magnesium upper motor mounts $98.00

Mosler Engines VW Conversion, 4 cylinder, 4 stroke, air cooled, 65 to 82 hp, single electronic ignition, direct prop drive, 168 pounds, 2.5 to 6 gph, electric starter, alternator. Prices range from $3253.14 to $6647.26. Options: this manufacturer offered so many options that available space would not cover their entirety.

This list of engines is just a sample of some of the ones that are available and the prices that are listed are from the manufacturers' latest catalogs.

AUTO CONVERSION ALTERNATIVE

Now we will examine what it would take to build up our own engine using the 1980 thru 1985 Subaru.

Subaru EA81 1800 cc 4 Cylinder, 4 stroke, liquid cooled, 79 hp @ 4800 rpm, 153 pounds, geared starter, 45 amp alternator, single carb. Price in salvage yards ranges from $50.00 to $1200.00, depending on condition and willingness to deal. Options: unlimited

I have found and some of Contact! readers already know that some of the foreign car parts dealers are now carrying used engines that are being imported from Japan. Most of these engines have less then 30,000 miles and come with a 6 month warranty and cost $775.00.

Let's review what it would cost to build an blueprinted Subaru 1800 cc engine. Last summer, I finished building a

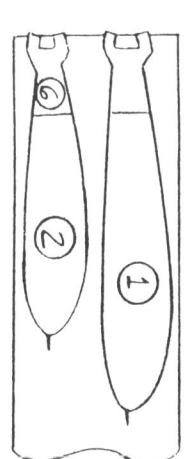
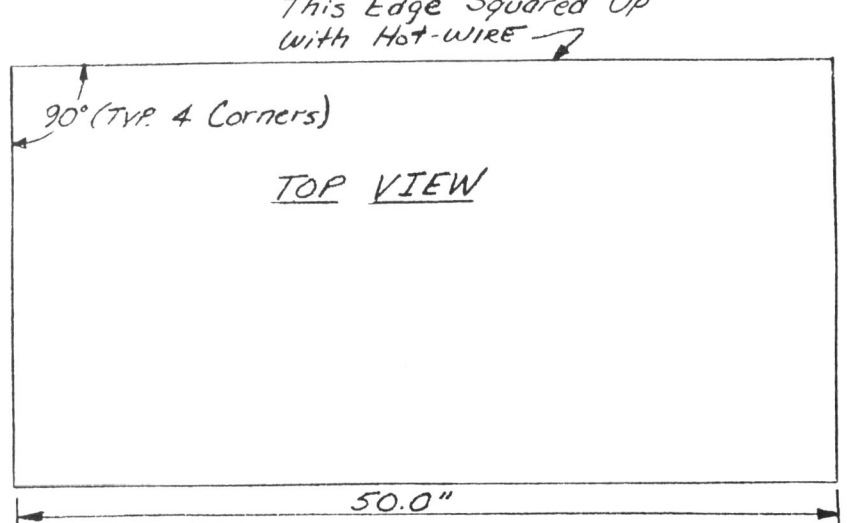
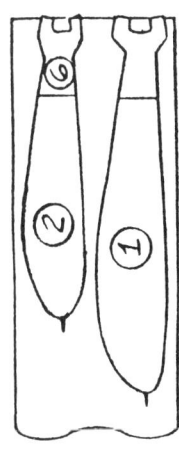

Typical Q2 lifting surface hot wiring guide with template orientation shown. Note two piece templates. The vertical cuts denote the shear webs created during application of the first two layers of UNI to the leading foam pieces. Trailing foam pieces are glued and skinned after lamination of the leading surfaces. This design minimizes alignment problems.

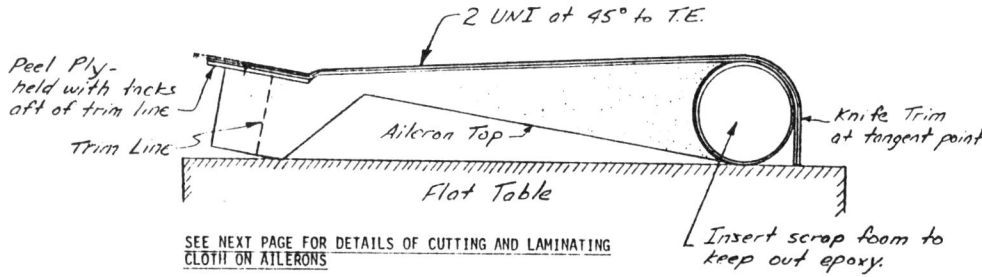

SEE NEXT PAGE FOR DETAILS OF CUTTING AND LAMINATING CLOTH ON AILERONS

Ailerons are constructed from hot wired foam sections, 6061 Al tube, and two layers of UNI glass. This view shows the glassed bottom surface. Remaining trailing edge foam will be sanded to the peel ply, the top surface glassed and the dip filled with micro.

300 hp small block engine for my 1964 Falcon sedan delivery and have found it to be very reliable so I am going to use the same techniques for building the Subaru engine. All the prices listed were quoted by a local Tucson machine shop.

To build this type of engine we will have the crank magnafluxed to check for any stress cracks or manufacturing imperfections. The crank is then reground to manufacturer specifications for the rod & main bearings, then is polished and balanced. The rods will be sized and balanced. New forged pistons and chrome moly rings will be balanced. The cylinders will be bored for the pistons we are using. We will have the cam reground so that the torque will be flatter across the rpm range. The heads will have a tri-cut valve job to give them the maximum seat area surface. The head surface and block surface will be milled to allow a perfect seal for the head gaskets and keep the compression to 8.5 to 1.

COST OF SUBARU ENGINE REBUILD

Subaru 1800 cc EA81 engine, used, 58,000 miles	$75.00	Forged pistons & Chrome moly rings	$274.00
Magnaflux crank	15.00	Rod bearings	26.00
Grind & polish crank	58.00	Main bearings	43.00
Balance crank, rods, pistons	70.00	Oil pump	79.00
Tri cut valve job	65.00	Lifters	47.00
Surface heads	40.00	Cam bearings	23.00
Surface block	50.00	Gasket set	68.00
Cylinder bore clean up	24.00	Geared reduction starter	52.00
Resize rods	40.00	Water pump	28.00
Replace cam bearings	20.00	Radiator	85.00
Reground cam	100.00	Hoses and clamps	9.00
Sub Total	**$557.00**	**Sub Total**	**$734.00**

USED PARTS	$557.00
NEW PARTS	$734.00
ASSEMBLY LABOR	$200.00
TOTAL COST	$1491.00

After studying the Subaru engines and going through the rebuild process I believe they will be the next generation powerplants to replace the VW engines and factory engines in the 65 to 200 hp range. They will give homebuilt aircraft the reliability of the certified engines at a quarter of the price of a certified engine. Even with the price of gas going up the average person will be able to afford to build a performance plane and, who knows, maybe the commercial aircraft industry will start building planes that the working person can afford.

The Subaru 1800cc engine, size and powerwise, seems to fill the bill for the TRI-Q. Next needed is a propeller speed reduction drive which many refer to as a REDRIVE

SPECIFICATIONS	TRI-Q
OVERALL	
span	17.8 ft
length	18.2 ft
height-level	4.1 ft
height-ground	2.8 ft
FUSELAGE	
seats	2
frontal area	8.5 sq ft
cockpit width	43.0 in
cockpit height	33.0 in
PERFORMANCE	
Vne	203 mph
Vc, 75% power	165 mph
Va	120 mph
Vs	50 mph
rate of climb	1000 fpm
service ceiling	18500 ft
takeoff, 50 ft obs.	1200 ft
landing, 50 ft obs.	2000 ft
range, 75% power	800 mi
fuel capacity	21.0 gal
wing loading	16.6 lbpsf
power loading	12.5 lbphp
G load+	4.4
G load -	2.0
WEIGHTS	
gross	1250.0 lb
payload	590 lb
baggage limit	20/70 lb
WING	
span	17.8 ft
area	36.7 sq ft
aspect ratio	9.7
chord-root	26.0 in
chord-tip	18.0 in
CG-fwd	
CG-aft	
airfoil-root	
airfoil-tip	
dihedral	2.0 deg
washout	0.0 deg
sweep	1.5 deg
incidence	3.0 deg
AILERONS (each)	
span	48.0 in
area	2.0 sq ft
def-up	23.0 deg
def-down	23.0 deg
type	plain
FLAPS (each)	
span	(none)
area	
type-def	
CANARD	
span	16.75 ft
stab area	38.7 sq ft
elevator area	4.5 sq ft
airfoil	LS1
def-up	12.0 deg
def-down	24.0 deg
incidence	0.0 deg
TAIL (vertical)	
span at rudder	3.0 ft
stab area	4.0 sq ft
rudder area	1.45 sq ft
airfoil	
deflection	28.0 deg
POWERPLANT	
make	Subaru
HP	100
max RPM	5600
max torque	130.0 lb-ft
fuel quality	89 LL
PROPELLER	
make	Warp
type	grnd. adj
material	composite
diameter	52.0 in
pitch	85.0 in

for simplicity. Homebuilders have several choices with respect to REDRIVES.

GEARS, BELTS, and CHAINS

The following is a list of some of the prebuilt redrives that are available to homebuilders. The prices are as listed at the time this article was written.

GEAR planetary (Ross Aero) 15 pounds $2500.00
Lou Ross is an unique individual who has designed and built engines for the US Government for their drones and has designed what I consider to be the best gear redrive on the market. Each unit is custom assembled from parts in stock. The housing is cast aluminum. Steel shafts and select steel planetary gears provide the basic speed reduction. The reduction housing mounts to a custom made bell housing which incorporates the starter mounting provisions. The flywheel is custom made aluminum with a shrink fit steel starter ring gear. A modified clutch disk is used to relieve the effects of torsional resonance in conjunction with the stock engine torsional dampener, as in manual transmission vehicles (see Contact! issue #1).

Optionally mounted in the flywheel are magnets which are used for the dual magneto pickup which are mounted in the bell housing and are mounted to be adjustable. For those of you that want to use electronic ignition you can specify leaving the magnets and associated magneto hardware out.

Three reductions ratios are available for this redrive at the present time: 3.17 to 1, 2.85 to 1 and 2.17 to 1. Now for those of you that don't need the larger unit Ross Aero is coming out with a smaller, lighter unit designed for the 1800 cc Subaru. This unit is approximately 25 percent smaller in size and weight. Even though a price has not been set yet it should be 25 percent less then the larger unit. Lou has done a lot of static tests on the larger unit and some are presently flying in Australia. Justin Mace (Contact! issue #6) has about 85 hours flying time in his Subaru Legacy powered Dragonfly. The Ross Aero Mooney RX-7 has flown about 20 hours.

If you are interested in this redrive give Lou or his son, Chris, a call (602-747-7877). Make arrangements to see them. You will find the visit to be an very educational experience as they do share their knowledge freely.

BELT cog type (RFI Publishing) 100 lbs $1600.00
This unit takes a very different tack on design. Instead of mounting the gears in a box every thing is mounted to a 1" thick steel plate which is mounted to the engine housing. The aluminum cog gears are mounted to two steel shafts which bolt to a aluminum flywheel and to the steel plate.

BELT cog type (Reductions) 22.8 lbs $1400.00
This unit was designed by Dave Johnson from Manitoba, Canada, using the HTD belt drive. You can get seven different gear ratios for this unit from 1.69:1 up to 2.37:1. Dave makes use of aluminum pulleys and mounting plates so that the weight could be kept down to the minimum without sacrificing strength and reliability.

This unit has been static tested for over 100 hours by various builders and a quite a few are now flying but not a lot of data has been kept on its performance or reliability. I do have to mention I was impressed by the information Dave has accumulated on converting the EA81 & EA82 engines and using various numeric combinations and different prop combinations. Dave will sell you just the plans or parts and pieces or the whole redrive ready to bolt together.

You will have to look far and wide to find a better belt drive. After talking to several people that have bought this unit they all had the same thing to say. Well designed & built! Now about the price it seems Dave has just signed an agreement to have this unit produced overseas which should mean the price will come down in the near future.

Now that I have looked at some of the prebuilt redrives I decided to look at the possiblity of designing my own using the Gates Poly Chain GT belt and gears. The following is the list price of the materials to build a 2.00:1 reduction unit.

Gates Poly Chain-GT belt part # 14-M-1120-125	$277.68
Gates upper gear part # 14MM-28S-125	166.68
Gates lower gear part # 14MM-56S-125	277.75
Upper bearings (2) 2" ID 3" OD	18.90
Lower bearing 2" ID 3" OD	18.90
1/2" 6061 T6 Aluminum plate 12x34 inches	290.00
1/4" 6061 T6 Aluminum plate 10x10 inches	65.00
3/4" 6061 T6 Aluminum plate 21x6 inches	180.00
2 inch x 2 foot 4130 steel shaft	40.00
Machine shop work	600.00
Total	$1934.31

Due to the liability factor Gates is not interested in providing support for the aircraft industry. They did offer that with the above belt and gears that the power rating would be 485 hp. Due to the price of the parts, materials and additional machining I believe that designing and building your own redrive with the Gates belt is not a viable alternative at this time.

Now that I have looked at the redrives available I am using the new, smaller Lou Ross package which weighs 22.0 pounds, total. First, I think the MTBF (Mean Time Between Failure) will be less on the gear type reduction systems. Second, he is located only 1 mile from my shop. This by itself gave me the support needed to get this conversion done in the shortest period of time.

I believe that both of the reduction units are very well designed and will fit the bill in the low budget market. My hats off to Dave & Lou for professionally designed and built redrives. Now that I have all the major parts together for the Ultimate Low Budget Plane let's take a look at the final cost figure:

TRI-Q	$1976.00
Subaru engine	$1491.00
Ross redrive	$1800.00
Total	$5267.00

Well, it looks like the Skunk Works and I are in good company. We both went over budget on our planes. At least, my overage is a lot easier to explain. In the future I will be adding full IFR to it and, yes, it will be a low budget installation.

The message is simple. There are still a lot of budget planes out there to be bought and finished. When I was looking for this plane I found a KR2 50 percent completed for $600.00, less then 2 miles from my house. So if you want to build a budget plane start looking. The next bargain may be just around the corner.

EA81 ENGINE ASSEMBLY

I like to set my work area with all the components situated in the order of assembly. Each moving part is lubed to prevent scoring of the parts. I personally prefer STP Oil Treatment. I have found that it will protect the surfaces for an extended period of time in case the engine does not get run as soon as it is finished. I rub strawberry Chapstick on the gaskets which make the removal of valve covers, oilpan and waterpump easier. I use the strawberry flavor as the wax is softer and easier to apply and my wife says that it tastes better. Water hoses are easier to install and remove by using a silicone based lube on the inside of the hoses and on the neck of the engine and radiator.

The first assembly step is to install the lifters in the two case halves using a generous amount of lube. Next, the rods are assembled to the crank using STP. The rods cap nuts should be torqued to 18-25 foot pounds. The main bearings are placed to the crankcase halves. At this time one gasket is installed at the top of the case for venting. The crank is placed into one case half and is followed by the cam. The crank gear and cam gear timing markings are aligned. The crankcase halves are slid together being careful not to scratch the cylinder bores with the rods. Before bolting the case halves together and torquing the bolts to 46-56 foot pounds don't miss the case bolt on the left side inside the case under where the head goes on. Now you can stand the engine on the head bolts so the pistons can be installed.

Lube the pistons generously as part of the lube will be lost on the ring compressor as the piston is tapped into the cylinder. Also lube the cylinder bore. Make sure that one wrist pin retaining clip is installed in the piston since that side of the piston cannot be reached from the inside. The piston is rotated to be aligned with the wrist pin access holes in the block.

Install one piston at a time and tap it in with a rubber hammer. Turn the crank so the rod lines up with the piston wrist pin and then tap the wrist pin into place while holding the rod end in position. Once started seat the wrist pin all the way down to the retainer clip and then install the second retaining clip. The last step in this procedure is to put the screw-in cover plates on. Be sure to use the new washers supplied in the gasket kit. The cover plates are only used on the front of the engine as the bell housing covers and seals the rear access holes. Make sure that the covers are tight as the right one is under the water pump.

Now the oil pickup tube can be inserted into the block and the mounting clamp tightened. The next step is to install the head gaskets over the studs. Now slide the heads onto the studs and install the pushrods. Then put the rocker arm assemblies in place making sure that the pushrods are in place on the cups. Tighten the mounting bolts down and torque the head bolts and nuts to 46-56 foot pounds.

At this time we will adjust the valve clearances by bringing each cylinder up to top dead center and adjusting the intake valve to 14mm and the exhaust to 16mm. After this adjustment the valve covers and the oil pan are installed. I suggest that time be taken beforehand to drill the bolt heads for safety wire. Next, install the water pump using Chapstick on the gasket. The front oil seal can now be put into place and the front single pulley can be put on and the bolt torqued to 47-54 foot pounds. The last item on the front to be installed is the oil pump which is held on by four bolts torqued to 8-12 foot pounds. Again, I would recommend that the bolts be drilled for safety wire.

Now we will turn the engine around and put the cam shaft retainer on. Make sure that the clips are put back into place for the bolts and torque the bolts to 8-12 foot pounds and then bend the tabs up to prevent the bolts from backing out. Now the rear seal can be installed on the custom bell housing. The bell housing is mounted in place and the bolts safetied together. The flywheel is mounted next and its bolts torqued to 51-55 foot pounds and then safety wired. The dampener assembly follows and these bolts are also safety wired. The gear reduction adapter plate is installed next.

The gear reduction is slid into place and its bolts installed and torqued to 47-54 foot pounds. Next, the starter can be installed and safety wired. The distributor can be installed, first bringing the number one cylinder to top dead center and then sliding the distributor into the block while aiming the rotor button to the number one position on the distributor cap. After the distributor is in the retaining bracket is installed, loosely tightened. The timing is adjusted when the engine is mounted in the airframe. The last two items to be installed are the oil filler tube and intake manifold. All auto anti-pollution hoses are left off and excess holes are plugged.

Now that we have an engine that will give us a lot of trouble free flying time we need a motor mount that will do the same. To do that we need proper vibration dampening. To achieve this I designed a four point firewall bed mount that uses 4 bolts that bolt into the bottom of the engine block, isolated by two rubbers per bolt held into place by mounting cups attached to the bed mount. The mount was built out of 5/8 inch 4130 chrome moly tubing.

To keep the firewall from flexing under high loads a top mount center support strut was added. It also uses a rubber doughnut to provide vibration isolation. To provide corrosion protection all the firewall mounting plates have been anodized.

With the engine mounted I decided to add a dual electronic ignition system. To provide the safety margin I wanted I chose the race proven Allison electronic LED type system. The pickups are small enough that two of them can be installed in the stock distributor 180 degrees apart. All the wiring has been brought back to the instrument panel so that I can switch between either ignition module or both at once. All the wiring for the removable instrument panel has polarized connectors so the panel can be disconnected and removed for maintenance. Yes, working behind the stock instrument panel on a Q Bird is a pain in the neck!

To provide fuel injection for this engine I used a single port throttle body from an EA82 engine. Due to the excessive height of the stock manifold I came up with my own design. I also could not use the stock computer as I did not have the same type of distributor as the EA82 and could not override the distributor inputs. I decided to keep the electronics simple so I decided to design my own fuel control system. I used the Throttle Position Sensor for the throttle control and cockpit mounted a rich/lean control pot. A future Contact! article will describe its function.

Now I will reveal the only problem I have discovered on the 1800cc Subaru EA81. The heads have unequal flow between the front and back cylinders. I had built an intake manifold for a single port throttle body injection. When I started to lean the engine down the front cylinders would become excessively lean and the back cylinders would still be rich. To correct this problem in production I found out Subaru had built up the inside of the manifold tube to force more air to the front cylinders. To compensate for this problem I redesigned the intake manifold so I could use direct dual port injection thus the air flow would not be so critical as the single port throttle body. My electronic control module can handle two injectors as easy as one so no modification had to be done to it.

THE PLANE TRUTH ABOUT EFI

The electronic fuel injection system can be broken down into three major parts:

#1 HIGH PRESSURE FUEL PUMP The fuel pump sends the fuel through a regulator which keeps the fuel at a constant pressure in the lines and the fuel injector. The optimum location is as close as possible to the fuel tank. The excess fuel is then recirculated back to the fuel tank.

#2 THROTTLE BODY The throttle body consists of a butterfly valve that is located downstream of a venturi which produces accelerated air flow. Attached to the throttle arm is the Throttle Position Sensor (TPS), basically a 1/2 turn potentiometer. The other item is the fuel injector which is mounted in the air flow of the venturi. The injector is a spring loaded valve which, when a dc voltage is applied, will open allowing the pressurized fuel to spray in a fine mist in the reduced air pressure of the venturi.

#3 ELECTRONIC CONTROL UNIT The last part of the fuel injection system is the electronic control unit (ECU). The principal job that the ECU preforms is a square wave oscillator. As the square wave goes positive (A) the injector opens allowing a fine spray of fuel to be released. When the square wave goes back to 0 volts the injector closes shutting off the gas flow. As the throttle (and TPS) is advanced the square wave changes frequency (B)) and turns on more often thus allowing more gas to be sprayed. At the same time, the butterfly valve allows more air into the engine thus keeping the air/fuel ratio the same but bringing up the RPM of the engine.

Second, to change the richness/leanness of the mixture all that has to be done is change the on time of the square

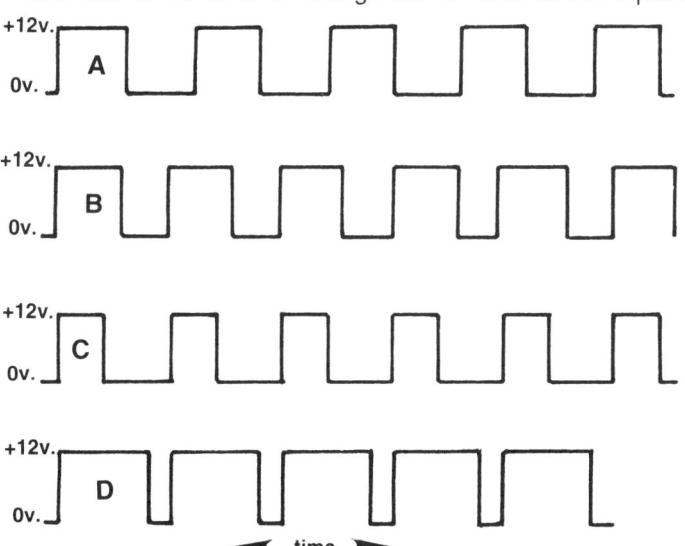

wave, narrower for leaner (C) and wider (D) for richer. Essentially, the above simplified description fits all modern fuel injection systems. However, due to the tough HC, CO and NOx standards set forth by the U.S. Federal Clean Air Act and CAFE fuel economy requirements the systems in today's automobiles are far more complex. O2 sensors, air flow sensors, knock sensors, coolant sensors and vehicle speed sensors are among the many pieces of additional hardware which, in combination, function to minimize

It is now May 1992. I'm running the engine (18 hours thus far), making a cowling, and modifying my exhaust system. As the plane is instrumented, painted and trimmed it appears the first flight will take place before August. If you have any specific questions while building up your Subaru EA81 please feel free to give me a call (I am a poor letter writer). I would be happy to pass on what I have learned. The ultimate success of auto power depends on the sharing of information among experimenters.

Bottom half of aft prefab fuselage panel is leveled in a cradle, the center and tail bulkheads are glassed in place, and the top panel is added. Upper halves of bulkheads are glassed next.

Cutouts in the forward fuselage are made to accept the wing, canard, and landing gear. Alignment is critical. Multi layers of glass tape distribute air and landing loads to the airframe.

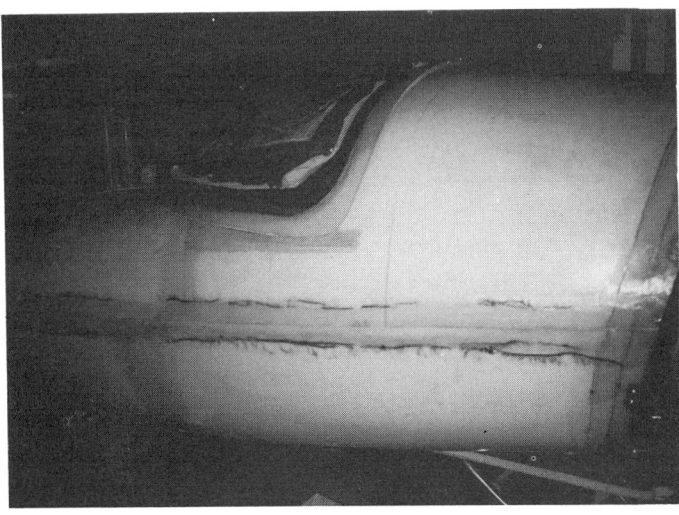
Forward fuselage panels are glassed. Parkman found it necessary to devise clamping plates to pull the surfaces together as the panel mating edges were warped.

Landing gear attachment between seat bulkhead and reinforcement panel is similar to Rutan designs. Ten tail cone attachment hard points permit removal and trailering.

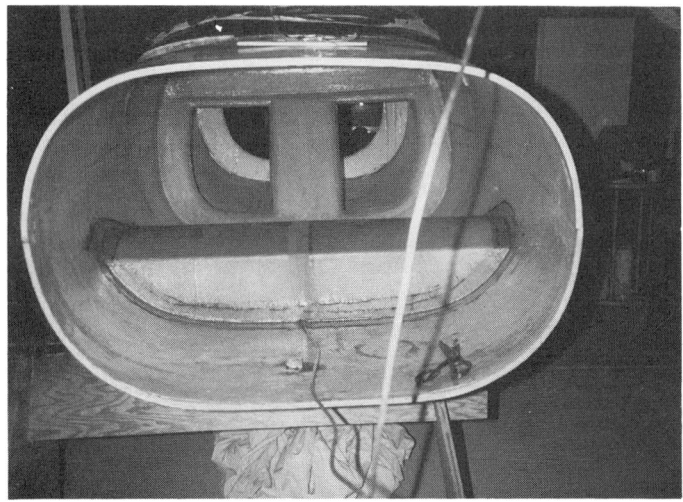
Forward end of fuselage without firewall. Seat type fuel tank is in foreground; seat back and rear bulkheads are also seen. Note thick fuselage composite wall and panel glassed joints.

Closeup of simple aileron control and reflexer. The circular plate contains an eccentric cam actuated by the lever arm which raises or lowers the ailerons collectively (reflexing).

Nothing fancy here: just good engine mechanic practice in keeping order during disassembly, essential marking of parts. The shop manual is referred to constantly.

Marks on the crankshaft flange and the camshaft gear are aligned to maintain proper engine timing. On the opposite end the stock torsional dampener is retained.

The Subaru EA81 crankcase is split vertically as with most horizontally opposed engines. Crank is balanced at the counterweights.

The wrist pin retaining clip must be installed in the inner facing end. The oil control ring has color coded segments which must be aligned for proper function.

Rods are installed according to their original locations taking care not to damage cylinder bores. Shop manual torque values are followed. With only one special tool overhaul is not difficult.

Parkman's TRI-Q Subaru engine mount follows original VW practice. A top center support strut was added later. Note simple nose gear attachment bracket.

Engine installation details. MG header tank and battery on firewall. Custom alternator brackets, intake manifold and racing grade plug wires are seen. Note stock bell housing.

View of left side of firewall. Two Allison ignition modules provide dual ignition redundancy. Directly below coil and resistor is Parkman's electronic fuel injection control module.

Ross Aero custom adapter plate and planetary redrive units are bolted to the stock bell housing. Engine oil lines feed the drive shaft needle and thrust bearings. Stock Subaru starter.

Subaru EA82 single port throttle body fuel injector. Fuel flow is automatically metered by the electronic control module, from pilot inputs to the TPS and rich/lean controls.

Overall view of installation. Valve cover breathers, throttle body, load resistor next to coil, engine mount and radiator are prominent. All wires are tie-wrapped neatly.

Cadillac air conditioner core serves as radiator.

SIX APPEAL

This 1988 CARCRAFT article is reprinted with permission to acquaint readers with the potential of the Chevrolet 4.3 liter V/6 engine. The wide availability of interchangeable parts from the small block V/8 make this engine an attractive aircraft powerplant for those needing 200 HP. Recommended as one of the best V/6 references by Fred Carter, his work on a 4.3 conversion was published in issue #30. MCM

Do you *really* need 600 horsepower to be happy? Countless magazine articles have fostered the mistaken notion that any engine with less power than a Pro Stock is hardly worthy of an enthusiast's consideration. But the reality of high-performance is quite different. Most Chevrolet enthusiasts will never have the experience of circling the Daytona Speedway at 200 MPH or free-falling through the Corkscrew at Laguna Seca in a turbocharged Indy car. For the Chevy performance fan with a street machine in his garage or a ski boat in his driveway, a 600-horsepower engine is as practical as a backyard nuclear reactor. So to all the Chevrolet enthusiasts who are looking for a reliable, responsive, and affordable high-performance engine: this V/6 is for you!

Like the original 265CID Chevy small-block V/8, the 4.3 liter (262CID) Chevrolet V/6 is an engine with unlimited potential. It has all the right stuff to appeal to innovative hot rodders. The V/6 owes its basic design to the small-block V/8, and many components are interchangeable between the two engines. The 4.3 liter V/6 has the same internal dimensions as a 350CID small-block V/8, with 4.00 inch diameter cylinder bores and a 3.48 inch stroke crankshaft. The smooth-running 4.3 liter Chevy is a true even-fire engine, with a uniform 120 degrees of crankshaft rotation between sparks. The V/6 is lighter and more compact than its V/8 counterpart: A complete V/6 engine assembly typically weighs 100 pounds less than a V/8, and the V/6 block is 4.40 inches shorter.

Chevrolet Special Products engineer Bill Howell championed the V/6's cause until his recent retirement. His enthusiasm and expertise made the Chevrolet V/6 a winner in road racing, oval track competition, and championship drag racing. Howell worked on projects ranging from V/6 powered sprint cars to the GTP Corvette's exotic turbocharged V/6. He even helped institute the ASA Gran Marque series that showcases Chevy's V/6 and provides an affordable alternative for circle track racers. But Howell didn't forget the "little guy" Chevy enthusiast during his V/6 investigations. One phase of Chevrolet Special Products V/6 development program was to explore the 4.3 liter Chevy's potential as a street performance engine.

The purpose of the test was to find out how the 4.3 liter V/6 would respond to traditional hot rodding techniques. Howell began the test procedure with a bone-stock engine with a Quadrajet carburetor, then ran a series of dyno tests that duplicated the steps a typical street rodder might take to improve his engine's performance. Howell's plans included testing a variety of factory and aftermarket components, such as dual exhausts, headers, camshafts, intake manifolds, and cylinder heads. It should be emphasized that these modifications are not emissions-legal; however, street rods and marine applications are exempt from emissions regulations in many areas.

The V/6 dyno tests were conducted at Katech, Inc. in Mt. Clemens, Michigan. Katech's dyno cells are usually occupied by IROC small-blocks and thoroughbred V/6 racing engines; a production motor outfitted with an air cleaner and muffled exhausts is a rare sight in this environment. Katech general manager Warren Frieze and his staff worked the V/6 hard, swapping intake manifolds, exhaust systems, cams, and cylinder heads dozens of times. The highlights of this extensive dyno program are summarized in the accompanying charts.

One of the objectives of the dyno test program was to determine the performance limits of the V/6's stock cast iron cylinder heads. All production 4.3 liter Chevy V/6 cylinder heads have "high swirl" intake ports; these heads can be identified by their raised rocker cover rails and valve covers with three central hold-down bolts. The high-swirl port design promotes turbulence in the cylinders, thereby enhancing combustion efficiency and suppressing detonation. The spark plugs are also centrally located in the combustion chambers to spread the flame front rapily throughout the cylinders.

The 4.3 liter Chevy requires significantly less spark advance

to produce maximum power than comparable engines without swirl-port heads. A 350CID small-block V/8, for example, typically performs well with 34 to 38 degrees of spark advance. The 4.3 liter V/6 dyno engine, in contrast, produced its highest power readings with swirl port heads with just 22 degrees of total spark advance!

The 4.3 liter 90 degree V/6 was introduced in 1985 in Chevrolet passenger cars and light trucks. Until 1987 it was produced in both carbureted and fuel injected versions; all production 4.3 liter V/6s are now equipped with two-barrel throttle body fuel injection. In 1988, the V/6/90 was introduced in S-10 pickups and Blazers. The engine used in the V/6 dyno marathon was an early model light truck engine with a Quadrajet four-barrel carburetor.

The initial dyno test established the V/6's performance baseline with its stock induction and exhaust systems. The little Chevy posted 172 horsepower at 4000 RPM. A Holley four-barrel aluminum intake manifold with a 650CFM Holley spread-bore carburetor was installed in Test 2; a set of street headers replaced the stock tubular exhaust manifolds for Test 3. These changes increased torque slightly between 2000 and 4000 RPM, but did not significantly improve the V/6's power above 4000 RPM. The conclusion: Although headers and a hot rod intake manifold may add to the visual appeal of a stock 4.3 liter engine, they won't add appreciably to its output without further improvements in the engine's breathing ability.

The camshaft change in Test 4 was more productive. The increased lift and duration of the GM marine cam profile added 17 horsepower and raised the power peak 800 RPM. Several other hydraulic camshafts were tested; the profile shown in Test 5 produced the best results-a dramatic 48 horsepower improvement over the baseline.

The cams used in the 4.3 liter dyno test were all reground stock camshafts. Chevrolet production flat tappet cams have induction hardened lobes. The heat treating on a stock cam is .100-inch deep, so the lobes can be reground to change the valve timing significantly. Although the selection of aftermarket cams for the even-fire V/6 is rather limited, many specialty camshaft companies can regrind a stock cam with a high-performance hydraulic or mechanical lifter profile.

The 1987 and later 4.3 liter V/6s are equipped with hydraulic roller tappets. Blocks used with roller lifters have longer tappet bosses with machined tops, mounting bosses for lifter guide retainers, and camshaft thrust plates. Chevrolet Special Products is currently evaluating several high-performance hydraulic roller cam profiles for the 4.3 liter V/6 which are scheduled to be released in late 1988.

A pair of heavy-duty aluminum Bow Tie cylinder heads (part number 14044802) were installed for Test 6. These first-design V/6 cylinder heads are similar to Phase 5 aluminum small-block V/8 heads. They have conventional intake ports, and the chambers are not a high-swirl design. The Bow Tie V/6 heads were outfitted with 2.02-inch-diameter intake valves and 1.60-inch exhausts.

Production 4.3-liter V6 cylinder heads have high-swirl intake ports. Raised rocker cover rails prevent oil leaks.

Intake runners in cast iron V6 heads are designed to create turbulence in the cylinders. High-swirl ports are effective at low-speeds, but they limit airflow at high rpm.

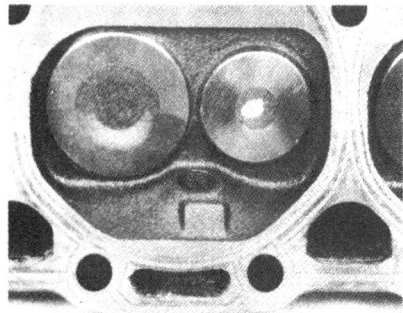

Centrally located spark plugs and high-swirl inlet ports lower the 4.3-liter V6's octane requirement. Cast iron heads have 1.94-inch-diameter intake valves and 1.50-inch exhausts.

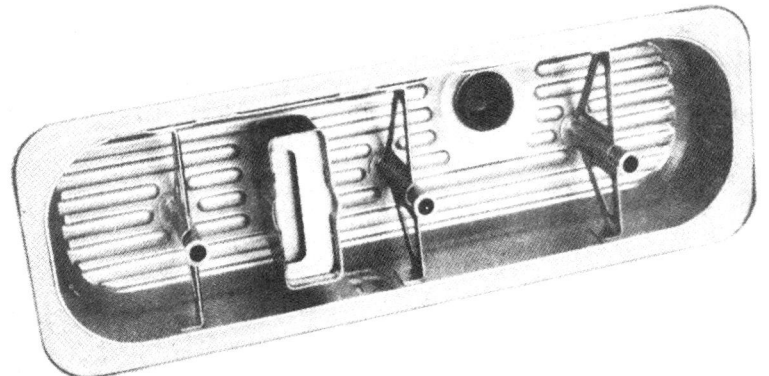

Rocker covers for cast iron V6 heads have central hold-down bolts which provide uniform gasket clamping and eliminate oil leaks.

"The runners and combustion chambers in the Bow Tie heads were untouched," notes Katech's Warren Frieze. "We did blend the valve bowls, but that was really just a cosmetic modification. The intake runners in the Holley manifold are designed to match the ports in a stock head. We built up the manifold flange by heliarc welding above the runners so the intake gaskets would seal with the taller ports in the Bow Tie heads." Katech technicians completed the aluminum head conversion with a pair of "Chevy Power" stamped steel valve covers (part number 14044826).

With the same exhaust manifolds and high-performance hydraulic cam used in the preceding test, the airflow improvement offered by the Bow Tie heads accounted for 31 additional horsepower at 5200 RPM. The switch to aluminum heads required an adjustment in the spark timing to unlock this horsepower, however. The engine produced maximum power with its spark advance set at 38 degrees BTDC.

A pair of high-performance mechanical lifter camshafts were the subjects of the next phase of the V/6 investigation. Increasing camshaft duration nearly 30 degrees (at .050-inch tappet lift) yielded an insignificant performance benefit with a muffled exhaust system, as shown in Test 7. Such a radical cam might also present serious driveability problems in a street-driven car.

A Chevrolet cross-ram intake manifold (part number 14044804) and a 600CFM standard flange Holley four-barrel were installed for Test 8. This cross-ram manifold complements the first-design Bow Tie cylinder heads, and requires no modifications for installation. The cross-ram's long intake runners fattened the torque curve above 4400 RPM, and added 13 more horsepower at 5600 RPM.

The mufflers were removed for the final test to see how the engine would perform with an unrestricted exhaust. The V/6 responded with its highest torque and horsepower numbers. With 273 horsepower at 5600 RPM, the 4.3 liter V/6 had gained 101 horsepower over its baseline--a substantial 59 percent increase.

Any Chevy enthusiast with a set of wrenches and some basic mechanical skills could duplicate this bolt-on performance program. Except for the

The 4.3-liter Chevrolet V6s installed in 1985 Astro vans and light trucks were equipped with cast iron Quadrajet intake manifolds (part number 14075660).

Stock induction hardened cast iron camshafts can be reground with high-performance hydraulic and mechanical lifter profiles.

Siamesed intake manifold runner feeds a pair of adjacent intake ports in high-swirl cast iron cylinder heads.

Aluminum Bow Tie cylinder heads produced a 31 horsepower increase over cast iron heads. Heads were not ported or extensively modified to increase airflow.

High-performance 650cfm Holley spread-bore carburetor (right) is a bolt-on replacement for stock Quadrajets.

Chevrolet cross-ram intake manifold produced a broad torque curve with aluminum Bow Tie cylinder heads. The carburetor is mounted sideways to provide clearance for a large-diameter HEI distributor cap.

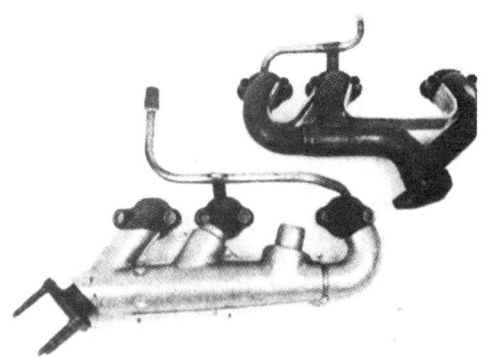
Free-flowing production tubular exhaust manifolds are ideal for street rods and engine swaps.

camshaft changes, the V/6 short-block was never touched throughout the entire series of dyno tests. It endured dozens of full-throttle power runs without a complaint and without a failure. That kind of reliability is hardly news to hot rodders, however. The 4.3 liter V/6 may be short a couple of cylinders, but it continues Chevrolet's long tradition of affordable performance. **CARCRAFT**

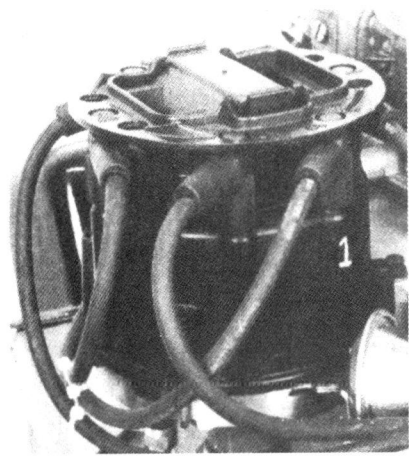

A production HEI distributor provided reliable ignition throughout the series of dyno tests. Cast iron heads required only 22 degrees total spark lead for best performance; timing was advanced to 38 degrees with aluminum Bow Tie heads.

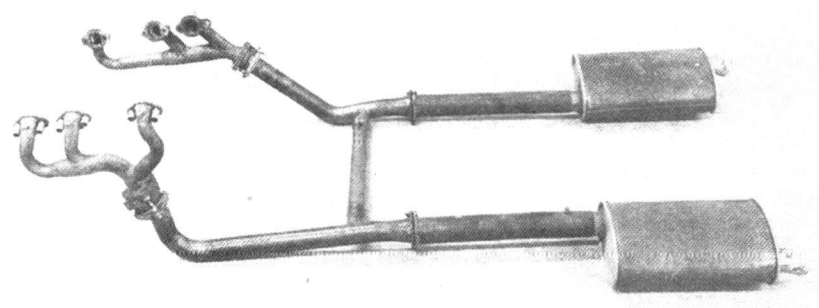

Unmuffled headers with a balance tube joining the collectors produced the highest horsepower readings in the V6 dyno session.

Dynamometer Test Of 4.3-Liter Chevrolet Engine

Test	Rpm	Torque	Bhp	Engine Configuration Or Change From Last Test
1	2100	**256**	101	Baseline: Stock 4.3-liter Chevrolet V6 with cast-iron heads, cast-iron intake manifold with Quadrajet carb and air cleaner. Stock steel tubing exhaust manifolds with dual exhaust, low-restriction Corvette mufflers and two-inch crossover ahead of mufflers. Twenty-two degrees total spark advance produced maximum power with swirl-port cylinder heads.
	2400	253	115	
	2800	251	134	
	3200	247	150	
	3600	240	164	
	4000	226	**172**	
	4400	203	169	
	4800	172	157	
2	2100	260	103	Changed to Holley Street Dominator intake manifold with 650cfm spread-bore Holley carburetor. Jetting is No. 65 primary, .055-inch power valve channel restriction, .076-inch secondary plate orifices.
	2400	260	119	
	2800	**261**	139	
	3200	254	155	
	3600	243	166	
	4000	227	**173**	
	4400	200	167	
	4800	170	155	
3	2100	256	101	Changed to street headers (1¾x29-inch-long primary pipes) with mufflers and balance tube. No carburetor recalibration required.
	2400	263	120	
	2800	**264**	140	
	3200	257	156	
	3600	245	168	
	4000	230	**175**	
	4400	202	169	
	4800	174	159	
4	2000	245	94	Changed to GM marine camshaft No. 14095449. No carb or timing changes required. Cam specs: 200 degrees intake duration, 214 degrees exhaust duration at .050-inch lift; .272-inch lobe lift, 110-degree centerlines with intake installed at 106 degrees.
	2400	244	111	
	2800	**254**	135	
	3200	235	154	
	3600	250	171	
	4000	244	185	
	4400	229	191	
	4800	212	**192**	
5	2000	244	92	Changed to street high-performance hydraulic lifter cam. Same headers and mufflers. Carburetor secondary orifices reduced to .070-inch, changed to No. 61 primary jets. Cam specs: 230 degrees intake and exhaust duration at .050-inch lift; .320-inch lobe lift, 109-degree lobe centerlines with intake installed at 105.
	2400	238	108	
	2800	256	136	
	3200	255	155	
	3600	259	177	
	4000	**263**	200	
	4400	253	212	
	4800	241	**220**	
	5200	222	**220**	
	5600	202	216	
6	2400	256	116	Installed Chevrolet aluminum Bow Tie cylinder heads No. 14044802 with Holley intake manifold and spread-bore carb. Changed to stock tubing exhaust manifolds with dual mufflers and crossover. 230-degree camshaft from previous test. No jet change made, but 38 degrees total spark advance required for maximum power.
	2800	245	130	
	3200	247	150	
	3600	255	174	
	4000	254	193	
	4400	**269**	225	
	4800	267	244	
	5200	254	**251**	
	5600	232	247	
7	2000	236	89	Changed to mechanical lifter camshaft used in ASA Gran Marque series. Reinstalled headers with dual mufflers and crossover. Cam specs: 258 degrees intake duration, 264 degrees exhaust duration at .050-inch lift; .345-inch lobe lift, 110-degree lobe centers, .025-inch valve lash (hot).
	2400	209	95	
	2800	227	121	
	3200	236	144	
	3600	236	161	
	4000	263	200	
	4400	**268**	225	
	4800	**268**	245	
	5200	242	239	
	5600	228	243	
	6000	222	**253**	
	6400	189	230	
8	2000	238	90	Installed Chevrolet cross-ram intake manifold No. 14044804 with 600cfm Holley carburetor (No. 64 primary jets, No. 74 secondary jets). Carb mounted sideways on Chevrolet manifold cover No. 14044803. Camshaft and headers same as preceding test.
	2400	207	94	
	2800	230	122	
	3200	246	149	
	3600	246	168	
	4000	262	199	
	4400	**273**	230	
	4800	268	245	
	5200	258	255	
	5600	240	**256**	
	6000	222	254	
9	2000	248	95	Removed mufflers; all other components same as preceding test. No jet or timing change required.
	2400	242	109	
	2800	247	131	
	3200	245	149	
	3600	253	173	
	4000	274	207	
	4400	281	235	
	4800	**282**	258	
	5200	272	269	
	5600	256	**273**	
	6000	235	268	

Octane Requirement and Your Experimental Airplane

Robert H. Yeakey P.E.
7921 Bellewood
Dallas Texas 74238
(214) 348 2947

You honestly believe your airplane needs the octane number fuel that you see on the engine data plate-right-wrong! The first and lower number on the Lycoming 180 hp is based on 100LL because that is the only suitable gas available. 91 octane is the correct and actual requirement for this particular engine. Because of unavailability 91/96 is not on the data plate.

As Technical Service Engineer for Humble Oil several years ago my duties included dealing with the situation created by trends toward ever higher compression ratios and combustion temperatures. Golden Esso Extra and Gulf Crest high octane (over 100 MON) fuels resulted from these formulation studies.

OCTANE DETERMINATION

How is fuel octane measured? The ASTM (American Society for Testing Materials) test is accepted throughout the world. A standard ASTM single cylinder CFR (Cooperative Fuel Research) variable compression engine is run on isooctane/heptane blended samples to establish incipient "knock" guidelines. One hundred percent isooctane produces an anti-knock quality of 100. A eighty eight percent isooctane, twelve percent heptane mixture produces an 88 octane anti knock quality and so on. Test and commercial fuels are rated against this standard measurement technique. At Southwest Research Institute we ran a test fuel in a flat head Ford V8. Running on a 70 octane blend test fuel the engine had an incipient knock. So any commercial gasoline of 70 octane would take care of this car's needs. Incidently, octane requirements over 100 are possible to be measured by the addition of TEL (tetraethyl lead) to pure isooctane. Above 100 these values are usually referred to as performance numbers (PN).

We have mentioned that 100LL is not the true engine requirement for the Lycoming 180 hp engine. Is the Lycoming 180 91 octane specification required all the time according to your engine manual? No-not true! Only once in a great while is 91 octane required. In one test I recall, Al Hundere, President of Alcor, tried to make the 180 knock using auto leaded regular (at 6,500 MSL, 40 degree F.) but failed.

REAL OCTANE FACTORS

Dallas is above sea level; that computes to reduced air density and octane need. We also have some humidity that also reduces the air/fuel charge and the octane requirement. The OAT is usually below 60 degrees F. which cuts the air/fuel weight entering the engine. At WOT standard procedure is to run full rich. This also reduces the requirement by cooling the combustion. Thus, it is quite unusual for the 180 to need fuel of 91 octane motor method.

PUMP OCTANE

Engines sometimes read differently than the CFR test engine, falling somewhere between the motor (MON) and the research (RON) method numbers. This difference is called the spread, usually 6 to 8 numbers. The number seen on pumps is an average of both method numbers. To get the motor method just subtract 4 numbers from the (R+ N) /2 pump number. Prior to EPA action gasoline was advertised heavily using the larger, RON number.

KNOCK MECHANISM

The actual detonation is an instantaneous combustion of the last portion of the air/fuel charge. When the spark plug ignites the mixture, the first 80 to 90 percent burns smoothly and the cylinder presseure rises in a nice pressure versus crank angle curve but as the flame front approaches the far reaches of the chamber the high temperature finishes off the remaining mixture with a bang. It is quite audible on most engines except the ones in aircraft. Knock causes overheating, quickly leading to holed pistons, and more. Liquid cooled engines are slightly more tolerant, having additional capability to remove excess heat.

ENGINE DESIGN FACTORS

Design of the combustion chamber influences the octane requirement. The following factors have significant effects: 1) distance from the plug to the most distant part of the cylinder 2) cylinder and exhaust valve temperatures 3) size of the combustion chamber quench area 4) ignition timing; the fixed timing of a magneto makes a higher octane specification necessary, electronic ignition with a knock sensor will largely eliminate this factor 5) coolant type-best is water with a rust inhibitor-next a ethylene glycol mixture, about 50/50-worst is air cooling 6) deposits which may induce preignition and 7) compression ratio, either designed or due to carbon buildup. Compression ratio also affects the requirement, but certainly, contrary to FAA preachments, is only one factor and not necessarily the most important.

There are two design features that cause many aircraft engines to demand gasoline of higher than normal octane:

Almost from the beginning, the aircraft engine was air

cooled. In small general aviation aircraft proper engine speed for substantial power output was ignored to accommodate the .8 Mach maximum propeller tip speed. This kept the rpm slowed down, to get by without the use of expensive and weight increasing reduction gearing. Looking at the engine comparisons table, the result of the design direction was a much larger engine with high octane requirement. Basically this octane was required - a worst condition basis - because of marginal air cooling and the large piston diameter. For example, the Lycoming 150 and 160 hp engines have 5 1/8 inch diameter pistons. The efficient car engines - the last four in the table - have water cooling and pistons less than 3 1/2 inches in diameter.

ENGINE REQUIREMENTS

ENGINE	HP	RPM	MON	CR	HP/IN^3
Lyc O-360	180	2750	91	8.5:1	.50
Lyc O-320	160	2750	91	8.5:1	.50
Lyc O-320	150	2750	80	7.0:1	.468
VW Quantum inline 4 110 in^3	88	5500	83	9.0:1	.80
Nissan Maxima inline 6 180 in^3	120	5200	83	8.9:1	.822
Nissan V6 180 in^3	152	5200	83	8.9:1	.844
Buick V6 225 in^3	160	4400	85	8.5:1	.71

One other factor working against performance is the magneto. The certified magneto ignition system causes a higher specified octane requirement. A system employing a knock sensor would give a far more economical solution.

The use of a more sophisticated and up to date ignition system together with lower octane number than the current ultra conservative one that you now see on the data plate would achieve a real reduction in fuel cost and overall operating expense.

There is no reason why super unleaded car fuel should not fully satisfy the current Lycoming 160 and 180 hp engines.

It would seem that design progress was made only when EAA lit a fire under the two aircraft engine manufacturers. Continental Teledyne brought out a water cooled version of the old O-200 and O-300 engines. It likely would never have happened without Dave Blanton's early experimentation program. His V6 Ford powered C-175 flies on 6.8 gallons per hour at cruise on super unleaded car gas! This V6 has a simple belt reduction propeller drive that slows the prop down and lets the engine work. The cost of this and other auto conversions make them very attractive.

CONCLUSIONS

A. Regular auto gas blended 66 percent with 34 percent 100LL will perfectly satisfy the current existing Lycoming 160 and 180 hp engine versions. This ratio also cuts the lead concentration to the optimum value, about .65 cc/gallon, thus beneficial valve lubrication is maintained with reduced lead fouling problems.

B. Auto gas alone will work beautifully in any 7.00:1 compression ratio aircraft engine. These are the most numerous in the general aviation fleet.

C. A change to electronic ignition is legal for experimental aircraft and will reduce the engine octane requirement enough to permit auto gas in most any experimental airplane.

Ross Aero engine mount fabrication method: 1) firewall attach points are defined on bottom plate 2) engine pulley/centerline is placed on located wood plug and steadied by hoist at prop flange 3) plumb measurements are taken to define thrust line offsets and 4) engine mount is fabricated. Yeakey's T18 Subaru XT6 mount is shown here.

Ford 3.8 Liter V/6 Engine Conversion Information

Bruce A. Frank
218 Landenberg Road
Landenberg Pennsylvania 19350
(215) 274 2168

The Dave Blanton designed Piper PA-22 tail dragger conversion powered by a Ford 3.8 liter engine was first flown in 1987. Its cog belt redrive was first tested in a Cessna 175 and appeared at Oshkosh in 1985. Since that time over 400 sets of plans have been sold and many of the type are now flying. Blanton has retired from support of his STOL design and is engaged in the development of a certificated four place bush plane called the Pegasus. Bruce Frank is a STOL builder, provides some conversion parts, and publishes an informative newsletter devoted to this design and the conversion of the Ford 3.8 liter engine. The following items are excerpted from his newsletters. These also contain much hands-on information on the conversion of the PA-22 airframe. Highly informative for STOL builders and recommended. MCM

ALTERNATOR

The need to slow the alternator was a problem that we have been trying to address for some time. After many tries a new five inch aluminum crank pulley was fabricated which reduces belt speed in combination with a 3.5 inch alternator pulley. Some 120 hours of running time on the Bayard DuPont Defiant have been trouble free, with no sign of alternator bracket cracking or loose water pump bolts.

FUEL PUMP

I have identified some AC Delco submersible fuel pumps (part number marking B1494-1336). Although they are called submersible I believe they need not be installed in that fashion. Both ends of the pump have nipple fittings so they can be easily adapted to aircraft use. My tests show that these pumps will make about 7 psi and a flow rate of 30 gph. These pumps are cooled and lubricated by passing fuel. If run dry the pump will screech and quit after about 45 minutes of running time!

ENGINE BALANCE

An important point to remember is the matter of engine balance. According to conventional wisdom factory engines are fairly well balanced. However, if the engine is disassembled it is easy to make sure that each piston and rod is within a couple of grams of its mates. Each engine is balanced externally at the factory. After re-assembly according to factory specifications the engine should be rebalanced. If your A&P has the equipment to balance a prop he can balance the engine at the flywheel by drilling holes and adding counterweight bolts and washers. The process is repeated at the crank pulley end of the engine. The engine must be balanced at both ends.

Some cog belt redrives (Blanton and Bassham) for the 3.8 liter engine use cast sprockets (also referred to as pulleys). In some instances, final machining does not clean up areas of these parts. Although the part ends up true and concentric a few grams of difference across the sprocket diameter may be sufficient to damage the prop shaft bearing seats or cause cracking of the flywheel plate. This is not speculation; I have seen these problems.

ENGINE COOLING

Incidences of engines blowing head gaskets have been reported. This problem is initially seen as a small coolant leak which manifests itself as a persistent pressure in the engine cooling system. As the aircraft is flown additional hours an increase in coolant pressure is evidenced. A pre-flight check showing 3-5 psi coolant pressure (no indication if normal) is another sign of head gasket leakage. If not corrected the coolant pressure will increase until the coolant filler cap is vented or coolant loss is excessive. If your gage indicates zero before start up it should also show zero after shut down and cooling back to ambient temperatures. On the 3.8 liter engine the leak usually develops between the end cylinders and the water jacket area at the end of the heads. It is apparent from experience that head gasket leaks will develop regardless of brand or care in torquing down head bolts unless the gaskets are "glued" on properly.

A method to prevent this problem is to use the old tried and true Kopper Kote spray. I recommend an abundant application of two to three coats, allowing complete drying between coats. The coating is applied to all surfaces, the heads, the block and both sides of the two gaskets. Buy two cans; I have used as much as a can and a half on one engine.

As a liquid cooled engine warms up the coolant dramatically expands. In most automobiles this expansion in handled in one of two ways; sometimes both methods are used.

One method is to keep the radiator full with little airspace in the top radiator tank and provide a catch/overflow canister. The coolant pressurizes until the cap lifts. The overflow flows into the canister and then is drawn back by atmospheric pressure when the engine cools after shutdown. The principal advantage of this system is that the radiator is full of coolant at all times so that heat exchange takes place at every square inch of the radiator fins. The disadvantage is that the repeated cross flow between radiator and canister introduces fresh oxygen into the coolant. Dissolved oxygen in the coolant causes rust. Coolant inhibitors fight this problem but, in time, are depleted causing the coolant to become acidic which accelerates the rusting process. Eventually, rust flakes clog radiator passages while aluminum radiator cores corrode and leak.

The other method is to provide enough air space above in the radiator to allow room for coolant expansion. This air space is compressed as the coolant expands. As long as the pressure does not exceed the radiator cap pressure rating the coolant remains contained.

Some auto manufacturers combine the overflow canister along with the "air space" system to allow for abuse such as pulling a trailer up Pike's Peak. Pressures go higher, exceeding the cap's rating and the canister catches the overflow. If everything works right the overflow returns to the radiator tank. However, if there is some air in the tank above the overflow as the cool down occurs this air expands to fill the volume of air space available and internal vacuum may not be sufficient to pull the coolant back into the radiator. Even when functioning correctly the oxygen problem is present. When working incorrectly, the radiator is not fully filled leading to overheating at normal power demand levels. I am sure one can visualize the consequences.

In homebuilt use the object is to provide enough expansion air space so that our high power demands never exceed the expansion tank capacity. For a given engine and radiator configuration the size of the expansion tank is inversely proportional to the coolant pressure. You may note that there is a "T" connector included with the expansion tank I offer. This configuration allows the connection of the expansion tank at whatever point desired. The "T" is made slightly asymmetrical to allow adjustment if needed.

Expansion tanks do not have to be at the highest point of the coolant system but a method for bleeding out air pockets trapped above the coolant filling level is essential. With the expansion tank mounted below some precautions are necessary. First, the hose connecting the tank to the cooling system must loop below the tank to prevent the air in the tank from escaping to the system high point, either the block coolant jacket or the radiator, whichever is higher. Second, the aircraft attitude must be considered during the location of the expansion tank. If incorrectly placed some maneuver could cause the expansion tank air to "burp" and flow to the block or radiator reducing cooling efficiency, or worse. Finally, the initial fill of coolant must be such that the expansion tank does not receive any coolant.

DUPONT DEFIANT COOLING SYSTEM

The rear engine has an expansion tank mounted high on the firewall. It is plumbed into the the upper water pump hose with a "T" fitting. The radiator is installed horizontally below the engine. The coolant can be added through the expansion tank. Virtually no coolant is in the tank when the system is cold since the tank is well above the engine block, allowing the expansion principle to function. Areas of the block which might trap air are bled with small diameter lines to the suction side of the water pump. (Some builders have omitted this method; care must be taken to "burp" the engine while filling). Small diameter lines are essential as too much flow through them may defeat normal block and head coolant circulation.

The front engine is set up with two radiators because of space constraints. One radiator has no filler cap and feeds in series through a second radiator with a pressure/filler cap. As both radiators were essentially at the same coolant level both tended to function with an expansion space in their top tanks. During running tests the flow would force the sealed radiator's air to the second down stream radiator and into the block causing cooling problems and the outflow of coolant at the pressure cap. After many futile attempts to solve the problem the solution was a custom expansion tank fitted against the cowling and located below the tops of the two radiator tanks. A fitting on the bottom of the expansion tank was connected to the overflow tube of the radiator's fill neck. A small line between the two allows free communication of pressure between the radiators and the expansion tank. The original pressure cap was replaced with a simple cap sealing the filler neck. The pressure cap was transferred to the expansion tank. Any minor displacement of coolant to the expansion tank during maneuvers is forced back by the increased pressure in the expansion tank.

DAVIDSON REDRIVE EXPERIENCE

After some 135 flight hours and his first Sportsman 2+2 airplane annual Bud Davidson decided to check the balance of his Blanton cog belt redrive and externally balance the engine. Working with Bayard DuPont they clamped the redrive to a work table and fashioned a electric motor to power the upper driven sprocket. The motor spun the cast sprocket at 2000 RPM, an appropriate speed for a 2:1 reduction design. At this speed the entire table jumped all over the floor. Balancing was accomplished quickly with the drilling of three 3/8 inch holes at the indicated spot on the web of the sprocket. The sprocket was re-spun with no sign of vibration other than that induced by the electric motor alone.

The Ford 3.8 flex plate mounting the starter ring gear (used instead of the cast iron flywheel for weight reduction) has been found in several instances to crack or fail. Some have theorized that the high thrust line relative to the engine mounts causes the normal gyrations of the propeller during flight to cause redrive oscillations about the crank centerline. Those minute displacements and gyroscopic forces on the thin flex plate stamping then cause it to vibrate leading to eventual failure.

A final balance check of Bud's engine was performed at 4000-4100 RPM. With the reduction drive front plate removed it was easy to observe the flex plate. As Bud retarded the throttle, at a point when the engine passed through 3800 RPM, Bayard saw the flex plate go through an oscillation which moved the edge of the starter ring gear over 1/2 inch from its normal track. That left no question that the flex plate can be excited to resonate at some RPM. The 3800 RPM number should not be construed as being of any significance since such harmonics will be very different with the complete reduction drive and propeller installed.

Since that check Bud, Bayard and I have collaborated to develop a machined aluminum flex reinforcement disk which replaces the back flange of the driver sprocket. This part extends out just short of the radiused area of the flex plate. Some additional machining may be required to fit the disk to compensate for redrive variations. The stiffness of the flex plate with the reinforcement disk is obvious. Bud Davidson ran the engine up and down through its operating range and no flexing was observed. Also, he felt that the engine ran smoother with the additional mass.

IGNITION COIL FAILURES

Some ignition failures have occurred likely due to heat or orientation. After a failure Bayard DuPont found a diode device at an auto parts store which allows two coils to be installed as in some auto racing setups. The part is made by MSD and costs about $60. This device permits two parallel coils to be activated selectively with no feedback through the coil not on line. Bayard's setup allows either coil to be run with either module and either battery. The MSD part number is 8210: AUTOMATIC COIL SELECTOR.

The ignition system is completely redundant except for the single pre 1985 distributor and single plugs. The Moroso company makes a flywheel mounted magnetic ignition sensor which is fool proof. Components can be found in most speed shops. With distributor or flywheel ignition sensing, dual ignition modules and dual batteries we are safer then the certificated engines, which run off a single distributor drive gear. **BAF**

MAGNETIC DISTRIBUTOR INSTALLATION

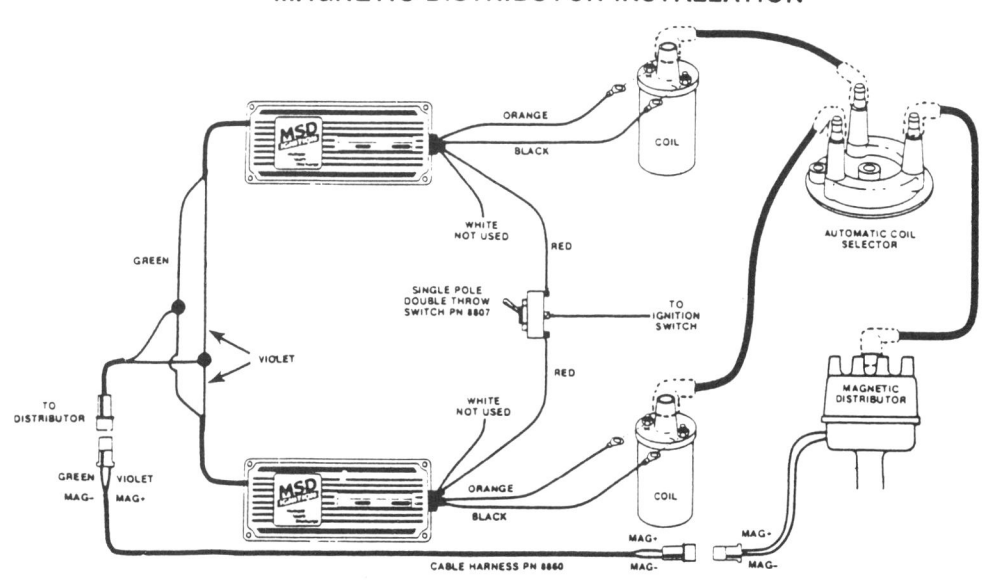

NOTE: In this installation, the two GREEN wires from the MAGNETIC CONNECTORS are spliced together then connected to the NEGATIVE side of the magnetic pickup.

Push-rods and Power in the Ford 3.8L V/6 Engine

Bruce A. Frank
Aircraft Projects
218 Landenberg Road
Landenberg PA 19650
(610) 274 2168 (H)

An engine mechanic and engineering technician with certification for pressure vessel and structural welding, Bruce in his spare time publishes the quarterly "Aircraft Projects Newsletter for the Ford 3.8L V/6 Engine and V/6 STOL Homebuilt Aircraft". His publication is the focal point for a large group of Blanton Ford V/6 STOL builders and fans. His personal involvement as a STOL builder extends to providing some special STOL parts to builders. Anyone building a Ford V/6 STOL should consider subscribing to his publication. MCM

Karl (Bud) Davidson first flew his 2+2 Sportsman in the fall of 1992. Bud is 6 foot 6 so there were some significant modifications to the airframe to accommodate his height and his other comfort and performance desires. One modification, which provided the most comfort to his wallet, was a radical exception to the plans: the selection of the Ford 3.8L V/6 engine rather than the recommended Lycoming power plant.

Per Dave Blanton's instructions, Bud obtained his engine from a local wrecking yard. When Bud approached the point where the engine was necessary, an auto machinist "friend" offered to machine and assemble the engine. Bud gave his friend all the acquired parts and the manual on the correct assembly.

Almost a year later (Bud had been in a hurry) the machinist called to tell Bud that the engine was ready. Bud was informed that were several deviations from the assembly instructions as the machinist "knew better from years of experience assembling race engines." A significant deviation was a substitution for the recommended pistons. Stock pistons, though adequate, had been found to provide varying compression ratios. This led to the instruction to use Wiseco 9:1 ratio pistons so we would all be working from the same baseline performance level. One reason Bud had agreed to his friend's building the engine was a promise to obtain the Wiseco pistons at "a significant cost savings."

After several hours of run testing, the function and power output seemed appropriate. The engine provided power through the 40 hour test period, requiring few adjustments. Then Bud's Sportsman began providing solid transportation for migration up and down the east coast.

At approximately 100 hours the engine broke a valve spring. There was no obvious reason for this happening so Bud chalked it up to just one of those things. But, upon disassembly, Bud found that the valve seats were cut much too deeply which actually recessed the valves into the heads. Bud did not trust the durability of new valve seat inserts in an aluminum head so the heads were scraped. Bud had acquired another rebuildable engine so its heads were pulled and reworked for use in the plane.

The engine ran as expected except that it now was using an excessive amount of oil, a quart every 7 to 8 hours. Before the new heads the engine was using only one quart every 15 to 20 hours. Other than the oil consumption, the engine continued to do its job with an occasional rough running episode which Bud could not ferret out. While returning from Florida to Pennsylvania in the spring of 1995, with a non-flying passenger, at 200 hours the engine broke another

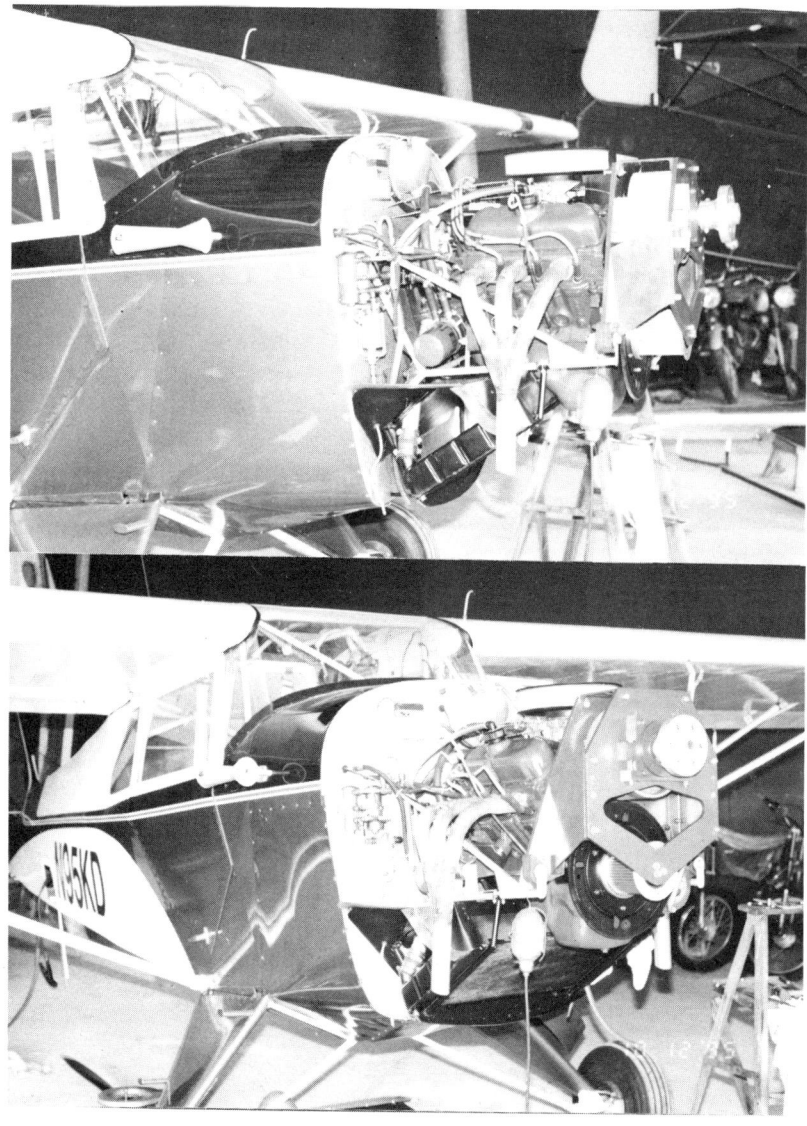

Two shots of Bud Davidson's new engine installation. His bottom mounted radiator has proven to be successful. The redrive is a reworked Blanton 1.6:1 unit. Note the high mounted header tank on the firewall.

valve spring, this one in a different location. Bud had been dodging thunder storms all morning but the engine continued to make power allowing him to make a straight in approach to a GPS located airport near Raleigh NC. The FBO was very helpful providing an A&P and transportation to the Ford dealer and other parts stores.

They found that not only had the spring broken but that the tip of the valve stem had sheared just below the keeper groove. The parts were found lying in the bottom of the valve cover. Repairs were made and Bud was able to continue the next morning.

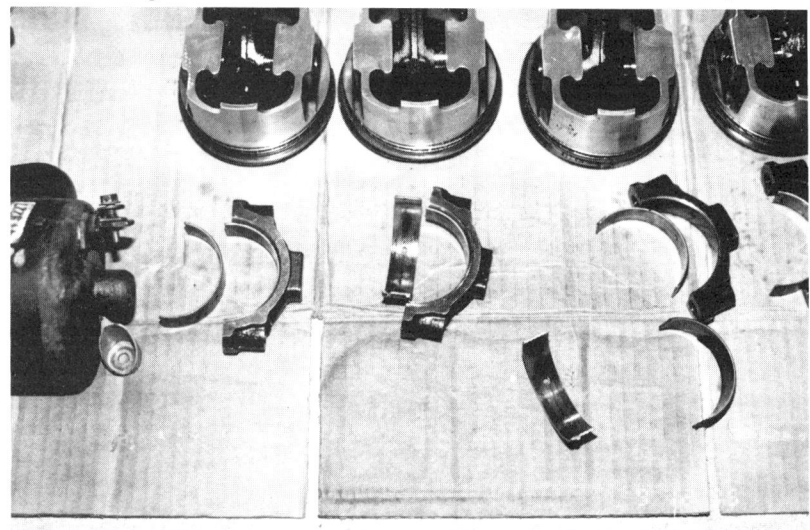

At disassembly, upper rod bearing shells were were found to be worn through to their copper backing. The rear main bearing also showed excessive wear, possibly due to the original Blanton belt non tensioning design. Metal from unusual lifter wear due to too-short push rods was the cause of this problem.

Once back home Bud found the engine continued to run slightly rough. This was another one of those problems that you just could not put your finger on. Since Bud had first built his engine we had become aware that the reground cam required longer push-rods. There had been some debate because many assumed, including Dave Blanton, that the hydraulic lifters had enough slack built in to allow for the reduced diameter cam billet. Brantly Harrison of Engines by Brantly, who, at the time, was building Ford engines for homebuilt use, informed Blanton of the need for a longer push-rod. To his credit Dave Blanton did publish the information in his newsletter. Brantly had told me that the too short push-rod allowed the engine to run well and make what seemed to be good power but that the engine just could not develop its full power potential. We had no idea how really serious this mistake could be.

Bayard DuPont replaced the push-rods in the rear engine of his Defiant with new ones of proper length, just before we departed for OSHKOSH 95. The engine ran flawlessly to OSH and back with two inches less manifold pressure than previously used at cruise RPM-a strong indication that the engine was breathing better and producing more horse power. Earlier, Bayard had checked his valve clearance by the Ford manual. He had found that his engine needed .050 inch longer push-rods to put the engine into the specified clearance range. Until that time Bayard had been using the original push-rods that came with the salvage yard engine. He had commented on several occasions about the need for more throttle (and thus higher manifold pressure) to match the front engine's RPM. We then thought that was just an idiosyncrasy of the engine in a pusher position.

Applying Bayard's experience, Bud did a clearance check and concluded that he needed longer push-rods. In the process of the usually minor disassembly required to install the yet to arrive push-rods Bud discovered the possible reason for his most recent valve stem failure. The hydraulic lifter for that broken spring was itself broken. The inside type "C" clip, which retains the button upon which the push-rod seats, was gone and had allowed the lifter to extend almost 3/8 inch beyond its normal length. With this information Bud concluded that the broken valve stem was probably caused by the rocker arm rocking past its normal position. This action would push the valve down too far causing the tip of the rocker arm to jam against the side of the stem's tip and generate enough side pressure (when the valve was probably forced back up by the piston) to shear the tip. Indications were that the valve had been hit by the piston, evidenced by a mark in the carbon on the piston's top surface. That blow bent the stem enough to hold the valve in the up position so there was no further conflict with the piston.

Bud decided to go deeper into the engine to see if there was additional damage and to locate the missing "C" clip. The next finding was that the cam lobe was spalled under the damaged lifter. About the same time Bud realized that the pistons were almost loose in the bores. The cylinders were not worn out: hone marks were still visible, but they were grossly overbored for the size pistons installed. As Bud removed the pistons he discovered that a wrist pin retaining clip had been left out, which allowed the pin to gouge a 1/4 inch deep groove in a cylinder wall. At this point the block was scrap.

All of the lifters showed significant wear, specifically at the point of button contact against the retaining "C" clips due to the too-short push rods. With all of this wear particle material circulating and possibly some oil break down (an experiment to reduce oil consumption with a lower viscosity synthetic) the rod bearings had been worn down to the copper on only the upper half, the pressure half. The lower half of the rod bearings looked like new. The mains also showed copper in many places with more excess wear on the rear main. The excess wear on the rear main may have been due to a defect in the Blanton built reduction drive that prevented proper belt tension adjustment.(Now corrected). Even the crankshaft showed a couple of gouges relegating it to the scrap heap also.

Bud then pulled the oil pump and found the missing lifter "C" clip embedded in its gears. When oriented just right the broken pieces of the clip could fit through the screen in the bottom of the pump pickup foot and had done exactly that. Worried that other large particles may have been lodged in the oil heat exchanger Bud scraped it too. There was not much salvageable from this engine.

Close-up shot of the Ford hydraulic lifters. The left part is normal; the right lifter shows the hyper-extended push-rod seat. This problem was created by too short push-rods and a faulty "C" clip which then caused a broken valve stem.

Bud began a rebuild with another engine he had. With Bud in direct control this time, all the specifications were followed to the letter. The decision was made to install the short push-rods for the ten minute flight to the East-Coast Fly-In location. The engine went together and ran. Then he hit into the proverbial brick wall; the reduction drive did not fit the engine. With three days to go and numerous other duties related to the fly-in, Bud had to admit that he could not make it.

After the duties of the East Coast Fly-In were over, Bud was able to make the minor changes required to get the reduction drive to fit his different model year engine. Since the engine was ready to fly, Bud felt that a few hours with the short push-rods would cause no problems so he decided to fly it some.. Bud was amazed. With the proper piston fit and valve guide seals (the steel clip lock down type provides best oil control) the engine had more power and smoothness than ever before.

A few days latter the .050 inch longer push arrived and were installed. To Bud's surprise, there was another, almost exponential, jump in power output. Bud found that his normal cruise RPM was now achieved at four inches lower manifold pressure than that of his original engine. An interesting effect was that static run up was now 4400 RPM rather than the 4100 Bud obtained from the original engine. The new engine with the short push-rods had also produced only 4100 RPM static. This gives us a direct comparison of the short push-rods versus the correct length ones.

If you built your engine with the recommended reground cam but you retained the original push-rods, you may be missing some horses. You may also be next in line for a short push-rod induced engine failure. I might end this article here but there were additional discoveries to be made with Bud's engine over the next couple of weeks. Bud was trying to get some testing time flown now before his annual return to Florida. After several hours of testing, Bud invited me to go flying. On climb-out I noted some heavy "bumps" in the engine. Bud said that he had not yet figured out what the bumps were .

We flew for about an hour and returned to the airport for Bud to give some other friends a ride. I went down the hill to the "Ghetto" hanger to work on my project. A few minutes later Everett DuPont came by the hanger to tell me that Bud had just declared an emergency over the Unicom. I stepped out to watch Bud land with what appeared to be an operating engine.

When Bud exited the plane he told me he had an engine-out just after leveling off after climb-out. After trying everything else, when the prop came to a stop, he hit the starter. The engine fired right up as if nothing had happened which allowed Bud to fly the pattern to land. It took about ten minutes before Bud got the shakes from the adrenaline let-down.

Several days of contemplation and discussion with Bayard and myself, led Bud to replace his ignition coil. We both got on Bud for not having switched to the dual coil and coil switcher set up. Bud did have the prescribed dual ignition modules in place. The new coil did not stop the "bumping." Next came the thought that maybe the problem was fuel flow.

After fiddling with fuel supply adjustments, Bud decided to try the 350 CFM Holley carb. Dave Blanton had originally said that nothing but the 500 CFM worked. Dave had done the tests himself on the dyno and, even though volumetric calculations showed that the 350 carburetor should work, it did not. Others, including Brantly, had done dyno tests that showed that the 350 did indeed work better. Take your pick. There were explanations that supported either side.

Bayard had done some early limited testing on the 350 and, after initial poor results, went back to the 500 CFM as it had been performing well on the Defiant. However, more and more experimenters were saying the 350 was better, so Bud, being in the test mode, installed the 350 CFM, with a leaning block, which I had on the shelf.

At some point over the last several years Bayard had discovered that the engine ran best when the float was set higher than specification and some leaning was used on takeoff. (This setup requires the aftermarket mechanical leaning block installation in the carb. The original 34-4412 Holley carb had an electric leaning device which proved

New valve springs were installed to cure the valve spring breakage problem. These were Crane parts which had the stock Ford dimensions and offered 30 percent more strength. The spring rate tester was used to verify compression rates.

inadequate). Bud found that the 350 also required the higher than specified float level with takeoff leaning to provide full fuel flow at all power demands (specific adjustment procedures are outlined in my newsletter). Everything looked great except that the "bumps" were still there and now even in level cruise flight.

Finally, after we exhausted all our collective stupidity, Bud said one day that he had induced another engine out. When he switched ignition modules the engine started again. A defective ignition module had mimicked an imminent coil failure.

Why this was not obvious to us after the coil was replaced we will never know. The fact that there have been very few module failures and several documented coil failures may have biased our logic. A few days later Bud made an uneventful flight to Florida.

As Bayard has recommended at his Oshkosh forums: do not fly without the dual coil and coil switcher setup! The Ford original equipment coils seem to be susceptible to failure due to vibration and heat (These failures are a serious problem and were reported in previous Contact! issues-MCM). The Ford ignition modules have had a good track record but Bayard has installed both his coils and modules inside the cockpit of his Defiant to protect them from heat and vibration. After-market, race-hardened modules and coils are available from your local speed shops. Make these changes so I do not have to write you up as a Ford engine statistic.

The fact remains that the 90 degree V/6 cannot be balanced to the extent of a V/8 or a 60 degree V/6. Some later Ford V/6s have a balance shaft whichs adds some 30 pounds to the engine. Based on observation and builder inputs I think that engines running with too short push-rods have higher than normal vibration amplitudes. I mention this vibration with some qualification because those with correctly assempled engines report vibration levels no worse than that experienced with certified engines.

Dave Blanton's initial recommendation was that V/6 STOL builders use the Macauley 8467 prop. Most since have found that 72 inches of pitch works better; some had gone to 76 inches. Several builders have installed three bladed props and have experienced smoother operation (both Warp Drive and IVO products). Even with careful dynamic balancing the metal two blade prop does not seem to attain the smoothness of these units. Both the Ford 3.8L V/6 and the Chevy 4.3L V/6 seem to benefit from the three blade props.

Australians Dave Sharples and Mike Burns report that their extensive dyno testing has shown that the Ford 3.8 produces a solid 195/200HP at 4800RPM. These numbers, along with Roger Mellema's analysis (Contact! #29), support Blanton's development efforts. I talked with Dave about two months ago and verified that he is marketing info packets and his Engine Builders Manual. The address reported in the December 1995 issue of Kitplanes is current. **BAF**

Bayard DuPont's Ford 3.8L engine conversion has a 2:1 reduction drive. Shown here with valve covers removed for replacement of the short push-rods. Note header design.

Converting the Subaru Legacy Engine

Kenneth R. Rogers
1450 Konnowac Pass Road
Moxee
Washington 98936
(509) 248 1413

Ken Rogers' auto power conversion is totally professional in appearance as well as function. The information he provides should save other experimenters considerable time and money. Ken plans to design and build an auto engine powered amphibian next. A scale design study and one of his early intake manifold designs is pictured in the Contact! brochure (lower photos). MCM

In 1989, I decided to install a Subaru Legacy engine in my ProTech airframe. The power output of the engine was in the ballpark, the price of a used engine was most affordable and I had machinist skills which would come in handy. After about three years of steady work on the plane I am now flying! The following information is offered to help other experimenters with their engine conversion projects.

ENGINE MOUNT

The first task was the fabrication of a suitable engine mount. The Subaru Legacy flat four cylinder, single overhead cam, 130 hp engine has a three point engine mounting system, typical of automobile configurations. It has two crankcase mounts (gel filled for vibration isolation) and a third point supporting the transmission and engine assembly. This setup was not designed to take engine thrust loads. I chose four new engine locations.

The engine mount fabrication method suggested by Lou Ross of Ross Aero was followed. They utilize a steel plate representing the firewall of the airplane lying flat on a work bench with the fuselage mounting points marked and located by weldments. The engine, with the flywheel end up, is placed over the plate in the correct location. Firewall clearances and any engine thrust offsets (angles) are incorporated in the spacer block supporting the crankshaft pulley which incidentally is aligned with the engine thrust line (this method does not apply to certified aircraft engines which don't have the crankshaft pulley).

In my case, I picked out a sheet of 3/4 inch plywood making sure it was absolutely flat. I laid out the firewall and its mounting points. I bolted six steel locator plates with 3/8 inch holes in position to match the six engine mount locations. The engine was blocked 2 inches away from the firewall base, basing this dimension on the published weight and balance. Once the engine was blocked up and restrained for safety, the job of locating the four engine mount points about twelve inches apart, fabricating engine mount pads, cutting and fitting tubing was taken on. I used eight 2 inch diameter 3/8 inch hole Sealed Power rubber bushings, part #270-2123, for my mount as recommended by Lou. Working around the engine and the bench was easy, I guess much easier than if the engine was suspended horizontally and moved into position against a leveled fuselage. I used 3/4 x .035 wall 4130 aircraft grade tubing throughout. The pieces were tack welded, the engine moved away and the assembly taken to a professional welder.

As it worked out, the engine could have been moved closer to the firewall but for maintenance purposes the extra space is really welcomed. The mount weighs 7.5

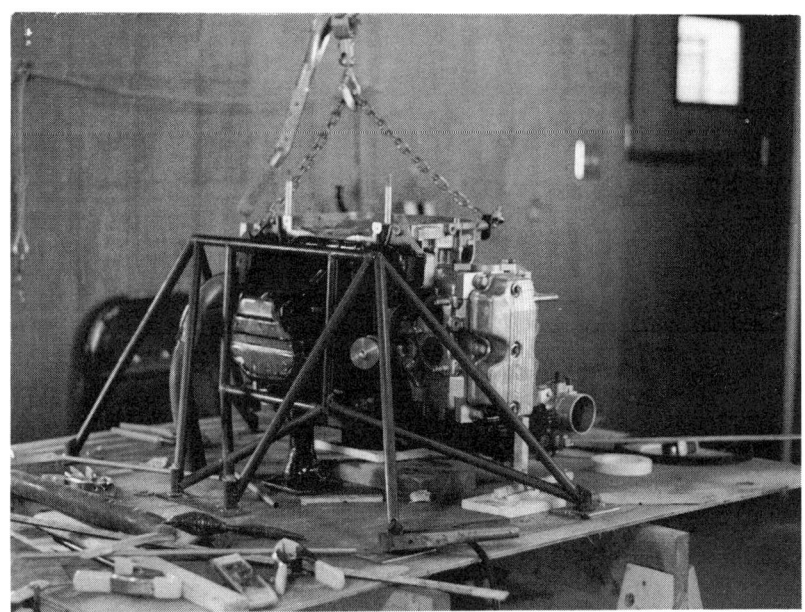

Rogers' engine mount fabrication setup. Drilled steel plates ensure accurate locations for firewall connections. Note safety restraint.

pounds and is rock solid. I started out with a bare engine without any accessories. My mount design worked out; I did not need to modify it to accommodate the other engine parts. For those of you thinking of auto power, engine mounting is one area which might cause you some headaches. The original engine installation plans or instructions should be studied beforehand. The typical mounts and fuselage attach points are most likely designed to accept specific factory engines and their engine accessories. Clearances have been factored in. Thus, when substituting a non-specified engine in a kit or plans built airframe it is prudent to use the fully dressed engine during build of the engine mount.

When plowing new ground mistakes can happen. I learned that it would have been a good idea to design the engine mount for the Subaru Legacy so that that the oil pan could be dropped without disturbing the engine mounting. I had two occasions where I needed to drop the pan. An extra 1/2 inch on the square bottom of the mount would have saved me a lot of extra work. So, when fabricating your mount, check your clearances to make sure that the pan can be pulled cleanly.

In designing the engine mount I neglected to consider engine torque effects on the ProTech. As you may already know most engines are mounted on an angle to partially counter act the effects of torque, particularly during takeoff. The Ross Aero redrive has a reduction ratio of 2.17:1 and the propeller rotation of this unit is reversed from standard. Couple the torque multiplication of the powerful Legacy engine with a comparatively light airframe and prior training to use right rudder and you can have a handful quickly. I don't think any pilot other than a professional test pilot would anticipate this, including high time pilots who may have fallen into the trap of doing things automatically. So your redrive conversion should address propeller rotation in terms of engine offset and you should be alert and expect any unusual torque effects to avoid running off the active or worse!

In flight, engine torque doesn't really matter much. I have a little tab on the rudder which neutralizes the torque just fine. On a take off run this engine produces a lot of torque especially going through that gear box. Hit the throttle hard and you can really feel the torque from the 130 cubic inches.

IGNITION/CARBURETION

I chose not to use the stock Legacy computerized ignition and fueling systems. For one, there were too many parts to deal with. Also, I was knowledgeable about distributor ignition and carburetion and felt more comfortable in adapting these conventional systems to this engine. By pure accident, I came across a distributor in the local salvage yard which appeared to fit the end of one of the cylinder heads. Those of you who wish to do the same with the Legacy engine will spot a cover plate on the right rear of the engine (car wise). When removed, the slot on the cam matches the distributor drive perfectly. It appears to be a Ford Escort part; an 81 Ford EXP tag was on it.

I originally installed a Marvel-Schebler side draft carburetor, angled for clearance. It worked but it wasn't that good because it was a single barrel with a 2 3/4 inch bore, far too large for correct fuel metering and did not work too well as the cylinders opposite the carburetor received most of the fuel. I then adapted a Weber side draft, two barrel 45 mm bore carburetor ordered from a catalog which solved the fueling problem. I fabricated a carburetor heat box over the left exhaust manifold. A cockpit inlet valve controls hot air flow into the firewall mounted, custom built air filter assembly which takes a Chevrolet Beretta filter. I believe that there is no point in feeding unfiltered air into the engine like some factory installations.

The final intake manifold feeding a plenum seems to work a lot better but probably is not optimized, since it still

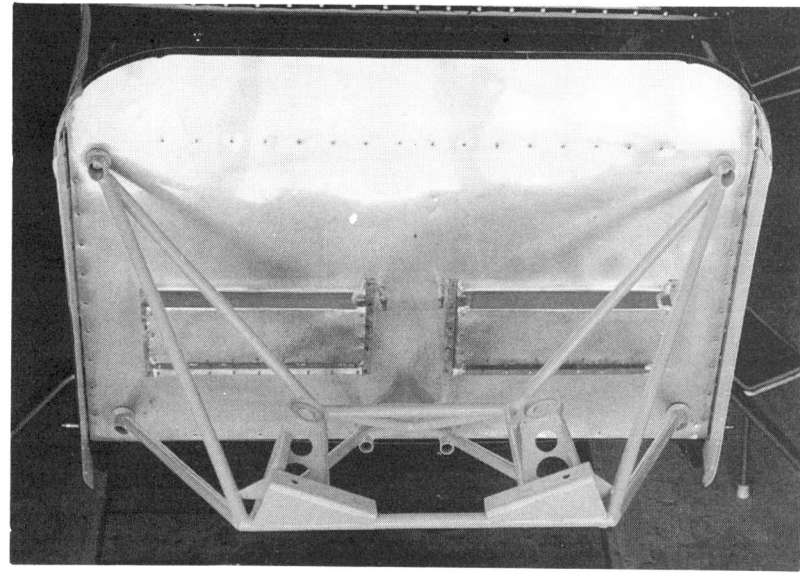

The six point firewall engine mount worked out by Rogers provides a clean, substantial saddle for the Subaru Legacy engine.

leaves a little to be desired in the way of equal fuel/air distribution. A four barrel downdraft setup would be ideal if cowling clearance was not a problem.

If I were to do it again I would seriously consider using four small carburetors, one on each intake port. This arrangement would follow the approach performance engines are setup. Some think you need to have fuel injection to get power out of an engine but the real reason the current crop of cars have fuel injection isn't for power; it's actually for mileage and emission controls. Fuel

The project at an early stage of engine dressing. The front and rear engine mount pads and rubber bushings are visible.

injection is definitely better for these requirements. But for simple power a good carburetor cannot be beat. Also, once you have the carburetor set up and running pretty good I think it's real hard to have it malfunction. Yes, you can get carburetor icing but carburetor heat isn't difficult to plumb or use anyway. My point here is: if a pilot cannot handle one extra knob he probably shouldn't be flying anyway. Elimination of engine electronics, computers, sensors or associated hardware should make the engine more reliable.

Angled manifold (top) caused poor fuel/air distribution. Final setup works well with the Weber, new plenum and 1.5 inch dia runners.

COOLING

The cooling setup took some lengthy experimentation. At the beginning, I was told that an aircraft application did not require much radiator capacity because of the increase in air flow during flight. I learned that if the radiator is not large enough for the engine power no amount of air flowing through it will compensate for the lack of cooling area.

My initial installation using a specially built radiator inside the cowling, just under the Ross Aero redrive, wasn't sufficient to fully cool the engine. I added two heater cores to increase the cooling area but this approach did not help enough. This arrangement cluttered the whole engine compartment since the oil cooler and the oil filter were also there. In retrospect, the special radiator likely should have worked had it been setup differently.

The plane now is flying with a 1987 Ford Taurus radiator mounted horizontally under the cowling with a scoop like housing feeding inlet air to a top side plenum. All Taurus radiators have the same external dimensions; the core dimension varies. Mine is 2 1/4 inches thick. With the shift of the radiator to the chin location I was able to move the oil cooler and oil filter forward, close to the nose bowl. This move made the whole engine compartment a lot neater and more serviceable, too. It works well; however, the ideal location would be inside the fuselage beyond the baggage area with a small belly scoop feeding air into a radiator plenum. This would reduce the drag somewhat and would eliminate my 7 pound tail ballast.

I experienced an unusual thermostat problem. Following recommendations I checked the function of my thermostat after 25 flight hours in boiling water to determine its opening and closing temperatures. Everything worked smoothly during flights. On one ground check my 50/50 coolant mix boiled over. The thermostat stuck in the closed position; this was with a new engine and a fresh OEM thermostat. Had this occurred in flight a forced landing would have been in order. Needless to say, that thermostat was junked and not replaced. I now fly with a cowl flap on the radiator scoop which I manually control from the cockpit. The summer weather has been hot so I have had no need to close it during this time.

PROPELLER MATCHING

I am now flying with a Performance Propeller as shown in some of the photos. I have also flown with a Warp Drive propeller. When dealing with unknowns such as airframe drag, engine power and redrive gearing, a ground adjustable propeller will save you a lot of time and trouble. For example, as you tweak the engine you can tweak the propeller to match engine power changes which is impossible with a fixed blade (but usually tried by builders because the initial investment was low). However, after tweaking and testing is done a fixed pitch wooden propeller is still a good bet. I like the solid laminated construction of a one piece two blade design, its low cost, and the dampening qualities of wood. According to both propeller manufacturers, Warp Drive and Performance Propeller, the engine is putting out in the vicinity of 115 horsepower at WOT and 5200 rpm. However, my current manifold setup is not working to the engine potential. I honesty believe that 150 horsepower (without turbocharging) can be obtained once the induction system is set up properly. The ProTech airplane has considerable drag. Any changes to the engine would not appreciably improve its current performance. Besides, I have accomplished what I set out to do and now it is time to fly. The urge to do more may come later.

LEXAN

I have included a picture of my windshield male form to expose readers to a nasty characteristic of Lexan. Many lightplane kits feature Lexan windshields because the material is strong, has negligible thermal expansion and can be drilled, riveted and the like. However, Lexan does not make for a good windshield material in my experience. As seen in the photo, the ProTech airplane has a windshield which wraps over to the top of the wing. I learned that Lexan is extremely sensitive to gasoline. It took me two windshields to discover that a few drops of fuel from my wing tanks on the stressed Lexan curved surface would suddenly shatter the entire part.

Gee-Bee Canopies of Seattle WA produced a tinted Plexiglass replacement for less than quoted for the replacement Lexan part. Unlike the original my new windshield is clearer, cleans up nicely and does not show scratches. My form is available to other ProTech builders who may wish to replace their factory windshields.

SHIMMY

Tail wheel shimmy was another unanticipated problem. Paul Seals, the designer of the ProTech, configured this plane to have an abnormal percent of the plane's weight on the tail wheels perhaps thinking that people not particularly proficient with tail wheel aircraft could handle it better with more weight on the tail wheel. However, the one problem overlooked was that these tail wheels, either a Maule or a Scott, were not made to take that much weight on them. As a matter of fact, they shimmied real bad on landing to the point where the whole tail of the airplane was a blur.

The airplane didn't handle too well on the ground. On two occasions the tail wheel springs were ripped off as the airplane ground looped. I didn't actually hit a wingtip but it was a wild ride! I then disengaged the free castering part. The airplane maneuvered somewhat better but would not free-caster. Some more rework was necessary but still didn't solve the problem. My solution was a custom built shimmy dampener which essentially did what it does for nose wheel airplanes. Very simple to make- two rod ends, some "O" rings, some spare aluminum and about an hour of lathe work. You may wonder about the additional link and cable attached to the tail wheel spring. It is connected to a winch at the forward end of my airplane trailer.

The 15x4.5 (13x2 throat) scoop covers the forward radiator tank and feeds air into the belly plenum. Effective turbo muffler is exposed.

For some reason, my tail wheel also came with lopsided springs. The spring on one side was twice the tension of the one on the other side. Perhaps there was a reason for it. None of the tail dragger pilots I have spoken with since agree with that system. The picture shows it has the two different sizes. I have since installed two springs of equal size. The springs are tighter. The airplane definitely handles better.

No more shimmy or play, the tail wheel just works perfect.

EXHAUST

I originally installed a muffler since we here in the Northwest appreciate the outdoors and quietness. Since I also wanted the minimum of engine back pressure I first chose a glass pack muffler. It ended up to be noisy and hanging out in the air stream. I replaced it with a turbo muffler costing twenty-five dollars, a generic unit 3.5x8.0x14.0 inches, overall. It didn't weigh any more and fit my installation much better.

It performs very well. Just to make sure I tested the airplane at wide open throttle tied down on my trailer, with the brakes locked up on the truck. I repeated the test with no muffler, with the glass pack and with the turbo muffler. I got the same RPM every time so the turbo muffler is costing me nothing in performance but it is so quiet. All I can hear in the cabin is the propeller whistling. It is really nice and is just about as quiet as a car. However, cars don't have propellers and propellers still make a fair amount of noise. I hear some experimenters considering making a custom Swiss muffler. Aside from the cost and time involved in making one I feel that twenty-five dollars spent on a turbo muffler will get your airplane as quiet as is possible. The propeller still makes so much noise there is really a limit on how much you are going to gain by putting a special muffler system on it.

A parallel exists in ground vehicles. In the 1970s the Federal EPA agency was pushing for low noise limits on trucks. They learned from tests that the majority of truck pass-by noise was generated by tires, that muffling of the engine compartment as proposed by some of their environmental activist regulators was ineffective. However, prompted by the test findings, truck and car tire noise has been reduced through changes in tread design. Most experts on noise generation will agree that more research is needed to reduce propeller noise.

COWLING

If you look closely at the photo of the left side of the uncowled engine you will notice some light streaks on the large SCAT intake hose. You are seeing some silicone RTV sealant which was applied to prevent the cowling from wearing against the hose in close quarters. Hoses are expensive to replace so I recommend that your installation consider this potential occurance.

EXPERIENCE FACTORS

One thing about an auto conversion that people who haven't done it before and may think it is a snap is that it requires an investment of time and money. If you are in any hurry to fly you would be better advised to just go and buy a serviceable certified aircraft engine. It will likely cost no more than you will spend getting your auto conversion to fly. However, the first time you need to buy a part for that Lycoming or Continental and see the bill you will discover why many are choosing auto power. You can build up a spare auto engine for the price of a aircraft cylinder and crankshaft. The operating costs of an auto conversion are just a fraction of aircraft engines because of the high cost of aircraft engine overhaul.

The reliability of the Subaru Legacy engine is pretty well established. At 5000 rpm the engine is absolutely smooth. It is not noisy. In fact, you can't imagine that that the engine is running at double the speed of a Lycoming. In my opinion, it just sounds like an electric motor sitting on a rubber pad with nothing hooked on it. A lot of parts are moving at 5000 rpm. Yet to be so smooth and quiet it's really amazing.

The question frequently asked is cost. I got a good bargain on the engine. I paid 1,000 dollars for it and it had only 145 miles on it. The car probably was running on the first tankful of gas. Most people are paying a little more than that. I talked to another experimenter and he bought one that had two miles on it, paying 900 dollars for it. I guess good deals are out there if you shop around a little bit beforehand. The Ross redrive was 2,500. The carburetor was around 300 dollars. The distributor was 25 dollars, the spark plugs were 97 cents, and I think I spent about 25 dollars for the premium racing ignition wire set. The oil cooler is a standard aircraft oil cooler. I think I paid about 150 for it.

The ProTech engine mount was factored in the price of the kit. Since I planned to use the Subaru Legacy at the outset I just asked the factory to send me the tubing instead of the mount. It was a pretty good deal for them so I received enough three-quarter inch tube to fabricate my own mount. Not counting all the mistakes I made and parts I had to throw away and the odds and ends needed, I estimate I have 4,500 dollars in the engine conversion at this time. You will have a tough time finding a new or low time aircraft engine for that price.

The plane's empty weight is the same as a Cessna 152 at 1140 pounds. My airplane is not particularly light; in fact, that's one of the problems I have with it. I installed a ballistic chute which added about forty pounds to the total empty weight. As far as I know I am the only ProTech

Installation Weights in Pounds

bare block	184.0
intake manifold/carburetor	9.0
alternator	11.0
distributor and wiring harness	3.5
Ross damper and flywheel	8.0
Ross Aero redrive	13.0
Ross housing adapter/ starter	21.0
Ross drive shaft	4.0
coolant crossover manifold	4.0
air filter andhoses	1.5
coolant recovery tank	1.0
coolant	16.0
radiator	5.0
oil filter/cooler	5.0
oil	10.0
engine mount	7.5
exhaust manifold	15.0
muffler	7.0
Sub-total	325.5
Performance Propeller	11.5
Total weight	337.0

builder who has done this. Structurally, the airplane was well designed, except for several attachments and some control system fittings. These were modified and reinforced. I felt that the emergency chute was a very good way to go and I still do.

If I were to install a Legacy over again I could do it in far less than half the time. If I was to do it on a totally different airplane with a different engine it would still take half of what it took me to do the ProTech. It was an educational process and I learned so much. The same holds true for airframe building; most fellows will say the next one could be built in half the time. However, if a person is new to auto power conversion and does not seek help from someone who has done one, that person can expect to spend a thousand hours doing it real easy. That estimate is above and beyond what an aircraft engine installation would take. My carburation and cooling systems were areas of major involvement and trial and error experimentation and set the project timing back. Most of that was due to listening to "experts" who didn't know what they were talking about.

A word of advice to all builders thinking of auto power and to those who claim to have expertise. If you have converted a powerplant and have actually flown it your objectivity and experiences will be useful to the next fellow even if he has a different airframe. If you are a builder seeking information take all non-qualified opinions with a grain of salt. Seek out people who have flown their auto conversions. Static testing alone, in my view, doesn't create expertise. Don't forget that the best proposed solutions on occasion don't work out the way conventional wisdom suggests. Airflow may not behave as expected. Engines make more heat then normally assumed. A lot of different factors can come into play together and make proper corrections difficult to define.

With an air cooled aircraft engine all the usual problems with cooling have been minimized over the years. With auto conversions we are at the ground level of cooling knowledge. Aircraft engines are known factors; engine performance is well defined relative to power output, propeller requirements, and fuel burn. Baffling, engine mounts and propeller matching have been pretty much sorted out, relatively speaking.

ENGINE WEIGHT

The tendency of people selling auto conversions is to publish optimistic weight and horsepower numbers. You would be surprised at the number of things that some of these people selling conversions can think of, to leave off the all up running weight numbers. For Subaru Legacy fans this engine installation weighs about 326 pounds. To summarize, this all-up weight includes oil, coolant, radiator, hoses, engine mount, alternator, starter, flywheel, and the reduction drive. When most other manufacturers publish weights (including the Lycoming and Continental factories), they come up with something totally optimistic and

Closeup of air filter and protective RTV streaks on the SCAT hose.

unrealistic. Builders immediately think "wow"; this combination is really good until they face reality, like putting oil in the engine (10 pounds), coolant (15 pounds), radiators (aren't really much heavier then the baffling but don't forget the coolant, hoses, clamps and pipes). Some manufacturers don't include the weight of starters and alternators. I have the standard factory alternator which weighs about 11 pounds and puts out 80 amp. This is more electricity than this plane needs, true, but there are light weight alternators that are in the vicinity of about a third of that weight and a third of that output which would

Closeup of Escort distributor which was happily discovered to fit the Subaru Legacy engine, saving much conversion effort.

be totally adequate (but cost enters into the equation). Some engine items can be lightened a bit; however, the geared auto starters are as light as you are going to get.

The Ross Aero redrive total weight is about 35 pounds, not including the flywheel. Available belt drives by the time you count all the parts are in the same ball park or heavier, weightwise. There is no particular advantage or disadvantage to either type of redrive in my estimation. With this horizontally opposed engine the Ross Aero unit just was absolutely perfect as you can see by looking in the pictures it looks like it all belongs together. For other

Rogers' special drape form for fabrication of Plexiglass windshield.

fast airplanes the 12 inch "prop extension" afforded by the gear box sure looks like it belongs.

If I were to use a belt redrive the two shafts would be about ten inches apart on centers. Keeping the propeller in the design location would have put the oil pan hanging below the plane's lower cowling line and destroy its looks. Dropping the smaller Subaru EA81 engine wouldn't be a problem in most planes but the Legacy is quite a bit bigger.

At 150 horsepower which the Legacy is fully capable of achieving it falls right in the weight range of a O-320 fully baffled and accessorized, for a fraction of the cost of both purchase, maintenance and operation on leaded aviation fuel. However, an aircraft engine is hard to beat in power to weight ratio since the auto engine must operate at high rpms. The technology may be fifty or sixty years old but the engine designers did do a good job in keeping the weight to a minimum.

Weight of an extra ten pounds in an automobile is not of significant concern. For example, it just doesn't seem to matter that the pulleys on the back of this engine are all steel, and that they are large. If a person was to make those out of aluminum and have them all hard anodized you could knock a few pounds off. The entire block is quite thick and obviously not optimized for aircraft use. That's probably what makes it a real durable engine, as demonstrated by the factory several years ago in top speed endurance runs. You can run it real hard and long. It holds up real well and it won't be affected by shock cooling because of its thickness which moderates thermal cycling. Shock cooling is not a major problem for water cooled engines but it does make for a heavy, solid durable block. Just accept the fact that it's heavier and that it was intended for a car.

LORAN PROBLEM
While sharing my experiences with the Subaru Legacy engine conversion I am taking the opportunity to mention my experiences with the Ray Jefferson LL400 LORAN unit. It works well on the ground but once my airplane moves it is useless. It doesn't doesn't work as intended. I mean it works just fine until the plane moves. I have met quite a few different people who said their installation didn't work either. They sent their units back to the factory and they still couldn't wouldn't perform as claimed. I got a GPS in the interim. My Loran was sent back to the factory and I hope the experts will solve this problem. I am curious if any readers bought a similar Loran and if they experienced similar or other problems. In my case, all I had to do was taxi as little as one hundred feet at five miles an hour and all the numbers disappeared. Please call me; perhaps together we can get some collective action going.

ICOM PERFORMANCE
I am using the ICOM hand held radio. It is plumbed into an outside antenna. With a ten watt linear amplifier inline it has the same power as most panel mounted units. The VOR function on it works as good as any I have used. However, it is a one and one-half system which means you can not listen or talk on an aviation frequency and have a VOR signal at the same time. This creates somewhat of a hassle but the VOR which is used most of the time works as intended. Also, I think the reliability on these hand held units are a lot better then panel mounts. I have never heard anyone having a hand held, particularly a ICOM, fail on them. It seems to me the people who have installed the panel mounts are spending time and money on them getting them worked on.

Last year I flew to Arlington WA with a friend in a rented 182 fully IFR equipped with dual NAVCOMs. I took my ICOM hand-held with its "rubber ducky" antenna. I laid it on top of the glare shield and it would track the VOR every bit as good as the panel mounted unit. Both radios would acquire the VOR at the same time without fail. Readings were within two to three degrees of each other. That to me was outstanding performance.

My airplane does really fly. Skeptics claim airplanes so powered are always trailered to air shows. I plan to change this perception and leave my trailer at home. At this time I have over 115 hours on the airplane, which includes a long (for me) cross-county flight of some 45 flight hours and 2800 round trip miles to Prescott, Arizona to attend the 21st CopperState Fly-In and a subsequent stop over in Bend, OR. Fuel burn averaged 6.2 gallons per hour at an engine rpm setting of 5200 rpm, using Jess Meyers' air bleed carburetor leaning method at altitude. At times my route took me up to 8600 MSL. I used the wooden 70 inch diameter 54 inch pitch Performance Propeller prop during this trip. The installation used just about a quart at the 35 hour interval, totally due to a gear box oil seal (problem now cured with new type of seal). I use Castrol GTX 20-50. I had no problems with the airframe or the engine, other than a crack in my custom alternator support bracket which was repaired at CopperState by a local EAA member.

It appears my engine development program is progressing well and I should accumulate an additional fifty hours before year end. My airplane was not designed for setting speed records nor was I expecting any great boost in performance. The engine is working nicely as I had hoped. I could have done a lot better with the conversion by keeping the stock fuel injection and removing all smog controls. I believe it is possible to get quite a bit more horsepower out of this engine then I'm getting now. In my opinion, the engine would really show its potential in a RV-6 or Lancair airframe.

WISH LIST

Additional conversion improvements will be postponed. In addition to induction system changes I have figured out a way to make a dual ignition system. It would have single spark plugs but all other ignition parts would be redundant, the backup system activated with just a switch. The chances of a spark plug failing with a high energy ignition source is pretty much zero. I have seen plugs badly burned still make sparks. I would also incorporate a metal fine mesh screen in the redrive return line. KRR

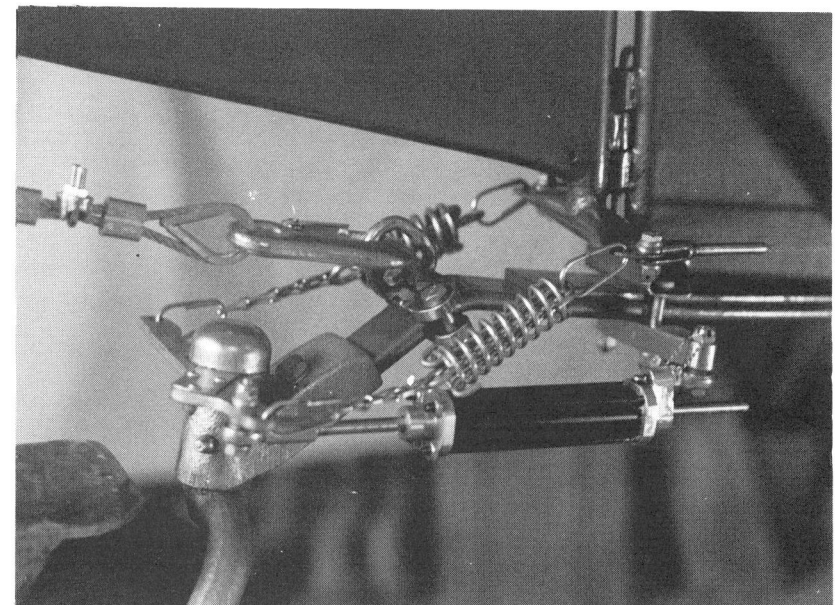

Analysis: Non Traditional Engines in KIS Aircraft

Vance W. Jaqua
7046 Quito Court
Camarillo CA 93012
(805) 484 9244

Some years ago I recall Lou Ross statically tested a stock 1986 Mazda rotary engine rated at 150 HP with his reduction unit. A Great American prop from a 150 HP Lycoming turning 2350 static was installed. The geared Mazda turned that prop to 2575 RPM. Vance Jaqua's analysis establishes the engineering basis for the experiences of many who have found better takeoff and climb performance using geared auto engines. MCM

At Tri - R Technologies, the home of the KIS airplane kits, one of the most frequent questions we hear is " Can I put a XXXXXXXXXX engine in the KIS?". The true answer for this and any other experimental aircraft is that if it falls within the design weight range, and makes enough horsepower for reasonable flight performance - of course you can put in anything you like. Most designers have a preference for a certain range of engines, and will also try to discourage the builder from combinations which he feels are unsuitable. The designer and kit manufacturer will also state that he can only provide support for a relatively few engine configurations with design information, engine mounts, and cowlings. In spite of this type of limitation the KIS two place, in its rather short existence, has been built up with more different types of engines than most any other design with the possible exception of the Pietenpol.

Most of our customers are building the two 2 place KIS kit with rather traditional aircraft engines from either Lycoming or Continental in the 100 to 130 brake horsepower range. However, this is not always the case.

The prototype aircraft was built and flown for over a year with a 2000 cc Limbach engine. This engine is derived from VW heritage, although it has virtually no actual VW parts. The Limbach family of engines are produced under strict quality control, being certified in Europe for motor gliders and other applications. The airplane flew very well with this powerplant providing a top speed of about 155 MPH and a cruise of 135 MPH. Easy starting and smooth operation reminds you of what you expect in an automobile but suffer through behind the usual aircraft engine. Climb rates at maximum loading were adequate but leisurely. Also the relatively light weight of this smaller engine made the airplane sensitive to potential aft CG load conditions. The selection of this engine for the prototype, in retrospect, turned out to be a bit of a tactical error since it left the undeserved stigma of not being a plane for "real" aircraft engines. However the use of the Limbach pointed out that this airframe is efficient and is suitable for a wide variety of engines, with the Limbach, or equivalent VW conversion being the low end of recommended engine size. There has been very little interest in either the Limbach or even the larger VW derived engines, although the 2.5 liter class would be excellent engines for the KIS.

The subsequent use of the Lycoming O-235 in the tail dragger version demonstrator did much to dispel the feeling that this airplane was only a toy, and provided a package that was capable of over 180 MPH top, and cruise in the 165 - 170 MPH range. This was the first airplane built from the actual production kit parts and was the second airplane in the series to fly. Even before this demonstration most of the customers were building with more traditional Lycoming and Continental powerplants (at least one builder is using a Franklin 125). The re-engining of the prototype tri gear

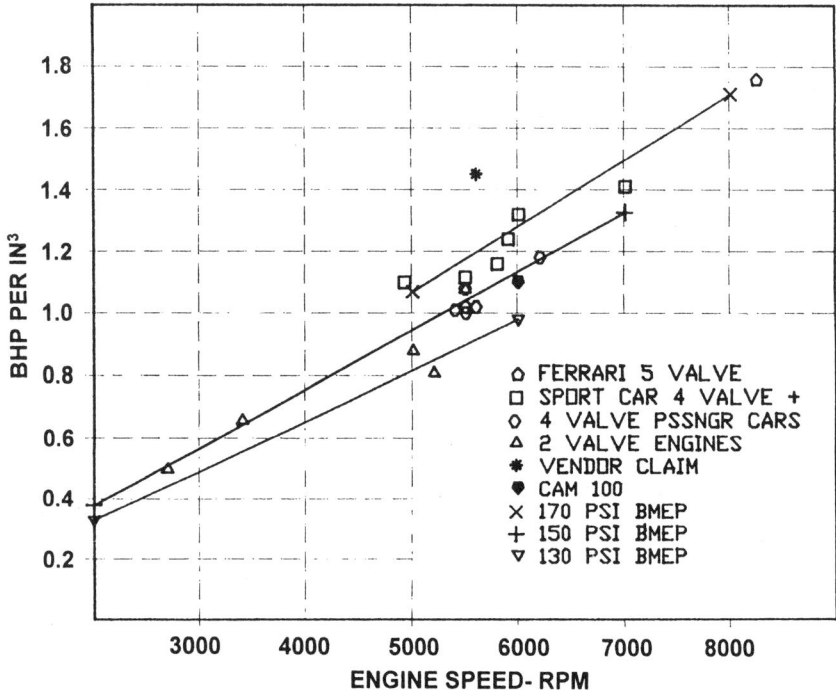

Plot of peak BHP per in^3 for various high performance engines compared to lines of constant BMEP. Note different ranges for various groups of engines and the fact that the CAM 100 data point appears to be a bit high for two valve pushrod engines.

aircraft with the new Continental IO-240 has put further emphasis on conventional selections, providing almost a 200 MPH top speed and cruise speed well over 170 MPH. The largest engine flying is the Lycoming O-290 (a converted ground power engine), and a couple of builders with high altitude short fields have been given the OK to use the Lycoming O-320.

With these larger engines the need for careful weight and balance has been stressed. Heavy items such as the battery must be moved rather far aft. The range of suitable engines, the way we describe it, is for an engine weight from roughly 180 pounds to about 280 pounds, with horsepower ranging from 80 BHP to 130 BHP. Lighter weight engines with the required power can be used with ballasting in the nose, but we do not recommend any increase in nose length because of aerodynamic stability considerations. We can provide cowlings and engine mounts for most of the Continentals and Lycomings in this range, as well as the Limbach and the CAM 100. However, the force of this article is to focus on some of the less traditional selections that a few of our builders are installing. Although the article refers to the comments and experiences of KIS builders this information would be expected to equally apply to similar installations in other aerodynamically clean aircraft designs in this size range.

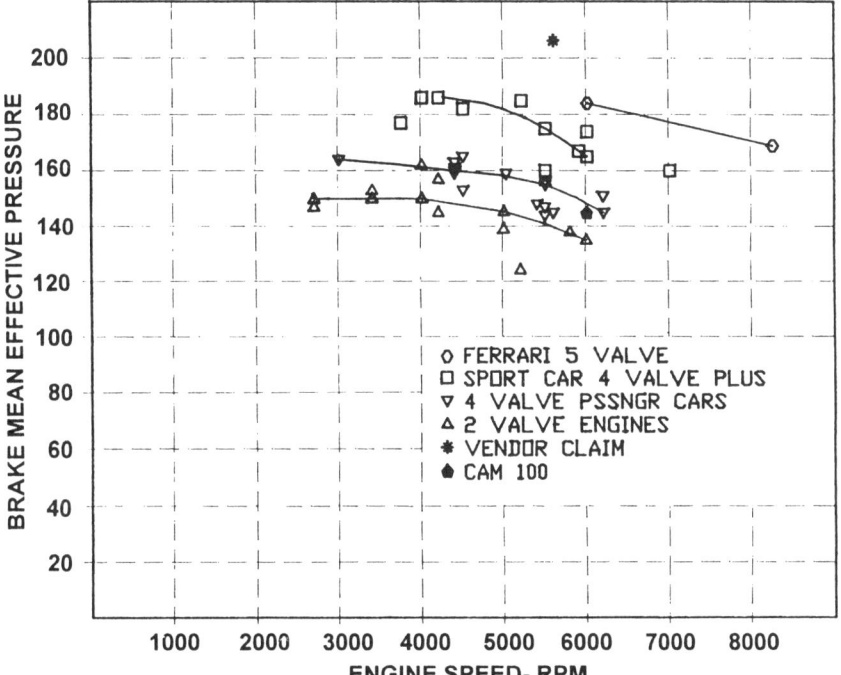

Plot of brake mean effective pressure for various high performance engines. This shows the increased power potential of multi valve high performance engines. The CAM 100 engine data point appears optimistic for a two valve pushrod configuration.

CAM 100

The use of non conventional engines for the KIS aircraft started very early, with the very first kit we delivered. This first kit was destined for our dealer in England. The cost of aviation fuel in England and Europe would strike real fear into our faint hearts, and this factor would seem to favor smaller displacement water cooled four stroke engines with their potential for more efficient consumption. For that reason, our dealer Brian Davies set out to qualify the CAM-100 (Honda Civic conversion) for the English and European Market. This conversion appeared to have solid backing, and was well into the development of a redundant ignition system to satisfy the desires of officialdom for something equivalent to the dual mags on most airplane installations. This engine is rated by the developer at 100 BHP with propeller speed of 2500 RPM, while the core engine turns at 6000 RPM. Specific fuel consumption ratings are very encouraging, and flight experience was being compiled in high wing aircraft in the "Piper Cub-like" design class.

Since this was for our dealer, and he was struggling for a very viable market, Tri-R supported this effort, designing a cowling, and an engine mount to accommodate this engine. This engine is a bit difficult to cowl on the small firewall associated with low drag higher performance aircraft. With the in-line 4 and the bulky cog belt drive, it is both quite tall, and rather long.

Originally we shipped him a cowl sized for the Lycoming O-235, but this was not at all satisfactory. We obtained a mock up engine from CAM and made a specific cowling plug for this very different shape. The cowling extends about 4 inches below the fuselage bottom, but Brian fabricated a sort of upside down Lamborghini rear window tunnel to visually and aerodynamically fair the line into the fuselage. This exit area was used to dump the radiator cooling air out the bottom of the cowling, and the exhaust system. Added inlet area was required to assure cooling at low speeds, and the cowling has a bit of the Hawker Typhoon look about it. The installed wet weight is on the high end of our range, running about the same or possibly more than the 240 cubic inch air-cooled certified engines. Since the advertised power rating is in the same range, it was felt that this was a viable package, and the fuel economy aspect remained the driving force.

This plane is flying, and indeed it would have been the first of our customer kits to fly, except that paperwork delays in the local certification process. These negotiations dragged on, and our Australian dealer was first into the air with his O-235 powered plane.

Flight characteristics with the CAM installation are barely satisfactory, and still to this day, performance is not up to the potential, at least partially because of the difficulty in providing a good engine/prop match. With the low rotation speed, and the clockwise rotation of this package, the supply of "off the shelf" suitable propeller designs is essentially non existent. Brian selected a 3 blade ground adjustable propeller from Warp Drive and the mechanical operation of this prop has been very satisfactory, but providing the right pitch for higher speed cruise without heavily sacrificing low speed thrust is still eluding Brian.

The plane has lots of static thrust, and outstanding climb rate, but top speeds have remained below 150 MPH, which is actually less than the prototype plane with the 80 HP Limbach. With 100 BHP this plane should attain a top speed of about 170 MPH, but the pitch that would be required at 2500 RPM would be over 75 inches. This has two problems, the high degree of prop airfoil stalling at low speeds, and the blades presently supplied by the prop builders do not have enough twist to operate near true helical pitch at these high pitch values. With the primary working portion of the blade pitched at 75 inches, the tip sections are over pitched. Matching of the engine to the propeller is always a problem with new designs, and these problems are aggravated when non-conventional engine installations are selected. Even with these problems it would still appear that the supplier's claim of 100 horsepower was very optimistic.

When we apply the tests outlined in my article on BMEP (Contact! Magazine issue #23) we find that the ratings appear questionable from at least two points. First of all, this is a higher power rating than the manufacturer ever claimed for this engine. The charts also reflect on the optimism since although the BMEP and HP per cubic inch versus RPM are not alarmingly high, they are definitely on the high end for two valve pushrod engines.

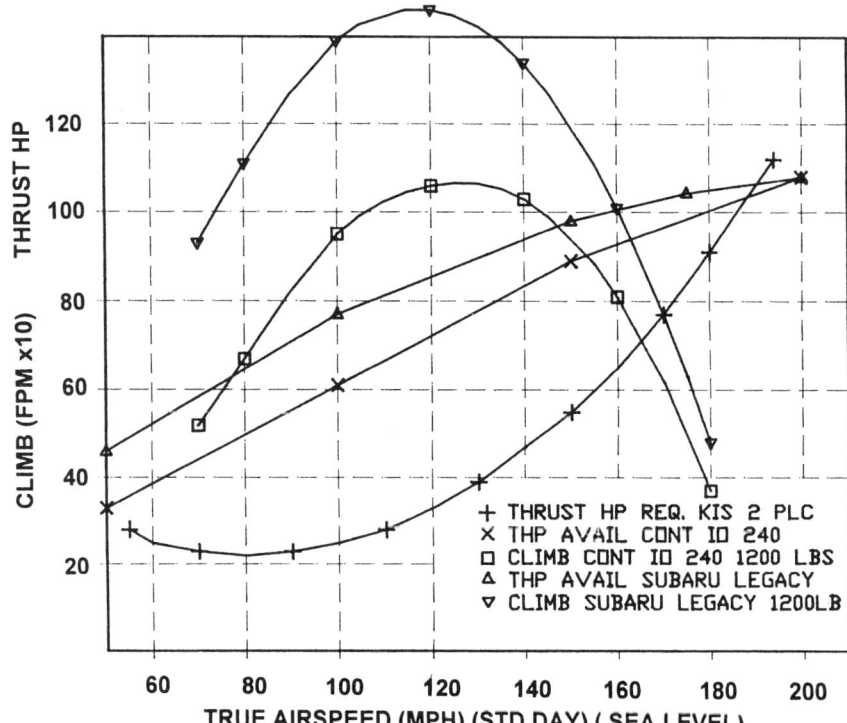

Plot of two place KIS required thrust horsepower as a function of true airspeed along with the available thrust horsepower from O-240 and EJ-22 Subaru Legacy engines and resulting climb rates peaking at 120 MPH.

SUBARU LEGACY

An even more exciting auto engine conversion project was accomplished by our second U.S. builder to fly. Ken McCormick of northern Minnesota chose to use a Subaru Legacy engine in his tail dragger version of the KIS. Ken is a very adept mechanic and fabricator who maintains, rebuilds and modifies industrial machinery for his primary living. His fertile mind has devised and accomplished modifications to machinery in the canning industry that have significantly improved their productivity. He has carried over these same skills to his airborne hobby, having built a gyrocopter, and a KR-2 prior to his Subaru powered KIS.

Ken searched out a late model Subaru wreck with less than 20,000 miles on the clock, which contained the engine model which he had selected for his project. This was the 2.2 liter Legacy engine with overhead cams and 4 valves per cylinder, rated at 130 BHP at a bit over 5000 RPM. This was not the first Subaru Legacy engine that has been used for an aircraft powerplant, so there was some supporting history. As we have intimated before, Ken is not one to follow the crowd, so his installation has several innovative twists which have a lot of promise for future users of this powerplant. First of all, he went against the crowd, and used the automotive computer virtually complete as designed. He reasoned (and I think rightly so) that there was little to be gained from reinventing the wheel. The computer operates a timed port injection system, and has altitude compensation up to 15,000 ft. It also runs the solid state ignition system with variable programmed timing and knock sensing. A possible drawback to this approach is that if you use 100 low lead aircraft fuel, some of the sensors may have reduced life - but many of us want to run auto gas anyway. The dependence on electrical power is also a bit

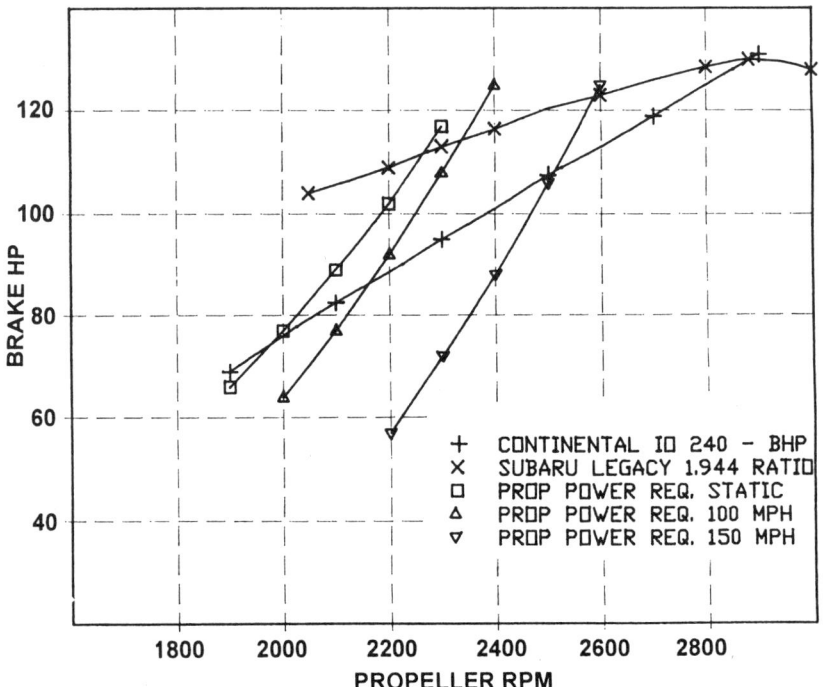

Comparison of brake horsepower curves between the Continental IO-240 and the EJ-22 Subaru Legacy engine geared at a 1.944:1 ratio for rated power at the same output shaft speed.

intimidating, so Ken is working on an automatically switched in back-up battery source.

The approach to the cooling system was also unique and fruitful. Two automotive air conditioning evaporators (the air coolers in your heater duct) were used, positioned behind each cowl inlet hole. This gives them high velocity cooling air flow, and virtually eliminates most of the sheet metal and rubber baffling work required for an air cooled engine. He fit the assembly into an O-235 cowling we provided, requiring only minor "bumping up" on the upper side, and he trimmed away a good deal of the excess volume in the underside. He set up a 4 into 1 exhaust system and computed a tuned length which protrudes a bit rearward under the cowl. A portion of this pipe was converted into a light weight glass pack muffler by drilling numerous holes, wrapping with fiberglass, and covering it with two shells from throw away propane torch cylinders. The result was a lovely fighter plane sound as he cruises by with the engine turning in the mid 4 thousands. Ken is an un repentant tinkerer and the last time I saw this plane the muffler was a more conventional auto part, and he had created a new composite low height intake system which actually looked like cast aluminum.

The reduction drive selected for this combination is a planetary system produced by Lou Ross, and this is part of the reason that the system packages so well. The bell housing adapter, and the housing of the reduction provide the same effect as prop extensions on the conventional aircraft engines, and the prop shaft centerline stays in line with the crankshaft. The reduction ratio is roughly 2.3:1 and results in clockwise rotation of the propeller. The low propeller RPM and rotation direction provides a similar problem as for the CAM-100. Ken also selected a 3 blade Warp Drive assembly which was provided with blades with a bit more taper and twist that their usual set up. With these blades set at the maximum pitch recommended by the supplier, he is over revving the engine at most flight points if he uses full throttle. He has already seen speeds approaching 180 MPH under these limitations, and indications are that this package will out perform the factory IO-240 plane when he gets everything dialed in properly. The first approach is going to be blades with more width in the outer section. Another option is that Ross provides a ratio of roughly 1.8:1 in this same reducer package and as mentioned for the CAM installation a bit higher prop speed might prove a better match for the system.

If you are as resourceful and adept as Ken, this provides a significantly cheaper route into the air, with an interesting high performance package. He has indicated that his out of pocket cost for the engine package was less than $4000. He picked up his kit at our 1992 Oshkosh show price, and has stated that he got into the air for less than $20,000 total (however this was probably aided by a transplant of some items from a previous KR-2 project).

His home video footage of early flights, with that P-51 sounding roar undoubtedly inspired a bunch of potential copies, as we showed it at our display tent at last years (1993) Oshkosh.

PLANE/REDRIVE MATCHING

Propeller designers keep telling reduction drive designers that slow propeller rotational speeds are always the way to go, but this is only partially true. At any single point design, the slower turning, larger diameter propeller will have the highest efficiency. However, in the real world, the diameter of the prop is limited, and you cannot stay on design "point" unless you have a variable pitch, variable twist propeller. For a fixed pitch (or ground adjustable) prop, a flatter pitch operating at a higher RPM may well have a wider useful operating range, particularly if blades with sufficient twist are not available. On the KIS aircraft (and with many other similar higher performance airplanes) a prop diameter of about 68 inches is a good trade between disk area and ground clearance.

A little understood fact is that geared engines operating in a breathing limited horsepower mode, such as auto engine conversions, are actually better suited to fixed pitch propeller operation than conventional aircraft engines. The BHP versus RPM curve for a typical aircraft engine such as the Continental O-240, is nearly a straight line, with power continuing to increase as RPM exceeds the manufacturer's rating (this fact is graphically demonstrated by F-1 race engines which put out roughly 150 BHP at about 4300 RPM from a "stock" O-200. Counter to this approach, the usual automotive rating is given at an RPM where the breathing limits further BHP increase, and BHP actually decreases as you increase RPM. This results in a curved BHP versus RPM plot, with a higher percentage of rated power being delivered in the mid range RPM values typical of static and climb power. The attached curve shows the theoretical relationship of a Continental IO-240 125 BHP conventional aircraft engine, and a Subaru Legacy geared at a ratio which will develop the rated 130 BHP at he same prop speed that the IO-240 would develop 130 BHP (about 2880 RPM or a ratio about 1.94:1). The data for the Subaru curve is based on service manual data for max BHP and max torque for the U.S. rating of 130 BHP, and this data is supplemented by a curve from a Japanese source for the 135 BHP Japanese rating. This second curve was published in the April 1992 issue of Homebuilt Rotorcraft, as pointed out to me by Mick Myal our intrepid publisher.

With a propeller optimized for a KIS or similar efficient aircraft installation these two engines would spin the same propeller at the same RPM at the same top speed, but not the same RPM at intermediate flight speeds. The plotted curves of available full throttle power are matched with computer predictions of the propeller load curves at static and several flight speeds, and the 195 MPH top speed attainable with a 125 BHP engine.

The first set of curves show the basic full throttle horsepower versus propeller shaft output RPM for the Continental, and the "geared" Subaru. Since both are rated at 130 BHP at 2880 prop RPM, you can readily compare the shape of the power curve at the lower output RPM values for the two engines. The added area under the power curve for the geared engine is quite evident with these plots. Also plotted to the same scale is the computer prediction of power required versus RPM for the selected propeller design, at several different aircraft speeds. The mid range speeds typical of climb conditions show the extra power to spin the prop at a higher RPM for increased thrust power in this mode.

The table below shows a comparison for rate of climb at different speeds that could be expected a clean, average Sunday afternoon loaded aircraft, similar to a KIS two place, with 2 people aboard and half tanks for a flight weight of 1200 lbs. Other loadings, and different drag characteristic would be expected to change these numbers, but the basic comparisons would still be valid.

CLIMB RATE (fpm)

A/C speed	IO-240	EJ-22
80	670	1110
90	830	1290
100	950	1390
110	1030	1470
120	1060	1460
130	1060	1440
140	1030	1340
150	940	1190
160	810	1000
170	580	780

This same data is shown on the second curve which is a plot of Thrust HP required to fly an airplane similar to the KIS two place at various speeds. This shows the classic fish hook curve shape for airplane drag, with the high drag from induced wing drag at low speeds decreasing till we get to the minimum value where the increasing parasitic drag (shape drag) takes over the curve and it swoops upward to where our total drag overcomes our power -and we can go no faster. The drag on this curve is plotted based on "thrust horsepower" required, and the shape varies a little from those curves plotted as pounds force of drag. Also plotted on this set of curves are the values of thrust horsepower that can be provided by these different engine systems, each with the same fixed pitch prop, and the curve of the respective rates of climb (multiply the numbers on the left by 10 to get feet per minute climb)

The results are fairly surprising, and show that the geared engine will have a better power match to performance requirements with a fixed pitch prop than a conventional direct drive aircraft engine. Significant gains are also noted in static thrust (which is not shown here), as well as the all important climb modes of operation. Design top speed would be the same, although with a slightly under pitched prop the IO-240 will deliver more power increase in the over rev condition. Obviously the climb and static thrust of either engine would be improved with the cost, weight, and complexity of a constant speed propeller, but surprisingly the "real" airplane engine needs this more than the converted auto engine. The biggest improvement with a constant speed prop would be the cruise fuel economy.

The shape of these power curves would also be expected to be true with the geared Rotax 912 series of engines as well as other well engineered auto engine conversions. The opposite side of this story is that a conventional engine installation can take advantage of the increased horsepower available in the overspeed of the engine at high speeds, if the shortened life expectancy is acceptable.

KIS CRUISER 4 PLACE

What about our new bigger plane, the KIS cruiser 4place now flying with the Lycoming 180 HP O-360 (carb model)? Can we come up with an engine conversion that would work this well for this plane? The discounted price for a new O-360 is about $19,000 which is a bit intimidating for the builder with a limited wallet. Staying in the Subaru "camp" there is that exciting 3.3 liter 6 cylinder SVX engine, but these mills are hard to find, and reportedly being held for high ransom by all of the salvage yards that have obtained them. The aluminum so called "small blocks" are also pretty pricey, and really are a bit large for this aircraft. A good possibility is moving further back in time and looking at the well known Buick/Olds/Rover aluminum V8s. The original factory ratings were pretty modest at about 150 HP, but as shown in "Contact" magazine issue #11, and further articles in issue #19, the engine responds well to rather simple modifications which can put it in the 200 BHP class without jeopardizing reliability too highly. The attached power curves are taken from the referenced article, and are shown plotted against shaft speed, and also a geared speed to compare with the 180 BHP Lycoming. Even the near stock power adaptation although short about 24 BHP at peak will fly the fully loaded Cruiser with a rate of climb only about 75 fpm below the big Lycoming because of the shape of the power curve. Top speed of course reflects the horsepower shortage, losing about 10 MPH. The modestly modified 180 BHP version wipes up the floor with the big Lycoming in the mid range climb characteristics and provides the same top speed.

Those of you that know me are aware that I am not a fan of rating auto conversions higher than factory claims. However, this engine was introduced as a breathing limited "cooking" version as our British friends put it, over 30 years ago. The potential remaining in this engine is supported by the Rover rating of 187 BHP at 5200 RPM,

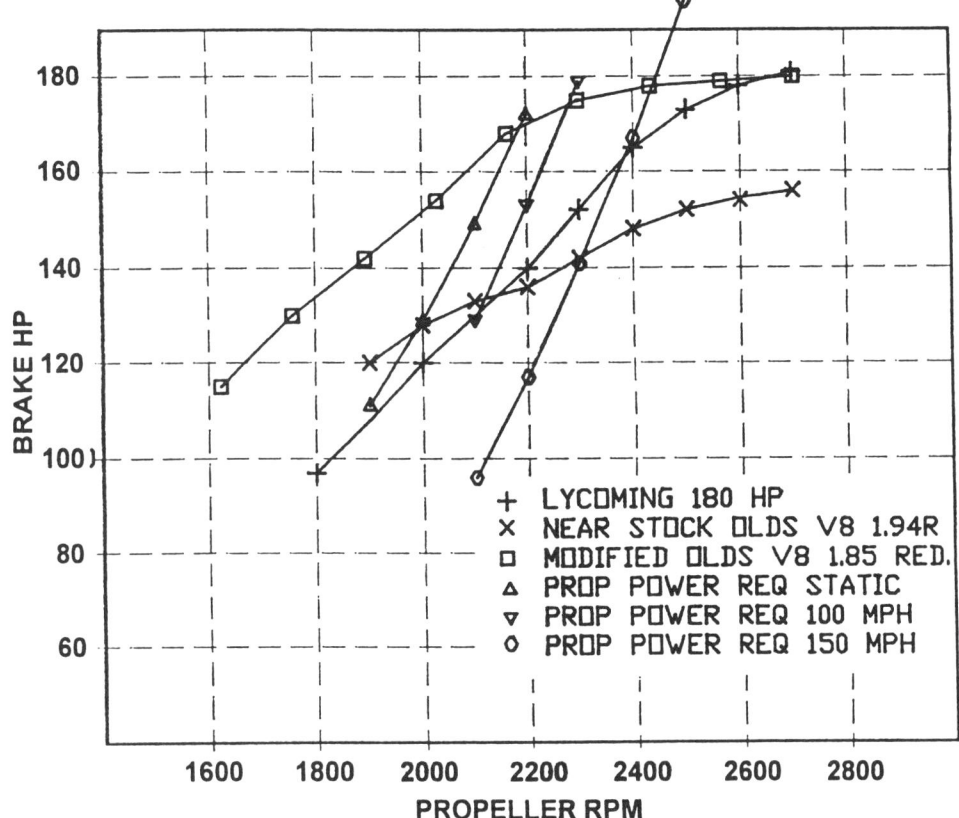

Comparison of power curves between a 180 horsepower Lycoming and two Buick/Oldsmobile aluminum 215 in³ engines (one near stock with 1.94:1 reduction)(the other modified with 1.85:1 gearing), both with shaft output speeds matched to that of the Lycoming.

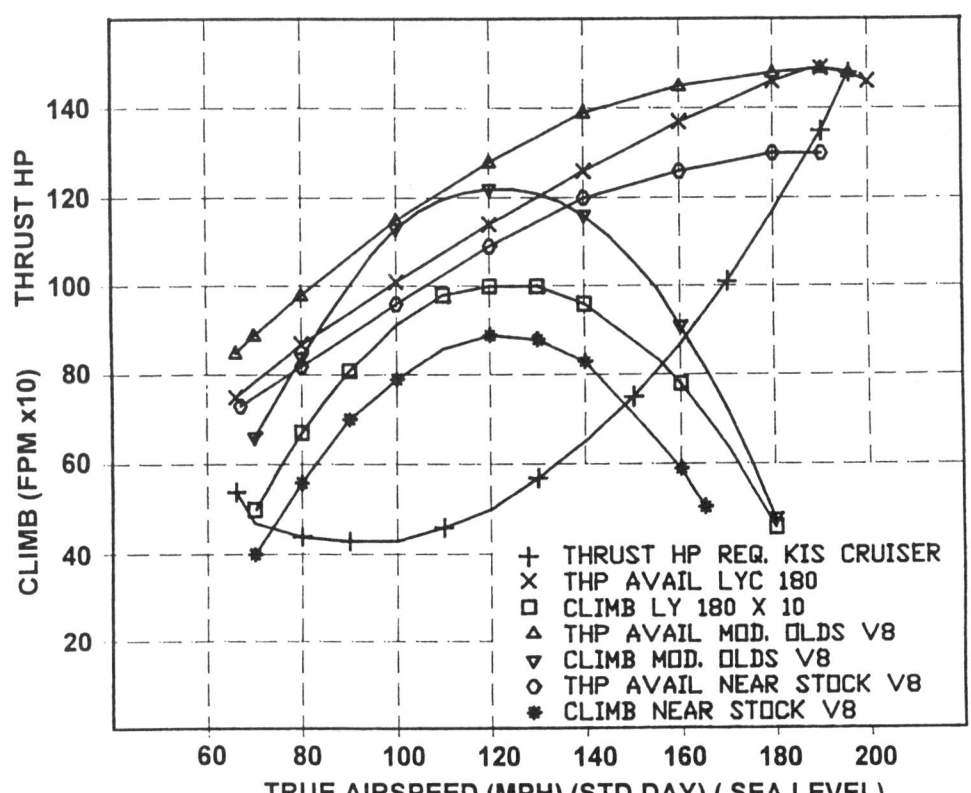

Plot of thrust horsepower required to fly the 4 place KIS Cruiser at various speeds and available thrust horsepower from various engines. Note the modifed 215 out climbs the Lycoming and matches it at the crossing of the power available and power required curves.

and the relative ease of the modifications in putting the power up into this range without going to extremes in compression ratios or RPM. The bore and stroke is slightly less than the Subaru, and the bearing sizes very similar, to give us confidence for good durability at these ratings. The two valve, pushrod valve gear will limit the breathing such that the specific output would be expected to stay below the Legacy, prompting a maximum rating about 180 BHP at 5500 RPM for our computed example. Using this engine as a "stand-in" for a 180 BHP Lycoming would appear to be a very practical consideration.

CONCLUSIONS

The bottom line of the anlysis is that an automobile engine conversion can outperform standard certified engines in terms of takeoff and climb and can match cruise speed numbers. The pure physics of geared auto conversions cannot be denied. However, ultimate success as achieved by growing numbers of experimenters is very much dependent on external processes such as cooling, induction, ignition and vibration as well as propeller matching. Basic consideration should also be given to the following:

● "Gear" your auto conversion to deliver shaft RPM (and hopefully rotation) very similar to the "aircraft" engine you are trying to replace.

● Do not "Hot Rod" the base engine into drag strip types of output (unless you are satisfied with drag strip type flight durations).

● Accept the fact that you might not be able to beat the weight "bogey" of the "aircraft" engine (eat less or pack light!) - but pay attention to your CG location.

Enjoy the fruits of the mid range power curve bulge, and enjoy the smoothness of a well engineered auto conversion. **VWJ**

Some Homebuilding Considerations

F. Folis Jones
4921 Fennell Lane
Suffolk VA 23435
(804) 484 3185

A high school dropout, a retired Senior Chief Machinist Mate after 20 years in the U.S. Navy Submarine Service, Jones received his GED at age 33. He continued his education at Virginia Wesleyan College, ending with a BA with Magna Cum Laude honors. A Masters degree in Clinical Psychology was received from Radford University in 1978 after which he was employed by the State of Virginia Department of Corrections and remains to the present time. His homebuilding experiences may save some reader grief and aggravation.   MCM

In 1989 I made the decision to work at two tasks. One was to get my Private Pilot license and the other was to build my own airplane. The acquisition of the license was pretty much a structured learning process; however, the aircraft construction project was a horse of another color. My initial knowledge of aircraft was limited to the basics one would pick up from movies and magazines.

After 25 years of building and racing various types of sports and formula cars I had developed a good foundation for approaching this new undertaking. Not surprisingly, I found the same BS factor existed in the airplane world as the auto racing world - only worse. The theorist and other all-knowing types abound and can postulate on every facet of the aircraft world until you ask them to show you exactly how to accomplish it. Then you get the "I never really did it myself, but my cousin knows someone that watched it being done". I assume I am like a lot of other homebuilders, eager and ready, but somewhat lost as to what direction to follow. With these historic disclaimers I have set the stage for the sequence of events that lead to our installing an EA-81 Subaru engine in my (name withheld) aluminum and fabric biplane from Chilliwack, B.C., Canada. Since I am an Irish-American, I would not want to deprive them of letting someone else experience building one as a "first time builder".

I knew all along I wanted a two-seater biplane and once I inspected the (Irish name) one I knew it was the one I wanted. Although my knowledge of aircraft engines was limited I had heard enough about Rotax engines to know I didn't want one. I was very adamant that I did not want an "Austrian hand-grenade" under any circumstances. I was assured by the factory that a Continental engine was one of their powerplant options. Much later, after I purchased the kit, they began to shy away from suggesting using one. It's funny how things change once the money is exchanged. Had I been told the Rotax was the only option, or any two-stroke, I would have looked elsewhere for a kit. This was probably the beginning of my loss of virginity as a "first time builder".

I asked my local EAA chapter Technical Counselor to come over and advise me on beginning this new project. His reply was, "call me when you are ready to cover". So, what you are about to read is the result of my own personal digging, asking, and experimenting. I wish I could say how much my local EAA Technical Counselors or members shared their obvious wealth of information, but it never happened. For those uninitiated to the home building world I am hearing the

same from other builders around the country. It is my view too many Chapters have become "chowder societies" for older pilots, some not even flying, to relive their grand old days with little regard for bringing in new members and sharing their tremendous stores of knowledge.

After much reading and research I was convinced the 1800cc Subaru engine was the answer. It had been flight proven in many applications and its longevity and power are legendary. I was fortunate enough to be introduced to Dave Johnson of Reductions Ltd. of Canada. I was, and still am, impressed by his methodical approach to designing and building his belt reduction drives. From him I purchased a complete EA-81 Subaru engine and reduction drive in 1989 at the very reasonable price of $3200.00 (US). I noted recently his price is still the same. The engine was a very stock U.S. version, as opposed the Asian models, with only the addition of the cog belt reduction drive and the removal of non-essential systems. It was shipped by truck, very well crated and just as advertised. I elected to have Dave put an SAE-1 hub on the prop shaft to alleviate future fitting problems with propellers. This proved to be a good move.

On adapting the engine to my airplane, I placed the fuselage at the level, in-flight attitude and positioned the engine exactly where I felt it should be. I then ran a yellow plumb-line down the center of the floor. From there another line with a plumb-bob hanging through the center of the crank pulley and one suspended through the center of the flywheel pulley. With the engine firmly in its correct position I was ready to fabricate the engine mount utilizing the mount hardware supplied by Dave Johnson. Prior to any welding or cutting of tubing I purchased a few feet of 3/4 inch wooden doweling to experiment with. I arrived at my design by going out in the shop with a cup of coffee at 5:30AM and trying different load paths by taping the doweling in various configurations until it "looked right". From that step on it was a only a matter of using the dowels as patterns for the steel. I chose 3/4 inch (.049) 4130 tubing for the primary structure although I was told it was a bit of overkill. What is "overkill" when safety is involved? I am sure I could have gotten away with a dinky mount as seen on a Cessna but I am not an engineer and would rather overbuild than underbuild. I fabricated steel bushings to go on the (Irish name airplane) engine mounting bolts. It was a simple matter to tack weld the tubing in place, remove it from the engine and fuselage, and weld it solid. I think if you are an "eyeball" engineer, such as myself, you eventually build a configuration that, as you look and visualize the load paths, it looks like it should.

By this time, the (Irish name aircraft company) was starting to squirm, telling me I could be building it too heavy and that they no longer suggested the Continental engine as an option. Thanks a lot, after assuring me prior to the sale it was safe. My Subaru weighs a lot less than the Continental. I think some people still belong to the "flat earth society"; i.e., if it is a Continental or Lycoming it can weigh 300 pounds because it is a "real" airplane engine. Even if your auto engine weighs 100 pounds less it is too heavy because it's not a "proper" engine.

Engine modifications were minimal. I strongly believe, based on 25 years caring and feeding racing engines, that reliability goes down the tube in direct proportion to the extent, or the degree, of modifications or "hopping up" to the engine. Therefore, I applied the "kiss" principle; i.e., keep it simple, stupid. We had previously installed the engine "as is" from Reductions Ltd. It had been inspected and found to be a true "low time" engine and all pressures and temperatures seemed within normal limits.

P-51 style belly scoop blends in with the classic fuselage shape. Built up of aluminum sheet the scoop location contributes to C.G. balance. Coolant tubes are contained in the fuselage.

However, after a few hours of test running the oil pressure wasn't quite what it should be, although it seemed to have gobs of power. We had installed a Weber DFE dual throat downdraft carburetor from a 2300cc Ford Capri. Otherwise, it was a box-stock 1800cc Subaru engine.

Meanwhile, I attended Oshkosh '92 and was fortunate enough to meet Bruce Arrigoni, then the future guru of Formula Power. As we talked at the (Irish named airplane)

Air is taken in to the Air Performance throttle body through this fiberglass scoop. Mounted on the fuselage aft of the firewall this arrangement allows for quick removal and installation of the engine cowling.

The air intake feeds air into a plenum chamber in the fuselage which supplies the air throttle body and the the cockpit heater.

booth, Bruce began to outline his plans to market a Subaru engine. At first I dismissed him as just another dreamer or fledgling rip-off artist. However, the more he talked the more it became obvious this guy had his stuff in one bag. His theory and approach were methodical, precise, and made sense. I have heard engine BS all my life and can usually spot it long before it smells. I was quite impressed with Bruce's ideas and began to take him seriously. We corresponded and he filled me in on the foundation of Formula Power and the progress he was making with dynamometer tests.

To put these conversations in perspective, ask some of the other auto engine conversion merchants about their dyno research or amount of dyno time they have. They will probably mumble something about what the "figures" show and totally avoid the recognition that a lot of dynamometer time is absolutely essential to any engine development program whether it is a racing engine or an aircraft conversion. There is a popular VW engine builder in North Carolina that routinely claims horsepower they do not have. In all fairness, I think there may be one or two other auto engine conversion vendors with extensive dyno time. I believe the people at CAM-100 are a good example of thorough research. I have responded to some of the advertisements for auto engine conversions and it is always immediately obvious what their game is - separate you from your money while you "field test" somebody's theory. The bottom line here is: if your engine supplier cannot prove he has extensive dynamometer testing to back up his claims, run the other way and make sure you have your wallet.

Unfortunately, the "non-engine" type person is going to get sucked in and put their life on the line playing development engineer and test pilot for these operators. If the engine builder of your choice does not have a thorough R&D program with proof of extensive testing, you are playing Russian Roulette with your life and your family's future. Most of these guys drift in, hose a few people with their tales of mystical horsepower, then fade off into the sunset carrying your money. If you are lucky, your aircraft will have survived the airborne abortion you bought.

What Formula Power does is take the stock American version Subaru and, as we called it in racing, "blueprint" it. This is the art of ensuring all critical components and dimensions of the engine are absolutely as precise as they can be and what the manufacturer calls for. No engine, as

Overall view of engine compartment. Engine is supported by mounts at the upper redrive housing and to fabricated plates secured to the sides of the Subaru engine. A ground adjustable Warp Drive propeller is used.

it arrives from the factory, is ever in a "blueprinted" state. As for the factory engine in the family car, this really doesn't matter and most wouldn't know the difference if it were. However, in a racing car or an aircraft, it becomes very critical. A blueprinted engine is going to run more efficiently, smoothly, and create less heat and internal drag than the engine in your car.

One of the real deficits in the Subaru 1800cc engine is its breathing. In stock form the intake system is choked off and restricted. This is good for the EPA and the Congressional mileage freaks but hardly conducive to efficiency and power generation. Formula Power's answer is to 'flow" the heads; i.e., place them on a flow bench to optimize and match each head to the other. By porting and polishing the inlets the amount of air taken in per intake stroke is equalized for each cylinder. Thus, the end result is that the engine breathes more, better, smoother and with greater efficiency than in its stock form. Need I mention all this equates to more horsepower? Now, on to the other end of the breathing mechanism, the valve train. The stock camshaft is reprofiled to move the torque and horsepower curves somewhere around 1000 RPM higher, right where you want it. The valves and associated parts are replaced with new or reconditioned stock components. No rough running, trick high-performance stuff here that breeds unreliability, just plain old basic factory components that are operating much more efficiently and in harmony.

At this point one can make several choices as to how to feed fuel into the engine. This, unfortunately, also equates to cubic dollars. Power costs money, no matter how you cut it. One may choose to use some form of carburetion or go with fuel injection. I chose what Formula Power recommends, the Airflow Performance complete injection system. I have spoken at length many times with the folks at Airflow Performance and find them to be thorough professionals and very dedicated to giving you the highest quality components as well as the best system available. They have an impressive history in fuel injection development; but I won't go into that, otherwise this article would sound like a commercial. I am not on the payroll of Airflow Performance or Formula Power in any shape, form, or fashion.

Both firms have excellent manuals and work very personally with you to ensure your system is correct for your application, a rarity in this business today. Simply put, the Airflow system injects fuel directly into each cylinder through fittings installed by Formula Power when the heads are flowed. I have dual (read that expensive) fuel pumps with the back-up pump wired directly to the battery. So if all else fails, I have direct current to the fuel pump and ignition systems. I have installed a two gallon header tank built into the pilot's seat. Both wing tanks drain into it and from here the two fuel pumps take suction from

Right side of Reductions redrive housing and upper mounting point is shown in this close up. Note alignment of propeller shaft thrust line with mounting point, cowling attachment anchor nut, and redrive bonding strap.

a common line. I have also incorporated an aircraft quality fuel filter that filters the fuel before it reaches either fuel pump. There is an isolation valve that shuts off the outlet line from the header tank in order to service the filter and pumps without having to drain the entire system. Curtis drains are installed in both wing tanks as well as one on the top and bottom of the header tank. The Curtis drain on the top of the

The lower engine attach point is seen behind the exhaust stack, below the valve cover. The stock starter is supported in place by the redrive frame. Disregard the Hamilton Standard decal!

header tank bleeds off any air that may be trapped ahead of the header tank. In the event both wing tanks are empty (only fuel left is in the header tank) a built in fuel warning light alerts the pilot he has two gallons or less remaining. This is placarded by a large, red "Low Fuel" light.

Starter is positively grounded to the crankcase, to prevent possibility of destructive arcing elsewhere (seen frequently on cars with inadequate grounding). Brass injectors and fuel resistant plastic lines feed the left cylinders. The valve cover is vented.

Engine gauges consists of oil pressure, oil temperature, water temperature and pressure, fuel pressure (the injection system needs between 20 and 30 psi to operate), EGT, oxygen sensor, ammeter, voltmeter, electronic fuel level indicators for both wing tanks, and the usual flight instruments. A remote compass is installed with its transmitter mounted in the tail. All fuel and electrical lines are routed through the cabane struts and therefore hidden. My tachometer was made by Westach and is programmed to read prop RPM instead of engine speed. My focus is on the prop output, and since it is mechanically connected to the engine, it makes more sense to me to read prop RPM. This keeps me oriented to the "airplane" mode rather than auto engine orientation. I merely told the nice folks at Westach what my reduction ratio was and they took care of the rest - and very reasonably. A simple solution to what could have been a complex problem. The tachometer was verified by a strobe-tach and found to be absolutely accurate. I put a small yellow dot on the tach for each thousand engine revs for reference, otherwise it indicates prop RPM, as any proper airplane tachometer should.

AUTO GAS EXPERIENCE

I tried using auto gas but for some reason this fuel caused the fuel pumps to become noisy and to produce 10 psi more. The consensus from Airflow Performance was that the "O" rings had swelled from the action of fuel additives. Formula Power said I was also losing about seven horsepower according to their dynamometer tests. Along with the ever present threat of the dreaded vapor-lock, I am now convinced 100LL is the only way to go. In my opinion, auto gas is of variable quality and content and, worst of all, will jell up and varnish the internals if left stored. I have also been told auto gas will literally "boil off" at high altitude. The AVGAS may be more expensive, but it is easily available and you can be fairly certain of its quality. For me, that last factor cinches the argument.

COOLING

I used a modified Volkswagen Rabbit radiator set just aft of the lower wing in much the same manner as the P-51 Mustang. I had a radiator shop alter the inlet and outlet to get the angle I wanted for fitting in my scoop area. I used a copper cored standard radiator rather than the aluminum/plastic ones. It was only a matter of a few pounds between the two and I could more easily alter the copper design. The coolant is conducted through two 1 inch aluminum tubes. The water system exits the engine via a 3/8 inch hose from the left Formula Power intake manifold to the "swirl pot", or expansion tank. The right cylinder water exits via another 3/8 inch hose to a small water distribution "manifold" that has two alternate paths. One is to feed directly, as the left cylinders do, to the

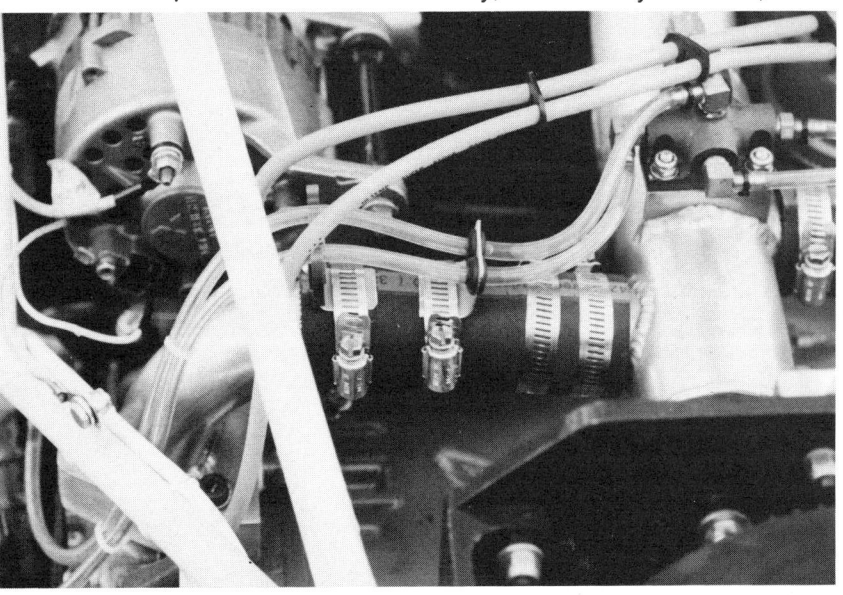

The intake manifold supports the fuel control block. Two intake runners are coupled to the manifold by hoses and clamps. A Mitsubishi alternator is seen in the background. Note tie-wraps and spark wire separators.

expansion tank. The other coolant path is directed through the automotive heater core mounted inside the front cockpit. This "cabin heat" arrangement is controlled by a standard mechanically operated automotive heater flow valve found at any parts store. The cabin heater core and plenum provides additional radiator surface should the need arise, as well as the heater outlet offering an alternate air source should the main intake become clogged. A pressure-stat is mounted on the top of the swirl pot to read water system pressure. Anyone who has ever raced automobiles will tell you a coolant leak isn't usually known until the engine seizes up. Any drop in coolant pressure should be looked at with great suspicion. As long as you have coolant pressure, you can be reasonably assured your water system is intact.

Overall view of the engine induction system with curved plenum and engine controls. Polished stainless steel firewall reflects Jones' workmanship.

VENDOR SUPPORT

Back to the basic engine package. My advice is whenever you buy an engine for your airplane, ALWAYS tear it down and have it gone through and blue-printed by a competent machine shop. When we tore my engine down to install the Formula Power cam and do a precautionary rebuild, we found all of the bearings totally worn out. Why, who knows? Thank God I got my engine and reduction from Dave Johnson of Reductions Ltd. Even though he owed me nothing in the way of a warranty from a legal sense, he still stepped in and paid half the bill. And this was an engine I had run for three years of testing. I was most appreciative, not only for his kindness in this matter, but in his staying in contact continuously since I bought the engine. Now that is what I call customer service. I would recommend Reductions Limited and Dave Johnson to anyone in need of a belt drive reduction unit. I have had the same quality of service form Bruce Arrigoni from Formula Power, no double-talk, no bull, just good customer service and doing all he can to make sure the customer is pleased and using his products safely and correctly.

I wish I could say the same for the (Irish name biplane) from Canada. I find they are reluctant to pass on the names of other builders, some living very close to you, and I cannot understand this. They have an excellent airplane (the biplane) although it is on the marketing back burner and their new Rebel is the focus. For those considering this project the biplane's plans are inaccurate, poorly drawn, and with omissions. The assembly manual, despite revisions, remains a poorly organized and poorly written manual and a source of irritation to those at its mercy. Every builder I have contacted, and so far I have names of ten builders, confirms the exact same irritation and disgust with using one. The only saving grace is that it has excellent performance and is an attractive aircraft. Oh well, you cannot have it all.

BUILDING PROGRESS

At this point in my project, we are finishing up the wing covering and doing a "dry run" of mounting them. We have not performed a weight and balance check as yet. The Subaru, with the Formula Power manifolds should be lighter than the 200 pounds estimated normal (stock) weight.

I would like anyone building a (Irish name) biplane or thinking of installing a Subaru engine to feel free to call or write if they have any questions. I am not affiliated with any manufacturer or vendor, so I have nothing to gain or lose in the deal. We are all in this for the sport and fellowship (I hope), and we should be communicating with each other for the benefit of all. I have had numerous phone calls from frustrated builders trying to interpret poorly written plans or vague instructions. With the "Spirit", I think (I hope) the big problems are behind me. From what I hear, it is a beautiful little bipe to fly. It's just a shame the builders are not organized and in touch with each other. I hope to cure this by forming a

The air control valve is the heart of the Air Performance fuel injection system. On the left is the ignition coil; the water "swirl pot" is on the right.

newsletter and "information bank" for current and future builders. I have over six hours of video tape of my project's construction.

I totally agree with a recent widely published article about the pit-falls of buying a aircraft kit. Ask the manufacturer and insist to be put in touch with other builders and those flying their product. Think twice about your choice if you are given the run-around. Then ask the builders hard questions about the quality of the components, the degree of customer support, and what they don't like about the kit. If at all possible, visit the factory. If this is not possible, find someone with this type of airplane and go look at it. Make friends with an owner and get yourself invited over for the weekend. You will then truly understand what you are in for. Never, never, buy one based solely on the manufacturer's hype or glowing magazine articles. I am beginning to believe the stories about some of the aircraft magazines always giving rave reviews that are less than objective because of advertising revenue they receive or other reasons. Don't let pictures and emotions rule your decision. Take it from someone who has been there, an airplane project is a major undertaking. Another big lie is the "build time". It's never as advertised unless you want to literally throw the thing together.

I hope to be flying this summer. However, if it takes until next spring in order to do it right, then that's the way it goes. I currently have 8.5 hours running time on the engine and all seems well so far. I believe my choice of the Subaru EA81 is a good one; many are flying today and are proving themselves to be reliable powerplants, outperforming O-200 installations as demonstrated by a recent Cessna 150 flight from Seattle to SNF. **FFJ**

Firewall end of the engine installation.

Custom panel reflects the builder's taste and close attention to detail.

One Hour Flight Test Program to Determine Aircraft Climb Performance

Bob Waldmiller
4400 Knox Avenue
Rosamond California 93560
(805) 256 6880

Bob Waldmiller graduated from State University of New York with a Bachelor of Science degree in Aerospace Engineering, was an USAF maintenance officer on the F-15E and currently is a B-2 Flight Test Engineer. He is also President of EAA 1000 at Edwards Air Force Base and is busy with his highly modified Corby Starlet project. This procedure should be included in any initial test program; besides, it can provide you with some fun flying while keeping current. MCM

This article was written not with the intent to make flight test engineers out of everyone but rather to show how a single flight test technique can be used to determine some basic aircraft performance.

The story begins when I had some doubts about my airplane's performance. These doubts started while departing the 1992 Copperstate Fly-In at Prescott Arizona. I knew I was going to fly the airplane heavy out of Prescott so I checked the operating manual to make sure it was a do-able thing. The takeoff roll was expected to be longer than normal which it was. The rate of climb was expected to be an acceptable 300 ft/minute. Once airborne, I discovered that it wasn't--it was more like 50 ft/min and I was about to write another chapter to Ernst K. Gann's book "*Fate is the Hunter*".

Nobody expects a Piper Cherokee 140's climb performance to match its phenomenal descent capabilities. I knew better too, but on another occasion, during a cross country between Lancaster, California and Phoenix, Arizona the airplane just "seemed off". It was probably my imagination but it just didn't feel right to me. With nearly 400 hours in type at the time, I should have been able to pinpoint my gut reactions but I couldn't. Confering with Piper's operating manual for the airplane left me with some serious doubts about my airplane so I aborted the flight and returned to base.

My initial investigation led me to believe that the engine was only producing about 65 percent power where I had expected it to produce 75 percent power. The RPMs were low, the rate of climb was really low, and even the cruise speed was a little off.

Time to check this thing over! The first thing I did was to give the engine a thorough inspection. Let's see, new spark plugs, new ignition harness, mag timing checked, cylinder differential pressure is in the mid 70s over 80 on all four cylinders, carb heat box rebuilt to replace a worn out seal and bushings, throttle plate moves to the fully open position, carb venturi looks ok, fuel and air filters all clean, and the mixture control operates normally. During run-ups the engine leans very smoothly like it always has; i.e., there is no engine shaking or backfiring as the engine is over-leaned which indicates to me that all four cylinders are getting pretty much the same mixture. Without the benefit of an EGT or a CHT it's difficult to be precise in my analysis, but I believe there are no defects in the engine itself. A tachometer check indicates that my tach is reading 50-60 RPM low throughout the entire operating range so I'm turning close to the required static RPMs although it's still 25 RPM low. Given the fact that we're 2300' above sea level while doing the run-up might have something to do with that however. I hereby give the engine a clean bill of health.

Now, what about the lack of climb performance? Time for the one hour flight test program! My objective is to learn as much as I can about the airplane's performance by doing a simple rate of climb check. Since I don't have calibration charts to correct for pitot-static system errors or instrument errors, I'll make the BIG assumption that the errors are reasonably small. Also, I presume Piper did a reasonable job of locating the pitot/static system on the airplane since certifying an airplane to Part 23 standards requires the airspeed system error to be within 3 percent or 5 kts--whichever is greater. Still, I'm making a BIG assumption here. To generate a little credibility however, I'll fly the airplane through a low speed ground course to verify my assumptions. 'Nuff said about instrument errors.

The procedure itself is simple. After setting the altimeter to 29.92, I'll climb at the best rate of climb speed (85 mph) from 500' AGL to 8000' pressure altitude. At 500 foot increments, I'll note the total elapsed time on the stopwatch (starting from a reference altitude) and the outside air temperature. During the climb, I'll keep adjusting the mixture to achieve best power on the engine and all the while the throttle will be wide open. Simple huh?

Still with me? Great! Before I started my climb, I performed an airspeed calibration test by flying both ways through a 4 mile ground course. The first two runs were done at 80 mph indicated in both directions and the second two runs were done at 85 mph indicated. A few minutes of electronic whiz-wheel time to calculate the average ground speed through the course along with my true airspeed revealed that my total airspeed system errors are less than 1 MPH at both 80 and 85 MPH! That's fantastic! How'd Piper do that?

Ok, back to the rate of climb data. I took the liberty and already did some number crunching in order to correct my data to standard atmosphere conditions (standard altitude = pressure altitude corrected for temperature). In addition, I calculated the actual rate of climb (ROCact) for each altitude based on the corrected altitudes and the stopwatch timing values. Since there is some scatter in the data due to vertical air mass movement during the test flight and altimeter errors, I applied a linear regression fit to the ROC$_{act}$ data to smooth it out (ROC$_{lr}$). Finally, I determined the horsepower required to climb at those rates using the following equation:

$$HP_{climb} = \frac{ROC}{33000} * Wt$$

Where *ROC* is the rate of climb in feet/minute and *Wt* is the aircraft weight in pounds. Table 1 is a summary of the raw flight test data and the calculated data.

Since the purpose of this exercise is to determine what the aircraft performance will be at 2150 pounds (gross weight) and compare it with the data that Piper published, I need to determine how much horsepower is consumed by aircraft drag in the climb configuration. Unfortunately, I can't measure drag directly nor do I know how much thrust the propeller is generating to measure it indirectly. Therefore, I'm forced to make a few more assumptions ... oh, oh, there's that word again! Conservatively, those assumptions are:

1. The engine produces 150 HP at sea level at 2700 RPM and 75% power at 7500' at 2600 RPM (per the operating manual).

2. The engine power output varies linearly with RPM from 2300 RPM to 2700 RPM.

3. The propeller efficiency is 75 percent and is constant with altitude, RPM, and true airspeed. This is not entirely true. However, changes should be relatively small and in fact will probably fall to something less than 75 percent at the higher true airspeeds. Therefore this assumption is very conservative.

4. The airframe parasitic drag is constant at 85 mph indicated in the climb configuration and only the induced drag will vary with aircraft weight. This is a good assumption until reaching the higher Mach numbers. (Come on now ... high Mach numbers in a Cherokee???)

First, I'll need to determine how much available horsepower I have at 75 percent power at 7500' standard altitude. From Table I we see that the engine is turning 2390 RPM at approximately 7554' standard altitude. From the above assumptions we defined the propeller efficiency as 75 percent and the desired RPM as 2600. So using the following equation,

$$HP_{avail} = 150 * \eta * \frac{RPM}{2600}$$

we find that HP_{avail} = 77.6 HP. From that we can subtract HP_{climb} at 7554' std altitude (20.4 HP) to get the horsepower required just to overcome the aircraft drag (HP_{drag}) which is 57.2 HP. Now, according to the fourth assumption, HP_{drag} is not dependent on altitude which allows us to do a quick check at sea level values. Adding HP_{climb} and HP_{drag} together gives 108.8 for HP_{avail} at sea level. Since I can only get about 2450 RPM at sea level at 85 mph, the HP_{avail} should only be 102.1 HP. Between the errors in the curve fit and my assumptions, I deem this 6.7 HP error acceptable.

The next step is to determine how much more horsepower I must give up at the higher gross weight to overcome the additional induced drag. To determine that, I must first calculate the lift coefficient at both weights. Using the well known formula, out pops the two numbers of $C_{l\,1670}$ = .603 for the 1670 pound airplane and $C_{l\,2150}$ = .776 for the 2150 pound airplane. (Oh, by the way, S = 150 ft², V = 124.7 ft/sec, and rho = .0023769 slug/ft³). The change in the induced drag coefficient can be expressed as follows:

$$C_l = \frac{W}{1/2 \rho V^2 S} \qquad \Delta C_{d_i} = \frac{C_{l_{2150}}^2 - C_{l_{1670}}^2}{\pi e AR}$$

Where e = Oswald's Efficiency factor of 0.8 for a rectangular wing, and AR is the wing's aspect ratio of 6.

The result is a change in the induced drag coefficient of 0.0158 which doesn't sound like very much but when expressed as a change in horsepower,

$$\Delta HP_{drag} = \frac{1/2 \rho V^3 \Delta C_d S}{550}$$

it works out to 9.9 horsepower, which is very significant! By adding this 9.9 HP to each HP_{drag} term, which in turn means there's 9.9 fewer HP for each HP\ term, we can calculate a rate of climb value for each altitude for the higher gross weight. Table 2 is a summary of that data.

After all this work, we can finally show all the relevant data in a single graph. Figure 1 allows us to see the original flight test data

_____	CALCULATED/PREDICTED DATA				_____
Std Alt	TAS	HP$_{avail}$	HP$_{drag}$	HP$_{climb}$	ROC$_{lr}$
0	85.0	108.8	67.1	41.7	640
4011	90.3				
4621	91.1		67.1	22.6	347
5174	91.9		67.1	20.4	313
5728	92.7		67.1	18.0	276
6337	93.5		67.1	15.6	239
6923	94.4		67.1	13.1	201
7554	95.3	77.6	67.1	10.5	161
8139	96.1		67.1	8.1	124
8547	96.7		67.1	6.4	98
8876	97.2		67.1	5.1	78
9316	97.9		67.1	3.3	51
9756	98.6		67.1	1.4	21
10196	99.3		67.1	-0.4	-6
10693	100.0		67.1		
11076	100.6			-2.5	-38

Aircraft weight = 2150 lbs

Table 2

at 1670 lbs, the linear regression curve fit applied to this data, the predicted data at 2150 lbs gross weight, and Piper Aircraft's data for a 2150 lb airplane as published in the operating manual.

So what conclusion can we draw from all this? Well, for starters, more test data at lower altitudes would improve the curve fit and would most likely change the slope of the lines a bit. Secondly, the gross difference between my predicted data and Piper's would indicate that Piper's test aircraft could produce more useable climb power at altitude than mine can. The only way this could be possible would be to either reduce the aircraft drag at high altitudes or increase the propeller efficiency with altitude. The first explanation isn't possible without changing the aircraft configuration, and the second explanation requires some really dramatic changes in propeller efficiency--like 75 percent at sea level to 91 percent at 16,500 feet (Piper's estimated service ceiling

RAW DATA				CORRECTED/CALCULATED DATA							
P-Alt	Time	Temp °C	RPM	Std Alt	TAS	Δt sec	ROC$_{act}$	ROC$_{lr}$	HP$_{climb}$	HP$_{avail}$	HP$_{drag}$
3000	0	19	2390	0	85.0			1020	51.6	108.8	57.2
3500	1:04.16	19	2370	4011	90.3	XXX	XXX				
4000	2:15.70	18.5	2397	4621	91.1	64.16	514	643	32.5		57.2
4500	3:12.59	18	2400	5174	91.9	71.54	515	598	30.3		57.2
5000	3:59.73	18	2380	5728	92.7	56.89	670	552	27.9		57.2
5500	5:09.80	17.8	2390	6337	93.5	47.14	612	503	25.5		57.2
6000	6:23.51	18	2390	6923	94.4	70.07	508	455	23.0		57.2
6500	7:42.48	17.8	2390	7554	95.3	73.71	478	403	20.4	77.6	57.2
7000	8:54.85	16	2385	8139	96.1	78.97	394	356	18.0		57.2
7500	10:59.86	13.5	2376	8547	96.7	72.37	224	322	16.3		57.2
8000	12:29.12	12	2385	8876	97.2	125.01	215	296	15.0		57.2
8500	14:08.14	10.5	2372	9316	97.9	89.26	280	260	13.2		57.2
9000	17:20.00	9	2370	9756	98.6	99.02	182	224	11.3		57.2
9500	18:30.00	8	2370	10196	99.3	191.86	215	188	9.5		57.2
10000	23:39.00	6	2375	10693	100.0	70.00	139	147	7.4		57.2
			2325	11076	100.6	309.00	XXX				

Airspeed = 85 mph indicated (instrument & position error < 1 mph)
Aircraft weight = 1670 lbs

Table 1

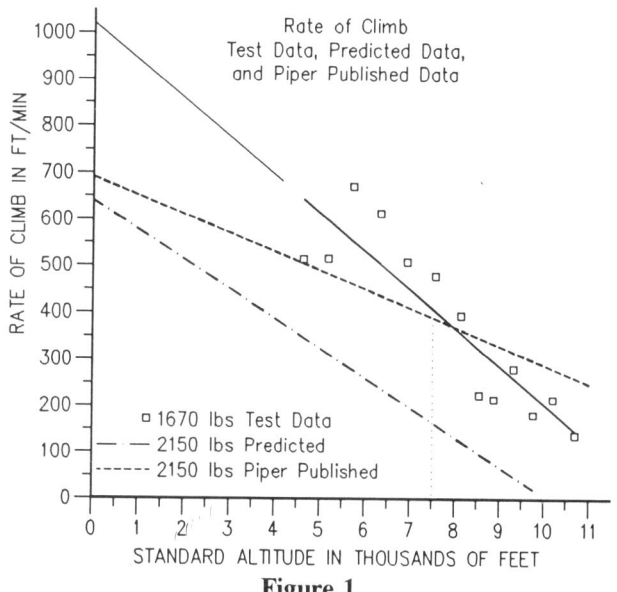

Figure 1

for the Cherokee 140)! I even gave Piper the benefit of the doubt by allowing them to use a climb prop to generate their rate of climb chart and I used their power charts as well. One last point. In Piper's Operating Manual, the rate of climb chart for the Cherokee 140 has the same slope as the Cherokee 180 except that it's offset 75 ft/minute lower. This difference might be valid at sea level but by the time both aircraft reach 7500 feet, the difference should be at least 250 ft/min in favor of the Cherokee 180 not the 75 ft/min that Piper claims. And this is using Piper's own data!!!

My conclusion at this point is that my airplane is pretty healthy considering it's 22 years-old. Also, the data in the operating manual is correct only for the Cherokee 180. At this point I discarded Piper's rate of climb chart for the Cherokee 140 and started using my own data.

The question I'm sure you've been dying to ask is: Why didn't I just load up the airplane to 2150 lbs gross weight and get all my test data there--and avoid all the mathematics? Boy, am I glad you asked that. The answer is: because I didn't know if it was the engine or the operating manual which was faulty. If indeed I had an engine problem, its effects were undocumented. By flying at the lighter weight, I could approach the problem more safely.

Now the story seems to end here but there is a sequel. So, as Paul Harvey would say: "Here's the rest of the story." In early July, as I was doing some routine maintenance on the Cherokee to get it ready for Oshkosh, I discovered the potential source of my dismal climb performance. I found a failed baffle inside the muffler. It took a while for the new muffler to arrive and once I got the plane back together, I knew it was going to perform a good deal better. On the initial test flight, a week before Oshkosh, I did all my usual preflight checks and was immediately impressed by the 100 rpm gain in static rpm. On climbout, it became blatantly apparent that this was not the same airplane I was used to. I was getting a good 1000 ft/min rate of climb and sustained it until reaching 5000'MSL ... WOW, I was impressed! Since I was low on fuel and flying solo I figured it would be interesting to quantify the impact of a failed muffler baffle on the airplane's rate of climb at gross weight. So the sequel to the story goes like this:

I basically duplicated the One Hour Flight Test Program as described above. I used all the same assumptions and equations to generate my new data. The only real difference was that my test weight was about 100 lbs heavier than before due to all the extra fuel I had onboard this time. Essentially I had excellent consistency with my previously computed data. For instance, the amount of horsepower required to overcome the aircraft's drag during the climb should be nearly the same for both tests. This is due to the fact that only change in the aircraft's configuration was the 100 lbs of extra fuel I was carrying the second time. My number crunching indicated that the horsepower required to overcome drag was less than I percent different than during the previous test--that's pretty good consistency! With confidence in my data, I then continued my data reduction to develop the following chart:

Immediately evident are three things. First the rate of climb is better than before which shows that the new muffler has a positive effect on the aircraft's performance. Secondly, even though the rate of climb at sea level is almost exactly what Piper published in their operating minual, at altitude the difference is still large. Thirdly, as I mentioned earlier, any change in climb power will change both the overall rate of climb and the slope of the line on the climb chart. Since Piper shows the same slope for the 150, 160, and 180 horsepower versions of the Cherokee, I again claim that Piper's methods for determining the Cherokee 140's climb performance are bogus and their data should not be used.

So how much horsepower did the failed muffler baffle consume? Well, if you look at the 7500' standard altitude values of the rate of climb, you'll see a 114 ft/min increase with the new muffler. To climb a 2150 pound airplane this much faster requires 7.4 more horsepower worth of useful work. Since I assumed that the propeller is only 75% efficient, this means the engine is now producing 9.9 more horsepower at 7500' than before. Imagine what I'd get if I installed those high compression pistons in my Lycoming O-320-E2A!!!

Without good data it would have been impossible to quantify changes in aircraft performance due to the muffler replacement. The techniques for determining aircraft performance are relatively simple and you may wish to duplicate the above test on your own aircraft. It can benefit you in at least two ways. First, you'll have accurate performance data for your airplane and second, you'll have the ability to quantify performance changes. Since most of us are always experimenting with different propellers, fairings, vortex generators, and other things, having good data to compare these changes will give you much more credibility when you tell everyone else how much better this fairing is over that one. There's no substitute for good data!   **RJW**

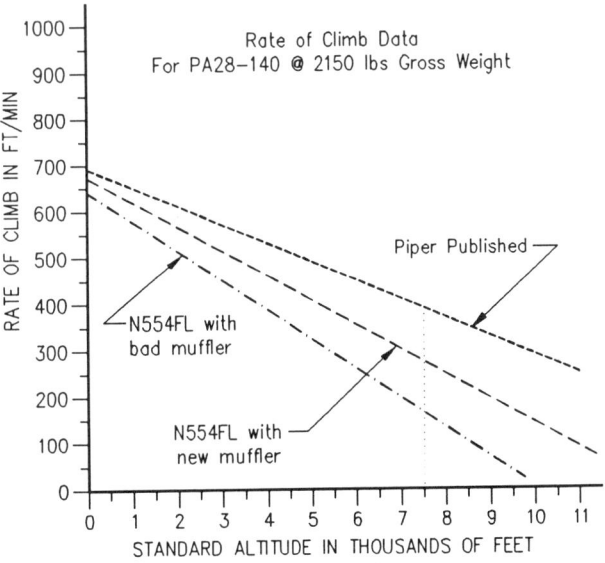

Legacy Powered KIS

Kenneth Mc Cormick
Route 3 Box 56
Hinckley Minnesota 55037
(612) 384 6876

Ken is one of those irrepressible experimenters who are compelled not to accept the ordinary or tried and true. He has built a Gyrocopter, a KR-2 and also has an original design under way. His KIS was built and flown within an nine month period. After nearly 100 hours of flawless flying time the KIS is back in the shop for some winter modifications intended to further improve its impressive performance. Knowing Ken's fervor for improvement Contact! will likely be publishing his revisions by this time next year. MCM

I really enjoyed building the KIS. The construction manual was very complete and easy to follow. The project was started October 15, 1992, and was completed in June of 1993. I estimate I spent about 500 hours building the airframe and about 300 hours on the engine/cowling installation. After a fruitless attempt to acquire a O-235 Lycoming engine at a reasonable price I finally decided to attempt the conversion of a Subaru Legacy engine because of its history of dependability, its fuel efficiency, liquid cooling, power to weight ratio, as well as lower cost.

AIRFRAME CHANGES

To be honest I made a valiant effort to avoid any modifications of the original factory kit but the urge to make changes overcame my initial resolve. The first change was to install an extra bell crank just forward of the rear fuselage bulkhead which allowed me to keep the tail wheel springs inside the fuselage for streamlining. This addition also gave me the opportunity to eliminate the external rudder cables and to substitute an internal push rod to move the rudder. All cable stresses previously applied to the rudder horn attachment are now taken up by the stronger bell crank mounted in the rear of the fuselage.

The next change was done to the rudder and vertical stabilizer. The more I looked at the original tall profile the less I liked it. The solution was simple and easily accomplished. The stabilizer chord was increased by the amount of the excess glass in the factory panels. The height of the profile was reduced some 8.0 inches causing the new, lower rudder counterbalance area to grow in proportion. As a result, less lead shot was required to achieve proper rudder balance. Not having flown the prototype airplane I have no idea if this change had any effect on directional stability. I sense no adverse stability or control problem at any speed.

Disliking the idea of stepping on the seats I found that by moving the instrument panel forward some 5.0 inches from the kit information my foot could reach the floor instead. The instrument panel was built from .25 inch Clark foam faced with 2 plies of glass on both sides. Instruments were mounted on .040 inch aluminum panel inserts, improving serviceability. A custom center console was built from .040 inch aluminum. The console completely covers the gas lines, vent, Pitot tubes and control cables. The console also offered sufficient space to mount additional control switches and circuit breakers. All electrical switches are wired as grounding circuits to control relays mounted behind the panel and on the firewall.

I revised the KIS fuel system to incorporate stock Subaru electric fuel pumps and Nylon filter socks in each of the wing tanks. Fuel flow is electrically controlled and check valves are used to prevent flow to opposite tanks. A second set of emergency switches were wired in as a safety item to override the engine controlled pump circuits. Excess fuel from the engine can be transferred to either tank by a manual control valve.

ENGINE SYSTEMS

The Subaru Legacy produces about 130 HP and 138 foot-pounds of torque at 4500 RPM. A dual coil waste type distributor-less ignition is controlled by a crank angle sensor and computer. An engine knock sensor is incorporated specifically to control any possible pre-detonation. Ignition is capable of up to 40 degrees advance for high speed operation and fuel economy. The mass air flow sensor detects flow of air in the intake system and the computer adjusts the air/fuel mixture to compensate for air density changes (altitude) and keeps the engine running should any sensor fail. Each cylinder receives a precise amount of fuel from its individual fuel injector according to computer commands, with pressure regulated at 33-46 PSI depending on power setting.

ENGINE CHANGES

An EJ22 Subaru Legacy 2.2 liter engine was bought from a salvage yard for $1200. I also picked up all of the vehicle wiring harness, sensors, and the computer controller. The engine portion of the wiring harness was saved. Some 90 percent of the wiring ended up being discarded. The Legacy has a sophisticated air induction system with tuned intake runners. The entire system adds some 8.0 inches to the height of the engine block proper. Typical aircraft powerplants place their induction components on the bottom of the engine, allowing production powerplant installations to have relatively high thrust lines. Needless to say a custom intake manifold was mandatory.

The intake runners were cut 3.5 inches above their engine block mounting flanges, retaining the stock port fuel injectors and enough material to connect them with short rubber hoses to preclude any possibility of hoses collapsing to a custom low profile manifold and the stock air throttle body. The stock crossover water manifold was replaced with two custom designed connectors which were bolted over the existing coolant inlets. These changes made it possible to retain the KIS supplied cowlings and to place the engine thrust line at the 38.0 WL. However, a modification to the upper cowl was required. A "U" shaped cut along the spinner projection of the cowl was necessary, making it possible to raise the opening 1.25 inches for engine clearance. The resulting gap was glassed in and filled, blending this change in profile to the stock fuselage. Doors were cut into the upper cowl for access to oil and coolant filler caps.

The stock lower cowl extends below the bottom of the fuselage leaving a large amount of vacant space below the engine. The saber saw came into play again with the result that the revised cowl is flush with the firewall except for a local fairing and opening for the custom engine muffler. A scoop was added to the lower cowl under the spinner for an oil cooler. The oil filter adapter plate is made from .75 inch aluminum plate, lathe turned to a 3.125 inch diameter and drilled and tapped for 3/8 inch oil lines. The center pipe was cut and threaded to accept a standard Ford filter. The Subaru Legacy filters are relatively expensive and have to be special ordered locally. A VW oil cooler is connected in series with the oil filter and engine.

The engine is cooled by two General Motors air conditioning evaporator cores originally found in 1980 and later model General Motors full size cars. They are connected in parallel. The stock KIS cowl and the radiator cross sectional areas combine to produce a diffuser effect which cools the engine very effectively. Temperatures never exceed 208 degrees F. A two quart coolant expansion tank is fitted with an 18 PSI pressure cap. The engine idle control valve is mounted on the firewall and adjusts idle speed by computer commands.

A custom air cleaner is made of 1/4 inch wire mesh shaped into a cylinder four inches in diameter and ten inches long which supports an open cell foam cover. The foam is a Shop-Vac filter replacement part which I bought at the local hardware for $1.39. Fuel filtration is accomplished through a Bosch diesel cartridge on the firewall.

I am using a 55 ampere Chevrolet Sprint alternator which weighs seven pounds. Considerable effort was spent on making a custom alternator support bracket that would not crack. I have about 60 hours on the current design. My engine computer wiring is completely shielded and all push/pull controls are grounded with custom grounding straps. Catalog items are expensive so I used some scrapped RG-8 cable instead. The outer plastic insulation is stripped off and the braided copper shield can be removed. If stretched the copper weave becomes a strap and if compressed the weave forms a tube up to 1 1/4 inches in diameter. Use of this material has reduced radio interference to a minimum.

The exhaust system is a "Y" type necessary for the O2 sensor function. The muffler is home made consisting of an inner pipe drilled with about a thousand .125 inch holes, then wrapped with fiberglass and covered with two propane tanks butted end to end and welded.

The engine cradle type mount is of my design, fabricated from one inch .035 wall 4130 tubing. It also has a upper hanger mount that can be adjusted to relevel the engine for any settling of the engine mounts. The engine installation is user friendly: the oil pan, air and oil filters, starter, alternator, thermostat, pumps, hoses, wiring and gas lines are easily accessible for inspection and service with both cowls removed.

REDRIVE

I am using the Ross Aero heavy duty planetary gear reduction drive and Subaru Legacy engine adapter housing. The unit is geared to 2.17:1. Lubrication is supplied by the engine oil system through a 1/8 inch I.D. copper line . A .040 inch metering jet provides sufficient lubrication and cooling. A 1/4 inch I.D. return line from the bottom of the redrive housing is connected to a fitting added to the side of the stock oil pan.

The complete engine, as installed, weighs 257 pounds. This weight includes the engine ready to run with all accessories, redrive, radiators and plumbing, coolant and engine oil included. Empty weight of my KIS taildragger is 830 pounds.

PERFORMANCE

I am quite pleased with the engine conversion and my slightly modified airplane. It is commonplace and expected for any development project to encounter some problem and spend time to make necessary changes to fix the deficiency. I am one of the very few not to have experienced any development problems as of this date. I had waited and watched for any signs of some potential problem but after almost 100 hours of flight time none have appeared.

The airplane with me and full fuel aboard climbs 1800 feet per minute at an indicated 80 knots, at 4700 RPMs (engine). Fuel burn is four gallons per hour at a 140 knot cruising setting of 4700 RPM. Top speed is 165 knots at 5600 RPM in level flight.

A Wrap Drive, three blade, almost constant speed, 68 inch diameter propeller is set at 76 inch pitch. At this time the engine is over revving in both level and climb flight. A set of wider blades is on order. **K McC**

Overall view of the engine compartment showing low profile Chevrolet Sprint alternator installation and stock air throttle body mounted on custom intake manifold.

The VW oil cooler is located facing the cowl scoop directly under the propeller. A lightweight Toyota starter is mounted to the adapter housing. Portion of radiator support is seen.

A pair of GM air conditioning evaporator cores are used as radiators. The secret to good cooling is the use here of leak free baffling to form a high pressure diffuser chamber.

Left side view of engine shows engine mount configuration, the firewall mounted custom machined oil filter base and other details of this successful conversion.

The Ross Aero redrive (left) and adapter housing also act as a prop extension to maintain the streamlined KIS cowl lines. Note radiator plumbing and the redrive oil feed line.

Coolant lines are tie-wrapped. Redrive oil drain line is seen. Engine internals were not touched after a careful inspection of engine conditions for poor maintenance or abuse.

Antifreeze and Coolant

Jean-Pierre Maes and Rich Armstrong
Texaco Incorporated
2000 Westchester Avenue
White Plains New York 10650
(914) 838 7502

INTRODUCTION

The popular definition of antifreeze is a liquid which prevents freezing when mixed with water in an automotive cooling system. At one time this definition was fairly adequate.

The modern antifreeze, however, does much more. It provides year-round protection of the cooling system: It prevents freeze-up in winter and boil-over in summer (especially in cars with air conditioning). It provides protection from rust and corrosion and does not harm rubber hoses and plastics. In addition, ethylene glycol-based antifreeze is relatively low in cost, is chemically stable, does not have an unpleasant odor and does not affect automotive finishes. Thus, the modern antifreeze is aptly called "antifreeze and coolant" (AF&C). For convenience, the term "AF&C" will be used throughout this article.

This article reviews the requirements, properties and characteristics of modern AF&C's, tests used to evaluate them and trends which will influence future AF&C development. For more historical information on AF&C's, see LUBRICATION, Vol. 65, No. 3 (1979).

AF&C REQUIREMENTS

The performance requirements of AF&C's became more severe during the 1980's. What was once a commodity product, primarily aimed at providing freezing protection for the cooling system of internal combustion engines, became a complex product containing a delicate balance of additives designed to meet many stringent requirements. The increased awareness of the importance of AF&C was prompted by the introduction of more efficient engines operating at higher temperatures, the use of light metals and plastics in the cooling system and a growing concern relative to the toxicological and ecological aspects of the AF&C itself.

The reduction of the overall mass of vehicles to improve fuel economy entailed extensive use of light materials such as aluminum and plastics for the construction of engine and cooling system parts. The volume of AF&C used was also drastically reduced to further reduce weight, subjecting the AF&C to high rates of flow, high temperatures and significant metal to coolant heat fluxes.

Today's smaller, efficient and powerful engines dissipate more heat, requiring that the AF&C keep the heat exchange surfaces in clean condition. In addition, corrosion, which in itself is of concern, can also result in the deposition of bulky corrosion products that will impede heat transfer.

Initial-fill user requirements and specifications are changing rapidly and contain demands for a cooling fluid that is:

-an effective heat exchange fluid, -capable of protecting freezing and boiling protection, -capable of protecting metals against corrosion, -compatible with plastics and elastomers, -chemically stable at low and high temperatures, -compatible with hard water, -low foaming and -ecologically and toxicologically acceptable.

These requirements are met by the development of multi-component AF&C's that provide a low freezing point, high thermal conductivity and specific heat, good fluidity, elevated boiling point, low toxicity, good chemical stability and a proper balance of supplemental additives. A corrosion inhibitor package is usually present at a concentration of two to five percent. Other additives, which may be present, include stabilizing agents to improve the hard water stability of inhibitors that form insoluble calcium salts, sequestering agents to inhibit deposit formation, antifoamants to inhibit excessive foaming and a dye to characterize the product.

ETHYLENE GLYCOL CHARACTERISTICS

Overview Water-ethylene glycol (EG) formulations are today's preferred AF&C's because the provide year-round, cost-effective freezing, boiling and corrosion protection. In addition, they are chemically stable and are compatible with elastomers and plastics used in the cooling system. The physical properties of water, methyl alcohol (CH_3OH),

TABLE I				
TYPICAL PHYSICAL PROPERTIES OF COOLING SYSTEM COMPOUNDS				
PROPERTY	WATER	CH_3OH	EG	PG
Specific gravity, 20/20°C	1.000	0.7924	1.1155	1.0381
Specific heat, cal/g -°C	0.998	0.600	0.574	0.600
Freezing pt. °C, pure	0	—97.7	—13.3	*
50% water solution	—	—44.5	—36.6	—33.0
Boiling pt., °C	100.00	64.50	197.30	187.20
Vapor pressure, 20°C, mm Hg	17.5	96.1	0.12	0.18
Flash point, open cup, °C	—	15.6	115.6	107.2
Viscosity, cP 20°C	1.00	0.60	20.9	60.5
40°C	0.65	0.46	9.1	19.3
100°C	0.28	—	1.8	2.6

*Supercools

1,2-ethanediol or ethylene glycol (EG), and 1,2-propanediol or propylene glycol (PG), the compounds considered as AF&C bases, are shown in Table 1. Ethylene glycol is the preferred AF&C base because of its high boiling point and flash point compared to methyl alcohol and its lower viscosity (better fluidity) compared to propylene glycol.

Many raw materials such as crude oil fractions, naphthas, and natural gases can be used in a light olefins unit to manufacture ethylene. Ethylene can be reacted with

SPECIFIC HEATS

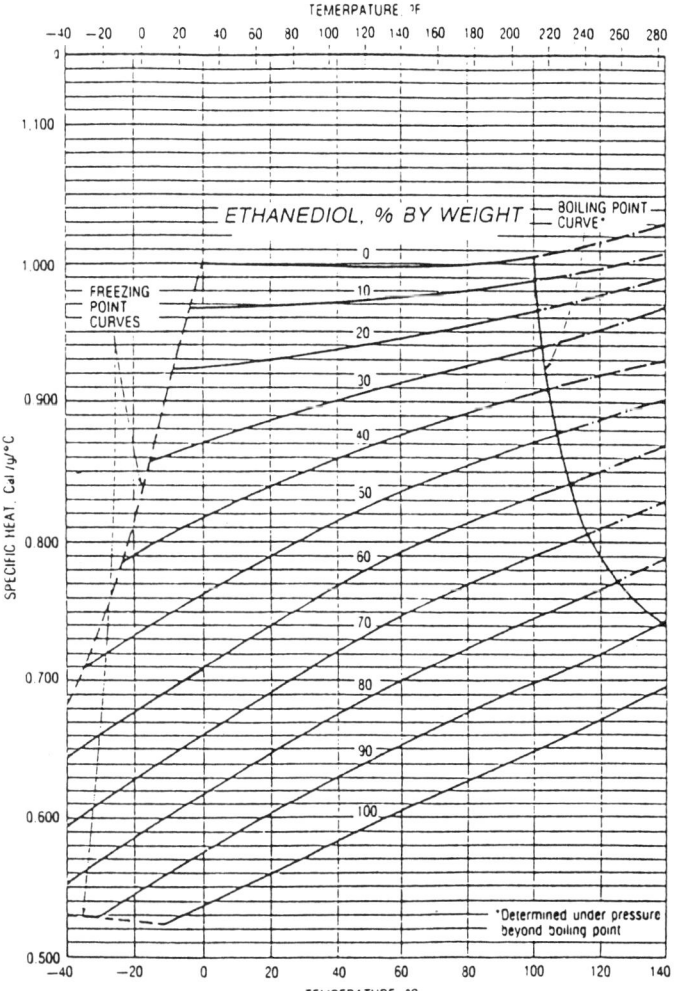

Figure 1 - Specific heats of solutions of ethylene glycol in water at different temperatures.

THERMAL CONDUCTIVITIES

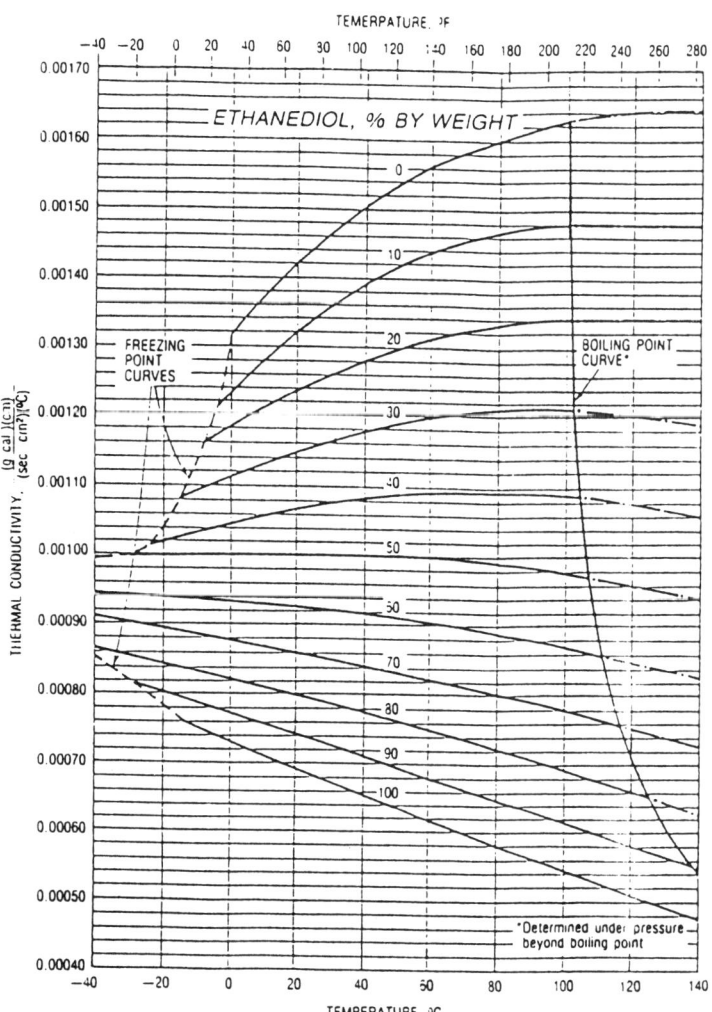

Figure 2 - Thermal conductivities of solutions of ethylene glycol in water at different temperatures.

oxygen to manufacture ethylene oxide, which, in turn, can reacted with water to produce ethylene glycol. About 10 million tons of ethylene glycol are manufactured worldwide annually for use not only as an AF&C base, but also as an industrial solvent and an intermediate in the manufacture of polymers.

Heat Exchange The capability of an AF&C to transport heat away from heat producing surfaces is expressed in terms of the specific heat and thermal conductivity of the fluid.

The specific heat of a substance is the ratio of its thermal capacity to that of water at 15 C (59F). Thermal capacity is the quantity of heat necessary to produce unit change of temperature per unit mass. It is expressed as calories per gram degree Centigrade (cal/g-C).

The thermal conductivity of a substance is the time rate of transfer of heat by conduction (cal/sec) through a mass of unit thickness across unit area for unit difference temperature. It is expressed as gram-calories-centimeter, per second-square centimeter-degree centigrade (g-cal-cm/sec-cm2-C).

Figure 1 shows the specific heats of solutions of EG in water at different temperatures. Figure 2 shows the ther-

mal conductivities of solutions of EG in water at different temperatures.

The heat exchange capacity of the EG/water solutions is reduced with increasing EG content. Water remains the better heat exchange fluid compared to any mixture of EG and water. A compromise between the required freezing protection and heat exchange efficiency has to be made. The viscosity of the cooling fluid is also a factor in evaluating the overall heat exchange efficiency. Lower viscosity (better fluidity) will aid heat transport.

Figure 3 shows the viscosities of solution of EG and water as a function of EG concentration and high temperature. Aqueous EG solutions have higher viscosities at higher EG concentrations. A better fluidity is thus obtained in solution containing less freezing point depressant.

Again, a compromise between freezing protection and fluidity has to be made.

Freezing Protection Because of its low cost and good heat exchange properties, water was used alone in the past as the coolant for internal combustion engines. However, its relatively high freezing point is a serious disadvantage. When water freezes, its volume expands

VISCOSITIES

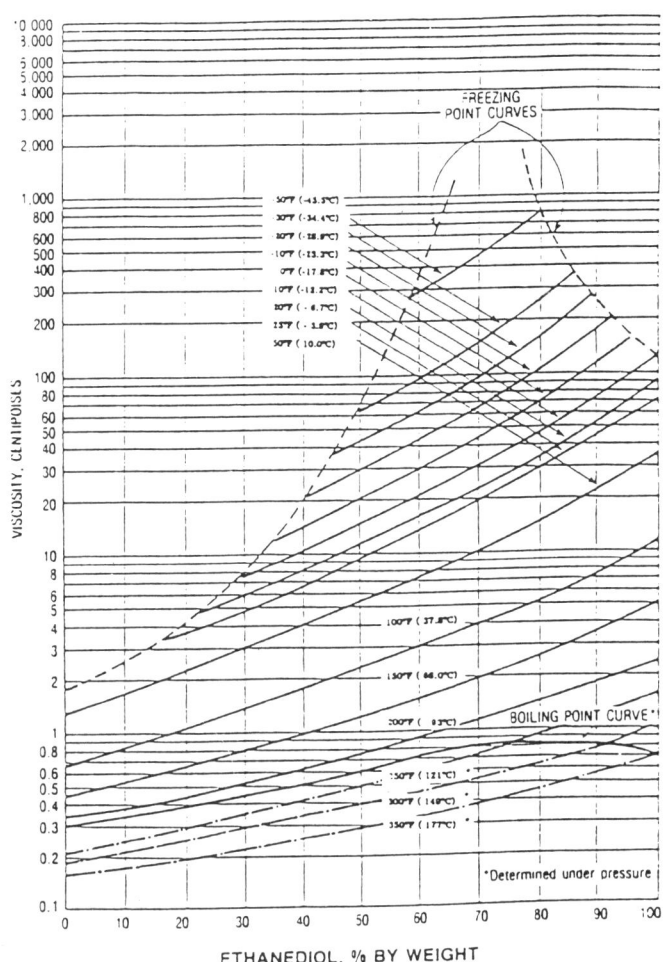

Figure 3 - Viscosities of solutions of ethylene glycol in water as a function of glycol concentration and temperature.

FREEZING POINTS

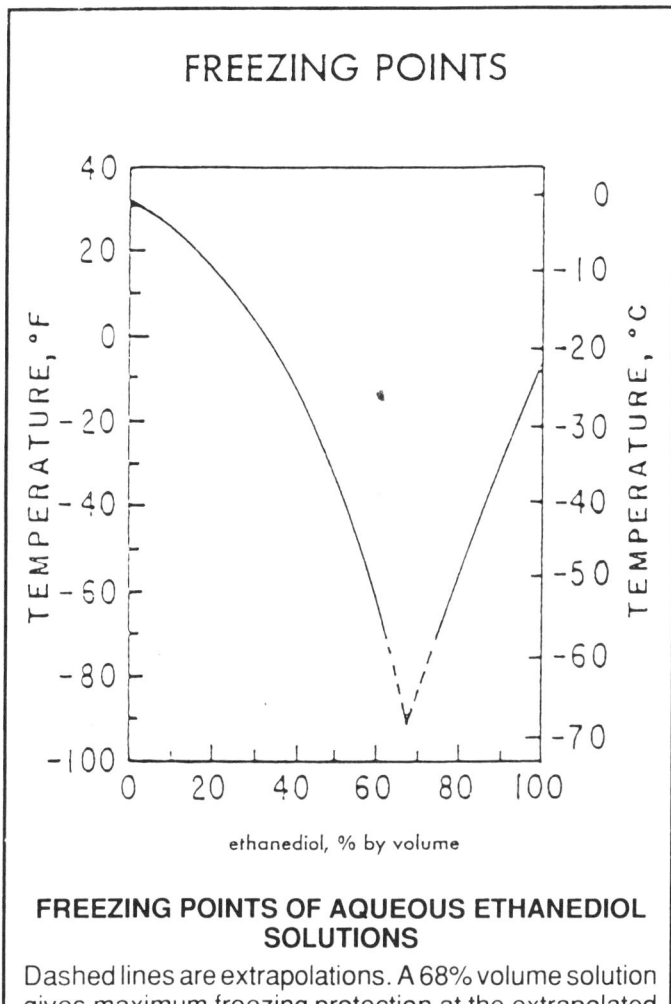

FREEZING POINTS OF AQUEOUS ETHANEDIOL SOLUTIONS

Dashed lines are extrapolations. A 68% volume solution gives maximum freezing protection at the extrapolated eutectic point.

Figure 4 - Freezing points of solutions of ethylene glycol AF&C in water.

about 9 percent. This change is enough to rupture a radiator or even an engine block.

The freezing point depressing properties of aqueous EG solutions are shown in Figure 4. At about 68 percent volume solution, the extrapolated eutectic point, freezing protection is at its maximum at about -69C (-92F). Solutions having a concentration either higher or lower than this composition offer less freezing protection. Pure EG has a freezing point of -13.3 C (+8F).

A formulated EG AF&C concentrate (before dilution with water for use) has a freezing point of approximately -18 C (0F), depending on its EG content. Apart from the EG base, it will contain corrosion inhibitors, defoamers, stabilizing agents, dye and some water.

EG solutions do not solidify when exposed to temperatures several degrees below their freezing point. After the appearance of the first ice crystals, the liquid portion becomes more concentrated and its freezing point is thus lowered. A further decrease in temperature will cause more crystallization until a thick ice slush is formed. The slushing phenomenon permits the AF&C to still flow as it expands. Although this behavior almost eliminates the

TABLE II		
BOILING POINTS OF VARIOUS CONCENTRATIONS OF ETHYLENE GLYCOL		
EG Concentration (Vol. %)	BOILING POINT	
	Atmospheric pressure	System pressure 103 kPa (15 psig)
33	104 C (219 F)	125 C (257 F)
44	107 C (224 F)	128 C (262 F)
50	108 C (227 F)	129 C (265 F)
60	111 C (232 F)	132 C (270 F)
70	114 C (238 F)	136 C (276 F)

Concentrations higher than 70 percent are not recommended; 68 percent provides maximum freezing protection, about -69 C (-92 F.)

FROST PROTECTION

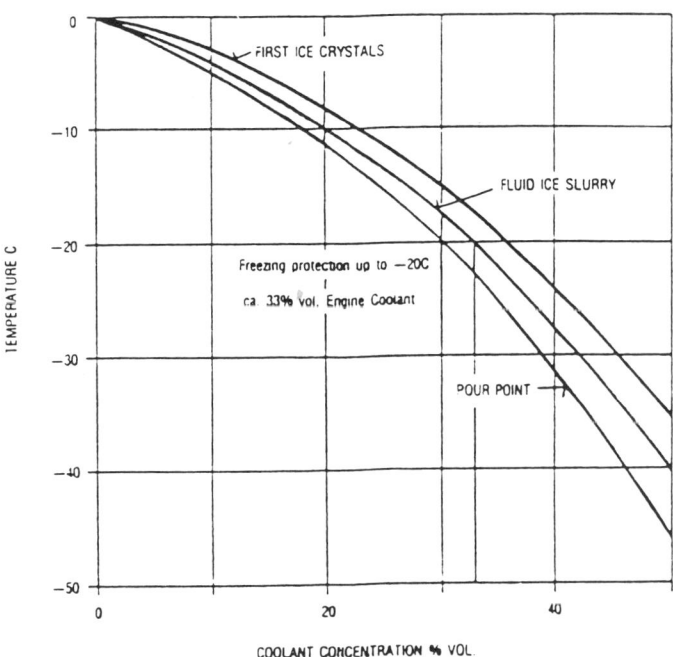

Figure 5-Frost protection by ethylene glycol AF&C solutions: temperature at which the solution is still a thin fluid ice slurry.

danger of freeze-cracking of the engine block, other cooling problems may result. For example, overheating, boiling and engine damage may occur if a thick slush forms that cannot circulate through the radiator. Consequently, the lowest temperature at which an aqueous EG solution provides freezing protection and properly functions as an AF&C is the temperature when crystallization initiates and the AF&C is still a thin ice slush.

Figure 5 shows experimentally determined freezing point curves for and EG AF&C. Curves are shown indicating the temperatures at which the first ice crystals are formed, at which the AF&C is a thin ice slush and at which the AF&C will not flow (at its pour point).

In practice, depending upon the climate, freezing protection ranging for -20 to -40C (-4 to -40F) will be required. EG AF&C is therefore generally used in concentrations ranging from 33 to 50 volume percent.

Boiling Protection As engine efficiency is increased, partly by increasing engine temperature, more heat must be rejected through the cooling system. Additional cooling can be provided by increasing the cooling system pressure and by allowing the AF&C to circulate at a higher maximum temperature. The elevated boiling point of EG AF&C relative to water is important because it reduces evaporation losses, water pump cavitation caused by flash boiling on the suction side of the pump and after-boil caused by residual heat from a shut-off engine.
Table II shows the boiling points of various concentrations of EG at atmospheric pressure and at 103 kPA (15 psig); Figure 6 shows the boiling points of EG at different concentrations in water at different pressures.

ADDITIVE TECHNOLOGY
Overview Uninhibited solutions of EG and water are cor-

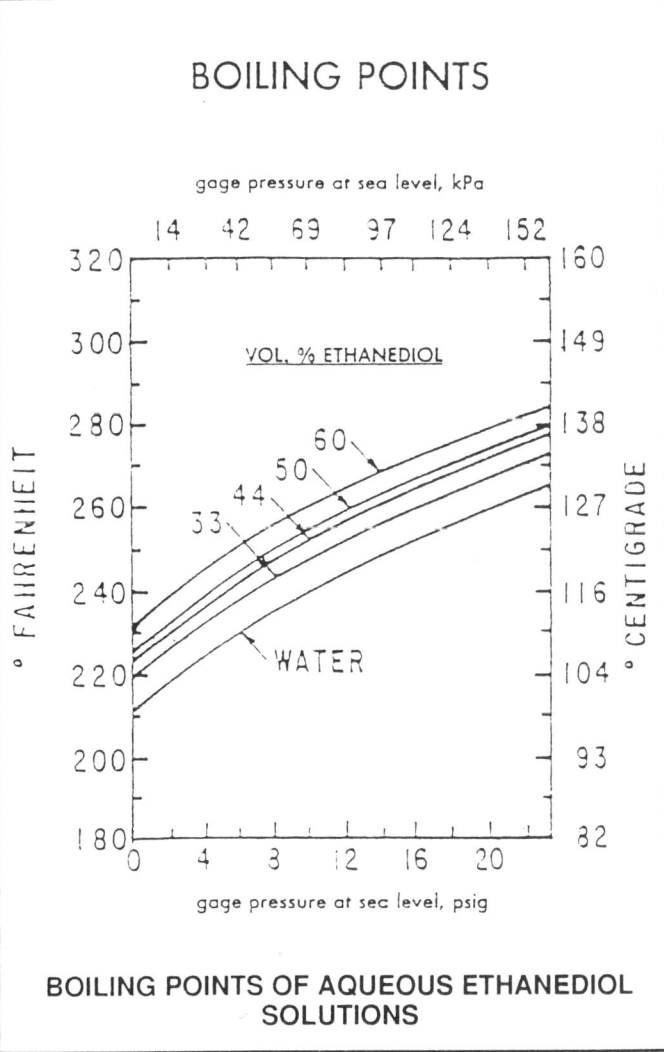

BOILING POINTS OF AQUEOUS ETHANEDIOL SOLUTIONS

Figure 6 - Boiling points of ethylene glycol solutions in water at different pressures.

rosive to the metals contained in engine cooling systems, requiring the addition of an effective corrosion inhibitor package. These additive treatments have to be compatible with the plastics and elastomers used as engine or cooling system components and should not form insoluble salts when diluted with hard water.

Corrosion in an engine cooling system will not only deteriorate metal components, but will also produce insoluble corrosion products that will tend to block radiator passageways, thermostat valves, etc. and impede heat transfer by deposition on heat exchange surfaces.

The metals that need to be protected are of four main classes:

1. iron, steel and grey cast iron
2. aluminum alloys in cast and wrought forms
3. copper and brass
4. lead-based solders

Grey cast iron has been the traditional material for cylinder blocks, heads and liners, but is being replaced by lighter aluminum alloys that have better thermal conductivity. Traditional copper or brass radiators are also being replaced by aluminum radiators with crossflow plastic tanks. However, heavy duty diesel engine systems continue to use the more traditional materials. Steel, cast iron

Development of a Turbocharged Subaru EA-81

Reg Clarke
Box 6896
Wetaskwin Alberta
Canada T9A 2G5
(403) 352-5001

As farm lads Reg and brother, Bud, learned mechanical skills early on. Despite friends' scary opinions to the contrary they decided to buy an airplane (Cessna 140) in 1976. Finding and scheduling a taildragger instructor for 5am sessions was a real challenge. Travel was the goal. Reg found friends were reluctant so he went alone, to the east, Toronto, south through Duluth to Arkansas, Texas and Arizona, then up north on the east side of the Rockies. He later bought a Cessna 120 while Bud continued to fly the 140. Always looking for more horsepower Reg put a O-200 in his 120; according to Reg it was a perfect match! Reg and Bud now live about 2.5 hours from each other (Xpresso hours); Bud is in Helena, Montana 1-406-449-7721.   MCM

Flying the Cessna whetted my appetite for travel. What I really wanted, though, was one of those new, fast homebuilts. I had been following the Q2 and the Dragonfly developments for some time. I then decided on a Dragonfly because of the larger wing area. Also, the design of the Dragonfly results in a very efficient airframe.

I just loved flying the Dragonfly; it was very comfortable and roomy. I could cruise at 145 MPH TAS behind a direct drive 60 HP VW powerplant having 1835 cc. On the negative side the airplane suffered from a lack of fuel capacity and needed more power. I flew to Oshkosh in 1992. It was very difficult to get above the scattered clouds to find the smooth thinner air. It was obvious I needed an engine with more power at higher altitudes.

ENGINE GOALS
These were my goals for the Subaru replacement engine:

1. economical to build (parts)
2. a tough little engine (I work it hard!)
3. likes to be turbocharged (above weather)
4. quiet and smooth
5. compact engine
6. has loads of power
7. very economical to operate (4.0-5.0 gal/hr)
8. has liquid cooling (more stable)
9. works great cross-country (100LL)
10. readily available
11. looks good (in my opinion)

That winter (-30 degrees F.) I decided to pull the VW and install a Subaru EA81 from a salvage yard, keeping engine internals stock. I was in the air by spring. The Subaru had about the same weight and power as my VW . Besides, it was smoother and had less fuel burn.

After some five hours of flying I decided to add a turbocharger and, with that change, the engine came alive! The climb rate tripled. I flew my conversion for about 100 hours. The compression ratio of that configuration was 9.5:1. I then disassembled the engine, plastigaged the bearings and measured all the parts. Everything was still within new engine specifications. One major change was the installation of turbo pistons giving a lower compression of 8.0:1. I took the additional step modifying the airframe to improve streamlining, control and performance. These changes included 60 degree wing tips, a new extended cowling, new wheel pants, an intake cooling scoop and auxiliary fuel tank, as well as 100 percent static balanced controls. The airplane again flew in fall 1993. The Dragonfly (Xpresso #4) is much quieter; the turbocharger acts like a muffler. It is very smooth. The airplane has lots of power to auger up through those holes in the clouds to find the smooth air. This is where the turbo really starts to work!

It didn't really hit me what an advantage a turbocharger was until I was flying formation with a friend in his Long-EZ powered with an O-235 Lycoming. At low altitudes we were very comparable in performance but as we went higher through 6000 to 9000 feet, I was really pulling back on the power. My friend is now talking about moving up to an O-320.

Here are some numbers which may interest readers. On the trip to Oshkosh in 1995 my true airspeed flying at 7500 MSL was 175 MPH. The fuel burn at the 75 percent power setting was between 4.0-5.0 gallons per hour. At 7500 MSL the figure is 4.5 gallons. In my estimation the Subaru is a very strong engine!

In keeping the original Dragonfly/VW direct drive concept which actually works for a lot of other airplane designs I have found it strange that people don't accept the Subaru running in this fashion. People have been telling me and others that it doesn't work, it won't work, that it has to have a prop-reduction unit on it. Well, just like the bumblebee, I didn't know that at the time!

If you calculate the tip speed on the smaller diameter propellers, it does work as shown more than adequately by the fellows flying Formula 1 racers. My 54 inch propeller is working great! As of October 28, 1995, the Subaru had 336.6 hours since its installation. The engine had about 30 thousand miles on it when retrieved from the salvage yard.

Since I first started flying with the Subaru I've made a lot of changes to improve performance. However, I want to remind readers that there is no glory in being the first one to do it wrong!

I feel that the little Subaru is a great engine. It is very comfortable to fly and I have a lot of confidence in the engine. Time will tell, but I plan on piling up the hours on it to see what it will do in the long run -- as I feel a lot of other people are wondering as well.

EA81 DETAILS
This Subaru is what is called the twin carb EA81, or Asian

engine. The difference is in the cylinder heads. The North American version has the exhaust valves next to each other in the center and the intakes on the outside so the ports to the valves are a little more restricted. You can have them ported and it will really help but you need to take them to someone who really knows how to do it. Use of a flow bench which checks the amount of air (CFM) moving through the head is recommended.

The twin carb engine has its intake valves in the center and the exhausts on the outside, same locations as the Subaru EA82. The other result is that the camshafts for the two versions are different to operate the valves correctly. That is the only difference that I am aware of. There were some teething problems to sort out in some of the systems but now they are all working good. My goal is to keep flying and put the hours on the Subaru. I don't baby this engine; I work it hard.

ENGINE OPERATION

Sometimes I operate up to an altitude of 12,500 feet because I live close to the Rocky Mountains. The engine is very strong that high up. I have been flying the Subaru in Xpresso #4 since Spring of 1993. I just love flying with the Subaru. It is very quiet and smooth. I have been tough on this engine because I and other people want to know what this engine will take. I have flown it all over the country -- Canada and U.S.A. In local air shows I have pushed it until there was nothing else to give on the flybys (speed, FAST) and it never complained once. My last test was to climb it to 10,000 feet from brake release before I took it apart. Airport was at 2509 feet ASL, temperature was at 55 degrees F. and indicated speed was maintained at 130 MPH.

Brake release =	:0 sec
Start climb =	:10 sec
3500 feet =	:49 sec
4500 feet =	1:26 sec
5500 feet =	2:00 sec
6500 feet =	2:38 sec
7500 feet =	3:18 sec
7500 feet =	cloud deck

OIL COOLING

My principal problem with the initial test flying was the engine cooling. I had a number of oil and water problems. The Subaru likes to see oil temperatures at about 200-240 degrees F. I built my own oil pan out of aluminum. In addition, I put some tubes through the bottom pan for more surface area to let air flow through. It dropped the oil temperature about 20 degrees.

The temperature of the oil and coolant in an engine are always linked. Once the coolant temperature climbs above 220 degrees F., the oil temperature soars. I found if you cool one you automatically cool the other, as all of the fluids see the engine's heat mass. Aircooled engines act the same. Oil temperature and cylinder temperatures are linked. You can partially cool an engine with oil, but it is not as efficient as water. Oil should run at 200 degrees F. at the minimum and a maximum of 250 degrees F. Synthetic oil can handle 380 degrees F. (Amsoil over 450 degrees F.); the bearings cannot. The Subaru is designed to use multi-viscosity automotive grades of engine oil. I use Amsoil.

Photo of direct drive Xpresso during its development was taken at Oshkosh 1994. This represents Version #4, the initial retrofit of a turbo to Clarke's airplane. Seen are the prop extension, modified coolant filler, intercooler housing, and muffler.

LIQUID COOLING

When I began the Subaru installation I didn't totally understand what it took to design an engine cooling system for an aircraft. I didn't know who to talk to about it so most of my effort was simple trial and error and doing a lot of reading and asking questions. With experience behind me I find it is quite simple and I could have saved myself a lot of grief if I knew then what I know now. It was my biggest nightmare. I repeat; there is no glory in doing it wrong!

One of the basic points in a successful installation is to keep air out of system. When trapped air gets hot, it expands, then turns to steam. It then either blocks the flow of the entire system or produces extreme pressure. Air can shut down your coolant flow and push your coolant out of the system. The engine ends up with hot spots; if in a cylinder head detonation will likely occur.

What worked best for me in the EA81 was having the radiators lower in the system than the engine. The coolant enters the engine from the water pump, goes through the block into the cylinder heads and out the top of each head into the header tank which feeds the radiator. I have installed a one-eighth inch pipe nipple on the top center of the engine block. It is at the engine's high point and it is pressurized from the water pump. I found if I ran a one-eighth inch line from that point to the top of the header tank it would clear any air out of the system and would be pushed out of the radiator cap. I suggest reading Contact! issue 28, Shirl Dickey's E-

Racer article. Also, there are other good articles in some of the back issues of Contact!.

Any air in the system should be driven to the header or tank, next to the radiator cap, because if it is trapped in the coolant somewhere it will make your life miserable.

The following illustration makes my point. In the old days we used to have what they called steam engines to power equipment because when they took water and heated it, it would turn to steam provided there was air in the system. Then it would create tremendous pressures to drive machinery.

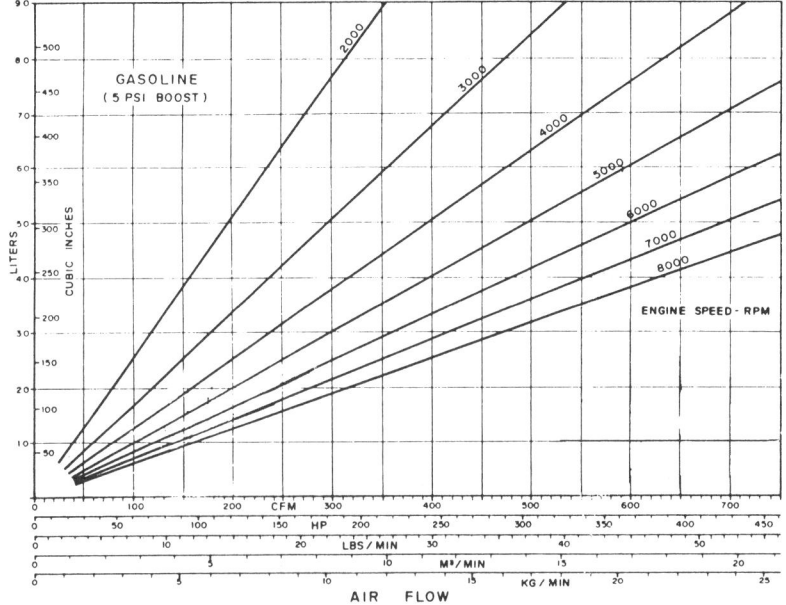

This displacement vs. air flow chart provided by Clarke is useful in determining horsepower and in sizing carburetors and electronic fuel injectors.

If you have a pocket of air trapped in the coolant passages you can probably circulate it out or suck it out if you made provisions for this. If you have an air lock, even a very small bubble of air, and it turns to steam it can and will push coolant out. Steam creates tremendous pressure. You will not cool your engine with this problem. At first it might be an air lock and it will shut some or all of the coolant flow. This makes the system hotter so eventually this air pocket turns to steam and then look out! We know that the higher the pressure the coolant system is under the higher the temperature can be before reaching the boiling point. That's why water boils at a lower temperature at higher altitudes. I recommend you don't use a super high pressure radiator cap because the higher the pressure the more violent the flow when your radiator cap releases pressure. I use a 13 PSI cap.

Remember air wants to go up. Your header tank needs to be up high. If a radiator or hoses are higher than the engine these may create air pockets. The solution is to suck the air out of the system. Remember air can get trapped in the top part of the radiator, turn to steam and make your life miserable. It needs a way out of the system before it has a chance to turn from air to steam. I put my Subaru through a lot of abuse just trying to get my cooling to work right. Now it just "keeps ticking" (purring). Bleeding off air from system high points is the secret. Coolant temperature at 190-210 degrees F. is perfect for this engine. I know some of you may think this is too hot. The Subaru is designed for this temperature. It is not as efficient if you run it cooler.

I spent a lot of time experimenting with different radiator configurations inside the cowling. Toward the end I achieved adequate cooling but my setup was cluttered. We finally made a belly cooling scoop that is 4 inches deeper than fuselage with a P-51 type of intake nozzle and a reverse NACA air duct in the back which works good. The advantage of a liquid cooled engine, in addition to fuel economy, is longer engine life from uniform operating conditions (no shock cooling). Of course, excellent cockpit heat is on everyone's list!

VIBRATION

I had some concerns about this after I installed the Subaru. I took a friend up for another ride. I didn't tell him I had changed from the VW to the Subaru. His comments were, "Why is your airplane so quiet now... I don't feel it shaking anymore." During the rebuild we balanced and blueprinted the engine, also match-flowed the cylinder heads and cc'd the combustion chambers.

PROPELLER

Xpresso #4 has a 6 inch prop extension from the engine crankshaft. The propeller is a 54 inch ground adjustable Warp Drive unit. It works good, a very strong, durable propeller. I had the propeller blade profile changed to a high speed blade so the blade now doesn't stall out at the one-third point of the blade. Also, it now pulls better at higher RPMs. I have taken it up to 4500 RPM at a few local air shows and it doesn't get really loud.

Gary Hunter is the crew chief of the Formula 1 racer, Pushy Galore. We are going to try a paddle blade design that he has on Pushy Galore. For progress and more information on this development please give me a call.

TURBOCHARGER

I am flying with a stock Subaru turbocharger. This was another topic I didn't totally understand - what it took to design an engine turbocharger system for an airplane. I made some early mistakes, such as sadly thinking I could bolt a used turbocharger on and go flying (surprisingly, some times that approach does work!). Normally, you can't just bolt on a turbocharger and go flying. I've learned this partly from trial and error.

One problem is the center bearing gets very hot because of the steady application of power and can quickly fail. Also, the exhaust can get hot if there is too much back pressure (that calls for a proper sized turbo). The intake side can get hot especially when you fly high. The pressure on the intake side can get high (that calls for adequate heat and pressure plumbing; you need to use the right kind of high pressure silicone hose).

The second turbocharger I bought new is a water-cooled turbocharger. This means there is a water jacket that goes around the center bearing. Coolant comes from the engine to the header tank. This center bearing housing is substantially cooler and it is very noticeably cooler when you let it sit after shut down.

A turbocharger can be very beneficial and reliable if operated properly. It should outlast the engine. A turbocharger needs time to cool down and slow down and stop turning before you shut off the engine because when the engine is shut off, the oil supply to the bearings stops. It needs a high quality clean oil. I don't know a better oil than Amsoil and that's another reason why I use it.

I have a manual waste gate so I can regulate the pressure power with a lever. With a turbocharger the intake system can see some high pressures. You need some good judgment to build it properly. How do you get good judgment? Apply lessons learned from bad judgment calls or learn from someone else's mistakes!

Properly tuned forced induction engines are capable of exponential power increases. However, mega horsepower potential also multiplies the consequences of mistakes. Once you have the tiger by the tail you had better know what you are doing, in this case the "tiger" is boost. Boost is the third engine management variable; the other two applicable to normally aspired engines are ignition curves and fuel supply. The three variables are interrelated. The total amount of engine timing is inversely proportional to the amount of boost, available fuel quantity and the engine's built-in static compression ratio.

Look at boost as a means to artificially increase the static compression ratio. Less dense air at altitude reduces the effective static compression ratio. I have learned that if you normally fly at higher altitudes you can start with a higher than normal static compression ratio which means the need for boost is less.

The arithmetic used in determining final compression ratio is straightforward:

Final CR = Static CR X (Boost PSI + Atmospheric PSI)/14.7

At sea level, with 10 PSI boost and a static CR of 8.0:

Final CR = 8.0 CR X (10 PSI + 14.7 PSI)/14.7 = 13.44

At 10000 feet, subtracting .5 PSI for each 1000 feet:

Final CR = 8.0 CR X (10 PSI + 9.7 PSI)/14.7 = 10.7

I've had three emergency landings due to a lack of turbo knowledge. My problems occurred during takeoff and 10 to 100 feet off the ground. When the induction system blew the result sounded like someone just threw a grenade in the cowling. Here are some pointers for a functional installation:

- use a proper intercooler; welded aluminum is best
- avoid plastic or Bakelite on ends of header tanks
- use high pressure silicone hose
- avoid large hose diameters
- avoid large surface areas; minimize buildup of pressure

INTAKE/EXHAUST

I have gone through making six different intake systems to get one that works well. Below are my schematics which will give readers some clues as to what worked and what didn't.

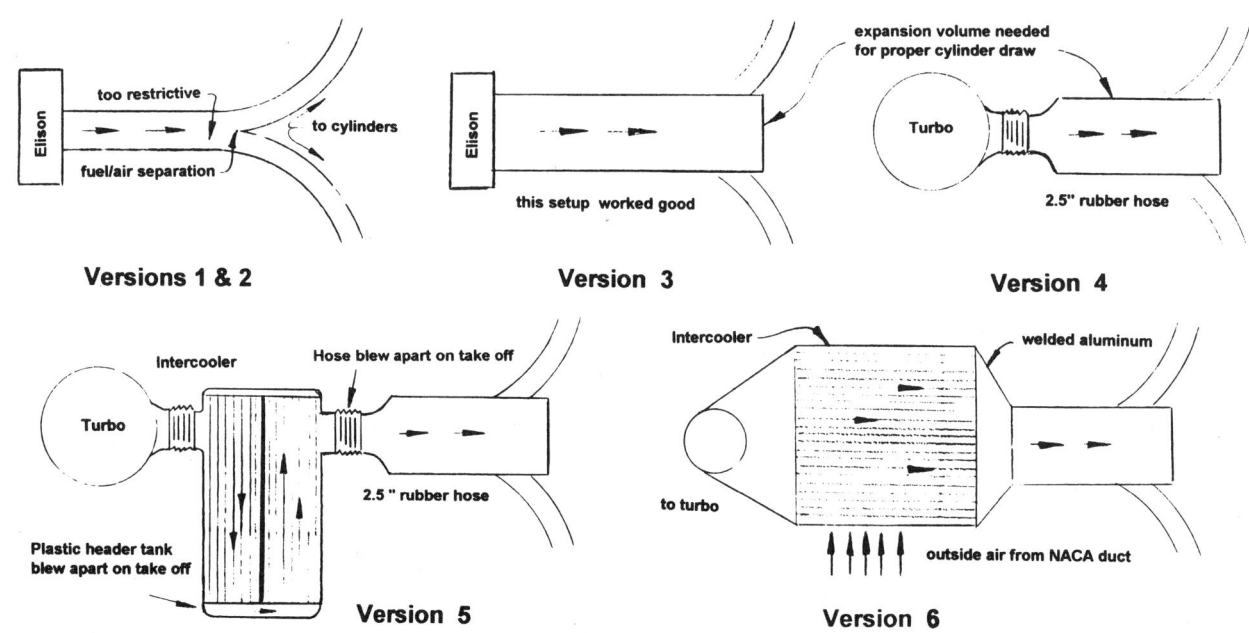

Versions 1 & 2

Version 3

Version 4

Version 5

Version 6

On the exhaust side of the engine I started off making my system out of ordinary automotive steel tubing. I did this because I was not sure if my design would work. Also, I wanted to see how it would stand up to the heat of the turbocharger system. I began to see some problems after about 75 to 100 hours. I am now in the process of changing my layout to stainless steel. I expect to have a more durable and lighter system.

FUEL SYSTEM

I use an Elison throttle body draw-through system. No matter what I boost it to, the Elison always can keep up and supply enough fuel to the air flow. We are doing some more experimenting with the Elison on fuel/air metering. We are also working on a multi-port fuel injection system on Xpresso #7. Bud is doing most of the work on this. We are also making some changes so the fuel intake system will work on a EA81 and EA82 turbocharger system.

INTERCOOLER

I have found that when you run the Subaru with a turbocharger down at low altitudes the fuel burn is low. As you go higher the turbocharger has to work harder to make up the difference for the thinner air. You are compressing more air. Whenever you compress air it makes it hotter. The engine needs more fuel to help cool the combustion temperature. I found that at 12,500 feet compared to 1,500 feet the engine would burn an extra 1.5 gal/hr. Now that I installed an intercooler my fuel burn has gone down and there is very little difference noticed between fuel burn and altitude. I would not even consider running a turbo without an intercooler if I was flying very high or boosting very much, now that I have tried both.

Cooling the induction air with an intercooler is one of the few things you can do to an engine and gain horsepower and at the same time take some strain off an engine. For each 11 degrees F. you can cool the intake air equals about 1 percent increase in horsepower.

IGNITION

I have used the factory ignition but I can adjust the timing manually: 25 degrees BTDC for take off, 40 degrees BTDC cruise (cooler EGT, less fuel burn). Detonation must be avoided so that is why I retard the timing during take off. I also have a knock sensor on my engine and a knock sensor gauge on my panel (MSD). We are working on a new, improved system on Xpresso #7. My brother, Bud Clarke, is doing most of the work on it. An adjustable timing kit is available.

Some rules of thumb that I follow:
- One inch of manifold pressure equals about .5 PSI manifold pressure, actually .491 PSI
- One PSI intake manifold pressure increase raises compression ratio about .5.
- Cool intake air 11 degrees F. equals 1% power gain
- Additional 4 inches of manifold pressure equals about 1.0 point on compression ratio.
- One atmosphere = 14.7 PSI
- 1000 foot MSL increase = about .5 PSI drop

AUTO CONVERSION FUEL

I often receive the question: "Do you use auto fuel?" We all are aware of the problems with aviation 100LL. Lead deposits build up on the pistons and in the combustion chamber of the cylinders, valves stick and, of course, the fuel costs are higher. On the other hand, it is so convenient to fly cross country, to stop and fill up 100LL and proceed on to the destination. I choose to use 100LL.

When I was checking the condition of the stock Subaru after the first 100 hours I found the combustion chamber had very heavy deposits in it and on the piston tops. We turned the cylinder heads upside-down, poured in some performance improver (Amsoil PI). Well, in the morning all the deposits were liquefied and I wiped the combustion chamber clean with some rags. Now I add about one ounce of PI with each 10 gallons of fuel and, to date, I have not experienced any problem associated with the use of 100LL.

I do know of a few cases of pilots using auto fuel and destroying all or part of their engine from bad fuel. Personally, I don't feel it is worth the savings to use auto fuel. For one, the fuel burn of my engine is so low it wouldn't make much difference in annual cost. Also, I don't want to take the chance of damaging my fiberglass fuel tanks. The turbocharged engine works good with the 100LL since I started using AMZoil's Performance Improver product.

CONCLUSION

Some readers may wonder why I like the turbocharged engine so much. Well, it has proven itself to be both functional and durable. I find that engine management is not that hard. At take off, I set the mixture on rich, advance throttle three-quarters and close the manual waste gate until I reach the power setting I want (40-45 inches MAP). As the RPMs come up the turbo comes in stronger. With experience I learned where to set the waste gate. I leave it there and use the throttle for power settings. Fuel management is easy when flying with the Elison throttle body. The fuel and air quantity work together so the only time I move the mixture is when I'm in cruise (EGT).

It is no problem to do some demonstration flybys under adverse conditions. When I took off from Cheyenne Wyoming (6100 MSL, 100 degrees F.) the airplane hardly noticed that it was high and hot. I returned from Oshkosh 1995 in about eight flight hours covering 1200 nautical miles. It was a great show and the organizers had set aside an auto power parking row which made it special.

I am probably like a lot of other homebuilders. I like to hear how these projects are doing. I know there's a lot of interest in the Subaru engine in homebuilts. A common question we hear -- "Is it tough enough for an airplane?" I think it is! My EA81 Subaru has 336.6 hours on it. It is a direct drive turbocharged intercooled conversion. It's working great. As with any development there were some teething problems to sort out with some of the systems but now they are all working well. Our goal is to keep flying and putting the hours on the Subaru.

We are always experimenting and trying new things and that means we are putting ourselves and an airplane on the line a little bit. Xpresso #7 will be ready to fly soon. Brother Bud is doing most of the work on this one. It has an EA82 (overhead cam) turbocharged and intercooled engine conversion with a Lou Ross redrive on it. We hope to make the 1996 Sun 'N Fun event; Oshkosh and Copperstate look good for both Xpressos. We will have more information as we proceed with more experiments (trial and error) and another health report on the turbo EA81 soon.

PRODUCTS

The auto engine conversion movement is definitely the most exciting aspect of experimental aircraft activities. Some experimenters, like us, are interested in development work and are willing to commit effort, time and funds to seek solutions to the high cost of flying. Many others are perfectly content, for a variety of reasons, to purchase complete firewall forward auto engine conversions or specific components.

We have taken the engine off the airframe because we are making up an information package and a 20 to 30-minute information video tape on this power plant and related systems. We are also opening up the Subaru again to see how it is doing because this is an experimental project. We will have more information soon.

In the future we will be able to provide additional products which are now in the test stage. We are considering making a video tape specifically applicable to cylinder head porting, turbocharging and cooling systems if there is enough interest. We believe this is one of the most difficult systems to design and apply with everything else.

To help satisfy the needs of these individuals my brother and I have decided to form AIR RYDER MANUFACTURING, INC. to specialize in high output Subaru engines.

We are currently set up to offer the following parts and services:

- propeller adaptors (direct drive), alignment dowels
- assembly of engines with reduction units. or direct drive
- instruction video tapes
- cooling systems (header tanks, hoses, fittings, radiators)
- intake and exhaust manifolds, intercoolers, silicone hose
- turbochargers
- synthetic lubricants/parts (oil, grease, antifreeze, oil and air filters, filter adaptors, oil/air separators)

Complete inspection and overhaul of the Xpresso powerplant was undertaken this winter. In the foreground is a torque plate used to reproduce cylinder head stresses during honing.

Weighing in of firewall forward engine components before mounting saves time and effort. Note box of loose components. Additional parts are weighed as they are added to the installation. The Xpresso 100 DT (100 HP) Subaru conversion weighs 182 pounds.

Bare engine shows off engine mounting method. The left lower mount member provides a cradle support for the block on two rubber pads. The upper engine mount attaches to a custom fitting bolted to the engine block (not installed in this view).

Right side view shows turbo compressor, hose connection and bottom of intercooler. The alternator support bracket is temporarily attached to the cylinder head. To its left is the water pump inlet.

Top right hand engine view. Behind and in front of the coolant filler cap is the starter support bracket. The intake port is connected to the inter cooler by a short length of coolant hose. A 3/8 inch Al slotted alternator bracket is also seen.

In the right foreground is the left upper engine mount attachment. Directly behind it is the firewall mounted header tank. Note the many fittings which are needed to make the cooling system work properly.

Viewed from the left side, the homebuilt intercooler adds considerable performance to the EA-81 engine. Below it is the turbo hot section before being plumbed to the exhaust. Also seen is the stock distributor and alternator.

The relatively small EA-81 and the 6 inch prop extension combine to produce a beautifully shaped front end, belying the outstanding performance of this experimental turbocharger application.

Reconsideration of Gyroscopic Forces and Torsional Vibration in Auto Conversions

Keith Spreuer
840 Chamberlain Place
Escondido, CA 92025
(619) 745-2218

There is a good article in November 92 issue of Sport Aviation by Bill Husa on "Reduction Drives an Engineering Perspective". Since I'm considering an auto (Subaru SVX) conversion for my Cozy Mark IV, I found it very interesting. The author is an engineer in the aerospace field as am I. I thought the article was well done and goes a long way to quantify some of the important issues to be addressed. I think, however, that some of the calculations use overly pessimistic assumptions.

The first area the article addresses are the gyroscopic forces generated by the propeller which have to be supported by the propeller speed reduction unit (redrive), the engine and the engine mount. Since the propeller is dynamically characterized as a weight rotating rapidly, it has very much the same properties as a gyroscope. In this case when ever the airplane pitches or yaws the propeller generates a force that is 90 degrees out of phase with the yaw or pitch motion. So, a yaw rate would generate a pitch moment and vice versa. The moment generated is proportional to the rate of the yaw or pitch motion. The yaw and pitch rates can get rather high in turbulence or during abrupt maneuvers typical of aerobatics. The other factor that determines how much force is generated by the propeller is the weight of the propeller and the distribution of that weight. This weight distribution is quantified by engineers and called inertia. The inertia is highest for a rotating body like a propeller when there is a lot of weight at the tip. In the Sport Aviation article the author uses an equation for inertia that assumes that the weight is uniformly distributed along the propeller. As you know, we all use designs that taper the blades so that they are as thin as possible at the tip. So the weight is not uniformly distributed. The equation in the article was $I_o = .6667 \times M \times l^2$. Since the propeller is tapered in both chord and thickness, I derived an equation for a uniformly tapered rectangle in both axes, the equation for this moment of inertia is:

$$I_p = 2 \int_0^R \rho A(R-x) B(R-x) x^2 dx$$

Where:
A = thickness @ root
b = chord @ root
ρ = material mass density
R = prop radius
I_p = prop inertia (both blades)
x = distance along radius

which results in $I_p = \rho A B R^3 / 15$.

For the 72", presumably, aluminum blade that the article uses, the inertia should be closer to 282 sl-in2 by this formula instead of the 806 sl-in2.

The article also assumes a 360 deg/sec yaw or pitch rate. I believe this is too conservative and I would use a rate of 60 deg/sec instead for a non aerobatic application. The equation for the resulting moment is:

$M = I \ast \Omega \ast \beta$ Where:
I is the inertia from the above equation converted to slug-ft^2
Ω is the rotation rate of the propeller in radians/sec and
β is the pitch rate or yaw rate in radians/sec
M is the moment generated in ft-lb

The resulting moments are then 644 ft-lb as opposed to 11,000 in the article. It should also be noted that the inertia goes down by the cube of radius, so that a 60" prop would have 58 percent of the moment compared to a 72" prop. Further, if the prop were a wood laminate (assumed density 0.0302 lb/in3) the 72" prop would have an inertia of only 87.6 sl-in2 and the resulting moment would be 200 ft-lbs. These values should be used with appropriate safety factors for the max load case. The article compares these loads to design allowables for fatigue purposes. Fatigue design allowables for aluminum are generally based on the load that material could stand for 10 million cycles. These gyroscopic maximum loads will not occur that frequently.

The article also brings up the issue of torsional vibrations. This vibration is evident many times on shut down or at very low RPM when the RPM matches the stiffness of the engine mounts and the whole airplane shutters. However a similar vibration can occur at higher RPM involving primarily the inertia of the prop, fly wheel and the crankshaft. The dynamic equations for this case involve the inertia of the components, the stiffness of the shafts, and the RPM of the engine. The problem is very complex from an analytical point of view, since it is further influenced by backlash in gears, and damping from friction and viscous sources. The stiffness of the components is not a piece of cake to establish either, since the geometry is constantly changing. The point that the article makes is a good one and that is that by changing the stiffness of the drive train, as is the case with the addition of a redrive, the torsional characteristics will change. It would take a very complex analysis to determine the magnitude of this problem. This is best analyzed empirically on an engine test stand; even this is beyond more than a cursory evaluation by most small manufacturers of redrives. So, for lack of any better information the article proposes a peak torque during a resonant torsional vibration of 800 ft-lbs. This is roughly about 4 times the maximum steady state torque of a 200 HP engine. The author seems alarmed by this mismatch of loads, however, crank shafts and the shafts in perspective redrives are not and should not be designed for the operational output torque of the engine. They must be designed for the peak transient load conditions. The load of 800 ft-lbs for peak loads due to transient torsional resonance and is well within the design criteria for most crankshafts. A typical crank shaft made from high strength steel (150 ksi), 1.5" diameter is good for 8300 ft-lbs of torsion. It should not be a burden to design the redrive for at least the 800 ft-lbs without excessive weight penalties. Even the smaller 1" diameter shafts in redrives are good for 2400 ft-lbs. Keep in mind also that the resonate conditions the article refers to are transient and again do not fall into a fatigue criteria.

There is another load that was not mentioned in the article that should be considered in redrive design. That is the yaw or pitch moment or combination of the two that occurs in high speed flight with a sideslip or an angle of attack. In this condition the air passes through the propeller disk at a skewed angle. If you envision the right sideslip case, the top blade (for counter clockwise rotation engines) has a reduced angle of attack while the bottom blade has an increased angle of attack. This produces a moment that is transmitted through the redrive that can be sizable. The calculations for this are complex and I don't know of a derivation for them, but I will work on it.

I think the article brings up excellent points and the design criteria of any redrive should be available to the builder/designer since these are critical issues. I hope that more people get

Electronic Fuel Injection Simplified

Steve Parkman
SWAG Aeromotive
2521 North Fairview
Tucson Arizona 85705
(520) 622 6910

For those of you that had a hard time programming your VCR (me included) just the thought of electronic fuel injection probably makes you break out in a cold sweat. Doubts that you could actually wire it up, lingering thoughts that you did it correctly, imagining the worst that when you turned the ignition switch on you would see smoke come rolling out. To allay these normal reactions I am going to give you a guided tour of a typical automotive multi-port fuel injection system and prove that you don't have to be an electronic engineer or trained technician to make it work. It may also ease your mind when faced some day with a car fueling problem. I will start with the various information input sensors and the functions they perform. I will then cover what the Electronic Control Unit (ECU) does with these signals. To keep the information organized I have included wire color codes and ECU connecting points associated with these sensors. In reality, these colors and connecting points differ from vehicle to vehicle and between manufacturers. Reference to respective shop manuals is necessary when dealing with specific vehicle ECU packages.

SENSORS

Throttle Position Sensor (TPS)
The TPS provides a voltage signal that changes relative to the throttle butterfly position. Signal voltage will vary from less then 1.25 volts at idle to about 5 volts at wide open throttle (WOT). The TPS signal is one of the most important inputs used by the ECU for fuel control and for many of the other ECU controller outputs. Acting like a rheostat, it is located on either the carburetor, single port throttle body, or air inlet throttle body, directly opposite the throttle plate linkage. An ohmmeter is used to verify its operation:

Connection	Wire color	ECU
TPS +5v.	blu/orn	c14
TPS	blk	d2(grd)
TPS varies	yel/blu	c13

Oxygen Sensor (O2)
The O2 sensor is found on the exhaust manifold near the engine exhaust ports. Acting as a battery, it generates a DC voltage as the tip is heated above 600 degrees F. The voltage will vary between 0.10 volts in a lean oxygen exhaust stream to 1.0 volt when sensing rich oxygen content. If the O2 sensor is below its normal 600 degrees F. operating temperature the engine goes into what is called a open loop condition. Thus at startup, the ECU ignores the O2 sensor signal and substitutes a pre-determined value programmed into the ECU, normally to provide a richer mixture. Some O2 sensors have heating elements built in to increase their sensing function:

O2	blu	d7
O2	blk/blu	d6(grd)

Coolant Temperature Sensor (CTS)
The CTS uses a thermistor to vary a signal voltage to the ECU. As the engine warms up the voltage will stabilize at 1.5 volt to 2 volts. CTS is used by the ECU to control fuel delivery & idle air control.

CTS+	gry/blk	c10
CTS-	gry/blk	a11(grd)

Intake Air Temperature Sensor (IAT)
The IAT sensor uses a thermistor to vary the signal voltage to the ECU. The ECU applies a voltage (4 to 6 volts) to the sensor. When the intake air is cold the sensor resistance is high therefore the ECU will see a high signal voltage. As the air warms the resistance becomes less and the voltage drops. The IAT helps control fuel delivery.

IAT+	blu/blk	c12
IAT-	blu/blk	d2(grd)

Manifold Absolute Pressure Sensor (MAP)
The MAP sensor responds to changes in manifold pressure (vacuum, or pressure in the case of turbocharging). The ECU receives this information as a signal voltage that will vary from about 1 to 1.5 volts at closed throttle idle to 4 to 4.5 volts at WOT (low vacuum, near atmospheric). This sensor will also signal the changes in altitude pressure. This input to the ECU adjusts the richness/leanness of the air to fuel ratio.

MAPsignal	gry/red	c11
MAP-	gry	a11
MAP+ref	blu/orn	c14

Crank Pulse Reference Sensor (CPR)
A variety of means are used to determine engine rotation. These on-off voltage signals to the ECU principally determine the rate at which fuel injectors open and close.

CPR	yel/red	b5

OUTPUT DEVICES

Fuel Injectors (FI)
These are spring loaded devices that open and close at a fixed rate depending on the throttle position and other inputs to the ECU. Fuel is fed to the fuel injectors (only one in the case of a throttle body injector-TBI) at a regulated value of pressure, typically about 36 pounds.

FI #1 and #2	blu/wht	d15
FI #3 and #4	blu/yel	c15

Intake Air Control Valve (IAC)
This electrical control valve allows air to be fed into the intake

---

Gyroscopic Forces cont

involved in this part of experimental aviation. It would be nice if there was a national clearing house for such information. I'd very much like to see statistics on the types of redrives flying with associated HP, hours of service, problems encountered etc. I'm also very interested in data that would help quantify the cooling requirements for liquid cooled engines in terms of radiator area, volume of coolant, and air mass flow rate as a function of horsepower. Do other builders use backup batteries for electronic ignition systems without magnetos? These are a few of the issues and I'm sure there are many more but it is rapidly getting to the point that the benefits will out weigh these concerns. If any of you know of sources for this type information I would be interested in hearing from you. KS

Contact! appreciates the permission to reprint this important analysis, originally published in the San Diego EZ Flyer newsletter. We encourage readers to call or write to Keith and share their thoughts concerning auto conversion issues raised here. MCM manifold to maintain a constant idle. This is controlled by the CTS and the IAT and the TPS.

| IAC | blu/blk | c12 |
| IAC | blk/wht | d2(grd) |

ECU WIRING

The heart of the ECU is a PROM, or Programmable Read Only Memory. When powered up the PROM recalls its memorized instructions and compares them to the signals being sent by the engine sensors. These instructions are complex by nature of almost infinitely variable driver demands, the engine design parameters, vehicle drag, and restraints imposed by fuel economy and exhaust emissions requirements. To achieve the optimum compromise for each specific vehicle model, engine control designers spend thousands of hours fine tuning the intricate PROM instructions. Running changes incorporating further improvements are common place.

Fortunately no one, except the PROM designer, needs to be concerned about the internal workings of the ECU. Short of a complete disruption of battery power the PROM goes on ticking under environmental extremes of temperature, humidity, and altitude. Performance PROMs are available in the hotrod marketplace but their advantages with respect to use in auto conversions for aircraft remain unproven.

For aircraft use the ECU can be powered up by an ignition key or a double pole single throw switch. This switch also powers the fuel injectors. The sketch shows the correct connections. Solid grounding of the switch to metal is important; the airframe, engine, engine mount, or the metal instrument panel can serve as suitable grounds.

Sensors are directly connected to the ECU according to the general ECU connection schematic. The ECU provides internal grounds for the various sensors (A11, A12, D2, D1, D6).

The ECU can be reset by removing the power totally. This causes the ECU to clear the memory and on the next power up it will go to the ROM (Read Only Memory) and start the instructions from there. On start up the ECU will look at the block temperature and determine if the block is cold and if it is it will increase the fuel flow to richen the mixture. At the same time it is looking at the TPS and the O2 Sensor. As the engine warms up the ECU will start leaning out the engine by reducing the fuel flow from the injectors. This is determined by taking samples from the IAT and the O2 sensors. As the RPM is increased the ECU will monitor the MAP and the TPS and use these readings and change the fuel mixture to give the maximum power output while leaning the engine to produce the smallest amount of unburnt fuel. Like the aircraft carburetor the electronic fuel injection can change the mixture at any time but it can do it with very minute changes.

When installing an auto conversion with electronic fuel injection controls it is virtually mandatory to refer to the respective shop manual for numbered and color coded connection instructions. These systems are subject to change so attention to the specific year is always prudent. Shop manuals are a great source of information; most local libraries will have recent model year copies which can put you in command of this technology. SP

From left: a typical EFI connector, Subaru, GM, Hyundai fuel injectors and Holly pressure fuel pump. SWAG injector base was developed to retrofit older model (carb) engines.

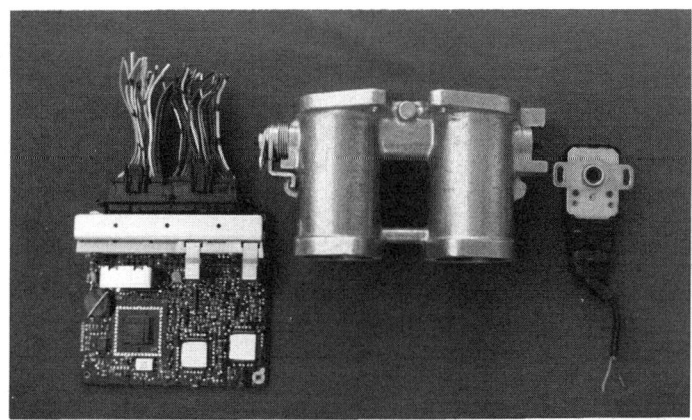

SWAG ECU computer board and air throttle body with TPS removed. Wires are color coded for connection ease.

Signal	Pin
Fuel Pump Driver	A1
Ignition Switched B+	A6
Switched Ground Reset	A10
CTS Ground	A11
System Ground	A12
B+ From Battery	B1
Ignition Timing Reference	B3
CTS Reference Signal	C10
MAP Reference Signal	C11
IAT Reference Signal	C12
TPS Reference Signal	C13
TPS 5 Volt Reference	C14
#1 & 3 Fuel Injector Drivers	C15
B+ From Battery	C16
System Ground	D1
TPS Sensor Ground	D2
O2 Sensor Ground	D6
O2 Reference Signal	D7
#2 & 4 Fuel Injector Drivers	D15

SWAG ECU connection diagram illustrates simplicity of automobile configurations. ECUs are appropriately labeled.

CONVERTING AUTO ENGINES FOR AIRCRAFT APPLICATIONS: AN INTRODUCTION

C. Hall "Skip" Jones
Post Office Box 42387
Kissimmee FL 34742
(407) 846 1244

Involved since 1972, Skip Jones' experiences cover a broad scope of aviation activities. From Chief Pilot for an international corporation, test pilot on the Mitsubishi MU-2 and MU-300, aerospace educator, he now operates an A&P and IA school and shop specializing in repair, rebuilding and restoration of certified airplanes and custom building services (airframes and auto conversions). He has first-flight tested some fifty homebuilts. MCM

What is required to convert a V6 or a V8 auto engine? Basic requirements involve very straight forward modifications. I will separate the engine into its basic functions and offer a few ideas on each. I will also include a few comments on propeller selection.

There are few topics in the experimental aircraft community that will generate as much debate among experienced builders as the conversion of auto engines for aircraft applications. The traditionalists will argue that the auto engine was never designed for the higher sustained power output generally demanded from an aircraft engine. They will also mention low direct-drive power availability necessitating the need for a heavy, expensive, and unreliable (in their opinion) prop reduction drive units and the potential problems arising from liquid cooling requirements. The more knowledgeable types will go on to discuss horsepower vs rpm, incorrect torque vs horsepower curves, incorrect ignition curves, and the lack of dual ignition and traditional aircraft-type mixture control capability. The question of operational experience and why there aren't more auto engines flying also seem to surface with stunning regularity. The issue seems to be primarily one of reliability with questions of weight and expense thrown in.

I had many of the same questions and reservations when I first began to work with auto engine conversions. My interest is primarily in the area of high horsepower engines for use on aircraft such as the larger scale WWII fighter replicas. These aircraft can demand very large amounts of horsepower and can easily handle the weight of the large cast iron block auto engines. In fact, they often require the weight for proper weight and balance.

The question of horsepower usually comes up very early in any discussion of auto engine conversions. A direct drive Lycoming 540 cubic inch air cooled (actually fuel cooled) aircraft engine that delivers 350 brake (prop) horsepower at 2,700 rpm (0.65 hp/cubic inch) is developing a certain internal cylinder combustion pressure (Brake Mean Effective Pressure -BMEP) to produce that horsepower. Using a 350 cubic inch V8 auto engine with a 2:1 prop reduction drive for comparison, the 350 V8 will have to develop substantially less BMEP to deliver 350 horsepower to the prop. Why? With a 2:1 reduction drive, the 350 cubic inch V8 is sweeping an engine displacement of 700 cubic inches per prop revolution as compared to the direct drive aircraft engines' 540 cubic inches per prop revolution. If the BMEP of the 350 V8 were raised to the same level as the aircraft engine, it would be producing approximately 420 horsepower (also 0.6 hp/ cubic inch - remember that we are sweeping 700 cubic inches per prop rpm). For comparison, a 454 cubic inch V8 operating at the same BMEP and using a prop reduction drive of 2:1 would deliver approximately 545 prop horsepower (still 0.6 hp per effective cubic inch). Now lets talk fuel consumption. The air cooled (actually fuel cooled) Lycoming 540 will require a specific fuel consumption (sfc) of 0.7 pounds per horsepower per hour, or a fuel flow of 28.6 gallons per hour at a cruise power setting of 70 percent power (245 horsepower). A liquid cooled auto engine operates at an sfc of 0.45 which would give a fuel consumption of only 18.4 gallons per hour at the same cruise setting of 245 horsepower, for a fuel flow reduction of 35 percent. The astute reader will see that the auto engine is actually producing 1.2 horsepower per cubic inch. This can be done due to the benefits of liquid cooling, higher compression ratios, and higher rpms as compared to an aircraft powerplant.

Torque is another subject that is often discussed. In the automotive application it is the torque that moves the vehicle form a standing stop. Horsepower keeps it moving. In a car, peak horsepower occurs at a much higher rpm than in an aircraft engine and peak torque occurs at a lower rpm. For this reason, the engine should be built so that the torque curve is moved upward and the horsepower is moved downward so that the two meet at the chosen operational rpm of the engine as it's being operated in the aircraft.

I consider myself very fortunate to have never had much interest in cars. As a result, I had no preconceptions of what could or could not be done to adapt an auto engine for aircraft use. After not having much luck in finding people with large auto engine conversion experience, I decided to look for the closest application I could find. The engine in an aircraft is operated very simply as compared to the engine in a car, and I found a very similar application in the off-shore boat industry. The off-shore boats operate in a manner that is very similar to an aircraft: engine start, brief warm-up, "taxi", and engine shut down. The off-shore boat engine builders have been working with very nearly the exact operational parameters that an aircraft engine experiences and have been doing it successfully for years.

If you're new to auto engines and you're planning a trip to your local junk yard to look over their selection of high performance engines (any make), think again. They have been picked over years ago. The days of finding a honest, factory high performance engine in a junk yard have been gone for at least a decade. The performance car builders and the backyard mechanics and would-be hotrod builders have picked the yards clean long ago. Combine that with the fact that Detroit hasn't built an honest, high performance engine for nearly two decades, and the situation becomes clear.

The best you can hope for in a junk yard today is to locate an engine with a high performance block on which to work your particular brand of aviation magic. Both the major auto engine manufacturers (Ford and GM) produce high performance engine blocks for use in RVs, off-road vehicles, and trucks. A high performance block will have 4-bolt main bearing caps, ports on the block for an external oil cooler, will usually have heavier cylinder walls, thicker water jackets, and will most often (but not always) have a stronger crankshaft. All these are very desirable features for an aircraft engine conversion.

There are primarily two alternatives when beginning an auto engine conversion project. The first alternative is to locate an engine with a high performance block at a local junk yard and build your engine on that block using as many (or as few) of the original parts as you choose. The second option is to locate a commercial engine rebuilder and buy a remanufactured "short block" or "long block" assembly from him. With a short block, the builder will supply the block, will have cleaned and inspected everything, and will have assembled the bottom end of the engine for you. The long block will include the above items plus the heads and the valve train. Depending on the exact source, you will have to add an oil pan, oil pump, intake manifold, carburetor, exhaust manifolds or headers, and all exterior accessories such as ignition, alternator, water pump, fuel pump, etc. Sources for these assemblies and all the required accessory items to build your engine can be found in ads in HOTROD and other performance car magazines.

If you locate an engine at a local junk yard, pay particular attention to two areas. Many automotive crankshafts are externally balanced using a dynamic damper on the front end of the crankshaft. The engine is balanced at the factory with its original vibration damper installed. Many junk yards remove these and throw them all in all pile. If this is the case, you must have your crankshaft and the damper you get with the engine rebalanced during the overhaul process. You will also need a ring gear for the starter. Two types are common. One is the heavy type used with standard transmissions. The other is a much lighter type used with automatic transmissions. Use the latter type to save weight. Again, have the crankshaft assembly balanced with this starter ring installed.

Be very careful in selecting engine mounts for your aircraft auto engine installation. The standard automotive engine mounts often don't have thru bolts. They use studs welded to a steel disc that is then bonded to each side of a rubber vibration damper. This works in the car since the engine weight is always down and there are no side forces on the mount. In aircraft, the prop thrust is perpendicular to these studs producing forces that the mounts were never designed to handle. Use only mounts with thru bolts. You can either buy them or make your own.

There are a number of general areas that should be considered in the mechanical preparation of an engine for aircraft use. First, under no circumstances should an engine ever be removed from a car and installed directly on an aircraft without a complete overhaul! To do so is to completely ignore not only mechanical requirements but also common sense. Walk out your front door and look both ways up and down your street and ask yourself how many of the cars you see are maintained in a manner that would make you comfortable installing that engine on an aircraft you and your family were going to fly in. Then compound the situation by having that engine experience the unknown effects of an auto accident (why else would the car be sitting in a junk yard for you to pull the engine out of it in the first place?).

If those two considerations are not enough, there is another very important reason for overhauling any auto engine being considered for aircraft use. Prior to flying behind any auto engine, everything on and in the engine should be safety wired or secured by cotter pins or other methods. The vibration patterns and frequencies developed by an engine operated in an aircraft are very different from those generated during operation in a ground vehicle. You will be amazed at the things that will vibrate loose that never came loose in a car. You must safety everything and you can't do that without opening up the engine.

Even if you are not interested in any performance modifications, your engine should be completely disassembles, cleaned, inspected and reassembled using all new bearings, rings, seals, and gaskets. To do otherwise is extremely foolish, especially considering the risk as opposed to the minimal cost and amount of work involved. Safety must be everyone's primary consideration in any aircraft work, and to fly behind any engine of unknown history and condition should be considered totally unacceptable.

Intake system The camshaft is a vital part of the engine intake system and should be considered for replacement before any other single part during an auto engine conversion for aircraft use. The camshaft is the part that is most responsible for the location of both the horsepower and torque curves of the engine and is very much responsible for the maximum horsepower and torque values produced by the engine. Stock automotive camshafts are designed for fuel economy, smog control, and street drivability, not for engine performance. A properly chosen after-market camshaft can offer very significant increases in both horsepower and torque with little or no negative effects on engine operation for aircraft use.

The stock intake systems used on today's car engines seem to be fairly efficient unless you are out to develop top performance for a given engine size. After-market aluminum intake manifolds are readily available for a very reasonable cost and so offer lower weight and increased performance potential, especially when combined with a few other basic modifications.

Carburetion is a subject that could be discussed at great length, but the basics are pretty simple. To develop maximum performance, you will require a carburetor that will efficiently flow about 2 cubic feet of air per minute per cubic inch of engine displacement. A 350 V8 will require a 700 cfm carburetor and a 454 V8 will require an 850 cfm carburetor. The Holley carburetors with the electronic mixture controls work extremely well on aircraft applications. If you don't choose to buy a carburetor with a mixture control, don't worry about it. You really don't need it until you start flying over about 10,000 feet. Be careful not to restrict the air intake with a restrictive air cleaner assembly. Completely remove all smog and PCV systems from your engine and positively block all vacuum ports. You won't use them on an aircraft engine intake or ignition.

A little time and attention to detail will go a long way in building your engine, and matching the intake manifold ports to the engine will be well worth your time and effort. Be sure to spring load your throttle to the full power position. Automotive carburetors come spring loaded to the idle position. You can always control your descent with the ignition in the event of a broken throttle linkage, but if the engine goes idle, it could create a less than desirable flight experience. Use a safety tray under the carb to catch any fuel that may leak. Make the tray from aluminum or steel sheet about 1 to 1.5 inches deep and run a drain hose from the tray down and out the bottom of the cowling. With the carburetor sitting on top of the engine, you don't really need leaking fuel running down over your hot engine.

You have two basic choices on how to set up the engine fuel supply system. One option is to use the stock engine driven mechanical fuel pump and run a fuel feed line to it from an electric fuel pump located downstream of all the fuel tanks. If this is done, be sure to check the mechanical fuel pump you choose. Many mechanical fuel pumps have a drain port located at the bottom of the pump case to drain fuel if the internal pump diaphragm ruptures. If this is the case, add a drain line and run it out the bottom of the cowling. Fuel leaking into your engine compartment during flight is a serious hazard. The second option is to remove the engine driven pump entirely and use two electric fuel pumps prior to the carburetor. The pad that was used for the engine driven pump than makes an excellent location for an additional crankcase vent.

The selection of fuel is pretty much limited to either premium automotive fuel or aviation grade 100LL (do not use aviation grade 80/87 in a high performance compression auto engine conversion). Either of these will work well if the engine compression ratio is held at or below 10:1 and the ignition timing and cooling system are set up properly. Some people choose to use a small "takeoff tank" filled with aviation grade 100LL fuel for takeoff, then switching to the main fuel system using premium auto fuel for the remainder of the flight.

Exhaust system Two don'ts: don't use the stock cast iron exhaust manifolds and don't use short stacks. The stock cast iron manifolds are too restrictive (especially for a modified engine), are very heavy and are not conducive to good engine cooling. Short stacks will give you every Excedrin headache that's ever been imagined all at once, especially with a large engine. Just because your buddy runs short stacks on his VW powered Sonerai don't even think about trying it on a 350 V8 powered scale P-51. A set of 4 into 1 tuned exhaust headers are very reasonable in cost, very light, can add up to 40 horsepower on a big engine over short stacks or stock manifolds, and they sound sooooo good.

Ignition system There are three very acceptable and very reliable choices. Use the auto ignition system that came with your engine (be sure to retrieve it all from the car when you pull the engine), use an after-market high performance ignition system, or use an after-market magneto ignition system. The ignition systems that have come stock with most cars in recent years are very reliable and provide good performance. The after-market high performance ignition systems are excellent and probably provide some additional advantages at an additional cost. A third method is to use an after-market high performance magneto ignition system that slips right into the stock distributor hole and is completely self contained. Any of these three alternatives will work well with an auto engine conversion as long as some attention is paid to the ignition system setup. First, disable any vacuum advance system that may have been used on the car. Have the mechanical or electronic advance mechanism redone by a qualified shop and set to an idle advance of 12 degrees with a straight line advance curve to a maximum advance of 38-40 degrees at around 2,000 engine rpm. The vacuum advance feature on a car engine provides for additional spark advance and therefore additional power during hard acceleration. This feature is unnecessary on an aircraft powerplant.

If the stock auto ignition system or an after-market electronic system is used, a "backup" system can be made by using two complete systems all the way up the distributor mechanism. The second system should be controlled by a switch and can even be connected to a small motorcycle battery to provide redundancy for the aircraft battery (assuming you remember to keep it charged). A system such as this will share only the distributor, high tension ignition leads, and spark plugs. Use only the best high tension ignition leads with solid core wire with high temperature silicon insulation material and don't run the wires next to each other or thru metallic wire looms. Due to the increased engine operating rpm and temperatures, the spark plugs will almost certainly need to be one range colder than the recommended auto plugs, and possibly even two ranges colder.

Electrical system Use an automotive alternator mounted just as in the car but reduce the size of the crankshaft belt pulley to bring the alternator rpm down to the same speed that it was running in the car (i.e. at a crankshaft speed of around 2,400 rpm). The aircraft conversion will be running much faster. Either use an alternator with a built-in solid state voltage regulator or use an external solid state voltage regulator. Do not use a vibrating points type regulator. It will eventually fail due to the vibration range found in the aircraft engine application. Install an "off" switch in the field circuit of the alternator to enable the pilot to turn the system off in the event of a voltage regulator failure. They always seem to fail in the max output mode rather than in the zero output mode.

Cooling system The liquid cooling system is one of the most critical parts of an auto engine conversion installation. Both coolant pressure and coolant temperature gages must be installed in the cockpit to constantly monitor the integrity and efficiency of the cooling system. The cooling system must be made to function flawlessly and efficiently. Severe engine damage can occur very quickly due to overheating and the resulting lubrication problems leading to seizure of metal components. The basic system functions exactly as it did in the car installation using the engine driven water pump assembly and an external radiator. The aircraft installation must also have a coolant header tank installed that is located at least 4-6 inches above the highest point of the engine. Use an aluminum radiator and a pressure cap of at least 10 psi. Use 100% antifreeze. The few pennies saved by using a water mix isn't worth the risk of even a little internal corrosion during idle periods on the ramp. Be sure to locate the radiator in a spot where differential pressure will force sufficient air flow thru the fins to provide adequate cooling. If the radiator is located aft of the cabin as in the P-51, run only metal tubing coolant lines thru the cockpit area, not hoses. A burst hose spraying hot coolant all aver the pilot will not do much toward contributing to a safe emergency landing.

Lubrication system The engine lubrication system operates exactly as it did in the auto installation. The oil pressure is provided by an engine driven oil pump supplied by a wet sump oil tank. Be sure to check the clearances on the oil pump during the engine overhaul and braze or weld the oil pump pick-up tube to the housing (most are a factory press fit and will vibrate loose at the vibration frequencies experienced in the aircraft). The oil pan should have baffles installed (braze or weld them in place) to prevent the oil from moving away from the pickup tube during slips and skids in flight. Also consider using a splash tray under the crankshaft to prevent the counterweights from spinning in the oil bath which wastes horsepower and disturbs the oil return to the sump. The engine should have an external oil cooler installed with a thermostatic bypass valve to ensure proper oil temperature control. The oil filter should also be externally mounted to prevent vibration failures. Connect both the oil coolers and oil filters to the engine using high pressure, high temperature fluid lines and fittings and safety all connections. Use either aviation ashless dispersant (AD) engine oil or automotive racing oil. Use 50 weight oil (aviation 100) for most engines. Remember that the rpm, bearing pressures, and temperatures will be higher for the aircraft installation than they were for the auto installation due to the higher power output. Install both oil pressure and oil temperature gages in the cockpit. Try to keep the operational oil temperature between 210-220 degrees with an operational red line at 245 degrees. Oil that is too cool will waste horsepower to drive the oil pump (as much as 15 hp) and oil that is too hot will not lubricate properly under load. Adjust the oil pressure relief valve to give 50-55 pounds of oil pressure. Less is risking poor lubrication and oil by-passing the rings and getting into the combustion chamber. Paint the inside of the engine block with Glyptal to aid the oil in returning to the oil sump. Also avoid the use of chrome valve covers. They look good (to the few people who will ever see them), but they don't cool worth a darn.

Power transfer systems The auto engine will not develop reasonable performance with the propeller bolted directly to the crankshaft as is done with direct drive aircraft engines. The auto engine must operate at a significantly higher rpm that an aircraft engine thus requiring a prop reduction drive unit of some type to keep the prop rpm at a reasonable level. The lower the prop rpm (within reason), the more efficient it will be and the quieter it will operate. For V6 and V8 engines, a reduction ration of between 1.6:1 and 2.4:1 will work well. Most V6 and V8 engines should be limited to a red line of around 5,000 rpm to maximize long term reliability (sounds high but is actually a fairly conservative figure for a properly set up and balanced auto engine). At an engine red line of 5,000 rpm, the 1.6:1 reduction would yield a prop rpm of 3,125 and the 2.4:1 reduction would yield a prop rpm of 2,083. The selection of specific ratio will depend on the length of the prop, number of prop blades, and the weight and anticipated speed of the aircraft. The longer the prop and the more blades it has, the slower it can turn and still generate acceptable thrust levels. Generally speaking, faster airplanes tend to have faster turning props of a smaller diameter and coarser pitch and slower airplanes tend to have slower turning props of greater diameter and finer pitch.

There are three viable types of prop reduction units available. Gear, chain, and belt. The gear and chain drives both require constant oil lubrication and an enclosed environment to run in. Both require somewhat heavy construction methods and are generally quite expensive. Gear drives offer an infinite selection of reduction ratios, can harness very large amounts of horsepower, are very smooth operating, and can be set up to operate constant speed props. Chain drives are also very strong, fairly quiet, and can handle significant amounts of horsepower. Many 4-wheel drive vehicles use chain drives to run the front wheel drive system. The belt drive is the simplest, lightest, most trouble-free, the easiest to work with, and can be made to easily handle any amount of power that will be generated by an auto engine, but cannot be made to accept a constant speed prop. Be very careful not to build a belt reduction drive ratio too close to 2:1 unless you make it exactly 2:1. A belt running just a few teeth off from exactly 2:1 will generate a vibration that is both obnoxious and dangerous and will also tend to wear excessively.

Propellers Propellers are somewhat of a problem area for auto engine conversions, especially high horsepower units. Fixed pitch wood props can be made in nearly any length or pitch (within reason) and can be made in two, three, and four blade configurations. Wood props are less efficient than metal props but run very smoothly, are less subject to vibration, and are fairly economical. Fixed pitch metal props are available to handle power outputs of up to around 250 horsepower but are available only in 2-blade design which is unacceptable for aircraft such as replica fighter aircraft requiring three or four props for realistic appearance. Constant speed props are available to handle any amount of horsepower desired and are available in 2, 3, and 4 blade configurations. They are also heavy, expensive, require a prop governor, and must have an engine/reduction combination set up to supply engine oil pressure to the prop hub to operate the prop pitch change mechanism.

Many people do not believe that a constant speed prop is worth the expense and the weight for high horsepower homebuilt aircraft. Most of these high horsepower type aircraft are operating with horsepower to weight ratios that are far in excess of any factory produced aircraft and don't need the constant speed prop for either climb of cruise. With a ground adjustable prop adjusted for cruise flight, the plane will still out climb anything that was ever born in Wichita or Vero BEach, and run away from it in cruise as well, while burning 2/3 the fuel.

Gound adjustable props can easily be made from constant speed props in one of two ways. The easiest way is to block off the oil entry port at the base of the prop and install a grease fitting in the hub in place of the air valve. Simply pump the hub full of grease to establish a new low pitch setting for the prop. Sounds strange, but pumping the hub full of oil is exactly what the prop governor does during constant speed prop operation. The grease merely takes the place of the engine oil. The second method is by shimming inside the prop hub with spacers to mechanically establish a new low pitch stop position. Either method will work well. The grease method has the advantage of being variable without having to disassemble the prop. By using a three or a four blade prop from an Airesearch TPE-331 turboprop engine (MU-2, Commander, etc.) any amount of horsepower can be handled easily and the blades are long enough to look scale on the larger homebuilt fighter types. These props routinely harness power levels over 1,000 horsepower, so your auto engine conversion isn't likely to strain it much. (Note: a prop from a Pratt Whitney PT-6 engine will not work - it has no low pitch stops).

It is not feasible to cover every detail of an auto engine conversion project in a single article or even a series of articles. Many details of the project are determined by the specific engine being converted and by the physical and aerodynamic considerations of the airframe in which the engine will be installed. An auto engine can be converted in an excellent, reliable, and very powerful aircraft powerplant if a few basic principles and sound shop practices are followed.

Legacy Power
A Clean Dragonfly Installation

Justin Mace
EAA 225212
7541 Shirley Lane
Tucson Arizona 85741
(602) 744 3532

It was 1983 when I decided I wanted to build a fiberglass airplane. It was the only type of construction I felt comfortable with. About 25 years ago I helped in the construction of two all fiberglass race cars. When I saw the snapdragon kit for the Dragonfly I decided to build it. I began construction in May of 1984 and completed the aircraft in March of 1986.

Not a pilot at the time of completion I also had to learn how to fly this airplane. I was not pleased with its performance. My first engine was a Volkswagen, 1835 cc HAPI of about 60 hp. The engine had 77 hours on it when I replaced it with an upscale 2276 cc version of the VW. I flew the second engine for 163 hours (240 air frame) when it broke the crankshaft (Contact! issue #1).

DECISION POINT

It was December 1989. I decided I was going to install an engine other than a Volkswagen. The airframe was designed for a flat engine. The Subaru auto engine was horizontally opposed, and water-cooled. The Subaru EA82 is an overhead cam engine and I thought that would be a pretty good choice although the distributor stuck up at the wrong point for the Ross reduction unit I wanted to use. The distributor was way out in front on the right hand side, and the cowl would have to have a large beauty bump to clear it. Not for me! It was about the same hp as the VW. I thought the airframe could handle quite a bit more power. Some home builders are power hungry, and I'm one of them.

Readers may recall in 1989 three Legacys set speed records of 138.8 mph for 17 plus days at a Casa Grande, Arizona test track. That equates to 100,000 kilometers or 60,000 miles at full power! That was the clincher. The horsepower was 130 at 5600 rpm; I decided I would operate at 120 hp (4600 rpm) and gain additional, desired longevity.

My problem was the fact that the engine was just introduced in the new 1990 models. With luck I found a Legacy engine at an auto recycler (wrecking yard) in Phoenix in January of 1990 with only 2800 miles on it. The price was $2,000; it was out of a station wagon that had been rolled over so there was absolutely no front end damage. I brought it home. The airplane also came home and the air frame was modified to accept the Legacy engine.

FIREWALL FORWARD

I stripped the engine down to its basic crankcase and heads with valve covers. The water pump was the only remaining part. The engine at that point weighed 188 pounds. I started weighing all the components I'd stripped off of it and the total weight was over 265 pounds.

To maintain ground clearance and cowling streamlining I had to fabricate a new intake manifold as well as the exhaust system. These were the major new components. The alternator had to be quite a bit lower than stock. A new alternator mount was made for the stock alternator. I chose to use a lighter Toyota starter in place of the stock Subaru unit. No modifications were made to the engine proper. It is still a stock engine. The gearbox was straight forward. I just let Ross Aero handle the gearbox.

The engine location relative to the Dragonfly firewall is critical. My CG calculations indicated that if the engine was set in the same place as the much lighter VW then I would need about 20 lbs of lead in the tail.

MOTOR MOUNT

The motor mount was a fun project. I had never built a motor mount. Lou Ross showed me how to get started. The motor mount was built on a horizontal plate the exact dimensions of the fire wall. The plate was laid on a work bench. The firewall bolts were put through the plate at the proper points. The standoffs were bolted to the plate. The engine was positioned vertically on the crankshaft pulley at the distance I wanted the engine away from the fire wall, in my case 1 inch. I determined which tapped holes in the engine case to use for the new motor mounts. I fabricated the pads that attached to the engine at four (4) points, two on top and two on the bottom. Then I started cutting the 3/4 inch X .035 wall 4130 tubes and tacking them together for final expert welding. The mount took about two days to fabricate.

COMPUTER COMPLEXITY

Due to the complexity of the computerized engine control system (fuel injection, engine timing, knock sensing, etc.) I felt it might be above my talents to make everything work properly. A friend of mine who is into computers and control systems said, "We can make it work." It was, as the FAA says, quite a learning experience. One of the key things I learned is that shop manuals are indispensable in a conversion, especially in dealing with modern electronic systems. The Subaru #2 electronics and #6 engine shop manuals are mandatory in a conversion of this type because they show what the various electronic modules do and define wire colors for proper connection. The Subaru manuals are very well written.

A problem in getting the engine to run was encountered. I had originally left the air by-pass valve out because there was no room for it. I felt that the engine could be made to operate without it. I discovered the problem and cure studying the trusty manuals. Without the air by-pass and the computer to make it run, the engine was hard to start and was erratic in idle. I found that the computer required a signal from the air by-pass valve. The air by-pass is actually a computer controlled idle circuit. I fooled the computer by plugging the air by-pass operating solenoid into the computer. It was not connected to the engine but the computer apparently was happy. Now the engine starts easily and idles well.

HARDWARE CHANGES

The intake manifold is approximately the same size as the original unit. It is arranged so that it is lower on the engine. I plugged in the stock PCV valve into the intake manifold at approximately the same position as in the automobile. The crankcase vents are also plugged in ahead of the throttle plate, just like it is on the car. The engine is running just like it is in a car. The throttle plate housing is heated by engine coolant to keep ice from forming on the backside of the butterfly. This engine warms up faster than anything I've ever seen. Start it up and run it at 2500 rpm for two hundred yards and the temperature of the water is up to 150.

The design of the cooling system is influenced by the Dragonfly airframe. My airframe could not handle the radiator and coolant weight forward. I used an air conditioner evaporator core from a 1986 Buick Electra for a radiator. This unit is about 14 inches wide, 11 inches tall, and 3.5 inches thick. Of all aluminum construction, it looks like a large aircraft oil cooler. It was put aft of the seat, on the bottom of the aircraft, ala P-51. This arrangement avoided cutting into the fuselage structure.

When the radiator was located, I preliminarily weighed the airplane with all the parts on it, and determined that the battery was also going to have to go aft, not into the tail, but way back. To avoid major rework the remote mounting of the radiator required external plumbing, consisting of .035 wall 1.5 inch aluminum tube. These tubes go from the engine back to the radiator and from the radiator

Heliarced .062 plenum (6.5x4.0x2.25 high), 2.0 dia .035 angled runners and 45 degree hose elbows connect to stock mainfold stubs and individual port fuel injectors. Internal baffles smooth air flow in plenum.

Coolant manifold rotated 180 degrees. Filler sectioned and modified to accept coolant hose. "W" tube routed inside of exhaust headers for cowling streamlining. Other coolant line connected to stock pump.

forward to the water pump. The connections are sections of automobile radiator hose, single clamped. The tubes require beads on the ends to keep the rubber hoses from slipping off. I fabricated a scoop housing to enclose the radiator. The inlet is 2 X 10 inches wide; the outlet area is variable, from about 2.5 X 9 to 9 X 9 inches.

The Legacy engine has an external crossover manifold to collect the coolant from both heads. The crossover was rotated 180 degrees for use in my installation. A Subaru XT-6 thermostat housing and coolant cap were welded to the outlet of the crossover. The cap allows for the use of a recovery tank and is the high point in the system. The opposite end of the crossover has a small line that supplies the heater. Wow! Consistent hot water heat, no more exhaust muff cabin heat.

The fuel system has been modified. The purge canister is gone. I kept the stock fuel arrangement. The fuel system on the Legacy delivers fuel to one side, flows through or past two injectors, crosses over to the other side, passes two injectors, goes to a regulating valve that regulates the fuel pressure at 40 psi to the injectors. Anything over 40 psi is discharged back into the fuel tank, in my case, the header tank. The engine will not vapor lock like standard aircraft fuel injected engines. Cool fuel under pressure passes the injectors at all times. They just use what's required. Very straight forward, a high pressure, high volume pump does the job. The new after market inline fuel pump I use as my primary fits many automobiles. My standby fuel pump is a used Toyota OEM pump. Outputs are paralleled for redundancy. A toggle center off switch allows selection of either one.

The ignition system is stock. The computer tells the igniter module when to squirt the electricity and the computer tells the fuel injectors when to squirt fuel. Crank angle and cam angle sensors tell the computer where each cylinder is at any given time. The sensors are bolted on externally to the engine. They are very small. This engine is also equipped with a knock sensor. If the computer detects a knock it will retard the timing 5 degrees and preset the absolute manifold pressure. This will protect the engine from damage, and only allow 3500 rpm at full throttle.

The computer requires a lot of input signals to operate the engine. These come from the crank angle, cam angle, and knock sensor, throttle position sensor, mass air flow sensor, and O_2 sensor. The engine also needs to know the engine coolant temperature.

The exhaust system, like all aircraft conversions, is dependent on the airframe configuration. I used the standard size pipe that Subaru used coming off the heads. The O_2 sensor is mounted in the system at the junction of the left and right pipes. The diameters are 1. 5 inches to the junction then the single tail pipe is 1.75.

ENGINE TUNING
The engine was set up to the original specifications. In fact, the engine required no set up on my part. I plugged in all the sensors, plugged the computer in, supplied the system 12 volts and put fuel in and it ran. That's the neat thing about these new engines that have computer control. If you want to play with them, you can go to the after market dealers and buy the horsepower chips or the high altitude chips which are available in some cases. Other than that there is nothing to mess with. The computer will also detect the failure of any system component and note that in its memory. The memory can be tapped to determine what component failed. The computer will revert to a limp-home mode if needed.

The electrical system on the engine is essentially stock. I plugged everything in using the connector plugs that come with the engine wiring harness. The idiot light works and unit charges the battery. The electrical system now allows me to have a landing light, taxi light, LORAN, radio, strobes, map lights, instrument lights, and most every light that I want to put on it. I've had no battery problems. The lack of a proper charging system was a continuing problem with the Volkswagen.

The ignition system of the engine draws about twelve amps. This ignition system uses a dual coil. One coil runs two spark plugs. It's a wasted spark system, so the off cylinder is getting spark whether it needs it or not. One coil runs the rear cylinders, and one coil runs the front cylinders. When the number one cylinder fires, the number two is not ready to fire, but the coil fires both cylinders. This is the wasted spark. It takes a lot of current to operate a wasted spark system, that is one of the reasons that you should use the stock alternator. The wasted spark system is a way to get around using a distributor.

COSTS
The total cost of the operating engine is about $7000.00. This includes all the custom parts, intake/exhaust, gear box, fuel pumps, motor mount, alternator bracket, heater core, hoses, wiring, gages, radiator, piping, props, custom built cowl for the engine and the radiator. The conversion took 18 months. The sound of the engine at full power is like no other aircraft that you have heard, unless you've heard a Lycoming turning 4500 rpm!.

RECOMMENDATIONS
If you purchase this or any other high-tech engine from a junk yard, get a fairly low mileage unit even if you have to pay extra money. Then you won't have to open the engine. My engine had 2,800 miles on it. Make sure you get all the parts associated with the engine. I didn't. I assumed that the junk yard knew what they were taking off, because that was their business. Well it was a new engine on a new model year car and they didn't know. The computer that they gave me was the ABS computer, (anti-lock brake system). I didn't know any better, and they didn't either. By the time I found out the rest of the car had gone to the east coast. It cost me an extra $500.00 to

get the computer, wires and igniter module. Plan ahead, know what you need when you go out and plunk down a couple of thousand bucks. Peripheral items on modern engines are in strange places. For example, The mass air flow sensor on the Legacy is in the air cleaner. The igniter module is mounted on the fire wall. It is easily overlooked: it's a small part 2 X 2 X 1/4 inches. If you want the stock fuel pump it's in the gas tank. The O_2 sensor is in the exhaust system. That will cost an extra $113.00 to replace. They don't normally sell the exhaust system with the engine so you may have to dig it out.

Thus, study the engine, buy the manuals, and know what you need when you go to the junk yard. It will cost you big bucks for electronic parts if you have to buy them separately, or new from dealer stock.

My long term objective was to have an engine that I did not have to work on. I wanted an engine that was stock, that I could go down to the local dealer and buy parts for. That's exactly what I've got now.

The Subaru Legacy engine installation and gear reduction meets Justin's demanding standards. However, the performance of the Dragonfly with its built-in propeller ground clearance limitation is further challenged by Tucson's summer density altitude. He now plans to concentrate future experimentation efforts in the areas of prop matching and cooling. The next issue of Contact! will report on the results of these tests which will establish additional auto conversion guidelines for other experimenters. Stay tuned-MCM.

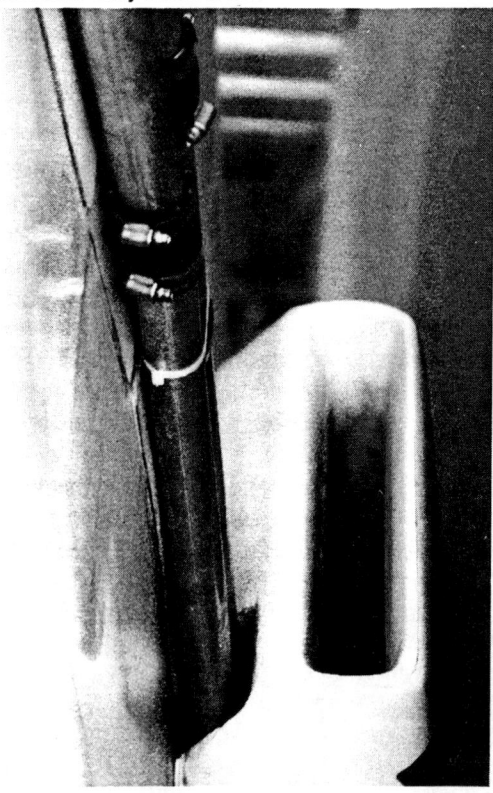

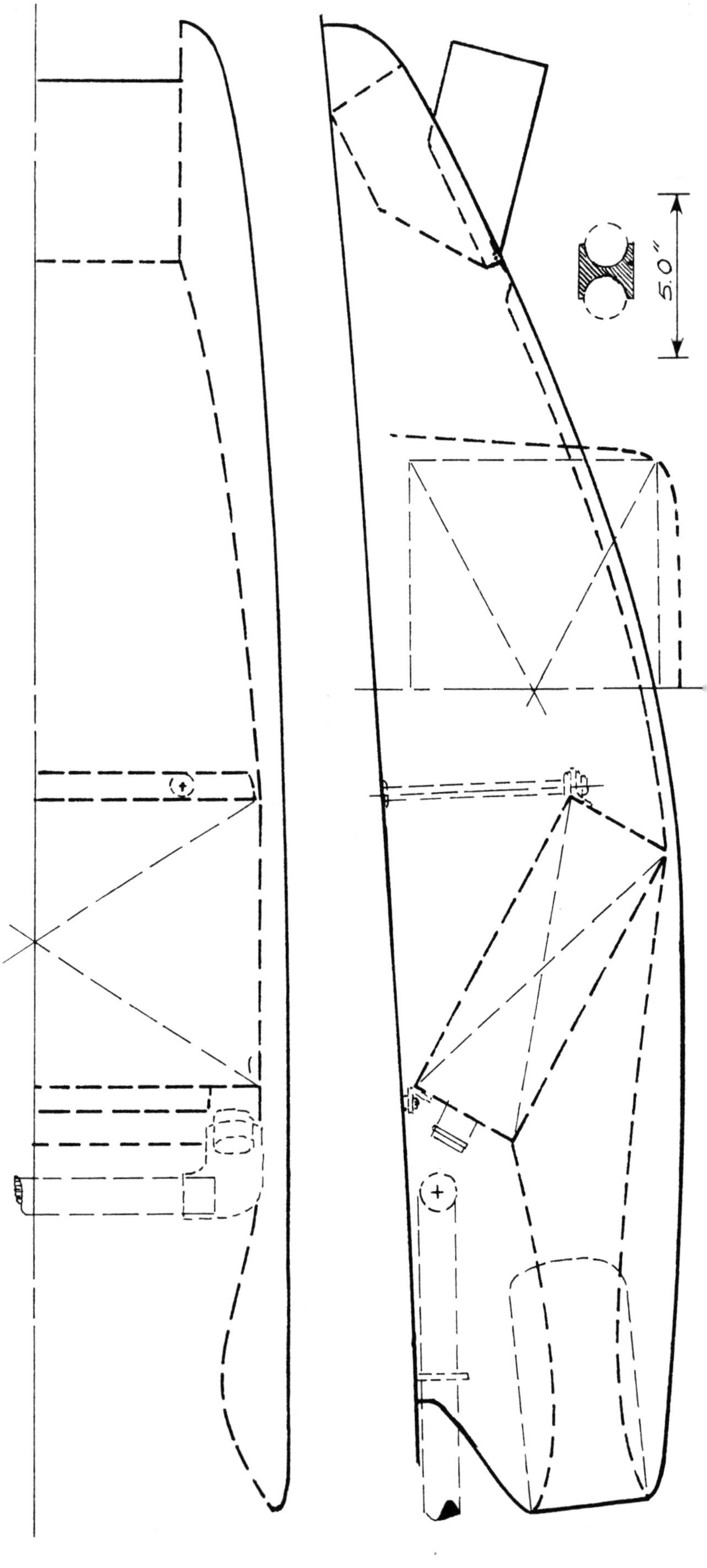

get the computer, wires and igniter module. Plan ahead, know what you need when you go out and plunk down a couple of thousand bucks. Peripheral items on modern engines are in strange places. For example, The mass air flow sensor on the Legacy is in the air cleaner. The igniter module is mounted on the fire wall. It is easily overlooked: it's a small part 2 X 2 X 1/4 inches. If you want the stock fuel pump it's in the gas tank. The O_2 sensor is in the exhaust system. That will cost an extra $113.00 to replace. They don't normally sell the exhaust system with the engine so you may have to dig it out.

Thus, study the engine, buy the manuals, and know what you need when you go to the junk yard. It will cost you big bucks for electronic parts if you have to buy them separately, or new from dealer stock.

My long term objective was to have an engine that I did not have to work on. I wanted an engine that was stock, that I could go down to the local dealer and buy parts for. That's exactly what I've got now.

The Subaru Legacy engine installation and gear reduction meets Justin's demanding standards. However, the performance of the Dragonfly with its built-in propeller ground clearance limitation is further challenged by Tucson's summer density altitude. He now plans to concentrate future experimentation efforts in the areas of prop matching and cooling. The next issue of Contact! will report on the results of these tests which will establish additional auto conversion guidelines for other experimenters. Stay tuned-MCM.

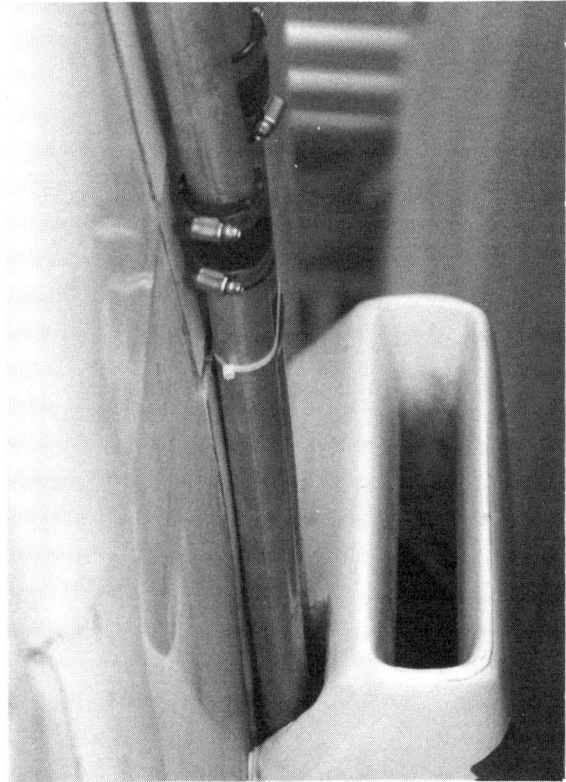

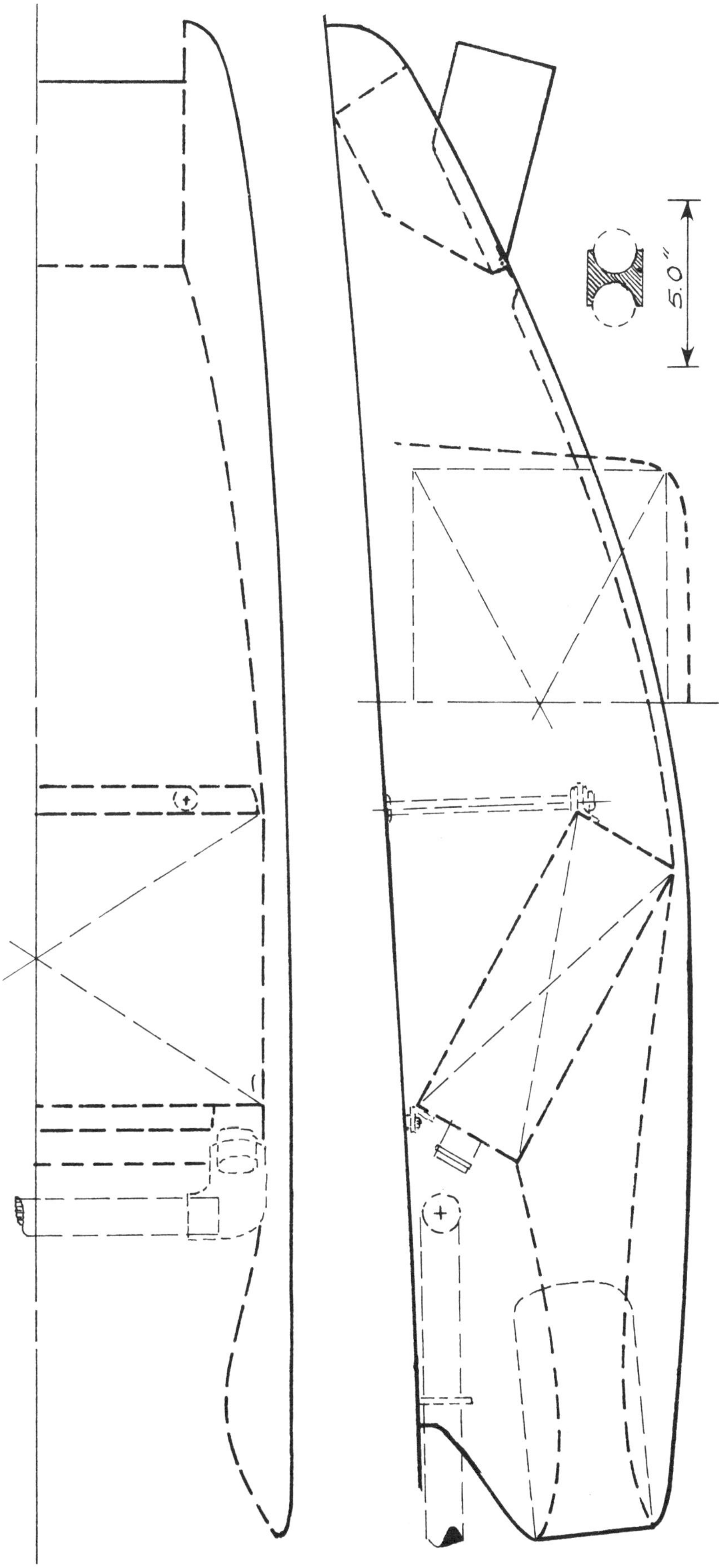

cooled. In small general aviation aircraft proper engine speed for substantial power output was ignored to accommodate the .8 Mach maximum propeller tip speed. This kept the rpm slowed down, to get by without the use of expensive and weight increasing reduction gearing. Looking at the engine comparisons table, the result of the design direction was a much larger engine with high octane requirement. Basically this octane was required - a worst condition basis - because of marginal air cooling and the large piston diameter. For example, the Lycoming 150 and 160 hp engines have 5 1/8 inch diameter pistons. The efficient car engines - the last four in the table - have water cooling and pistons less than 3 1/2 inches in diameter.

ENGINE REQUIREMENTS

ENGINE	HP	RPM	MON	CR	HP/IN^3
Lyc O-360	180	2750	91	8.5:1	.50
Lyc O-320	160	2750	91	8.5:1	.50
Lyc O-320	150	2750	80	7.0:1	.468
VW Quantum inline 4 110 in^3	88	5500	83	9.0:1	.80
Nissan Maxima inline 6 180 in^3	120	5200	83	8.9:1	.822
Nissan V6 180 in^3	152	5200	83	8.9:1	.844
Buick V6 225 in^3	160	4400	85	8.5:1	.71

One other factor working against performance is the magneto. The certified magneto ignition system causes a higher specified octane requirement. A system employing a knock sensor would give a far more economical solution.

The use of a more sophisticated and up to date ignition system together with lower octane number than the current ultra conservative one that you now see on the data plate would achieve a real reduction in fuel cost and overall operating expense.

There is no reason why super unleaded car fuel should not fully satisfy the current Lycoming 160 and 180 hp engines.

It would seem that design progress was made only when EAA lit a fire under the two aircraft engine manufacturers. Continental Teledyne brought out a water cooled version of the old O-200 and O-300 engines. It likely would never have happened without Dave Blanton's early experimentation program. His V6 Ford powered C-175 flies on 6.8 gallons per hour at cruise on super unleaded car gas! This V6 has a simple belt reduction propeller drive that slows the prop down and lets the engine work. The cost of this and other auto conversions make them very attractive.

CONCLUSIONS

A. Regular auto gas blended 66 percent with 34 percent 100LL will perfectly satisfy the current existing Lycoming 160 and 180 hp engine versions. This ratio also cuts the lead concentration to the optimum value, about .65 cc/gallon, thus beneficial valve lubrication is maintained with reduced lead fouling problems.

B. Auto gas alone will work beautifully in any 7.00:1 compression ratio aircraft engine. These are the most numerous in the general aviation fleet.

C. A change to electronic ignition is legal for experimental aircraft and will reduce the engine octane requirement enough to permit auto gas in most any experimental airplane.

Ross Aero engine mount fabrication method: 1) firewall attach points are defined on bottom plate 2) engine pulley/centerline is placed on located wood plug and steadied by hoist at prop flange 3) plumb measurements are taken to define thrust line offsets and 4) engine mount is fabricated. Yeakey's T18 Subaru XT6 mount is shown here.

Subaru Powered Dragonfly

160 Flight Hours On This 2.2 Liter Legacy Installation

Justin Mace
EAA 225212
7541 Shirley Lane
Tucson Arizona 85741
(602) 744 3532

The verdict is in! The Subaru Legacy engine is capable of powering an aircraft. I say that after accumulating over 160 flight hours, at least six of them at an altitude above 10,000 feet. The engine operates the same at 11,500 feet as it does at 500 feet, thanks to automatic altitude compensation (leaning) provided by the engine's stock electronic fuel control. The only difference is the reduction in the amount of power output at altitude which every aircraft experiences with normally aspirated engines.

The engine is equipped with the Ross Aero planetary redrive based on heavy duty Ford truck planetary gears, an integral vorsional damper and a 256 heat treated aluminum case and engine adapter housing. The unit has been opened up for inspection every 40 hours. No indication of wear or any potential problem was found. Short of any unforeseen problem the redrive will be run without any other inspections. I am convinced that the Ross unit is a non-issue and will be as trouble free as the typical automobile transmission.

The engine is essentially stock with the exception of custom intake and exhaust manifolds, necessary to cowl the installation efficiently. A description of the installation was published in issue #6 of Contact! published January of 1992. Shortly after that article was written I sensed a slight vibration while flying (my passenger didn't). On the ground a diagnostic check of the computer electronics showed that the O2 sensor had been activated. One plug was coated with carbon; the other plugs were clean and had the typical coloring of clean firing. Plugs, ignition wires, fuel rails and injectors were swapped with no effect.

It took some time to trace the problem to the intake manifold and the rubber hose elbows. Apparently, the hose elbow feeding the rich running cylinder would partially collapse at certain RPMs slightly changing the amount of air entering the cylinder. The engine, not knowing that the air supply to that single cylinder was reduced, continued to call for fuel based on the demands of the other three cylinders causing the rich cylinder condition. The problem was easily cured with light gage steel inserts in the rubber elbows.

My custom alternator bracket (also needed for a clean cowling) required two subsequent modifications to cure a fatigue cracking problem. If you read Contact! issue #9 dealing with vibration you will appreciate the fact that any change to a stock engine installation will require a close watch on custom parts. Vibration is an inherent characteristic of all engines and all manufacturers spend vast sums to design, fabricate and prove out the durability of accessory support brackets.

I share my experiences so that other builders of auto conversions consider all possible effects impacting specific changes and monitor closely any custom parts.

PROPELLER MATCHING

The engine operating range typically has been at 3600 RPM at economy cruise to 5600 RPM at takeoff (1660/2580 RPM at the prop). I am now flying a five (5) bladed propeller; yes, the number of blades is not a typo. The installation of a powerful engine in this airframe with a 2.17 redrive introduces the problem of maximum torque usage. The Dragonfly, due to to its short legs limits the length of the propeller to 54 inches. This not enough diameter to allow maximum propeller efficiency and to absorb the almost 300 foot pounds of torque at 2,000 prop RPM.

I had operated the engine at above 5000 rpm for about 50 hours using a 3 bladed wooden propeller. I was not happy with the high engine RPM and set about to lower it.

I feel engine longevity will increase by operating it at its peak torque range rather than its peak HP range. Maximum HP is developed at 5600 RPM; the peak torque is developed at about 4500 RPM. I am now cruising the airplane at 4500 RPM at 160 MPH ground speed using the five blade propeller.

After trying out two designs of three blade wooden propellers the performance improvement with the Warp Drive five blade setup has been convincing. The blades are solid carbon fibers and are ground adjustable. It is the smoothest of the three I have tried. I believe my Dragonfly and specific engine modification is at the outer limits of propeller design theory. I would recommend the use of Warp Drive propellers for any original aircraft design which is a departure from known aircraft configurations (speed, power, propeller clearance).

COOLING CHANGES

The engine is being cooled by a 50/50 mix of distilled water and automotive antifreeze. The cooling system now holds eight U.S. quarts. The first radiator was actually an aluminum air conditioner evaporator core out of a large Buick vehicle. This unit worked well and would have sufficied for temperatures in the Northern tier of States. It appeared to very efficient in the original P51 style belly scoop. I measured the water inlet temperature to be 193 degrees F. The inlet air was 70 degrees, the outlet air was 173 degrees and the coolant return was measured at 118 degrees. Measurements were taken at 140 MPH indi-

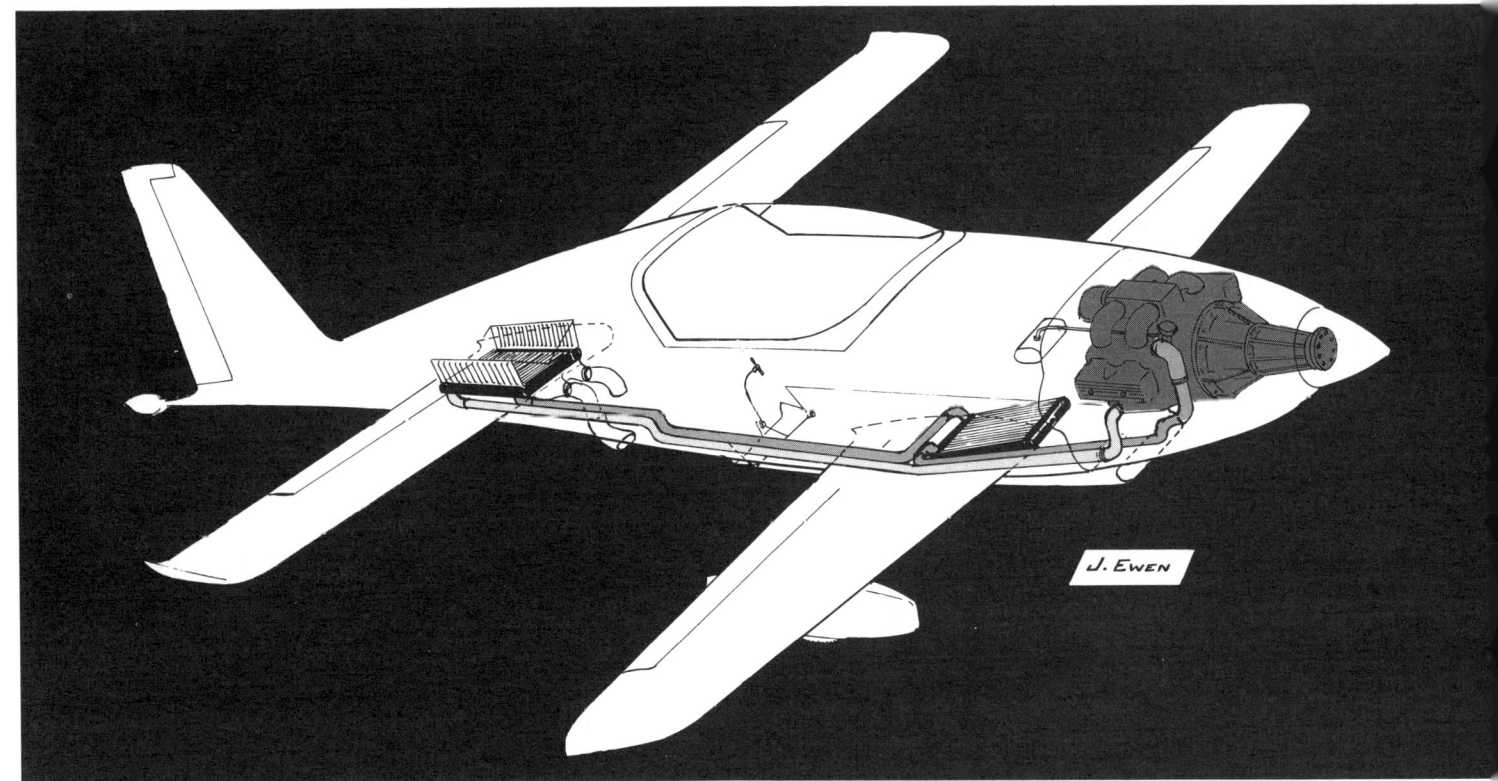

Dragonfly design was originally powered by Volkswagen power of 45-80 HP. The Subaru in stock form produces 130 HP and is substantially heavier. The C.G. was managed by locating the engine next to the firewall and the use of two VW Rabbit aluminum radiators (5 lb each). Cooling is more than adequate for hot Arizona summer conditions.

cated. This system was not quite up to the task of dealing with hot Arizona summers.

I removed the evaporator core from the belly and installed a VW Rabbit radiator inside the fuselage with air inlets under the wing roots. I noted "no" increase in speed with the removal of the original belly scoop which was somewhat surprizing since the frontal area presented by the scoop was approximately 130 in^2. However, the Rabbit radiator was designed for the VW1.8 liter engine and was not up to cooling the 2.2 liter Subaru at full power.

I am now using two Rabbit radiators. This radiator uses an aluminum tube, two pass core with plastic header tanks. The second radiator is mounted under the fuselage in a new belly pod. The radiators are connected in series; that is, the coolant in the belly unit is cooled first and then flows to the rear radiator for additional cooling. Each radiator has its own air supply. This arrangement works satisfactorily. The coolant temperature has never gone over 185 degrees, even during a full power climb out on a 105 degree day. The stock engine thermostat was retained and is calibrated to be wide open at 193 degrees. Per automotive practice a coolant overflow tank is installed inside the cockpit. Needless to say, my cooling problems are history.

OBSERVATIONS

A recurring question when talking to many people about auto conversions in general is "what about dual ignition?".

The best answer I can give regarding using a "stock" auto engine is that the manufacturer did not consider it necessary (except in the case of the Mazda RX-7 rotary engine which has a long flame front). Thus, dual plugs are missing from most auto engines. Plug durability is established; methods for providing ignition redundancy are known. The logic of implanting another plug in a thoroughly tested cylinder head and disturbing coolant flow is fuzzy.

All new technology engines are computer controlled to meet increasing stringent fuel economy and and exhaust emissions standards. There are several schools of thought on converting these engines. One is to install one or two of the new solid state ignition systems and a carburetor. Another is to redesign existing computer systems. Yet another is to leave the original systems alone and allow the computer to control the engine.

My opinion on this is shared by a growing number of experimenters. In my view, the original designers of the specific engine spent countless hours and many dollars (yen, deutsch marks, etc.) to develop these computer controllers. To toss out that technology and revert back to 50 year old (aircraft) means or to design replacement computer systems seems illogical.

As mentioned earlier, my stock engine is altitude compensated. I can only assume that the stock Subaru vehicle can make it to the top of Pikes Peak (14,100 feet) without quitting. In addition, it does not require power robbing carburetor heat. To alter the system, to add mixture control and carb heat, seems expensive and time consuming. The homebuilt movement has and should continue to advance the state of art, which means engines as well as airframes.

One of the neat things about going flying with the stock auto engine is the run up, or I should say the lack of it. If the engine can make it out to the active runway there is nothing to check except those systems my CFI called "killer items", such as fuel on, controls free and correct and canopy down and locked.

The only drawback with using the "stock" auto engine is that it requires unleaded fuel which may not be available at your next stop. However, you can remove the O_2 sensor, replace it with a plug or bad unit, and fly on with your engine on 'rich". As an alternative it is possible some experimenter will come up with a solution for using 100LL by bypassing the O_2 sensor and adding a separate mixture control.

Last September I flew over to Olathe, Kansas, to attend the equal span canard get together, an annual event organized by fellow Dragonfly builder, "Spud" Spornitz. Total distance covered was in the neighborhood of 2000 miles. The fuel burn was right at 5.3 gallons per hour. Most of the flight hours were flown above 8500 feet. As noted earlier the engine did not give any indication that it cared what altitude it was at. The computer made all the fuel adjustments. It sure was nice to fly the plane and navigate, not to have concerns about leaning or being careful about pulling power too fast during descents. Flying this trip made it pleasurable knowing that the air inlet butterfly had a water heated jacket at the bottom side to preclude any ice build up in the induction system. Very comforting to know that ice won't be building up when you pull the throttle in a high humidity environment. Some of the trip was in rain at 50 degrees F., I experienced no hint of an engine stumble due to ice.

The engine and redrive is performing well. I use Mobil1 15/50 automotive oil

EFI ensures perfect fuel/air mixture to each cylinder. Carbureting would have required considerable experimentation with the intake plenum to obtain balanced fuel/air distribution. Aluminum box, tubes and hoses connect to stock EFI ports.

and change it every fifty hours. The redrive is lubricated by engine oil under pressure. A #53 drill inlet orfice limits the amount of oil entering the gear box. A 1/4 inch line to the engine sump provides adequate drainage.

Oil consumption is minimal: I have used about a 1/2 quart in the first 100 hours of flying.

Needless to say, I am pleased with the performance of the Subaru Legacy engine. It should give me many years of worry-free service and equal the results of the 1989 Subaru conducted WOT 17 day endurance tests. **JM**

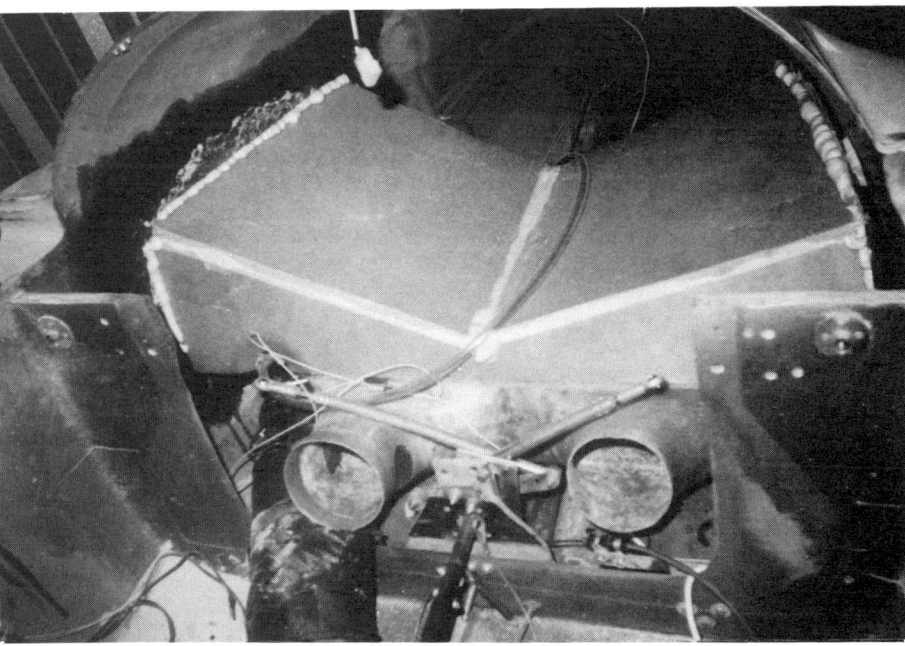

Rear radiator (not visible) is completely shrouded by a sandwich exhaust plenumbox and glass air intake openings. Tests showed need for only one cooling air inlet scoop which is located .

Separating the BS from BHP Using BMEP

Vance W. Jaqua
7046 Quito Court
Camarillo California 93012
(805) 484 9244

A graduate engineer with about 40 years of experience in gas turbine and rocket propulsion the author holds several international patents in aerospace propulsion and related fields. He was honored as Rockwell's "Engineer of the Year" in 1980. Vance is an avid participant in experimental aircraft activities, heading up the LA area "Design Group" for many years and as member of both EAA Chapter 40 and 723. He claims he is retired but is fully involved in the engineering support for the KIS programs. Contact! appreciates his timely article concerning auto engine conversions.   MCM

Probably some of the most controversial claims in the homebuilt aircraft market are the horsepower ratings of the various engine conversions being offered. I personally take a very jaded view of conversion salesmen that claim more delivered horsepower from their product than was ever claimed by the auto maker's advertising department. Automotive advertising departments are not particularly noted for conservative claims concerning the power output of their engines. Virtually all of us grew up during the classic Hot Rodding age, and I do not dispute the fact that one can modify an existing engine to provide more horsepower output. However, this is almost always accomplished by compromising reliability at higher RPM values, and higher compression ratios, not particularly well suited to aircraft use.

BHP

BHP is the shortened expression for "Brake HorsePower", and the number quoted should be based on actual output power of the engine. Power is the rate of doing work, and making power is what you brought that noisy, smoking thing along for. Do not be misdirected by those that claim that torque or static thrust is the real measure of an engines output because they are about to try to sell you a "bill of goods". Good old brother Watt wanted a uniform measure of power to rate those newfangled machines that were coming out. So he watched some underfed horses pumping out some mine water (which was also the job these new steam engines were designed to do), and decided 550 foot pounds per second (or 33,000 foot pounds per minute) would be called one horsepower. This means that if you raised 550 pounds up one foot in one second, or if you raised 110 pounds 5 feet in one second, you would be working at a rate of one horsepower during that one second. It is very possible that you can. Now most self respecting horses can work lots harder than that - but those are the numbers we use (our metric friends use Kilowatts, each one of which holds a bit more than a horsepower).

Brake Horsepower is the common term, because a common way to measure it for the old slow moving steam engines was to use a device called a Prony Brake. This was simply a friction brake on the flywheel that was connected to an arm resting on a scale to measure the torque in foot pounds (the force on the scale times the lever arm length in feet). Now one foot pound of torque means that if you would have a windlass drum of one foot radius (2 feet diameter) a one pound weight would be raised roughly 6.28 (2 times Pi) feet per each revolution of the shaft. Therefore, to compute horsepower using measured torque you simply multiply the torque times 6.28 times the revolutions per second and divide by 550 (or use RPM and divide by 33,000). Gearing an engine to make more output torque does not increase power since the RPM rate of the output goes down in the same ratio as the torque is increased, and the properly computed power stays the same (except for the added friction loses in the gearing). People will often use the term SAE horsepower to impress the novice but this simply means that they have taken advantage of correction factors such that the number that they are quoting may be significantly

Vehicle	disp cu in	BHP	HP cu in	RPM	BMEP (psi)	torque foot-lbs	RPM	BMEP (psi)
Ford Contour SE	155	170	1.10	6250	139	165	4250	160
Honda Accord EX	134	145	1.08	5500	156	147	4500	165
Nissan Altima GXE	146	150	1.02	5600	145	154	4400	159
Toyota Camry LE	134	135	1.01	5400	148	145	4400	163
Acura Legend LS	195	230	1.18	6200	151	206	5000	159
Lincoln Mk VIII	281	280	1.00	5500	144	285	4500	153
Mercedes E320	195	217	1.11	5500	160	229	3750	177
BMW 325I	152	189	1.24	5900	167	181	4200	180
AUDI Cabrolet	169	172	1.02	5500	147	184	3000	164
Olds Aurora	244	250	1.02	5600	145	260	4400	161
BMW 540I	244	282	1.16	5800	158	295	4500	182
Porsche PFM3200	193	212	1.10	5300	164	n/a	n/a	n/a
BMW M3	182	240	1.32	6000	174	225	4200	186
Lamborghini Diablo	348	492	1.41	7000	160	428	5200	185
Ferrari 355	213	375	1.76	8250	169	260	6000	184
Chevrolet 350	350	285	0.81	5200	124	337	4200	145
Buick 215 (mod)	215	189	0.88	5000	139	231	4000	162
Buick 215 (hi-mod)	215	230	1.07	6000	141	n/a	n/a	n/a
VW Jetta III	170	172	1.01	5800	138	177	4200	157
Continental O-200	200	100	0.50	2700	147	n/a	n/a	n/a
CAM 100	92	100	1.09	6000	144	n/a	n/a	n/a
Limbach 2000	122	80	0.66	3400	153	n/a	n/a	n/a
ROTAX 912	74	80	1.08	5500	156	75	4800	153
Vendor Claim	**146**	**213**	**1.45**	**5600**	**206**	**n/a**	**n/a**	**n/a**

Maximum HP and maximum torque data acquired from published manufacturer and vendor information.

higher than the actual measured value. The SAE (Society of Automotive Engineers) define the standards for engine equipment (SAE 1349-ed.), and give you factors to correct your measured value to a possibly higher value which you would have measured if it had been a standard 65 degree day at standard humidity and barometric pressure. This can be viewed as somewhat like correcting to true air speed.

BMEP

BMEP, which stands for Brake Mean Effective Pressure, is

a great tool for reviewing published engine performance and can be used somewhat as a de-liar on horsepower claims. For a normally aspirated engine (one which has no super charging) there is a very real practical limit or the amount of air being packed into the chamber at the end of the intake stroke. This filling of the combustion chamber before compression is defined by the term volumetric efficiency. At low speeds the charging efficiency (Vol. Eff.) is impacted by valve timing, backflow, and leakages. As RPM is increased, the flow resistance through the intake system reduces this volumetric efficiency and the resultant BMEP until finally a "breathing" limit is reached at maximum horsepower. Maximum volumetric efficiency and maximum BMEP is reached where the engine delivers the maximum torque (significantly below the maximum BHP RPM). For well designed engines, this value of maximum BMEP stays within a relatively narrow band. More highly developed engines will generally increase the RPM where this maximum value can be obtained, and also raise the breathing limited RPM resulting in higher BHP per cubic inch.

BMEP is a representation of the average pressure in the cylinder during the expansion of the power stroke, as derived from the brake horsepower measurement. This value can be computed from power ratings by using the formula below. The (12) changes foot pounds to inch pounds of work, and the (2) in this expression allows for the fact that there is only one power stroke per cylinder in two revolutions of a 4 cycle engine.

$$BMEP = \frac{BHP \times 33000 \times (12) \times (2)}{RPM \times Displacement(CU\ IN)}$$

As an interesting historical aside, there is also a value known as IMEP, or Indicated Mean Effective Pressure. Many earlier steam engines had a direct pressure measurement into the cylinder, which would trace the pressure vs. stroke curve directly on a graph called the indicator card. This would give a real time indication of how hard the engine was working. The averaged value of this pressure is called IMEP. With both measurements, the difference between IMEP and BMEP is a measure of engine internal friction losses. IMEP is very difficult to measure in a modern, high speed internal combustion engine, so it is rarely used.

The chart and plot show the BMEP values plotted against RPM for both the maximum torque case (where data is available) and for the maximum horsepower point for several modern engines. A very suspect data point is shown for a horsepower claim for the premium engine model of a well known vendor of auto conversions. The BMEP value indicated for this engine is grossly above the "state of the art" for non-supercharged engines on standard fuels. This point is well above the curve for premium 4 valve per cylinder sports car engines It is even about 10 percent above the 5 valve Ferrari 355, which is considered to be the highest specific output normally aspirated piston engine on the market. Plotting the maximum power per cubic inch versus RPM data shows the same level of disparity with the vendor claims.

There is no way a customer can realize the performance inferred by this rating when he purchases this engine. Many of the engines used in compiling this chart are among the auto industry performance leaders, with high tech injection and ignition systems on engines with double overhead cams and four valve heads. For this reason, one would not expect to see much improvement over these values with the usual cam, porting, or induction modifications. Make your own calculations based on the vendor claims, put the point on the chart, and decide if you can accept his stories.

SUPERCHARGING

Under conditions of supercharging all bets are off for BHP limits. The upper power limits are set by engine durability. You can cheerfully increase the power to your heart's content, to the point where your engine lies in smoking ruin. Word nit pickers are trying to separate the terms supercharging, and turbocharging but the truth is that "super" and "charging" are the operative terms here. They refer to any form of pumping inlet air such that the inlet manifold pressure is above atmospheric. Turbocharging is just a type of supercharger which is driven by a turbine harnessing expanding exhaust gas products. As a result of this higher manifold pressure, you can "charge" the cylinder with more air, so you can burn more fuel, and make more power. Supercharging equipment can be engine driven with belts, chain or gears, or it can be driven with an exhaust turbine, the result is pretty much the same. The amount of power that you can derive from the power stroke in your cylinder is a direct function of the weight and temperature of the combustion gases at top dead center, and the expansion ratio of the power stroke (as modified somewhat by the thermodynamic properties associated with the chemical composition of those gases) . Some small amount of supercharging can actually be accomplished by tuned, resonate intake passages. Exhaust tuning is much less effective with a classic four stroke (four cycle) engine than it is for high performance two stroke engines.

Energy releasing fuel additives such as the various "Nitro" compounds fall into somewhat the same area as supercharging, such that power output is more a function of courage and the availability of replacement engines, than any other factor. Power outputs of racing engines are incredibly high. Often, more than 50 percent of them finish the race without failure! If you are satisfied to finish just most of your 3 hour flights, go ahead and modify your airplane engine to this level - you are a braver man than I am-Gunga Din.

RECOMMENDATION

Unless your primary use is racing, pick a reputable supplier, and tell him you are more interested in reliable power than a flash in the pan (or a flash under the cowl) super powerplant. Work within the smooth and ample power provided at low cost by the well engineered auto conversions and happy flying days to you.   **VJ**

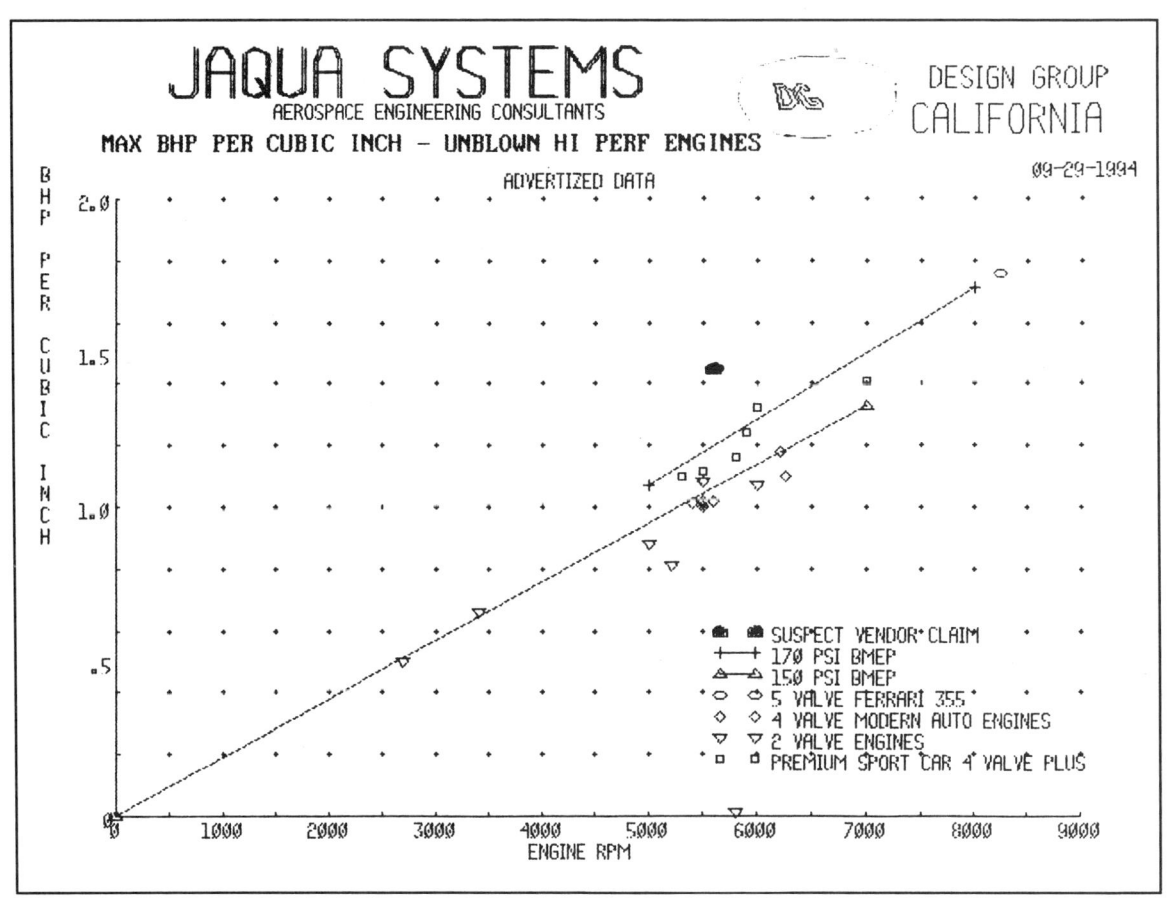
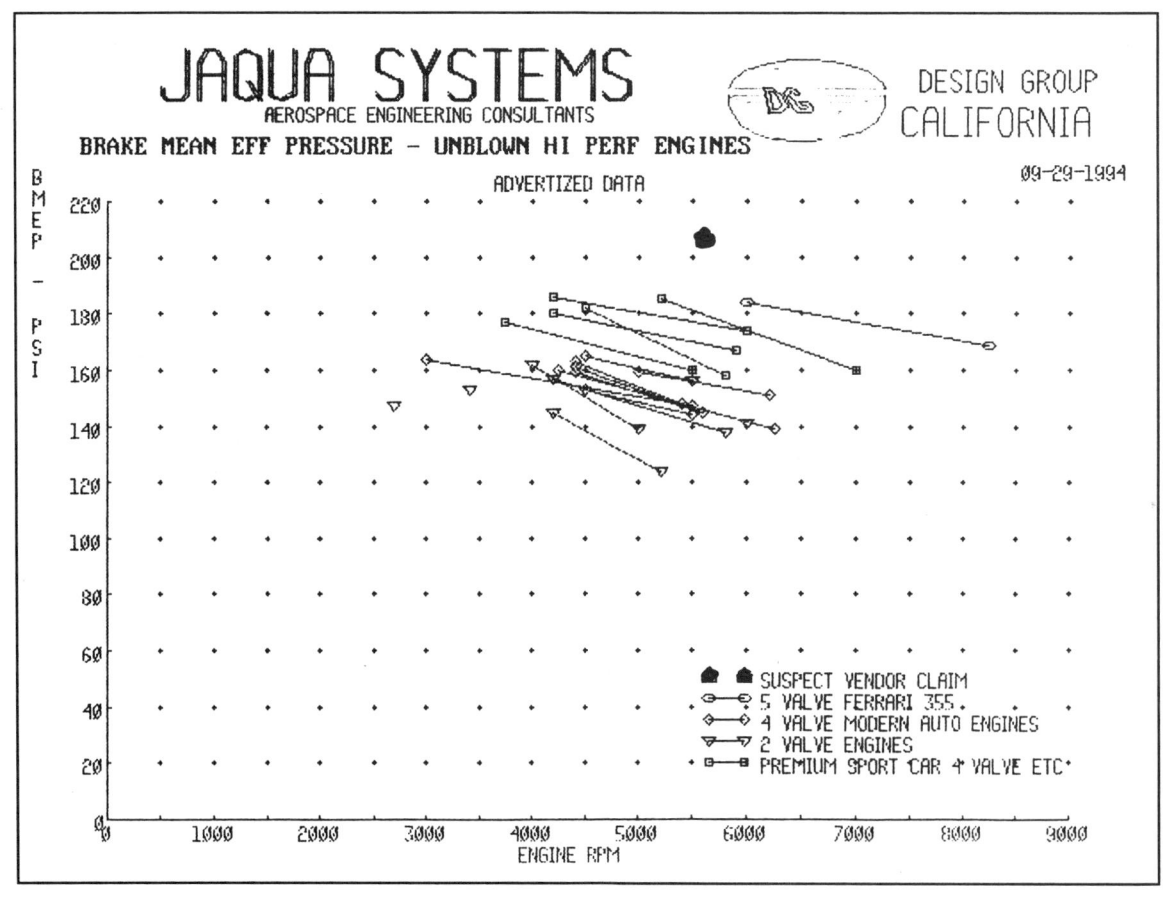

Mazda 13B Powerplant Installation in a Long EZ

Ron Gowan
316 Darrell Road
Roanoke Texas 76262
(817) 491 4646
Long EZ N86RG

I received my A&P in 1981 and have been working for Delta Air Lines since that time in flight line maintenance. In 1983, I made my first flight in a Continental C-85 powered Quickie Q2 I had built. Flown and repaired a few times due to a damaged canard and after a second broken canard, I decommissioned the plane and cut it up into a bunch of pieces. In 1985, I purchased plans for a Long EZ. Two years later I was flying. My Long EZ is built per plans and was originally powered with a Lycoming O-235 C2C.

The only problem in the entire project was related to the engine. I had purchased a used Lycoming O-235 with 430 hours logged since new. After I put some 300 hours on it in the Long it needed a top overhaul. Since I knew that the engine had sat around for a while the need for overhaul came as no big suprise. What I didn't expect was a $2,200 bill. Later, some 400 hours since that top overhaul, I was flying along fat, dumb and happy, minding my own business, and the engine began to run rough. Since it was February, and I was flying in some cold rain, I at first thought the carburetor had picked up some ice. Addition of carb heat did no good. I milked the plane home and found a dead cylinder. I yanked it off and found a hole between the intake and exhaust valves. That experience was enough to make a grown man cry.

The lesson to be learned from this experience is that used engines, aircraft or auto, can be bargains or can be expensive. Particularily, the aircraft kind. Engines that sit around likely are not pickled and can acquire premature old age. Spray can overhauls seem to attract the unwary buyer.

Before the Lycoming blew up I was working on another plane of my design, a composite canard configuration, a twin engined four place pusher (for project photo, see Contact issue #11-ed). I planned to install two Mazda rotary engines on it and had already purchased two for my "Mini Starship". When the Lycoming gave out I figured it would be best to install one on something I had already flown. Although the Mazda installation is flying in my Long EZ the principal objective still remains to refine this powerplant installation to suit the "mini starship."

I chose the best of the engine litter. I paid $1000 each for 1987 and 1989 vintage engines. The 1989 had only 13,000 miles on it so this was the one to push my airplane around. I purchased a Ross Aero redrive, adapter bell housing and one of their side saddle oil tanks to allow me to rotate the engine 90 degrees for better cowling clearances. In hindsight, the original engine orientation may well be used in the Mini Starship.

After removing the Lycoming and system hardware I removed the entire firewall from the Long EZ, and installed a new one. I then hung the rotary from the garage ceiling over a duplicate dummy firewall placed on my work table. I used 5/8 inch PVC pipe and a hot glue gun to then design the engine mount structure. When I was happy with the design I welded up a duplicate mount using 4130 steel tubing. Wall thickness varies following the stock Long EZ mount design.

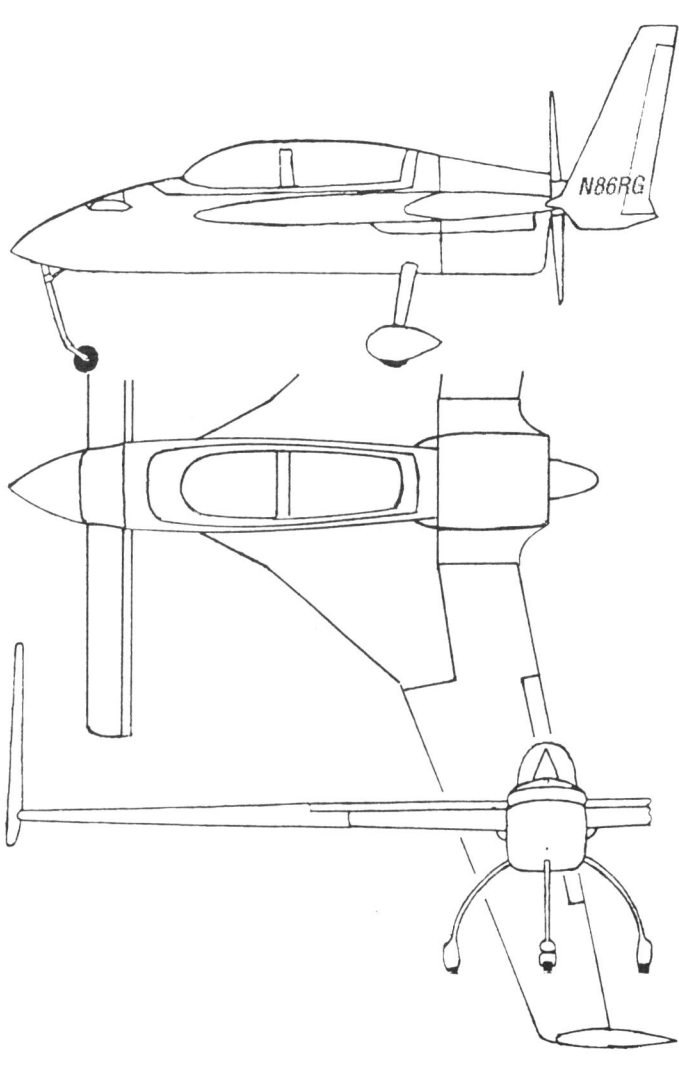

I chose the Marvel Schebler HA-6 aircraft carburetor for my installation. A side draft design, it is about as light as high CFM flow carburetors get. It feeds an aluminum intake plenum box 3 x 3 x 6 inches long. To get around expensive bending I used parts of six 1 1/2 inch steel sink drainage pipes held together with 1 1/2 inch ID radiator hose and hose clamps to make my intake manifolding. The length of the intake runners from the plenum to the bottom located intake ports is about 24 inches. The air filter is mounted in front of the carburetor and a ram air valve is on the firewall.

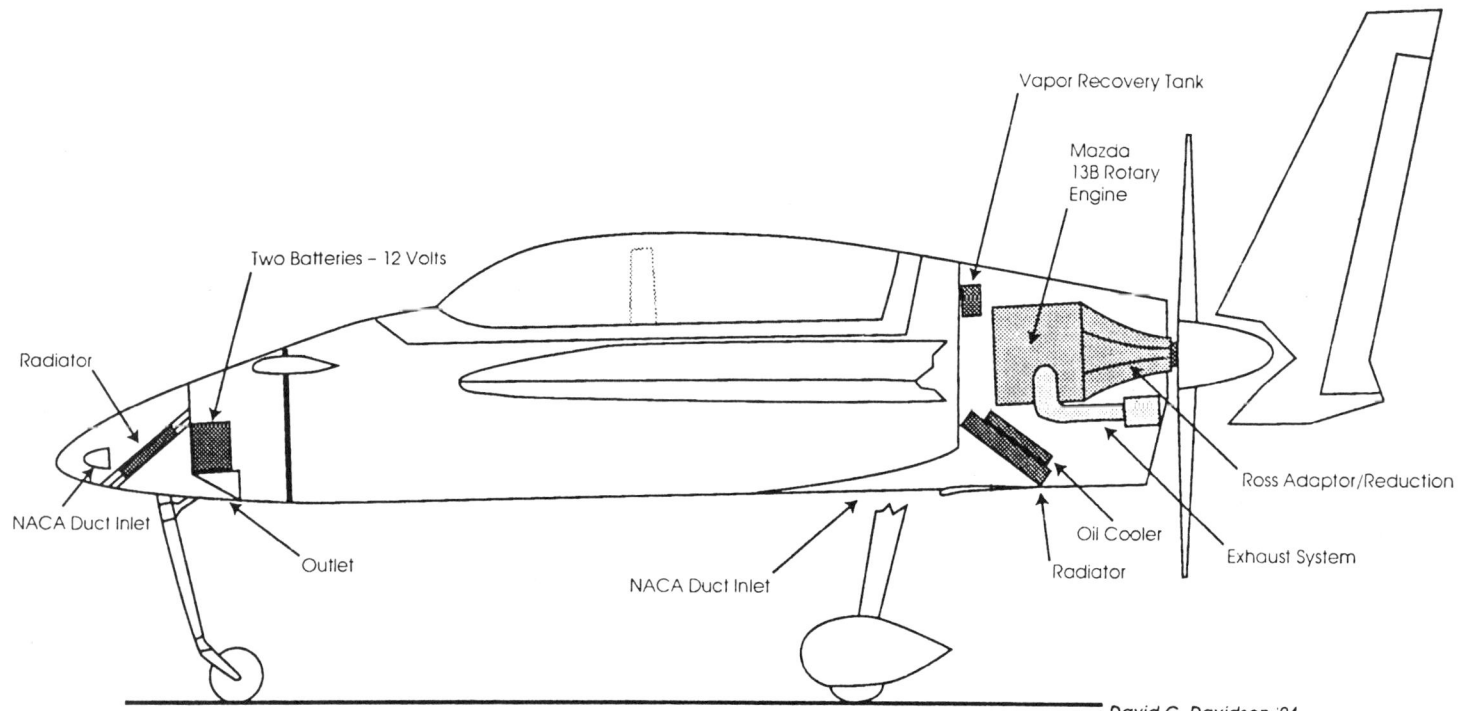

There isn't much distance from the exhaust ports to the pusher prop in the Long EZ so I had to come up with something short in the way of an exhaust system. My first design was simply two stainless steel open pipes. The noise even at idle was terrible so I needed some kind of muffler system. I welded up the ends of the two pipes, drilled a bunch of 1/2 inch holes near the ends of the pipes, and built a 4 inch long steel welded shroud over the holes, allowing about 1/2 inch clearance all round the two pipes. To minimize engine compartment heat the pipes were wrapped with tape from J.C. Whitney. My static RPM, believe it or not, increased from 5300 to 5400. The engine exhaust is much quieter and acceptable to most people.

The vacuum advance distributor with point ignition is a stock 1985 Mazda. Two Mazda ignition coils are mounted vertically on the firewall. The four plugs are stock Mazda items. They are expensive and have the look of aircraft plugs. I use a Honda Civic radiator. The oil cooler is from J.C. Whitney. Both are mounted and sealed in underneath the engine, just behind the NACA scoop, at about a 45 degree angle. There is also a small radiator in the nose, in front of the batteries, with 5/8 inch aluminum lines going back to the engine. I threw out the thermostat and control because thermostats have been known to fail in the closed position. There is a lot riding on a $5 thermostat. Engine temperatures are controlled manually with a moveable door on the NACA scoop. A plastic coolant overflow bottle is mounted on the firewall above the engine. Entire cooling system is filled with 5 quarts of standard 50/50 coolant mix. The engine coolant at cruise typically runs at 13 pounds of pressure. Coolant temperature varies with OAT. On a 100 degree day the cooling system can reach 200-210 degrees down low at full power. On a cold day I can fly at full power down low and barely reach 175 degrees. The NACA duct and radiator position (see sketch) form an inlet diffuser much like the P-51 setup.

ELECTRICAL SYSTEMS

Since this engine is different from a Lycoming or a Continental, several things needed to be changed, mostly so I could sleep better. The engine is "electrified" so 12 volts DC is very important to its reliability. For this reason, I have installed two small batteries in the nose. Each battery is independent and both are charged through an isolator circuit. I purchased a battey isolator from an RV shop. Motor campers that have more than one battery use this device. Two Facet electric fuel pumps, as recommended in the Rutan Long EZ plans, are installed since there is no engine driven pump. I use one as my backup.

As my main concern was to save weight I installed a GEO Metro alternator instead of the original Mazda unit and saved 3 pounds and a little space. This alternator fits the engine just like it was made for it.The stock engine will run for a while without its alternator belt but this belt also drives the water pump. To add some additional reliability I purchased a special pulley from Racing Beat in California for the crankshaft. This pulley drives two belts and is smaller than the original to slow down the water pump and alternator at high RPM. One belt loops from the alternator to the water

Top: Gowan's new cowling shapes are the only clue to the additional power of his Long EZ. Note 2 bladed propeller.

Middle: The original NACA scoop feeds the aft mounted radiator. Sufficient cooling is produced by this configuration except for ground taxi operations. Additional development is underway to solve the electric fan blocking problem.

Bottom: With upper and lower cowlings removed, the radiator is exposed to view. The center hose is connected to the engine water pump inlet. The small hose is routed to the forward radiator core. Inlet and exhaust pipes are also seen.

Top: 3/4 rear view of the Mazda installation. At the left is the Ross Aero 2.17:1 redrive and bell housing adapter. Left hand starter is mounted facing the custom flywheel. Overall induction system is pictured.

Middle: Kitchen sink tubes are light and eliminate runner fabrication! Aluminum plenum is prominent. The clutch plate bolt can be seen behind the adapter.

Bottom: Close up view of the well matched HA-6 carburetor, plenum, air cleaner, and fresh air supply. This set-up is working well; like most conversions cooling requires the most attention.

Top: Looking at the right side of the engine, a portion of the air cleaner, fuel line and carburetor can be seen. The oil filter is a aftermarket unit. Below it, the cable to the starter is bonded to the adapter.

Middle: Left 3/4 view of installation. The saddle type oil tank, dip stick, and redrive oil return are seen. Note the new propeller which has vastly improved the performance of the rotary Mazda.

Bottom: The unique exhaust system works well to reduce the bark of the engine. Note the brace between exhaust and the redrive.

Top: Ignition system is stock Mazda. Carb air is drawn from the cockpit; carburetor heat is not installed as front radiator feeding cockpit produces warm intake air. Ignition coils (2) are mounted on the firewall. Plastic coolant overflow bottle is also mounted to the firewall at the high point location.

Middle and Bottom: Overhead shots show off wiring and plumbing. Where possible, all parts, routings and connections are stock Mazda. Note cooling system pressure cap, four plug wires and top engine mounts. The oil tank is vented to the carburetor plenum to eliminate any oil system pressurization.

Mazda 13B
1/5 Scale

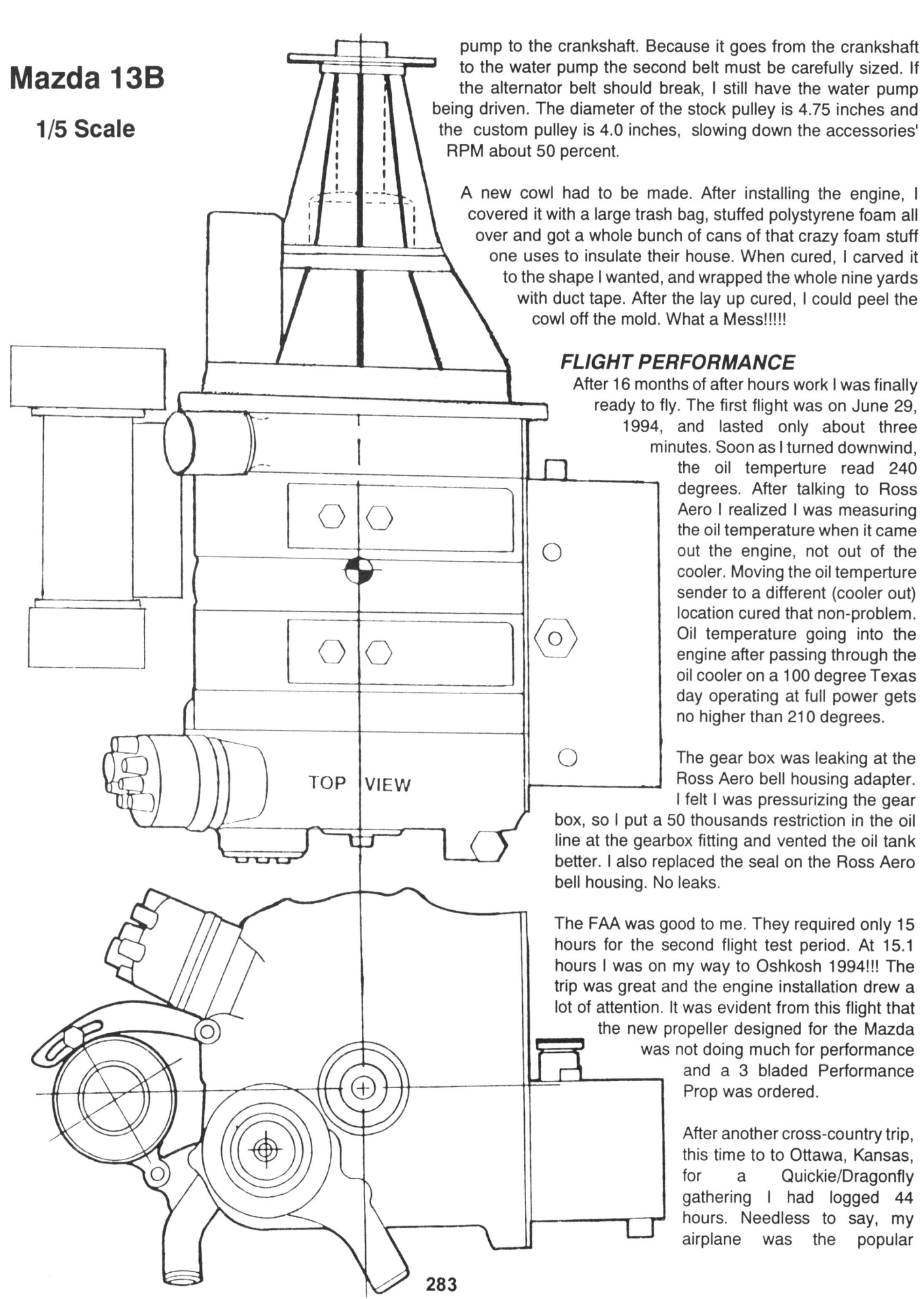

TOP VIEW

pump to the crankshaft. Because it goes from the crankshaft to the water pump the second belt must be carefully sized. If the alternator belt should break, I still have the water pump being driven. The diameter of the stock pulley is 4.75 inches and the custom pulley is 4.0 inches, slowing down the accessories' RPM about 50 percent.

A new cowl had to be made. After installing the engine, I covered it with a large trash bag, stuffed polystyrene foam all over and got a whole bunch of cans of that crazy foam stuff one uses to insulate their house. When cured, I carved it to the shape I wanted, and wrapped the whole nine yards with duct tape. After the lay up cured, I could peel the cowl off the mold. What a Mess!!!!!

FLIGHT PERFORMANCE

After 16 months of after hours work I was finally ready to fly. The first flight was on June 29, 1994, and lasted only about three minutes. Soon as I turned downwind, the oil temperture read 240 degrees. After talking to Ross Aero I realized I was measuring the oil temperature when it came out the engine, not out of the cooler. Moving the oil temperture sender to a different (cooler out) location cured that non-problem. Oil temperature going into the engine after passing through the oil cooler on a 100 degree Texas day operating at full power gets no higher than 210 degrees.

The gear box was leaking at the Ross Aero bell housing adapter. I felt I was pressurizing the gear box, so I put a 50 thousands restriction in the oil line at the gearbox fitting and vented the oil tank better. I also replaced the seal on the Ross Aero bell housing. No leaks.

The FAA was good to me. They required only 15 hours for the second flight test period. At 15.1 hours I was on my way to Oshkosh 1994!!! The trip was great and the engine installation drew a lot of attention. It was evident from this flight that the new propeller designed for the Mazda was not doing much for performance and a 3 bladed Performance Prop was ordered.

After another cross-country trip, this time to to Ottawa, Kansas, for a Quickie/Dragonfly gathering I had logged 44 hours. Needless to say, my airplane was the popular airplane on the field.

The Performance 3 bladed propeller with a 62 inch diameter x 72 inch pitch performs quite well! At 1500 feet above sea level, I am indicating 190 MPH at 5900 RPM, which is my max cruise setting. With the old propeller I was indicating 190 MPH at 6200 RPM. Everything they say about the Performance prop is true. Also, it is much quieter and smoother than the two bladed variety. Clark Lydick claims he can cut it down some and get some more speed with higher RPM. Some additional numbers; on the trip to Ottawa, I was at 12,500 feet indicating 160 MPH at 5500 RPM. Fuel burn at this setting is about 8.5-9 gallons per hour. Fuel burn is not that high compared to a Lycoming O-320 of 160 HP. According to Performance Propeller estimates I am getting about 160 HP out of the rotary engine. I still need to fly along with a 160HP Lycoming Long EZ to establish a comparison although at this point I feel performance should be about the same.

After the Ottawa KS trip, my auxiliary cooling fan quit. I guess it was windmilling too fast. I finally fixed my redrive leak. I replaced the seal for the fourth time, but this time I used a double edge seal instead of a single edge seal. I also attached the top oil tank vent to the intake manifold to create a slight suction so the oil from the gear box will flow back to the tank better. I believe this minor change to encourage return oil flow from the redrive is the solution to pressure buildup in the redrive. It has cured the problem.

The airplane powered by the O-235 Lycoming weighed 825 pounds at the time of its first flight. This was a basic, bare Long EZ with no starter or wheel pants, basic VFR instrument package and in paint primer. The airplane now weighs 975 pounds fully equipped (and with a second paint job). This weight is average for a Long EZ with a 160 HP Lycoming O-320. The CG is in the specified mid-range location, with the addition of a 5 pound ballast in the front seat. I believe the rotary is a viable substitute for the O-320 weight wise and offfers the homebuilder a simpler, cost effective powerplant alternative.

At this date (February 1995) I have over 76 hours on the Mazda installation. One problem needs more attention; ground cooling is pretty poor, especially after a flight when the engine is hot. However, I am quite happy with the results. I know I won't be blowing any expensive Lycoming cylinders which started me on this development.

The principal reason this engine installation is a success is because of people like Ross Aero and support from other homebuilders. Total cost of this installation is about 4500 dollars, or a little over $28 per HP.

Please look for my plane, N86RG, at Sun 'N Fun, Oshkosh, Copperstate and other events, weather permitting of course. I will be happy to answer any question not covered in this article. **RG**

More on Mazda Rotarys

Some other examples of Mazda Rotary engines using Ross Aero redrives are solid evidence that the engine deserved the support that it received when we originally combined the engine with a reduction drive back in 1978. Our original concept centered on the internally unmodified "box stock", or slightly modified automotive engine, in this case, the Mazda 13B Wankel Rotary.

Here are some others who are developing a rotary information base. Jim Mayfield is operating his aircraft type 2PL gyroplane with a 4 port 13B Mazda with a 2.85:1 Ross redrive engine. The engine is internally standard with no special porting work. As detailed in an earlier issue of CONTACT! magazine Jim is happy with the conversion. HP is approximately 160. Total time now is 680 hours. The engine just now beginning to use a wee bit of oil, which Jim says is comparable to typical aircraft engine consumption. Inspection and analysis including bringing the drive back to Ross for a check up is scheduled.

Others are using late model "6 Port" 86 through 92 non-turbo 13B engines obtained at automotive salvage yards, or are remanufactured. We received a nice phone call from Tracey Crook describing successful initial flights of his RV-4 with a 1988 engine with a 2.17:1 redrive unit. He has developed his own ignition system using some late model RX7 parts and his own controlling electronics. Duplicate ignition hardware will be tested by Ross Aero. Tracey is only just now expanding his flight test envelope. He reports some exciting performance with his engine at low power settings which seem to make good on the promises of the rotary engine. Here are some numbers-lift offs at less than full power, 3800 engine RPM, 1600 FPM climb at 4500 RPM, 95 MPH at 2800 RPM and 155 MPH at 4500 RPM with much throttle opening remaining! How much? We'll have to see when he makes his next report. (expect a write-up in CONTACT!).

Ted Ruffli in Alaska reports a total time of 12 hours in a Piper Super Cub with powered with a 1989 Mazda using a 2.85:1 Ross Aero redrive. His test pilot (who is a former USAF Thunderbird pilot) pronounces the performance to be equal to that of a 180 horsepower Super Cub and he ought to know. Some background, Ted blew up an engine on the ground due to overheating but stuck with the rotary concept. He obtained a remanufactured 1989 and got it together. He will enter a contest in Alaska where they see whose bush plane takes off in the shortest distance. With the thrust (780 lbs.) afforded him by the 2.85:1 gearing he has a good chance to do well.

Andrew Venable of Utah has a Christavia Mk4 powered by a 4 port 13B, 2.85:1 redrive ratio. He is in his early test stage and reports same excellent results. First flights at a somewhat high field elevation (4400 MSL) reported a surplus of power.

Surprisingly, all the above mentioned people feel maximum fuel consumption is 9 GPH, comparable to an aircraft engine. The rotary engine is liable to make a very strong showing for itself and may even become the preeminent alternative flying engine of the 90s and beyond. We are aware that many are planning installation of Mazda rotarys into an extremely wide variety of projects including Cozy Mk3s and 4s, RV-4 and -6 and others. Anyone wishing to discuss using a rotary engine in a project can call Chris Ross at Ross Aero on Saturdays (520) 747 7877 for further information. **CR**

Programmable EFI for Auto Aircraft Engine Conversions

Ross Farnham
SDS-Racetech Engineering
Bay G, 1007 55th Avenue N.E.
Calgary Alberta
Canada T2E 6W1
(403) 274 0154

Electronic fuel injection became available on automobiles over 25 years ago in the form of analog Bosch D Jetronic systems. These systems worked quite well and paved the way for the digital systems introduced in the eighties. Today, virtually every car built In the world today is equipped with digital EFI because of fuel economy and emission requirements. Using a carburetor would be unthinkable to almost any contemporary auto engine designer.

Certified aircraft engines continue to be equipped with carburetors and crude 1950s era mechanical fuel injection systems which match their own ancient design technology.

With the tremendous upsurge in adapting auto engines for aircraft use in the past few years is the disturbing fact that many of these great conversions have removed the EFI systems that were designed specifically for these engines and replaced them with carburetors, surely a step backwards. Although a few automotive EFI systems are not entirely suitable for aircraft use, most are removed by people who are afraid of this "new" technology because they don't understand it. This is amusing in a way because most people don't fully understand how to work with carburetors either.

Once EFI systems are understood it is actually easier to diagnose and fix problems on them than on old fashioned carbs. Digital EFI will be the wave of the future on aircraft just as it has become on cars.

All EFI systems regulate the fuel flow in relation to airflow by controlling the amount of time that solenoid injector valves remain open. Fuel pressure developed by an electric pump is held at a constant pressure by a regulator. Various sensors relay information to the computer which determines correct on-time for the injectors under the engine conditions present at that instant. Extremely accurate fuel metering is the result.

Today, there are alternatives to the OEM EFI systems found on automobile engines. These are programmable systems which replace of most of the original electronic components while still using the essential mechanical parts of the OEM system such as injectors, fuel rails, regulators and throttle bodies.

As the name suggests, these systems are designed to permit the easy change of fuel flow values for a given parameter unlike all OEM systems which have fixed fuel values for any given engine operation condition. As such, the programmable system can be used to control injectors on any engine when fitted with suitable software. Many of these units require a laptop or PC to re-write values in the system's PROM chip. However, several new systems have come on the market recently with built-in programming capability offering cheaper, faster and easier to understand changes. This article profiles the unit produced by Simple Digital Systems based in Calgary, Alberta, Canada. SDS is now being tested on aircraft automotive conversions.

DEVELOPMENT

Initial SDS development began in 1988 with the first digital prototype being tested on a 4 cylinder car in early 1990. The system was originally designed for the performance automotive market and was extensively tested on many racing cars as well as in tens of thousands of miles on street driven vehicles in Canada's harsh environment. Design goals were to develop the simplest, most reliable programmable EFI system at a realistic price.

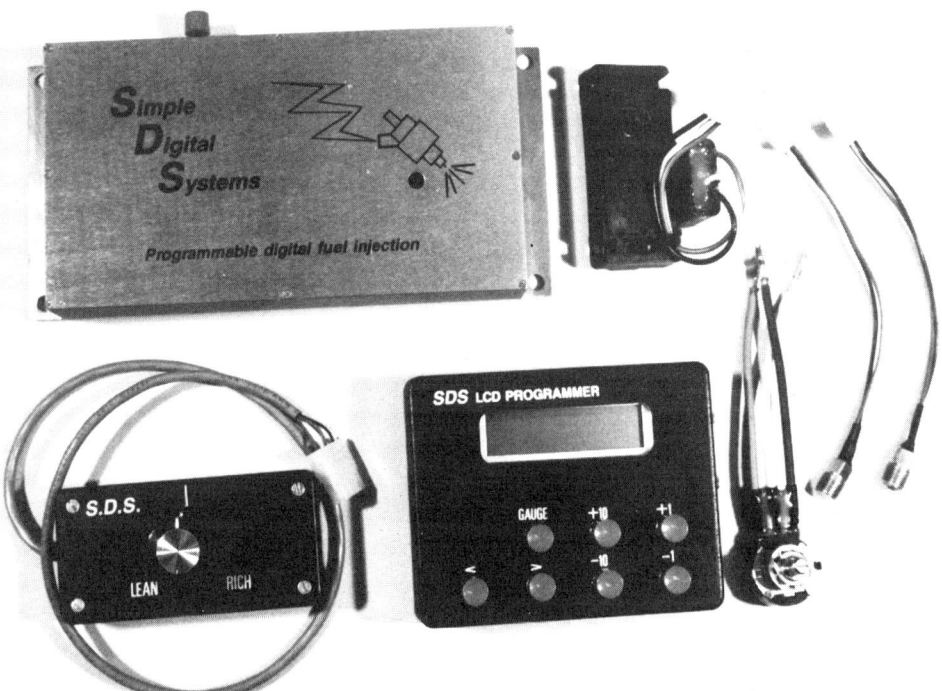

BASIC COMPONENTS

SDS consists of six main components:

- ECU- this is the computer or "black box." (It's actually gold in this case.)
- LCD programmer- permits user access to the PROM or memory in the ECU.

Injector driver- transistor triggering package driving injectors via wiring harness.
Mixture control knob- permits manual richening or leaning of all parameters.
Main wiring harness- Connects ECU to sensors and controls.
Sensor package- includes MAP, TPS and temperature sensors.

THEORY OF OPERATION

The SDS unit is a speed/density type of system using a piezoelectric pressure transducer (similar to the pressure sensing device in an encoding altimeter) to measure manifold pressure. Ignition pulses are read from the primary side of the ignition coil to determine RPM. From these two main parameters, engine airflow can be determined by the ECU. Air and water temperature sensors also relay their information to the ECU so it can determine corrections for induction and coolant temperatures. Finally a throttle position sensor relays rate of change information to compensate for rapid throttle movements.

The ECU takes all sensor inputs into account and pulls the appropriate value for each parameter from memory then performs the necessary computations with its microprocessor to determine injector on-time. A square wave output signal of exact duration is sent to the injector drivers resulting in a precise amount of fuel being injected.

PROGRAMMING THEORY

SDS programming is accomplished with its integrated LCD programmer. This unit allows you to change any fuel value relating to MAP, RPM, water temperature, air temperature and accelerator pump parameters. There are 64 MAP locations, 64 air temperatures, 32 water temperatures and RPM is adjustable every 250 RPM.

By calling up the appropriate parameter and range in the LCD window, the fuel value at that location can be changed in memory to any number between 0 and 255 by pressing plus or minus buttons on the programmer. For example:

Let's assume the engine is too lean at 3500 RPM. You call up RPM 3500 in the window by using the left or right scrolling buttons. The fuel value reference number at this location is displayed as 130. By pressing the +1 or +10 button you increase the value to 140. The value at 3500 RPM has now been reprogrammed from 130 to 140 thus the computer will richen the mixture at 3500 RPM. Conversely, if the mixture is rich the programmer can be used to lean the mixture.

The programmer also has a gauge mode which displays the 4 main sensor outputs simultaneously in the LCD window in real-time allowing the user to see where the engine is presently operating. Mixture ratio can be determined by an optional mixture (EGT) meter hooked to a EGT probe or a stand-alone oxygen sensor.

ADVANTAGES OVER CARBS AND OEM EFI

Port type fuel injection offers cylinder to cylinder mixture distribution that carbs cannot duplicate because only dry air is now flowing through the manifolds. Air will turn corners that fuel will not. Manifold runners need not be heated to keep fuel vaporized because the fuel is injected near the valve head. This allows higher charge density thus more power as well as better fuel economy because all cylinders should be equally lean at cruise.

A straight bore throttle body can be used with EFI resulting in less restriction and eliminating the need for carb heat. EFI is more compact than carbs because the throttle body can be located anywhere and it is physically smaller than a carb. Cold starting is superior because the fuel is well vaporized going into the cylinder.

SDS offers automatic altitude compensation via its absolute referenced MAP sensor as well as manual leaning via the mixture knob once cruise power is set. Over rev and over boost conditions are protected against by setting limits in the ECU.

Turbocharged applications are not compromised by poor mixture control under boost as with carbs. Any mixture curve under boost is possible with SDS. Changes to engine airflow with regards to camshafts, porting or intake manifolds is easily corrected by reprogramming.

The LCD programmer's gauge mode displays RPM, MAP, water and inlet air temperatures. The programmer can be panel mounted and left in gauge mode for most operations, saving the cost and space for separate instruments. The fuel/air mixture can be determined with a standard EGT gauge, or a SDS meter connected to an automotive type oxygen sensor. The SDS meter displays a lean, stoichiometric or rich condition via 10 multicolored LEDs according to the voltage delivered by the oxygen sensor. The DC voltage varies as the amount of free oxygen in the exhaust stream. Too much oxygen indicates a lean condition and vice versa.

Reliability of the solid state components should be superior to mechanical devices. Failure of water, air temperature or throttle position sensors will not cause major running problems as these components' electronic outputs to the ECM are of minor impact to system operation. Failure of the MAP sensor could be compensated for via the mixture knob.

Finally, cost of the system is comparable to some of the good carbs used today.

DISADVANTAGES

The computer, injectors and electric fuel pumps need electrical power to work. A working battery and alternator is essential. If the wrong wire breaks you are a glider. This situation is probably comparable to breaking the float arm in your carb or ice in your carb. In both cases, you are a glider. Anything COULD fail on almost any system. Redundant electrical systems could easily be installed at additional cost to cover this eventuality.

ENGINE MAPPING

An engine map as shown below consists of the values stored in the computer memory for each parameter and range. Each value can be changed with the LCD programmer to alter the amount of fuel injected at that point. The computer multiplies the RPM value with the manifold pressure value then adds the water temperature value to correct for a cold engine and the air temperature value to correct for density changes not sensed by the MAP sensor. This final composite number determines how long the injectors are energised to remain open.

It is important to note that the frequency of the injectors opening is proportional to the RPM so that at 4000 RPM you will have twice the number of injections as at 2000 RPM regardless of the values entered. The slope of the RPM values only compensates for the volumetric efficiency (Ve) or breathing capability of the engine. Since Ve is always highest at the torque peak, this is where the highest RPM value will be. In this case between 5750 and 6000 RPM. The higher the value the longer the injector will remain open.

MAP stands for manifold air pressure which is the air pressure in the intake manifold. The more the throttle is opened or the higher the boost pressure at a given RPM, the higher the MAP will be. Since RPM times MAP approximately equals airflow or air mass flow these are the two main parameters determining how much fuel should be injected. Note that engine map values proportionally increase with increasing MAP.

Since RPM and MAP values are multiplied by the computer, entering 0s or 1s for RPM and MAP values, will effectively shut off the fuel whenever these points are crossed. In this case, fuel would be shut off at 7500 RPM and at MAP values corresponding to high vacuum, closed throttle conditions and at boost pressures over 7.98 psi.

The water temperature values tell the computer to supply extra fuel when the water temperature is cold. As the temperature warms up, fuel delivery is tapered off until no extra fuel is injected with a fully warmed engine, indicated by entering 1s at that point.

Since the density of air varies with temperature, air temperature values tell the computer to alter the injector pulse width so that mixture strength stays constant when the induction temperature changes. This is especially important on turbocharged engines which operate over a wide range of induction temperatures.

Finally, the accel value determines the amount of fuel injected when the throttle is rapidly opened. Once the proper values are entered in the engine map the engine should run flawlessly under all conditions without altering the position of the mixture knob except to lean for maximum cruise efficiency. Engine map values are retained in hard memory even with power switched off.

SYSTEM INSTALLATION

Installation of the electronics is simple and straightforward. The ECU and programmer would be mounted in the cockpit away from potential moisture. The main wiring harness

SDS EM-1 Engine Map 4AGT On M-85

RPM		MAP		WATER TEMP		AIR TEMP			
1000	131	-24.4	1	-40	255	-50	95	83	24
1250	130	-23.5	1	-25	240	-45	94	85	22
1500	130	-22.6	1	-20	235	-35	92	90	21
1750	130	-21.8	11	-10	225	-25	89	93	19
2000	130	-20.9	12	0	215	-20	87	95	18
2250	128	-20.1	15	5	205	-15	86	100	16
2500	127	-19.2	17	10	200	-10	84	105	15
2750	130	-18.4	19	15	180	-7	83	110	14
3000	130	-17.5	20	17	170	-5	82	115	12
3250	130	-16.6	22	20	155	0	81	120	10
3500	130	-15.8	24	25	120	3	79	125	8
3750	130	-14.9	26	28	100	5	78	130	7
4000	130	-14.0	27	30	80	7	76	135	6
4250	130	-13.2	28	35	50	10	75	140	3
4500	131	-12.3	29	40	30	12	74	145	2
4750	133	-11.5	30	42	20	14	72	150	1
5000	135	-10.6	32	45	10	15	70		
5250	137	-9.76	35	to 105	1	17	69		
5500	145	-8.90	38	115	0	20	67		
5750	150	-8.04	41			22	66		
6000	150	-7.18	43			23	65		
6250	140	-6.32	46			25	63		
6500	110	-5.46	49			27	61		
6750	100	-4.60	52			28	60		
7000	100	-3.74	55			30	58		
7250	100	-2.88	58			32	57		
7500	1	-2.02	61			35	55		
		-1.16	63			37	54		
		-0.30	65			38	52		
		-0.18	68			40	51		
		0.61	71			41	50		
		1.04	74			43	49		
		1.47	78			45	48		
		1.90	82			48	46		
		2.33	86			50	45		
		2.76	89			52	43		
		3.19	93			53	41		
		3.62	97			55	40		
		4.05	100			57	39		
		4.48	104			60	37		
		4.91	108			61	36		
		5.34	112			63	34		
		5.78	122			65	33		
Accel		6.22	130			67	31		
		6.66	137			70	30		
50		7.10	141			73	28		
		7.54	146			75	27		
		7.98	1			80	25		

connects the engine sensors to the ECU through the firewall. The injector driver box would be mounted on the back side of the firewall. The injector harness connects the driver to the injectors themselves on the engine. Power wires are connected to the master switch and the various negative wires go to ground. A vacuum hose connects the MAP sensor to the intake manifold. The temperature sensors are screwed into 1/8 NPT holes tapped into the cylinder head and induction system then plugged into the main harness. The green wire from the harness attaches to the negative terminal of the ignition coil to supply an RPM signal to the computer.

INJECTORS

The SDS unit is intended to operate one injector per cylinder which is referred to as port fuel injection. Many different types of electronic fuel injectors are available today. Our preference is Bosch or Nippondenso pintle style injectors. These types have been proven in 25 years of automobile use and are more resistant to clogging than the newer disc style units widely used today. There is also a multitude of fuel rail mounting methods. Some use a barb fitting on the injector to take push on high pressure hose and a clamp while others use an "O" ring to seal the connection. Each has its advantages. The solenoid windings on the injector also have different impedances depending on the driver circuit used. The SDS driver is compatible with most common injectors from 2.5 to 12 ohms. Injectors are available in a wide range of flow rates to suit different applications.

Flow rates are a very important consideration on any application. If the injector is too small, either the engine will run lean or the injector may overheat due to high duty cycle times. Injectors in an aircraft application should never be run at duty cycles over 80 percent continuously. Duty cycle refers to the percentage of time the injector is open in relation to the time available before the next injection cycle begins. At 100 percent, the injector is spraying continuously because the triggering pulses come together offering no oft time. This is then the maximum amount of fuel that can be delivered from the injector.

Flow rates are expressed in ccs/min. or lbs./hr. at a constant fuel pressure, usually 35-38 psi, with the injector spraying continuously. As a rule of thumb, on gasoline, a piston engine will require about 5.7 cc/min. per HP; i.e., a 300 HP engine would burn about 171 0 cc per minute at full throttle. (300 X 5.7). Total fuel flow divided by the number of injectors will give you the minimum flow rate needed from each injector. Say we have a 300 HP 6 cylinder engine. Take 1710 divided by 6 = 285. 285 divided by .8 (our 80 percent) gives us 356. This would be the minimum flow rate needed from each

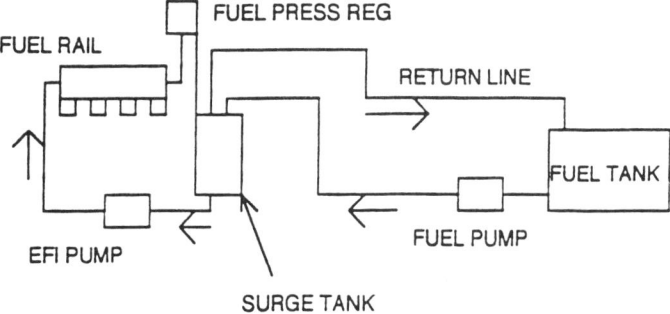

injector. Used injectors should always be checked for leakage, matched flow rates to each other and proper spray pattern as well as mounting compatibility for the specific application.

FUEL SYSTEM

EFI fuel systems differ from many conventional systems in that a constant volume (excess) of fuel is delivered at all times to the fuel rail. Fuel not injected is passed through the pressure regulator back to the tank. The regulator is pressure referenced to manifold pressure so that the pressure differential between fuel and manifold pressure is held constant. Pressure and flow rates are increased or decreased by varying the quantity returned to the tank. At idle most of the fuel delivered by the pump is sent back to the tank; at full throttle smaller amounts are returned. Obviously the fuel pump must always be able to supply some excess amount of fuel above that demanded by the engine or the fuel pressure will drop and the engine will run lean.

A Bosch electric EFI pump would be our choice to feed the fuel rail. These are available in many flow rates and configurations. The EFI pump must have a constant supply of fuel as they do not pump air or prime well. A high volume low pressure pump or gravity feed header tank should be used to ensure an uninterrupted supply. In the case of aircraft with multiple tanks, some arrangement would probably have to be made so that fuel returned from the rail is returned to the tank selected for feeding to avoid having fuel returned where not intended. Pumps, lines and injectors must be tested to ensure adequate fuel flow for the intended application. If adequate fuel is not available at the injector, no amount of programming will make the engine perform properly.

PROGRAMMING THE SYSTEM

In an aircraft application it will be necessary to put the engine on a test stand or tie down the aircraft securely with engine and propeller in place and progressively increase manifold pressure and RPM while altering map values for smooth running. Satisfactory operation should be obtained on the ground before fine tuning in the air.

Engine mapping is usually approached from an over rich condition, slowly leaning until no excess fuel is being delivered at each point. This lean point can be determined by leaning with the mixture knob until a stumble appears at that range while in gauge mode then returning the mixture knob to the neutral position and leaning the appropriate value with the programmer. With the many value slots available, this can be a fairly time consuming process for the novice.

Rapid transition between gauge mode and the parameter you are programming is possible by depressing the gauge button again. The computer will remember where it was and return there so you can confirm where the stumble was and correct it quickly without scrolling through all the ranges.

CONCLUSION

This article covered many of the steps necessary to install a programmable EFI system on an engine. Systems are tailored with different hardware and software for a particular engine type and application. For instance, a unit for a 6-cylinder turbocharged engine would be different from one for a 4-cylinder naturally aspirated engine. Compatible fuel system components are also important. Check with knowledgeable personnel before purchasing any component. Like any other building project, a complete understanding of the entire system should be gained before undertaking the task. **RF**

Stratus Engine Development

Reiner Hoffmann
Stratus Incorporated
7750 Twelfth Avenue N.W.
Seattle Washington 98117
(206) 783 3845

The general aviation fleet is aging. Certified replacement engines exceed the cost of Classic Age trainer airframes. Should airworthy airframes be held hostage to 50 year old rules? The application of auto engines to these airframes using Supplemental Type Certificate (STC) procedures is an needed alternative. Contact! applauds Stratus efforts in demonstrating once again the viability of professional auto engine conversions. MCM

After about 20 flying hours, I grew to hate the Rotax 532 that came with an Avid Flyer I had purchased pre-built. The Rotax was extremely loud and vibrated so much that my feet actually grew numb after a few hours of flying time. It also had a reputation for being unreliable. These factors led me in late 1991 to convert a Subaru EA-81 turbo engine (see Contact issue #12) and install it in my Avid. I flew the engine for over 220 hours, including an altitude test flight over 14,410 foot Mount Rainier. I liked the performance of the Subaru so much that I decided to found Stratus Incorporated, a company that converts normal aspirated Subaru engines and makes them available to kitplane owners.

It was obvious after going through the necessary modifications and successful development of this installation that a suitably converted Subaru engine would outperform almost any engine available to kit builders. But it also seemed to me that this Subaru engine would be an ideal replacement for the aging O-200 engines in certified aircraft such as Cessna 150s. I set out to prove my theory by installing a Stratus production engine in my own Cessna 150. I, like many readers, was tired of seeing auto engines that were bolted to trailers and demonstrated at air shows, but never actually flew.

I finished installing the Stratus engine in the Cessna late in 1993. Since then, the engine has accumulated more than 246 hours, including a round trip flight from Seattle, Washington, to Lakeland, Florida for Sun 'N Fun '94.

THE ENGINE

At Stratus, we start out by buying low-mileage Japanese engine cores that we completely disassemble, clean, and inspect to make sure they meet OEM tolerances. We bore the cylinders to first oversize (.025 inch), and then assemble the engine using all-new pistons and rings, bearings, a new oil pump, etc., to make a true zero-time engine.

We port the cylinder heads for better breathing and change the camshaft profile to include a 250 degree duration on the intake and exhaust lobes. We fit the engines with a custom, lightweight intake manifold using two Bing altitude-compensating carburetors of 32mm bore (part # 62-32-94). I have tried and tested other makes but find that these Bing carburetors are the best I have ever worked with.

Front end of the Stratus EA-81 powered Cessna 150F as seen at the 1994 Sun 'N Fun Fly-In. Undisturbed cowling sheet metal is noteworthy, made possible by careful positioning of heater cores in the nose bowl openings. A 70 inch ground adjustable Warp Drive propeller is used.

Our engines always start on the first revolution, hot or cold. One of the nicest things about this carburetor is that, because it has no venturi to speak of, there is no need for carburetor heat. We have flown for many hours in Northwest conditions that make most carburetors susceptible to icing, but have never encountered the problem with Bing carburetors.

Engine compartment exhibits ample use of tie-wraps for security. Two Bing carburetor air filters (by alternator) provide clean air to each intake port. The redrive sprocket mounts a propeller extension to clear the cowl cheeks.

Before they are delivered, Stratus engines are completely assembled and test run. Each engine assembly includes a reduction drive, electric starter, air filters, an ignition coil a fuel pump and a choice of prop extensions. Because the engines are completely overhauled engine break-in procedures should be followed.

Some readers may wonder why the turbo version is not offered at this time. Although the Avid turbo installation proved successful it was the fact that proper engine management was and remains another element in the pilot/airplane equation. Enough articles have been written regarding the specific care and feeding of turbo installations, as well as problems because of misinformed use. In my experience, turbo-charged engines call on pilots to watch the engine fueling parameters so much that they can miss the pure enjoyment of sport flying. I find the normal aspirated engine as in my Cessna is a lot easier to operate, essentially no different than that pilots experience with factory certified engines. Another factor against turbo installations should be mentioned. The fuel consumption of the turbo motor was very high when I ran it under boost, necessary to keep the engine combustion within limits.

THE REDUCTION DRIVE

We build a belt reduction drive that features two 30-mm-wide HTD belts. This has proven to be a very good setup. The ratio of 2.2:1 brings the prop speed to less than 2,500 RPM. We use two belts to provide redundancy. If one should break, the other can still drive the propeller.

The Stratus rear redrive housing contains one additional bearing. This bearing is designed to fit over the crankshaft flange. It prevents belt torque loads from loading the crankshaft main bearing as in some other cog belt reduction drives. Both aluminum redrive sprockets are hard-anodized to provide long service life. The propeller flange is machined to SAE # 1 hub dimensions. The ready to mount Stratus redrive, with flywheel, weighs 32.0 pounds.

The belts' tension can be adjusted via cams on the hollow prop shaft. For the first 20 hours or so of running time, we find that the belts seem to stretch a little. They should be adjusted once after 20 hours or so, but do not need to be adjusted again for the service life of the belt. We recommend that belts be replaced at 500 hours, or five years, just to be on the safe side. The belts typically run for thousands of hours in industrial applications. However, we are dealing with an

Two 1979 Ford heater cores provide adequate cooling surfaces. Baffling seals are tightly fitted. SAE #1 flange pattern is used on the 4 inch extension.

Light weight fiberglass cuff captures cabin heat air. A butterfly valve dumps heated air when not needed, allowing the radiator to flow at all times.

Hose routing. Top hose flows coolant to other radiator in series. Middle hose feeds primary flow from water pump to engine when cold. Bottom hose carries heated coolant from engine to radiator.

airplane environment and we feel that a $70 dollar investment in new belts every 500 hours is worthwhile.

ENGINE COOLING

The size and placement of radiators varies from one aircraft to another. In the Avid, I used a VW Rabbit radiator mounted on the bottom of the fuselage at about a 15-degree angle, and a scoop that guided air through it. It was not the most aesthetic setup, but it worked very well. However, I did not want to modify the stock and expensive Cessna cowling, so I decided to install the radiators in the stock air inlets to the

This firewall mounted 1974 Dodge heater valve is used to manually lean the carburetors. The upper hose is tapped into the intake manifold; the lower hose is connected in "Y" fashion to the float bowls.

left and right of the prop spinner. This has proven to be a good location for cooling. It also saved a lot of time since the installation was fairly simple without any interference from surrounding parts. The radiator cores measure about 6 x 8 x 2.5 inches (heater cores from a 1979 Ford automobile) and have the capability of maintaining an 180 degree F. coolant temperature in the engine during cruise. Climb out condition are usually critical. With an OAT of 85 degrees F. this radiator installation, under full-power climb-out at about 80 MPH, keeps the coolant at 195 degrees .

Oil cooling proved to be more of a challenge. A Stratus engine typically runs at a lower power setting in an Avid Flyer than it does in the C-150. The reason is that the C-150 is a much heavier airplane and requires a higher power output to achieve the same cruise speed. As a result, no oil cooler is necessary for the Avid. I knew the C-150 would definitely need an oil cooler. In Subaru EA-81 engines, the oil return galley passes next to the exhaust port, which means the oil basically comes in contact with the heat of the exhaust gases. The first oil cooler I installed proved to be too small, so I installed a used one from a yard that measured 10 x 5 x 2 inches, which keeps the oil at about 220 degrees. In modern car engines, the oil temperature can easily reach over 300 degrees, but I believe lower oil temperatures increase the life of the engine.

IGNITION

We use a stock Subaru distributor, which is all-electronic and has no points. We set up the engines so that the distributor's mechanical advance is fully advanced to 34 degrees BTDC. Although a 34-degree advance is efficient, a 28-degree advance would yield a little more top-end power. The drawback to a 28-degree advance is that it consumes more fuel in cruise.

In the Cessna 150, I installed a dedicated ignition battery that is connected with the main system via a diode, so electricity can flow only into the battery. The ignition switch draws electricity from this battery.

We are currently working on a crank-fired CDI ignition. One electronic module will contain one coil per spark plug, resulting in four independent ignition systems. All Stratus Inc. engines delivered to date will be retrofitable to this ignition system.

ENGINE OPERATION

Starting a Stratus engine is just like starting your car: you turn the ignition key and the engine comes to life. The carburetors use a built-in choke when the OAT is below 45 degrees. The fact that the engine always starts on the first revolution is pretty impressive compared to updraft carburetor fed Lycoming and Continental engines.

I left most of the instrument panel unchanged. I put new engine instruments where avionics used to be. It took me about 200 hours to build the

The design of the side draft Bing carburetor minimizes carburetor icing. Sheltered, slightly warmed air also helps reduce icing problems. An auto voltage regulator is mounted on the firewall. Note tie-wraps.

The Exide battery is dedicated to the ignition system. Above it is a ADC oil filter and to the left is a Carter 6 psi fuel electric fuel pump.

Note mounting of muffler and O_2 sensor used to measure fuel/air mixture.

Two inch muffler end inlets with single 1 3/4 inch center exhaust. Highly modified "T" configuration could be reason exhaust noise is noticeably low.

motor mount and complete the installation of the engine. The airframe structure was left stock and the same engine mounting points were used as the engine weighed 30 pounds less than the Continental O-200.

To minimize installation problems we chose the smallest muffler we could find at the local auto parts store. It quiets engine noise dramatically. It is unbelievably quiet inside and outside the plane, making a headset unnecessary for hearing loss protection. In fact, the quietness of the Cessna's engine generally attracts a group of people when I stop to fuel at airports that I haven't been to before. People sense that something about my Cessna just doesn't sound quite "right." The quietness of the engine makes it a good choice in areas where noise pollution is a problem. To date, I have put more than 200 hours on the C150, all trouble-free. On typical flights, I burn an average of 4.2 GPH and normally cruise at about 100 MPH indicated.

This spring, fellow pilot Jerry Dietz and I flew our Cessnas to the 1994 Sun 'N Fun Fly-In Convention. His Cessna has a Bolen Taildragger conversion and is powered by an O-200. Although my three point Cessna is quite a bit dirtier, my fuel consumption averaged 4.3 GPH compared to Jerry's consumption of 5.9, a 27 percent fuel savings (looking at it from the auto engine perspective the fuel burn of the O-200 is 37 percent greater!). Overall, the performance of my Cessna was quite a bit better. Jerry radioed me several times to say, "Slow down!"

STRATUS PERFORMANCE

To date, George Thiel holds the record for the most time accumulated on a Stratus engine. The engine in his Avid Flyer (N4371J) has logged more than 400 hours without any reliability problems. I am confident that Stratus engines will achieve a better TBO than certified engines when given the same, close servicing attention that certified engines normally receive. But even when the time does come to overhaul a Stratus engine, it will cost only a fraction of what it costs to rebuild a certified engine.

For an aircraft, a liquid-cooled engine is a far better choice. Because there is no shock cooling, there is less stress on the engine. Liquid-cooled engines also run cooler than their air-cooled counterparts, which also should lead to longer service life. Relative fuel

SPECIFICATIONS

Engine type	all-aluminum, four-cylinder, four-stroke, liquid-cooled, pushrod, normally aspirated
Displacement	1781 cc (109 in^3)
Power output	100 hp
Bore	92 mm (3.62 in)
Stroke	67 mm (2.64 in)
Fuel	unleaded gasoline
Weight	182 lbs
Reduction ratio	2.2:1
Direction of rotation	clockwise
Reduction system	two 30-mm wide HTD belts
Cooling	water-glycol mixture
Ignition	single electronic, single spark plugs
Alternator	12 amp, optional 50 amps
Carburetion	dual Bing altitude-compensating carburetors
Fuel consumption	0.48 lb/hp/hr at 75 percent power
Starter	electric gear-reduction

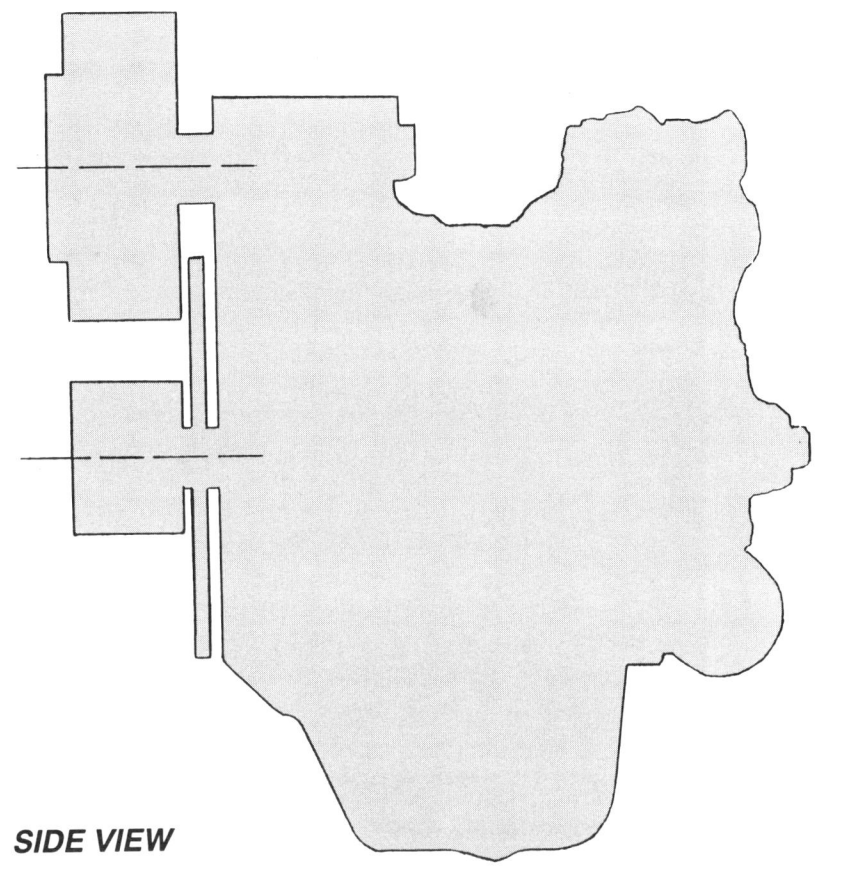

SIDE VIEW

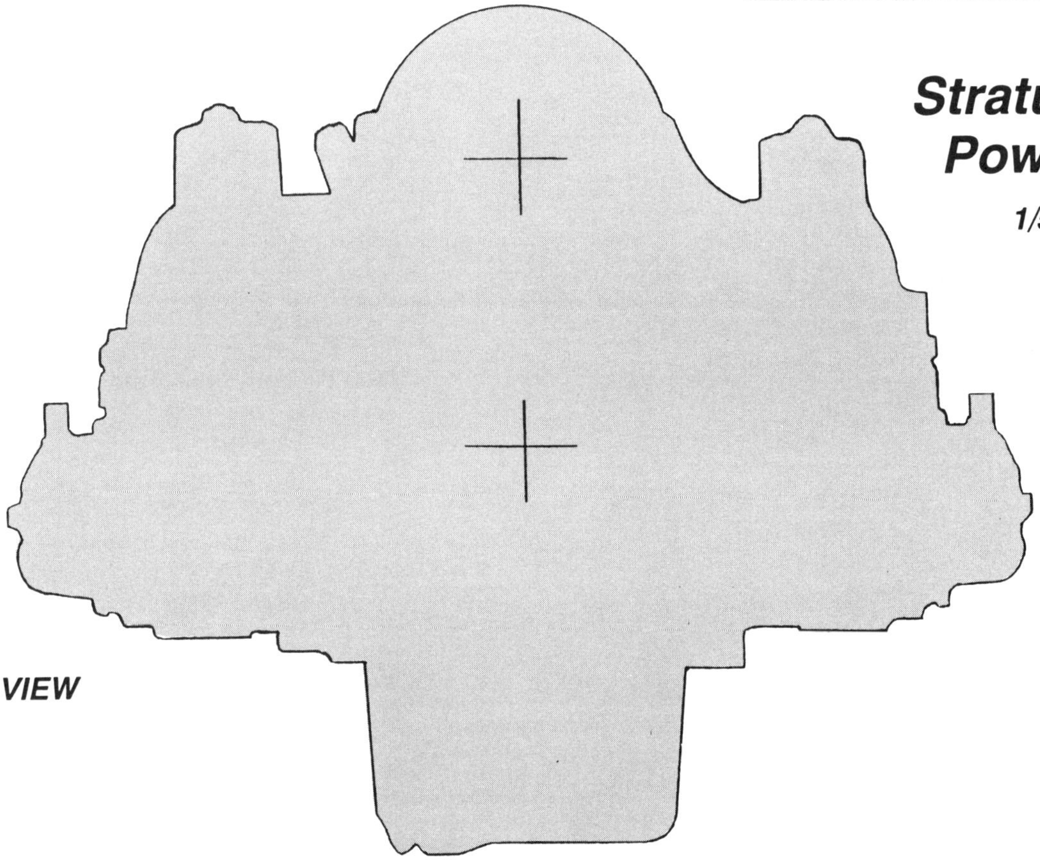

FRONT VIEW

Stratus EA-81 Powerplant

1/5 Scale

efficiency is notable. All things considered, I believe the Stratus conversion is a better powerplant than the Continental O-200 for the Cessna 150.

PAPERWORK

Because the Cessna now had a non-certified engine in it, it had to be licensed in the Experimental category. The process is simple in Washington State. After I completed the engine installation and calculated the weight and balance, I called the FAA and set up an appointment for inspection. When the FAA inspector arrived, he looked the plane over very carefully and checked the Cessna's serial number to see if all my paperwork matched. After he inspected the plane and found everything to his satisfaction, he gave me a new experimental air worthiness certificate. For about 20 hours, I was restricted to a 50-mile radius around Arlington, Washington. Now I can (and do) fly anywhere I want to. The 20-hour restriction is the same one that is applied to home-built aircraft. The only difference is I am required to renew my air worthiness certificate on a yearly basis.

PROP MATCHING

I have been using a 70-inch 3-bladed Warp Drive propeller with good results. The prop is ground adjustable, which is a nice feature in tuning the prop to the airframe. I once ran the C-150 metal prop on the converted engine, and to my surprise, found that the engine turned it 140 RPM faster than the O-200 did. I expected the EA-81 to be similar to the O-200. I never flew the metal prop on my conversion because I expected that the gyroscopic forces caused by the high prop inertia would be too much for our reduction drive.

COMPONENT WEIGHTS

The complete Stratus engine weight of 182 pounds includes: propeller speed reduction unit, alternator (12 amps), starter and flywheel, two carburetors, distributor, motor mounts, and exhaust manifold. Not included in the engine weight are the following items totalling 32 pounds:

4 Quarts of oil	8.2 lbs
1.5 Gallons of coolant	11.8 lbs
Radiators/supports	5.0 lbs
Ignition coil	3.0 lbs
Muffler	4.0 lbs

STRATUS vs. O-200

The following table summarizes my test results and provides a comparison of performance figures between the Stratus engine to the Continental O-200. These figures are based on a stock Cessna 150F with no wheel pants; sea-level conditions; a take-off weight of 1,600 pounds; outside air temperature of 55 degrees; and humidity of 68 percent. These tests were performed at Arlington Airport, Arlington, Washington, in January of 1994:

	Stratus EA-81	Continental O-200
Continuous rate of climb at sea level	690 FPM	610 FPM
Top speed, indicated	130 MPH	120 MPH
Fuel burn at 100MPH, indicated	4.0 GPH	5.5 GPH

RH

Panel modifications. Below key, left: Hobbs hour meter, large battery voltmeter, EGT, fuel/air mixture. Below key, right and center: fuel flow meter, tach, coolant pressure, coolant temperature, oil temperature.

The stock appearing Stratus Cessna as seen at SNF 1994. Hoffmann plans to fly the airplane to the 1000 hour mark before scheduling its overhaul. Engine parts should still be within limits at that interval.

I first met Reiner at Arlington 1992. He had just completed his Avid Flyer and advised me of his intention to produce firewall forward Subaru EA-81 conversions. His meticulous attention to engine cooling, fueling, ignition and exhaust details has resulted in a succesful conversion that, in my estimation, equals that of the highly tested CAM 100 unit. Contact! will periodically report on the progress of this effort. MCM

The LPE Engine: Alternative High End Power

Darus H. Zehrbach
Light Power Engine Corporation
Post Office Drawer 3350
Morgantown WV 26505
(304) 291 3843

Leading edge technology is the hallmark of these engines. Shown in various configurations for several years at Oshkosh and Sun 'N Fun, LPE's modest aircraft engine manufacturing effort is largely supported by its principal activity, that of furnishing special engines to endurance ocean going power boat racers, powering boats commonly known as the "Cigarette" and "Diablo" classes. Contact! issue #12 focused on the design considerations leading to the current production confuguration. Several Cirrus homebuilders have chosen the LPE engine for their aircraft. MCM

LPE chose the 90 degree V/8 configuration due to its compact size and weight. Cast from A-356 aluminum in silt sand and treated to T-6 condition, the unique engine block features 6 bolt cross bolted mains, replaceable cylinder sleeves, and all stud fasteners. In addition, all oil and water galleries are plugged with snap ring locks over the plugs. This block is intended to withstand much higher load demands than would be experienced in aircraft applications.

"ZM" engines also feature a new, dual plug, lean burn head design. This increases efficiency while providing the utmost in reliability. The spark plug tip is extended into the chamber rather than being recessed. This allows the engine to run hot at low speeds and loads in order to prevent fouling. When the engine speed and load are increased, the plug runs cooler due to the air flow over the plug tip.

The pistons used in the "ZM" engines use gapless piston rings. This type of ring significantly reduces blow by gases and oil leak down on inverted models. Cleaner oil, less oil consumption, and an increase in fuel efficiency are other benefits. In addition to the gapless rings, The customer hasa choice of compression ratios in order to run on lower octane fuel or on 100 LL. Gapless rings, historically used in Diesels, allow tighter piston fit.

An aircraft can induce severe torsional and flexural forces and vibrations to its drive train. LPE addresses this fact by balancing the entire engine both internally and externally, and by designing the components to withstand this treatment. As described above, the engine block is sufficiently strong to endure the harsh conditions of an aircraft drive train. In addition, the crankshaft, the one part that ultimately must withstand and transmit all power, is formed from a 4340 alloy steel forging. This selection of material greatly increases torsional rigidity while the design of the shaft is also responsible for its superior strength.

Some additional features of the "ZM" engines include a large base circle, gear driven cam, an all roller valve train, and extremely long connecting rods. A roller valve train requires less lubrication and less power and remains cooler than plain bearings. Side thrust exerted on the valve stem is eliminated through the use of roller rocker arms. As an additional feature of the inverted engine designs, the entire valve is constantly immersed in oil during operation.

A multiple pick up, dry sump oil system is used on all "ZM" engines. These systems are noted for doubling the life of internal bearings as they de-aerate and cool oil in the collection tank. The oil cooler is a heat exchanger to the water. The water thermostat regulates the oil temperature. The heads get hot first so the oil lubrication is improved. At peak power, the oil is cooled by water.

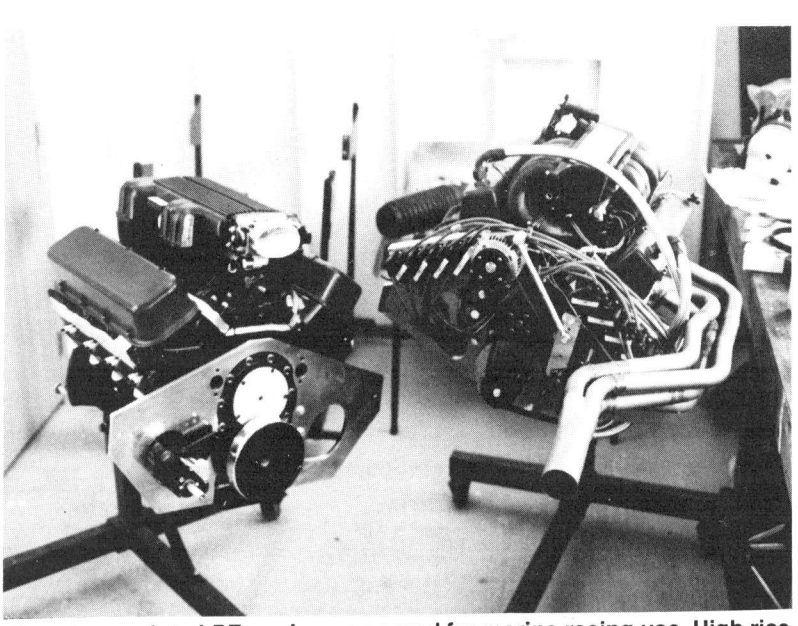

Two heavy duty LPE engines prepared for marine racing use. High rise induction systems feature tuned intake runners.

Engine cooling is certainly a major factor in designing an aircraft engine. On a dynamometer, an air cooled engine lasts as long as a water cooled engine. However, in actual aircraft situations, water cooled engines excel in performance. Water cooled engines rise to operating temperature rapidly, temperature fluctuations are controlled automatically, and thermal shock from quick descents and emergency power reductions are eliminated. Water cooling also enables hot water cabin heat, reducing the danger of carbon monoxide poisoning.

Electronic fuel injection is utilized for efficient use of the available fuel and to avoid operating problems due to carburetor ice. Electronic fuel injection offers maximum fuel efficiency at all times and prohibits the pilot from destroying the engine by running excessively rich or lean. In addition, the computer based injection system can be programmed for all operating conditions. The mixture control is eliminated. Fuel pressure at 42 PSI eliminates vapor lock and improves atomization.

In addition to electronic fuel management, LPE's "ZM" engines feature completely automatic electronic ignition. Containing no moving parts, this system is absolutely maintenance free while still producing more energy per horsepower consumed than any other ignition systems currently used in this application. The electronic ignition systems used on the "ZM" engines constantly adjust over a 50 degree range in response to load, temperature and engine knock. These features combine to provide the most fuel efficient engine of this type. The ignition has no distributor cap or rotor.

All accessories on a LPE "ZM" eight cylinder engine are driven by toothed belts that are selected for 50 times the actual applied load. This design eliminates conventional belt slip, absorbs vibration, costs less and is more quiet than gear drives. These engines have a total of five accessory drive points. There is a 1:1 prop governor drive point, two belt drives for alternators, and two belt drives for other accessories.

The V/8 engines are designed to operate at any speed up to 4,500 RPM in geared engines or up to 2,900 RPM direct. Light Power Engine recommends 3, 4, or 5 blade propellers which reduce prop induced vibration, promote longer engine life, and provide higher cabin comfort levels. Rated power is at 2700 direct and 4300RPM geared.

The cost of overhaul is another advantage of LPE's "ZM" engines. These engines are some of the easiest in the world to repair. The crankshaft and all bearings can be replaced without splitting the engine cases. The cam can be replaced without total engine disassembly. Average rebuild cost for a "ZM" engine is less than $900. The 500 HP twin turbo direct drive engine can be rebuilt for a cost of $5000, including the turbo units. For comparison, the major overhaul of a Lycoming or Continental engine of comparable power will run anywhere between $15,000 and $25,000, depending on engine condition and pricing policies.

In order to increase the time between overhauls, space-age, dry-film coatings are applied to most wear surfaces.

The resulting package at equal displacements to horizontally opposed engines has at least 40 percent less frontal area at 10 to 25 percent less weight (wet) installed.

The performance, low cost of operation, and the ease and low cost of rebuilding, along with all of the other features of this design make the "ZM" V/8 engine by Light Power Engine Corporation a viable alternative to the conventional choices.

DESIGN GOALS

Light Power Engine Corporation is committed to the continued advancement of the "ZM" line of engines. We state that the "ZM" aircraft engine line is the most advanced in the world. We intend to keep them in that position. "ZM" test engines have already run the next generation of advancements. Cost control efforts are being made now to start phasing in each new development as its cost comes under control. We are already successfully running:

- 10.2:1 CR engine at 6 PSI boost
- Carbon fiber push rods (0.7 oz. each)
- Carbon fiber roller lifters
- Fluorocarbon head gaskets
- Carbon fiber engine blocks
- Composite material valve covers
- Variable duration and lift valve trains
- Carbon pistons - the ultimate tight fit
- Variable vane turbochargers - no waste gate
- Ceramic cylinders

THE CNC ENGINE

Premium aircraft engine re-builders have repeatedly demonstrated their engines superiority over factory rebuilds by "blue printing" engines. In short, they attempt to re-work the Lycoming and Continental parts to make them the same in weight, shape, and performance. By doing so they attempt to make all of the cylinders produce equal power.

"ZM" engine parts are all equal straight from the factory because only LPE produces their aircraft engine parts on CNC machinery. Even our combustion chambers are milled out - not cast as is. The result is that you get a premium blueprinted engine straight from the factory - without the excessive costs of a custom engine.

CAM DESIGN

"ZM" engines are all V/8 (or based on V/8) designs with the camshaft located high in the V as compared to typical auto engine camshafts. This reduces the pushrod distance from the rocker arms to the cam. In the "ZM" design most of the direct valve accuracy and lightness of an overhead cam design is achieved without the complexity.

Compared to an opposed engine the "ZM" high V design runs very short, very light push rods. A typical "ZM" push rod is less than 6.5 inches long. Compared to the opposed engine the push rods are less than 1/2 of the opposed engine rod length, 1/4 of the weight, and 4 times stronger.

ROLLER VALVE TRAIN

Hydraulic roller lifters are used. They run with very little oil supply and reduce friction for "free" power or less fuel burn. A roller can follow a cam profile much tighter so that cam profiles can be altered to yield faster opening and closing with less engine parts strain compared to flat tappet cams which skid while operating. On cold starts or any time lubrication fails the roller is vastly superior and won't wipe out a lobe. Normal flat tappets have an off center bevel to turn the lifter to prevent wear in one spot. That also means that the load is concentrated and it jams the cam to one end of the block. As flat tappets wear the surface which started out convex becomes concave. That height difference shows up as altered valve timing, valve lash, etc. Roller wear is negligible. Rollers sharply reduce oil/water heating to wring more efficiency from the engines.

VALVE TRAIN

The valve train is the big power eater in a reciprocating engine. Power is absorbed and lots of heat is made. Major engine failures occur in the valve train so any improvement is of major importance. To make sure that the valve train runs as smooth and as cool as possible roller rocker arms are used. Both the fulcrum and the tip are roller. The fulcrum creates great heat in non-roller tappets. The roller tip stops the side loading on the valve stems so valve guides don't get egg shaped and suck oil.

Reduced friction and heat result in more power and/or fuel efficiency. A 5 percent gain is normal with an all roller valve train. Less heat means less cooling drag.

INVERTED ENGINE

The inverted engine offers many design benefits besides prop ground clearance. Steam pockets don't form in the heads to disturb cooling. The head self drains any liquids. The valve train runs in an oil bath. Valve springs which are normally heat soaked in the coils near the engine are cooled uniformly by the oil bath so that they don't fail. The heat of the valve train is immediately drained out of the engine, not fed back into the engine. The last added heat from the hottest part of the engine goes directly to the oil cooler for maximum thermal efficiency.

In opposed Continental/Lycoming engines the cam lies high in the casing above all oil. Although the bearings are pressure oiled, the lobes and lifters are not. The sole oil on the cam face is mere slung oil flying around from the crank parts.

In contrast, the cam for the "ZM" engines is in the crankcase sump. All of the oil coming off of the entire bottom end goes over the cam. It runs in a constant flowing bath of oil under the crank. Camshaft spalling is obviously not a problem. In addition, the roller cam lifters need only a fraction of the oil needed by flat tappets. The oil bath keeps all parts at an uniform temperature.

DRY SUMP LUBRICATION

Piston oiling is controlled by special drilling and grooves. Scraped and flung oil is pulled through the center galley by up to 8 inches of vacuum on the dry sump pump. It flows through the push rod galleries into the valve cover where a standpipe sets the level to flood the springs and rockers in a bath before being drained from the engine. Oil is literally sucked out of the engine, not merely pumped. In effect a "wind" blows right to the pump pickup carrying the oil.

COMPACTNESS

A 90 degree V engine is simply the tightest package for large cubic inch engines. Rods on an opposed engine can't be as long as they should be and strokes can't get too long or the engine gets too wide. The long exhaust system under an horizontally opposed engine makes it twice as deep as the bare engine. Bare engine specs are deceptive.

The scale drawing of the "ZM" and the Continental 550 engines dramatically points out the size advantage, especially in the critical frontal area. The turbine-like pointed nose of the"ZM" can contribute to aircraft performance and visibility. The propeller air swirl is not clipped by the cowling. The LPE design is available in custom length nose drive units to avoid propeller spacers and their unsupported loads. Up to 6 extra inches can be added.

LPE COMBUSTION CHAMBER

"ZM" engines feature ultra modern lean burn technology. Compression ratios of up to 14 to 1 can be run without detonation. By comparison, the conventional opposed engines are "knock limited" engines. Their compression and /or spark advance, and thus power output, is limited by the onset of destructive fuel detonation. Current generation opposed engine heads have the spark plugs at the extreme edges of the heads to try to get good flame propagation across a very wide piston. The "ZM" engine has its two plugs located in the combustion chamber center/top in a "semi-hemi" configuration with mixture homogenizing features throughout the chamber. All of this is why Lycoming will run 20 to 22 degree ignition advance and a "ZM" engine has 50 degrees of advance capability in its system. The "ZM" V/8 head design will deliver more power on less fuel. It does this by running much leaner and fuel efficient mixtures at high compression. The result is that more power is squeezed out of each unit of fuel. Higher compression also allows the fuel to burn more completely and quicker while lowering exhaust gas temperatures.

Modern heads have very small combustion chamber volumes. The smaller the chamber the less surface area there is to absorb heat; therefore, the engine runs cooler. Less surface area also means less fuel wetted surface for more efficient fuel burn and lower emissions.

- **Recessed plug inhibiting flame ignition**
- **Lower plug can fill with oil and foul**
- **Poor flame propagation due to plug positions**
- **Large, open chamber inhibits fuel mixing**
- **Large surface area absorbs heat**
- **No vibration damping on valve springs**
- **Standard rocker tip promotes guide wear**
- **Lack of valve stem cooling**

LPE has thrown away all the conventions of old World War II aircraft cylinder heads and incorporate what is the latest in reliability and efficiency in its cylinder heads. The last five years have had evidenced considerable refinement in combustion chamber design. Readers should understand that the mysteries of what really goes on in a combustion chamber are still being learned.

The primary thrust of LPE has been to increase fuel mixture atomization and distribution and even burning in all parts of the chamber. Post operation teardowns have checked for detonation and the tell tale deposits that indicate incomplete fuel burn. Research has shown that the smaller combustion chambers are better for efficiency and less heat absorbed into the head. Thus, the engine can stand more ignition advance and leaner mixtures without detonation. LPE chambers all use concave pistons wherever possible - never a domed piston. The compression is created with the small chamber which results in a very large squish area around the piston and an idealized combustion pocket.

The "ZM" head has a very small chamber volume. The valves are not parallel at 23 degrees intake and 15 degrees exhaust to form the famous cross-flowing hemi-head. The ports are smooth and straight with cooling water jackets right to the valve seat. The piston squish area surrounds the entire pocket. No valves are shrouded by the cylinder wall. Spark plugs are located at the center of the chamber and in the swirl pocket for maximum uniform burn. Conventional engines have retracted tip plugs that rely on their retracted position to try to stay cool. On a water jacketed plug the water temperature sets the plug temperature. A projected tip plug is used on LPE engines. The incoming air blast cools the plug. Better still, since it is sticking into the chamber the tip heats up fast to stop fouling.

DUAL/SINGLE PLUGS

The dual plug LPE head has 95 cc for a 600 cubic inch engine. New, smaller diameter plugs allow dual plugs without compromising cylinder head cooling around the plugs.

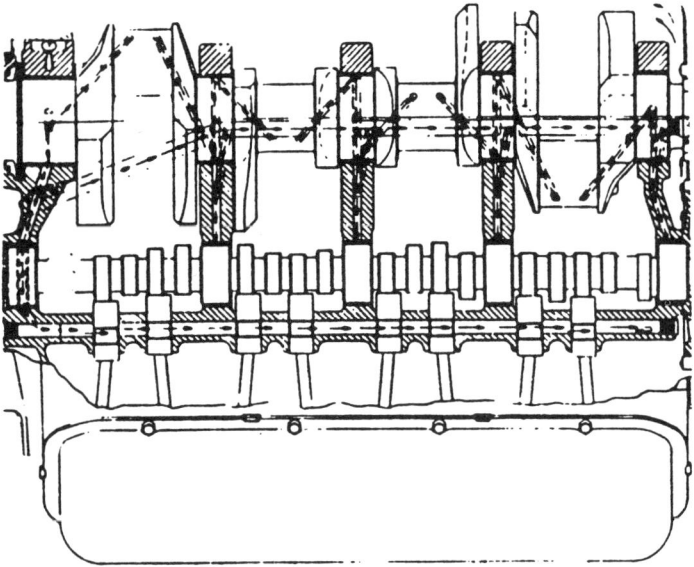

Inboard view of inverted LPE engine showing oil passages in crankshaft, to camshaft bearings and roller lifters. Tighter bearing clearances require less oil pressure.

Engine cylinder pressures vary during the four stroke Otto cycle. These pressure variations are the prime cause of torsional vibration. Uniform fuel mixture, ignition, and combustion minimize these variations. LPE engines show little of these variations in comparison to other aircraft engines. Part of the cylinder pressure variations are caused by exhaust contamination/scavenging. LPE chambers use a cross flow design that approach a hemi-head design with the valves splayed wide apart. The exhaust valve is canted toward the exhaust pipe and moved versus the piston center toward the pipe to reduce heat absorption. The intake is canted in the other direction. This has the effect of straightening out the runner passages for good breathing. New heads being tested reduce chamber size to 70 cc. Valves have more cant.

ELECTRONIC IGNITION

LPE engine safety is ensured by dual electronic ignition. These systems are totally redundant. Even the FARs for engine certification allow that systems other than dual mags and dual plugs can be substituted (FAR Part 33.37). The consumer has the option. System reliability is just as good with one plug or two. The reason is that the same force that would destroy one plug will kill the second plug, too. That force is detonation. LPE engine detonation is controlled by the knock sensors and automatic feedback systems. Detonation will either knock a hole in the piston top or knock the tip off the spark plug. LPE stops it before damage is done. If you must have damage it is better to ruin a plug than a piston.

The loss of one plug, for whatever reason, in a V/8 engine is far less significant than that occurring in a four cylinder aircraft engine. Plug fouling is a result of a cold engine and a too rich mixture. LPE water cooled engines warm up fast and the EFI prevents fouling mixtures. Even if a plug was fouled LPE's ignition system would fire it.

"ZM" engines run distributorless electronic ignitions that automatically adjust ignition timing for knock, load, temperature, and gasoline quality. They also enable more complete combustion for more power on less fuel flow. By lighting the mixture with a high power spark the time interval between ignition and maximum pressure can be reduced. Therefore the spark advance can be reduced and the rising piston does not have to fight against rising combustion pressure.

It takes more horsepower to spin dual magnetos than to run an alternator (considering all drive losses). By using high efficiency alternators to create the electricity for the spark, horsepower is saved, consuming less than one HP to keep the electrical system at full charge. "ZM" engines can adjust spark timing advance over a 50 degree range. Cold engines and high altitude require 8 to 12 degrees of additional advance. Magnetos cannot do this - LPE's "ZM" engine ignition system can.

LPE ignition systems are self-adjusting for zero maintenance. LPE also uses two independent ignition systems for redundancy. Each independent system has eight separate coils. If a control unit fails, the other will maintain 100 percent power. A separate bus and battery for the second ignition system is the means of creating two totally independent systems.

VALVE GUIDES

The compression and ignition advance of an engine is linked to the valve guides. The reason is that oil contamination of the incoming fuel charge will cause detonation. LPE engines run Teflon valve stem seals that thread on for absolute retention and no oil contamination.

Because LPE "ZM" Series engines are liquid cooled they can run exceptionally tight valve guide clearances. The guides are honed to fit each valve in a near interference fit. The result is minimal oil consumption, extra long engine life, and compression can be raised for more power and efficiency. Raising the compression increases the life of the valves, seats, and guides. When compression is raised the fuel burns more completely so the exhaust gas temperature is lowered to reduce engine component stress levels.

RING DESIGN

LPE "ZM" Series engines use gapless rings. The piston ring ends overlap. When brand new conventional rings are fitted an excellent seal is a 4-6 percent pressure loss (leak down). The gapless design will be zero to 2 percent. That translates into 4 percent more power, or 4 percent less fuel burn when engines are new.

The more a conventional ring wears the larger the gap becomes and leak downs soar. The gap less design never gets a gap so that on used engines the gapless design can have a 10 percent advantage in fuel efficiency or power.

Gapless rings keep oil out of the combustion chamber. But more importantly, they don't let the hot combustion gases into the crankcase, or below the piston top. The oil stays a lot cooler; the oil doesn't get carbonized and the piston/cylinder wear is reduced along with glazing. The piston can be fitted tighter for even longer wear.

LPE uses moly rings. Total break-in takes 30 minutes, not 30 hours. The moly rings make super slick, low drag (friction) walls possible. LPE cylinders are honed to fit and then polished. The rings obviously will last a long time. Moly wears better than iron.

LPE also uses steel (not iron) second and oil rings that are specially designed to conform to the cylinder walls. An extremely rigid ring will not follow the wall surface. Even the cylinder vibrations upset the rings. The LPE design with siamesed and pinned cylinders stops cylinder ringing for a better ring seal.

FUEL INJECTION
Light Power Engine Corporation's electronic engine management systems are what enable the "ZM" engine line to perform at the highest levels in the industry. These systems check the engine's operating parameters every one-third of a second. Adjustments are made automatically as needed to maintain maximum efficiency and performance.

Compared to carburetors, current generation aircraft mechanical fuel injection is a major improvement. But these MFI systems are now 50 years old and are a major block to increasing engine efficiency. The conventional system merely runs fuel to a "spider" distribution block and squirts fuel to all of the cylinders at the same time. Cylinders get fuel they don't need, increasing fuel consumption. Other problem areas are:
- **Small Diameter Fuel Lines Clog Easily**
- **Fuel Pumps Vaporize Fuel**
- **Vapor Lock**
- **Injector Nozzles Drip Fuel**
- **Poor Fuel Atomization**

"ZM" electronics monitor all engine inputs, supplying the proper amount of fuel at every possible condition. Light Power Engine Corporation's electronic fuel injection (EFI) improves engine reliability! "ZM" engines start easier in all conditions, run smoother, and provide more power.

Electronic fuel injection also conserves fuel. Converting to EFI causes a 10 percent power increase at 10 percent less fuel burn. Current generation EFI does much better than this. High pressure systems and multiple orifice nozzles finely atomize fuel to sub-100 micron particles. Brake Specific Fuel Consumption (BSFC) of "ZM" engines is 0.45 at *full power* versus 0.55 for current generation Lycoming and Continentals. LPE's EFI incorporates a "Limp Home Mode" that the system adapts if something fails. This mode creates a full rich situation to provide adequate power to reach an airport. Long runners and fuel injected directly at the valve opening make LPE engines very smooth and responsive. Fuel specifics are .39 at cruise.

ACCESSORY DRIVES
Unique among aircraft engine manufacturers is the intent of LPE to eliminate or reduce engine drive points as part of overall engine design philosophy. The reasons are several fold. The primary intent is to increase engine reliability by eliminating moving components and total parts and to eliminate oil seal/gasket potential leak points. All of the magneto and accessory case gears and seals are eliminated in the "ZM" design.

The secondary intent was to increase accessory and related system reliability. We found that accessories only lasted 1/2 as long as they should due to being subjected to engine heat and vibration. This ties in with our and the U. S. Armed Forces findings that electromechanical devices are more reliable than mechanical devices. We believe that the vacuum and fuel pumps should be driven electrically and remote mounted for maximum reliability.

We believe in exposing all maintenance areas and making them exceptionally easy to inspect and/or repair. The cog belt accessory drive(s) is an indication of this philosophy. In a typical gear case everything is hidden and nothing is known about gear drives until failure or teardown. Gear cases contain all of the possible drives - even if you don't want or need them, which add to final engine cost and weight.

By contrast, the accessory drive belts that LPE uses on "ZM" engines are exposed for inspection, cheap to replace, and isolate expensive accessories from the damaging heat and vibration of the engine. This increases the reliability of these accessories and eliminates the heating and contamination of the engine oil from the drives for these accessories.

Time to belt failure is 1,500 hours at 220 degrees F. LPE specifies belt replacement every 1,000 hours for $40 instead of adding an extra $1,000 to an engine's maintenance cost with gear case work and accessory replacement. Just extending the life of one vacuum pump will buy from 12 to 20 belts.

EMISSIONS/FUEL
"ZM" engines are extremely fuel efficient with very clean fuel burn. This translates into very low exhaust emissions. The entire "ZM" engine line will pass most EPA emission requirements today without a catalytic converter and will pass all of them with one installed.

"ZM" engines are designed to run on unleaded fuel or leaded fuel of I 00 octane. Our engine can be set up to run 92 octane premium unleaded fuel at a 5 to 10 percent power loss, if requested.

NOISE REDUCTION
Noise levels both in the cockpit as well as outside the aircraft are becoming increasingly important. To address this concern, Light Power Engine Corporation makes every attempt to reduce the noise levels emanating from the aircraft. There are four major areas that LPE has concentrated on to achieve a significant reduction in engine created noise.

LPE's "ZM" engine configuration is made up of less moving parts than other designs. This is due in part to the design characteristics of all V/8 engines as well as LPE designed features. Specifically, all accessories are driven by toothed belts that make very little operating noise. In addition, the use of electronic ignition eliminates magnetos and the associated drive mechanisms which create even more engine noise. Even the interconnected cylinder barrel design aids in noise reduction by reducing the barrel vibration. These areas alone significantly reduce the amount of mechanical noise created by the "ZM" engines.

The design of the air intake system is another major area in which LPE has drastically reduced the noise created by these aircraft engines. The air charge in a "ZM" engine is introduced to the cylinders from a series of plenum chambers rather than directly from the atmosphere. This reduces the amount of audible noise created by the intake air surges. To further reduce the air pulses, the eight cylinder design takes in the same amount of air as other designs, but does it in smaller and more frequent pulses. This reduces the amplitude of the pulses while increasing their frequency leading to a smooth sounding engine.

The fact that these engines are liquid cooled aids even further in reducing the noise created as compared to air cooled engines. By eliminating the cooling fins on an air cooled engine, the associated "ringing" is also eliminated. Liquid cooling also allows for tighter tolerances on internal engine parts due to the uniform and predictable temperature throughout the engine. The tight tolerances prevent parts from rattling and making noise as well as increasing wear characteristics.

Lastly, the selection of a propeller is greatly overlooked as a noise consideration. LPE suggests the use of a three blade propeller, or even more if possible. The theory behind this is the same as the intake design discussed above. With a multi-blade prop, the vibration pulses are smaller in amplitude and more frequent. These factors lead to a smooth sounding propeller.

LPE takes every step necessary to make these engines the most reliable, efficient, and customer oriented engines on the market. 'Me reduction of noise and vibration levels is one more step along this direction..

PARTS REDUCTION
Consider the diagram from a Lycoming manual. Thirteen gears, one eccentric and a push rod are all grinding away in these engines. The backlash and vibration from all of this thrashing around can be considerable. These are all eliminated on the "ZM" engines except for the cam drive (3 total) for a 14 piece (plus housings) - 16 piece total parts reduction.

Now consider the comparison of a 6 cylinder horizontally opposed engine to an inverted V/8, as shown in the relative parts count; less parts mean more reliability:

CERAMICS AND DRY FILMS
LPE engines feature ceramics in combustion chambers and exhaust ports to increase power and thermal efficiency. Heat is contained in the chamber. It does not go readily into the piston and head. Cooling drag and cooling system weight are therefore reduced. The cooler piston and head can handle more ignition advance and more compression without knock. Power is increased 5 percent for every 1.0 point of

	"ZM" V/8	HO Aircraft
Crankcase	1	2
Cylinders	0	6
Heads	2	6
Valve covers	2	6
Gaskets	2	6
Pushrod tubes	0	12
Seals	0	24
Gears	3	13
Head gaskets	2	6
Cyl gaskets	0	6
Part Count	**12**	**87**

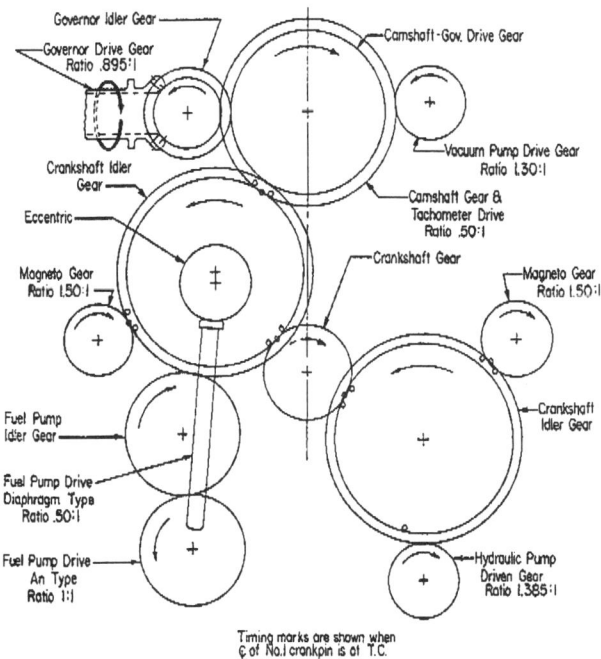

Lycoming engine accessory drives and associated parts.

compression increase (or reduction of fuel burn at equal power). A Continental IO-470 runs at 8:1 compression. A "ZM" IIV-440 runs at 10.5:1, or a 2.5 point increase.

The ceramics work in connection with the EFI, electronic ignition, and water cooling to make this possible. A "ZM" 600 with its special combustion chamber can run 16:1 compression on 100 octane without knock.

Now that the ceramics let the piston run cooler we can fit the piston tighter. The piston is coated with dry film lubricant to help it out in start up, low oil pressure situations. All of the "ZM" engine valves, plain bearings, and pistons are coated. If it doesn't have a roller on it, it gets coated.

We have raised combustion efficiency with the ceramics. But since the head is cooler we can run leaner still for another 3 percent power or fuel economy gain. The offshoot is that combustion is now more complete - exhaust gas temperature goes down. Less EGT means that turbos can live with "ZM" engines (plus they have water cooled bearings.)

SERVICEABILITY
LPE's "ZM" Series are designed for the ultimate in service ease. To check, pull, replace crankshafts or bearings in an

opposed engine you must do a total teardown. By only removing the crankcase cover plate these can he serviced in the "ZM" series. The thrust/radial load drive end can be completely dismantled and serviced without touching the rest of the engine. The inverted position keeps the lifters in place so that the cam can be pulled through a special circular access hatch. The cam drive gears are also accessible through this service plate.

Cylinders can be replaced as they are pressed-in dry sleeves. Pistons and rods can be pulled without a total teardown. Lifters can be removed by only lifting off the intake manifold for access. No engine dismantling is required. Valve springs can be replaced without removing the head.

CRANKSHAFT/CRANKCASE STRENGTH

When analyzing Continental, Continental and Lycoming engines it was found that the crankcase halves moved around causing fretting, wear, and oil leaks. The "ZM" one piece block does not have that problem.

Opposed engine crankcase failure was generally in the first bearing web due to bending loads from the prop. As these engines aged they were increased in power but crank diameter remained the same at 2.25 inches. Only the low horsepower "ZM" engines have such small crankshafts. Engines from 140 to 270 HP have 2.25 OD cranks, rod journal and 3.0 inch main bearings. All engines above that HP feature 2.75 inch OD cranks and bearings for a tremendous increase in rigidity. Bearing area is increased significantly at a given width by a 20 percent increase in ID. This crank thickness also helps control torsional vibration.

For maximum load stiffness "ZM" engines use a separate radial and thrust load section designed solely for that purpose. This takes the bending loads off the engine and protects it.

OIL COOLING

The temperature of oil and coolant in an engine are always linked. Once the coolant temperature climbs above 220 degrees the oil temperature soars. Cool one and you automatically cool the other as all of the fluids see the engine's heat mass. Air cooled engines act the same. Cylinder temperatures and oil temperatures are linked. You can cool an engine with oil but it is not as efficient as water. LPE certified, air cooled, inverted engines are cooled this way.

LPE goes a step further by deliberately interlinking the oil and water heat exchanger. The advantages are many. The small exchanger mounts anywhere and does not need air flow. That means less drag, less duct weight and latitude in weight and balance. The combination helps prevent blowing oil coolers with thick oil. The exchanger transfers the heat to the water so only one air intake is needed for the engine. Resulting weight reductions are worth 7-15 pounds on most aircraft.

The big advantage is to cause the oil and water warm up equally. On a cold start the water warms up first which immediately warms the oil. This increases oil flow to all parts of the engine to reduce wear and seizure. Engine life is increased because temperature variations throughout the engine are relieved. Stresses are therefore reduced.

Oil should run at 200°F at the minimum and a max of 250°F. Oil gage temperature lags bearing temperature by 30° to 50°. Synthetic oil can handle 380°F (the bearing can not). Our engines are designed to use multi-viscosity automotive grades of engine oil which greatly reduce the engine warm-up problem.

Now you can understand the true importance of liquid cooling and why engines fail at takeoff. On opposed, air cooled engines, idling rich, it is hard to get them hot enough for takeoff, particularly in cold weather. A thermostatically controlled, water cooled engine which warms up fast is the safest engine and suffers less wear.

A side benefit of tight clearances is more power and fuel efficiency. Tight bearings require less oil flow volume. Less oil "leaks" out. Oil pumping losses are lower and oil in the crank windage is reduced which lowers oil temperature. We believe every aircraft engine should have an oil heater which solves many operating problems. They are cheap and they don't weigh much - get one.

BALANCE/VIBRATION

LPE engines are engineered to be smooth. The V/8's more frequent 90 degree firing pulses in contrast to the 120 degree of an opposed 6 cylinder help as do the smaller pulses of a given horsepower engine. The up and down motion of the piston and the restraining of the piston at its travel limits

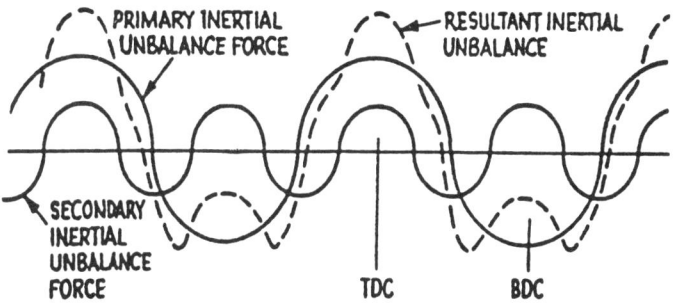

causes inertial imbalance in engines. This is in proportion to piston and rod weight. The piston size of an 8 is smaller than that of a big 6 (4.5 vs. 5) so inertial weight is reduced as are imbalance forces and primary unbalanced forces (once each rev) in an LPE engine. Secondary unbalanced forces (twice each rev) add to the primary forces at the top of the stroke and subtract at the bottom as shown in the chart.

Differences in piston speed occur over a piston's travel. It moves further over the last 90 degrees of crank travel at the top of its stroke and moves faster over that distance. The speed difference is controlled by rod length at a given stroke. The longer the rod the less speed difference. "ZM" engines feature long rods of up to 7.25 center to center to decrease rod angularity and piston speed differences.

The result is a sharp drop in torsional vibration and secondary unbalanced forces. A huge side benefit is lower friction from rod angularity loads for more power and longer engine life. Longer rods by reducing piston speeds also reduce the loads at TDC. Now the rod and piston can be made lighter to further lower primary imbalance.

Torsional vibration is linked to the cylinder pressure variations cylinder to cylinder and before, during, and after combustion. LPE defeats these forces in several ways. LPE

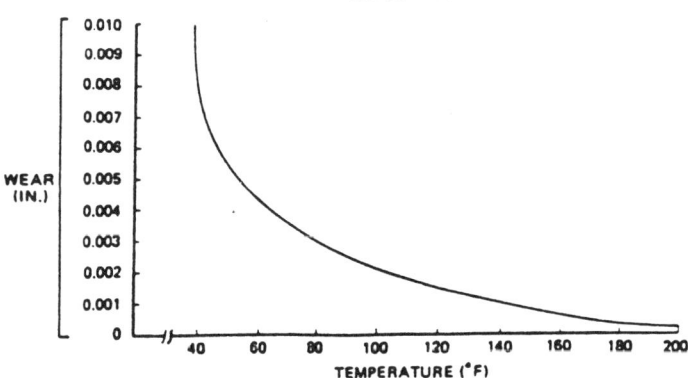

Wear/temperature tests support need for preflight warmup. The coolant temperature gage is a far better indicator than oil pressure as a Go/No Go device.

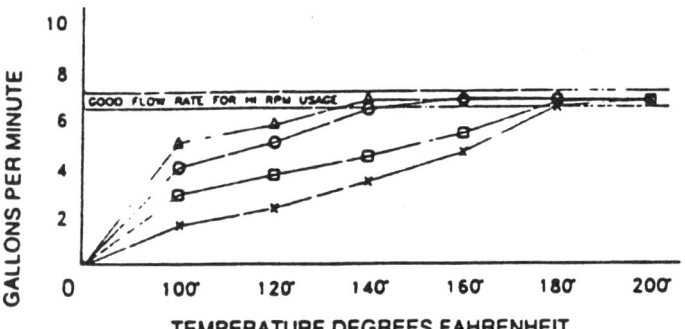

Synthetic multi, 10W40, 30, and 50 weight flows (top to bottom) as they relate to cold start and wear effects. At 140 F. the synthetic flows at 200 % the volume of the 30/50 oils.

cranks are unusually thick SAE 4340 forgings. They resist twisting. The stiffness of the crank raises the vibration frequency out of the engine speed range. V/8 cranks are short and therefore stiffer yet. V/8 cranks have less throws per cylinder so cranks are less flexible and shorter.

Lastly, if cylinder to cylinder pressure variations are reduced vibration drops sharply. Partial misfires caused by poor ignition and poor fuel atomization is the primary culprit. LPE engines with their high power ignition systems and finely sprayed fuel contribute to reduced torsional vibration.

To ensure smoothness all LPE engines use an inertial ring, free floating, set in silicone fluid on the crankshaft end to soak up as much as 5 degree of crank twist. These dampers are amplitude responsive and are not frequency or RPM specific. They clip the amplitude spike out of any crank vibration by increasing resistance opposing crank twist and soften crank deceleration. All cranks have a resonant frequency. Only the frequency and duration will change with a change in amplitude. Other frequencies coming from piston speed, camshaft movement, vacuum pump imbalance and other moving parts etc. can compound or cancel vibrations. LPE engines are the only aircraft engines in the world that have a vibration damping system that cancels

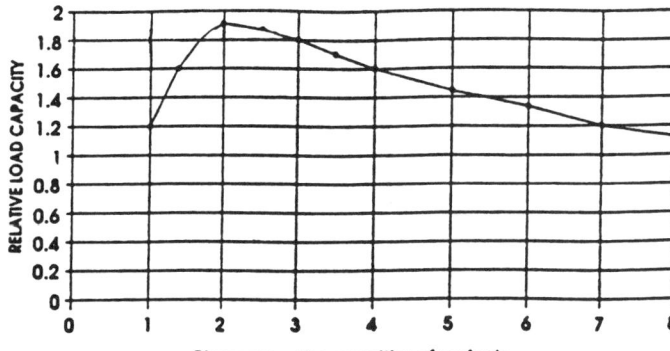

Tight bearings handle more load but require multi viscosity oils. Large bearing clearances require heavy oils which require more pumping capacity (horsepower).

vibrations of all frequencies and amplitudes, produced at engine operating RPMs.

The virtual elimination of torsional vibration is a real LPE strong point. The oil temperature falls, and bearing life increases. Since the cam and ignition always drive off of one end of a crank every 1 degree of twist equals 2 degrees of ignition and valve timing error. By taming vibration LPE nets more power and fuel efficiency.

In LPE engines the crankshafts are fully counterweighted. That means that each piston/rod/throw has its own set of balance weights. This is unique. Most opposed engines have balance weights only on the rear cylinders. Auto V/8s only have them on both ends but not in the middle. Fully counterweighted cranks suffer less flexing and torsional vibration. Stresses produced at one cylinder are taken care of there, not passed on through the crank to the crank end where a balance has to do double duty. **DHZ**

LPE 500 HP engine firewall forward package for a Lancair IV, Oshkosh 1995.

Auto Engine Conversions
Custom Airplane Designs
Experimenter Reports

Bimonthly Contact! magazine is a year around forum for homebuilders, experimenters and designers to share their experiences. Each issue contains 20 pages of in-depth articles, printed on coated quality paper so black and white photos are as sharp as any in the business. The editorial back page contains late breaking news such as forum schedules, safety alerts, and some commentary. Advertising is not carried, so the text flows easily from page to page. The magazine is supported entirely by subscription.

I also publish technical articles on airplanes and airframes on occasion, particularly one-off designs which will be of interest to most experimenters. I do get a complaint now and then because a reader would like exclusive attention paid to auto engines. Because this area of homebuilding is relatively new articles are hard to come by. Many people are working with auto conversions now so I believe you can expect more and more pages of each issue devoted to the coverage of flying conversions.

Contact! is published on the fifteenth or the following Monday of each odd month (Jan, Mar, ...Nov). U.S. subscriptions are mailed out at standard non profit organization bulk rates which means about 10 days enroute (according to the USPS). Canadians get theirs via airmail while overseas subscribers have a choice between surface and airmail service. I am proud and also thankful I have not missed a mailing date in the last five years of publication. You may have gathered by now that I enjoy working with fellow experimenter/authors !

I find magazine renewal notices are a real irritant; you may feel the same as I do. My solution is simple. Each mailing label contains the last issue number right after the last name. A simple match and it is time to renew!

You have seen a sampling of articles from the first five years. You can expect the same emphasis on useful information in future issues. The price is right; one article alone could save you a bundle and perhaps much more.

Save the coupon for the next reader! A simple note along with your check, money order or credit card information will do perfectly. If you wish you can place your order on the 800 number - 1(800) 823 0692.

Mick Myal   Editor/Publisher of Contact! magazine

☐ Sign me up for a subscription (six issues/year)

☐ Sign me up for two years (twelve issues)

☐ Payment $_____

Charge it!   VISA ☐   MC ☐   exp date_____

name_____

address_____

city/ state_____ zip+4 _____

Contact!
2900 East Weymouth
Tucson AZ 85716-1249

☐☐☐☐ ☐☐☐☐ ☐☐☐☐ ☐☐☐☐

signature of cardholder and date_____

Subscription (U.S. Funds)	1 year	2 years
U.S.A.	$20.00	$36.00
Canada (air)	$27.00	$50.00
Overseas (surface)	$29.00	$54.00
Overseas (air)	$38.00	$72.00

Michael C. Myal (Mick) was born in 1930. He graduated from the General Motors Institute in 1953 with a Batchelor of Mechanical Engineering degree. He served three years in the U.S. Army. His thirty-five year career at General Motors included assignments in body production, styling, human factors, vehicle safety and international government regulatory activities. He received certification as a Registered Professional Engineer in 1967.

An EAA member since 1959 and Detroit area Chapter 13 officer for several years, aircraft involvement included consulting work on two engine installation STCs and the building of a Minicab and a 2/3 scale Mustang. He successfully completed and flew a Varieze in 1980. During that period, he also volunteered his time to serve as president of a DC-7B and Lockheed Electra private air travel club based at Detroit Metro. He is the author of several Sport Aviation articles, including *Ultimate Glue, Eagle1-Ultimate Airfoil* and *Cockpit Design Simplified.* He was awarded a patent for a vehicle occupant packaging tool, the principal part of a design system used today by all road vehicle manufacturers.

Retired since 1988, his main interest is the publication of non profit Contact! magazine. He also serves as an EAA Technical Counselor and auto power forum organizer for the annual Sun'N Fun and Copperstate Fly-ins. In his spare time he is designing his concept of a practical, two place, side-by-side cross-country airplane.